Foundations for Soul Care

A CHRISTIAN PSYCHOLOGY PROPOSAL

Eric L. Johnson

An imprint of InterVarsity Press
Downers Grove, Illinois

InterVarsity Press
P.O. Box 1400, Downers Grove, IL 60515-1426
World Wide Web: www.ivpress.com
E-mail: email@ivpress.com

InterVarsity Press® is the book-publishing division of InterVarsity Christian Fellowship/USA®, a movement of students and faculty active on campus at hundreds of universities, colleges and schools of nursing in the United States of America, and a member movement of the International Fellowship of Evangelical Students. For information about local and regional activities, write Public Relations Dept., InterVarsity Christian Fellowship/USA, 6400 Schroeder Rd., P.O. Box 7895, Madison, WI 53707-7895, or visit the IVCF website at <www.intervarsity.org>.

Design: Cindy Kiple
Images: Clay Patrick McBride/Getty Images

ISBN 978-0-8308-2567-7 (hardcover)
ISBN 978-0-8308-4054-0 (paperback)
ISBN 978-0-8308-7527-6 (digital)

Printed in the United States of America ∞

green press INITIATIVE *InterVarsity Press is committed to protecting the environment and to the responsible use of natural resources. As a member of the Green Press Initiative we use recycled paper whenever possible. To learn more about the Green Press Initiative, visit <www.greenpressinitiative.org>.*

Library of Congress Cataloging-in-Publication Data

Johnson, Eric L., 1956-
Foundations for soul care: a Christian psychology proposal / Eric Johnson.
p. cm.
Includes bibliographical references and index.
ISBN-13: 978-0-8308-2567-7 (pbk.: alk. cloth)
1. Christianity—Psychology. 2. Bible—Psychology. I. Title.
BR110.J558 2007
253.5'2—dc22

2007016679

P 21 20 19 18 17 16 15 14 13 12 11 10 9 8 7 6 5 4 3 2 1
Y 32 31 30 29 28 27 26 25 24 23 22 21 20 19 18 17 16 15 14

To Rebekah,

My wife, friend, and fellow sojourner

on the way to the City of God

Contents

Preface

THERE ARE ONLY A FEW TOPICS ABOUT WHICH Christians have more disparate ideas and are more deeply divided than that of psychology and soul care. What is it about this area of thought and practice that makes it so contentious? Early on, this book tries to offer an explanation. But most of our time will be spent on a more constructive agenda: a proposal for a fundamental framework for Christian soul care (a broad category that includes psychotherapy, counseling and spiritual direction, and in fact encompasses the main tasks of the church). The various Christian approaches to soul care have all made important contributions to the debate. Though some criticisms of current Christian approaches to soul care will be presented, this book is clearly indebted to that work. This model is inevitably something of a response, and in turn is put forth as a proposal—to be engaged with and criticized itself. It is, therefore, also an invitation to enter into this ongoing dialogue, in order for all of the interested parties in the Christian community to make more progress in our common cause of serving Christ, one another and humanity in Christ's name.

However, this book is undeniably a *Christian psychology* proposal. The project of a Christian psychology is not yet widely understood, and there will always be different notions of just what it is (as there are of modern psychology). Most of its proponents, however, I think would agree that it aims at the development of a distinctly Christian *version* of psychology: a wise science of individual human beings that includes theory building, research, teaching, training and various kinds of practice, including the care of souls. This science flows from a Christian understanding of human nature and therefore can be distinguished from alternative versions of psychology based on different worldviews.

At first glance it may appear that "Christian psychology" is a poor candidate to unify a fractious field, especially since the term means different things to different people. Some think it an oxymoron (MacArthur, 1994); others have used it to label any activity in the field of psychology or counseling done by a Christian. Nevertheless, the term has a worthy pedigree and there are good reasons to think it a fitting label for what this book is about. Let us consider some of the background to this term to gain our bearings.

Depending on how one understands it, the Christian psychology paradigm might be said to have three historical "moments." First, psychology of some kind can be found throughout the Bible and the writings of the Christian tradition. The fact that for most of that history the term "Christian psychology" was not used does not mean it did not exist. Few of these writings are scientific in the modern sense, but they nonetheless contain many insightful Christian descriptions of human nature and the care of souls, and I will suggest that they ought to provide the foundation and heart of a contemporary Christian psychology. Second, Søren Kierkegaard identified himself as a Christian psychologist, and described what he was doing as Christian psychology, though his work was not empirical in the way modern psychology is (Evans, 1990; Kierkegaard, 1834/1946a, 1847/1938, 1849/1980). Before Freud was born, Kierkegaard put together in his many writings a profound description of human beings and their development from a thoroughly Christian standpoint. Third, a contemporary approach to psychology and counseling has begun to develop what amounts to a distinctly Christian version of psychology—including some preliminary psychological theory-building, research and models of soul care—through a reinvestment in the canonical, historical and contemporary resources of the Christian tradition, as well as through a Christian reinterpretation of the work of modern and postmodern psychology. Though the most recent, this third moment is not very well known. While few have used the label "Christian psychology," its contributors rightly include Vitz (1994, 1988), White (1979, 1982, 1987), Van Leeuwen (1982, 1985), Evans (1977, 1989, 1990), Roberts (1987, 1993, 2000; Talbot, 1997), Watson (1993, 2004, 2005; along with Morris, Hood & Hall, 1985; Morris & Hood, 1988a; and Morris, Loy, Hamrick & Grizzle, in press), Johnson (1996a, 1996b, 1997, 2000), Crabb (1987, 1988, 1993, 1997, 1999, 2003, 2006), Crabb and Allender (1996), Allender and Longman (1990, 1993, 1995), Allender (1999, 2005), Payne (1991, 1995, 1996), Langberg (1997, 1999), Wilson (1990,

1998, 2001), and Clinton and Ohlschlager (2002) (and undoubtedly others). For a summary of the third moment's history, the reader is directed to the introductory chapter of *Christianity and Psychology: Four Views* (Johnson & Jones, 2000).

In light of these three moments, and in spite of the misgivings that attend its use, the term "Christian psychology" is considered by the author to be the best label in this era for the kind of work grouped together above and found in this book.

Toward a "Worldview" for Christian Soul Care

By any reckoning, a Christian psychology that aims at being counted scientific is in its infancy (if not still in gestation). Where is work most needed? One worthwhile candidate would be a description of what a Christian worldview for soul care might consist of—what we might call a Christian *edification framework.* The term *edification* has metaphorical origins: its Old English root means "temple" or "house" (from which we derive *edifice*). It is also used in the English Bible to translate the Greek word *oikodomē* (Rom 15:2; 1 Cor 14:3; Eph 4:29), which denotes spiritual strengthening or "building up" (Arndt & Gingrich, 1957). Soul care has as its aim the construction or the upbuilding of the soul. In this sense all religions and forms of psychotherapy aim at some kind of edification. As a result, the term *edification framework* (E.F.) will be used to refer to the "set of a therapist's articulable cognitive-axiological-volitional structures relevant to improving the state of a person's well-being" (Johnson & Sandage, 1999, p. 2). It is made up of a few components, including a narrative structure within which to make sense of the stories of clients, as well as many beliefs about human nature: its composition, important features, soul-problems and their causes, and solutions for those problems. A subset of these beliefs are normative and include assumptions regarding values, goods, virtues, desirable goals and morality, as well as the overarching goal toward which humans are to aspire, the human *telos.* This book provides a description of some of the main features of these foundations for a Christian understanding of soul care.

Core Distinctives of This Soul-Care Model

A few novel aspects of the model presented in this book should probably be explained.

It is doxological. Christianity is a God-centered system of life and thought. God is the Lord of creation and the Lord of the covenant (Frame, 1987, 2002; Horton, 2002), so Christians owe him absolute fealty, loyalty and love. For those set free by his grace, he is easy to love, because of his great beauty.

> One thing I have asked from the LORD, that I shall seek:
> That I may dwell in the house of the LORD all the days of my life,
> To behold the beauty of the LORD. (Ps 27:4)

From a Christian standpoint, "beauty is a category indispensable to Christian thought; all that theology saw of the triune life of God, the gratuity of creation, the incarnation of the Word, and the salvation of the world makes room for—indeed depends upon—a thought, and a narrative, of the beautiful" (Hart, 2003, p. 16). Christians throughout the ages have recognized that God is intrinsically beautiful, as well as the source of all created beauty. Jonathan Edwards, for example (1765/1960), described God as "infinitely the most beautiful and excellent" being (p. 14), "the foundation and fountain of all being and beauty" (p. 15).

A more common word for beauty, in Christian parlance, is glory. The Greek word for glory *(doxa)* signifies brightness, splendor or radiance (Arndt & Gingrich, 1957, p. 202), and the glory of God has been defined as the outflowing or radiance of his beauty, that is, the manifestation of his glorious attributes—his holiness, righteousness and love (Balthasar, 1982-1991; Barth, 1957; Bavinck, 2004; Edwards, 1765/1998; Muller, 2003). From the standpoint of Christianity, God's greatest beauty may be the infinite love the triune God shares among Father, Son and Holy Spirit.

Because God created all things for his glory (Is 43:7; Rom 11:36; Eph 1; Rev 4:8-11), it might be expected that the well-being of his image-bearers would be coordinated to their celebration and expression of and participation in that glory. In a virtuous human being, "God's glory is revealed as something communicable and intrinsically delightful, as including the creature in its ends, and as completely worthy of love" (Hart, 2003, p. 17). What is the fitting human response to God's glory or beauty? Worship and love and emulation. The soul that sees something of God's infinite beauty cannot help but utter praise, feel drawn toward that beauty, desire to participate in it and resemble it, and seek to live to exalt it.

As a result, a Christian soul-care model ought to be *doxological* (Yates,

1997), that is, it ought to aim to interpret and conduct everything in order to best foster the human appropriation and manifestation of the glory of God. It ought to act so as to draw others into an increasingly closer orbit around God, a greater love of God and others (in imitation of the Trinity), and a greater likeness to God. Needless to say, this is a radically different framework for soul care than that which governs modern psychotherapy and counseling.

It is semiodiscursive. Another way to think about glory is meaning. God's glory consists of the infinite weight of his greatness and goodness; it is all the meaning that he possesses—his meaning-fullness. Semiotics is the discipline that deals with the representation of meaning. The most basic type of representation is the sign. As Augustine (trans. 1997) noted, a sign is anything that refers to something else. Signs are "pointers" that represent or "stand for" other things. While almost anything can be a sign of something else, soul care is interested in the referential function of various aspects of human life: language, emotions, mental images, actions and other people, and texts in general, including narratives.

Like a painting that inevitably "points" to the one who painted it, God created a world that signifies him. It all bears his imprint, but some creatures represent God more clearly than others. Humans, for example, are made in the "image" of God, indicating a relatively high degree of semiotic correspondence. As image-bearers, humans are supposed to resemble God; the greater the likeness, the better. God created signs of himself, for the purpose of manifesting something of his glory, over time, in the creation. The soul care model of this book is aimed at helping humans become better signs of God.

Words are also signs of meaning, so linguistics is considered by some to be a branch of semiotics. A language is the most complex and powerful formal sign-system we know of, so it can communicate meaning with great sophistication (compared to facial expressions, for example). However, a language in the abstract is inert; it only "enters into the world" *in use. Discourse* is the actual use of a language by an author (a speaker or writer) to communicate meaning. "God is a communicating Being" (Edwards, 1994, p. 410), so it is no surprise that discourse figures prominently in God's agenda to communicate his glory through his image-bearers. To start with the creation, we learn from the Bible that the created order is a function of God's speech, and so we can infer it is endowed with meaning, which science uncovers or explicates: everything created is constituted by the word of God. Second, consider how foundational language is to human development, making possible the realization of reason, complex emotions, social relations, moral responsibility, even spirituality. Unless raised up within a discursive community and educated within its forms of speech, it appears that humans cannot attain to any form of human maturity. Third, God revealed himself and his plan of salvation in the inspired and explicit discourse of the Bible.

In very different ways, discourse, then, is constitutive of created, human and Christian reality, and Christian soul care is interested in the reconstitution of all three. However, we are also concerned with discourse in this book for two other, practical reasons: first, because, the formulation of Christian psychological theory and practice is directly concerned with texts—the Bible and relevant Christian literature, and the massive body of discourse known as modern psychology; and second, because the care of souls is fundamentally discursive; it inevitably involves conversation (Martin, 1994)—even behavior therapy requires speech explaining the use of various techniques.

So Christian soul care is semiodiscursive: it concerns itself with meaning—ultimately with glory—expressed in signs, utterances or texts. As a result, this model is unavoidably hermeneutic, that is, it involves the interpretation of discourse (including the "texts" of others and the events of their lives).

It is dialogical/trialogical. But discourse has a deeper goal: interpersonal relationship. Discourse is communication, and communication is for the purpose of communion. Through discourse, humans engage in dialogue, in order to relate to, inform, influence, and enjoy one another. According to Bakhtin (1981, 1986), however, dialogue is more than humans talking together—it is foundational to human nature. Humans are "co-beings" (Holquist, 1990). The self is necessarily related to the other; it cannot develop or exist alone—even the hermit was formed by dialogue and carries on a dialogue with himself. The social space each individual inhabits has already long been inhabited by others, and they have spoken and are in some sense still speaking (through written texts, as well as in the continual, ongoing transmission of discourse everyday). Out of the discourse of others, new human discourse arises. The utterances of one initiate responses in the other, which in turn prompt further utterances from others, and so goes the dialogue in which human life consists.

Adult dialogue in particular can be edifying. When two persons meet together, each may know things the other does not and each may see things about the other that the other does not. So if they love each other, dialogue between them inevitably leads to the enrichment and building up of each other. Human dialogue is supposed to be a concrete model of divine communion. The triune God eternally exists in a dialogue of interpersonal love and mutual glorification (Jn 17:3, 21). Dialogue is fundamental to the life of persons, and humans image the Trinity in loving, reciprocal, upbuilding conversation. Moreover, human image-bearing is especially realized in dialogue with the living God, who is speaking to us one way or another through Scripture (most clearly), through the creation and through our dialogue with others.

Christian soul care, according to this model, promotes relational communion through dialogue. God is a dialogue partner in the Christian healing of the soul, and we are always situated in the midst of a history and matrix of human conversations, one of which is that between counselor and counselee. Understood rightly—by faith—Christian soul care is always a *trialogue,* involving counselor, counselee and the omnipresent God (Kellemen, 2005b; Sphar & Smith, 2003).

It is canonical. This model is also biblical. The Bible is the Text of texts, the Discourse of discourses. Because it is God's inspired word in human language, it offers Christians God's semiodiscursive key to interpreting the universe, particularly the meaningfulness of human life, and through it the triune God meets with and dialogues with his people. Since the early centuries of the church, the Bible has been referred to as *canon.* The term *canon* comes from the Greek word *kanōn*, meaning rule, measure or standard (Packer, 1988). So the term identifies the Bible as the authoritative rule for the Christian life. "The canon is the norm for Christian language, thought, and action" (Vanhoozer, 2005, p. 217). As a result, it serves as the foundational "rule" or "guide" for Christian soul care, revealing to us how human life can best promote the glory of God. Given the Bible's status, Christian soul care should have as its primary aim the training and edification of its counselees in "canonical competence" (Vanhoozer, 2000), a way of seeing and living, shaped by the Bible.

This is especially important in the twenty-first century, since for the past 125 years the field of psychology and soul care has been almost entirely composed of texts generated out of a secular framework. This requires of Christians the development of a canonically based hermeneutics of such texts, so that they can be interpreted Christianly. The canon of Scripture provides the "spectacles" (Calvin, 1559/1960) by which we read and make sense of those texts, as well as human nature in general.

It is psychological. But in what way can the model above be legitimately considered *psychological*? This whole book is an attempt to answer that question, but a succinct response is to point out that the primary object of our interest here is not mathematics, chemistry, or society, not God, and not even the Bible, but the nature of individual human beings and their psychopathology and recovery, and the name for the science of those concerns is currently *psychology*, the study of the soul. Christian soul-care providers study the Bible not for its own sake but for the light it sheds on the nature of human beings and their well-being and improvement. A comprehensive Christian version of psychology should be rigorously empirical, experiential, philosophical and biblical, and it will have to deal with a vast range of topics, like brain-soul relations, genetics, beliefs, memory, rationality, emotion, motivation, social relations, virtues, developmental processes, the image of God, human agency, sin, personality, narrative and the effects of redemption, because these sorts of things constitute and shape human beings.

Some will resist calling the above discipline psychology. It could be called anthropology (as in the fields of philosophy and theology). But according to the majority of scholars currently working on the study of individual humans, their problems and their remediation, *psychology* is the designated term. So we will call this model psychology; it is just an example of *Christian* psychology.

The Nature of Human Nature

Perhaps a book with the above subject matter should somewhere have a thorough discussion regarding the ontology of human beings that underlies it. The reader will find some consideration of such matters within (especially in part two). However, less time will be spent on such matters than may be desirable. This is at least in part due to some skepticism on my part regarding our ability to resolve some of the conundrums regarding human nature. I suppose I am something of a "New Mysterian" (see McGinn, 2000)—one who questions whether humans have the cognitive capacity to be able to explain satisfactorily the relationship between the brain and the soul (though perhaps all I am questioning is whether *I* shall ever be able to understand it!). But I acknowledge that something needs to be said, before we embark.

The Bible and "common sense" have convinced me that the felt dichotomy between body and soul (including brain and mind)—universally common to human experience—is a fundamental distinction (Johnson, 1998a). Furthermore, there seems to me no way to make sense of this dichotomy, particularly the existence of the soul in the intermediate state (after death, but before the resurrection of the body), without a notion that the soul is some kind of immaterial substance. However, on the basis of a great deal of brain research, it would appear that God has established that in this age (in contrast to the intermediate state), the soul is thoroughly brain-dependent, by which I mean that everything the soul experiences (perceives, thinks, feels) and does has a physiological basis or correlate.

Nonetheless, positively, I also want to assert that both soul and brain are characterized by semiodiscursiveness, that is, somehow brain and soul are both a function of the speech of God. The creating-sustaining God holds all things together—material and immaterial—by the word of his power (Heb 1:3; see also Jn 1:3; Col 1:15). (As the reader will discover in part two, I believe that adult humans are actually constituted by four "orders of divine discourse.") Consequently, my position bears some similarity to that of Bishop George Berkeley and Jonathan Edwards, both of whom seemed to believe that everything in the creation was a function of the *ideas* of God.

In addition, the soul, though in some respects simple (e.g., it cannot be cut into parts), also appears to develop throughout life into a (metaphorically) "larger" and more complex dynamic structure—evidenced over the life span by an increasing number of memories and skills, greater knowledge-base, more complex reasoning processes, emotions and traits, a strengthening of virtues and so on, that altogether constitute an individual human being. In fact, as the structures of the soul develop, increasingly complex levels of organization appear to emerge, which can in turn influence lower levels, including brain-states, so that adult experience is qualitatively of a different order in certain key respects than childhood experience (most importantly, ethical and spiritual experience). Yet, somehow, all of the above complexity is still dependent in this life upon the maturation and experientially driven organization of the brain. Exactly how information in the brain is correlated to information in the soul and vice versa, and how it is passed from one to the other, no one today knows. Though it may be beyond our capacities to understand, we ought to work toward understanding the relationship between body and soul as well as possible.

As if this is not complicated enough, the Holy Spirit is the ultimate efficient cause of all this, an activity we call providence, and furthermore, he could intervene in these systems whenever he wants. But most of the time, he seems to be content to work with the created structures as they are, gradually transforming them by the facilitation of incremental Godward human activity (Phil 2:12-13). Consequently, the Holy Spirit is ultimately responsible for all human goodness in body and soul. Beyond these rather sketchy positions (and the elaborations in the book), I currently hesitate to go.

Outline of the Book

The book is divided into four parts and eighteen chapters. Part one examines the intellectual background to the current state of affairs in Christian soul care. In chapter one the Bible's claims to be God's teachings given to address the needs of the soul are presented, and it is concluded that the Bible is the primary soul care text for the Christian community.

The Christian tradition's use of the Bible is examined in the following chapter, from the early church fathers to the modern era, to show the reliance on the Bible that characterized historic Christian soul care, and also that the discomfort with the Bible demonstrated in the modern pastoral care movement—at its zenith in the mid-twentieth century—was fundamentally due to the influence of the modernist worldview and so was a radical departure from the Christian tradition. However, it is admitted that the modern pastoral care movement was attempting to respond to the increasingly impressive achievements of modern psychology, which were creating an epistemological and soul-care crisis for the contemporary church that has still not yet been adequately addressed.

In chapter three we examine the two major evangelical approaches to counseling that arose in the last half of the twentieth century. We might say they responded to that crisis in opposite ways: the integration movement sought to incorporate the discoveries of modern psychology in its soul care, while screening it with an evangelical theology (in contrast to the liberal theology that undergirded modern pastoral care), whereas the biblical counseling movement essentially rejected modern psychology and relied instead solely on the Bible for its soul-care resources. It is argued that both approaches have strengths the other lacks.

Part two attempts to develop a method for proceeding. There are two sets of texts that are important to the project of a Christian psychology in our day: the Bible and classics of the Christian tradition (based largely on the Bible) and those of modern psychology. The problem, of course, is that most of the contending parties assume that these two sets of texts are in certain respects incompatible. Chapter four defends some radical and contestable disciplinary claims: the study of the Bible must be understood again as a metadiscipline that addresses all of human life, in one way or another, and psychology must be less restrained by the methods and assumptions of naturalism and positivism than modern psychology conceives of it, and defined as simply the study of the nature of individual human beings—and open to any legitimate method of inquiry into its object. Such changes would free Christian psychology to use Scripture to aid in the study of its focus (admittedly a scandalous position from the standpoint of modern psychology). Rather than beginning with a dichotomy between psychology and theology or the Bible, in the approach taken in this book the real dichotomy facing the contemporary Christian soul-care provider is that between the modern and Christian *communities*. Having different worldviews (and disciplinary matrices and edification frameworks), both communities should view the task, sources and methods of psychology and soul care substantially differently from each other.

A major issue facing the project of a Christian psychology is figuring out how to properly interpret the most relevant texts. As established in chapter one, the foremost text for the Christian is the Bible. In chapter five, some of the features of Scripture, identified in the Reformation and post-Reformation eras, are examined for their relevance to the contemporary debate in the Christian counseling community regarding the role of the Bible. The Bible's authority and necessity in soul care, sufficiency in matters of salvation, and primacy in reference to other soul-care texts will be affirmed.

Given the primacy of Scripture, the next two chapters address some of the hermeneutics of reading: first, how to read the Bible with a view to the science of psychology and to contemporary soul care concerns (chap. 6), and second, how to read modern psychology texts Christianly and then how to translate them, where necessary, into Christian discourse (chap. 7). Part two ends with a short postscript exploring how a Christian psychology might arise and fit into the contemporary psychology scene.

Part three makes an ambitious attempt to describe a *semiodiscursive* model of created reality, as the expression of the Word of God and composed of signs and texts. For all its complexity, it is believed that such a model offers a promising way to understand human beings and their development, soul-problems and soul-healing *holistically*, and that will allow us to avoid the faulty dualisms that have haunted other Christian approaches to these matters. In chapter eight, the triune God's agenda of self-glorification is described as a communicative endeavor: God spoke into existence everything in the universe (sin excepted) and still maintains it by the word of his power. Upon close examination, the creation, then, would seem to be characterized by semiodiscursiveness: it is all a function of and signifies the Word of God.

The semiodiscursiveness that constitutes human life is examined in more detail in chapter nine, beginning with its simplest elements (words, emotions, images and actions) and culminating with its narrative contexts, the largest of which is the momentous drama of history that God is ultimately authoring, but within which normal adults are free, responsible actors and coauthors.

The next two chapters outline a multidimensional, holistic and hierarchical model of human nature. It will be suggested there that human beings are composed of four orders or levels of semiodiscursive meaning: biological, psychosocial, ethical and spiritual. It is believed that the structural dynamics of normal adults can be understood in terms of all four orders, and that the orders themselves are interrelated and interdependent.

The hierarchical relation of the four orders to each other is addressed in chapter eleven. The lower orders provide the grounding for the higher orders, which emerge out of the lower. However, the higher have greater significance in the eyes of God, since their meaningfulness is more explicitly related to him and his glory. There it will be suggested that Christian soul-care providers should work at the highest levels possible, but at the lowest levels necessary.

Part four is the real heart of the book, the most practical section in this theoretical work on Christian soul-care practice. Chapter twelve explains the foundational involvement of the Trinity in Christian soul care through the child of God's relation with the Father, union with the Son and indwelling by the Holy Spirit.

The following four chapters address aspects of the interior nature of Christian soul care. First, the encouragement of the Bible and the Christian tradition to "journey inward" is examined. This move of inwardness has three aspects, discussed in the next three chapters. The first involves the illumination of the current state of one's soul through self-examination. The next chapter concerns the recognition and dismantling of previously existing barriers that inhibit self-examination and the internalization of the signs of God. Human psychopathology is interpreted as a function of problems within the four, semiodiscursive orders: physiological deficits, psychosocial damage, ethical wrong-doing and sin. The third, discussed in chapter sixteen, entails the promotion of the internalization of the expressions of God in Scripture and the gospel, through the form of Christlike humans, submission to God's will and dipolar self-regulation skills.

In chapter seventeen we consider the immanent goal of Christian inwardness: the outward manifestation of Christlikeness in one's life, actions and relationships. Through the dialectical processes of inwardness and outwardness, the believer develops into the form of Christ, becoming more and more a living sign of God's glory. The final chapter addresses the major modalities that are available to Christian soul care that together provide a comprehensive set of means for delivering the word and form of God for the purpose of Christiformity: biomedical, cognitive-behavioral, relational, family-systems and group, symbolic/narrative, psychodynamic, experiential and character therapies, as well as spiritual direction. Let us begin.

Acknowledgments

It WOULD HAVE BEEN IMPOSSIBLE FOR ME to have written this book without the help of many others. Though intellectual influences are nearly impossible to trace, I want to mention (or confess) a few in order to give the reader some clues as to some of the places through which we will be traveling.

We must begin with the Bible. Sometimes the biblical writers are not recognized as authors by orthodox Christians, so strong is our persuasion that the Bible is God's Word, but it needs to be stated that the project guiding this book finds its earliest expression in the prophets and the apostles, with Paul's psychology being particularly valuable. Next, mention should be made of Augustine's philosophy of Christian thought and of God's salvific transformation of the soul, and his impact on Thomas Aquinas, John Calvin, Martin Luther and Abraham Kuyper, all of whom have profoundly affected my understanding of things. Many of the Puritans too have shaped my thought about the Christian life and the role of Scripture in healing the soul, as well as some of my practice, and Jonathan Edwards's influence can be seen throughout the book. It is hard to estimate the impact his thought has had on mine. Encountering Søren Kierkegaard in my thirties changed my life, and I am still recovering. At the same time, Cornelius Van Til's system of thought (particularly his notion of "limiting concepts") continues to have a significant impact on my thinking—though my embrace of Van Til's reformed fundamentalism was nearly cured by Kierkegaard. While I am ambivalent about Karl Barth's system as a whole, his stunning grasp of major features of God's nature and his revelation in Christ and Scripture have compelled me to appreciation and study. In addition, over the past half decade Hans Urs von Balthasar's corpus has been both rewarding and stimulating to me. I admit that it is hard to imagine a discussion among this diverse group of people, but, thanks to reading, just such a dialogue explains a good part of my intellectual journey.

I also admit that many modern psychologists have contributed to my thinking, but the four who have probably impacted me the most, both directly and through those whom they influenced, are Lev Vygotsky, Jean Piaget, Albert Bandura and, yes, Sigmund Freud. While I have always sought to read them critically—as a *Christian* reader—these brilliant thinkers and investigators have undoubtedly shaped me constructively in what they discerned and wrote about human beings and their development. On the other hand, in spite of tremendous theoretical and methodological differences, they were unified in their commitment to the development of a modern, *secular* psychology, so their influence on me can also be seen in their motivating me to work toward a psychology that is ultimately very different from theirs.

Of those living authors whose writings have helped me, I must single out John Frame, Alvin Plantinga, Alisdair MacIntyre, Charles Taylor, Paul Vitz, Kevin Vanhoozer, David Bentley Hart, Ellen Charry, Jay Adams, Gary Collins and Bruce Narramore. I am even more indebted to the teachers who have shaped my thinking in one way or another, beginning with John Piper, Amar Djaballah, Mary Van Leeuwen, Mary Vandergoot, George Marsden, Evelyn Oka and James Gavelek. Of special importance is Wayne Joosse, who has been a tremendous encourager over the years. Among great conversation partners who have enriched me, I would like to mention my wife, Rebekah, to whom this book is dedicated, Richard Plass, Chuck Hannaford, P. J. Watson, Diane Langberg, Keith Whitfield, Sam Williams, Timothy Sisemore, Phil Monroe, Bryan Maier, Stan Jones, C. Stephen Evans, Leigh Conver, Mike Mangis, Steven Sandage, Dee Reju, Crista Holt, Unhye Kwon, Lia Vassiliades, Robert Cheong, Nate and Sarah Collins, and Don Johnson. Special thanks are due to my friends at IGNIS, the German Institute for Christian Psychology, especially Kathrin Halder, Werner and Agnes May, and Wolfram Soldan. Their labors for eighteen years before we in America ever came to know of them have been an inspiration to me. My apologies to others that I should have mentioned, but did not.

I am also grateful to those who have given me feedback on parts of this book. Of singular note are Robert Roberts, Ray Anderson and Siang Yang Tan, who read through the manuscript and gave me pointed advice (much of which I heeded). Robert Roberts's significant influence goes back much further. Though a philosopher by trade, he took on psychology as an avocation and has been pointing the way toward a Christian psychology for a couple of decades. He and Steve Evans were the first to challenge me to consider the viability of the project of a Christian psychology. David Powlison gave me an extraordinary amount of feedback on a couple of chapters I was struggling with; I was stunned by his kind lavishness. I am also indebted to the following persons for giving me comments on chapters or sections: Keith Whitfield, Mark McMinn, Sam Williams, Tom Schreiner, Bob Kellemen, Bruce Ware, Timothy Sisemore, Ed Welch, Russell Moore, Nathan Joyce and Joshua Creason. I also want to express my appreciation for the many Southern Seminary and Psychological Studies Institute students who read various chapters in my classes over the past five years but must go nameless. Special mention should be made of those who helped with the indexes: Nate and Sara Collins, Brett and Rachael Vaden, and Carrie Beohm; and with the bibliography: Rebekah Johnson and Unhye Kwon. The editors of InterVarsity Press, especially Joel Scandrett, Allison Rieck and Andy LePeau, have been a delight and encouragement all the way. And I also want to thank Dr. Albert Mohler and the trustees of the Southern Baptist Theological Seminary for granting me a sabbatical during which time I worked on the manuscript.

PART ONE

Background to the Current Predicament

THE BIBLE SHOWS THAT THE CARE OF SOULS has been an ongoing concern of Jews and Christians ever since God began calling people to himself. The Bible itself provides the basic soul-care framework for the Christian church, and one of the church's most important tasks has been the application of the Bible's teachings to the ongoing needs of believers throughout the ages. In the modern era, the church abdicated much of this role, while modern psychiatry and psychology usurped it, and this has led to an epistemological and soul-care crisis for the church. Over the last fifty years this has developed into what might be called the Christian counseling wars, as Christians of various stripes have come to different understandings of how the Bible ought to operate within Christian soul care in light of the enormous literature put out by proponents of modern psychology.

1

A Place for the Bible in Christian Soul Care

WHAT SINGLE BOOK HAS HAD THE BIGGEST IMPACT in the history of Western civilization? It is hard to think of a more viable candidate than the Bible.[1] Some of its influence may be hard to trace, but think of its direct effects on Western theology and philosophy; cultural forms like art, music and literature; the creation of social roles like monk and nun, priest and pastor, and religious settings like monasteries and churches; ethical proscriptions regarding homosexuality and abortion, and prescriptions regarding the care of the poor and the mentally ill; and then consider its indirect effects on the development of social institutions like hospitals and universities; the spread of literacy after the Reformation; the advances of the scientific revolution; the rationale for democracy; and liberation movements like the abolition of slavery and equality for women. In the words of MacCulloch (2003), the Bible has been "an explosive, unpredictable force in every age."

Over the centuries, however, one of the Bible's most significant roles in the West has been its influence in the care of souls. As we shall see, the Bible claims to be a soul-care book, and over the nearly twenty centuries since its completion, it has consistently fulfilled that claim in the minds, hearts, lives and relationships of Christians. The subtext of this book consists of an exploration of the Bible's relevance for soul care. However, the main concern of this book is broader: a description of the major foundations of a specifically Christian model for interpreting and researching human beings, their problems in living and the care of their souls—a model informed by a careful reading of all relevant texts (including those of modern psychology) but guided throughout by a Christian hermeneutic. The Bible is given great attention in this book because of its pivotal role in this larger undertaking, since, according to Christianity, it provides the hermeneutical key for the rest of life, especially the care of the soul. On the way to developing a modest, yet ambitious *Christian* model of psychology and soul care (modest because it is necessarily incomplete; ambitious because it aims at being scientific), I will also examine the current state of Christian counseling; a rudimentary Christian philosophy of psychology; and a general hermeneutic for critically interpreting non-Christian psychology texts. Hence, the size of this book. In this first chapter, we will hear from the Bible itself regarding its role in such an endeavor.

The Soul-Care Agenda of the Bible

The central, underlying thrust of the whole Bible is an articulation of the glory of the triune God (see Edwards, 1765/1989; Balthasar, 1989a, 1991). From Gregory of Nyssa and Augustine through Bernard, Aquinas, Julian of Norwich, Luther, Calvin, van Mastricht and Edwards, to Bavinck, Barth and Balthasar, the classical Christian tradition has recognized that this goal, though strictly speaking extrinsic to human nature, is nonetheless wondrously realized through human participation in its actualization. According to Edwards (1765/1989), for example, the *true* happiness of human beings is directly correlated to their sharing in the manifestation of God's glory, finding their ultimate fulfillment in relationship with God.[2] Julian of Norwich (trans. 1977) put this succinctly: "[my] intention was . . . to live more for God's glory and my profit" (p. 133). When the Bible is read this way, its theocentric agenda is understood to be a project that simultaneously (though secondarily) promotes human well-being.

What unites these dual goals is the conformity of believers into the image of Christ. Jesus Christ, the Son of God, is *the* image of God (2 Cor 4:4; Col 1:15), the radiance of God's glory and the exact representation of God's nature (Heb 1:3). All humans were created in God's image, but this is a developmental goal as well as a feature of human nature (Pannenberg, 1985), and human sin damaged the image, causing fallen humans to resemble God much less than is God's design. As the Real Man (Barth, 1960; Bonhoeffer, 1955), Christ is the human ideal, so he is the Form toward which human beings are supposed to be moving (Balthasar, 1982-1991). The Bible is a postlapsarian book (written after the Fall into sin), given in part to help *re-form* the damaged human, not just into a more accurate image of God, but into resemblance with Christ, the perfect Form of humanity. This scriptural re-formation provides a singular display of God's glory.

One must concede that the genres of the Bible are such that its soul-reforming agenda is not always self-evident. One can conceive of a more explicit, comprehensive and systematic soul-care text, perhaps organized around specific disorders, personality constructs or therapy modalities (e.g., see Bonger & Beutler, 1995). But classical Christians take the inspired form of the Bible with great seriousness, doing their best not to force it into some alien mold. It is what it is, so there is nothing for Christians to do but relish the challenge its actual form presents and endeavor to read it appropriately in pursuit of a biblically based, scientifically sophisticated model of Christian soul care for the glory of God. In what follows, we look at three lines of evidence for the Bible's pervasive soul-care agenda.

A Brief Biblical Theology of Soul Care

The entire canon shows a concern with human well-being with reference to God. To begin with, the Bible was composed by writers who were deeply aware that something was radically wrong with humanity. We read first that God ordered the lives of the first humans with both positive directives ("Be fruitful and multiply, and fill the earth, and subdue it; and rule over [it]" [Gen 1:28]) and negative ("from the tree of the knowledge of good and evil you shall not eat" [Gen 2:17]). Following the word of an alternative way, they disobeyed, and as the consequent judgments of God make clear (and also symbolize), on account of their newfound, relative independence from God's word, humans will live in great distress. The first psychological outcomes of the Fall mentioned in the text are shame and defensiveness (blame-shifting). Cain's story shows that when fallen humans interpret God's actions antagonistically—in self-destructive ways—they experience a perverse anguish, which leads to violence against others. Within a number of generations, God grew greatly disheartened by the tragic and morally deformed psychological state of humanity: "The LORD saw that the wickedness of man was great on the earth, and that every intent of the thoughts of his heart was only evil continually. The LORD was sorry that He had made man on the earth, and He was grieved in His heart" (Gen 6:5-6). This very early passage tells us God experienced "pain in his heart" (Hamilton, 1990, p. 274) upon seeing into the human hearts of that time. God's reaction flowed from his own nature (the verb *'atsab*, in a Hithpael stem, indicates that God brought it upon himself), and he responded with punishment (on that occasion, the flood), because of his intrinsic abhorrence of human unlikeness to himself and the resultant compromise of his glory—we can surmise from the rest of Scripture.

Nevertheless, after the flood, in spite of the ongoing pain God would have kept feeling (things, after all, did not really get better), he continued to speak words of hope and words of judgment to humans. The rest of the Bible tells of how God, in a variety of ways, rescues and heals humanity from their psychological and spiritual predicament.

Soul-healing through the Old Testament: Preparation by a divine ethics. The text of the Old Testament was written after God had established a special covenant with the people of Israel, with that covenant laid out in the Torah (the first five books of the Old Testament) and the rest of the Old Testament based upon it. To understand the Old Testament properly for our purposes, we need to consider its formative function in the history of humanity and how it was appropriated throughout the pre-Christian era. Primitive humanity had to contend with its desires, some that were largely biologically based (e.g., for pleasure and away from pain, and for food, sex and attachment) and others that were more socially constructed (for power, possessions and relationship), but all of which were grounded in a created human nature that was corrupted by its fallenness. As a result, humans sought out gods other than their Creator and were inclined to follow their desires with some abandon. So to prepare humanity for his primary soul-healing intervention (the coming of the Son of God to earth), God established his covenant with Israel through his giving of the *law*—normative language that also reveal in part humanity's purpose and fulfillment in God. The text of the Torah included civil, ceremonial and moral codes to regulate thoughts, desires and human relationships in a theocentric direction, as well as narratives describing the struggles and progress this covenantal revelation and relationship engendered in the lives of the Israelites.

The process of receiving and internalizing the law of God was slow and halting, and it ultimately failed. Specific individuals sought to embrace the law as best as they could (e.g., Moses, Joshua, David and the prophets), but as a people the Israelites struggled morally throughout most of the time period recorded in the Old Testament, a story, painstakingly described in long narratives, that is useful in revealing God's character, the various human responses to God's word and the consequences of those responses. In continuity with the Mosaic law, the prophets were raised up to restate and elaborate on God's law to his people in light of their current actions, and to call them back to the covenant. These nouthetic teachers cried out against Israel's idolatry and sins, and called them to self-examination and repentance, further revealing God's holiness, as well as his fidelity to his covenant-people in spite of their waywardness. The Old Testament canon reveals that God is *for* his people, by being vehemently opposed to that which undermines his glory and destroys their well-being. The emotional tone of much of the Old Testament is decidedly negative, but it aptly communicates the desperate psychospiritual situation of sinful humans before God and challenges readers to engage in searching self-examination. At the same time, the prophets also gave hope, by pointing to a better era and covenant to come (Jer 31:33). The fact that much of the last half of the Old Testament looks ahead to a coming messianic redemption provides an underlying degree of optimism in the face of the overwhelming failure of the Old Covenant (Dempster, 2000).

What was the Old Testament's soul-care significance? Manifold. First, its norms and narratives consistently made plain the centrality that God and his glory were to have in the human heart and community, as well as God's relentless opposition to his diminution by humans. In a diversity of ways, the Old Testament declared that there is no more important value for human well-being than God's supremacy. Second, many of the law's cultic regulations underscored and gave divine sanction to the sense of uncleanness and brokenness that is endemic to humanity. Third, the Old Testament documents gave divine hope by making clear that God was covenantally bound to the Israelites and that he would pursue them with all his might for the sake of their well-being (in spite of their resistance to him!). Fourth, the account of this pursuit offered an elaborate narrative in which later Israelites could see themselves, a rich and significant story that doubtless contributed to the formation of their identity, individually and corporately (and into the present). Fifth, the law provided a well-articulated moral framework that could be disseminated throughout the community and would aid in the inhibition of the self- and other-destructive possibilities of unchecked, fallen human desires. Sixth, the law prepared the way for Christ by providing a description of the ideal human form toward which fallen humans were to move (love of God and neighbor), so that the ultimate failure of the Israelites (recorded in the exilic narratives) to fulfill that ideal cast a pall upon human nature that was supposed to have fostered greater self-awareness and that pointed to the need for divine forgiveness and transcendent help. We are told in the New Testament that the law was given to show us our lostness (Rom 7:7-25; Gal 3:23-24). But this last point also makes clear the insufficiency of the Old Testament, in and of itself. It is not the complete canon; it required a complementary and fulfilling text. As a preparatory word, it necessarily fell short of the clarity and fullness of the revelation of the gospel found in the New Testament (Vos, 1949). Even so, as the inspired record of the "covenant of law" (Robertson, 1980) and the history of its appropriation by the Israelites, the Old Testament is supposed to be formative for the development of later believers.

Soul-healing through the New Testament: Fulfillment by a divine gospel. One of those Israelites was Jesus Christ (Work, 2002). As a human he was shaped by the texts he inspired as God, and these words, along with his genetic endowment, life experiences (especially his family life) and choices, contributed to his becoming a perfected human (Heb 5:9), the blessed Form of humanity, the loving, obedient Child of God. In contrast to Adam and Eve, he endured a rigorous, soul-building forty-day period of temptation, after which he embarked on a ministry that manifested the Form: teaching reparative truth, loving sinners and the weak of this world, opposing the betrayal of God by religious hypocrites, and healing the sick. This last "sign" (see Jn 4:54; 6:14; 12:18) would seem to be symbolic of his overall salvific mission of restoring body *and* soul to wholeness. The Gospels describe the Word narratively and portray him as a shepherd of sheep (Mt 9:36; Jn 10:11), a physician of sinners (Mk 2:17), a friend (Mt 11:19; Jn 15:13-15), as well as a prophet who aggressively resisted religious pretense (Mt 23; Jn 2:13-17), one who held forth the highest imaginable standards of care for others (Mt 5; Lk 6:27-38) and exemplified a resolutely theocentric approach to his own suffering. Such is the Form of the God-human, the preeminent manifestation of God's character and human well-being.

As the Old Covenant texts revealed and the Gospel texts underscored, humans have fallen short of God's law and design and are incapable in themselves of making the kinds of changes necessary for Godward wholeness. A new way, a new covenant, was promised in the Old Testament. It involved a spiritual transcription of the law on the heart (Jer 31:31-34; 32:38-40; Ezek 36:25-32), but all that this entailed was not clearly revealed until after the evil blindness and bondage of humanity was most fully manifested in the death of Israel's (and the world's) Messiah. The Gospels and the rest of the New Testament depict in a variety of ways the nature of the New Covenant in Christ. The good news of the gospel is an articulation of the free gift of divine salvation and soul-healing, accomplished through Christ's life, death and resurrection and offered to all who consent to it from the heart.

It was the task of the apostles to further develop the psychotherapeutic (soul-healing) import of Christ's actions on our behalf in their letters to the earliest churches (see e.g., Roberts, 2001). More than simply manifesting the Form of God, Christ's life, death and resurrection *communicated* the Form to humans through union with Christ and faith in the word describing it. By believing the gospel, humans are united with Christ in his death and resurrection (Rom 6:1-11) and so are brought into a radically different place of meaning and significance. They are regenerated and renewed (Tit 3:5); their sins are forgiven (Heb 9); they are given the righteousness of God as a gift (Rom 5:17); they are adopted into God's family (Rom 8:15-17; 1 Jn 3:2); they are indwelt by the Holy Spirit; they are chosen, holy and beloved (Col 3:12); they are a part of the new creation (2 Cor 5:17) and aliens of the old (1 Pet 2:11); and they are becoming lovers of God and of neighbors. Such descriptions and expositions of the meaning of Christ's life, death and resurrection, if taken seriously, are explosive in their soul-care significance: they legitimize an exchange of self-definitions, from broken sinner to holy sojourner—traveling in this life from brokenness and sinfulness to greater wholeness in God. They provide the God-breathed basis for a radically new set of relationships, identity, story (past, present and future), attributional framework and motivational orientation. These descriptions are given to in-form and re-form the souls and lives of those who believe.

The Old and New Testament Scriptures together are what Charry (1997) calls *aretegenic*, that is, they have a virtue-shaping function as the textual means of realizing the ethicospiritual excellence known as the Form of Christ. With the Holy Spirit's aid, the Word of God reconfigures the minds of believers, recalibrates their hearts and reshapes their lives, moving them, communally, into an increasingly theocentric way of life that gradually comes to resemble, as individuals, the Form of Christ and, as a body, the communion of the Trinity. Preaching, teaching and counseling are needed for this reformulation because "becoming a Christian [is] a confusing undertaking, for one must sort out one's old self from one's new, God-given status" (Charry, p. 43), a process of distinguishing that continues throughout this age.

The Bible's Teachings About Its Own Aretegenic Function

The Bible is not silent about its soul-shaping value. However, before examining those self-attestations, we should think through the *discursive* implications of Genesis 2—3.

As mentioned above, God issued a number of commands to the first humans. The prohibition not to eat from the tree of the knowledge of good and evil (Gen 2:16-17) seems to have been given as a test of belief (Vos, 1949). Throughout the Scriptures, God's words are assumed to be trustworthy, since he is absolute goodness. The serpent's temptation was hermeneutic in nature and consisted of calling into question the veracity of God's words and the goodness of his intentions. Until the serpent spoke, there was one word and one way (Bonhoeffer, 1955). The serpent's words articulated and constituted an alternative way of interpretation, one that reframed or recontextualized God's words. On account of the serpent's interpretive distortions, the tree looked different. Now, instead of being a tree from which it was unthinkable to eat or touch (Gen 3:3), "the woman saw that the tree was good for food, and that it was a delight to the eyes, and that the tree was desirable to make one wise" (Gen 3:6). Words can alter our perceptions and attitudes. As many Christians have noted, the first sin was instigated by disbelief in God's word (a *dissent*) and disobedience to his command, made possible by belief in an anti-theistic word that posited meaning contrary to God's interpretive system. God's speech is of fundamental importance to human well-being. Humanity committed the most egregious action when it rejected God's word and cast itself into misery (Gen 3:16-17; both the man and the woman experience *pain* as a result of their sin, the same root word that describes God's response to sin in Gen 6:6). In contrast, human well-being is found in hearing, accepting and obeying God's word (Anderson, 1982). This foundational teaching-narrative that there is a linguistic basis for psychopathology undergirds all that follows in Scripture and helps to explain Scripture's restorative force.

Psalm 19. After referring to the nonverbal "speech" of God's creation in Psalm 19:1-6, the psalmist wrote of God's covenantal speech to his people:

> The law of the LORD is perfect, restoring the soul;

The testimony of the LORD is sure, making wise the simple.
The precepts of the LORD are right, rejoicing the heart;
The commandment of the LORD is pure, enlightening the eyes.
The fear of the LORD is clean, enduring forever;
The judgments of the LORD are true; they are righteous altogether.
They are more desirable than gold, yes, than much fine gold;
Sweeter also than honey and the drippings of the honeycomb.
Moreover, by them Your servant is warned;
In keeping them there is great reward.
Who can discern his errors? Acquit me of hidden faults.
Also keep back Your servant from presumptuous sins;
Let them not rule over me;
Then I will be blameless,
And I shall be acquitted of great transgression.
Let the words of my mouth and the meditation of my heart
Be acceptable in Your sight,
O LORD, my rock and my Redeemer. (Ps 19:7-14)

The psychospiritual benefits of God's words are here highly extolled. The references to law, commandment and precepts show that the psalmist is referring to the Torah. The fact that God's law (Ps 19:7) is treated synonymously with the fear of the Lord (Ps 19:9) suggests that all of these verses refer to the received and implemented words of God that issue in the fear of the Lord, the beginning of wisdom (Prov 1:7). We would expect to read that God's commands enlighten and make one wise, soul-states having great therapeutic significance; but perhaps more notable is their ability to restore the soul (Ps 19:7; see also Ps 23:3) and rejoice the heart (Ps 19:8). The psalmist believed God's words heal the soul and bring it to its happy fulfillment. According to this passage, if one thinks rightly, one sees God's words as the greatest of blessings. The psalm concludes by linking these blessings with the self-reflection of the psalmist. God's words enlighten and provoke the receiver to confession. "Cleanse my unconscious," he says to God, in so many words, "so that my meditations may be pure enough for you." It shows an unusual degree of self-awareness—promoted, it would seem, by the glad reception of God's directives.

Psalm 119. Psalm 119 is an even longer digest of striking affirmations of God's words. We will only look at a selection.

How blessed are those whose way is blameless,

Who walk in the law of the LORD.
How blessed are those who observe His testimonies,
Who seek Him with all their heart. (Ps 119:1-2)

This psalm opens with a declaration that human well-being (blessedness) is found in adhering to God's written words—especially his commands—and seeking him from deep within. These sentiments are reiterated in other places:

I have inherited Your testimonies forever,
For they are the joy of my heart. (Ps 119:111)

and

Trouble and anguish have come upon me;
Yet Your commandments are my delight. (Ps 119:143)

God's law is a supreme source of human happiness, even in the midst of distress. Psychological consolation is derived from his Word:

This is my comfort in my affliction,
That Your word has revived me. (Ps 119:50)

I have remembered Your ordinances from of old, O LORD,
And comfort myself. (Ps 119:52)

O may Your lovingkindness comfort me,
According to Your word to Your servant. (Ps 119:76)

My eyes fail with longing for Your word,
While I say, "When will You comfort me?" (Ps 119:82)

If Your law had not been my delight,
Then I would have perished in my affliction. (Ps 119:92)

In various ways, God's words and commands provide security and peace, and the psalmist's reflections on them constitute a type of coping strategy.

The words of God also lead to a theocentric focus:

Let my lips utter praise,
For You teach me Your statutes. (Ps 119:171)

They lead away from sin (the biblical concept of psychopathology).[3]

Establish my footsteps in Your word,
And do not let any iniquity have dominion over me. (Ps 119:133)

Yet, in spite of the strongly legal tone of this psalm, the psalmist sees a surprising interdependence between God's law and God's love. Both are sources of encouragement in distress:

> Revive me according to Your lovingkindness,
> So that I may keep the testimony of Your mouth. (Ps 119:88)

> I am exceedingly afflicted;
> Revive me, O LORD, according to Your word. (Ps 119:107; see also Ps 119:154)

> Revive me, O LORD, according to Your lovingkindness. (Ps 119:159)

The psalm ends on an unexpected note:

> I have gone astray like a lost sheep; seek Your servant,
> For I do not forget Your commandments. (Ps 119:176)

In this great worship song, we learn that the law leads to self-examination, humility and confession.

We find in Psalm 19 and throughout Psalm 119 an affirmation of the role of God's moral statutes in fostering human well-being. This emphasis on commandment is typical of the Old Testament (and of course not absent in the New). This teaching is foundation building, in that it underscores God's centrality and lordship over his people, while providing moral structure that has to be internalized for human maturation to occur, and this emphasis on morality is a necessary preparation for the gospel. But more broadly, these two psalms are a scriptural assessment of the soul-care value of an earlier portion of Scripture.

2 Timothy 3:15-17. Centuries later, the apostle Paul gave a strong commendation of the soul-care value of the entire Old Testament:

> From childhood you have known the sacred writings which are able to give you the wisdom that leads to salvation through faith which is in Christ Jesus. All Scripture is inspired by God and profitable for teaching, for reproof, for correction, for training in righteousness; so that the man of God may be adequate, equipped for every good work. (2 Tim 3:15-17)

The pastoral epistles, from which this passage comes, deal with foundational teachings for the church, and here we have the most important of the Bible's self-attestations in the New Testament, and instruction that implies the Bible is directly relevant to counseling (Adams, 1979; Jones & Butman, 1991; Mack,

1997). In the context, Paul was warning Timothy that false teachers ("imposters," 2 Tim 3:13, *goētes*) would be coming to deceive the church. In contrast, Timothy was told to "continue in the things you have learned" (2 Tim 3:14), which were based on the Old Testament, the "sacred writings," texts that were human but nonetheless "holy" (meaning "set apart"). Their unique status is due to their being *theopneustos,* a word often translated "inspired" but which literally means "God-breathed." Scripture is the product of God's creative breath, composed of expressions that proceeded, as it were, right from God's own mouth (Murray, 1946). While Paul recognized the human authorship of Scripture (e.g., Rom 10:5, 19), the "sacred writings" were absolutely unique among human books: they consist of the very oracles of God. And why were they given? In Scripture is found the wisdom that leads to salvation (*sōtēria,* "deliverance"; Arndt & Gingrich, 1957) in Christ. The Old Testament consists of wise teachings that point to Christ and guide us to eternal life (when read *Christianly*: through faith in Christ; see Hanson, 1982).[4]

Paul next expanded on this general commendation. The Old Testament, he said, is profitable (or useful, *ōphelimos*) for a range of soul-improving activities: teaching, reproof, correction and training in righteousness. Paul taught Timothy that reading the Bible is beneficial; it is good for the soul. It would make him adequate *(artios),* that is, "complete, capable, proficient, or able to meet all demands" (Arndt & Gingrich, p. 110), which, when combined with the phrase "equipped *(exērtismenos)* for every good work" reveals the Scripture's primary aretegenic Form-function: it is supremely useful for the reformation of character; it is an agent of virtue, contributing to the ability to act in a godly way in every type of condition or situation.

Paul extols the Bible's vital importance for human maturation (and so for Christian counseling). Four specific uses of the Bible follow: *teaching (didaskalia),* that is, instruction regarding God, the human plight and salvation; *reproof (elegmos),* the identification of error or sin; *correction* (*epanorthōsis,* restoration, improvement), we might say, revelation regarding the ways of life that exemplify godliness or Christian maturity; and *training in righteousness* (*paideia* [giving guidance] *tēn en dikaiosynē* [uprightness]), guidelines for how to attain godliness in this life. Understanding Scripture promotes our understanding of God, ourselves and the way of salvation, so it is indispensable for our psychospiritual well-being (and for Christian soul care).

2 Peter 1:2-4. In another passage often cited in conjunction with 2 Timothy 3:16-17, the apostle Peter[5] stated:

> Grace and peace be multiplied to you in the knowledge of God and of Jesus our Lord; seeing that his divine power has granted to us everything pertaining to life and godliness, through the true knowledge of Him who called us by His own glory and excellence. For by these He has granted to us His precious and magnificent promises, in order that by them you might become partakers of the divine nature, having escaped the corruption that is in the world by lust.

In this grammatically complicated passage, Peter wrote that everything necessary for life and godliness is gained through the knowledge of God and Jesus, all of which God has promised. Since the Bible is the primary textual repository of the knowledge of God, as well as of God's promises, the Scriptures should be understood to play a central role in the spiritual growth to which Peter referred. However, Scripture is not explicitly referred to. Calvin (1578/1979) suggested that the source of the knowledge of God and his promises referred to in this passage is the gospel.

Regardless, the real emphasis of this passage is on God's power. Peter says *that* is the *source* of everything important that we need in order to grow in grace, so that Calvin (1578/1979) believed that the "everything" which we have been granted consists of "the peculiar endowments of the new and spiritual life" (p. 369). So then, the knowledge of God is the *means* of God's power in the Christian life as well as the communication of God's characteristics (*physis*, nature). And since Scripture best reveals such knowledge, we can properly infer from this passage that preaching and prayerful meditation on Scripture should promote Christlikeness in a corrupt world.

Romans 15:1-4. Just prior to this passage, Paul had argued that believers who are strong in their faith must have regard for those who are weak, who could stumble at the more mature behavior of the strong. Then he wrote:

> Now we who are strong ought to bear the weaknesses of those without strength and not just please ourselves. Each of us is to please his neighbor for his good, to his edification. For even Christ did not please Himself; but as it is written, "The reproaches of those who reproached You fell on Me." For whatever was written in earlier times was written for our instruction, so that through perseverance and the encouragement of the Scriptures we might have hope.

Paul here appealed to the Roman Christians to live their lives with the well-being of their brothers and sisters in mind, and he pointed to the example of Christ, who bore the suffering of the cross for the sake of his people (Dunn, 1988). Christ's life is "a pattern and model for the church" (Schreiner, 1998, p. 748). Paul quoted an Old Testament Scripture that he applied to Christ, and then he drew the more general observation that such Scriptures were given to teach us, for the purpose of promoting our continuing in the faith (and so developing proven character, Rom 5:4) and granting hope through a sense of consolation (or strength and comfort), psychospiritual blessings that derive from the teaching of Scripture (*graphōn* is a genitive of source). Again, we see that Paul understood the Old Testament to be the means of communicating positive affective dynamics that led to Christlikeness manifested in the mutual love of others in the body of Christ.

Colossians 1:25-29. Paul discusses another important mode of the word of God in Colossians 1:25-29.

> Of this church I was made a minister according to the stewardship from God bestowed on me for your benefit, so that I might fully carry out the preaching of the word of God, that is the mystery which has been hidden from the past ages and generations; but has now been manifested to His saints, to whom God willed to make known what is the riches of the glory of this mystery among the Gentiles, which is Christ in you, the hope of glory. We proclaim Him, admonishing every man and teaching every man with all wisdom, so that we may present every man complete in Christ. And for this purpose also I labor, striving according to His power, which mightily works within me.

Here Paul points out that his apostolic ministry involved preeminently the preaching of the word of God. However, this preaching did not consist of quoting Old Testament texts, but rather refers to a verbal exposition of the message of Christ, the *kerygma* (Mounce, 1986), the word that had not been fully revealed in the past but was manifested now in Christ's life, death and resurrection (see also Acts 13:5, 46; 18:11). We learn here that the word of God is not to be identified exclusively with Scripture; in this usage the "word of God" is the central message of Scripture, the gospel of Jesus Christ. Paul then highlights what for him was a core theme of this verbal condensation of the word of God: the indwelling of Christ in the believer (and among the body of Christ, the church). Paul calls the abiding of Christ in the believer the "hope of glory," that is, Christ's indwelling is the ground for the believer's eternal participation in the glory of God. So the gospel provides a sense of security and stability that is an anchor for the soul. Paul also vigorously proclaimed Christ and his work, and the goal of this teaching was to "present every man complete [*teleion,* perfect] in Christ." Therefore, teaching about Christ brings about soul change, eventually leading to a complete conformity to the image of Christ in heaven, as a result of union with Christ (a bilateral union: the believer in Christ and Christ in the believer). So here we learn that the spoken gospel brings immense and everlasting benefits to the human soul.

Ephesians 4:11-16. This is the last passage we will look at in this section. After bringing up the topic of gifts to the church, Paul wrote:

> And [God] gave some as apostles, and some as prophets, and some as evangelists, and some as pastors and teachers, for the equipping of the saints for the work of service, to the building up of the body of Christ; until we all attain to the unity of the faith, and of the knowledge of the Son of God, to a mature man, to the measure of the stature which belongs to the fullness of Christ. As a result, we are no longer to be children, tossed here and there by waves and carried about by every wind of doctrine, by the trickery of men, by craftiness in deceitful scheming; but speaking the truth in love, we are to grow up in all aspects into him, who is the head, even Christ, from whom the whole body, being fitted and held together by that which every joint supplies, according to the proper working of each individual part, causes the growth of the body for the building up of itself in love.

Paul does not mention the Scriptures here, but the gifts to which he refers are all "Ministers of the Word" (Barth, 1974, p. 482), either those who themselves wrote Scripture (apostles and prophets) or those who are called to communicate its message (evangelists, pastors and teachers). So we may infer, at the very least, that when Paul wrote of what God gave the church to help foster its maturation, he had in the back of his mind the content of Scripture, the inspired, infallible record of the message of these gifts to the church. Consider further the fruit of their labors: "the equipping of the saints for the work of service, to the building up of the body of Christ" (Eph 4:12). The ministers do this through their teaching, and the goal of that teaching is knowledge, that is, the "knowledge of the Son of God" (see also Jn 17:3; 2 Pet 1:3-4). Paul went on to say that the outcome of that ministry is a maturity and wisdom that keeps the saints from being tossed about by "every wind of doctrine, by the trickery of men, by craftiness in deceitful scheming"; instead, they will have learned to speak "the truth in love." Paul is teaching that the truths of the gospel lead to Christian discernment, growth and maturity. So, while the Scriptures are not explicitly mentioned, we are warranted in concluding that when the final New Testament canon would be formed, the writings it contained would perform the same functions as its authors and the other deliverers of its soul- and community-changing message.

Earlier in the chapter Paul pleaded with the Ephesians to maintain their unity as the body of Christ. Paul continues with that theme in Ephesians 4:11-16 by arguing that the ministers were given to promote unity through the maturation of the saints. This developmental goal is variously described as attaining to "the unity of the faith" and "the knowledge of the Son of God" (Eph 4:13), growing up "in all aspects into Christ" (Eph 4:15), and becoming a whole body, each part fitted together and properly working, causing "the growth of the body for the building up of itself in love" (Eph 4:16). The goal of Christian and pastoral soul care then is thoroughly interpersonal. It entails a communal unity in faith, through the personal, sweet knowledge of Jesus, such that we all grow into his likeness, everyone moving, little by little, into his image, helped by each other's love.

Paul was thinking developmentally and encouraging the Ephesians to grow in unity by becoming increasing alike through a co-transformation, by the truths of God's Word, leading to a mutual, reciprocal edifying of one another in love. The dual importance of God's Word and the church in the fostering of psychospiritual development could hardly be more strongly stated. The canon is now closed, and we look to the Scriptures as the permanent, inerrant record of God's Word to us, but, in addition to the Scriptures, there is a fundamental role that both Christian teachers and laypersons play in promoting this Christlikeness. The mature Christian pastor, counselor and layperson are all supposed to communicate and promote both truth and love.

Let us turn next to examine some of the biblical teachings relevant for this task.

Some Explicit Soul-Care Teachings in the Bible

The last focus of this chapter concerns the many themes derived from the content of the Bible that lead to the resolution of some of the main problems of our souls as well as the experience of positive affect and the practice of virtuous behavior, as we learn how to embrace such themes more fully and deeply. Helping others go deeper with these teachings is, of course, what makes distinctly Christian soul care a *practice* (MacIntyre, 1984; Murphy, Kallenberg & Nation, 1997)—if not an art—that itself requires virtue, rather than just the communication of intellectual information.

The perfectly good God. First and foremost, Scripture teaches us about God. Paul wrote of "the glorious gospel of the blessed God" (1 Tim 1:11). The Greek word for "blessed" *(makarios)* conveys something akin to "happy" (Arndt & Gingrich, 1957) or "perfectly blissful" (Guthrie, 1957), and the Bible portrays God as being completely content, fulfilled and joyful: "enter into the *joy* of your master" (Mt 25:23, italics added). There is no hint of deficit in him, no emptiness, neediness or misery. On the contrary, in the words of theologians, God is self-existent and self-sufficient (Bavinck, 2004), and the source of all else. "In Him we live and move and exist" (Acts 17:28). "From Him and through Him and to Him are all things. To Him be the glory forever" (Rom 11:36). To God belongs "all power and riches and wisdom and might and honor and glory and blessing" (Rev 5:12). Therefore, God is able "to enjoy what is most enjoyable with unbounded energy and passion forever" (Piper, 1991, p. 24). He is the plenitude of reality, beauty, greatness and goodness, and so is the source of all true happiness and aid.

At the same time, God's infinite capacities enable him to be perfectly concerned for human well-being. We noted that the Bible portrays God as grieved and angry over human evil, but it also shows him to be the Savior and Protector of the weak, the poor and the suffering (Ps 12:5; 68:5-6; 113:5-9; Prov 19:17; 1 Cor 1:27-28). God is "compassionate and gracious, slow to anger, and *abounding* in lovingkindness and truth" (Ex 34:6). It is his nature to be moved with compassion at the sight of human suffering and victims of evil, traits clearly displayed in Christ (Mt 9:36; Mk 6:34; 8:2; Lk 19:41; Jn 11:35, 38), who demonstrated a steady love for sinners and the broken, concretely manifesting that the triune God is love (Jn 15:9; 1 Jn 4:8).

Both these aspects of God are wondrously relevant for soul care. The infinitely joyful God is alone capable of supplying human blessedness, because he alone is filled with overflowing blessedness. And he himself is inclined to do so, because his blessedness consists in part in perfect compassion towards humans, including his design to rescue them from their suffering and brokenness and their sin and condemnation. His glory is manifested in his love as well as his infinitude. These corollary truths provide the bedrock that undergirds Christian soul care.

God, the soul healer. Flowing from his good character is God's active care for the psychospiritual well-being of his people. The Bible tells us God comforts the downcast (2 Cor 7:6; see 2 Thess 2:17), sustains those who fall and raises up all who are bowed down (Ps 145:14), preserves the souls of his godly ones (Ps 97:10), hears the cries of his people and saves them (Ps 34:15, 17; 145:19), restores the souls of his "sheep" (Ps 23:2-3), delivers the righteous from their afflictions (Ps 34:19), heals the brokenhearted, binds up their wounds and supports (or relieves) the afflicted (Ps 147:3, 6). God said to the distressed that he would build them up as a fortress of jewels (Is 54:11-14). The psalmist was encouraged that "when my spirit was overwhelmed within me, You knew my path" (Ps 142:3). God grants his people to be "strengthened with power through His Spirit in the inner man" (Eph 3:16), a strengthening of their hearts in every good work and word (2 Thess 2:17). The psalmist declared to fellow-believers that

> [God] delivers you from the snare of the trapper,
> And from the deadly pestilence.
> He will cover you with His pinions;
> And under His wings you may seek refuge;
> His faithfulness is a shield and bulwark. (Ps 91:3)

These metaphors comfort by reminding readers that the all-powerful God is on their side and committed to their good. This feeds a transcendent sense of optimism, a trait that many have identified as crucial to human well-being (Carver & Scheier, 2002; Seligman, 1991; Snyder, 2000).

Christ's work is soul healing. According to the Bible, the most important soul-healing event of all time was the death and resurrection of Christ, an event that has many ramifications for the soul. The most important outcome was that Christ's death propitiated the wrath of God against sinners (Rom 3:25) and made possible their reconciliation with God (2 Cor 5), which in turn made it possible for God to be the believer's soul-healer, Father and friend, all roles that bring comfort and create unique forms of religious coping for the Christian. Humans are said to be alienated from their Creator, but the gospel declares that through faith humans are granted divine forgiveness because of what Christ accomplished on the cross (Col 2:13-16). But this objective forgiveness also has subjective benefits. The experience of guilt and shame, signs of alienation from God, are ubiquitous and debilitating (especially shame,

Tangney & Dearing, 2002). The blood of Christ, we are told, is able to "cleanse your conscience from dead works to serve the living God" (Heb 9:14), so that we can experience the divine forgiveness and be released from a futile, works-oriented religious regimen. This experience, in turn, can assist Christians in forgiving others (Eph 4:32), an activity that itself likely reduces one's own distress (McCullough, Pargament & Thoresen, 2000).

While speaking to the seven churches in Asia Minor, Christ said to the Sardis church: "Buy from Me gold refined by fire so that you may become rich, and white garments so that you may clothe yourself, and that the shame of your nakedness may not be revealed; and eye salve to anoint your eyes so that you may see" (Rev 3:18). In rich metaphor, Christ informed the church that his death and resurrection procured abundant spiritual wealth, a perfect standing before God that covered their psychospiritual uncleanness and gave them wisdom to see the reality beyond appearance. We are told in Hebrews that Christ's death specifically addresses a particular kind of anxiety: he died to deliver from their slavery those who struggle with fear of death (Heb 4:10). But Christ's work relates more broadly to all soul-disorders in a fundamental way: "by his bruises we are healed" (Is 53:5), pointing ahead to the transcendent, all-encompassing soul-healing accomplishments bound up in the suffering of the coming Messiah.

Christian salvation is soul healing. The Bible informs us that when the believer is brought into Christ, a host of psychospiritual benefits become available to him or her. Paul sounded something like an early Christian cognitive therapist when he told Christians that because of their union with Christ, they could let go of certain vices, like sexual immorality, evil desire, anger and malice (Col 3:1-8)—dispositions that all have psychopathological implications—by setting their minds on the realities in Christ that are above: their union with him, their new selves, their new standing and status, and so on. In fact, Paul taught that God is constructing within Christians a "new self" through their faith and requisite internal activity (known as mortification and vivification; Eph 2:10; Col 3:9-10; 2 Cor 5:17; see Calvin, 1559/1960, Vol. 1, pp. 595-602). He pointed explicitly to the word of God's grace that was "able to build you up and to give you the inheritance among all those who are sanctified" (Acts 20:32), a "building up" of inner resources for living the Christian life. However, he also understood the psychospiritual impact of Christian experience, pointing to the peace of God as something capable of guarding the hearts and minds of believers (Phil 4:7). The indwelling Holy Spirit produces this peace, along with other soul-fulfilling states of mind and traits of character like love, joy, patience, kindness, gentleness, long-suffering, goodness and self-control (Gal 5:22-23). Though Paul did not give a comprehensive model of how to develop these Spirit-fostered virtues, he constantly directed the attention of his fellow believers to their transcendent, omnipotent, attributional source: God in Christ. On account of such realizations, he understood that Christianity produces an unbounded optimism in one's spiritual competence in Christ: "I can do all things through Him who strengthens me" (Phil 4:13).

Other apostles taught similarly. According to John, knowing and experiencing the love of God enables one to overcome fear (and perhaps its cousins, anxiety and shame?): "There is no fear in love; but perfect love casts out fear, because fear involves punishment, and the one who fears is not perfected in love" (1 Jn 4:18). Peter encouraged his readers to endure their sufferings knowing they have an imperishable inheritance awaiting them in eternity (1 Pet 1:3-7). The Bible teaches that Christian salvation has secured abundant psychospiritual resources for Christians.

Human life has a christocentric maturity goal. Given the Christian's God-established standing and new life, the Bible points to the goal of this life, the Form of Christ. This Form is in view in the Bible's many admonitions and exhortations to be a person characterized by humility, gentleness, and patience, courage in the face of adversity (Acts 4:1-21), forbearance of one another in love (Eph 4:2), concern for the weak and disadvantaged (1 Thess 5:14; Jas 1:27), quickness to listen and slowness to anger (Jas 1:19), joyfulness (Phil 4:4), freedom from the love of money (Heb 13:5) and from anxiety (Phil 4:6), the bearing of other's burdens (Gal 6:2) and a radical love (1 Cor 13). The Bible's description of Christian virtues provides a template for one's character, the transformation of which is the goal of human life and Christian maturity (and so Christian soul care). This goal is summarized well in two distinct but corollary ways: as the love of God and the love of neighbor (Mt 22:37-39; see O'Donovan, 1986, ch. 11) and as conformity to the image of Christ (Rom 8:29; 2 Cor 3:18).

Historically, the traditions flowing from the Reformation have labeled the gradual realization of this conformity "sanctification," with the implication that one's life can be increasingly "set apart to God." Unfortunately, many Christians have interpreted sanctification superficially and relegated it to little more than a legalistic program of conforming one's beliefs and behaviors to the belief system and moral code of one's church. However, if this process entails an increasing conformity to the image of Christ—the ideal Form of human life—it must also include an inward dimension, affecting the depth structures and activities of the heart (Crabb, 1988; Powlison, 2003; Narramore, 1984; Roberts, 1997; Tripp, 2002), and encompassing affective dispositions, attitudes, motives, loves and hates, and character traits (i.e., virtues), a much more profound change than mere cognition and behavior work alone could provide.

Christian soul-healing has an inter-human dimension. It is impossible to read the New Testament epistles carefully without recognizing the interpersonal nature of the salvific process. The epistles themselves are the work of anointed human beings communicating the gospel, at least in part, to address the soul-care needs and concerns of communities of other believers. Thus, the form of Scripture itself involves human-to-human interaction and psychospiritual support through its written discourse.

In the Scriptures, the local church is envisioned as a site of significant social support, shaped by the example and power of God in Christ. "Be devoted to one another in brotherly love; give preference to one another in honor; . . . contributing to the needs of the saints, practicing hospitality. . . . Be of the same mind toward one another; do not be haughty in mind, but associate with the lowly. Do not be wise in your estimation. Never pay back evil for evil to anyone" (Rom 12:10, 13, 16-17). "Admonish the unruly, encourage the fainthearted, help the weak, be patient with everyone" (1 Thess 5:14). "[God] loved us and sent His Son to be the propitiation for our sins. Beloved, if God so loved us, we also ought to love one another" (1 Jn 4:10-11). Implementing such admonitions and encouragements leads to the creation of communities with high and holy standards that simultaneously provide loving, patient and accepting environments. Communities such as these can best help their members mature into the kind of Christian personhood that is increasingly able to engage in self-examination, take responsibility for one's actions and behave in ways that promote the welfare of others. At the same time, there are biblical limits to the acceptance of the community. Unruliness, for example, is to be admonished (as just mentioned); unrepentant sin is not to be given unconditional positive regard (see 1 Cor 5). But it is precisely the existence of such interpersonal limits that constitutes a part of the soul-healing value of the biblical community. If maintained with deep humility and grace, they will encourage struggling believers to hang in there and seek higher ground.

Christians should take care of their souls. One of the sages of Proverbs wrote this classic self-care maxim: "Watch over your heart with all diligence, for from it flow the springs of life" (Prov 4:23). We discover there that the wise person pays attention to her heart, listens to it and seeks to improve its condition, since the heart is of central importance to human well-being.

Two examples of such care of one's heart in the Psalms demonstrate a prescient use of self-regulation found in what might be called "theocentric self-talk," used for manifestly therapeutic purposes:

> Why are you cast down, O my soul,
> And why are you disquieted within?
> Hope in God; for I shall again praise him,
> My help and my God. (Ps 42:11 New Oxford Bible)

> Bless the LORD, O my soul;
> And all that is within me; bless His holy name.
> Bless the LORD, O my soul,
> And forget none of His benefits;
> Who pardons all your iniquities;
> Who heals all your diseases;
> Who redeems your life from the pit;
> Who crowns you with lovingkindness and compassion;
> Who satisfies your years with good things,
> So that your youth is renewed like the eagle. (Ps 103:1-5)

These passages illustrate a specific soul-care strategy recorded in the Bible: when feeling bad, one should try to take a more spiritual posture and address the distressed "parts" of one's soul as a "dialogue partner," in order to summon more of the soul into conformity to God's word. Many centuries later, contemporary cognitive therapists would make use of similar "self-regulation" strategies; what is different today is that they are typically implemented apart from a theocentric context.

Most of the time, however, the biblical authors give more *general* encouragements or illustrations regarding the care of one's soul. For example, consider how some of the biblical authors approach anxiety, a common malady of the soul. "When my anxious thoughts multiply within me, Your consolations delight my soul" (Ps 94:19). We are not told exactly what the consolations were, but the preceding verses refer to God helping his people and to his love holding them up. Such reflections helped the author in overcoming his worries and filled him with delight. The psalmist wrote, "Cast your burden upon the LORD and He will sustain you" (Ps 55:22). This is similar to the New Testament admonition to cast "all your anxiety on Him, because He cares for you" (1 Pet 5:6-7). Believers are taught here that they can "cast" their psychospiritual struggles on to God, and through this activity they will experience relief. In his Sermon on the Mount, Christ gave his followers a number of reasons to help them overcome anxiety about whether their basic needs would be met: there are more important things with which to concern oneself; God cares for birds and flowers; he will care for you; if you seek God first, you will have no wants; take one day at a time (Mt 6:25-34). Paul later told the Colossians to "let the peace of Christ rule in your hearts" (Col 3:15).

Such passages teach that believers have access to a spiritual contentment that undermines anxiety, and they are encouraged to pursue it. However, let us conclude this chapter on the Bible's self-attested value as a soul-care book by acknowledging that all these instructions are quite general in nature. Nowhere, for example, is it spelled out exactly *how to* cast burdens or anxiety on the Lord. Such "how-to" procedures are not self-evident, and this kind of task is particularly challenging for some, depending on their proneness to anxiety. The Bible is characterized by this *general* level of strategic sophistication. Perhaps we can infer from this observation that God desires the Christian community to continue to develop its understanding of human beings and come up with more specific, detailed and comprehensive guidelines—strategies and treatment protocols, based on good Christian theory—to help people apply and fulfill the more general soul-care principles that he specially revealed in the Bible, much as he sanctioned later trinitarian reflection.

The specific strategies given in the Bible, combined with the multitude of general, therapeutically oriented encouragements and admonitions, together convey God's revealed agenda that his children need to care for their souls biblically. However, the texts themselves would also seem to leave open the possibility of developing *further* Christian thinking about human beings and soul care, leading to an even richer and more comprehensive system of soul care (e.g., with detailed strategies for particular disorders), all to be realized within the theocentric guidelines found in the Bible. The sampling of biblical soul-care teaching that we have examined makes a persuasive case that it is God's intention that the Bible have a secure place as the main text for Christian soul care in his church. We turn next to consider how the church has used the Bible in its soul-care thinking and practice.

Notes

[1]For various types of evidence, see Cook and Herzman (1983), [illegible] (1997), Jeffries (1996), Kuyper (1898a), Levy (1992), Lindberg & Numbers (1986, 2003), MacCulloch (2003), McGrath (1999b, chap. 14), Prickett (1986), Schweiker (2002), Stark (2003), Torrance (1984) and Van Til (1959).

[2]This thesis has been developed popularly by Piper (1991, 1998).

[3]As we will see, the Bible has its own psychopathology framework that centers on alienation from God as the chief human psychological disorder, which all humans share. Later in the book we will attempt to make sense of other forms of psychopathology within this theocentric context.

[4]And “there was room within the term ‘sacred writings’ for the New Testament to be considered by later Christians as included in this assertion” (Oden, 1989, p. 24).

[5]Peter’s authorship is disputed, but not universally.

2

The Bible in the History of Christian Soul Care

THE BIBLE CLAIMS TO BE THE SOUL-CARE GUIDEBOOK for God's covenant community, and it conveys essential Christian soul-care information. So it is no surprise that throughout the history of the church Christians have looked to the Bible for their main guidance in the healing of souls. "The theme of Christianity as therapy runs throughout Christian theology" (Charry, 1997, p. 11). In this chapter we will examine some of the church's understanding of the Scripture's relevance to soul care, concluding with an exploration of how this orientation was severely compromised with the advent of modernism and its effects on modern versions of Christianity.

The Bible in Classical Christian Soul Care

The very early church. During the first centuries after the biblical writings were completed, Christian authors (and presumably preachers and teachers) evidenced a concern for the education and reformation of the soul, and the Scriptures were assumed to be foundational to these tasks.[1] The reading of Scripture was a central focus of the gatherings of the very early church, and sermons based on scriptural texts were common (Young, 1997). Christians were encouraged to stay at home reading Scripture, rather than to be out "roaming the streets" (see the *Apostolic Constitutions* 1.4-6).

The unknown author of the *Didache* (written before A.D. 150, Staniforth, 1968) provides a list of moral admonitions given to direct the reader to "perfection" (p. 227), many of which were quotations from or paraphrases of the eventual New Testament. "The Way of Life is this: 'You shall love first the

Lord your Creator, and secondly your neighbor as yourself'; and you shall do nothing to any man that you would not wish to be done to yourself" (p. 227). The earliest Christian writers, like Clement of Rome (c. A.D. 96), sought to base their teaching on Scripture, and that teaching usually had a life-reforming ethical agenda (Staniforth, 1968). As an example, Clement wrote, "Mutual admonition is wholly good and beneficial, for it leads us into conformity with the will of God. The sacred word says . . ." (p. 52), followed by the quotation of a number of Bible passages.

Much of this very early Christian literature is called *paraenesis,* the genre of moral exhortation (Young, 1997). This form of writing consisted of many quotations of Scripture as well as scriptural allusions, so that, at points, the works amounted to little more than collocations of Scripture. Also common was reference to scriptural heroes of the faith, used as moral examples that the early Christians were encouraged to emulate.

Somewhat later, *hagiography* became an increasingly common Christian genre. This consisted of stories of the lives of saints and martyrs (Young, 1997). Grounded in scriptural forms of story-telling, these stories were written to present exemplary moral models to the reader. Implied in them was the invitation to imitate the saints in fulfillment of the same Scripture that shaped them. Also important in the early church was the process of *catechesis*, the education of new converts and Christian youth in the church's teaching. This consisted almost entirely of biblical instruction (Schneiders, 1989).

This teaching and writing contributed to the formation of a subculture within the Roman Empire, constructed in large measure through reliance upon the Hebrew and Christian Scriptures. This subculture developed its own identity that involved a distinct morality and lifestyle (Young, 1997). Because early Christian education consisted largely in moral exhortations and the use of moral examples, its soul-care agenda rarely moved beyond rules for Christian living. Nonetheless, given the ongoing spread of the church in the first few centuries, no one can deny that this teaching contributed to a notable reformation of individuals' thinking and behavior that led to a growing subcommunity distinguished by a certain way of life shaped by Scripture. Let us survey next a few early church fathers regarding the role of Scripture in their views of soul-reformation.

Some fathers of the early church. In continuity with the earliest writings of the church, the desert fathers (late 200s-400) and many of the other fathers of the early church made use of the Bible's teaching and narratives, either to promote high ethical standards or to teach doctrine, so that the Bible's soul-healing functions continued to be mostly relegated to moral guidance and education, foundational uses to be sure, but certainly not reflective of the range of soul-care teaching in the Scriptures, particularly regarding the role of grace.

In his most important theological treatise, Gregory of Nazianzus (330-389) advocated the processes of "being molded and molding others by Holy Scripture" (1956, p. 136). The task of guiding others into Christian virtue was called by Gregory "the art of arts and the science of sciences" (sec. 16, *Flight from Pontus*). Using a metaphor common in his day, he saw the pastor as a "physician of souls" who has to treat a sickness found within "the hidden man of the heart" (quoted in Purves, 2001, p. 19), a task more difficult than that of the medical physician, because it deals with "the diagnosis and cure of our habits, passions, lives, wills, and whatever else is within us" (sec. 18, *Flight from Pontus*). Opening the Scriptures to others gives to them the mind of Christ, treasures that make them able, in turn, to enrich others (sec. 96).

Chrysostom (c. 350-407) was perhaps the finest preacher of the early church. The bulk of his recorded sermons consisted of expositions of books of the Bible. The content of those sermons suggests he sought "to foster in his hearers the life of faith which is set forth in scripture" (Young, 1997, p. 249). In *On the Priesthood*, he also compared the pastor's role to that of a physician, with the preaching of Scripture being the main healing instrument. "By means of this, we raise up the soul when prostrate, and cool it when fevered, and cut off what is superfluous, and fill up deficiencies, and do everything else which contributes to the health of the soul. . . . When the soul is sick by reason of false doctrine, then the preaching of the word is very necessary" (p. 92).

Augustine (354-430) has been reckoned by many as one of the greatest of the church fathers. The course of his Christian writings itself shows a profound intellectual and spiritual development, so one witnesses "a mind increasingly formed by the reading of scripture" (Young, 1997; see Van Til, 1959). In the absence of the beatific vision of God, he believed that the Scriptures constitute the very "countenance of God" (quoted in Brown, 1967, p. 262). He wrote of the great benefits that attend the reading of the Bible: "By these means wayward minds are corrected, weak minds are nourished, and strong minds are filled with pleasure, in such a way as is profitable to all. This doctrine has no enemy, but the man who, being in error, is ignorant of its incomparable usefulness, or being spiritually diseased, is averse to its healing power" (Letter 137.18). Since one's spiritual development was dependent on one's understanding and experience of God's Word, he prayed, "Let your Scriptures be my chaste delights" (1948, Vol. 1, p. 184). He once noted that he had too quickly rebuked others as an inexperienced priest: having "learned my infirmity, my duty is to study with all diligence all the remedies which the Scripture contains for such a case as mine, and to make it my business by prayer and reading to secure that my soul be endued with the health and vigor necessary for labors so responsible" (Letter 21). He knew that the Bible "could form a man for all he needed in this life" (Brown, 1967, p. 263).

Augustine wrote his great autobiography, the *Confessions* (1948, Vol. 1), to some extent, as a testimony of the power of Scripture to change a life. In it he argued against the classical ideal of the perfectibility of human nature and in favor of the inability of humans, even Christians (in marked contrast to earlier Christian hortatory writing), to become more ethical and spiritual themselves, making the case through his own story that all need the grace of God for soul-reformation. But an important part of God's grace toward humans was the Bible. Augustine was himself subdued, he said, by God's books, and his wounds were touched by God's healing fingers (7.20). He documented that his conversion was elicited by the reading of Scripture, and throughout the *Confessions*, he described how his life and thought came to be marked by a growing incorporation of scriptural ways of understanding and loving (O'Donnell, 1999; see e.g., 6.5, 7.20).

So important was the Bible for Augustine (1997) that he wrote a treatise on its interpretation, *On Christian Teaching*, where he presented a number of what have become standard hermeneutical principles for reading the Bible (and along the way lauded the use of the liberal arts, including logic, dialectic, historical enquiry, natural science, technology and so on—in spite of their pagan origin—to aid in exegesis, see book 2). But the main theme of the book is that the words (or signs) of Scripture lead to God and godliness: "the fulfillment and end of the law and all the divine scriptures" is the double-love of God and neighbor (pp. 26-27). Though sometimes hard to interpret, Scripture is the means "by which assistance is provided for the many serious disorders of the human will" (p. 32).

By Augustine's time, private and family Bible reading were being encouraged by Christian leaders and were a commonly accepted practice (Chadwick,

1967, pp. 242, 272). According to Cameron (1991), no small part of the success of the early church's conquest of the Roman Empire was due to its being word-oriented and text-based. Its discourse—that is, its doctrinal and moral teachings and symbolism based in the Bible—constituted a new dominant cultural world, within which its members were to be transformed into increasingly orthodox and virtuous persons. Their lives and Christianity's Scriptural rationale eventually became so persuasive that it took over Western cultural imagination and hope.

The medieval era. "The Bible was far and away the most influential and important book for the Middle Ages" (Cook & Herzman, 1983, p. 3). As a result, much of medieval life was structured in relation to it. Because of this orientation, it is no exaggeration to say that the Middle Ages were more universally concerned with the care of the soul than any other era before or since, at least among the intellectual leadership. The movement of the soul toward God and Christlikeness was avowedly of paramount importance, and one of the culture's most influential class of institutions—the monasteries—was expressly devoted to promoting such growth. Understanding the monastic tradition and its reliance on the Bible, then, is necessary for understanding the soul care of the Middle Ages, but for this we need go back to its roots in the days of the early church.

Beginning with the desert fathers in the late 200s, certain Christians had felt led to leave behind the culture of their upbringing and devote their lives to the pursuit of God and the transformation of their souls. By the late 300s a strong monastic movement was underway, setting the pace for spiritual development for the rest of Christianity. From the beginning, Scripture was the primary text used to promote soul change. Cassian (360-432), for example, an early monastic leader, advocated consistent memorization of Scripture and a ceaseless pondering upon it (1985, p. 164). Every monastic order had a "Rule," its own guidebook for monastic life, but it was considered subordinate to the Scriptures (Spearritt, 1986), and the Rule itself typically required much daily exposure to Scripture through reading, preaching and hearing, praying and singing (see e.g., Meisel & Mastro, 1975). As a result, a good portion of a monk's day was spent meditating on Scripture (Schneiders, 1989). With this foundation, the Scriptures came to play a profound regulative role in medieval discourse regarding the spiritual development and care of an elite class of believers.

Monasteries were set up to be essentially Scripture-based soul-care institutions, where younger members were trained by older in the transforming ways of the faith. Since most of the great Christian authors during the Middle Ages were members of or associated with some monastic community, the Bible inevitably became the dominant text throughout that period. At the same time, one must not overlook the social dimension of the monastery, which provided the interpersonal milieu within which soul change was fostered. It was understood that the members were to contribute to each other's well-being through word and example (Bynum, 1979). One Rule from the early 1100s put it this way:

> Let [the monks] love the juniors spiritually, honor the seniors; entreat in the love of God for their enemies; love each other; let them minister to each other in turn according to the order of charity; let them maintain gravity not only in speaking or acting, but also in walking or standing; let them have beauty of character, sanctity, and honesty not only of deeds but also of words; let them season all with whom they associate with the salt of wisdom and draw them to better things by their examples. Finally let them confess and believe, serve and teach all things which the sequence of the Old and New Testament relates. (quoted in Bynum, 1979, p. 38)

The Text of Life—the Bible—and the text of their lives were supposed to form a seamless context for the fostering of the individual's and the community's conformity to Christlikeness.

One of the most influential monastic leaders of the Middle Ages was Bernard of Clairvaux (1090-1153). Intensely focused on the love of God, his stage theory of the development of Christian love (see Bernard, 1983) would seem likely to withstand empirical scrutiny, were it tested. He believed that advancing in this love was dependent upon meditating, reading, praying and obeying (Bernard, 1953, p. 53), and that only such love could fulfill the human soul. In his widely appreciated sermon series on the Song of Songs—which he interpreted allegorically, as a love poem between Christ and his bride, the church, as was common until the modern era—he demonstrated a thorough familiarity with the Bible by constant cross-referencing of other passages. Bernard "drew the inspiration for his spiritual doctrine from Scripture, directly by meditation on the Bible and indirectly by reading the biblical commentaries" of the church fathers (Aumann, 1985, p. 97).

Bonaventure (1221-1274), an early leader in the Franciscan order, wrote works that "are Christocentric, saturated with Scripture, and learned in the Fathers" (Thorne, 1974). Bonaventure believed theology should lead believers to eternal life. His (1946) short treatise on Christian doctrine, *Breviloquium*, opens with a lengthy description and purpose of the nature of Scripture. He quotes Ephesians 3:14-19 and said Paul's prayer for the love of Christ discloses "the source, growth, and result of Holy Scripture" (p. 3). Its source, he wrote, is the Trinity, its growth is the increase of human capability, and its result is the fullest human happiness. The Bible provides a knowledge sufficient for salvation, comprehending the breadth, length, height and depth of all that is important in the universe, and "it is written not only that we may believe, but also that we may possess eternal life, in which we shall see and love, and our desires will be completely satisfied. . . . This, then, is the end and this the intention with which Holy Scripture should be studied, taught, and even heard" (p. 5). With regard to the main focus of the Bible, Bonaventure stated, "The subject of Scripture, so far as it is a substance, is God, so far as it is virtue, is Christ, and so far as it is an operation, is the work of reparation" (p. 12).

Eastern Orthodox soul care. We are concentrating on soul care in the West, but all-too-brief mention should be made of the Eastern church's equally heavy investment in soul change. As was noted above, the monastic tradition actually began among Greek-speaking Christians, the desert fathers, and monasticism thrived in the Orthodox church throughout the Middle Ages (Gribomont, 1989), and—as in the Catholic tradition—soul care flourished most in the monasteries, where they too were devoted to fostering Bible-based likeness to Christ.

In the Orthodox church, spiritual direction became a refined art, and its centuries of practice and reflection upon it provide an enduring, Christ-centered tradition of soul care (see, e.g., Allen, 1994; Ware, 2000). Throughout its history, Orthodox soul care held Scripture in high esteem, a fact evidenced by consistent reference to Scripture in its classic works. The *Philokalia*, for example, a compendium of Orthodox spiritual counsel from the early church to the fifteenth century (Palmer, Sherrard and Ware, 1782/1979-1984), is pervaded with scriptural teaching, reference and allusion. Though the Eastern church has long emphasized seeking a direct experience of God's energies beyond words, ideas and images, its greatest soul-care writers have always sought to base their understandings of the spiritual life in large measure on the Bible's teachings.

Much more could be written about further developments of Catholic and (especially) Orthodox soul-care teaching and practice, but enough has been said to indicate the importance of the Bible in these classic Christian traditions. We turn next to examine the Bible's role in the soul care of the Reformation traditions.

The Bible in the Reformation era. The impact of the Reformation on soul care in the West was enormous. In the twentieth century even the Catholic Church implicitly conceded that many of the Reformation's scriptural correctives were valid (evidenced by many of the changes of Vatican II; see Noll & Nystrom, 2005). Most important for our purposes is the high view of Scripture that the leaders of the Reformation enjoined for the improvement of the soul.

As we have seen, pre-Reformation Christians had a profound respect for Scripture. However, over the centuries, the writings of the church fathers and other church leaders came to be increasingly esteemed for their wisdom, originally merely as aids in interpreting Scripture but eventually as authoritative in their own right, resulting in a "dual-source" model of textual authority (McGrath, 1999b). In addition, while monks and nuns read Scripture (in Latin), ordinary believers were unable to read or hear Scripture, because, in most countries, until the Reformation the Scriptures were not translated into the vernacular (though the illiteracy of most Christians likely contributed to the lack of much impetus to do such translation). There were many causes for the cultural paradigm shift in Northern Europe during the Reformation (McGrath, 1999b), but one of the most important was the Reformers' aim to bring the entire church "back to the Bible" as the ultimate authority for Christian doctrine and practice. In the process, the Reformers clarified the role of Scripture in Christian thought and life and its relation to other texts.

Martin Luther's story (1483-1546) is the Reformation's defining narrative and is extremely relevant to our agenda. As a young monk, Luther struggled in his vocation, knowing himself to be a sinner and unworthy of God's love (Bainton, 1950; McGrath, 1999b). He multiplied his efforts to improve his spiritual state but could find no solace. From 1515 to 1517, as teacher of Bible at the University in Wittenberg, he lectured on the books of Romans and Galatians. Through those studies he began to realize that God's righteousness cannot be attained by humans; it can only be given by God as a gift. Luther's grasp of the gospel message of Scripture brought about a radical change in his soul, replacing his anxiety and depression with a deep sense of confidence with God.

Luther found that the appropriation of Scripture could address deep, pervasive distress of a degree that would be labeled psychopathological today (Erikson, 1962). For him, more than most other historical Christian figures, the Bible was the means of a seismic change in his psychospiritual well-being, and his experience shaped his understanding of the function of Scripture. He taught that the Bible deals with sin in two ways: the word of the law reveals and condemns sin, and the word of the gospel forgives it. The gospel "heals the corruption of human nature" (Luther, 1962, p. 348) by persuading us of God's favor and the gift of his righteousness. "This grace effects a true peace of mind eventually, so that a man is healed of his disease and knows in addition that he has a gracious God. This puts marrow into the bones. This brings back a conscience that knows joy and security and stands without fear. There is nothing it will not dare, nothing it cannot do, and in such trust in God's grace laughs even at death" (pp. 348-49).

The word of God of greatest importance to Luther was the gospel declaration of the sinner as righteous through justification, which the Christian must believe in order to receive. Luther used this biblical teaching to help the souls of others:

> The preaching of the gospel is nothing else than Christ coming to us, or we being brought to him. When you see how he works, however, and how he helps everyone to whom he comes or who is brought to him, then rest assured that faith is accomplishing this in you and that he is offering your soul exactly the same sort of help and favor through the gospel. If you pause there and let him do you good, that is, if you believe that he benefits and helps you, then you really have it. Then Christ is yours, presented to you as a gift (1989, p. 108).

The high value Luther placed on the Word of God was underscored by his regular preaching and writing on the Scriptures and his own translation of the Hebrew and Greek Scriptures into the German tongue.

The Reformation's leading theologian, John Calvin (1509-1564), similarly understood that the Bible was given to help the soul. In the preface to the *Institutes of the Christian Religion*, he stated his aim was to teach the "pure doctrine of godliness" (1559/1960, p. 5), which is nothing other than a summary of religion as it is revealed in the Scriptures. He had little patience for speculative, philosophical talk of God; he wanted his teachings to lead God's people into greater resemblance to God, the *imago Dei* (Charry, 1997), which, for Calvin, is the true human essence. Charry, in fact, considers him more of a pastoral theologian than a systematician.

Calvin suggested the Bible was the believer's "spectacles," given to teach us about God, ourselves and the created order. The headings of the first two books of the *Institutes* focus primarily on the knowledge of God (Book 1: On the Creator, and Book 2: On the Redeemer). But he noted that the teaching of the Bible also convinces us of our "primal worthiness" as well as "our foulness and dishonor" (Vol. 1, p. 242); both teachings, Calvin argued, are necessary for the kind of accurate self-knowledge that leads to Christian wholeness: "From this source arise abhorrence and displeasure with ourselves, as well as true humility; and thence is kindled a new zeal to seek God, in whom each of us may recover those good things we have utterly and completely lost" (p. 242). Believers, "when humbled by a true knowledge of themselves," die to their old selves, are slain by the sword of the word of God (Heb 4:12), and flee to Christ (Calvin, 1979, Vol. 22, p. 100). Scripture encourages believers with declarations of God's sure love for them and his promises regarding their spiritual well-being in the present and the future, so that "earthly miseries and calamities . . . cannot hinder his benevolence from being their full happiness" (1559/1960, Vol. 1, p. 574).

The Bible provides a "pattern for the conduct of life" (Calvin, 1559/1960, Vol. 1, p. 684), the goal of which is likeness to God (p. 686), and the realization of this pattern through obedience yields the greatest human happiness. Perfect happiness, according to Calvin (and Bernard before him), is union with God (Vol. 1, pp. 988-89). So our growing resemblance to God, constituted by Scripture and aided by the Holy Spirit, fulfills our nature as well as our divinely appointed destiny. Calvin's belief in the value of Scripture for soul care was similar to that of Luther and was evidenced by his careful expository sermons based on many books of the Bible, as well as his exemplary commentaries on most of those books (Haroutunian, 1958).

The Puritan era. Many Christians are unjustly being left out of this discussion, but reference must be made to the Puritans, a group of pastors who bequeathed the greatest treasury of soul-care literature written in the English language (Packer, 1990a). With the advantage of a few more generations of reflection and practice, they brought the soul-care genius of the Reformation to its zenith. The Puritan pastors were among the most highly educated persons of their day, and they devoted their erudition to the care of souls, preaching frequently—and some also writing voluminously—to help people glorify God and enjoy him forever. The Puritans had their weaknesses. Which age does not? But, at its best, the Puritan movement provided us with great role models of how to bring Scripture to bear on the soul-care needs of God's people.

To begin with, in contrast to modern views of theology as an academic discipline, the Puritans understood it to be preeminently a practical discipline, necessary for the formation of a godly life. For example, two early Puritan leaders defined theology as "the doctrine or teaching of living to God" (Ames, 1983, p. 77) and "the science of living blessedly for ever" (Perkins, quoted in Packer, 1990a, p. 64). So the Puritans "read the Bible as a book of normative experience, no less than of normative doctrine" (Packer, p. 68). Packer (1990a) concluded from this that the Puritans were basically pastoral theologians. Most of their works were expositions of Scripture, directed to comfort and encourage believers in their soul struggles, for example, *A Bruised Reed* by Richard Sibbes, *A Lifting Up for the Downcast* by William Bridge, *An Ark for All God's Noahs* by Thomas Brooks, *Pilgrim's Progress* by John Bunyan and *The Duty of Being Spiritually Minded* by John Owen, to name just a few.

Richard Baxter (1615-1691) was exemplary in his application of Scripture in the care of souls. A pastor of tremendous energy, he wrote, preached and counseled tirelessly throughout his life. His most famous work, *The Reformed Pastor*, laid out the "counseling program" he used in Kidderminster, where he labored for many years. Baxter spent a portion of a typical week going from house to house to counsel the members of the household, sometimes individually and sometimes as a group, with the purpose of covering the entire parish on a regular basis. He used this time to encourage and test Scripture and catechism memorization (the catechism being a summary of scriptural teaching), deal with doctrinal questions and misunderstandings, and assess the soul-needs of his parishioners. His use of Scripture to advance the well-being of the souls under his watch set a high mark for pastoral care for all time (Purves, 2001).

He also wrote a great deal, an output collected in four massive volumes. One of these volumes is called *A Christian Directory* (1673/1990), and it takes well over a million words to present the "sum of practical theology" (from its subtitle). It was intended as an encyclopedic "how-to" guide to godliness (much longer than the "how-to" "self-help" guides of our day!), covering spiritual growth, progress over the psychopathology of sin, the control of one's thoughts, passions and behaviors, and prosperity in marriage, child-rearing, business, and church, discussions all based on Scripture. It was a soul-care compendium of the scriptural wisdom of his day (Packer, 1990b).

Over two hundred years before the rise of psychoanalysis, the Puritans demonstrated an avid interest in the heart and in self-deception (Packer, 1990a, chap. 4 refers to their "affectionate practical theology")—based on their massive knowledge of the Bible and an earnest commitment to make that knowledge life-changing. The Puritans saw pastoral ministry and preaching as soul-healing and the church as a hospital, and they believed that "all Christians need Scripture truth as medicine for their souls at every stage" (Packer, 1990a, p. 65). While our era far outstrips theirs in terms of an understanding of the created mechanics of human development and soul change, ours is dwarfed by theirs with regard to the more important expertise of applying the Bible to the greatest needs of the soul.

For evangelicals, the Puritan era has to be reckoned as a high point in the history of Christian soul care, and it continued to reap fruit into the next century through people like Jonathan Edwards and John Newton, on into the 1800s through Archibald Alexander, Octavious Winslow, John Colquhoun and Charles Spurgeon. However, its tendency toward contentiousness and scrupulosity festered in some quarters and led to a distaste for all things Puritan, even among most late-nineteenth-century religious conservatives. Tragically, this declension was correlated with the increasing influence of rationalism, empiricism and secularism that came to be known as modernism. But before considering the impact of modernism on the church and the church's soul care, the influence of the scientific revolution in the West must be discussed.

Christianity and Science

Many forces were an impetus to the development of science in the West, but certainly one of the most important was the Christian faith (Brooke, 1991; Butterfield, 1957; Cohen, 1990; Goldstein, 1980; Hooykaas, 1972; Lindberg & Numbers, 1986; Livingston, Hart & Noll, 1999; Pearcey & Thaxton, 1994; Pearcey, 2004; Stark, 2003). A large part of the reason for this was the Bible's teaching regarding God as Creator and providential guide of the creation, and the creation itself as a reflection of his wisdom, greatness and glory. Such truths led many Christians to engage in scientific research and theory building, reasoning that since the regularities found in the natural world were the product of God's hand, their discovery brought him glory. This framework, in turn, provided a metaphysical basis for the development of the natural science methods of observation and experimentation necessary for deducing these lawful regularities (Brooke, 1991). Many of the early leaders of the scientific revolution were Christians of various stripes, including Roger Bacon, Copernicus, Kepler, Francis Bacon, Galileo, Newton, Boyle, Pascal, Descartes, Ray, Linnaeus and Gassendi. Puritan scientists, in particular, like Boyle, are instructive role models for contemporary Christians, since they used Scripture in their scientific writings and sought in various ways to articulate the underlying harmony of natural and revealed truth (Cohen, 1990; Webster, 1986). Historically, Christians regarded science as fundamentally a good gift from God.

At the same time, the scientific revolution contributed to an unprecedented upheaval in the West's conceptions of the universe, and Christianity was at the center of the controversy. Perhaps most important was the discovery that the earth belonged to a heliocentric planetary system, in contrast to the received geocentric model of the classical and medieval worlds. This discovery appeared to contradict some biblical passages (though orthodox Christians could be found on both sides of the debate). Furthermore, the mechanistic view of the universe that came to dominate the West's science can be based on a belief in God's creative sovereignty (as taught by a theist like Newton), as well as in the autonomous, mindless laws of nature (as taught by an atheist like La Mettrie) (Deason, 1986; Holton, 1973; Roger, 1986). As a result, a broad fracture gradually opened up in Western thought, dividing naturalists and supernaturalists. Ironically, while Christianity contributed to the development of the scientific revolution, that revolution came to be increasingly linked to an alternative worldview: modernism.

The Rise and Reign of Modernism

Depending on one's reckoning, the roots of modernism may go back into the medieval period, the 1300s (Milbank, 1997), but its founding is generally considered to be somewhere between 1600 and 1700 (Gilson & Langan, 1963). At that time the Christian worldview still undergirded Western thought. It is not surprising, then, to learn that many of the forerunners and founders of modernism considered themselves to be Christians. They nonetheless instigated ways of thinking that in subsequent centuries contributed to the demise of Christianity's intellectual supremacy in the West. Writing in the seventeenth century, Descartes and Locke were two of modernism's most important founders. Both came to center their respective philosophies in the human subject but engaged in very different analyses of the subject's experience and knowledge. Together their work formed much of the basis of the Enlightenment, a broader, more popular intellectual movement limited to the 1700s (Brinton, 1967), that itself typified modernism and contributed to its advance. Both movements culminated in the unifying work of Kant, who instituted a fatal division in modernist thought between the empirical or scientific realm and the metaphysical (labeled the phenomenal and the noumenal, respectively). By the beginning of the twentieth century, modernism had taken over Western thought, decisively replacing Christianity as the West's dominant worldview.

The major themes of modernism and the Enlightenment are tightly interrelated around the individual subject. Tradition, metaphysics and revelation were eschewed as sources of knowledge. Reacting against the medieval reliance on tradition (and all its contradictions), and the danger of skepticism, modernists rejected knowledge claims that could not be independently verified by the thinking individual. As a result, human reason (using logic and mathematics) came to be favored as the primary adjudicator of genuine knowledge, bolstered by the impressive accomplishments of the natural sciences, the increasing power of observational research, and technological progress, leading to a growing confidence that increasing knowledge and human improvement were virtually guaranteed. Allied with the experimental method, pure human reason (separated from morals and values) was believed by modernists to offer a sounder basis for obtaining indubitable knowledge about the universe and humanity than the teachings of biblical revelation. As a result, though initially a defender of Christianity, modernism eventually became a fundamentally secular movement of thought and practice. However, like Christianity, it aimed at a universal understanding of reality—though now based on reason and experiment—with which all rational parties could agree.

Another important theme of modernism, and something of a reaction to rationalism and scientism, was the importance of the individual subject's *experience.* This experience came to be regarded as authoritative in certain segments of modernism. Kant's notion of the categorical imperative; romanticism's exaltation of emotion, intuition and the arts; and later, existentialism's and humanism's focus on creative freedom illustrate the movement within modernism towards expressive individualism (Taylor, 1989). Though seemingly opposed, the dialectically related twin sources of authority in modernism—reason and experience—are the two major pillars of the worldview of the autonomous Self.

At core what distinguishes modernism and Christianity as ways of thinking about human life are their different ultimate commitments. Christianity assumes a God-centered worldview in which the individual self (with its *submissive* reason) is seen as relatively important in relation to the rest of creation but relatively unimportant in comparison to the infinite God. In such a framework, science is a noble task done first for the glory of God and second for the benefit of humanity, a good means to a greater end. Modernism inherited the self of Christianity, but without its God to keep things in proper perspective, the *self* became the center of the universe (an anti-Copernican revolution!), eventually regarding its own experience, together with its autonomous reason, as the foundations of truth and morality. In a modern framework, science and human experience become themselves norm producing, the means by which the Self discovers and realizes itself, overruling sources of knowledge that call into question the Self's autonomy, like testimony, revelation and tradition (except for its own tradition! Taylor, 1989). Consequently, individualism—and not relationship—was established at the base of the modern worldview. Aided by higher standards of living, individualism manifested itself in the last half of the twentieth century in consumerism, the so-called therapeutic culture, contemporary art and music, and such social trends as sexual promiscuity and variant forms of sexual expression, a high divorce rate and transience in employment and residence.

This negative assessment, however, cannot adequately explain modernism's rise to power. Had not the Christian West failed miserably to achieve social and religious harmony—as evidenced in the Thirty Years War (1618-1648)—modernism might never have gotten off the ground. The paradox of the religion of the Prince of Peace embroiled in seemingly intractable conflict, combined with the repressive, anti-intellectual traditionalism of many of its proponents, made the search for an alternative inevitable. The need to question one's traditional assumptions and subject them to some rational critique seemed to many self-evident. In addition, much of modernism's intellectual agenda could be embraced by Christians: its reliance on reason and scientific methods to discover truth, its suspicion of religious hypocrisy, its recognition of the value of the individual over against unjust and unrepresentative regimes, and its eventual promotion of human rights have led to constructive changes in the West—and made the case for modernism compelling. From 1650 to 1950 a battle of ideas was being waged in the West, and modernism carried the day. More and more intellectuals left the faith of their fathers and mothers and converted to this new worldview that promised peace, justice and progress forevermore—without the spiritual encumbrances of Christianity. Eventually a clear majority of the West's best minds favored the modern mindset over the Christian. Over three centuries, modernists of various kinds had put together a persuasive textual tradition of autonomous rationality that seemed indefatigable and unimpeachable, certainly by a failed tradition from out of the Dark Ages.

The Bible and modernism. The clash between Christianity and modernism was to some extent a clash of authoritative texts. As the texts of modernist proponents were read and their teachings believed, the value of the Christian canon and classics from its tradition was correspondingly undermined. It was only a matter of time until modernist epistemological assumptions and methods would come to be applied to the Christian tradition. In fact, central to its agenda was the rejection of the Bible. "Enlightenment critique is primarily directed against the religious traditions of Christianity—i.e., the Bible. . . . This is the real radicality of the Enlightenment compared to all other movements of enlightenment: it must assert itself against the Bible and dogmatic interpretations of it" (Gadamer, 1975, p. 272). As a result, the Bible itself became an object of scientific scrutiny by critics examining the Bible from a supposedly neutral, rational standpoint (see Plantinga, 2003), and an increasing number of scholars came to believe the Bible was nothing more than a set of human documents, flawed if not mostly mythological (Bray, 1996; Rogerson, 1988). Skepticism regarding the historicity of the biblical accounts became the accepted stance in certain circles, and a rejection of the Bible's "objectionable" teachings followed close behind (Reventlow, 1985). Most problematic, if reason based on empirical research provides the best account of things, what are we to think of topics that cannot be studied empirically, for example, God, morality and salvation? Positivism, the radical wing of modernism, concluded we can say nothing about them; in fact, some positivists allowed their favored method of determining knowledge (empirical science) to determine what may or may not exist at all, and so came to question the reality of the whole spiritual realm. From the opposite quarter, expressive individualism questioned the authority of truth outside one's experience. "What meaning can the resurrection of Christ have for me, since I didn't witness it?"

All these dynamics contributed to the growth of the last important constitutive theme of modernism that we will mention: secularism. As skepticism about the Bible and God grew, and the influence of religion and the church waned, increasingly large segments of Western culture came to be marked by an absence of belief in or reference to God or religion in public discourse, a trend known as secularism. Eventually, secularism became a hallmark of modernity (Levy, 1972).

Christian responses to modernism. Reactions to modernism varied among Christians. The conservative response was twofold. Protestant theologians in America like Charles Hodge, B. B. Warfield and Gresham Machen mounted a vigorous defense of traditional Christian beliefs and the Bible, while perhaps unwittingly making use of some modernist assumptions and methods (e.g., Hodge's empiricist discussion of the method of theology, 1995, Vol. 1, pp. 1-3). However, a less intellectual and more antagonistic fundamentalism reacted against modernism by simply withdrawing from interactions with more liberal Christians and from cultural engagement in general (apart from a few ethical issues of importance, like temperance), concentrating instead on evangelism, missions and the maintenance of a Christian subculture. Either way, conservative Protestantism in the nineteenth and twentieth centuries did not provide a compelling challenge to modernism (Noll, 1995).

A more favorable religious response to modernism, known as liberalism, arose in the state churches in Europe and what became the mainline denominations in America. These churches tended to accommodate themselves in varying degrees to modernity without relinquishing all of the Christian vernacular. Individuals and institutions differed in terms of their degree of accommodation. A theologian like Paul Tillich (1886-1965), for example, continued to use scriptural terminology (e.g., God, Christ, sin and salvation, 1957b), while substantially reinterpreting it in ways more compatible with modern experiential sensibilities, as merely religious symbols of universal phenomena (e.g., sin as existential estrangement), since (following Kant) we have no cognitive access to the noumenal. Tillich believed that a reliance on the Bible as a source for theology had to be balanced with a reliance on church history, history of religion, cultural studies (including art and science) and human experience. He developed the correlation method for relating theology to culture (1951), suggesting that culture asked the questions to which theology provided the answers (questions and answers being correlated), but this method mandated that the communicative agenda for theology was derived from and dictated by contemporary culture's concerns, thus minimizing the reforming or prophetic role of the Christian faith though (Cooper, 2006, suggests that Tillich himself was never so linear).[2] Later theologians influenced by Tillich include Tracy (1975, 1981), Farley (1982), Kaufman (1993) and Gustafson (1981, 1984), and they, like Tillich, make "enlightened" use of the Bible, recognizing its cultural-historical limitations and therefore its limited authority (for example, see Farley, 1982, for an extended apologetic for such a view of the Bible).

At the other end of this continuum was the neo-orthodoxy of Karl Barth (1886-1968), who reacted against liberal theology by taking seriously the Bible as an instrument of the revelation of God and seeking to base his theology solely on Scripture. Barth rightly realized that liberal theology was bound by its modernist allegiance to human reason and experience, and so was unable to hear from God (Molnar, 2000). At the same time, Barth's doctrine of Scripture rendered it more of a witness to revelation, than revelation itself, subtly evading the implications of a "scientific," historical-critical approach to the Bible, while maintaining an allegiance to Scripture as a *medium* of the word of God, a stance that would undoubtedly have puzzled historic Christian thinkers. Though his interpreters are divided, a logical consequence of Barth's position has seemed to some to be that the Bible and its study had *no* correlation with contemporary culture and the scientific study of the creation (Webster, 1988; McGrath, 2001).

As already mentioned, Kant's epistemology had severed any link between the phenomenal world, accessible to human knowledge through scientific research (the empirical; how reality appears to us), and the noumenal world beyond human knowledge (the metaphysical; how reality is in its own right). As the implications of Kant's dichotomy sunk in during the twentieth century, what were modernists to think about God? In effect, Tillichian liberalism opted for the phenomenal over the noumenal, limiting human knowledge of God to empty symbols of "God," the validity of which we have no way of assessing, a stance that profoundly undermined scriptural authority in its churches. Neo-orthodoxy, on the other hand, sought to side-step the crisis in knowledge of the modern era by favoring the noumenal, as mediated by the word of God, but assuming the same Kantian epistemological gap—now between biblical truth and the empirical study of the natural order—it could not offer a vigorous corrective to liberalism. At best, it served to underscore the isolation and perceived irrelevance of the Christian faith from the "real," empirical world (Spykman, 1992; though as McGrath, 2001, points out, T. F. Torrance has shown that Barth's project can be harmonized with the natural sciences).

The Bible and modern pastoral care. By the late 1800s, modernism had basically preempted the scientific revolution at the very time it came to be applied to the study and care of human beings, effectively replacing a massive Christian tradition of reflection on human beings and soul care, leading to the founding of modern versions of psychology and psychiatry that had as their aim a universal knowledge of human beings (Alexander & Selesnick, 1968; Cushman, 1995; Rieff, 1966; Toulmin & Leary, 1992; Vandenbos, Cummings & DeLeon, 1992), and the development of a new tradition of soul care—a *secular* one—devoid of reference to alleged metaphysical entities, supernatural assistance and moral discourse. Along with many other Western intellectuals, most of the leaders of modern psychology and psychotherapy were consciously moving away from the Judeo-Christian religions and became contributors to that movement, including such major figures as Wundt, Titchener, Galton, G. S. Hall, James, Thorndike, Baldwin, Ladd, Dewey, Angell, Freud, Adler, Jung, Horney, Fromm, Rogers, Maslow, Piaget, Pavlov, Watson and Skinner. Eventually, "psychology came to be seen by many of its participants, and increasingly by the culture at large, as providing an authoritative replacement for the pronouncements of the Bible, the pope, and church tradition (cf. Watson, 1925)" (Johnson & Jones, 2000, p. 29). As a result, by the middle of the twentieth century, secular psychology and psychotherapy was firmly entrenched as the only legitimate approach to the study of human nature and to soul care. Rightly interpreted, modern soul care should be seen as the chief religious competitor to Christian salvation in the West (Adams, 1970; Vitz, 1994).

Given liberal Protestantism's greater willingness to accommodate to modernism and its own historical-critical skepticism regarding Scripture, it is no surprise that within liberalism's ranks there arose those interested in soul care who were persuaded that modern psychology's resources were more valuable than Christianity's. In 1905 the Emmanuel Movement became the first attempt to shape pastoral care by "the sciences" rather than by "tradition" (Holifield, 1983). However, a few decades passed before this new approach became more widely influential. Involved in the Emmanuel Movement from its earliest days, the Unitarian Richard Cabot, along with Russell Dicks, wrote *The Art of Ministering to the Sick*, published in 1936, where they "defined God as a power of healing" and advocated listening and looking for the "better parts of the person's mind," so that the minister could help persons "discover the direction in which [the] immanent divinity was carrying them" (Holifield, p. 237). With support from Cabot, Anton Boisen (1876-1965) spearheaded the development of Clinical Pastoral Education, a program of supervision and training of ministers in modern pastoral care, relying on the best of modern psychology. A former mental patient himself, Boisen (1936) advocated taking seriously the lives and experience of those with whom caregivers worked. He called patients "living human documents," recognizing the scientific and therapeutic value of narrative and the textual nature of human life, but also exemplifying the modern preoccupation with the individual subject. Scripture was virtually absent from his work.

Modern pastoral care, however, came into its own with the next generation. A cadre of resourceful authors and leaders arose who created a pastoral-care literature heavily influenced by the psychotherapy theory of their time, while maintaining a distinctively religious perspective. They included Hiltner (1943, 1949, 1958, 1972; and with Colston, 1961), Johnson (1953), Wise (1951, 1980) and Oates (1953; 1959; 1962), and in the sixties, Clinebell (1966). All of them showed an aversion to a "biblical-didactic" approach to counseling (as often practiced by premodern pastoral caregivers) and a preference for the methods and understandings of the modern psychotherapy movement, particularly psychodynamic and client-centered therapy (see Patton, 1990). Though most of them taught at seminaries or divinity schools, Holifield (1983) has made a good case that the underlying, unifying theme of this body of work was self-realization.[3]

Seward Hiltner and the modernization of Christian soul care. Hiltner provides as good a representative as any of modern pastoral soul care. In his first major work (1949), he noted that he studied with Boisen and Wise and worked with Dicks. He also cited Erich Fromm and Carl Rogers (among others) as being especially helpful in the development of his psychological thinking and Tillich as one of the three major influences on his theology. Hiltner (1949) described the aims of pastoral counseling in orthodox terms: "bringing people to Christ and the Christian fellowship, aiding them to acknowledge and repent of sin and to accept God's freely offered salvation, helping them to live with themselves and their fellow men in brotherhood and love, enabling them to act with faith and confidence instead of the previous doubt and anxiety, bringing peace where discord reigned before" (p. 19). However, biblical teaching was less evident than one might expect in a book on pastoral work. Instead the emphasis was on "understanding" (p. 20), helping the other to help himself (p. 21), ethical issues (p. 22) and respect for the parishioner (p. 23). He argued that the pastoral counselor should promote a special kind of "inner release" (pp. 28-30), the ethical liberation of genuine human needs that have been restricted by damaging social forces. Wherever the counselor sees this inner liberation, it should be reckoned as the work of the Holy Spirit, but the methods used for this "liberation" seem far more dependent upon current psychotherapy theory than Scripture. As Oden (1984) pointed out, Hiltner made frequent mention of Freud, Jung, Rogers and Fromm, but nobody from the classical pastoral-care literature. Even more telling, throughout this classic work ("the most frequently used text in pastoral care courses" in American seminaries in 1956; Holifield, 1983, p. 300), the content of Scripture is never seriously engaged.

In a chapter on "religious resources," Hiltner (1949) states that "the pastor will use the Bible in counseling, *as he understands it* and as it applies to particular situations with which he is dealing" (p. 202, italics mine). But the three examples he gives demonstrate a limited and awkward use of the Bible that feels unpersuasive. First, he cites a case where a parishioner comes with a question about the Bible's teaching, to which the pastor responds with sensitivity and gentleness. The pastor, he noted, "does not moralize, generalize, coerce, or divert. Instead he understands, accepts, clarifies, and helps to consolidate" (p. 207). This is far from Richard Baxter!

In the second example, to help a recently returning veteran make sense of his struggle about whether to stay at home with his parents or live on his own, a pastor makes an allusion to Paul's teaching in Romans 7 about the internal war in his members. Not recognizing that Romans 7 is dealing with a very different topic—the ethicospiritual struggle of human inability before the law of God—Hiltner says the example shows that "the Scriptures *are* relevant" (p. 208). But then he goes on to warn against using Scripture in this way if it would lead the conversation away from the parishioner's situation toward more familiar territory to the pastor (the Bible).

He saves his best example for last: recommending the giving of a short scriptural text to a troubled parishioner, discussing its meaning, and perhaps writing it on a card, so that the text can be pulled out should the parishioner later be tempted to drink or engage in self-pity, allowing the creation of a new perspective to enter the mind. He comments, "There seems to be validity in texts used in this way, if handled with discrimination and if used in an eductive and not a coercive or moralistic way" (p. 209). *Eductive* was his term for drawing out the solution to problems from the "creative potentialities of the person needing help" (p. 97), rather than mere teaching. He concluded the section by recommending that biblical scholars should explore the many possible uses of the Bible in pastoral work. But the fact that such work does not occur to him as central to his own mission as a pastoral theologian is indicative of his greater interest in another set of texts than the Bible, those of secular psychotherapy (Oden, 1984; Purves, 2004). A new era had indeed dawned in Christian soul care: the eclipse of the Bible as the premier soul-care text and nothing less than a shift from the centrality of God to the centrality of the Self.

Hiltner later recognized the thinness of the theology of his earlier work and sought to remedy his previous neglect of Christian content in two later books: *Preface to Pastoral Theology* (1958) and *Theological Dynamics* (1972). However, only in the latter does he really begin to interact with Scripture. Even so, we find there a theological reinterpretation of biblical teaching that accords with modern understandings of well-being far better than with the faith once delivered to the saints.[4] Perhaps we have seen enough to understand why he took the Bible so lightly: he did not recognize it to be the word of God, at least in the way it had always been viewed prior to the modern era. In his system there were other textual authorities that functioned canonically. Rather than the Bible serving as system-guiding spectacles for soul care, Hiltner's understanding of human well-being was derived from mid-twentieth-century existentialism and humanism, and the primary resources for soul healing were those of modern psychotherapy.

Hiltner's approach, unfortunately, is hardly unique among the other, early leaders of the modern pastoral-care movement. Very rarely is Scripture mentioned in the works of Wise, Johnson or Clinebell, and when it is, it is usually used illustratively rather than canonically.[5]

An assessment of modern pastoral care. In retrospect, we can see that Scripture exercised a negligible influence on the modern pastoral-care (MPC) movement. With modernism in general, liberal theology shared the belief that a new era had come and the old traditions, including a genuine reliance on relics like the Bible, must be viewed with some suspicion. If it is to be used at all, the Bible must be "demythologized" of its supernaturalism and reinterpreted according to the more rational and empirical canons of modernist epistemology, and, in general, modern pastoral care simply traveled along with the rest of the liberal crowd they were in. They looked to the heralds and prophets of this new era—the secular psychological scientists and therapists—rather than to the Bible for their primary inspiration, and they did their best to "sanctify" their body of work so that it retained a mildly religious flavor that pleased the palates of some of their peers. In this they well exemplified the correlation method of Tillich (Holifield, 1990; Purves, 2004), which in their hands allowed the questions of secular psychology to shape the modest answers that a nebulous, liberal practical theology could offer.

Tillich's influence continued to pervade MPC after Hiltner, for example, in the work of Pruyser (1976), Patton (1983, 1993) and Olson (1997), and the monumental *Dictionary of Pastoral Care and Counseling* (Hunter, 1990). MPC today continues to look for its inspiration outside of orthodox Christian resources in one of two directions: either to modern psychology (like Hiltner)—then seeking to "enrich" it with a dollop of religious sensibility—or to some variant of modern theology, "revisioning" the care of souls with "the latest" theological trend, for example, process (Grant, 2001) or feminist theology (Gorsuch, 2001). Either way, the Bible's influence has been minimal, and those committed to historic Christianity will have to look elsewhere to develop a robustly Christian version of psychology and soul care.

Nonetheless, orthodox Christians can acknowledge that the MPC movement has provided a service to the church, both positively and negatively. Positively, MPC has always attempted to take seriously the individual's state of soul, rather than being driven exclusively by a concern to educate (Capps, 1990a). Human subjectivity was not unimportant in premodern Christian soul care, and unfortunately, many hyper-conservatives in the twentieth century (outside Pentecostalism) developed an antipathy to experience—even experience grounded in Scripture—focusing instead on adherence to orthodox doctrine and legalistic behavior codes. While the turn to the Subject of modernism has had devastating consequences, the rationalistic/educational overreaction that characterized the seminary training of the fundamentalist/evangelical movement over the past century betrayed a closer identification with elements of modernism than it was aware—in comparison with its own Puritan and pietist roots! At any rate, becoming a mature soul caregiver requires an advanced kind of empathic perspective-taking that is able to grasp something of what the world looks and feels like to the counselee. The experiential emphasis of the MPC challenges classical Christians to take seriously the subjectivity of their counselees and adjust their communication accordingly.

On the other hand, generally speaking, the MPC movement teaches those committed to historic Christianity that a low view of Scripture leads, unsurprisingly, to low formative impact of Scripture on counseling theory and practice, and as a result, little that is qualitatively different from secular psychology. There is rarely reference to redemption—either God's special forgiveness or adoption of believers or the supernatural work of God in the believer—and little consideration of the impact of one's personal relationship with Christ, both of which have marked classical Christian experience and soul care from the Bible onward. In fact, the MPC in general diverges sharply enough from historic Christian pastoral care that one must wonder about the degree to which many of its practitioners ought still to use the term *Christian* to refer to their models of soul care. At a certain point, the variance becomes so great that some other label is called for.[6]

Tillich's influence fostered some of the worst excesses in modern pastoral care. Because his correlational method takes its questions from contemporary culture (in pastoral care, from secular psychology and psychiatry), it makes a methodological virtue out of allowing non-Christian thought to set the stage for how Christians should think about human nature, psychopathology and its treatment.

The Barthian soul-care alternative. In stark contrast to Tillich, until recently Karl Barth had minimal influence on pastoral counseling. As noted above, Barth attempted to base his theology on the word of God, which, for him, required a responsive dependence upon Scripture. Most of the pastoral-care leadership in America viewed Barth and his followers with some disdain, clearly preferring Tillich over Barth in citations (see, e.g., Clinebell, 1966; Hiltner, 1972; Oates, 1962; Oden, 1967; Thornton, 1964; Wise, 1980). Nonetheless, an early example of Barthian pastoral care can be found. Eduard Thurneysen (1962), a Swiss pastoral theologian and friend of Barth, developed a model of pastoral counseling that eschewed secular counseling models and sought to ground its entire program on the delivery of the word of God, an agenda consonant with the soul-care traditions of historic Christianity. Thurneysen believed the task of pastoral care consists of the sanctification of the whole person for God, and this task was fostered by the word of God. "We shall really understand man only when we understand him from the Bible" (p. 205). A true self-understanding is only possible in response to the word of God. Scripture teaches that sanctification involves repentance and forgiveness of sins in Christ, said Thurneysen, and only within that context can genuine soul-healing occur. God's word radically changes one's perspective on one's psychological predicament.

Thurneysen (1962) thought that secular psychology and psychotherapy were auxiliary sciences to pastoral ministry, valuable, even necessary, for a proper understanding of created human nature, but they did not go far enough in addressing humanity's core religious need: the forgiveness of sins. Yet, following Barth, Thurneysen also assumed a significant divide between the created order (and the scientific texts of psychology) and divine revelation (and the biblical text upon which pastoral counseling is based), and showed no appreciation for the fundamental worldview differences that distinguish modern and Christian soul care. For example, he wrote, "The attempt to establish a 'Christian' psychology pursued by Christian scholars is senseless. As there is no Christian zoology or physics, there is no Christian psychology either. Nor is there any need of it. What is needed is a Christian use of psychology, an application of its results in the pastoral care of the Christian church. And that is something else" (p. 209). This would seem a valid, if extreme, deduction from Barth's post-Kantian understanding of the word of the God and his radical dichotomies between reason and revelation, and creation and redemption. Unfortunately, it provides no Christian hermeneutic for interpreting secular psychology, and it ends up legitimizing a simplistic and tragic division in one's understanding of soul care that inevitably compromises the extent to which one can envision human nature theocentrically and redemptive-historically, and therefore holistically. So, while Thurneysen's Barthian counseling model was markedly more Christian in content than those approaches that used Tillich's correlation method, it offered no help for developing a critique of modern psychology or a holistic, Christian approach to soul care that can do justice to the complexity of the created structures of human nature, as well as its fallen and redemptive dynamics, within a single coherent framework.

The postmodern critique. Likely cheered by Thurneysen, a number of pastoral theologians have sought to distinguish themselves from MPC. This trend was initiated by Thomas Oden, one of the first MPC authors to react against the movement's accommodation to modernity, at least in part as penance for his own earlier contributions (1966, 1967, 1972; and see his retractions in 1983, 1990). In his now classic exposé, Oden (1984) examined a number of the most important MPC texts and found that they were far more inclined to reference modern psychologists than earlier leaders in historic Christian pastoral care. In a later book, Oden (1990) became perhaps the pastoral care movement's first author to label himself *post*-modern, and in so doing, presaged a new direction in the pastoral care movement, an approach that will be designated *Postmodern Pastoral Care* (PPC). Since that time, Oden (1987-1992, 2003) has embarked on a second major career as a leader among those wishing to reinvest in the classical resources of Christianity.

No participant in the pastoral-care movement has done more to overcome the deficiencies of MPC than the pastoral theologian Don Browning. He has offered constructive critiques of the movement's weaknesses from the standpoint of ethics (1983) as well as of the modern psychologies upon which it was based (1987, 2006; Browning and Cooper, 2004) and has made significant theological contributions to pastoral care himself (1966, 1990, 2006). Recently he has been working with a cadre of like-minded theologians, psychologists and sociologists toward the articulation of a Christian postmodern view of the family (2000, 2003; Wall, Browning, Doherty & Post, 2002).

One of Browning's (1990) greatest contributions to pastoral care was his discussion of the importance of hermeneutics to the broader discipline called *practical theology*. He utilizes a version of Tillich's correlational method developed by the Catholic theologian David Tracy (1975, 1981). Immersed in the general hermeneutical theory of Gadamer and Ricoeur, Browning deftly argues that Christian practical theology—the systematic articulation of Christian practice—is grounded in and itself contributes to the Christian community's self-understanding, which is also fundamentally shaped by the classic texts of the Christian tradition. Browning's project has as its aim the development of Christian communal wisdom exemplified in Christian practice, which he tested empirically through case studies of three congregations.

In a number of ways Browning sets a high standard for Christians interested in the care of souls. First, his life project has been exemplary in its use of multiple modes of inquiry, including empirical investigation, engagement with Scripture and careful philosophical reflection, in the service of improving Christian practice. In his substantial critique of the implicit ethics of the various psychologies, from which he also wishes to learn (2006; Cooper, 2004), Browning's intelligent engagement with scholars outside the Christian faith offers a powerful example to evangelical psychologists and counselors of all stripes. His choice of ethics as a point of contact with those in the broader culture was brilliant. Moreover, in contrast to most works in modern psychology and theology (whether liberal or conservative), he recognizes that theory and practice are interdependent and that knowledge claims should be subject to criticism that is based on their practical, ethical implications. For most of the twentieth century, evangelical theology was largely divorced from soul-care practice, evidenced in the almost universal neglect of such matters in systematic theologies during this period (though the work of theologians like Ferguson, 1981; Lewis and Demarest, 1996; and Vanhoozer, 2005, may presage the renewal of such an orientation). Such neglect would have been unthinkable in premodern Christianity (Charry, 1997), and most importantly, in the theological sources of evangelicalism itself (Noll, 1995; e.g., Ames, 1983; Calvin 1559/1960).

However, the value of Browning's body of work is mitigated by his resolute commitment to a post-Kantian epistemological paradigm that is insufficiently subject to Scripture and Scripture's God. Though more interested in Scripture than MPC authors, the specter of the Enlightenment still haunts his work, depriving Scripture of its historic role as *primary* in the formulation of Christian theory and practice. It is not enough to affirm the "classic" texts of Christianity (1990); one looks in vain in his work for decisive guidance from Scripture for the church's practices. The recent dialogue he and Cooper (2004, chap. 11) have initiated with evangelicals is noteworthy and deserving of greater reciprocation than can be accomplished here, but their distaste for evangelicals' "positivist view of scriptural authority" (p. 265) suggests that our disagreements may lie in the modernism/postmodernism that remains uncritically correlated to their Christianity. One wishes there were greater appreciation for classical Christian views of Scripture and the sophisticated realism of contemporary Christian epistemologies like Plantinga, Alston and Wolterstorff, or a theologian like McGrath. While laudably seeking to promote

Christian intellectual influence in the contemporary world, Browning's conceptual framework would seem to have seriously weakened access to what most importantly distinguishes Christianity. Most problematic, throughout this body of work is the lack of a theocentric *gravitas*—such as one finds in the best premodern Christian literature. There is little discussion of the Christian God who exists beyond our constructions and has revealed himself in Christ and in Scripture, and—given its pastoral aims—surprisingly little reference to God's saving agency in human life and recognition of the soul-healing value of a personal relationship with God, as characterized the work of Augustine, Julian of Norwich, Martin Luther or John Wesley.

These limitations are likely also related to Browning's apologetic agenda. Browning and Cooper (2004) are right to challenge evangelicals to be less resistant to genuine dialogue with intellectuals outside the faith (pp. 252-53). However, evangelicals will wonder whether the desire to speak with those who are not "confirmed believers" (p. 2) has so driven their agenda that the more basic task—dialogue among Christians around the canon and its traditions—has been too much neglected, a task so necessary to clarify and deepen a community's distinctive self-understanding and identity. In some sense, this needs to happen "before" we speak with modernists and postmodernists, lest we "lose ourselves" in the worldviews of others. Genuine dialogue does not require either party to accommodate core features of its identity to the other or to weaken its commitment to persuade (Bakhtin, 1981).

For a variety of reasons, not least of which are his exemplary contributions, much of the work in pastoral care over the past three decades has demonstrated a greater willingness to integrate Scripture with secular psychology than was typical in Modern Pastoral Care (see Capps, 1981, 1987, 1990a, 1990b, 1993, 1995; Gerkin, 1984, 1997; Grant, 2001; Howe, 1995; Hunsinger, 1995; Lester, 1995, 2003; Olthuis, 2001). Of special interest are those works that focus especially on the use of Scripture or theology in pastoral care and counseling (Capps, 1981, 1990a; Oglesby, 1980; Stone, 1996; Wimberly, 1994). Though it is now over twenty-five years old, Capps's (1981) discussion of the use of the Bible in pastoral counseling is still the best available from a mainline perspective. Ahead of his time, Capps argued that one must consider genre if one is properly to interpret and apply a passage of Scripture.

While the pastoral care works in the "post-Hiltner era" are *generally* more open to Scripture than was typical in classic MPC, this contemporary pastoral care is still basically accommodating: it just accommodates to postmodernism. Olthuis (2001), for example, strenuously rejects the evils of modernist therapy but then goes to the postmodern philosophies of Levinas, Kristeva and Irigary for his therapeutic agenda rather than to historic Christian resources. Lester's (1995) narrative model of pastoral care is almost devoid of theological considerations, aside from the observation that Christianity is future-oriented, so influential is the secular existential and narrative theory that dominates it. In spite of a greater interest in the Bible, the MPC tendency to look primarily to contemporary non-Christian thought would seem to be alive and well in Postmodern Pastoral Care.

A postliberal recovery? More encouraging is the growing number of contemporary theologians in mainline denominations who have an interest in soul-care issues that is fueled by a serious engagement with Scripture and a respect for its authority to a far greater degree than is typically seen in MPC and PPC approaches (see Anderson, 1982, 1990, 2000; Brown, 2002; Ford, 1999; Hauerwas, 1983, 1990; Hunsinger, 1995; Jones, 1995; Loder, 1998; Price, 2002; Purves, 2004; Volf, 1998; Volf & Bass, 2002). These authors give evidence of a desire to see Scripture transform the Church and are unwilling to allow modern and postmodern psychology to set the church's soul-care agenda. Some of them are pastoral theologians, and some are not. As we might expect, much of this activity can be traced to the continuing influence of that early postliberal, Karl Barth. Though the efforts of postliberals and other Barthians tend to be hampered by the same post-Kantian epistemological dualism that afflicted Barth, their openness to the Word of God in Scripture has resulted in their thought, like that of Barth, being more robustly informed by Scripture than anything since Thurneysen.

Hunsinger (1995), for example, has offered a provocative model of pastoral counseling that assumes an "interdisciplinary" dualism regarding psychology and theology, but grounds it in the Chalcedonian statement regarding the two natures of Christ. She rightly criticizes Thurneysen for so emphasizing redemption that he was unable to appreciate adequately the contributions of psychological science. However, she maintains that the disciplines of theology and psychology have their own "'indissoluble differentiation'; they are seen as concepts which belong to their own respective disciplines and which have a kind of irreducible integrity within their own context. They are not to be confused with each other; theological concepts are not to be changed into psychological ones or vice versa" (p. 103). On the other hand, they must not be separated. Both perspectives are to be unified in the caregiver's practice, in order for the most comprehensive care to emerge. As a result, Hunsinger is better able to appreciate and make use of psychological science than Thurneysen. However, her model maintains a fundamental antithesis between the languages of psychology and theology *based on the doctrine of Christ's two natures* (perhaps providing a soul-care analogy to the Nestorian heresy[7]). While offering a Christocentric model for Christian soul care, it ultimately perpetuates the disciplinary dichotomy that modernity reified (while uniting the methods of Barth and Tillich!).

Quite different is the recent work of Andrew Purves (2004), trained in the neo-Barthian thought of T. F. Torrance. Purves is sharply critical of the theological vacuity of Hiltner and presents a model of pastoral theology deeply shaped by Scripture and grounded in the work of the triune God and the Christian's union with Christ. The work is pervasively Christocentric, and classical Christians will find much on which to feast. However, reminiscent of Thurneysen and Barth (and in contrast to Hunsinger), there is almost no engagement with contemporary psychological literature, resulting in a new Barthian model that, contrary to his intentions, continues to reinforce a dichotomy between the book of Nature and the book of Scripture. Another student of T. F. Torrance, Ray Anderson (1982, 1990, 2000, 2003) has done a better job of applying the scientific orientation of their teacher to the science of soul care. As a result, Anderson skillfully combines a submission to Scripture with a willingness to interpret psychological research and theory theocentrically. Anderson has written to evangelical counselors and pastors (1990, 2001), but his works require patience and diligence. Were they not so challenging, his prolific pen would have had much greater impact than it has had so far. But both Purves and Anderson have written more theologically profound treatments of soul care than can be found in the vast majority of evangelical counseling literature.

Conclusion

While, for the most part, MPC offers little of value to evangelicals interested in biblically based soul care, the postmodern and especially the postliberal/Barthian reengagement with Scripture presents a challenge that should provoke evangelicals to develop better soul-care models. To begin with, the substantial quality and intellectual rigor evident in their work, particularly that of people like Browning, Capps, Purves and Anderson sets the bar high for excellence in Christian soul-care theory and practice. Moreover, some have incorporated certain insights or models in contemporary psychology into their soul-care theory and practice, while maintaining a strong commitment to Christian truth. Generally speaking, evangelicals have developed relatively little that matches the caliber of this work.

But there remain concerns. Many commentators have suggested that postmodernism and modernism have far more in common with each other than they differ. The rejection of absolute truth joined to the absolute affirmation of the values of each community are an incoherent result of the objectivist, critical values of modernity turned back upon itself. As a result, the postmodern critique, including the postliberal reengagement with Scripture, contains some of the same problems that compromised the MPC movement. For one thing, we find within PPC a wide range of theological commitments, some of which deviate considerably from orthodoxy (though this cannot be said of the neo-Barthians and postliberals). As a result, while classical Christians must applaud PPC's greater emphasis on the Bible and theology, we must lament the theological softness, if not heterodoxy, of some of this work.

One example is the consistent undermining of the substitutionary theory of the atonement in works as diverse as Browning (1966) and Purves (2004), indicating a tendency to minimize the human predicament, both theologically and psychologically. Related to this is the discomfort of some of the PPC and postliberal authors with the classical understanding of sin as an offense to God that legitimately provokes his wrath towards the individual sinner (see Jn 3:36; Eph 2:1-3; Rev 16:1; Calvin, 1559/1960; Hill & James, 2004). When Christians downplay the offense of sin, an agenda alien to Christianity is operating somewhere, and the glory and greatness of God and his redemption from sin are inevitably correspondingly compromised. At its worst, postmodern accommodationism resembles too closely the theological agenda that one finds in MPC literature.

Perhaps no soul-care issue is more revealing on this score than that of homosexuality. Wherever Christianity has entered a culture, it has taught on the basis of the Scriptures that homosexuality is a sinful abnormality and has sought to bring healing for it in the name of Christ. Today, of course, there is intense pressure from our culture for Christians to accommodate to the autocentric framework of the expressive individualism of modernism/postmodernism that affirms individual preference regarding one's sexual object (and gender identity) over any other consideration (even evolutionary norms of reproductive success). Consequently, while there are many important ethical issues in our day, this issue in particular is a contemporary litmus test regarding scriptural authority, and one that is especially significant for soul care. As we would expect, liberal and postmodern pastoral care has reached a consensus that homosexuality must be accepted (see the ethics standards of the American Association of Pastoral Counselors; as well as Forward, 2000; Grant, 2001; McCarthy, 2000).

But evangelicals, along with others pursuing historic Christian orthodoxy, must follow Scripture, so they love persons who engage in homosexuality, while teaching its incompatibility with both human nature and the Christian faith, and working with those who struggle (Grenz, 1998; Jones & Yarhouse, 2000; Payne, 1996; Schmidt, 1995; Thompson, 2004). One might hope that the return to Scripture by postliberals and others influenced by Barth will lead them to fidelity regarding this momentous ethical issue (as seen in Anderson, 2007). So far, the signals are mixed (e.g., among theologians who have expressed their opinions, Childs [1985] and Gagnon [2002] have publicly supported the classical position, but others have shown slippage [see Brueggemann, Placher & Blount, 2002, in *Struggling with Scripture,* a fascinating title]). Concerned Christians should be praying that God will continue to foster a deeper reengagement with Scripture in this movement, and through that reengagement, grant a genuine and thorough revitalization in mainline pastoral care along increasingly biblical lines.

Notes

[1]This assertion is complicated by the fact that the formation of the New Testament canon was occurring during this time period. Most of the books of the New Testament were recognized as canonical by the late second century, but the final form of the New Testament canon was not settled until as late as the fifth century A.D. (Metzger, 1965; Bray, 1996).

[2]See Cooper, 2006, for a fascinating discussion on the role Tillich and his correlational approach played in dialogues concerning religion and psychology in the mid-twentieth century.

[3]Fueling and being shaped by this growing literature was an increasing national interest in pastoral counseling in the fifties. For example, early in the decade the new periodical for pastors, *Pastoral Psychology,* reached a peak of sixteen thousand subscribers; in the fifties almost seven hundred full-time chaplains worked in general or mental hospitals (an enormous increase over the previous decade); and by the end of the decade there were eighty-four Protestant counseling centers in the U.S. (Holifield, 1983), to say nothing of the counseling done in local churches by pastors influenced by this movement.

Notably, in addition to Hiltner and Oates, *Pastoral Psychology* had on its founding editorial board Rollo May and Carl Rogers. Both studied at Union Theological Seminary, where May likely began his appreciation for the thought of Tillich and graduated with a B.D. He affirmed a Tillichian/existential approach to religion (1953, p. 209), but the minimal presence of religious themes in his works (see e.g., 1953; 1967; 1969) would seem to illustrate the modern trend of secularization (if not also the influence of Tillich). Rogers left Union without graduating, furthering his movement away from the fundamentalist faith of his family-of-origin, and he said nothing about God or religion in his major writings. Indeed, he once described himself as "too religious to be religious" (Evans, 1975, p. 73). Both May and Rogers explicitly advocated self-realization as the primary goal of human life (Vitz, 1994), an expected orientation for Subject-oriented modernists. Their presence on the board of *Pastoral Psychology* indicates the deep appreciation the modern pastoral care movement had for the thought of these two guiding lights of modern, secular psychotherapy.

[4]For example, in his first chapter he addressed the subjects of freedom and destiny, categories themselves that are obviously more reflective of existentialism than the Bible or the Christian tradition. There he defined freedom as self-fulfillment, self-direction and self-transcendence, a profound contrast to the historic Christian understanding that true freedom is experienced in responsive obedience to God (Anderson, 1982; Bonhoeffer, 1955). He went on to say that "Paul saw that it was much more important to be a liberated man than a good man" (p. 19), implying a perverse divide in his system between virtue and freedom. In the next chapter, on grace and gratitude, he defined grace as "God has done something for us that he did not have to do and that we did not have coming to us in the contract" (p. 39). But he did not give this christological or redemptive content. On the contrary, grace seems to have morphed into providence: "The doctrine of grace, therefore, is a declaration that God is involved with the movement and progress of what he has created, and does not stand aloofly above or aside from his creation" (p. 41). However, the biblical authors understood grace to be directly related to sin. Grace, for Hiltner, was simply God's goodness toward us. Thus he tragically equated common grace with redemptive grace and undermined the true glory of both. In his chapter on sin and sickness, sin was said to be committed when "there is movement away from human fulfillment" (p. 82). The biblical teaching about sin, according to Hiltner, is not fundamentally about humans being evil and worthy of judgment, it is about our being responsible for our impairment and therefore having hope because we are responsible and therefore able to move toward being repaired (by grace, he says, but it sounds a lot like the "grace" of Pelagius).

Chapter eight focused on word and sacrament, so here we get the final form of Hiltner's views regarding the word of God. He calls the word of God a helpful metaphor (p. 166) that points toward the message that God is for us and desires our fulfillment. But he calls it a metaphor to make clear that humans have no access to the actual words of God. The great problem in church history on this score, he wrote, is to confuse the words of the Bible with the word of God. "Fundamentalists of all kinds and in nearly all ages have committed this heresy" (p. 173), a broad brush that essentially accuses all the major leaders and writers of the Christian church prior to the modern era of heresy and fundamentalism (see Bavinck, 1956; Gerstner, 1979; Preus, 1979; Reid, 1957; Warfield, 1970a), an allegation that obviously tells us more about Hiltner than anything else.

[5]Oates (1953, 1959) would be the major exception here. In a book (1953) devoted to the Bible's use in counseling, he seemed to be speaking to his pastoral-care colleagues (in a critique of Carl Rogers's nondirective techniques), "The pastor who uses the Bible realistically in his counseling ministry cannot be dominated by secular concepts devised by men who have little or no knowledge of the Bible or concern for its place in culture and in the instruction, patience, and comfort of distressed people" (pp. 71-72). He encouraged pastoral counselors to exercise their authority as knowledgeable Bible interpreters in order to relieve religious anxieties and concerns, provide moral guidance and mediate com-

fort to those suffering. When persons are in distress, "The Biblical revelation has almost a startling relevance when the pastor (who has steeped his own mind in the thought forms and encompassed his spiritual perceptions in the redemptive design of the whole Bible) confronts the critical situation that occurs between him, and a person in need, and the living God when he ministers to the needy person in his crucial hour" (p. 89). Looking back on his career years later, Oates (1986) wrote that whereas many pastoral counselors found the "centers" of their counseling work in the therapy systems of various schools, he always sought to make his center the presence of God as revealed in Scripture (1986).

In comparison with his peers, Oates was the exception within the modern pastoral-care movement and dispositionally closer to the use of Scripture within the "Great Tradition" of pastoral care that we examined above. Yet, in spite of his advocacy of the Bible, he tended to use it in piecemeal fashion, as a source of insights or a book of maxims to give persons something to comfort or guide them. This is certainly legitimate, but it is a far cry from seeing the reformative, canonical role of the Bible that we have seen practiced throughout church history, especially in the churches of the Reformation. He cited Tillich and the Tillichian pastoral-care leaders approvingly and demonstrated a much better understanding of modern psychotherapy than of classic Christian theology. One has to wonder why Oates's own fidelity to Scripture did not alert him to the problems in the modern pastoral-care movement and the move of its canonical center to that of secular therapy systems, and why he was content to so identify himself with and participate in that movement throughout his life.

[6]Of course, to raise this issue will seem uncharitable to some, and I realize that only Christ is ultimately worthy of the label Christian. But both the Old and New Testaments make it clear that covenantal discourse entails talk of boundaries, even as we unite around the Center, the triune God (Erickson, Helseth & Taylor, 2004).

[7]Historically the Nestorian heresy has been considered the belief that the individual Jesus Christ is composed of two persons: one divine and one human.

3

The Bible and Current Evangelical Soul-Care Paradigms

MODERNIST CHRISTIANS HAVE TENDED TO EMBRACE modern psychology and therapy rather uncritically, and to the extent they related their faith to modern therapy, it was a "modern" faith. But there have been a number of other ways Christians have approached modern psychology and therapy, depending on their training, professional and vocational context, and theological orientation.

The Levels-of-Explanation Approach and Scripture

Probably the approach held by most Christian academic psychologists over the past hundred years has been the "levels-of-explanation" approach (Myers, 1978, 2000), or perspectivalism (Evans, 1977). It has been exemplified by nonclinical psychologists like Jeeves (1976, 1997), Mackay (1982), Myers (1978, 1996, 2000), Myers and Jeeves (1987), and Boivin (2002). Proponents have argued that the languages of faith and of science offer distinct forms of explanation that cannot be brought together without distortion of one or the other. Theology and psychology provide two valuable approaches to reality, they say, and each has something significant to offer us in the development of a full understanding of human nature: theology addresses issues of ultimate meaning and purpose, whereas psychology provides a careful description of empirical human beings and causal relations between human phenomena. However, these two perspectives ought not to be confused; psychologists and theologians are working on different projects with different objects. As a result, the Scriptures should never be considered relevant for the scientific work of the psychologist or, by extension, the clinical work of the psychotherapist.

While this approach tends to be more popular among Christian academic psychologists and professors than among Christian counselors, it would be naïve to think that there were not many Christian therapists who essentially subscribe to this view. Even some who call themselves integrationists seem in practice to hold to this approach. We should begin by acknowledging that this model is based on some valid intuitions. Divine causality is not the same as natural causality; God's Spirit ought not to be identified with psychological processes. Moreover, as this view's proponents frequently point out, understanding the more mechanistic aspects of human nature (e.g., memory schemas) is not much altered by faith concerns (in contrast, say, to psychopathology or counseling). In order to understand human nature accurately, some "perspective-like" distinctions are called for (though we will view them considerably differently in chapters ten and eleven). However, its proponents often fail to appreciate the significance of their model's compatibility with most of the core assumptions of modernism. By assuming a modern, neopositivistic philosophy of psychology, its valid concerns are confounded by control beliefs that are alien to Christianity. One consequence is its incapacity to offer a comprehensive, holistic approach to human beings. Its radical separation between psychology and theology allows Christians to practice counseling according to the current standards of the mental-health community, which are largely secular, and thus avoid the cognitive dissonance that more reflection and a more explicit utilization of one's faith might entail. They can do this by cordoning off their religious beliefs and norms from the rest of their beliefs and practices. Myers, for example, exemplifies this tendency with his long-standing acceptance of homosexuality and his questioning of the Christian community's historic prohibitions against it (see Myers, 2000, 2003; Myers & Jeeves, 1987; Myers & Scanzoni, 2005).

Christians in counseling who hold to a levels-of-explanation approach will likewise have no need to consult Scripture with reference to their work. Working within secular scientific and mental-health environments presents serious challenges for Christians, but this solution seems extreme to most self-identified Christian counselors (for example, those involved in the American Association of Christian Counselors and the Christian Association for Psychological Studies). As a result, we will spend more time discussing two evangelical counseling approaches that grant Scripture more of a role.

The Integration Approach and Scripture

The integration model of Christian scholarship was developed by evangelicals in the last half of the twentieth century. In reaction to the perceived intellectualism of theological liberals from whom they were separating, fundamentalists in the early twentieth century had eschewed more scholarly approaches to the Bible and started forming their own institutions of higher learning (Bible colleges) that concentrated on the Bible and tended to neglect other studies, except insofar as they provided practical, vocational training (Noll, 1995; Ringenberg, 1984). By mid-century, evangelicalism had arisen as a reaction to fundamentalism and was more open to scholarship that sought to reengage the intellectual world of the day. In order to receive advanced training in various disciplines, Christians began to reenter the academic realm (that had by now been entirely taken over by modernism), and they discovered that much of the knowledge being taught was valid and useful, in spite of the fact that there could be no public reference to God or faith. Yet there was a nagging sense that faith should have some role to play in that knowledge. The concept of integration was formulated to help deal with this issue.

The task of integration was based on a recognition of the "all-embracing truth of God" (Gaebelein, 1954, p. 8). Gaebelein, an early evangelical proponent of integration, was one of the first to sound the cry that "all truth is God's truth" (p. 20). The foundation of all truth is the fact that it is revealed by God. This revelation is found primarily in the Bible, but it is also manifested in the natural world, so that the Bible and nature can be called God's "two books." Gaebelein offered his ideas about what integration might look like in a few different fields (mathematics, literature and music) and suggested that it involves studying the subject matter in light of what the Bible has to say about it, recognizing that its beauty and complexity come from God, and engaging in its activity (e.g. musical performance) as service for Christ's sake.

Gaebelein's little book was seminal for an evangelical movement reacting against fundamentalist isolation and anti-intellectualism. Over the next fifty years, some of its statements would become shibboleths of academic orthodoxy at major evangelical liberal-arts colleges, as Christian scholars attempted to relate their faith with the learning they obtained in the secular graduate schools they had attended (see Holmes, 1977). Reflection on integration has continued throughout this time, so that our understanding of the integration project today is significantly more sophisticated than when Gaebelein first outlined the task (see e.g., Hasker, 1992; Wolfe, 1987; Wolterstorff, 1975, 2004).

At the time Gaebelein penned his classic, evangelical soul care had largely disappeared. In contrast to the rich heritage of classical soul care and the growing modern pastoral-care movement, fundamentalists and evangelicals gave scant attention to the well-being of the soul after it was converted to Christ. The first evangelical group to recognize this void consisted of evangelicals who had studied counseling at secular universities and believed their training could aid the church. Looking for a rationale, they became some of integration's most enthusiastic supporters. Their numbers included Clyde Narramore (1960), Bruce Narramore (1973) together with Carter (1979), Collins (1969, 1977, 1980, 1981), the early Crabb (1975, 1977, 1987), and perhaps most famously James Dobson (1970, 1979). The sixties and seventies could be called the golden age of integration work among Christians in psychology. Since that time there have been many significant contributions. Some of the most important include Kirwin (1984), Narramore (1984), Farnsworth (1985), Jones and Butman (1991), Collins (1994, 2000), Tan (1987a, 1991, 1996); Dueck (1995), McMinn (1996, 2004), McMinn and Campbell (2007), Worthington (1989, 2000), Shults and Sandage (2003, 2006), Hall and Porter (2004), Beck and Demarest (2005), and many others that cannot be mentioned. The movement has sought to take legitimate research and theory from contemporary psychology and cultivate a psychological and clinical sophistication in their understanding of people, in order to help promote the well-being of Christ's people.

However, once one gets beyond the general goal of "integrating faith and psychology," one finds the integration movement is strikingly disparate. There are significant differences in the quality of integration done, and most notably, in the understanding of what integration actually is. To help navigate this variability, a few integrationists have devised a matrix of integration models, by which the extant types can be categorized, compared and contrasted (e.g., Carter & Narramore, 1979; Collins, 1981; Eck, 1996; Farnsworth, 1985; Jones & Butman, 1991). There was value in this endeavor, but it has also likely contributed to some of the confusion surrounding the concept, since it forced all the models of relating faith and psychology into an integrationist mold.[1] This tendency to construe all the approaches that Christians take to psychology as various forms of *integration* is very common and may indicate that some of its proponents are so embedded in an integrationist mindset that it is hard for them to recognize the distinctiveness of the alternative models.[2]

Consequently, rather than use any of the extant matrices of "integration," we will concern ourselves in what follows with what seem to be *pure* integration models and attempt to distinguish between different subtypes of integration: first, between different kinds and qualities of what is termed here conceptual integration, and second, between conceptual and ethical integration. We will finish the discussion with a critique of some of the planks in the general integration platform.

Conceptual integration. The majority approach among genuine integration models considers integration to be an intellectual project concerned with bringing together and harmonizing the concepts of the theology and philosophy of the Christian faith with those of contemporary psychology. Consequently this approach will be called "conceptual integration." As just suggested, there are great differences in how and to what extent integrationists integrate concepts from the two (or three) disciplines. The state of the art is illustrated in the *Baker Encyclopedia of Psychology and Counseling* (Benner & Hill, 1999), a significant resource that has as its goal "evaluating the concepts, theories, and research findings (of the rapidly expanding body of knowledge in psychology) in light of biblical teachings" (p. 7). However, we find within an enormous diversity in the quality of the conceptual integration present.[3] Of course, some differences are unavoidable in an encyclopedia, but given its stated goal, the wide variance may signify the lack of a genuine consensus regarding what integration is, and it demonstrates the extent to which its different proponents believe integration can be attempted. As a result, conceptual integration has to be further distinguished between high quality or *strong* conceptual integration and poor quality or *weak*. Simply put: strong integration approaches can be easily identified by evidence of a substantial impact of Christian belief on the discourse. On the other end of the continuum, weak integration is demonstrated by a marginal to negligible impact.

Strong conceptual integration. When most people think of the integration of faith and psychology, strong conceptual integration is likely the ideal they are thinking of. However, even here, not everyone is agreed, for among its best proponents, there are two different formulations of integration: interdisciplinary integration (II) and worldview integration (WI).

The dominant understanding of conceptual integration is usually termed "interdisciplinary" or just "disciplinary" integration (Beck & Demarest, 2005; Bouma-Prediger, 1990; Gorsuch, 2002; Shults & Sandage, 2003; Worthington, 1994), and it consists of the integration of the two disciplines: theology and psychology. Its advocates understand theology to be the study of the Bible (though it may also include philosophy and church history)—which is divinely inspired and is *special revelation*—and psychology to be the empirical investigation of human beings—which is considered *general revelation* (see e.g., Collins, 1977; Carter & Narramore, 1979; Farnsworth, 1985; Larzelere, 1980; Timpe, 1999b). According to Carter and Narramore, "Theology represents the distillation of God's revelation of Himself to humanity in a linguistic, conceptual, and cultural medium people can understand," whereas "psychology is primarily concerned with the mechanisms by which people function and the methods to assess and influence that functioning" (p. 49). Interdisciplinary integration, then, is the attempt to "unite or combine aspects of two different disciplines" (Bouma-Prediger, 1990, p. 23). "The aim is to compare and contrast, and if possible, reconcile and unite the assumptions, conclusions, methods, and so forth, of two distinct disciplines so as to combine them in some fruitful way" (p. 24). Consequently, the task of interdisciplinary integration ostensibly involves reflection on the propositions of modern psychology and the propositions of theology (and the Bible) in order for Christians to end up with discourse that includes both theological and psychological propositions and that is logically consistent with the Christian faith. This would seem to be an extremely laudable goal. However, most proponents admit that it has hardly been realized. Most of the best examples of interdisciplinary integration are popular books aimed either at Christian counselors or lay Christians.

Another approach to conceptual integration—and one of the best examples by most accounts—is *Modern Psychotherapies* (Jones & Butman, 1991), a thorough, systematic critique of twelve major models of modern psychotherapy in light of a Christian worldview (reviewing each model's philosophical assumptions; models of personality, abnormality, health and psychotherapy; and demonstrated effectiveness). In terms of its knowledge of the discipline at the time of its composition, it compared favorably with the best of the pastoral-care tradition (in contrast to the more popular level of most interdisciplinary integration literature); but in terms of its Christian critique, it exceeded almost everything else.[4] In contrast to most integrationists, Jones and Butman do not consider integration to be interdisciplinary. They believe that psychology and theology are "two distinct conceptual disciplines" (p. 19), and they should therefore *not* be "fused together." Instead, following Wolterstorff (1975), they believe the task of integration involves "the explicit incorporation of religiously based beliefs as the control beliefs that shape the perceptions of facts, theories and methods in social sciences" (p. 20). The fact that most integrationists view integration as interdisciplinary and yet still consider Jones and Butman to be leading proponents of their position is more evidence that there may be some unresolved confusion at the heart of the integration project. But worldview integration shares in common with interdisciplinary integration the assumptions that psychology and theology are to be sharply distinguished from each other and that their disciplinary boundaries as drawn in the modern era are legitimate. Where worldview integration differs from interdisciplinary integration is in the former's advocacy of the "incorporation" (or integration) of *Christian worldview beliefs* (presumably derived from Christian theology and philosophy)—*rather than biblical or theological propositions per se*—into the thinking of Christians regarding psychology. Jones and Butman are clear that they want to avoid a final product that is an invalid hybridization of two distinct disciplines. However, the chief problem of this position is that it would seem to exclude the use of the Bible by Christians in psychology; at best, it can be used to formulate a Christian worldview. Nevertheless, Jones and Butman are widely recognized as leaders and exemplars of integration by most Interdisciplinary Integration advocates, probably because they do such good integration in *Modern Psychotherapies*.[5]

Jones and Butman (1991) distinguish between a *critical evaluation* stage of integration, in which current secular psychology is carefully studied and assessed and the valid is retained and the invalid (from a Christian standpoint) is rejected, and a *theory-building* stage, where Christians develop their own research and theories, shaped by work from the first stage and Christian worldview beliefs—but not by biblical content directly. Their own book, they acknowledge, is only an example of critical evaluation. The authors warn of the dangers of accepting the secular biases of modern psychology and incorporating false speculations posing as science, but they respond to integration's critics by arguing that non-Christians are capable of discovering scientific truth about human beings, and Christians interested in human beings must make responsible use of such knowledge. The quality of their integrationist scholarship has not been surpassed.

The strengths of both types of strong conceptual integration (SCI) are considerable. First, in contrast to the levels-of-explanation and modern pastoral care models, SCI holds an evangelical commitment to Scripture and therefore maintains a belief in its relevance to psychological understanding and counseling. As a result, when Scripture conflicts with modern psychology, SCI has maintained Christian orthodoxy (e.g., rejecting the belief that homosexuality is a legitimate option for human beings, see Collins, 2000; Jones & Yarhouse, 2000), and the best SCI literature makes reference to Christian realities that are beyond the capacity of secularists (and theological liberals) to recognize, like the role of the Holy Spirit, the evil and destructiveness of sin, and the healing power of a supernatural salvation (see e.g., Anderson, Zuelke & Zuelke, 2000; Cloud & Townsend, 2001; Collins, 1994; McMinn, 2004; among others). Second, evidencing their training in modern psychology, SCI demonstrates a knowledge and utilization of sophisticated psychological theory and research, and many have worked hard to benefit the church and Christian soul care by applying the best science of human beings available. Third, their familiarity with the current field has also helped a few strong conceptual integrationists contribute to the contemporary field of psychology, using modernist, scientific discourse standards to address issues of importance to Christians. In this way they have broadened the scope of the discipline and increased its validity. Their contribution has included work on the value of religion as a dialogue partner for psychology (Jones, 1994), the role of values in counseling and therapy (Tjeltveit, 1999; Worthington, 1993), the psychology of religion (Gorsuch, 1988; Spilka, Hood, Hunsberger & Gorsuch, 2003) and the use of horizontal forgiveness as a counseling strategy (Worthington, Sandage & Berry, 2000). It must be admitted, however, that such work is also compatible with a levels-of-explanation approach and is also promoted by the proponents of that model (see, e.g., Myers, 1993, 2000, 2003).

Weak conceptual integration. However, as suggested above, not all conceptual integration is of high quality. One of the difficulties we face here, however, is that poor quality is to some extent in the eye of the beholder, and, of course, no one labels himself as a poor integrator. Consequently, we will limit ourselves to a description of a few examples of weak conceptual integration (WCI) and finish with some evaluative remarks.

One kind of WCI is the illustrative use of the Bible, where the integration consists of finding illustrations of psychological phenomena in the Bible. An example of this was seen in a panel discussion on bipolar disorder at a recent national conference of Christian counselors (Carter, Okamoto, Barnhurst & Rheinheimer, 2003). The first speaker opened the two-hour presentation with a case study of King Saul as a possible biblical example of someone with bipolar disorder. Then, the following discussants—a psychiatrist and two psychotherapists—provided helpful medical and clinical information regarding the causes and treatment of the disorder, but without any mention of the Bible or theology, let alone reference to King Saul! The integration therefore was extremely limited. But one can question whether it is even appropriate to use Scripture in this way. Does the Bible's main contribution to psychopathology lie in narrative examples of particular disorders? What if we cannot find an example? Does the Bible have nothing else of importance to say regarding the nature and experience of psychological problems? The well-intentioned presenters did not appear to understand the Bible to be a worldview-constituting text, which lights our path (Ps 119:105) by giving us a way of seeing things differently (Jones & Butman, 1991; Powlison, 2004). Many integrationists are rightly motivated to bring the Bible into their work, but without an adequate conceptual framework for interpreting secular psychology and the Bible and relevant theological literature, they are unable to accomplish what they sincerely desire to do.

Another kind of WCI is the use of the Bible and Christian theology strictly as a set of epistemological standards, to screen modern psychology and evaluate it for glaring contradictions with Christian thought. Conceived in this way, at best, integration consists of little more than the rather mechanical intellectual task of comparing propositions of psychological content with those having biblical or theological content, regardless of their original worldview context. In such cases, WCI amounts to little more than a simple *comparative* task requiring relatively superficial categorical organization, rather than a complex *interpretive* task, that seeks to understand what the author actually meant (Collins, 2000, pp. 115-18; De Vries, 1982; Johnson, 1997a). Most of the time, when used by itself, this "rule-book" approach to the Bible (Bookman, 1994b) results in the uncritical reception of almost all of modern psychology, since blatant, explicit contradictions of biblical teaching are relatively infrequent in secular psychological discourse, which was developed in part to avoid reference to metaphysics.

The rather superficial discussions typical of WCI tend to obscure significant differences in linguistic meaning, while conveying the false impression that some unity of truth has been forged between the disciplines. When propositions are treated as mere "atoms of thought"—and pulled from their respective texts—to be compared with each other (or just laid aside each other!), their original meaning within their semiotic "field"—the sociolinguistic context within which that meaning is to be found—is impossible to grasp. Complex theoretical terms, constructs and practices must be understood within their original context if they are to be properly understood.

A Christian reading and interpretation of the texts of modern psychology must always keep in mind their grounding in a modern, secular ideological surround (Watson, 1993). Counseling concepts, in particular, are loaded with connotations shaped by worldview beliefs. Notions like mental health, psychopathology, positive psychology, self-actualization, self-esteem, locus of control, unconditional positive regard, assertiveness, narcissism, sexual orientation and even spirituality are not autonomous intellectual atoms but are subtly modified by the larger sociolinguistic context within which they are used and therefore are unavoidably embedded with worldview significance. Since WCI does not typically explore these kinds of complex interpretive issues, their integration work is rendered more or less suspect. This is why, all too often, the work of WCI proponents differs little from that of their secular colleagues, even in areas where we would expect substantial differences. For example, weak conceptual integrationists may write on "religion," "spirituality" and even "God," but do so as mere theists, rather than distinctively Christian trinitarians. This is appropriate when secularists and other theists are the intended audience—some adjustments are usually necessary when communicating with those in other communities. But weak conceptual integrationists use this generic way of speaking throughout all of their writings, even in Christian journal articles and books. One is forced to conclude that at least some understandings of integration entail a linguistic/conceptual capitulation to modernism, so that one fails to speak the "language of Zion" even when the audience is the people of God. Ultimately, this move is destructive to the Christian psychological community's self-understanding and has effectively sundered much of its ability to think creatively—for itself—about psychology and counseling. As a result of these problems, weak conceptual integration deserves the label "pseudointegration" (Wolfe, 1987).

Ethical integration. Integrationists themselves have acknowledged there has been a lack of substantive integration work since the foundations were laid in the sixties and seventies (Collins, 2000; Sorenson, 1996a; Worthington, 1994), and many have suggested that there is a need to broaden the scope of integration beyond a conceptual orientation and make the ethical, relational, experiential or sociocultural dimensions central to the integrative project (see Bouma-Prediger, 1990; Canning, Case & Kruse, 2001; Canning, Pozzi, McNeil & McMinn, 2000; Collins, 2000; Dueck, 1995; Farnsworth, 1985; Gorsuch, 2002; Sorenson, 1996a, 1996b, 2004; Worthington, 1994). The fact that one of the movement's founders, Gary Collins (2000), is strongly advocating such a reappraisal signifies that a major shift in emphasis may be underway (though it must be pointed out that he himself acknowledged the personal dimension of integration long ago [1981, p. 83], as did Carter & Narramore, 1979, in their influential work). Similar to the Romantic movement's reaction to the intellectualism of the Enlightenment (and somewhat influenced by today's postmodern reaction to modernism), these authors argue, in different ways, that the task of integration should not be considered primarily a logical, conceptual enterprise. This, they rightly recognize, was a function of modernist influence. Instead, they believe that integration involves, fundamentally, the bringing of one's Christian values, beliefs and relationship with God into one's personal and professional life such that Christian counselors act with integrity and coherence throughout their faith and life.

This *ethical* integration (see Jones, 1986; Jones & Butman, 1991) reflects the overriding concern of the New Testament that one's faith in Christ should permeate and transform one's entire life and relations with others, and the importance of this concern to God is inestimable. This agenda should be central to every Christian involved in counseling and therapy, regardless of how they relate their faith to psychology (see Johnson & Jones, 2000, pp. 244-45). Yet, in reference to the subtext of this book—articulating the role that Scripture should play in our counseling theory and practice—the ethical integration (EI) agenda offers little help. Ethical integrationists point counselors to the high ethical-spiritual norms of Scripture: Spirit-led service to Christ (Collins, 2000; Farnsworth, 1985); care of others, especially the poor (Collins, 2000; Canning, Case & Kruse, 2001; Dueck, 1995); cultural sensitivity (Collins, 2000; Dueck, 1995); personal and spiritual wholeness, integrity, inner consistency and congruence (Bouma-Prediger, 1990; Sorenson, 1996a, 1996b); and gratitude and joy (Sorenson, 1996b). However, it offers little direction in how to allow Scripture to inform theory or practice beyond these broad ethical principles (most of which are equally compatible with other philosophical or religious frameworks). They are right to note that psychology and especially counseling has essential ethical implications. Yet psychology is also essentially a rational-linguistic, scientific project that has produced an enormous set of texts, so the rational-linguistic side of integration cannot be neglected. The valid desire to move beyond the intellectualism of conceptual integration may lead in the minds of some to a pragmatic "solution" that offers little help and hope for a genuine alternative to modern psychology.

As already mentioned, many integrationists recognize that the dichotomy between conceptual and ethical integration is false (e.g., Carter & Narramore, 1979; Eck, 1996; Tan, 1987b, 2001). Hall and Porter (2004) have made some progress by uniting the "conceptual" and the "experiential" models of integration into a single, complex model. Especially promising is the "integrative psychotherapy" model of McMinn and Campbell (2007), which develops a sophisticated Christian cognitive-relational approach to therapy, as well as the "relational integration" of Shults and Sandage (2006, p. 26), who have explored forgiveness (2003) and spirituality (2006) from their respective interdisciplinary vantage points (Shults: theology, Sandage: psychology). More work like this needs to be done by strong conceptual integrationists, if the integration project is to make the progress that its founders originally envisioned.[6]

Questions About Integration

As the foregoing shows, there is a great deal of diversity among those who call themselves integrationists. Such variety and the relative paucity of rigorous, academic integration literature raise some questions about the integration project itself. Gaebelein's original ideal of integrating all knowledge unto God would seem to be deeply Christian, but there are some reasons to believe that the common, contemporary understanding of integration may be intrinsically flawed, perhaps contributing to the stagnation the movement has faced since its golden age (Collins, 2000; Sorenson, 1996a; Worthington, 1994).

Integration and the antithesis principle: The relation of the Fall to knowledge and practice, part 1. Church fathers like Tertullian and Augustine taught that at their core Christian thinking and living diverged sharply from non-Christian. They based this stance on biblical teaching regarding a fundamental contrast between the thinking and living of the people of God and those who remain alienated from him (2 Cor 6:14-18; Eph 2:1-3; 1 Jn 2:15; 5:19; Jas 4:14). Augustine (1949), in the *City of God*, described a basic motivational disparity between the two groups: there are those who love God and despise self, and there are those who love self and despise God. Augustine rightly understood that such crucial differences in the heart lead to radical differences in understanding God, humans and the rest of reality. Throughout the history of Christian thought, a basic religious division in humanity has been assumed, termed by Abraham Kuyper (1898a, 1898b) the *antithesis*. Kuyper taught that *regeneration* was responsible for a radical change in Christians, who as sinners have lived primarily for themselves, but now—because of regeneration—seek to live primarily for God. Kuyper argued further that this antithesis leads to two different types of sciences that operate according to different fundamental principles. Since then, the term *antithesis* has been used by many in the Dutch Reformed tradition (Dooyeweerd, 1979, 1984; Mouw, 2001; Runner, 1982; C. Van Til, 1972; H. Van Til, 1959; Walsh & Middleton, 1984; Woltiers, 1985). As Stob described the antithesis (quoted by Mouw), there is a "real and uncompromising, although uneven, contest being waged between God and Satan, between Christ and antichrist, between the seed of the woman and the seed of the serpent, between the church and the world" (p. 15). Accordingly, there is no neutral standpoint by which we can live and understand reality. One's ultimate religious allegiances color everything one interprets and does. We might state the antithesis principle this way: *Non-Christian thought and life are alienated from God and operate in ways that are fundamentally opposed to Christian thought and life.*

The antithesis that divides humanity into two ultimate groups has numerous, significant psychological effects, including distorted thinking, motives, feelings, attitudes, values, choices and actions, and so ultimately even plans and programs. The so-called noetic effects of sin (Moroney, 1999; Nash, 1988; Westphal, 1990) lead to misunderstandings regarding reality so serious that they obscure our interpretations and warp our descriptions of important aspects of God and his creation. In fact, the closer the particular discipline is to the central issues of life, the greater the distortion (Brunner, 1946). These distortions can only be undone by the illuminating work of the Holy Spirit (1

Cor 2), yet because of indwelling sin, Christians can never assume that the noetic effects of sin have been completely eliminated from their own minds. Consequently, Christians must also regularly examine their own thinking and living, so that they can reduce the influence of the antithesis on their own thought and life.[7]

If such an antithesis exists anywhere, one would expect it to show up in models of soul care, where basic beliefs about human nature (including abnormality and treatment) are being utilized and implemented all the time. As noted in chapter two, modern psychology arose within an intellectual context where beliefs in God and the spiritual realm were being increasingly called into question and removed from scientific discourse. Modern soul care deals with the core religious issues of life—human meaning, fulfillment, abnormality and recovery—but it is secular and grounded in evolutionary theory and naturalism or humanism, and it assumes the Self as the source of morality and recovery and its well-being as the ultimate value. In various ways, modern soul care is based in, perpetuates and fosters a fundamentally human-centered orientation (Cushman, 1995; Holifield, 1983; Johnson & Sandage, 1999; Vitz, 1994).

So, at its core, modern soul care is directly antithetical to Christian. The fact that such matters are often not even addressed in their literature would suggest that some integrationists are naïve about the intellectual conflict that has been waged over the past few centuries and have underestimated, on the one hand, how profoundly non-Christian worldview assumptions distort the research choices, data interpretations and conclusions, and theoretical formulations of modern psychology, and on the other, the tremendous soul-care resources organic to Christianity (with the exception of the recent renewal of interest in Christian spirituality, e.g., Benner, 2004a; Moon, 2004). In contrast to modern pastoral care proponents, integrationists did not "modernize" their theological beliefs, but like them some have tended to seem more interested in the achievements of modern psychology than in the Bible and the Christian tradition. (Could this be a main difference between weak and strong integration?) To help rekindle the movement, integrationist models across the board will have to reflect more of the kind of antithesis awareness seen in Jones and Butman (1991) and McMinn and Campbell (2007).

Is psychology really a product of general revelation? One reason the antithesis principle may have been neglected is that most integrationists believe that the facts of psychology are the product of general revelation (Carter & Narramore, 1979; Collins, 1977; early Crabb, 1977; Guy, 1980; Hurley & Berry, 1997a; Timpe, 1999b). As Timpe suggests: "The task of integration involves explicitly relating truth discovered through general or natural revelation to that disclosed in special or biblical revelation, of interrelating knowledge gained from the world and knowledge gained from the Word" (p. 192). The core intuition is valid: God is the ultimate source of everything good (Jas 1:17), so somehow he is *involved* in the development of scientific truth. But should that be called *general revelation*?

Historically, Christian theologians have understood the term "general revelation" to refer to God's ongoing revelation of *himself* through the created order (Rom 1:20-23) and not to the activities of humankind. Think about it: if psychological science were general revelation, what exactly is being *revealed?* Perhaps we could say, truth about human nature. But if so, how exactly is *God* doing the *revealing* in the course of someone's research study or the writing or reading of a text? It is certainly not like what he did in the burning bush or the inspiration of Scripture.

The major problem with labeling psychology "general revelation" is it implies that the texts of psychology and the Bible are *both* products of the direct activity of God (perhaps leading to the conclusion that psychology texts have a validity and authority equal to that of the Bible. Bookman [1994b] calls this the *falsely perceived validity fallacy*). But God's activity with respect to psychology is not directly causal; he does not *inspire* psychology research or texts. The latter are socially constructed attempts to describe human nature based on research and a set of worldview assumptions, and as we all know, the assumptions may be flawed, the research more or less faulty, and the texts may contain some falsehoods. In contrast, the Christian faith understands the Bible to consist of human writings that are simultaneously *divinely authored.* This dual-authorship renders the Bible unique, gives it an authority over human life that no other text has and also guarantees that it is free from deception and error; therefore, its assertions and worldview assumptions are uniformly and permanently correct, something that cannot be said of any set of scientific texts. As Bookman (1994b) notes, to use the term "general revelation" to refer to knowledge-formation in science is simply a category mistake.

Some integrationists (e.g., Farnsworth, 1985) have more carefully noted that *both* psychology and theology are socially constructed disciplines, and therefore neither can themselves be considered direct revelation nor authoritative over the other. This rightly reminds us that both disciplines are necessarily limited and partially distorted versions of reality. However, this point also obscures the unique nature of Scripture as verbal revelation from God—which gives *it* a unique authority that is mediated in human rearticulations of its content. The Bible is a *text* that "projects a world"—it offers a divinely inspired interpretation of reality. The created order *contains* meaning—we could say it is constituted with meaning by it's Creator God (e.g., the human genome)—but that meaning was not *communicated by God to humans.* It remains embedded in the created order, unless human activity "pries" it out through some investigative procedures (like careful observation with special instrumentation).

Avoiding the term "general revelation" for psychology is especially important in our day, since the secular psychologies that currently dominate the field are grounded in modern worldview assumptions that in certain respects are fundamentally incompatible with Christianity. Consequently, the Christian interpretation of the texts of modern psychology is in some ways more problematic than the interpretation of the Bible. The worldview bias of modern psychology is recognized by strong integrationists (see e.g., Jones & Butman, 1991, chap. 1), but it is rarely acknowledged in much integrationist writing, leaving readers to speculate about an author's lack of awareness of such matters. Integrationist authors in the future will have to do a better job convincing their readers that they are reading secular psychology critically *as Christians.* In light of these considerations, "common grace" is a better theological term to refer to God's involvement in scientific research and the writing and reading of texts, since it refers to God's active goodness manifested in good human activity and its products, without implying that they flowed directly and infallibly from his mind (see below).

All alleged truth is not necessarily God's truth. The belief that psychology is based on general revelation is tied closely to another common theme in the integrationist paradigm, its favorite motto: "All truth is God's truth." No Christian, of course, can deny the statement (even Jay Adams, 2003, affirms it), if by it one means that, since God is the omniscient Creator of the universe, he knows all things and both the universe and truths about it belong to him. A problem arises, however, when "all truth" is equated with all the texts of human scientific activity. The history of scientific research makes clear that scientists have often believed certain states-of-affairs to be the case which in fact were not so (Butterfield, 1957; Goldstein, 1980; Kuhn, 1962, 1977a; Toulmin, 1972). And given human finitude and the antithesis principle, Christians ought to expect that human scientific activity will yield some distortions in human understanding, particularly when dealing with issues of ultimate significance (Jones, 1986; Kuyper, 1898b; Westphal, 1990). As a result, perhaps the phrase "All truth is God's truth" needs to be elaborated: "All truth is God's truth, but not all texts express God's truth." Unfortunately, that is not quite so pithy. Nonetheless, not all the assertions of modern psychology are true.

Consider, for example, the role evolutionary theory has played in modern psychology, a fact that has become more evident in the evolutionary explanations offered for an increasing number of psychological phenomena over the past fifteen years. It is a fact that orthodox Christians disagree about the means God used to come up with human creatures made in his image. However, orthodox Christians cannot countenance the reductionism intrinsic to the naturalistic worldview of hardcore evolutionary psychology. For one thing, it is committed to the belief that the unique psychological phenomena that characterize contemporary humans arose in their environment of evolutionary adaptedness (EEA), somewhere between one hundred thousand to one million years ago (depending on the ancestor of interest). The burdensome consequence of this assumption is that evolutionary psychologists must explain *every* unique psychological characteristic in terms of its adaptive fitness for life as a hunter/gatherer on the African savanna (or as an adaptation of another characteristic). Now there is plenty of evidence for the adaptiveness of many lower-level psychological characteristics with clear reproductive or survival value—for example, those relating to sex differences, mating strategies, attachment behaviors and social affiliation (Buss, 1999)—but it is far more difficult to explain how the formal logic and advanced language modules, and complex personalities of homo sapiens arose by means of genetics and natural selection in the EEA (though modern psychologists are certainly trying). However, the highest capacities of humans are impossible to explain in terms of the pressures in the EEA, features like philosophical and higher mathematical reasoning (like calculus), musical ability, aesthetic awareness in general, narrative sense, the *experience* of ethicospiritual guilt and shame, human morality and responsibility and religion. This is due to the inability of lower-level mechanisms (like reproductive success) to really explain the existence of higher-level dynamics (like consciousness or belief in God). There is no possible set of laws that could provide a causal link between genetic changes naturally selected within the EEA with the extraordinary phenotypic capacities expressed, say, in a Wagner opera (or even our enjoyment of the harmonic changes in a simple folk song). How could such complex musical ability which was not to be realized until much later be selected for in the savanna? Of course evolutionary psychologists are also trying to explain these higher features; they have to. However, their explanations fall far short of compelling, and they are so necessarily—though an a priori commitment to the modern worldview obligates modernists to accept them. On the other hand, all orthodox Christians can at least minimally agree that God is behind the existence of unique human features, and with his own purposes in mind—purposes that go beyond mere survival and reproduction. The influence of evolution on modern psychology is just one example,[8] but it shows that assertions commonly found in modern psychology literature are not necessarily true from a Christian standpoint, requiring us to use the phrase "All truth is God's truth" cautiously.

Conversely, Christians recognize some psychological features that modernists would not, for example, the image of God,[9] indwelling sin, the influence of the Holy Spirit, ethical and spiritual absolutes for human life, the believer's union and communion with Christ, the new self/old self dichotomy and demonic possession, among others. Their worldview does not permit modern psychologists to recognize these psychological features, and this too raises questions about the phrase "All truth is God's truth." A faulty understanding of the maxim might seem to imply that all psychological truth is to be found within the modern version of psychology. Consequently, integration cannot be the only distinctive task that Christians in psychology practice. Otherwise, our understanding of psychological truth will be entirely constricted by the affordances of modern assumptions.

The problem of training to read. Good conceptual integration requires equal psychological and biblical and doctrinal sophistication (and perhaps some schooling in philosophy). Strong conceptual integration literature is distinguished by a more complex use of the Bible and theology (see, e.g., Jones & Butman, 1991; McMinn, 1996, 2004; McMinn & Campbell, 2007; Tan & Ortberg, 1995), but a simplistic reading of the Bible and doctrine remains common in integration literature. The problem here is twofold. First, the academic training of many integrationists provided them with a complex understanding of modern psychology but a poor grasp of their faith (a problem recognized by many integrationists, e.g., Sorenson, 1996b, 2004), and therefore, they were taught to read modern psychology texts as modernists do, and not as Christians.

The best integrationist training programs have added significant coursework to their requirements in order to try to address these problems.[10] But limited resources can hamper these laudable obligations. Often the required Bible and theology courses are taught by *theological* faculty, which will not teach students how to integrate; on the contrary, in some cases such courses underscore the irrelevance of academic theology to the care of the souls. Fortunately, these programs usually offer some integration courses taught by psychology faculty. The only issue here is whether those faculty practice weak or strong conceptual integration. What has dogged the integration movement over the past forty years is the fact that psychology education in America requires the mastery of complex modern psychology texts and offers little to no help training people how to read them *as Christians*, with one's worldview highly salient, so the texts can be interpreted in light of the antithesis, for example. (Of course, we do not expect modern institutions to offer this training, but even Christian institutions have not adequately recognized the hermeneutical problems here.) That is why simply adding theology or integration courses is not the only answer (though such courses are better than nothing). Until the majority of a department's faculty are competent, strong conceptual integrationists who have developed a clinically oriented understanding of the Bible and theology as rigorous as their understanding of modern psychology and are skilled in the Christian reading of modern texts, the department will be unlikely to help their students move much beyond the intellectual constraints of a modern worldview. This discussion is not meant to be a casting of stones at brothers and sisters—God knows how difficult this work is—but something more is needed if, after forty years of integration, Jones and Butman's (1991) call over fifteen years ago for a second stage of integration work that produces "new and different theories" has hardly been attempted, let alone realized.

Christian counselors who practice modern soul care in the name of integration. One of the greatest dilemmas in Christian counseling today is the fact that across the United States there are counselors who represent themselves to the Christian community as Christians but whose counseling is indistinguishable from that of secular therapists. Were one to do a discourse analysis of the content of their speech over ten sessions, there would be no reference to anything Christian—not even a prayer. Instead, their theory, practice and ethics are entirely derived from modern psychology, which they learned during their training. Furthermore, by helping people get better solely with human resources, such Christians may actually, unwittingly, be working in opposition to the soul-healing agenda of the kingdom of God.

Some people object to such concerns by drawing a comparison between counseling and medicine or plumbing, and noting that the latter do not necessarily use specifically Christian resources. One could respond by noting that the vocations of *all* Christians ought to be understood from within a Christian worldview and practiced for the glory of God, and conscientious Christian doctors and plumbers likely give more thought to the Christian implications of their work than many realize. However, in contrast to most other vocations, the care of souls is *essentially* a religious task (Johnson & Sandage, 1999), and *Christian* soul care is a direct function of Christ's work of redemption. Consequently, the Christian soul-care provider is under a special obligation to work self-consciously and explicitly *as a Christian,* whenever and wherever possible.

Of couse, Christian counselors can do much good that does not necessarily utilize Christian resources directly, including the treatment of phobias, learning disabilities, marriage communication, conflict resolution and so on. And certain settings have more restrictive requirements than others that must be respected (though there may also be some places Christians therefore cannot work). But to use techniques that are less "worldview-dependent" while counseling as a self-identified Christian (e.g., in one's informed consent form) is quite different from conducting one's entire counseling practice without ever disclosing anything of one's ultimate orientation and without ever working with any Christian resources.

There are complex cultural, institutional and financial reasons why this makes sense to such counselors, which we cannot go into here. However, at least some such counselors would claim to subscribe to an "integration" model. This is, of course, pseudo-integration, and their practice is really closer to the "levels of explanation," model, so it would be patently wrong to conclude that such dissociated practice is a necessary result of integration thinking. But some milder questions can be raised. How is it that some supporters of integration are able to work as secularists and not wrestle more with their Christian identity and sense of integrity? Could the sharp division between theology and psychology that undergirds the integration paradigm subtly reinforce this kind of dualistic living?

Regardless of the answer to that question, the integration label is being used by some to rationalize a false dichotomy between one's faith and one's professional life. McMinn and Campbell (2007) have recently acknowledged this problem, arguing against such a dichotomization and offering an impressive counterexample of what robust Christian integration looks like. Other strong integrationists need to follow suit and widely publicize their solutions so that such dichotomizing distortions become increasingly rare. Secular counseling in Christian garb is especially tragic, because it would seem to imply to its Christian counselees that the Christian faith is irrelevant to the healing of their souls. The compromise that such misrepresentation renders the glory of God and the long-term harm that such experiences have caused the church of Christ is incalculable.

Conclusions. In spite of the above criticisms, there are many encouraging signs of progress within the integrationist movement, too many to cite them all. As already noted, of great significance is the growing interest of many integrationists in Christian spirituality (see, e.g., Benner, 2004a; Moon, 2004; Moon & Benner, 2002). McMinn's (2004) discussion of sin, psychology and counseling is a great example of "antithesis integration," and his work with the Center for Church-Psychology Collaboration has pointed the way for a novel and very practical kind of integration (McMinn & Dominquez, 2005). Long overdue attention is being paid to attachment from a Christian standpoint (e.g., Clinton and Sibcy, 2002; and the work at Abilene Christian University: Beck & McDonald, 2004; McDonald, Beck, Allison & Norsworthy, 2005; Beck, 2006). Models of integration based on a radical reformation model look promising (Dueck & Lee, 2005), as does the work of the Society for the Study of Psychology and Wesleyan Theology. There is excellent evangelical assessment of the research on homosexuality available (Jones & Yarhouse, 2000; Jones & Kwee, 2005) and a novel approach for treatment (Yarhouse & Burkett, 2003). And the recent significant collaborative efforts of Hall and Porter (2004), Beck and Demarest (2005), and especially Shults and Sandage (2003, 2006) and McMinn and Campbell (2007) may be leading to a new era in integrative thinking. Such developments as these may portend the transcending of what seem to be limitations in the integrationist paradigm.

However, in the current social climate of psychology, where secularism is so dominant, one wonders if the integration paradigm itself may be capable of yielding the kind of radical, qualitatively unique version of soul care that one might think Christianity could supply, because it begins its task with psychology as already defined by modernism. Weak conceptual integrationists, in particular—who read modern texts without much mindfulness of the antithesis—are unwittingly incorporating more secularity than is their intention and are paradoxically eroding from within the very project of a Christian integration. The goals of integration are good; it is motivated by the deeply Christian desire to affirm God's truth wherever it is found. But the ideal of integration will only be realized as the Christian psychological community obtains both greater intellectual independence from modernity and greater interpretive sophistication, so that modern psychology texts are read *Christianly.*

We turn next to look at an evangelical counseling movement that operates out of a very different orientation. Taking the Bible's self-attestation of its soul-care purposes very seriously, the proponents of this approach seek to base all their psychological theory and therapeutic activity on the Bible's teachings alone.

Biblical Counseling and Scripture

Beginning with the nouthetic counseling model of Jay Adams (1970, 1973), the biblical counseling movement (BCM) has vigorously argued that the Bible should be the Christian counselor's sole textbook for counseling (Adams, 1975). The identity of the movement has also been defined, to some extent, by its reaction to integrationism. Adams wrote after the integration movement had begun and in response to it, and he and those he has influenced have strongly criticized the Christian appropriation of secular psychological theory, research and practice, believing that the faith has been compromised through syncretizing biblical thought and unbelieving thought under the misleading banner of "integration" (see Adams, 1970, 1973, 1979; Almy, 2000; Babler, 1999; Bobgan & Bobgan, 1989a, 1989b; Buckley, 1994; Ganz, 1993; MacArthur, 1991, 1994a; Powlison, 1992, 1997, 2003).

In contrast, Adams's nouthetic model is an attempt to base one's counseling program entirely on biblical resources. The term nouthetic is derived from the New Testament Greek word *noutheteō*, which means to admonish, warn or instruct (Arndt & Gingrich, 1959). Consequently, in marked contrast to the secular, client-centered model so popular in the sixties and seventies, Adams defined Christian counseling as consisting primarily of instruction in biblical truth and confrontation of the individual's sin (see 1970, chap. 4). And in a time when fundamentalist and evangelical seminaries were largely ignoring counseling, Adams argued that counseling should be seen as a primary responsibility of ordained ministers trained in the Scriptures (and therefore not laypersons trained in secular psychology) (Powlison, 1996b). Finally, in his counseling theory, he tended to focus on behavioral dynamics like personal discipline, dehabituation and rehabituation, and practical homework (Adams, 1973).

The most important theme sounded by Adams and the movement he founded is the belief that God must be recognized as the center of the counseling enterprise (Adams, 1979, chap. 4; Bookman, 1994a; Powlison, 1994a, 1996b; Welch, 1997b; Powlison, 2003). God and his salvation are the matters of greatest concern to the Christian, and Christian counselors must see everything in that light. Consequently, sin is the greatest soul problem there is (Adams, 1973; Powlison, 1994a, 1996b), and God's deliverance through Christ is the supreme solution to that problem (Adams, 1970; MacArthur, 1991; Powlison, 1994a, 1996b).

Because modern psychotherapy and counseling discourse make no substantial reference to God and sin, counseling by Christians largely based on that work will not rely on God and the power of Christ's salvation in its soul-healing, and so will unwittingly contribute to the substitution of the Christian religion with another, secular religion. The very glory of God is at stake here, and the BCM has seen itself as on a prophetic mission, challenging God's people to choose God and his salvation for the cure of the soul rather than rely on secular (that is, merely human) counseling strategies.

Many of their critics have not understood that the BCM emphasis on sin is a function of its theocentrism. Sin is so important because it is contrary to God's purposes, and his purposes are more important than anything else. This theocentric emphasis also leads the BCM to interpret the field of counseling largely in terms of the antithesis principle, seeing a radical divide separating the counseling agenda of the world from that of the church (though BCM authors do not typically refer to this principle). The BCM believes that the noetic effects of sin have severely distorted secular psychology and that therefore Christians cannot blindly trust its theories and research (cf. Buckley, 1994;

Mack, 1997; Powlison, 1997). The BCM also holds that modern therapy and counseling theory is fundamentally humanistic and self-centered, and so offers an alternative religious framework to heal the soul. The BCM recognized more quickly than the Integrationists the significance of the intellectual conflict at stake in the reception of many of modern psychology's theoretical assumptions and how radically different is a Christian framework. Beginning with Adams's (1970) first volley, the BCM has criticized the reductionism of naturalistic psychiatry and psychology that implies humans are not responsible for their soul problems, which are solely a function of biological and/or environmental influences. Taking seriously the Bible's emphasis on human responsibility, the BCM holds counselees responsible for the sin that contributes to their struggles and for seeking their recovery in Christ. Though such an emphasis can become moralistic and insensitive, it offers more hope to the client than naturalistic determinism.

As one would expect, the antithesis principle also leads the BCM to be skeptical of the modern mental health system and its training, certifications and licensure. The BCM believes that the church must reembrace its calling as the major cultural institution of the care of souls (hence Adams call to pastors to take counseling more seriously), so it rejects the idea that Christian counseling should be a profession shaped to any extent by a secular agenda alien to its own salvific missions to evangelize and promote sanctification. Perhaps some of this orientation is due to the fact that the BCM originated in and is supported by conservative seminaries, Bible colleges and churches and is promoted by theologians and pastors, a social-institutional context very different from that of the integration movement (Powlison, personal communication, July 8, 2005).

The BCM's commitment to use only the Bible in its counseling theory and practice and its general rejection of modern psychology are based on the theological assumption that the Bible is entirely and singularly *sufficient* for counseling and psychotherapy (Mack, 1997); in fact, the concept of the sufficiency of Scripture has become a rallying cry for the BCM (see Hindson & Eyrich, 1997; IABC, n.d.; Powlison, 2002). This exclusive reliance on the Bible is understood to be an essential safeguard, protecting the church from the unrecognized secular assumptions that the BCM believes are far more influential than Christian assumptions in determining the practices of integrationist counseling (Powlison, 1997, p. 60).

The strongly biblical stance of the BCM has enabled its adherents to make some singular contributions to Christian soul care, including the reminder that God is the ultimate counseling environment and prayer is a Christian necessity (Adams, 1979); the role of idolatry in psychopathology (Powlison, 1986, 1995a)—particularly in social anxiety and perfectionism (Welch, 1997b)—union with Christ for counseling (Maddox, 1994); and Welch's (1998, 2005) discussions on the relations between neuropsychology, biochemistry, human responsibility and sin. Also of interest is the special issue of the *Journal of Biblical Counseling* on Ephesians (Vol. 17, No. 2), which provides an excellent demonstration of how to mine a book of the Bible for soul-care purposes. The BCM has done much to further the development of a distinctly Christian counseling approach.

Different Approaches to Counseling Based on the Bible Alone

In spite of much broad agreement, there are at least three orientations that can be distinguished among Adams's intellectual heirs.

Traditional Biblical Counseling. The origins of the largest group can be traced to 1976, when Jay Adams (along with his colleague at Westminster, John Bettler, and others) formed the National Association of Nouthetic Counselors (NANC), an organization that continues to certify counselors and hold annual meetings. A closely related tributary is the work of an early follower of Adams, John Broger, who founded the Biblical Counseling Foundation in 1977 to help train biblically based counselors. In 1992 Master's College decided to replace their psychology department with a "biblical counseling" department (headed by Wayne Mack, a former student and colleague of Adams), and then John MacArthur and Mack edited *Introduction to Biblical Counseling* in 1994, the best overview of the movement's agenda. Another organization in this tradition is called the International Association of Biblical Counselors (IABC) and is headed by Ed Buckley. Recently, supporters of this approach started a new periodical called *The Journal of Modern Ministry*, with Jay Adams as the editor. Though there are exceptions, by and large, most of the members of these institutions and organs adhere very closely to the emphases of Jay Adams. Consequently, this approach will be called *Traditional* Biblical Counseling. It forms the dominant model in the movement.

Progressive Biblical Counseling. Jay Adams began writing about counseling while a professor of practical theology at Westminster Theological Seminary.

Together with Bettler, a biblical counseling program was begun, with a number of additional faculty being hired over the ensuing years. Adams also started a counseling center known as the Christian Counseling and Education Foundation (CCEF) across the street from Westminster, which was eventually headed up by Bettler, where the faculty would typically do some counseling.[11] In addition, Adams founded the *Journal of Pastoral Practice* in 1977. It was renamed the *Journal of Biblical Counseling* in 1992 and is also a part of CCEF. At present it is under the editorship of David Powlison. In addition to this journal, members of Westminster/CCEF have put out many pamphlets and books dealing with counseling issues (e.g., Powlison, 1995b, 1999b, 2004; 2005; Tripp, 2001, 2002; Welch, 1997b, 1998, 2000, 2001b, 2003, 2005). In recent years (and in response to some of the criticisms of Integrationists, Carter, 1975; Collins, 1977, 1993; Hurley & Berry, 1997a; Narramore, 1984), they have tried to distinguish their approach from that of their founder in a number of ways.

To begin with, they have noted that Adams's model of people-helping had a tendency to focus more on doing than on being, more on behavior than on the heart (Powlison, 1988, 1996a; Welch, 2002). Consequently, Westminster/CCEF began addressing the dynamics of the heart, particularly the problem of idolatry (Powlison, 1986, 1995a; Tripp, 2001; Welch, 1997b, 2001b). Whereas TBC focuses almost exclusively on the role of sin in psychopathology, the Westminster/CCEF group and Kellemen are developing a more complex model that combines a primary focus on sin with a theology of suffering and examines the biological and social contextual factors that are interwoven with sin in the human heart (Emlet, 2002; Kellemen, 2005a[12]; Powlison, 1988, 1996a; Tripp, 2002; Welch, 1998, 2002, 2005), so that some allow for a discerning use of psychotropic medication (Emlet, 2002; Kellemen, 2005b; Welch, 1998, 2005), something uncommon in TBC. In addition, the Progressives typically place greater positive value on the role of the counseling relationship than does TBC (Kellemen, 2005a, 2005b; Tripp, 2002; Welch, 2005). One also notices a more irenic tone among the Progressives and a greater willingness to interact with others as compared with Adams's generally confrontational stance toward Christians with whom he disagrees (see Powlison, 1996a). Given this willingness to move beyond Adams's nouthetic model in certain respects, this approach will be termed *Progressive* Biblical Counseling (PBC).

The Psychoheresy Awareness Network. The most reactionary approach to descend from Adams is seen in the work of Martin and Diedre Bobgan (1985, 1987, 1989a, 1989b, 2004). Their activities are marked by a strongly adversarial spirit exceeding that of their mentor (e.g., on the Bobgan's website <www.psychoheresy-aware.org> there are articles critical of Dobson, Crabb, Willow Creek, Cal Thomas, Hank Hanegraaf, Philip Yancey, Ronald Nash and R. C. Sproul, as well as those they are presumably closest to in philosophy, e.g., Westminster Theological Seminary/CCEF, Master's College and Seminary, IABC, and NANC!). The Bobgans have written a book provocatively titled *Against Biblical Counseling: For the Bible* (1994), which signals their move away from most others influenced by Adams. The Bobgans reject all parachurch counseling institutions, timed sessions, fee-based counseling and nearly all psychological terminology. However, they would appear to have relatively little influence outside of a small group of like-minded extremists. Consequently, the following discussion will concentrate on the other two groups. Suffice to say that the Bobgans serve as a tragic reminder to conservatives of what can happen when Christians become consumed by the antithesis, to the point that they cut off everyone in the body of Christ, except those who are in total agreement with themselves.

Questions About Biblical Counseling

There can be no doubt that the BCM has made an invaluable contribution to the dialogue within the evangelical counseling community (noted by integrationists like Collins, 2000; Hurley & Berry, 1997a; McMinn, 2004; McMinn & Campbell, 2007; and Tan, 1991). Yet legitimate questions can be raised about aspects of the BCM model, particularly the TBC approach.

Biblical counseling and the creation grace principle: The relation of the fall to knowledge and practice, part 2. Taking the exact opposite position of the integrationists regarding the work of secular psychology, the BCM has come to define itself implicitly almost entirely in terms of the antithesis principle. In so doing, however, the BCM has tended toward an isolationist, "against-culture" mind set (Niebuhr, 1951). TBC in particular often seems to assume what logicians have called the "genetic fallacy" as an argument against the validity of the psychological knowledge of non-Christians, that is, since modern psychology originates from non-Christians, it all must be invalid (see Noll, 1995; Carpenter, 1998, for a discussion of this tendency in fundamentalism).

This argument is sometimes bolstered by the beliefs that (1) psychology itself is not really a science but a pseudo-science; and (2) since psychology and counseling deal with spiritual realities, non-Christians cannot understand them at all (Almy, 2000; Buckley, 1994; Ganz, 1993; MacArthur, 1994a; Quinn, 1994).

The first argument is due to the somewhat common misapplication of natural science criteria and methods to the human sciences. But the scientific basis of most of contemporary psychology is beyond dispute in contemporary academia, because of its now voluminous, well-documented and replicated studies in areas like neuropsychology, cognition, motivation, emotion, social psychology, personality, as well as psychopathology and psychotherapy, a judgment confirmed by scientists in other disciplines (e.g., psychologists are regularly invited to contribute to representative science periodicals like *Scientific American*). The second criticism would seem to conflate the study of human nature with the study of Scripture and also misjudges the extent to which spiritual truth bears *directly* on *all* psychological and counseling topics *equally.*

This issue appears to distinguish the two major groups in the BCM. For the most part, Traditionalists tend to reject non-Christian psychological work across the board (see MacArthur, 1994a, p. 19, 1994b; Madtes & Hyndman, 1997; Quinn, 1994) though Adams has always acknowledged the legitimacy of science and psychology, *rightly understood* (Adams, 1970,[13] 1982; Powlison, 1988; Adams even allows for integration [1982], so long as it is not considered *necessary,* and "it does not conflict with biblical principles or practices," p. 6). Following Adams on this point, the Progressives are not opposed to all non-Christian psychology; but they all strenously object to the encroachment of the field of psychology (by which they actually mean modern psychotherapy and counseling) upon territory that belongs to Christian ministers who are ordained by God to counsel according to God's Word (see Powlison, 2000; Welch & Powlison, 1997a). As noted above, Welch, in particular, has made positive reference to research regarding the biomedical features of psychological conditions and treatment, and Powlison has repeatedly offered a cautious theoretical justification for such openness.

Typical of the Traditionalists is point five of the membership covenant of the National Association of Nouthetic Counselors: "We deny that secular theories and practices are manifestations of General Revelation or Common Grace. We affirm that they are, in fact, attempts to substitute the 'discoveries' of rebellious human thought for the truths revealed in Scripture, and are, therefore, in competition with a proper interpretation of General Revelation and with biblical counseling. They cannot be integrated with the Faith once for all delivered to the saints" (NANC website, retrieved August 27, 2005). Mack (1997) goes even further: "Because of our finiteness and sinfulness, our understanding of man and his problems can be trusted only when our thoughts and insights reflect the teaching of Holy Scripture. We simply are not able to ascertain truth apart from divine revelation" (p. 43). Unless it is just carelessly worded, this is an example of "scriptural positivism," and it would seem to necessitate the rejection of all information not found in Scripture (for example, information about anorexia nervosa, neurotransmitters and personality traits).

Such extreme pessimism about human reason, however, is foreign to the greatest thinkers of the Christian tradition. Calvin (1559/1960), for example, recognized both sin's mental distortions as well as the preserving, blessed effects of God's common grace on non-Christian thought[14] (Is 28:24-29; Mt 5:45; Acts 14:17; Rom 2:4, 15; see Kuyper, 1998; Mouw, 2001; Murray, 1977; C. Van Til, 1972; H. Van Til, 1959; for more recent discussion of common grace). Since Calvin's day, the term "common grace" has been used to refer to God's goodness to all humans in common, that explains the goodness, truth and beauty of human morality, culture, the sciences and the arts, in spite of human sin and apart from personal salvation. I will use the term "creation grace," however, rather than the more popular "common grace."[15] For our purposes, we will formulate the creation grace principle this way: *Unredeemed humans are capable of accurately understanding aspects of God's creation (including human nature, psychopathology and facets of its remediation)—except insofar as it requires spiritual illumination—and this understanding is the gift of God.*

The terminology of creation grace and redemptive grace roots these concepts in the grand events of redemptive-history (what Dooyeweerd called the "Christian ground-motive"): creation, fall and redemption. But some Christians have so emphasized the fall and redemption that they have lost sight of the fact that both are grounded in the creation. Humans are part of the created order. Studying human nature, therefore, is to take seriously God's handiwork. Though Calvin (1559/1960) frequently warned of the noetic effects of sin regarding spiritual matters (see the *Institutes* 2.1.8; 2.2.18-25), he also extolled the abilities of unredeemed human reason to obtain truth apart from special revelation. "If we regard the Spirit of God as the sole foundation of truth, we shall neither reject the truth itself, nor despise it wherever it shall appear, unless we wish to dishonor the Spirit of God" (p. 273). "Shall we say that the philosophers were blind in their fine observation and artful description of nature? . . . No, we cannot read the writings of the ancients on these subjects without great admiration" (p. 274). "But if the Lord has willed that we be helped in physics, dialectic, mathematics, and other like disciplines, by the work and ministry of the ungodly, let us use this assistance. *For if we neglect God's gift freely offered in these arts, we ought to suffer just punishment for our sloths*" (p. 275, italics mine).[16]

Calvin (1960) admittedly affirmed non-Christian contributions in logic and the natural sciences more than in morality and religion. In fact, Calvin criticized the reasonings of "the philosophers" on many points (by which he meant the ancient Greek and Roman philosophers as well as the medieval; see pp. 64, 192-94). But what would he say about the human science of psychology? Because psychology and counseling were not around in their present (scientific, modern) forms, it is impossible to say for sure. However, in Calvin's day it was "the philosophers" who had written more about psychology than anyone else. In a discussion on the basic components of the soul (what we call psychology today), Calvin noted their analysis: "I leave it to the philosophers to discuss these faculties in their subtle way. . . . I indeed agree that the things they teach are true, not only enjoyable, but also profitable to learn, and skillfully assembled by them. And I do not forbid those who are desirous of learning to study them" (p. 193). The majority of contemporary psychology concerns itself with the same kinds of created structures of interest to "the philosophers": memory, reason, perception and motivation (though contemporary psychology is frankly far more sophisticated and detailed in its descriptions, largely due to the application of well-developed empirical methods). On these matters at least, Calvin would surely have approved of the study of modern psychology. He even on occasion appreciatively quoted ancient philosophers like Seneca and Cicero regarding elements of their moral and spiritual thought (e.g., Vol. 1, pp. 53, 55, 57-58, 257, 688, 711, 715; similar to Paul, Acts 17:23, 28)! However, on *these* matters, where the Scriptures have much more say, Calvin is unsurprisingly more critical. The intricacy of Calvin's evaluation follows from his balanced understanding of and commitment to both the principles of the antithesis *and* creation grace (though the terms themselves had not yet been coined). Following Calvin's example today, Christian psychologists ought to be more critical of secular *psychopathology* and *counseling* theory and practices than of research on memory and personality, but they should be eager to identify whatever truth modern psychology contains, so as not to despise the Holy Spirit's gifts.

Calvin was a complex thinker. He could affirm the insights of non-Christians, while simultaneously warning of the noetic distortions caused by sin, particularly in matters of morality and religion. The demand for such cognitive complexity is common in biblical thought, for example, the doctrines of the Trinity, Christ's two natures and the relation of God's sovereignty and human responsibility (Johnson, 1996b, 2002). Though hard to grasp their relation, the Bible teaches both sides of these paradoxes (termed "mysteries" in church history). The antithesis and creation grace principles provide a similar paradox. They pose an apparent contradiction: either non-Christian understandings can be trusted or not. But some have tried to resolve this paradox too easily by overemphasizing one side of the dilemma at the expense of the other.

In the present debate, the BCM tends to focus on the antithesis between secular and Christian thought in counseling, whereas Integrationists tend to emphasize the creation grace evident in modern psychology (though calling it general revelation). But the creation grace and antithesis principles are corollary truths, *both* of which must be fully affirmed, in spite of the difficulty we have in reconciling them (Frame, 1987; Poythress, 1987; Johnson, 2002). They are an example of what Van Til (1972) called "limiting concepts," linked to each other and necessary to each other to restrain the extreme conclusions that can be deduced from a one-sided, imbalanced approach to the problem. The two principles complement and entail each other; therefore, they cannot be understood in isolation from each other. To overemphasize either one will rob God of some of his glory, either by ignoring his creation grace or undermining the significance of redemption from sin. So, in the Christian reading of modern psychology texts, it is necessary to take seriously creation grace as well as the antithesis. Creation grace, particularly God's goodness to those who oppose him, gives God tremendous glory, and if *Christians* minimize or neglect it, who will glorify God for that grace? Non-Christians will not. This is perhaps the most important reason why Christians in psychology and counseling should be eager to discover the genuine truth and goodness available in non-Christian psychology: to claim it for the God to whom it belongs and rejoice in him for his remarkable goodness and wisdom.

At the same time, the BCM is understandably suspicious about creation grace, because interest in it can replace an emphasis on redemptive grace. In affirming God's goodness in culture, Christians must never lose sight of the fundamental, though usually unconscious, antithetical opposition of humanity against God. So the two principles are not equivalent. The antithesis principle has a fundamental axiological and eschatological priority over the creation grace principle, since the final judgment will be based on the antithesis and not ultimately on creation grace. The antithesis in human history is moving toward divine judgment, and Christian soul care must never lose sight of this ultimate, soul-care end. By so emphasizing the antithesis, the BCM has rightly called the Christian counseling community to recognize the fundamental redemptive agenda of human history that Christ's death and resurrection has brought about.

On the other hand, sinful saints (like ourselves) can tragically use their love of God and the Bible as a source of self-aggrandizement. Ironically, because of their remaining sin, well-taught Christians can unconsciously serve sinful purposes through their vigorous criticism of the sin and limitations of others and even in defense of the Bible's supremacy. An excessive devotion to the antithesis is often related to an overidentification of oneself (or one's movement) with the perfect God, and this will tend to be manifested by the "works of the flesh," for example, in enmities, strife, disputes, dissension and factions (Gal 5:20); such divisiveness is paradoxically often promoted by those who hold to the highest Christian ideals. Bible-believing Christians like those in the BCM can guard against this tendency by expending greater energy fighting against their own flesh—what we might call the "internal antithesis"—than they do the counseling inadequacies of their brothers and sisters.

As we conclude this section, we should note one way in which the antithesis and creation grace are harmonized. In some of the most sophisticated discussions of creation grace, Kuyper (1898b; 1998) and his heirs (Bavinck, 1989; Dooyeweerd, 1960; Murray, 1977; Runner, 1982; C. Van Til, 1972; H. Van Til, 1959) have argued that it is God's intention that creation grace serve redemptive grace and the church. Taking into account the redemptive goals of Scripture, these authors suggest that the development of culture and social stability due to creation grace can contribute to the spread of the gospel and the flourishing of the church. Consequently, if there are legitimate treasures of God's goodness in psychology and even soul care that can be made use of *in the service of redemptive grace and the improvement of the church for God's glory,* then it is legitimate and desirable (even if not *necessary*) for the church to "spoil the Egyptians" (Augustine, 1950; Crabb, 1977). But what might this imply about our doctrine of Scripture?

The sufficiency of Scripture. We have seen that the Bible proclaims its value for Christian soul care. However, TBC proponents teach that Christian soul care must be based *exclusively* on what the Bible teaches and have suggested it is heterodox to make positive reference to contemporary psychological research and theory and argued that it compromises the adequacy of God's revelation in the Bible.[17] Mack (1994d), for example, has written that "everything we need to know to live successfully is found within the pages of God's Word" (p. 251). He (1997) believes that "we do not need any extrabiblical resources to understand people and their problems and help them to develop the qualities, attitudes, desires, values, feelings, and behavior that are proper for relating to living before God in a way that pleases and honors Him" (p. 52). Then he suggests a little later that if any novel information that would help others live successfully is found outside the Bible, the truthfulness of the whole Bible is undermined. As a result, he concludes: "Secular psychology has nothing to offer for understanding or providing solutions to the non-physical problems of people. When it comes to counseling people, we have no reason to depend on the insights of finite and fallen men" (Mack, 1997, p. 53).[18] Bookman (1994b) demonstrates a similar logic when he argues that the whole project of integration implies that "there is some intrinsic inadequacy or imperfection in the Scriptures demanding that insights be gleaned from secular psychology that will redress those deficiencies and enable Christian counselors to more effectively help hurting people" (p. 93). The Bible claims sufficiency, he says (referring to 2 Tim 3:15-17; 2 Pet 1:3), and Christians relied on the Scriptures for centuries without modern psychology's help, so Bookman says we should be suspicious of Christian models that assume there is some "demerit or deficiency . . . intrinsic to those scriptures" (p. 93). Late in life, Adams (2003) made the shocking claims that "when a Christian seeks to discover Truth about man's problems through the empirical method he denies the sufficiency of the Bible and ends up sinning against God and his neighbor. . . . The integrationist cannot discover in nature what God has already provided in the Scriptures. Observation, experience, and experimentation will never elicit Truth about man" (p. 48).[19] Quinn (1994) likewise defends the remarkable assertion that "biblical counselors refuse to use information from science and psychology" (pp. 371-72).

The positive function of this rhetoric is to affirm the *guaranteed* truth value of the Bible—which TBC supports in common with the historic Christian church—but there is nothing in a Bible-based counseling model that necessitates the further deduction of TBC that accepting extrabiblical soul-care information or doing research implicitly denigrates the Bible.[20] That is like saying that a fellow who wishes that a beautiful piece of music would not have ended as soon as it did was being critical of it.

Though it may not be their intention, ultimately this position would seem to imply that God's exhaustive knowledge of human beings and soul care is to be identified entirely with the biblical text. But is it possible that the omniscient God knows some additional, albeit secondary information about human beings, which is not necessary but is relevant and helpful for soul care, that he did not include in the Bible? And if it is, is God within his rights to share it some other way (like through creation grace)? TBC proponents apparently believe that God will not give such gifts, because he has already said in the Bible that *it* is entirely sufficient for soul care. But is that really what he said?

Let us look again at the two passages often cited by TBC proponents to make the case for their position (Adams, 1973, 1975a; Mack, 1997). The first is 2 Peter 1:2-4:

> Grace and peace be multiplied to you in the knowledge of God and of Jesus our Lord; seeing that His divine power has granted to us everything pertaining to life and godliness, through the true knowledge of Him who called us by His own glory and excellence. For by these He has granted to us His precious and magnificent promises, so that by them you may become partakers of the divine nature, having escaped the corruption that is in the world by lust.

We noted in chapter one that this passage ought to encourage believers to read the Bible to promote godliness, since Scripture is God's permanent textual record of the knowledge of God and his promises. However, it has to be pointed out that Scripture is not mentioned here, and good exegetes differ as to what exactly is being referred to by "everything." At the very least, it provides no sure basis for the conclusion that the Bible contains all the information one may use in psychology or counseling, and excludes all other sources. That inference is a non sequitur; it does not follow from the passage.

More relevant is 2 Timothy 3:15-17:

> From childhood you have known the sacred writings which are able to give you the wisdom that leads to salvation through faith which is in Christ Jesus. All Scripture is inspired by God and profitable for teaching, for reproof, for correction, for training in righteousness; that the man of God may be adequate, equipped for every good work.

As we observed, this passage teaches that the Old Testament[21] is invaluable for soul care, because its doctrine, moral and religious standards, and instruction in how to live rightly before God clearly and sufficiently describe the immanent goal of salvation: a thoroughly God-centered, virtuous life. Matthew Henry (n.d.) summarizes the passage this way: "[The Bible] instructs us in that which is true, reproves us for that which is amiss, directs us in that which is good" (p. 847). But what exactly was Paul's communicative intent? He was extolling the supreme value of the Bible for the realization of Christian ethicospiritual maturity. But, again, he does *not* say that the Scripture contains *all* the soul-care information there is—*all* the knowledge *that God has* regarding the care of souls—or that all extrabiblical information that bears on human nature and counseling is irrelevant or useless or sin. Those are completely different points, far removed from the evidence in this passage and any proper inference from it (Hurley & Berry, 1997a; Jones & Butman, 1991, p. 26).

Anyone familiar with the contemporary science of psychology recognizes that there are countless soul-care issues that are not directly addressed in Scripture. To argue from this passage that the Bible should be considered a "counseling textbook" (Priolo, 2005) or that it contains a "comprehensive system of theoretical commitments, principles, insights, goals, and appropriate methods for understanding and resolving the non-physical problems of people" (Mack, 1997), would seem to be an egregious misunderstanding of both the form of the Bible and of psychological science. It is always much easier to deduce what is being positively asserted in a text than it is to know for certain what is actually being ruled out. Ultimately this "absolute sufficiency" position is based on an argument from silence. So what *are* we warranted to conclude from this passage? That the Bible contains what might be called the *first principles* of soul care—the *most important truths* for the maturation of the soul—and so it provides the God-breathed *foundation* for a radically Christian model of soul-healing.

These are the two best passages that TBC proponents cite, and neither teaches that Christians are required to reject all extrabiblical knowledge about human nature and soul care. Such an implication is simply foreign to the original intentions of the biblical authors. Absolute-sufficiency advocates have read into these texts their own considerations in light of the contemporary context.

More problematic for an absolute sufficiency position is the fact that the Bible itself appears to incorporate material from outside the Bible. To begin with two rather obvious points, the Bible was written in languages that existed prior to its enscripturation, and it makes reference to the created order, human experience, social structures and even the good of nonbelieving cultures (1 Kings 7:14, good that was used to help build Solomon's temple)—so there is a world outside the Bible that gave rise to the Bible (previous languages) and that the Bible itself affirms. But more importantly, the Holy Spirit also seems to have "borrowed" treaty-forms, text and terms from extrabiblical sources in the Bible's composition (Hurley & Berry, 1997a). For example, the suzerainty treaty form used as a literary framework for the formal restatement of the Mosaic covenant in Deuteronomy (Kline, 1972). There are also some sayings in the book of Proverbs (Prov 22:17—23:11) that are very similar to those in *The Instruction of Amenemope,* an Egyptian collection that some believe was written before Solomon's time (e.g.,Waltke, 2004, though Westermann, 1995, argues against any dependence). Here we have wise observations about human life that may have been written first by those outside the covenant people, and then incorporated into the canon of Scripture, but *recontextualized as reflecting the wisdom of Yahweh.* If we could be sure that the sages of Proverbs did such "integration" of texts of moral reasoning *into the canon* it would appear to authoritatively legitimate incorporating into Christian psychology the valid texts of non-Christian scientists dedicated to describing psychological features of human beings. But this cannot be established at present. Regardless, even if *The Instruction of Amenemope* was derived from the book of Proverbs or they were composed independently, the fact that an Egyptian community codified similar proverbs still strikingly underscores that image-bearers outside the canonical community can recognize moral truths that God authorized in Scripture (as well as in the human heart, Rom 2:12-13). Any explanation, it would seem, leads to the rejection of a simplistic notion of the sufficiency of Scripture.

Mention should also be made of Paul's positive use of the insight of some Greek poets (Acts 17:28). And perhaps most remarkable is John's radical reinterpretation of the term *logos* in John 1:1-14—where it is applied to the Son of God!—though it had a long prior history in Jewish and Hellenistic religious philosophy (Carson, 1991; Ferguson, 1993). This example, more than any other, clarifies the task of such incorporation, since it shows both the benefits of utilizing a term previously defined in more or less alien contexts that nonetheless enriches our understanding of Christ (what transforming accommodation!) as well as the thorough redefinition of that term christologically. If all integration was so clearly redefined, its critics would be silenced.

Of course there is a tremendous irony in the metaphor of God "borrowing" something in the inspiration of Scripture, since all truth first came from God, regardless of when and where it was first written by humans, but if the sovereign God himself role-models such redemptive "incorporation" in his own inspired authorization of the canon, ought we not imitate him? Should we not *live canonically* and take captive valid contemporary psychological science to the obedience of Christ (2 Cor 10:5) and let the context of Scripture and a Christian worldview transform it into a science that better reflects God's comprehensive, infinite, theocentric understanding? And would not a high view of Scripture require us to do so? Integrationists who have done good Christian recontextualization have simply been following God's example.

Good intentions and progress in biblical counseling. If the Bible itself does not exemplify a biblical exclusivity, where did the TBC stance come from? I would argue that it is a faulty deduction based on good, Spirit-led intuitions (though for an additional philosophical explanation, see appendix one). Those intuitions are right: the Bible's teachings bear on all of soul care, and the Bible has a textual supremacy over all other texts (an argument that will be developed in chapter five). We saw in the first two chapters that such intuitions follow from Scripture's self-attestations, and their implications have been explored throughout church history. The problem occurred when these legitimate intuitions were faced with the scientific revolution's advance into soul-care territory by modern psychology in the twentieth century. Reacting to the encroachment of secularism into the sphere of soul care—aided by modernist psychological research (and speculative theorizing by Freud among others)—it is understandable that Bible-loving Christians would reject any insinuation that the Bible and Christ and salvation are irrelevant to soul care. However, TBC overreached in its response. Its extreme sufficiency position would seem to entail that the Bible is adequate as a scientific text, that it is *scientifically* sufficient, having the same level of precision, specificity and comprehensiveness regarding psychological and soul-care topics that one finds in good contemporary psychological textbooks and journal articles, and that is obviously not the case.

The Progressives, on the other hand, have recognized the inadequacy of this position (e.g., Powlison, 1997, 2000; Tripp, 2002; Welch, 1997a). Powlison, in particular has argued that science, along with any legitimate part of the created order and human culture (including personal experience, counseling cases, literature and philosophy) can be used for positive reasons, confirming and illustrating the truth. However, he (1994b) cautions that extrabiblical resources should never play a "constitutive role" in the core of a Christian system of counseling, and asks,

> Do secular disciplines have anything to offer to the *methodology* of Biblical counseling? The answer is a flat no. Scriptures provide the *system* for Biblical counseling. Other disciplines—history, anthropology, literature, sociology, psychology, biology, business, political science—*may be useful in a variety of secondary ways* to the pastor and the biblical counselor, but *such disciplines can never provide a system* for understanding and counseling people. (p. 365, italics mine)

Powlison's admittedly strident language may lead some to miss his point and his concession: the Bible alone must provide the *system* (or *edification framework*) for Christian soul care, but he also allows for a role for extrabiblical literature, and he recognizes that the Bible cannot be understood as "an encyclopedia of proof texts containing all facts about people and the diversity of problems in living" (2000, p. 19). The fundamental difference between Traditional and Progressive Biblical Counseling may actually be hermeneutic, having more to do with *how to interpret the Bible for soul care,* than anything else (Tripp, 2002, pp. 24-28; Ed Welch, personal communication, November 15, 2006).

PBC proponents believe that the Bible does not provide an exhaustive discussion of Christian soul care, but it is *comprehensive in scope*, since it reveals the major soul-care principles that *cover all the details of life* (see Powlison, 1997, p. 92, 2000, 2003, 2004; Tripp, 2002; Welch, 1997a; a position that is actually much closer to that of the strong integrationists, at least theoretically, than PBC has ever officially admitted; see Collins, 1977, 1994; early Crabb, 1977; Hurley & Berry, 1997a; Jones & Butman, 1991; McMinn & Campbell, 2007; Tan, 1991). As Powlison (2000, 2004) has repeatedly put it, the Scriptures provide us with a "gaze." The PBC position, following Calvin, leads to the use of the Bible as "principle-spectacles" through which one can critically read and interpret all of life (including the psychology texts of other communities; see Horton, 2002, p. 15).

The actual sufficiency beliefs of the TBC. One hopes that Progressives (besides Welch) will put their greater openness into practice and demonstrate for others—more than they have so far—how to interpret the texts of secular psychology and soul care constructively in biblical ways. But their position legitimizes the use of valid terminology derived from extrabiblical sources. More surprising is the fact that even many Traditionalists are willing to use terms (with great misgivings) that are not found in the Bible, and many of which are derived from contemporary psychological discourse, for example, anorexia nervosa (Fitzpatrick, 1999), child development (Street, 2005), dehabituation (Adams, 1973), depression (Mack, 1978), blended families (Street, 2005), emotion (Adams, 1973) and sexual abuse (Baker, 2005).[22] The most amazing evidence of this openness (and ambivalence) is a recent book titled *The Christian's Guide to Psychological Terms* (Asher & Asher, 2004), which examines and critiques 208 psychology labels.

Officially, most BCM authors remain critical of such discourse (see e.g., Babler's [1999] critique of the DSM-IV), and they usually make it clear that they use the terms more by way of concession to the contemporary context than by affirmation ("Many [psychological] terms are integrated into common use," so we have to become familiar with them; Asher & Asher, 2004, Preface). But a careful examination of the above articles and books forces one to conclude that even some Traditionalists recognize *some* value in scientific labels not found in the Bible but developed in the twentieth century by secularists (Carter, 1975). "A psychological diagnosis is unnecessary and may not be correct, but the ability to translate psychological labels into specific attitudes and behaviors helps the counselor to know what questions to ask during the data gathering process" (Asher & Asher, Preface). As a result, TBC itself appears to have benefited, to some extent, from the increased conceptual precision that has resulted from scientific research and theorizing in psychology, and that they are therefore doing *some* integration (something the Bobgans have noted). While warranted by the Progressive position, this fact does not seem to square with the rhetoric of the Traditionalists regarding the absolute sufficiency of Scripture for soul care, their avowed rejection of modern psychology and their severe criticism of those who integrate. No doubt TBC authors would say that when using such terms, they are "redefining them using biblical terminology" (Asher & Asher, Preface). That is granted. But how different is that from the goals of the strong integrationists, who are trying to do essentially the same thing? Given their strengths and training, biblical counselors might do a better job of redefinition, and integrationists should welcome their help. But intellectual integrity demands that they abandon their extreme sufficiency-of-Scripture rhetoric and embrace the more nuanced position of the PBC proponents since, according to their own standards, they are themselves guilty of implying that the Bible is not solely sufficient for soul care, just to a lesser degree.

What the BCM is after—what all orthodox Christian counselors are after—is *God's understanding of human nature and counseling*. God's understanding *alone* is complete, final, comprehensive and exhaustive (Bavinck, 1951; Frame, 2002; Van Til, 1955); so it is God's mind that contains the ultimate psychology: all the knowledge there is that is relevant to human nature and to counseling, in all situations, with all persons, whatever the disorder. Theological liberals risk turning the Bible into an irrelevant, merely human book; however, conservatives risk turning it into a fourth member of the Trinity (Vanhoozer, 2005, p. 227). As the inspired, inerrant, enscripturated Word of God, the Bible reveals principles of eternally abiding value and validity, particularly for soul care, but it must not be equated with God's infinite understanding of anything; otherwise, irony of ironies, Bible-loving conservatives may become guilty of bibliolatry. Were all biblical and Christian counselors to take more seriously the BCM emphases on the importance of Scripture and the noetic effects of sin and understand them more *personally*, so that we read the Bible more to illuminate our own hearts (Heb 4:12-13) and to expose the remaining sin that we all have there, we would be more likely to work together rather than against each other. Since its inception, TBC has boldly and rightly stood for truth. But when sinners, even saved sinners, identify themselves so much with the truth, the risk of other sinful distortions (like pride) becomes peculiarly great. As it is now, in spite of obvious formal differences, TBC has tended paradoxically to have more in common in the heart than it is aware with the human-centered counseling to which it is so virulently opposed.

Conclusion and Introduction

For many reasons this chapter was by far the most difficult to write. To begin with, God knows I am guilty of just about everything I have criticized in others, at one point or another in my life (in some cases, on into the present). At the same time, the criticism of the positions of others is a necessary part of scholarship, and ideally it ought to be a worthwhile part of serious and genuine dialogue. Nonetheless, it becomes especially problematic when one weighs in on what has been something like a Forty Years War in evangelical counseling. The goal in this book, however, is not to announce the formation of another party of combatants. By the time it is finished, it should be clear that this book could never have been written without the help of both schools of thought and practice.

What do we learn from this intellectual conflict? First, the facts that both groups are composed of those who love Jesus Christ, believe the Bible to be authoritative and want to help the souls of others and yet that both hold such differing positions make clear that the evangelical counseling community has been for some time in the midst of a significant epistemological and soul-care crisis (MacIntyre, 1977, 1990). Second, both groups have better and poorer representatives of their respective positions, a factor that must be kept in mind when evaluating them. Third, both groups have considerable strengths, and together they reflect more of the all-knowing wisdom of God than either by itself. Perhaps *together* they point the way forward.

In part two, we will try to develop a hermeneutical framework for a Christian science of psychology and soul care that will allow us to avail ourselves, in a principled way, of the insights of both groups, and so of *all* the resources God has given us for the task, and that may help us find a resolution of this conflict.

Notes

[1]As an example, Carter and Narramore (1979) write of the parallel model of "integration": "Integration [here] consists of finding the concepts that are parallel (equivalent) in the other discipline (sphere)" (p. 99). Yet, they note that within the parallel model psychology and theology are seen as very distinct disciplines, so that its proponents seek only to discover similarities or correlations between them. But this means that the parallel model is not an integration model at all and is probably better understood as a "levels-of-explanation" approach.

[2]One purpose of the book *Psychology and Christianity: Four Views* (Johnson & Jones, 2000) was to promote such recognition.

[3]To cite just a few examples, the *Encyclopedia* contains many fine articles that well exemplify interdisciplinary integration, including two on counseling and psychotherapy (Hall & Peters; Ellens), and others on depression (Lastoria), sexuality (Jones), the self (Evans), locus of control (Welton), psychoanalytic psychology (Narramore) and spiritual and religious issues in psychotherapy (McMinn). But there are many major articles on topics that one might suppose would illustrate the model that are

essentially devoid of integration, for example, those on abnormal psychology (Al-Issa), attribution (Hill), developmental psychology and moral development (both by Clouse), family therapy (Peters), love (Rottschafer), motivation (Bolt), object relations theory (Edkins), self psychology (Johnson), personality disorders (Berry) and personality and social psychology (both by Timpe).

[4]Browning and Cooper's *Religious Thought and the Modern Psychologies* (2004), Roberts's *Taking the Word to Heart* (1993), and the works of Shults and Sandage (2003, 2006) are in the same league, but *Modern Psychotherapies* is the most systematic and comprehensive of them all.

[5]Perhaps we could say that the scope of the belief-set Jones and Butman are integrating into psychology is more limited than that envisioned by proponents of II: simply foundational beliefs that bear on the nature of human beings, rather than actual theological disciplinary content. This narrower scope permits them to continue to define psychology in a way that is compatible with modern rules of discourse (for example, that psychology aims at universal description and therefore is ideally a community-generic discipline, influenced by worldview, but not constitutionally worldview dependent), enabling worldview integrationists to contribute to mainstream psychology publications and advocate for a dialogue between *religion* and psychology (see Jones, 1994).

[6]Some integrationists have suggested that postmodernism may help overcome some of the problems of a modernist model of interdisciplinary integration (Dueck & Parsons, 2004; Ingram, 1995, 1997; Lee, 2004; Sandage, 1998; Shults & Sandage, 2003, 2006; Sorenson, 2004). Without endorsing the radical relativism of hard postmodernism, these authors share a postmodern skepticism regarding the intellectualism, individualism and scientism that pervades modern psychology and psychotherapy, and they believe that some postmodern emphases offer a necessary corrective for evangelical models of therapy (and integration), including an interest in narrative, a suspicion of absolutist and universal models of knowledge, a concern with dominance and power over others, a willingness to dialogue with others including the client, and an openness about one's communal membership and perspective. These themes have merit, and the present author shares many of the concerns of a postmodern critique of integration, most importantly, an interest in affirming "the Christian tradition as that community which shapes the grammar of our language and praxis as psychologists" (Dueck & Parsons, p. 242).

Conceptual integration has taken for granted many of the assumptions of modern psychology: that it is a discrete science—distinct from theology and philosophy—that rightly aims at context-independent, perspective-free, universal knowledge, rather than viewing the modern psychologies as simply particularly sophisticated versions of psychology that, for all their validity and value, are still socially constructed within a secular ideological surround (Watson, 1993; also see Danziger, 1997, who has made a compelling case that even the labeling of psychological categories in modern psychology has been shaped by sociohistorical forces). However, thus far, postmodern integrationists assume the same disciplinary division between psychology and theology that will be diagnosed as problematic in the next chapter. For example, Dueck and Parsons (2004) argue that a postmodern approach leads to a reticence to force an integration of psychology and theology, since each discipline's integrity must be respected. "Psychological theories and theological approaches provide us with two very different universes of discourse. The language games or rules that shape them seem very different. Hence the reduction of one language to the other would be neither possible nor encouraged" (Dueck & Parsons, 2004, p. 243). But why this dichotomy? Where did it come from? Could it too be a result of the intellectual fragmentation of modernity? Perhaps postmodern integrationists have not gone far enough in their critique of modernity and its influence on the integration project. A more radical critique might examine the assumptions undergirding the concept of "integration" itself.

[7]Runner (1982) called the incorporation of thought and practice that is antithetical to the Christian worldview into the thought and practice of Christians, *synthesis*.

[8]For Christian philosophical critiques of naturalism and evolutionary theory see Beilby (2002) and

Dembski (1998, 2002), and for a critique of evolutionary psychology, see the two special issues of the *Journal of Psychology and Theology*, edited by Christopher Grace (2001, 2002).

[9]How is this term any less useful than "personality" or "self" as a label for the whole person? It is conceptually different, of course, but also more meaningful from a Christian standpoint.

[10]For example, among the longest running evangelical programs, Fuller Theological Seminary requires the most: almost an M.A. for its Psy.D. and a complete M.A. for its Ph.D. with 20 and 16 credits respectively in integration classes, and they have tailored a couple of theology classes just for their psychology students. Rosemead Ph.D. and Psy.D. students must take 17 theology credits at Talbot Seminary and another 14 in integration seminars. Wheaton's Psy.D. requires 22 hours of biblical and theological studies, though over half appear to be taught outside the psychology/counseling department. George Fox University's Psy.D. program appears to require 14 credit hours of theology outside the department and a 1 credit integration seminar.

[11]Most of the following history is recorded in Powlison, 1996a.

[12]Though Kellemen teaches at Capital Bible Seminary, his model of biblical counseling is far closer to that of Westminster/CCEF than that of TBC.

[13]"I do not wish to disregard science, but rather I welcome it as a useful adjunct for the purposes of illustrating, filling in generalizations with specifics, and challenging wrong human interpretations of Scripture, thereby forcing the student to restudy the Scriptures" (Adams, 1971, p. xxi).

[14]On common grace, Calvin followed Augustine. See Augustine on the Manichees: "Much that they say of the created universe is true, but they do not religiously seek the Truth, the architect of the created universe" (1942, p. 71).

[15]I prefer the term *creation grace* to describe this reality for a number of reasons. First, it underscores the connection this grace has with the first, foundational event of redemptive history, the creation. Creation grace proceeds from the same purposes that brought the universe into being. Just as God made everything for his glory, so he continues to hold everything together for his glory (Ps 8; 104; 148). Creation and providence are directly related. It may be easier for Christians to focus on the significance of the fall and redemption. After all, sin leads to eternal destruction, whereas salvation leads to eternal life. In contrast to these realities, creation grace may seem insignificant. However, Christians cannot afford to neglect creation teaching, for the outworking of the fall and redemption is only made possible by being situated within the created order. Creation grace is the necessary ground and context for the realization of God's redemptive purposes. It must not be despised or neglected.

Second, just as the original goodness of creation was a function of God's goodness (he cannot do evil), to call this dynamic *creation grace* shows the continuity of God's goodness that is still the source of whatever good there remains in the creation (even in the relatively good, but ultimately bad activity of sinful humans). God's goodness in the creation cannot be destroyed or overturned, and Christians are to praise him for it. Third, there is an underlying unity between God's grace toward the nonhuman creation and the human creation. Rain blesses plants and animals as well as people (Ps 104; Mt 5:45). Finally, the term *common grace*, while useful for making clear that this grace is common to all people, regardless of their relation to God (in contrast to "*special* grace"), might imply either that it is neutral once it is given or that it is not of supernatural origin. To call it *creation grace* makes it clear that it proceeds from the Creator's hand and always bestows on the recipient a responsibility to use it for God with gratitude. It will be contrasted with *redemptive* grace, which is enjoyed only by believers.

[16]Calvin sounds something like an integrationist, except that he adds that "this capacity to understand [in the non-Christian] is an unstable and transitory thing in God's sight, when a solid foundation of truth does not underlie it" (p. 275).

[17]Before discussing this teaching, it might be mentioned that the strict Bible-only position of the TBC

bears a curious resemblance to the stance of Barth and many of his followers, regarding the deep division between biblical thought and science and reason (already mentioned in chapter two), based in the lingering influence of Kant's phenomenal-noumenal distinction on Barth (see also Thurneyson, 1962). One reason for this similarity may be the roots of both Barthianism and the TBC approach in Kantianism. The TBC link to post-Kantian Idealism is discussed in appendix one.

[18]Admittedly, he does follow PBC in allowing that extrabiblical resources may be used in *illustrative* or *provocative* ways, but they are *unnecessary* (see also Adams, 1986, p. 37).

[19]The International Association of Biblical Counselors (n.d.) states in a position paper, "We affirm the Bible to be the indispensable textbook on human and divine relationships and behavior," "We deny that there are other voices of God ('truths') other than God's Word," and "We deny that the counselor can build a 'Biblical' system of counseling that syncretizes secular sources and the Holy Scriptures."

[20]Earlier in his life, Adams (1973) permitted the discerning use of non-Christian resources, at least theoretically: "In the common grace of God, unbelievers stumble over aspects of truth in God's creation. They always distort these by their sin and from their non-Christian stance toward life. But *from the vantage point of his biblical foundation* the Christian counselor may take note of, evaluate, and reclaim the truth dimly reflected by the unbeliever so long as he does so in a manner consistent with biblical principles and methodology" (p. 92). Much of my book could be considered an outworking of this statement. Unfortunately, throughout most of Adams's literature, as with the rest of TBC, it appears difficult to find almost anything in modern psychology that can be reclaimed. Adams effectively took back his previous concession in a footnote at the bottom of the page: "From a biblical foundation, upon which a house of biblical methodology has been constructed, a Christian counselor may view the surrounding landscape. But he must not construct his foundation or house out of any non-Christian materials."

[21]Christians have rightly deduced that Paul's claim should be extended to the New Testament, but it is somewhat ironic in the present context that when Paul wrote this the New Testament canon was not yet formed, so technically Paul was referring to the sufficiency of the Old Testament.

[22]See also, action (Adams, 1973), behavior (Adams, 1973), data gathering and homework (Adams, 1973), empathy (Adams, 1973), learning disabilities (Alspaugh, 1978), PMS and menopause (Mack 1997), psychosomatic problems (Smith, 1977), schizophrenic behavior (Adams, 1973; Mack, 1997), self-esteem (Adams, 1979), sexual frigidity (Eyrich, 1979), panic attacks (Propri, 2005), transsexualism (Mack, 1997) and the use of proper nonverbal communication in counseling (Mack, 1994b). The position of the Progressives allows them to make use of extrabiblical terminology, which they do: ADHD (Welch, 1998), alcoholism (Welch, 1998), codependency (Welch, 1997b), cognition, affection and volition (Emlet, 2002), defensiveness (Powlison, 2004), identity (Welch, 1997), neurotransmitters (Welch, 1998), obsessions and compulsions (Emlet, 2004), adonis complex (Powlison, 2004), self-injury (Welch, 2004) and sexual abuse (Freeman, 2003).

PART TWO

Texts and Contexts

IN THE NEXT SECTION WE WILL EXAMINE the major practices required for a scientific discipline, particularly reading. However, the first step, in chapter four, will be a reconsideration of the content and boundaries of psychology and theology, which have been distorted by sociohistorical factors, rather than constrained by their actual objects of inquiry. It will be suggested that the object of psychology is individual human beings (*individual* human beings to distinguish psychology from sociology and other human sciences), and that they can be studied using all relevant resources, which for a Christian psychology include the Bible. Consideration will also be given to the components of a Christian disciplinary matrix for psychology. In the next chapter, we will consider how the Bible ought to function in a Christian psychology: as its primary text. The final two chapters of part two concern how to read the Bible and other relevant texts for the purpose of forming a Christian psychology. The Christian community's greatest current challenge is hermeneutic: how to read and interpret the most important available texts that describe human beings. Modern psychology has a largely uncontested and shared agreement about the basic values and methods that should guide and shape a science of human beings, and its practitioners have authored the largest set of texts describing individual human beings ever composed. However, Christianity has always assumed that God's special revelation in Scripture was paramount for understanding human beings properly and caring for their souls well. In addition, the Christian tradition contains centuries of reflection on human beings in the light of Scripture. The Christian psychology community needs to develop a sophisticated hermeneutical framework for reading these three sources aright (Scripture, the Christian tradition and modern psychology), in order to compose a Christian scientific literature that describes human beings in a more comprehensive way than any of these sets of texts alone would provide, and in a way that allows the Bible to be the controlling interpretive guidebook. As that literature grows, research programs will be spawned that will study aspects of human beings from distinctly Christian perspectives, the results of which will increasingly add to and improve this body of literature. Christian soul care will become wiser and increasingly sophisticated as its content and practices are shaped by this growing body of Christian psychology discourse.

4

Objects of Disciplines and Their Contexts

IN DIFFERENT WAYS, THE MAJOR APPROACHES that most Christians have taken to psychology and soul care have assumed a disciplinary dichotomy between psychology and theology that has made it difficult to understand human nature holistically, through both empirical research and what the Bible teaches. Embedded in the modern conceptual framework that makes this particular disciplinary division plausible, a more foundational questioning of this dichotomy has been simply inconceivable. But we must ask, from where did this disciplinary division arise? Does the dichotomy exist in reality, or was its development more a function of sociohistorical and epistemological factors, so that we may legitimately entertain an alternative scientific framework? After examining how the disciplinary dichotomy came to be, we will discuss how we might reconstrue the discipline of psychology and its knowledge sources along lines more consistent with a Christian worldview.

A Brief Archaeology of Two Disciplines and Their Objects

In order to understand what led to the current disciplinary boundaries, it is necessary to consider their respective sociohistorical backgrounds. This kind of exploration is admittedly somewhat unusual, since those working within an existing discipline typically assume the received understanding of that discipline's boundaries and its corollary methodological assumptions, in order to do their work. However, some postmodern thinkers have shown that an investigation of the sociohistorical origins of conceptual and cultural institutions, like modern science, can bring to light some of the implicit dynamics that legitimate them and help us gain some understanding of that which is taken for granted in our present ordering of the world (e.g., Foucault, 1970, 1972; Lyotard, 1984; MacIntyre, 1988, 1990; Taylor, 1989, among others). Foucault (1972) termed such foundational investigations an "archaeology of knowledge." For centuries theology and psychology have been understood to constitute two distinct fields of study having different sources of data, methods of investigation and objects of study. Let us examine each in turn.

The object of theology. Anglo-Americans typically understand the term *theology* to refer to the discipline or science concerned with the Bible's teachings (see, e.g., Erickson, 1983-1985). But the term has not always been used in precisely that way. *Theology,* of course, is derived from the Greek words *theos* (God) and *logos* (knowledge). As the etymology would suggest, the term has often been used to refer simply to the study of the nature of God (e.g., Gregory of Nazianzus [1956], Oration 2; see also the discussions on theology of Congar, 1968; Whaling, 1981; and Wright, 1988). Pastors and teachers in the church, however, were responsible to expound the whole Bible to other Christians. Given the pressing needs of God's people to understand the written word of God, there arose in the early church intellectual leaders who became experts in the study and exposition (and preservation) of the Bible and its teachings (Bray, 1996; Young, 1997).

Eventually a formal discipline arose that was dedicated to the study of the Bible (Wright, 1988). By the high Middle Ages, it was understood to be a science that dealt with *all sacred doctrine,* which meant *everything that God revealed in the Scripture:* teachings regarding the triune God, his nature and works, as well as all things directly ordered to or pertaining to God (Thomas Aquinas, 1945). Consequently, many topics addressed in the Bible in addition to God and his works were included within its disciplinary boundaries, including doctrine itself, the nature of angels and human beings (e.g., the soul, appetites, will, intellect), sin, grace, faith and the sacraments (see Bonaventure, 1946; Thomas Aquinas, 1945). By the time of the Reformation a large body of literature existed that focused on and summarized all the teachings of the Scriptures, and given their own pastoral and ecclesial concerns, particularly the training of ministers, the Reformers accepted this discipline as it was defined. They simply contributed to this literature according to *their* understanding of biblical teaching, elaborating especially on topics where they differed from Catholics, for example, salvation and the church.

English-speaking cultures have tended to call this discipline *theology.* But given that the object of this discipline is not God per se, but the Bible, the term *theology* is something of a misnomer, a historical artifact, as often happens in the temporal, diachronic transformation of a word. As a matter of fact, the label "theology" for this field of study has never been universally accepted. Other terms used to cover this area include "first principles" (Origen), "sentences" (Lombard), "common places" (or "loci communes," Melanchthon), "the Christian philosophy" or "Christian doctrine" (Calvin), the "Christian faith" (H. Berkhof), and (quite common on the European continent) "dogmatics" (Bavinck, Barth, Weber). But regardless of what it is called, since the first few centuries of the early church, a discipline has existed that focused on the Bible's teachings.

The Bible *is* a complex object of study in its own right, consisting of a set of books of different genres, written by many different authors in either Hebrew or Greek, and its study produced large bodies of Latin and Greek literature (and now German and English) regarding its interpretation that also needed to be studied carefully. It deserved its own specialists. Moreover, it makes some conceptual sense to group together all the material in the Bible, since it is all information that was specially revealed by God. Given these considerations, it was inevitable that the Bible would be an object of intellectual study having its own discipline of inquiry.[1] Nonetheless, today we can more readily appreciate one of the negative intellectual consequences of this state of affairs.

Most important for Christians in psychology and counseling, the existence of a distinct discipline that had the Bible as its object of focus (instead of God) inadvertently isolated the study of the Bible from other disciplines that focused on objects within the created order. This becomes a fateful problem in the modern era, as the modern understanding and organization of intellectual disciplines was being formed. For example, Christians believed that *theology* concerns "supernatural revelation"—something equated in the modern era with the Kantian notion of the noumenal—and this effectively cordoned off its content from *science,* which studies "the empirical"—or what Kant termed the phenomenal. As a result, in marked contrast to the science of the Puritans (Cohen, 1990; Webster, 1986), modern Christian scientists and scholars interested in aspects of the created order had no rationale for including the Bible within the sphere of their work, even when the disciplines had as their objects of study subjects with which the Bible *also* dealt (as in the human sciences and humanities). This radical dichotomy is powerfully illustrated in the work of that great Reformed theologian Herman Bavinck. A few decades after completing his *Reformed Dogmatics*—where he spent hundreds of pages expounding the Bible's teaching about human nature—he also wrote a book about psychology (1923, translated 1981), where he described human nature without any reference to those biblical materials!

During the Middle Ages, there fortunately arose a compensating recognition that theology, together with philosophy, addresses matters of relevance to *all* the intellectual disciplines. Theology and philosophy came to be seen as what we would call today *metadisciplines,* those that could offer foundational principles and actual content (more or less) to all the sciences (in this vein, theology was considered the queen of the sciences). We will return to this topic in a moment.

The natural sciences were the first to develop in the scientific revolution of the early modern era (in astronomy, physics and chemistry), and this undermined the notion that biblical study constituted a metadiscipline because it became increasingly clear that the Bible would not contribute very much *directly* to the content of those disciplines.

Complicating matters were the growing number of secularist thinkers and scientists in the West who in their personal lives had left, or at least were moving away from, the Judeo-Christian framework of their culture (or their own childhood). For them, the Bible was obviously a historical document of great influence on the West, but one that had little relevance to their scientific work (and their own lives). By the time the scientific revolution had reached the study of human beings—in sociology and psychology in the late 1800s, *disciplines where the Bible had much more relevance*—the intellectual control of the West had already shifted into the hands of the nominally religious or the secularist (see Marsden, 1994; Stout, 1988; Turner, 1985). It was self-evident to the founders of the modern versions of psychology and sociology that the Bible had no role to play in their disciplines.

Two other rather abstract reasons led even Christians to believe the Bible was unrelated to other disciplines in the twentieth century. First was the modern penchant for analysis and the trend toward specialization. Analysis is a reasoning skill that breaks down something into its component parts. The value of this activity was well demonstrated in chemistry through the isolation of the basic elements of the material universe, organized into the periodic table. A major theme of modernism is the assumption that everything is either an element or composed of elements (a theme that touched early modern psychology; see, e.g., Thorndike, 1905, *The Elements of Psychology*). As a result, many modern scientists sought to identify the basic elements or categories of the object of their discipline, understood most purely apart from their relations to each other and other things (MacIntyre, 1990). A sense of the unity of being that permeated a Christian worldview (Gilson, 1940), and even the classical Greek worldview, gradually came to be replaced with an atomistic and splintered view of the universe, resulting in a fragmentation of knowledge into a multiplicity of discrete sciences (each of which continue to multiply into subdisciplines and sub-subdisciplines through ever increasing analysis and specialization).

Second, also during this period of time, the "encyclopedia" was seen as a major, unifying intellectual achievement: the attempt to organize, categorize and present all of human knowledge in a single multivolume work. The value of a comprehensive compendium of knowledge is obvious, but such a project had a special attraction to moderns and certain modern assumptions were built into it that have not really been overturned, and its vision of knowledge reinforced and expressed the secularizing tendencies already present in the academy (MacIntyre, 1990). For example, the modernists of the encyclopedia project assumed that human reason could successfully understand all aspects of reality (including all matters of human nature and religion), in such a way that all interested and rational parties could agree on the findings, resulting in a timeless, ahistorical, universal and objective account of the universe (MacIntyre, 1990). In addition, with the demise of metaphysics, as a result of the growing influence of positivism and the success of the natural sciences, it also came to be assumed that all data or truths were fundamentally equal. There was no privileged standpoint by which one idea, perspective or category of knowledge could be seen as more important than another. Consequently, all data and all disciplines were to be laid side by side in the organization of knowledge. One consequence of this trend was a cultural incapacity to recognize the deep relations and interconnections between things and knowledge about them, including hierarchial relations between them.

In this context, theology and philosophy could have no place of preeminence as metadisciplines, so at best they too were placed alongside all the other discrete aspects of human life. Such categorizations were eventually reified and thought to be the actual state of affairs in the universe. As a result, deposed from its throne as the queen of the sciences, theology became a commoner, one discipline among all the others (eventually devolving into that tepid modern discipline known as "religious studies"; see Marsden, 1994). As if this were not troubling enough from a Christian perspective, when logical positivism eventually came to dominate much of the intellectual life of the West in the early twentieth century, reference to supernatural objects to which the Bible refers was ruled to be meaningless, and secularism was soundly established as a pillar of the intellectual framework of the West. Consequently, in the twentieth century most Christian scholars—trained in the secular institutions of higher learning, as they had to be if they wanted to work in the academy—accepted the dominant ways of construing their disciplines and so found it difficult to entertain seriously how biblical teachings related in any meaningful way to their disciplines.

In our day, just how much of these historical developments can be aptly judged to have been unfortunate and misleading? The isolation of Scripture study, combined with the dethroning of theology in modern thought, convinced many Christian scholars outside theology that the Scriptures were not directly relevant to their scientific tasks. In such a context, integration is at best considered secondary to the real work of science—a hobby perhaps—leaving many others with the feeling that it is superfluous.

In light of this reading of history, let us entertain a proposal. A distinct science of biblical study is obviously needed, first because of the complexity of such study and, second, for the training of ministers (necessitating institutions of biblical study known as seminaries). However, since the biblical text is of such tremendous epistemic importance and broad relevance to Christians in a variety of disciplines that deal with aspects of the created order (particularly in the human sciences and humanities), let us revive the notion that biblical study is also a *metadiscipline* (like philosophy). Scriptural study and reflection on it must be done by Christians in *all* relevant scholarly disciplines if the Bible's full epistemic value is to be realized by the respective Christian scholarly communities in each discipline.[2] This would allow the biblical text and reflection upon it to contribute foundational principles *indirectly* to all the disciplines and, second, content *directly* and *internally* to any relevant discipline, as appropriate, rendering such study scientifically respectable (at least according to the Christian community's understanding of science).

The object of psychology. But we are getting a little ahead of ourselves. What about the focus of psychology? It is also well known that the term psychology comes from *psyche* (soul) and *logos* (knowledge). The term was coined in the premodern era, when thinkers in the West still believed humans had an immaterial aspect that could be described, if not observed (Johnson, 1998a). Before psychology became a distinct discipline, theologians and philosophers were the only scholars who discussed the nature of the soul (see Brett, 1953; Watson & Evans, 1991). Philosophers in the pre-Christian era, like Plato and Aristotle, wrote a great deal about the soul and human nature, cognition and virtue, based on personal experience, the writings of others and logical analysis. The value of this body of work began to be reappropriated in the Middle Ages by monks working in monasteries. But given their callings, the study of human nature was rarely engaged in for its own sake, independently of ecclesial and spiritual concerns. During the Renaissance and after, learned individuals, encouraged by their own study of ancient philosophy, began writing about the nature of the soul themselves. Gradually, a group of intellectuals arose in the West who composed their own discourse on human nature (among other things), focusing on topics like reason, memory, body-soul relations, habit and morality, work that resembled more closely that of ancient Greece and Rome than that done by Christians in the Middle Ages, since its considerations were little shaped by religious doctrine and the teachings of the Bible. These "philosophers" were either independently wealthy (e.g., J. S. Mill) or were employed as tutors or teachers (e.g., Descartes), or worked on philosophy in their spare time (e.g., Hume) (Brett, 1953; Murphy, 1949; Viney & King, 1998; Watson & Evans, 1991).

Eventually, in the late 1800s the scientific revolution hit the study of human beings, and mathematics and the research methods of the natural sciences began to be applied to the empirical study of humans. Given the assumptions of the positivism that was influencing the thinking of many, the psychology of that time eschewed any reference to things metaphysical, ethical or supernatural (see, e.g., James, 1890). A central dynamic of this movement was the desire to progress beyond the superstition and speculation of the past and base the "new psychology" solely on the facts of human nature as they were discovered empirically (Danziger, 1990; Toulmin & Leary, 1992; see Watson, 1925). As a result, from the beginning, these "new psychologists" strove to study human nature from a value-neutral, "objective" standpoint, free from any assumptions about the facts, particularly any metaphysical commitments, so that the "pure" psychological facts could be examined on their own. Scientific terminology had to be developed that would be more precise and objective than normal speech (e.g., prosocial behavior instead of love), for the purpose of developing a more complex and univocal description of human nature, but that also systematically excluded certain topics (e.g., the soul, free will, one's relation to God and the virtues). While the ideal of objectivity is a necessary goal of science, Christians recognize that the modern ideal was also motivated by an implicit, unconscious antireligious dynamic that was a function of the antithesis.[3]

At any rate, modern psychology came to be conceived by its founders as an empirically based study of individual human beings that had successfully replaced the theological and philosophical discourse on human beings of a bygone era. In the 1930s logical positivism provided an influential basis for this transition and insisted that reference to anything metaphysical was meaningless nonsense and therefore could not be considered knowledge. By the time modern psychology began to come into its own as a major cultural force, sometime between the 1930s and 1950s, the relevance of the study of Scripture for its formation was utterly inconceivable.

From a historical standpoint, there was value in the attempt to develop a psychology defined by stringent positivist requirements. For one thing, negatively, it showed what such ideological extremism can lead to. But modern psychologists have demonstrated a laudable, scientifically minded discipline that pushed researchers to listen as carefully as possible to the object and avoid reading into human nature features that were not there, and not to say more than their research would allow them to say. Nevertheless, the standards of the "cult of empiricism" (Toulmin & Leary, 1992) are undeniably excessive by Christian epistemic standards. As the logical positivism of the first half of the century softened into the neopositivism of mainstream psychology in the second half, it still required researchers to avoid the appearance of taking ethical, ontological or religious perspectives in interpreting the data (so, spirituality is now okay, but not Christianity or Islam), and it still prohibits appeal to anything beyond the publicly verifiable. These modern discourse strictures make it impossible for Christians to describe Christian experience using Christian forms of discourse, for example, referring to an improvement in a person's psychological well-being after Christian conversion as a result of the work of the

Holy Spirit. The prohibitions of modernism profoundly reinforced the assumption that psychology and theology were entirely distinct, unrelated disciplines, so that the combined force of the sociohistorical influences examined so far in this chapter made the dichotomy between them a self-evident truism for Christians and non-Christians throughout the twentieth century.

Other Explanations for Disciplinary Dualism Among Christians

It is easy to see why secularists would affirm the current disciplinary dichotomy that divides the study of human beings and the study of Scripture. But, as we noted earlier, Christians have long believed the Bible was relevant for their understanding of human beings and soul care. And even today, most Christians in psychology and counseling sense intuitively that the biblical content of their faith should make some difference in their understanding. Yet, this faulty disciplinary dualism has gone largely unchallenged. The breadth of the current gap between psychological and biblical discourse is currently so great that there must be additional factors beyond the sociohistorical dynamics we have examined. Let us consider some possibilities.

A methodological explanation. The most common explanation given is the fact that they use different methods: psychology is derived from research that uses various empirical methods to study human beings (including skilled observation, surveys, experimentation and interviews), whereas biblical studies involves the reading and interpretation of biblical texts, and the systematization of their teaching (Carter & Narramore, 1979). However, this explanation begs the question of what it is attempting to prove, for who decided that psychology ought not to include reference to the Bible in its discourse?

But let us think a bit more deeply about this methodological distinction, for modern psychology may have more in common with biblical studies than one might think. Viewed one way, a science consists of a set of texts written to describe some object. Of course, modern psychology authors seek to base all their assertions on empirical research done on human beings at a specific time, using sanctioned methods, but the fact remains that undergraduate and graduate psychology education mostly involves the reading of authoritative texts that describe features of human beings. The issue is, what makes them authoritative? Well-designed empirical research is one good standard, but so is the testimony of humanity's Creator, revealed through the prophets and apostles. Studying the Bible (and the Christian tradition) to aid us in the development of our psychology is simply to be reading the most important authoritative texts of the Christian research tradition.

Some might object that there are no research studies upon which these authoritative texts are based, as there are in modern psychology. But even here some rethinking is necessary, for really all empirical studies of human beings require the use of discourse to understand the nature of the object being studied—research using interviews, questionnaires and case studies requires the study of discourse as data, and even experimental studies that engage in quantitative analysis still must be understood linguistically (and eventually written up into a text). But perhaps the current psychology research method most relevant to the study of the Bible and the Christian tradition is qualitative research methods like discourse analysis. In some areas of the field, it is now considered legitimate to do psychology research focusing on texts like personal journals, stories and essays in order to understand some aspect of human beings. At the very least, Christians can consider biblical and theological studies to be a kind of discourse analysis, necessary to understand human nature most accurately.

At least in these ways, the idea of there being a huge methodological gap dividing biblical and theological studies and psychology is somewhat misleading. Modern psychologists will consider reading the Bible to be illegitimate for their psychology, but why should Christians?

An educational/institutional explanation. Another fact that maintains this disciplinary dualism is that modern psychology and soul care have been developed within a secular educational context by a largely secular community, within which most Christians are trained (or, in the case of Christian programs, by those who have been at least influenced by modern psychology). As a result, most Christians in the field have been socialized to work within the rules of the secular establishment. Psychology and soul care are both crafts that are taught by experts who pass on to their students a knowledge base that includes the rules of the craft (MacIntyre, 1981). Those rules are the result of years of practice, and they are usually based on some good reasons and evidence, but we must not assume that they are all necessarily valid. Christians in the field will need to call into question the "received rules" of the secular community's version of psychology and the soul-care crafts before we as a community will be able to develop our own knowledge base and rules of the craft that flow from a Christian vision of human nature and soul healing.

A vocational explanation. One of the strongest factors intensifying the contemporary disciplinary dichotomy is the fact that most employment in human services (including the highest paying jobs) exists in avowedly secular establishments, supervised and regulated by secularists trained in secular soul care. If Christians want to work in the current mental-health field, their odds for getting hired are to some extent increased as the Christian quality of their thinking and practice is diluted and as their acceptance of secular rules for soul-care discourse and practice is strengthened. Those of us who have worked in the public arena in the human-services sector know that the antipathy toward Christianity among some mental-health professionals is great. Such realities create enormous pressures for sincere Christians who want to help people. One hopes that the influence of postmodernism on the field may open up positions for Christians at *pluralist* centers (rather than *secular*) to be employed *as Christian* counselors. But it will take decades for such a rethinking of the field to become widely understood and embraced in American culture.

A neuropsychological explanation. The following explanation is somewhat speculative, but it is also plausible, given current understandings of neuropsychology. We know that some categories of information are stored in distinct neural regions, for example, animate and inanimate objects are stored in separate locations (Schacter, Wagner & Buckner, 2000). Perhaps information from the Bible (learned in "theology" classes, church or on our own) forms a distinct neural network of associated knowledge, while information regarding human beings (learned in secular psychology classes or books) forms another neural network. Unless a good deal of time is spent relating these two bodies of information, there is little opportunity for neural pathways to be created connecting the respective neural regions (Friston, 2005), so they remain dissociated. With regard to training in Christian programs, there need to be multiple opportunities to promote conceptual/neural linkages throughout the curriculum (and cerebrum), without which the possibility of cross-fertilization of the respective subject matters/neural regions is lessened, and the gap between "theology" and "psychology" is maintained rather than undermined. One "integration" class at the end of one's education will not do. To bridge the conceptual/neural gaps, students need to be mentored in how to develop an understanding of human nature that is holistic and brings together all the relevant information at their disposal into one framework. They need a single, complex, interrelated system of truths that promotes a corresponding highly associated and interactive set of regions of the brain.

A Summary of the Problems with a Psychology/Theology Disciplinary Dualism

Soul care and the study of human beings are not the only arenas where a faulty dualism has caused problems for Christians. There has been a perennial tendency in the church to divide the creation, culture or human life into two fundamentally different kinds of things in a way foreign to their actual created nature. In such cases, those aspects of reality that relate explicitly to God are deemed religious (e.g., church, prayer, witnessing), and those aspects that do not (e.g., factory work, sexual intercourse, recreation) are deemed to be either void of religious significance or radically inferior to the religious aspects. We will call such an approach *religious dualism.* This problem will be discussed in more detail in chapter eleven.

The traditional understanding of theology's object of study and the modern approach to psychology both seem to have contributed to some other faulty dualisms: either the kind of hard-core religious dualism that underlies the levels-of-explanation and weak integration understanding of both disciplines; or a softer religious dualism that leads most biblical counselors to strongly favor theology (the virtuous study of the Bible) over psychology (the intrinsically tainted study of human beings). Strong integrationists, to their credit, have sought to overturn or undermine both of these dualisms.

However, a milder form of religious dualism would seem implicit in the integrationist acceptance of the current disciplinary division between modern psychology and biblical studies, with the positing of *two* different objects of study that should be integrated (theological or Christian worldview beliefs and empirical research of human beings). It must be admitted that there is a certain plausibility to the traditional way of construing psychology and theology; it has a kind of tidiness. But this way of conceptualizing these disciplines has created a number of conceptual and practical problems that are not easy to remedy. First, as we have seen, it fosters and reinforces a conceptual chasm between the biblical text on the one hand, and the texts of psychology and the practice of counseling on the other. This chasm becomes mentally, neurologically and practically difficult, if not impossible, to adequately bridge. Second, it implicitly reinforces a separation of life into the religious domain (where the Bible is relevant) and the nonreligious (where it is not). But the Bible itself teaches that the whole universe belongs to the Lord and is related to him—not just the Bible—so the traditional disciplinary boundaries inherently foster, to some extent, a secularizing view of human life. Therefore, third, it would seem that the current disciplinary ordering strongly encourages the formation of a psychology that is intrinsically secular and anthropocentric—since it must exclude reference to God (which integrationists then try to remedy by integrating faith back into it).

Actually, a telling violation of theology's traditional disciplinary boundary has long occurred in theology, and this violation could help to undermine the chasm between theology and other disciplines. As we have seen, theology has traditionally focused on the Bible. Nonetheless, it is widely accepted that theologians must also give due consideration to God's general revelation of himself in the creation, if they are to avail themselves of *all* the information there is about God (Ps 19:1-6; Rom 1:19-20). But if theologians do not restrict themselves exclusively to the study of their traditional object of inquiry (the Bible), maybe Christians in psychology do not have to restrict themselves to empirical research on human beings either.

But perhaps the most important reason to throw out the traditional disciplinary dichotomy between theology and psychology concerns the function of Scripture in the Christian's life (Frame, 1987; Vanhoozer, 2005; Work, 2002). Scripture is not just an object of knowledge, comparable to other objects. Its texts provide a vision of the world: a worldview. It offers a divinely inspired interpretation of reality and history, a theocentric way of thinking and valuing everything, in which we learn to enter through reading, understanding and receiving the Scriptures in mind and heart. Wherever it speaks of empirical objects—including human beings—it must be allowed to shine on, that is, illuminate the object, enabling us to see its actual nature more clearly. And that, after all, is the aim of all true science.

The fact is that the disciplinary division between theology and psychology is not necessarily part of the order of things. It is a sociohistorically constructed dichotomy that, upon reflection today, may not have been in the best interests of the Christian community. One can imagine a psychology less constrained by the methodological presumptions of modern psychology. What we need today is a single, comprehensive, holistic discipline that seeks to understand individual human beings, using all available and relevant resources. Some label is necessary for this area. Of all the available terms, I would suggest this single discipline be called psychology—the study of the soul—and then we ought always to use an adjective (like *Christian* or *modern* or *Buddhist*) to distinguish the specific version under consideration.

Toward a More Comprehensive and Holistic Discipline of Psychology

A science consists of a set of communally established practices for elucidating the nature of some object of inquiry and how it changes, leading to a resulting body of complex discourse that records and organizes that knowledge. Modern psychology has produced an enormous set of texts that are the result of a massive and highly successful effort in the twentieth century to describe individual human beings using the research practices of the natural sciences within the intellectual context of modernism (Toulmin & Leary, 1992; Viney & King, 1998). But what if it is the responsibility of the Christian psychology community to redefine psychology in a way that corresponds more faithfully to its understanding of the universe?

Let us suppose that there is really only *one* object of study for Christians in psychology and soul care—individual human beings—but there are multiple modalities that can be used to help us discern the nature of that object, including research on humans using natural science methods, as well as first-person articulations of human experience, philosophical reflection and analysis, human science research, research on humans using natural science methods, literature, the Christian intellectual tradition and most importantly Scripture.

This way of drawing the boundaries of psychology is bolstered by seeing the Christian's epistemological goal to be to understand reality the way God does (Van Til, 1955). This is a necessary implication of the Christian belief in an all-knowing God, who therefore is the "Ideal Knower" or "Omniscient Observer," and who provides an epistemological ideal for our understanding.[4] "Truth, in the general, may be defined after the most strict and metaphysical manner: the 'consistency and agreement of our ideas with the ideas of God'" (Edwards, 1980, pp. 341-42). To put it in a more rigid formulation: necessarily, for any proposition *p*, *p* is true if and only if God believes *p* (see Plantinga, 1993a). Believing in the existence of a comprehensive, unitary knowledge and appraisal of reality in the mind and heart of God follows from the classical Christian view of God (Frame, 1987, 2002; Pearcey, 2004; Stoker, 1971; Van Til, 1955, 1969), and it permits us to think about science in a very different way than that dictated by modernism (which assumes that human understanding is all there is).

The triune God has a perfect knowledge and accurate appraisal of everything there is to know about human beings, since he made them and he knows all things, past, present and future (Ps 139; 1 Jn 3:20; Heb 4:13). This guarantees his comprehensive understanding even of aspects of humans he did not create (for example, sin). So we can aim no higher in our knowledge of human nature than the goal of thinking about and evaluating it the way the omniscient (and perfectly emotional) God does. We, of course, are incapable of duplicating that knowledge and appraisal in its entirety, lacking the necessary prerequisites of omniscience and perfect emotions. No creature can replicate God's understanding, since his alone is exhaustive and comprehensive (Frame, 1987; Van Til, 1969). However, the *ideal* of a single, holistic understanding and appraisal of human nature, analogous to God's, could be used to guide a Christian undertaking of psychology, even if we know humans will forever fall short of it. God has created our minds and hearts such that they may know a finite portion of knowable reality (Plantinga, 1993a, 1993b, 2000) and care about it, and so can share in God's knowledge and love. There are then, "two levels of interpreters of our created universe: (i) *God*, who interprets absolutely, and (ii) *man*, who must be a reinterpreter of God's interpretation" (Stoker, 1971, p. 56).

Assuming the existence of such an epistemic ideal is important for many reasons. First, we will be less inclined to accept the current human understanding of human beings as the only, right way to understand reality. Believing in the existence of that ideal should help Christians be more objective about current understandings of psychology and recognize they are simply *versions* of psychology. This makes it easier to entertain alternative construals, without necessarily rejecting everything that the extant versions offer. Second, knowing of the ideal should incline us to be perpetually open to questioning aspects of our own current understanding of human nature, since we know we do not have the perfect understanding that God does. Third, it will keep us from becoming ideologues and affirming only one model of the truth (e.g., cognitive-behaviorism, the medical model or even *the* biblical model), since God's understanding must always be larger than any single human system. Lastly, holding that God has the perfect knowledge and appraisal of human beings leads quite naturally to the recognition that the divinely inspired Bible—his revelation of himself and the first principles of human life—would be helpful to get a better grasp of God's exhaustive understanding. God's perfect, comprehensive and exhaustive knowledge and appraisal of human nature provides a unified epistemological and axiological goal toward which Christians should aspire, recognizing that our representation (ectype) will always only be an approximation of God's perfect representation (archetype) (Johnson, 1997a; see Muller, 2003, Vol. 1).

So, rather than the Bible being the sole object of study as it is (appropriately) in biblical counseling, or psychology and theology constituting the two objects of study as is assumed in integration, the Christian psychology community has a single object of psychological study—individual human beings—knowledge of which can be obtained by multiple sources (including the Bible and the Christian tradition), and there is a perfect understanding of that single object already in the unified mind and heart of God toward which we strive. Given how controversial the claim, let us spend some more time justifying the inclusion of the Bible in a Christian psychology.

Philosophical warrant for using the Bible within a Christian psychology. The idea that the Bible should be a part of psychology is patently scandalous from the standpoint of modern psychology. Intrinsic to modern science is the requirement that any scientific assertion must in principle be publicly verifiable, that is, capable of being subjected to tests that can be conducted by any interested (or better, disinterested) party—so that all researchers would obtain the same finding with experiments done in various locations by different, unbiased researchers—and only if it passes such tests can it be counted as genuine knowledge, worthy of incorporation into a body of scientific discourse. As a result, according to modernism, unfalsifiable beliefs that Christians hold, which non-Christians do not hold, cannot be counted as knowledge.

But is this true? Or are there also rational grounds for using a source like the Bible within a Christian psychology? To begin with, belief in God can be considered a *basic* belief by Christians, that is, one of a number of beliefs that form the doxastic (belief) foundation for all of one's conceptual activity and life, functionally equivalent to beliefs in an external world, other minds, memories, perceptions and the reliable testimony of others (Alston, 1991; Nash, 1988; Plantinga, 1981, 1983, 1993b). Contemporary epistemologists have come to the conclusion that it is not possible to *prove* any of these kinds of beliefs. For example, Plantinga (1993b, 2001) and others (Alston, 1991, 1996; Audi, 1998) have shown that modernist standards for what counts as knowledge are far too high for most of our basic beliefs. It is not possible, for example, to prove that other humans are not well-disguised aliens or that we are not all subject to mass illusion as in the Matrix. If some of the most fundamental beliefs that normal persons take to be true are not capable of being thoroughly proven according to modernist (or foundationalist) criteria, then perhaps human knowing in general is quite different than modernism (and scientism) supposes, and maybe belief in God is fundamentally no different from any other basic belief.

One way of thinking about knowledge is to suppose that people are warranted in holding beliefs to be true (to be *knowledge*) if they are produced by reliable belief-producing mechanisms situated within appropriate environments. For example, we are warranted in believing what we see if we have no reason for suspecting that our vision-processing system is malfunctioning or the environment we are viewing has been distorted in some way (Plantinga, 1993b). According to Calvin (1559/1960), humans were created with a *sensus divinitatis*, a mechanism (or module) for perceiving God, so that humans ought to count their belief in God as knowledge, so long as they have no reason to suspect that that mechanism is faulty. It is true that one's noetic equipment may malfunction, resulting in a false belief, when one does not know it, but there are no good grounds to conclude from this *possibility* that all human knowledge claims are thereby rendered equally suspect.

Furthermore, there is also a rational basis for counting many of the core truths of Christianity as *knowledge* and not as mere subjective opinions (e.g., the Trinity, the image of God, human depravity, the death of Christ for our sins and justification by faith) (Plantinga, 2000). According to Calvin (1559/1960), the *clear truths* of Scripture are self-authenticating; ultimately they are as worthy of being considered knowledge as any other clear truths, like the proposition "George Washington was the first president of the United States," and my recollection that I visited Texas in 2003. According to a Christian epistemology (specifically a Reformed epistemology), Christians are justified in considering a teaching of the Christian religion *knowledge*, if four conditions are met: (1) the knower has properly functioning noetic equipment (like reasoning and reading ability), aimed at truth, in an environment for which it was fitted; that is, if the knower has warrant, (2) there are adequately clear texts of the Bible that teach the truth, (3) the Holy Spirit illumines the knower so he is persuaded of its truth, and (4) the knower, in fact, believes it to be true (has "faith") (see Plantinga, 2000).

If this is so, even distinctively Christian beliefs are fundamentally no different and just as rationally justified as beliefs derived from one's perception, reason, memory and reliable testimony from others (Audi, 1998)—sources that provide the grounds for beliefs in the veracity of scientific research and discourse about it. The dissemination of scientific knowledge itself requires that most people accept the testimony of the researcher. Audi (1998) points out further that scientific knowledge is by definition approximate. Even well-established knowledge, like Newton's laws, has been shown to have limited application (it explains planetary movement, but not the universe as a whole). Scientific knowledge can only be approximate, because it consists of generalizations made at a certain level of precision. According to a postfoundationalist account, psychological knowledge based on careful, replicated research (which itself is based on perception, memory, reason, the setting up of research procedures and the testimony of the scientists) is not *more* worthy of the name *knowledge* than are the deliverances of any legitimate forms of knowing. Rather than scientific knowledge being some ideal, purified form of knowledge that has been *proven* to be true—vastly more sure than "lay knowledge"—it is simply human knowledge derived from a set of logically warranted procedures that we are justified to believe procure knowledge in *hard-to-get-at regions of the world.* These procedures are practiced by professional knowledge-gatherers called scientists but are still fundamentally akin to other legitimate lay methods of human knowledge-formation, like looking, asking and reading.

No disparagement of scientific research is intended here. Its techniques obviously produce knowledge that would be unobtainable by lay methods. But this account does bring scientific pronouncements down from their pedestal and shows that in terms of its trustworthiness, scientific knowledge is no different than other forms of human knowledge.

As a result, Christians are within their epistemic rights to reject some modern research rules for science and develop broader, Christian research rules that comport better with their worldview. Psychologists in the Christian community are free to define psychology as a careful, disciplined, but fallible inquiry into the nature of individual human beings that may make use of all appropriate information-gathering methods to form the most comprehensive and accurate psychology possible. According to Christian teaching, humans are created and known perfectly by God, and God has revealed some truths about humans in Scripture that are necessary for the most accurate understanding of human beings possible. If that is true, the most rational thing to do is to include the reading of Scripture as an information-gathering method in one's psychology. Of course, rules are needed for reading Scripture *appropriately* for a Christian psychology, just as there are rules for running an experiment appropriately. But Christians in psychology should be able to use the Bible as a part of their own version of a science of human beings and soul care.

The necessary ingredients of a Christian psychology. Christians in psychology should use *all* the means at their disposal that will yield the greatest amount of relevant information about individual human beings, regardless of their previous assignment to a separate discipline. Psychology, in that case, would be *the integration of all these findings*. This use of integration, however, makes it a *discipline-constituting* activity, rather than a post-hoc activity conducted *after* psychology has already been formed (by modernism).

What should be the formative ingredients of a Christian psychology? To begin with, it should include the use of statistics and natural-science methods of research (e.g., naturalistic observation, questionnaires, case studies and experiments). These, of course, are the favored methods of modern psychology, but that is because of their strengths: they yield findings of unusual clarity, in which one can obtain a relatively high degree of confidence (depending on the quality of the research), that itself can be measured (e.g., with obtained p values and effect sizes). This has been called "research in the third person"—understanding human beings from a "distance"—that requires bracketing our presuppositions about and sympathies with the object of inquiry and engaging in a kind of detached observation of and manipulation of the experience of humans, which—when combined with quantitative analysis—yield replicable and easily comparable findings. In addition to the traditional research topics that can be studied with these methods (like neuropsychology, cognition, personality traits and group dynamics), Christians should use them to study phenomena unique to a Christian vision of human beings, for example, Christian spiritual experience using questionnaires (rather than generic "spirituality"), Christian self-representations, perceptions of sin, shame, guilt and divine forgiveness, and uniquely Christian treatment strategies (as some integrationists have done). But with only these methods, modern psychology is limited to the study of features of human beings that can be identified by these methods, and there is more to a full accounting of human beings than that.

So, in addition, Christian psychology should use human-science methods, including ethnographic, narrative, phenomenological and discourse analysis, since some facets of human nature can only be examined by taking into account human subjectivity and actual human experience. This has been called "research in the first and second persons" (e.g., see Varela & Shear, 1999)—understanding human nature through trust and dialogue—by means of our preunderstanding and relationship with the object of inquiry. These interpretive methods usually take longer to gather data and yield a lower degree of confidence in the findings and lower generalizibility, but such approaches provide essential insights into human life *as it is lived*, from "within," so to speak, for example, the experience of personal agency (see Giorgi, 1970; Taylor, 1985a, 1989; Van Leeuwen, 1982, 1985; Varela & Shear, 1999). In addition to studying universal human experience this way, Christians can use such methods to examine Christian spiritual experience "from the inside" (interviews about believers' daily experience with the Holy Spirit or their personal relationship with God over their life span), Christian virtues, the perceived relation between the law and the gospel, and the dynamics of change in Christian maturation.

Critical human-science methods also require interpretation, but their goal is to examine *unconscious* dynamics, whether related to power, economics, gender, family-of-origin or spiritual issues (Apel, 1984; Bhaskar, 1986; Bernstein, 1985; Fay, 1987). In contrast to the qualitative methods mentioned above, this approach distrusts the Subject's self-awareness and understanding, and seeks to get "beneath it," by subjecting conscious material to critical examination. Given their doctrine of sin, Christians would expect such research would be necessary. Natural- and human-science methods all have their strengths and weaknesses. As a result, some researchers will want to use multiple methods in the same study.

Philosophical work is also necessary in all the sciences. This is especially true for the human sciences, given their complexity, in order to clarify terms and concepts, develop and criticize arguments related to research findings and theory, articulate and illuminate seemingly intractable problems (like soul-body dualism), develop research questions and compare information from other disciplines. Good psychology will come from good philosophical analysis.

Biblical teachings about human nature and salvation should also be included as legitimate psychological information. Such information legitimately belongs in psychology—not in a discipline that studies the Bible for its own sake. Modern seminaries have sometimes tended to treat theological study almost as if it were an end in itself. But this is akin to some astronomers devoting their energies to understanding the nature of the telescope. Christian psychologists should approach the Bible as a research instrument that enables them to see human beings in ways they cannot without its aid. Closely allied to the study of the Bible for psychology, is the study of the history of Christian thought regarding human beings and their care. Centuries of soul care and serious reflection on Scripture in a variety of sociohistorical contexts have yielded a storehouse of valuable psychological information. All of these ingredients are needed in a comprehensive Christian psychology.

Modern psychologists understand that statistics and research design are an integral part of psychology. Therefore, all psychology faculty are supposed to have received some training in these areas and are expected to have a working knowledge of them, and most large psychology departments also employ an expert who specializes in the application of statistics and research design to the study of human beings and teaches required courses in those areas with psychology in mind. Psychology departments are typically not content to send their students to study statistics in the math department, recognizing that that would not equip the psychology students to apply their statistical knowledge to their own discipline.

In the same way, it should be expected that all faculty in Christian departments of psychology and counseling have training in and a working knowledge of biblical and theological studies, and these departments should also employ a "doctrine" expert—one who specializes in the application of Scripture to the study of human beings and teaches required hermeneutics and biblical studies courses, *but with psychology in mind*—and not simply send their students to the Bible department. Likewise, just as some statistics and research design is taught and assumed throughout many of the other courses in the curriculum, Christian psychology departments should do the same with biblical research. Until biblical study is seen to be an integral and pervasive part of a Christian psychology/counseling program, the integration project will be fundamentally compromised.

An objection. The claim for the Bible's inclusion in psychological science will surely strike modern theologians and psychologists as ridiculous, and no doubt some Christians in psychology would also object. For example, they might point—with good reason—to the early modern controversy concerning the relative positions and movement of the sun and the earth, and argue that the literary contents of the Bible are nonscientific and simply cannot be legitimately utilized in scientific discussion.

Clearly there *are* serious risks involved in such an openness to Scripture as is being suggested here. Bringing the Bible into psychology might seem to open the door of science up to any kind of bogus input: for example, astrology or communication from aliens. It is likely this kind of concern that led Wolterstorff (1975; and Jones & Butman, 1991) to limit the influence of Christian considerations in science to the formation of Christian *control beliefs* (about what constitutes a good theory and good data), but not as *data* themselves. Christians, it must be conceded, will make egregious epistemological blunders if they read the Bible with communicative expectations that do not correspond to God's communicative intentions (as was done in the 1500s in astronomy).

At the same time, we must not overreact to that earlier conflagration. There are good Christian reasons to suppose that the Bible provides some information necessary for a human science like psychology, where worldview beliefs necessarily constitute significant aspects of one's understanding of the object (compared, e.g., with astronomy). Neglecting this source of information in *our* scientific work may simply be a capitulation to control beliefs foreign to Christianity. Who made up the positivist rules that exclude a serious consideration of Scripture in the *human* sciences? Modernists. So why should Christians submit to those rules, *at least* when discussing psychology among themselves? Of course modernists and postmodernists will not subscribe to the Bible as a source of psychological data, but why should Christians do likewise, given their faith-commitments regarding the Bible?[5] How can they? We must accept that a Christian disciplinary framework for psychology will likely have some rules that differ from those having other worldviews.

For psychologists and counselors who affirm the divine authorship of the Bible and its authority over life, it is eminently rational to make use of biblical teaching in their work. Alvin Plantinga (2003) makes this point with the following illustration. Suppose someone says to a friend, "I am curious about your whereabouts last Friday night: were you perhaps at The Linebacker's Bar? Perhaps I could find out in three different ways: by asking you, by asking your wife, and by examining the bar for your fingerprints (fortunately the bar is never washed)" (p. 46). Plantinga asks if there would be something immoral or illogical in using any one of these methods when one of the others was available, and he concludes there is not. Similarly, from a Christian perspective, there are simply no compelling reasons why Christians in psychology should not be able to make hermeneutically responsible use of the Bible in their psychological and soul-care work. Such an option is especially necessary for Christians in psychology, since they have no other access to some of the information they need (e.g., the nature of sin, the work of the Holy Spirit). Let Christians then incorporate the Bible into *their* psychology and soul-care work, soberly and carefully, as a communal enterprise that subjects their assertions to at least three kinds of hermeneutical critiques: empirical, philosophical and exegetical.

Toward a Christian Philosophy of Psychology

At this point, it might be a good idea to consider what a Christian understanding of philosophy of human science might look like and how it might differ from the dominant neopositivist models regnant in secular psychology.[6]

What is a science? Each science has its own object of inquiry that is believed to have a discernable dynamic form (or structure) and identifiable influences on that form (Polanyi, 1958). Therefore, each science is a hermeneutical discipline that seeks to elucidate the meaning of its object by obtaining an increasingly accurate and comprehensive description, explanation and understanding of it (Bernstein, 1985). Like all complex human activities, a science is constituted by its tradition—the history of its beliefs, practices and institutions through which the science has been realized. This means a science is necessarily situated within a history and a cultural community, and therefore, it is always limited by the finite capacities of its practitioners and their sociohistorical location. A science is then also a communal enterprise, comprising all those who share the science's foundational beliefs and are skilled in seeking to understand its object (including researchers, theoreticians, authors and teachers); a discursive enterprise, made up of all the available texts that describe its object well (of particular importance are the authoritative texts—those that are considered exemplary); and a pragmatic enterprise, consisting in the practices and methods of its researchers used to obtain their understandings. A Christian understanding of science adds that the ultimate composer of science is the God of all truth and grace, who already knows each object exhaustively and who sovereignly grants knowledge to those made in his image through the excellence of their knowledge-gathering practices (for a more detailed discussion of some of these themes and for what follows, see Bhaskar, 1975; Chalmers, 1982; Kuyper, 1898b; Ramm, 1954; Ratzsch, 1986; Suppe, 1977; Torrance, 1984, 1989).

Because it is a communal activity, a science can have more or less different versions, due to the existence of scientific subcommunities that differ among themselves regarding certain basic assumptions, depending on historical and communal particularities (within contemporary psychology, e.g., the main neopositivist approach can be distinguished from a postmodern school). According to MacIntyre (1977, 1988, 1990), when one subcommunity offers a more compelling version of a discipline than another, the vulnerable community is thrown into an epistemological crisis. Its very existence is threatened unless it can successfully respond to the challenge by providing an even more persuasive account—at least in terms of its own standards of rationality—by addressing satisfactorily the problems the alternative version raised. The community of Christians in psychology and soul care is in the midst of such a crisis.

Regarding the discourse of the science, its texts will include *observational statements* (which may also include mathematical formulas and analysis) that are intended to represent faithfully (or objectively) some actual feature of the object, and *theoretical statements* consisting of models, abstract generalizations or broader explanatory principles that are used to represent faithfully actual relationships between features of objects. *Lower-level* theoretical statements are directly related to the data and are conceptually united to form theories, which are used to interpret the observational statements. *Higher-level* theoretical statements include one's fundamental beliefs (or control beliefs, Wolterstorff, 1975) about the object, which often cannot be proven but must be assumed and provide the largest context within which the science's texts are composed. The set of these latter statements has variously been called a worldview (Naugle, 2002), an ideological surround (Watson, 1993), a disciplinary matrix (Kuhn, 1977b), and a research program (Lakatos, 1970). As we will see, contemporary philosophy of science supports Quine's (1963; Ullian, 1978) insight that observational and theoretical statements are interdependent and together form a web of interrelated and interdependent beliefs.

The epistemological context of human knowledge: worldviews. Much of the knowledge that humans possess comes from other humans, through listening to others or reading texts. Even perceptual concepts and our experience are mediated by language, and all language is historically constituted. As a result, mature thinkers find that their terms/concepts are already in use. They come prepackaged, as it were, already situated within an ideological surround, preinterpreted by others and already understood in certain ways. While simple observational terms/concepts offer fairly straightforward representations of objects, relatively unaffected by culture (e.g., yellow, banana, food), certain abstract terms are especially loaded with culture-specific meaning (e.g., freedom, happiness, folly, God and so on). Such words are not culture-neutral. When used in discourse, they are being interpreted by the author in a certain way. And if such words are never neutral, texts that use such words are never neutral. This is why a general hermeneutic is necessary for understanding all of human life.

General hermeneutic theory (as developed by Heidegger, Gadamer and Ricoeur) suggests that human knowledge is always situated within a preinterpreted, sociolinguistic context or tradition. As children develop into personal agents (or interpreters), they come to participate creatively in their community's intellectual tradition. Their tradition is the medium within which they know. All humans approach every situation with a given *preunderstanding*. It is simply not possible to enter a new situation without any presuppositions derived from one's familial, cultural and intellectual traditions. "Understanding, since it is an historically accumulated and historically operative basic structure, underlies even scientific interpretation; the meaning of a described experiment does not come from the interplay of the elements in the experiment but from the tradition of interpretation in which it stands and the future possibilities it opens up" (Palmer, 1969, p. 182).

The folly of modernism (and modern psychology) is seen in its epistemological ideal of a perspective-free, universal knowledge, devoid of any prejudgment. No human is capable of such knowledge. Only God has exhaustive, comprehensive knowledge, which guarantees its entire validity. But this realization does not obligate one to take a relativist stance towards human knowledge. Our preunderstanding need not be a hindrance to knowledge (or truth); it can be (and usually is) the necessary means of our obtaining knowledge (Polanyi, 1959). A primary goal, then, of human knowledge must be the acquiring of the most valid preunderstanding possible, that will be the most effective in securing an understanding most like the way the world really is (the way God understands it). Faith, according to Christianity, is a fundamental component of one's preunderstanding; it is a Christian way of construing reality, and this faith is shaped by Scripture (Dooyeweerd, 1984; Powlison, 2003; Van Til, 1971).

Of the entire set of beliefs that make up one's preunderstanding, one's *worldview* constitutes the most important subset. "A worldview is a conceptual scheme by which we consciously or unconsciously place or fit everything we believe and by which we interpret and judge reality" (Nash, 1988, p. 24). It consists of those beliefs that are the most influential within one's entire noetic structure and includes beliefs regarding God, metaphysics, epistemology, a metanarrative, ethics and human nature. Given the nature of human belief formation, worldviews are basically sociocultural phenomena, drawn from one's familial or intellectual community (or both), and are usually implicit. Christians in the modern era have reflected deeply about worldviews, because, being an intellectual minority, they needed to reflect on those preunderstanding beliefs that distinguish their thought from that of the majority culture (see, e.g., Dooyeweerd, 1984; Henry, 1976; Kuyper, 1898a, 1898b; Nash, 1988; Naugle, 2002; Orr, 1904; Woltiers, 1985). As the Christian canon, the Scriptures provide the key contribution to a Christian worldview, since they describe a divinely interpreted world into which we enter by reading, that, in turn, alters our vision of the world around us.

Though a worldview consists of a set of abstract beliefs that can be analyzed by reason alone, a worldview is simultaneously rooted in the deepest parts of one's being. This becomes clear when one changes one's worldview. Such a change is called a conversion (regardless of the worldview one comes to accept), and it is often precipitated by some degree of emotional turmoil (Spilka, Hood, Hunsberger & Gorsuch, 2003). To alter one's worldview entails an uprooting of one's deepest commitments and a radical change of heart. If deep enough, any conversion in worldview is fundamentally a religious act—an act of faith—and because of its centrality, it touches on everything one does and thinks. If all this is true, the worldview of scientists colors their work in a fundamental way.

The epistemological context of scientific knowledge. As a matter of fact, in the last half of the twentieth century, philosophers of science have come to agree that scientists require some kind of conceptual scheme that orients their work. One of the most influential, Thomas Kuhn (1970, 1977a, 1977b), argued that scientists are guided by what he first called a *paradigm* (1970) and later termed a *disciplinary matrix* (1977b), a mental structure, shared by members in good standing within the disciplinary community, that includes ontological assumptions and values, a vocabulary and symbolic generalizations relevant to one's discipline, judgments about what needs to be studied and explained, standards for good scientific practice and exemplars ("exemplary concrete puzzle solutions," Bird, 2000, or definitive scientific models; this last characteristic is what he now calls a paradigm, 1977b; Bird, 2000). A disciplinary matrix is essentially the set of beliefs and conceptual tools most important for scientists, those that ground and give shape to their understanding and practice of their discipline, so it is functionally the scientist's worldview (Suppe, 1977).

One of the important implications of Kuhn's somewhat controversial work, now universally accepted, is that observations are shaped by theory (or are theory-laden). Theories are needed to direct attention to important research questions, to guide the formulation of hypotheses and, most importantly, to recognize and interpret the data. So complex is the object of a science that, without theory, there is no way to sort through all the information at hand. Theory steers the scientific enterprise. So theoretical assumptions are the necessary means for making sense of observational statements.

More controversial is Kuhn's claim that disciplinary matrices (DMS) set their own standards of what constitutes good science (through exemplars or paradigms). Because observations are shaped by theory, it is not possible to get outside of a DM to form a conclusion about the data. Communication between DMs, then, is incommensurable (they cannot be fairly compared). Kuhn has been frequently chastised for this claim (Chalmers, 1982; Shapere, 1977), because it seems to suggest that there are no rational grounds for choosing a DM, implying that science is based on purely subjective, if not arbitrary, factors. A related assertion of Kuhn's is that science changes significantly only when a research community abandons one DM and adopts another. This is precipitated by the existence of a significant number of anomalies in the data for which the current DM is unable to account. Because a disciplinary matrix makes possible one's interpretation of the data, individual scientists usually do not switch them; typically they continue to interpret the anomalies as relatively insignificant and work on repairing their DM. According to Kuhn, DMs are changed only when the old scientists die out and the younger scientists who are more troubled by the anomalies recognize the greater power of the new DM to explain the anomalies, and so switch to it, thus creating a disciplinary-wide "scientific revolution."

Reacting to Kuhn's perceived relativism, Lakatos (1970) developed a modified and more realist model of science, in which he refers to something analogous to DMs as "scientific research programs." Such programs include a *core theory* that provides "a general view of the nature of the entities being investigated"

(Murphy & Ellis, 1996, p.11). This is sometimes called the "hard core," and it is assumed and beyond question (and so most like a worldview in Lakatos's model). Surrounding the core is a "protective belt" of "auxiliary hypotheses." These are lower-level theories, which support the core theory but can be adjusted without rejecting the core theory (showing how significant scientific change can occur without shifting to a new DM). The data in turn are supposed to provide support for the auxiliary hypotheses. Lakatos also addressed the problem of incommensurability by suggesting that over time scientists could objectively evaluate research programs in terms of their ability to predict and account for an increasing number of phenomena (called a "progressive" research program) and those that were having less such success (called "degenerative").

Lakatos's (1970) model of science is an improvement over Kuhn's because, while it acknowledges the existence of research traditions and conceptual frameworks, it allows for a greater role for human reasoning to assess the superior plausibility of one tradition over another. Following Lakatos (as well as evangelical theologian McGrath [2002] and ethical philosopher MacIntyre [1988, 1990]), and against a radical postmodernism, realist psychologists will want to maintain belief in a "trans-tradition rationality" that makes possible communication between traditions that promotes their respective understanding and can even lead to conversion.[7]

A scientific worldview has also been termed an *ideological surround* (Watson, 1993, 2004, 2005; Watson, Morris & Hood, 1990, 1992; Watson, Morris, Hood, Milliron & Stutz, 1998). According to Watson (personal communication, September 2, 2006), two features distinguish this concept from the others. First, among other things, an ideological surround possesses a normative dimension, that is, scientific worldviews contain usually implicit norms to which the science should conform (including what Christians would call ethical norms). As heirs of modernity, Kuhn and Lakatos make such considerations less salient in their discussions; Watson argues that all scientific communities are guided by norms that regulate scientific practice and discourse. Second, the term implies a measured skepticism toward any community's set of normative assumptions (including one's own). Though science necessarily operates within an ideological surround, because of its foundational nature, it can also blind researchers to their distorted understandings of the object and their biases toward the work of other communities.

A diagram of science influenced by the foregoing discussion can be found in figure 4.1. The main point of the diagram is to show how the object of a science and the observational statements used to describe its basic features are always situated within a larger discursive context that provides the conceptual means for interpreting and making sense of the object. From the human standpoint, the object of inquiry becomes meaningful only within some such context. Without these larger conceptual schemes, a science does not exist.

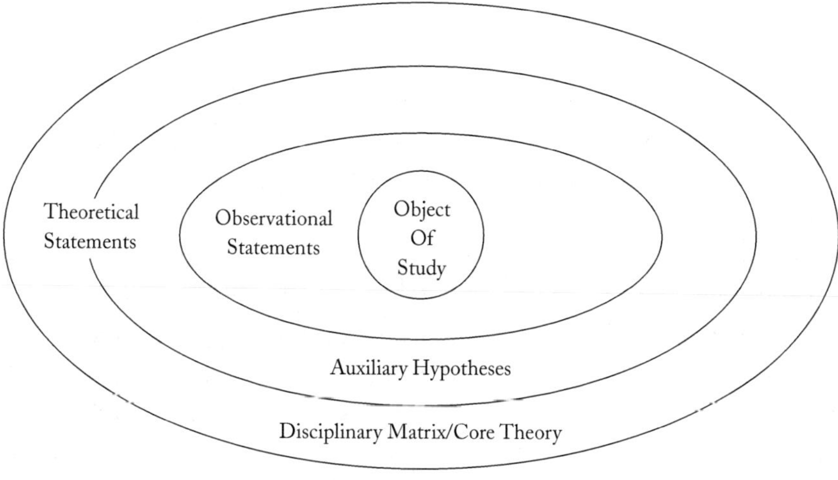

Figure 4.1. Texts and contexts of scientific knowledge

A conflict of intellectual/scientific traditions in the field of psychology. If scientific worldviews are relevant to the natural sciences (as was the focus of Kuhn and Lakatos's work), how much more applicable are the above considerations to the human sciences—like psychology and soul care—where assumptions about human beings are constitutive of some of the very facets of human life we seek to study (Taylor, 1966, 1989)?[8] For example, naturalistic assumptions in a modern disciplinary matrix lead some to believe and treat humans as if they were merely biologically and socially determined, so they do not "see" personal agency and will be therefore less likely to foster the formation of people into personal agents. The secular worldview assumptions of mainstream modern/postmodern psychology and soul care differ in some key respects from those of historic Christianity. In light of Kuhn and Lakatos's models, we see that such assumptions lie in the disciplinary matrix/core theory of modern psychology, so it is naïve to think that one can simply lift observational statements and especially lower level theoretical statements from a secular web of beliefs and "integrate" them with Christian beliefs, since the former statements are conceptually shaped by the larger meaning context within which they were originally composed (though Strong Integrationists are aware of this problem, Jones & Butman, 1991; Larzelere, 1980).

At the same time, we must not conclude that worldview beliefs affect interpretations of different observations to the same extent. Depending on the degree to which the human feature under examination is itself *constituted* by worldview beliefs, its interpretation would understandably be more affected by worldview beliefs. For example, we would expect differences in interpretation in the study of aspects that are the most subject to sociocultural influence, the most complex, the most existential, and the understanding of which are the most value-laden are the most likely to be so constituted (e.g., uniquely human motivation, personality, psychopathology, soul care and social relations).[9] On the other hand, interpretation will be less confounded by worldview issues in those areas that are the most predetermined genetically, the most elemental, the least existential and the understanding of which are the least value-laden (e.g., neuroscience, cognition, emotion and organismic motivation). Psychological features would seem to lie on a continuum from weak-worldview-impact to strong-worldview-impact. As a result, while all psychological understanding is conditioned to some extent by one's disciplinary matrix (DM), differences in DM will not markedly alter how some human features are understood (the timing of neurotransmitter reuptake), whereas they will have a profound impact on how others are understood (the nature of a flourishing human being). However, even in areas where worldview assumptions presumably affect observations very little, one's DM is still permeated by one's ultimate concerns and impacts such factors as the weight one gives to an observation and how one interprets its significance (e.g., the finding that homosexuality has biological correlates).

Even more importantly, competing research programs strive to make sense of the same set of data. Modern psychology has to be understood as a research program that exists in fundamental (antithetic) competition with the (embryonic) research program of the Christian community. Decisions for or against a DM are based on such things as the amount of data it is able to take into account and the fewer number of anomalies it possesses. From a Christian standpoint, the modern psychological research program is unable to adequately account for some of the most important aspects of human life, for example, human alienation from God and related human violence, a Christian's relationship to and dependence upon God, and genuine spiritual development. Such are anomalies for Christian psychologists, and they should drive us to better articulate our own disciplinary matrix. It must be a matrix that critically utilizes many of the same natural-science and human-science research assumptions and methods developed by modern psychological communities but that also uses the study of the Bible, Christian classics and philosophy as additional epistemological resources. And it must be a matrix that is permeated by faith in the Christ of Scripture from beginning to end.

Some Christians in psychology already committed to a *modern* disciplinary matrix will complain that it is not possible to develop a genuinely Christian scientific research program, because uniquely Christian features of human nature taught about in the Bible (e.g., sin, regeneration, the new self and the indwelling Holy Spirit) are not accessible to empirical validation. However, by now the reader would expect this objection to be ruled misleading and ultimately false by this author, since it is based in modern assumptions, and not Christian. While it is true that such realities are not *observable* in the sense that they are not *material*, that does not mean they do not belong in a scientific theory of human nature and soul care, and that they cannot be empirically studied. Any genuine feature of an object warrants being included in a science concerned with that object. The fact is that even in the physical sciences unobservable entities or properties are posited and their effects studied (e.g., quarks and strings; Klemke, Hollinger & Kline, 1988, p. 156), and psychology has long done research on "constructs" like personality and intelligence. Each of the above Christian doctrinal terms refers to a configuration of features identifiable within a Christian DM and so subject to research, but admittedly impossible to recognize within a modern DM. Given how little work in Christian psychology has yet been done, we really have no idea just how much distortion of human nature is perpetuated by modern psychology. Let us consider how a Christian DM might alter our understanding of one psychological topic.

A self-representation is the sum of a person's self-beliefs or self-perceived characteristics, or "how one describes oneself" (Harter, 1999, p. 4), and is a construct as psychological as one could find (see Leary & Tangney, 2003). But what of the *Christian's* self-representation? Ted describes himself as a fairly bright English teacher, hard-working, a decent tennis player but poor in mechanical aptitude. Yet Ted is a Christian, and he also believes that he is a sinner declared perfectly righteous in Christ.

Now how is the modern researcher to approach Ted's self-representation? Are aspects of it outside the purview of psychology? Modern studies of self-representation only deal with self-beliefs based on characteristics that modernists can identity (like intelligence, physical appearance and social skills). One, of course, cannot blame secularists for not identifying features of *Christian* self-representations. But what exactly is the psychological truth, from the standpoint of a Christian?

How might an integrationist approach Ted's complete self-representation? Perhaps the alleged division between psychology and theology that integrationists assume would lead them to divide Ted's self-representation into *psychological* characteristics (self-perceptions about tennis playing and mechanical aptitude, that modernists also recognize) and *theological* characteristics (his standing as a sinner and in Christ), since the latter features of his self-representation are distinctive to Christianity and were ultimately derived from the Bible (supposedly the object of the nonpsychological discipline of *theology*). But Ted's self-representation has no such division, to begin with. Second, the *sources* of the beliefs that compose Ted's self-representation are irrelevant to their being psychological phenomena. Whether derived from social feedback, personal experience or the Bible, all of Ted's self-beliefs are *psychological* entities through and through—they are all cognitions and the legitimate objects of the science of psychology.

The point being raised here is actually not all that controversial from an empirical standpoint. In fact, Ted's uniquely Christian self-beliefs *are* empirical in at least three ways: (1) Ted holds these beliefs about himself and can report them, (2) they are psychological beliefs that that can be found in the Bible and studied with discourse analysis there; and (3) other Christians can express them in their conversations with Ted, constituting a social source for the beliefs, the communication of which can also be documented. Presumably, upon reflection, even a fair-minded secular psychologist would have no good reason to regard Ted's uniquely Christian self-beliefs as *nonpsychological.* Christians in psychology or counseling really have no reason not to study them, publish studies about them and encourage them in their counselees.

More controversial is the Christian claim that Ted's uniquely Christian self-beliefs are *true*—just as true as his valid beliefs about his intelligence and conscientiousness—because they reflect the reality of *God's assessment of Ted in Christ.* But from a Christian standpoint, Ted's uniquely Christian self-beliefs are *truth-based representations about himself* announced in the Bible, even though their truth-value with respect to Ted is itself transcendent and beyond empirical validation—unlike intelligence or mechanical aptitude. However, since the Bible is considered a legitimate source of psychological knowledge within a Christian psychology—which has as its goal to think about and appraise humans the way God does—the Christian psychologist will reject the philosophical assumptions of neopositivism and argue that uniquely Christian self-beliefs can correspond to reality just as truly as beliefs about one's conscientiousness and tennis playing, and that Christians are warranted in believing them (just as they are warranted in holding other Christian beliefs that secularists would not affirm; see Plantinga, 2000).

The assertion of the validity of such beliefs is especially important to Christian soul care. For Ted to become a more mature and healthier Christian, his beliefs about himself in Christ need to become more deeply ingressed into the core of his own hierarchically organized self-representation—it should become more and more "weighted" by such considerations (Harter, 1999). A Christian counselor would want to help him appropriate these beliefs as deeply as possible and—here is the rub—the depth of that ingression is contingent upon their being perceived as true. So, the truth value of uniquely Christian self-beliefs is also a factor of interest to a Christian psychology and soul care, even though their transcendent validity itself cannot be established empirically—*beyond the declarations of the Bible,* as well as Ted's self-report. For the Christian striving for integrity—and an integrated self before God—the complete truth about Ted's self-representation lies ultimately in the mind and heart of God, and it is that *whole* account that is the goal of a Christian psychology. If Ted is a believer, he really is righteous in Christ. That is his *real self* (Johnson, 1997); Paul calls it the *new man* (*kainos anthrōpos;* Eph 4:22-24); and the Christian psychological researcher or counselor is called by God to think about and appraise human beings in ways that correspond as closely as possible to *God's* understanding and appraisal, as best as can be discerned, with all the information at our disposal, regardless of whether it lies outside the scope of a secular version of psychology.

From the preceding, it should be clear that a traditional integrationist paradigm, which makes a sharp dichotomy between psychology and theology, might obscure the actual psychological state-of-affairs in the case of Ted's self-representation. An a priori discontinuity between beliefs based on test results or social evaluation and those based on Scripture is an assumption derived from modern biases that are alien to a Christian disciplinary matrix, and if forever accepted by Christians would lead to serious distortions in their science of the way things really are.

Conclusion

We noted in an earlier chapter that among intellectuals in the West the modernist worldview came to be seen as more persuasive than the Christian worldview. Since that ascension to power, the Christian soul-care community has had a difficult time determining its response. Some soul-care workers decided to reject modern psychology in toto, and others, drawn in by its tremendous accomplishments, uncritically embraced too many of its ideological norms.

Christians must concede that the twentieth century was the modernist century for psychology. But perhaps the early twenty-first century would be a good time for a radical recommitment to a Christian worldview and a reinvestment in the unique resources of the Christian tradition. At the same time, Christian psychologists need to be willing to contend and interact with the intellectual powers that reign in our culture by developing a more comprehensive and scientific Christian version of psychology and soul care than has ever been seen. From the standpoint of a Christian disciplinary matrix/research program, contemporary secular psychological theory regarding the whole person, including motivation, the self, personal responsibility, psychopathology, treatment and social relationships, is distorted in its core theory. Consequently, it is unable to describe adequately, holistically and comprehensively human functioning in a way that coheres with all the knowledge that a Christian possesses, since it leaves out that which is most important about human beings. For Christians in psychology, this constitutes a set of anomalies of such enormous proportions as to be a "defeater" of secular psychological theory and renders the modern psychology disciplinary matrix a degenerative research program. From a Christian standpoint, it is intrinsically incapable of accounting for all that Christians understand and are able to see about human beings.

Of course, modern psychology is the reigning paradigm in the field, and it has attained its position by its remarkable scientific achievements and extensive, sophisticated literature (all consistent with its DM). Consequently, Christians must learn from and be challenged by their work, reading and appropriating it critically from the standpoint of our own disciplinary matrix. This will be necessary if Christians are ever to construct a research program that does a better job of accounting for the nature of human beings and soul healing—from a Christian standpoint—than does the modern, and develop a scientific literature that is just as rigorous. Research must be done. But we have learned in this chapter of the importance of getting straight our preunderstanding and developing a distinctly Christian disciplinary matrix for psychology. As a result, some of the first work that needs to be done is the reading of already available texts. We must read—and learn how to read—the texts that are the most relevant for our task. In the next chapter we shall consider the precise place of Scripture in this project.

Notes

[1]Generally speaking, most scientific disciplines are labeled according to their object of study: physics, the physical world; chemistry, chemicals; biology, life; sociology, social structures and institutions (though that is not always the case: e.g., economics, anthropology or mathematics). If the discipline under consideration here were labeled according to its object, perhaps "systematic biblical studies" would have been more fitting (in the modern era, needless to say, "biblical studies" has been applied to a subdiscipline that focuses particularly on the interpretation of the texts of the Bible). An unfortunate outcome of labeling that discipline concerned with all biblical teaching "theology" is that it relegates God to merely being one locus within a series of the other main topics treated in the Bible. But on reflection, when one considers all the disciplines that have been developed by humanity, surely the infinite, triune God ought to be considered the object of study of the utmost importance, and worthy of an entire discipline dedicated just to understanding, loving and worshiping him. Theology *proper,* as is well known, is the usual label for that subdiscipline of theology, but strictly speaking, the term *theology* would make the best label of the science of God (see Thomas Aquinas, 1945; Torrance, 1969). Of course, there is no point, I realize, in trying to change such widespread usage of a term.

[2]Milbank (1990), for one, advocates returning theology, broadly defined, to its reign as the queen of the sciences (p. 381).

[3]One could argue that modern psychology does have a place for religion—in the subdiscipline called the *psychology of religion,* which has as its focus the religious beliefs and behavior of human beings. However, in this typically modern subdiscipline, the psychologists are still avowedly neutral with respect to the validity of the religiousness they study, so it is a peculiarly modern investigation of religious experience from a universal standpoint, cleansed of any particular community's "ideological surround" (Watson, 2002). But from a Christian deconstructive standpoint, the fact that this kind of *psychology* of religion has developed in modern psychology is instructive. Apparently, it is permissible for psychologists to study humans in relation to their religious objects of devotion, so long as it is done from a modern, neutral standpoint—so long as the scientist does not "take sides." Given modernism's worldview, that is perfectly understandable. But if it is legitimate for some modern psychologists to study humans in relation to their religious object of devotion from a universal standpoint and still call

it *psychology*, why would discourse about Christians' relation to God (say, their union with Christ) be considered a topic in theology? The reasons for this double standard are sociohistorical and simply a function of modernist assumptions.

[4]This epistemological goal was assumed for centuries when a Christian worldview was adhered to, and more recently by exponents of common-sense realism. For a justification of this move see Gilson (1940), Horton (2002), Johnson (1997a), Plantinga (1993a, 2000), Reid (1785/1969). In contrast to Kantianism, traditionally a Christian epistemology understands human knowledge to be analogical to God's—not identical to God's but similar, more or less, in at least some respects.

[5]Let me add that I think Christians are free to conform their epistemological/scientific practices to those that are accepted by their modern colleagues—so long as they do not deny any core tenet or practice of the faith in their teaching or writing—for a wide variety of legitimate reasons (e.g., they may wish to serve God by teaching at a state university). Christians must allow other believers the Christian liberty to discern their own calling, so long as the faith is not being denied. But the point here is that Christians do not *have to* conform to the standards of modern scholarship. Moreover, they *should not* in their discourse within the Christian community (including their reflection within their own Christian minds), given the internal, rational coherence of the broader discursive standards of the Christian community that should include the canon of Scripture.

[6]A somewhat more thorough treatment of these issues can be found in Johnson (2007). Some of the following is derived from that article.

[7]Space prevents us from examining Polanyi's (1958, 1966) important contributions to the position being described here. And a fuller discussion would also have to incorporate the work of MacIntyre (1981, 1988, 1990) into an understanding of how intellectual traditions develop, are maintained and strengthened, and communicate profitably with and learn from each other.

[8]I am defining soul care as the applied science of the "repair" of the soul (Stoker, 1971, p. 44). Some might object that soul care is better understood to be an art or a skill. But the two definitions are not incompatible. The field of medicine is an applied science, based on pure biological science and its own research, and being a good medical doctor is an art and a skill. Soul care is applied science, based on psychological science, that engages in its own research. Being a soul-care provider, like a pastor, has been rightly likened to being a physician of the soul.

[9]Christians have noted that the greater the existential import of the subject matter, the more sin is likely to distort one's understanding of it, a problem Westphal (1990) calls the "law of inverse rationality" (see also Brunner, 1946; Jones, 1986).

5

Properties of Scripture and Its Relation to Other Texts

HAVING ESTABLISHED THAT TEACHING FROM THE BIBLE and the classics of the Christian tradition belong within the boundaries of a Christian psychology, we turn to consider some of the Bible's characteristics to help us determine its relation to other texts (particularly those of the Christian tradition and of modern psychology). Thirty years ago, McQuilkin (1977), then president of Columbia Bible College, challenged Christians in the behavioral sciences to work under the authority of Scripture in their disciplines and as practitioners. Since that time the interest of Christians in psychology and counseling has exploded. Yet McQuilkin's call has not been correspondingly realized. As we have already noted, the primary stumbling block for Christians is that, far and away, the most significant work in the behavioral sciences is done without any reference to Scripture, within a disciplinary matrix that does not permit such reference, and most Christians in the behavioral sciences have been trained and practice within such a disciplinary matrix. As we have seen, this sociohistorical context has led to some very different Christian approaches to the relation between the Bible and psychology.

An understanding of one of the debates in the historical period known as the Reformation (ca. 1500-1650) may give us some clarity regarding that relation. During that time, the Reformers raised questions about a number of the teachings of the late medieval Catholic Church. Next to justification by faith, perhaps the most important issue was the relation of Scripture to the Christian tradition that had developed over the centuries. As they reflected on this issue over the next two hundred years, Protestant theologians identified a number of the properties of the Bible that helped to make clear the Bible's importance and uniqueness. As we saw in chapter three, the biblical counseling movement has drawn attention to one of those properties (MacArthur & Mack, 1994; Hindson & Eyrich, 1997)—the sufficiency of Scripture. In the interest of advancing McQuilkin's argument, we will take a look at that property, along with three others that also have significance for Christian psychology and soul care.

The Authority of Scripture

Think of the billions upon billions of texts that have been written since humans became literate (notes, letters, poems, essays, stories, books and now e-mails). However, not all texts are created equal. Christians believe that one text is "God-breathed" (2 Tim 3:16). Although the Bible was written through the medium of human authors, Christians hold that the Bible is "inspired by God in such way that he can be said to be its principal author" (Plantinga, 2000, p. 206; see Heb 3:7; 4:7; 2 Pet 1:20-21; Berkouwer, 1975; Dockery, 1995; Murray, 1953; Warfield, 1970; Wolterstorff, 1995; Young, 1957). Consequently, Christians have historically recognized that the Bible is a text with unique and distinct authority to which they must submit (Braaten, 1984; Erickson, 1983; Muller, 2003, Vol. 2; Weber, 1981). As Barr (1980) has acknowledged, "The Bible has authority because its authority, in some form or other, is built into the structure of Christian faith and the Christian religion" (p. 52). It is the nature of a Christian to recognize and submit to the authority of Scripture. But what is the nature of this authority?

When we think of authority in interpersonal relations, it usually implies two orders, a superior and an inferior, with the latter in some way relinquishing autonomy to the former. The correlative to authority is obedience (Weber, 1981, p. 269). Scripture is not a person, but since its ultimate author is God—a person of absolute authority—the Bible possesses its authority by virtue of its being *authorized* by God. It is the inscribed speech-acts of God, and therefore is in some sense the expression and extension of God's authority (Frame, 1987; Geldenhuys, 1958)—just as the written edict of a king is authoritative in his kingdom. Christians submit to the triune God as their master, absolutely and unreservedly, and they regard the Bible as the designated proclamations of their master. Consequently, Christians pay special attention to Scripture, affirm its teachings and obey its covenantal commands.

One can also consider scriptural authority epistemologically, in regard to Scripture's status as a source of knowledge. We speak, for example, of a scientist being a noted "authority" in her field or of a certain handbook being "authoritative." Such expressions convey the person's or book's epistemological value as a source of valid information in a particular area and imply that what the scientist or book states in the area of expertise should be accepted. God, Christians would say, is the ultimate authority in this sense, since he created the universe and knows all things. As God's authoritative discourse, Scripture becomes a textual authority (akin to an acclaimed scholarly handbook). Divine inspiration rendered it "infallible" and preserved it from error, so that the Bible is, far and away, the best written record of certain significant truths—the world's authoritative volume with respect to God's nature, core features of human beings and God's program of human salvation.

There are at least two experiential aspects to this authority. First, Scripture should be honored and revered in Christian hearts (Calvin, 1559/1960, 1.7.1; Wallace, 1953). This is a gift of the Holy Spirit who bears an inner testimony of the authority of Scripture (Berkhof, 1939; Calvin, 1559/1960; Plantinga, 2000). This testimony produces in believers a desire to understand and abide in Scripture (1 Jn 2:12), so that it would fulfill its purposes in their lives, conforming them to the image of Christ, and equipping them for good works (Eph 2:10; 2 Tim 3:17). This leads to a second experiential aspect of the Bible's authority: the actual conformity of Christian minds, hearts and lives to its teaching.

Because of this Christian experience and the Bible's self-attestation (2 Tim 3:16, 17; 2 Pet 1:20, 21; Jn 10:35), Scripture can be seen as the church's "normative authority" (Lecerf, 1949; Weber, 1981). Scripture is the norm, rule or canon of the Christian life, the standard by which all other texts and norms are to be evaluated (Johnson, 1992). Luther referred to the Bible as the "proper touchstone" by which all teaching is to be tested (Wood, 1969, p. 122), an "unregulated regulator" that was to be seen as the judge of everything, but was to be judged by nothing (Wood, p. 120). This has also been called Scripture's "juridical authority" (Weber, 1981) or "canonical authority" (Muller, 2003, Vol. 2). The Bible calls into question our previous beliefs and practices and calls upon us to reject them insofar as they depart from scriptural revelation. "It is through this checking and questioning role that the Bible exercises its authority: the Bible queries the tradition of its own interpretation" (Barr, 1980, p.63).

Beyond this "deconstructive" function, at the same time, Scripture would seem to exercise a special authority in human knowing. As the words of God, it is knowledge "from above," available here below in the words of humans. So humans are not left to their own finite, historically conditioned understandings (contrary to the opinions of various skeptics) that would leave us with nothing but a self-referential language system impossible to break out of to assess its correspondence with reality. In spite of Scripture's human authorship and historically conditioned human origins, divine inspiration means that some of its content simultaneously originated in some sense from *outside* a human frame of reference. Consequently, the Bible provides a divinely appointed textual reference point, a set of signs/utterances within human language, that offers a transcendent epistemological-discursive frame of reference by which all other human discourse is established and can be evaluated.[1] This primal authority makes all other texts necessarily subordinate to Scripture, since only one set of texts is so inspired and has this legitimizing relation to all other texts.[2]

The comprehensive scope of scriptural authority is seen in the fact that it reveals certain universal truths (e.g., that Christ died for sinners), and it expresses (and implies) norms that relate to every aspect of human life for all time (e.g., all human activity should glorify God, loving others is more important than self-gratification, and so on; Frame, 1987), so we can conclude that scriptural authority applies *indirectly* to all of human life, including every discipline and practice (Frame, 1987; Van Til, 1967; even mathematics, Poythress, 1980). Its divine origin gives Scripture a general, fundamental authority in relation to all other texts and knowledge, uniquely legitimizing, criticizing, guiding and healing.

The special authority of Scripture in psychology and soul care. However, Scripture's authority is also specially manifested in what it says positively about the most important things in human life: God's nature, human nature, God's norms and goals for human life, and God's way of healing humanity's disorders. Scriptural authority is evident "in the manner in which it teaches persons to understand themselves, the world, history, and the future in the light of the God and Father of Jesus Christ. It is on account of this clarity of the Scripture that it is an ever flowing book of knowledge and life and that it teaches wisdom to the simple" (Ridderbos, 1978, p. 34). Perhaps most important for soul-care purposes is what we might call Scripture's salvific or therapeutic authority. Since Scripture reveals the primary purposes of human life, its ideal goods, values and norms, and the God-ordained way of recovery from its ills, and is itself the cognitive-discursive means of their realization, Scripture has a salvific/therapeutic authority over human life. In essence, the Bible is God saying, "For your own soul's good, know *this*, believe *this*, live *this*, be like *this*." The Scriptures direct our attention to God's therapeutic goods for the soul, so they are very much like a physician's authoritative instructions to help the patient recover from his bodily disease (Work, 2002).

So, within its conceptual purview—those areas where Scripture in fact speaks authoritatively—it is *especially* authoritative. Since it reveals so much that is important about human nature, it is an especially authoritative text for Christian psychology and soul care. The authority of Scripture in relation to psychology and soul care simply means that *the Bible has ultimate authority over all of psychology and soul care and is the most significant source of knowledge about human beings and their psychospiritual problems.*

Such an understanding of scriptural authority need not undermine the value of extrabiblical knowledge or imply that it has no use in soul care (even that which bears on the concerns of Scripture, e.g., genetic influence on aggression). No Christian argues that the Bible is directly authoritative in surgery or plumbing, since it does not address such topics. Scriptural authority cannot be asserted irrespective of the relevance of God's communicative agenda (Vanhoozer, 2005), nor can it be affirmed in isolation from other forms of epistemological authority. Christians submit to scriptural authority within a complex web of interrelated authorities—most importantly that of the Holy Spirit, but also perception, memory, conscious experience, reason and the testimony of other humans (including human "authorities" like scientists, as they report their research; Audi, 1998). Without this larger authoritative context, Scripture could not itself be comprehended. To understand the phrase "the Lord is my shepherd" one must know what a shepherd is and must have already submitted to the "authority" of one's perception, memory and reason, and (for city folk) the testimony of others.

So while Scripture has a special authority, it is not the only or absolute authority (only God is that), and it cannot be abstracted from other knowledge authorities. For example, developmentally speaking, one's submission to scriptural authority is preceded by submission to an indefinite number of epistemological authorities, including parents, teachers, dictionaries and so on. Imagine some perverse parent who, while teaching his child word meanings, changed those meanings every day: "But I thought that was a bird." "No. That's a chair." "But yesterday you called that a bird." "No, that's always been a chair." Such conversation would likely permanently warp the child's trust in others and render unstable his understanding of the world. Proper human mental development (and human knowledge) relies on a history of consistent authoritative testimony from others (as well as one's perception, memory, experience and reason). These other sources form the larger epistemological *authority-network* that Scripture enters into (from the standpoint of the developing child), of which Scripture comes to form a singular part, through the believer's growing submission (Frame, 1987).

Scripture's differential authority by (sub)discipline. The Bible's authority also varies depending on the subject matter. Scripture's authority increases in proportion to the extent that Scripture explicitly addresses a particular topic. Scriptural authority, then, is most pressing in reference to God and his salvation, the most important features of human beings, their soul problems and the salvific treatment of those problems.

To illustrate such distinctions, figure 5.1 contains a diagram of a continuum of scientific disciplines and psychology subdisciplines which differ in terms of how much the Bible explicitly addresses their concerns.

We noted in previous chapters that Scripture provides a set of glasses through which Christians view the entire world. But given God's communi-

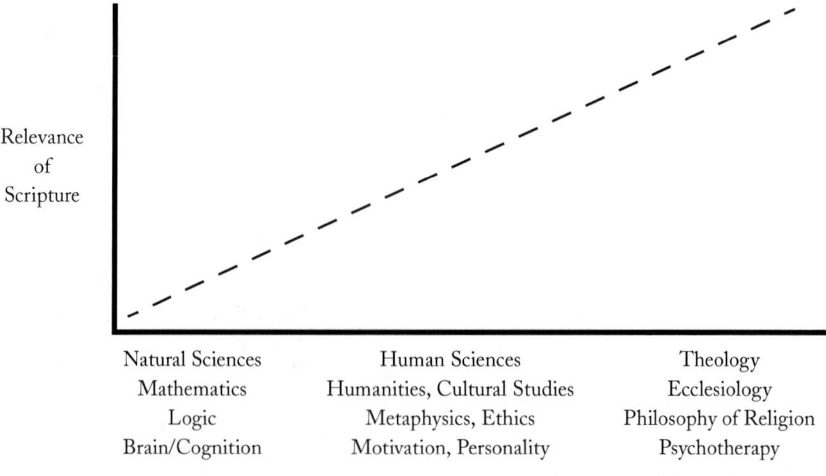

Figure 5.1. The relevance of Scripture to various disciplines and subdisciplines

cative agenda in the speech-acts of the Bible, those disciplines that deal with topics the Bible directly addresses will need to rely more on Scripture for their disciplinary matrix and content than those that do not. Consequently, scriptural authority in the various disciplines will be weighted differentially. For example, the Bible has relatively little to contribute *directly* to subjects like mathematics and the natural sciences (e.g., physics, chemistry, astronomy and biology), and their applied disciplines (e.g., technology), though even in these disciplines, truths like God's creatorhood and moral norms are relevant and necessary. At the other end of the continuum, the Bible is the most important source of information regarding the nature of God and topics like the polity of the church. In between, the Bible will contribute more or less, depending on the precise topic under consideration. Scriptural themes will be substantially influential in shaping Christian understandings in certain areas in philosophy (ontology, ethics, philosophy of religion), the humanities (e.g., literary interpretation and criticism), cultural studies and the human sciences.

Within psychology, individual subdisciplines will vary in terms of their dependence on scriptural input. Given the complexity of human nature, psychology has to cover a broad range of topics, some that are more mechanical and biological in nature and others where ethical and spiritual dynamics are more influential. This reminds us that some psychological topics are more worldview-dependent (see chap. 4) and others topics are less worldview-dependent (though even here teaching about Christ's lordship is relevant).[3] So, with regard to a science of human nature, the Bible's contribution to the understanding of neuropsychology and cognition will be relatively less than its contributions to motivation, personality, psychopathology and soul care.

The Necessity of Scripture

The Bible includes a record of events and truths of momentous importance that are essential for human well-being in this life. Certain truths indispensable for understanding God and human beings were not built into human nature or the creation in such a way as to be readily accessible, without some explicit discursive revelation (Van Til, 1955). This problem of access was intensified by the noetic effects of sin, which made it even more difficult to discern certain truths in creation without aid (a fact demonstrated in the enormous variety of views of human nature found in different religions and philosophies, e.g., Stevenson, 1974). So, for our sake, God needed to reveal many truths in a fixed textual form that humans could go back to, again and again, in order to find their way in the world and to make sense of themselves. In light of this need, Reformation theologians argued that another characteristic of Scripture is its necessity (Muller, 2003, Vol. 2; Osterhaven, 1971). Humans need a divinely inspired written record of the most significant teachings and events that concern human life to which they can have ongoing access.

The special necessity of Scripture for psychology and soul care. This is especially the case in psychology and soul care. We have already noted that the Scriptures are *profitable* for the realization of ethicospiritual maturity (2 Tim 3:16-17). This renowned self-definition is the beginning of a formal case for the necessity of the Bible for the Christian soul-care task, since such maturity is the highest clinical goal toward which a Christian counselor can work.

Excursus: The Necessity of the Created Order and Some Knowledge About It

We are focusing in this chapter on the importance of Scripture for a Christian model of psychology and soul care. This is because of the controversial nature of the claim that the Bible is relevant for psychology in our day. However, in some circles the controversy concerns the value of empirical research on human beings. So something here should be said about the necessity of extrabiblical knowledge about human beings with reference to Scripture.

To begin with the obvious, Scripture itself does not exist in a vacuum. Before any of it was written, God had created a world and a human race, and had established many kinds of knowledge about the created order and language systems that were used to describe that order and accomplish things in it. Second, the Bible itself refers to the created order on every page. Consequently, third, there is no way we could make sense of any part of the Bible without having some previous knowledge about the created order. This means that the created order and *some* knowledge about it are *just as* necessary as Scripture for Christian psychology and soul care.

This is not as controversial as it might sound to some. Van Til (1953) pointed out that natural revelation is necessary to make sense of special revelation. The tree of the knowledge of good and evil in Eden was a necessary part of the realization of God's plan and his prohibition regard-

There are many important facets of human nature, life and recovery that are either not available in the creation (including within humans natively) or are so distorted by the psychic effects of sin that we do not have reliable access to them apart from their being in a permanently fixed form, including such themes as the centrality of God to human life; the triune nature and attributes of that God; the relation of God to all things; humans as the image of God; the nature, power, guilt and deceptiveness of sin; the role of union with Christ and his cross and resurrection in human recovery from sin; the existence and power of the indwelling Holy Spirit; the old and new selves; the terms of the Christian community's covenant with God; the major norms of Christian morality; the grand metanarrative of redemptive history; countless themes of encouragement that facilitate coping; forgiveness with God; the importance of

ing it obviously could not be grasped apart from it. Likewise, the fifth commandment requires families and the eighth and tenth commandments, possessions, and so on. The created order and *some* knowledge about it provide the necessary context for Scripture to be understood and for its divinely intended communicative purposes to be realized in human life. Frame (1987) suggests that knowing the meaning of a sentence in Scripture entails "being able to *use* the sentence, to understand its implications, its powers, its applications" (p. 67). He concludes that "facts are laws in a sense; they have normative force" (p. 67), so that, with regard to our understanding, knowledge of the creation is interdependent with knowledge of Scripture.

As a result, while *scientific* knowledge about human beings and soul care is not *necessary* in order to live godly in Christ Jesus—after all, Christians got along without such knowledge for centuries—the *more* we know about human beings and soul care, the better job we can do applying Scripture to the interpretation and soul-healing of human beings as they actually are. And this says nothing of the doxological legitimization of science in general: God receives glory when his image-bearers discover evidence of his wisdom in the created order and magnify him because of it. To summarize this brief discussion: the more precise and comprehensive our psychological and soul-care knowledge—the more it conforms to God's—whatever the source of the information, the better we can fulfill God's purposes for us to glorify him and enjoy him forever.

repentance and mortification; vivification and the raising of the new self from out of the deadness of sin; the way, story and nature of salvation; and the possible futures of humanity, just to name some of the most important.

The Bible also communicates the Christian's system of goods for human life (Adams, 1999; Van Til, 1955). There are an immense number of possible goods, and the Bible provides an inspired record of what God thinks is good, including a relative ranking of illustrative particulars. Related to that, the Bible also reveals God's primary intentions for humanity (where we are supposed to be heading on our journey). We suggested earlier that the Bible's teaching is *aretegenic* (Charry, 1997). Its content provides the primary cognitive means by which believers develop into virtuous persons, as its truths are healingly and empoweringly embraced, internalized and appropriated, and then embodied, performed and expressed. The articulation of such maturity ideals is necessary for the realization of proper human maturation and provides the fundamental goals of Christian counseling. Simply put, the Bible reveals to us the wisdom we need to live our lives the way for which God designed and redeemed us.

One way to think about the Bible's necessity is to consider it as the map we need for life. The Bible shows us "where" God is and how to return to him, as well as how to "find ourselves"—to understand who we are and where we are going (see Taylor, 1989, chap. 1); without it humans are hopelessly lost and ignorant of some of the most important truths we need in order to realize the fulfillment of our nature. Life is a journey and counseling is like orienteering (Johnson & Sandage, 1999), and the counselor is supposed to be a skilled orienteer. The counselor should be able to read the signs necessary to help clients find their way from where they are to their maturational destination. There are the signs of the trail (hard to identify if there is a lot of brush), and there are the signs on the map. The Bible is the Christian counselor's trail guide or map, drawn up by God, the great cartographer of life. It includes a description of some of the major features of the landscape of human nature (including the best trails—those that lead to the greatest glory for God and well-being for humans), that give us an idea about where we are, where we are to go and how best to get to the proper end of our journey. Like a typical map, it does not provide every detail of the landscape (e.g., every tree). Maps are meant to provide a *summary* representation of the landscape and offer the *essential* information (the major streams, levels of elevation and trails) needed to locate one's present position and to help one get to where one is supposed to go. But a map is a necessity for one who hopes to make some progress and cover some ground. The necessity of Scripture, then, in relation to psychology and soul care means, *the Bible is essential for properly understanding human beings and properly addressing their psychospiritual problems.*

The Sufficiency of Scripture

The issues surrounding this property of Scripture as developed in the Reformation are especially relevant to our predicament as Christians in psychology and counseling in the early twenty-first century. By the late 1400s, many in the Catholic Church were persuaded that writings from the Christian tradition provided a necessary complement to the sacred Scriptures regarding what constituted divinely revealed Christian truth and morality (Evans, 1985; McGrath, 1988). Not only did the Christian tradition guide the interpretation of the Bible, but it was believed to supplement the Bible's teachings, through the ongoing revelatory work of the Holy Spirit in the church. As a result, the Catholic Church came to believe that two sets of texts were utilized by God for the communication of divine revelation, and these two sets were therefore equal in authority. This view was formally ratified by the Catholic Church at the Council of Trent (1545-1547).

The Reformers, in contrast, taught the sufficiency of Scripture, that is, Scripture alone *(sola scriptura)* was divine revelation and therefore was by itself adequate for the task of formulating the church's doctrine and morality. The Reformation was a "Back to the Bible" movement, and it uniformly taught that the Bible alone was divinely inspired and preserved from error, so that it alone could function as the ultimate textual authority for the church. No *additional* input from the Christian tradition was *necessary.*

But the Reformation was composed of more than one faction. It is well known that the Reformation began with the protests of an Augustinian monk named Martin Luther, who was calling the Catholic Church of his day back to the teachings and practices of the Bible and the early church. Soon, others joined him in his protests, including Zwingli, Bucer, Bullinger and later Calvin. Because they also sought to work with, persuade and ultimately submit to the ruling civil authorities (the magistrates), their movement has been termed the magisterial Reformation. Part of this orientation originally included the assumption that child baptism was a necessary part of the preservation of the social order. On the other hand, the leaders of the radical Reformation—people like Grebel, Sattler, Hubmaier and later Menno Simons—saw Christianity as more of a countercultural movement and so were inclined to separate themselves from the civil structures of their communities and practice a more radical form of Christianity that involved believer's baptism (an Anabaptist was one who had been "rebaptized") and nonparticipation in civil society (like government and the military). Such a stance caused them to be perceived as a threat to the social stability of Catholic, Lutheran and Reformed communities, and resulted (unfortunately) in their vigorous persecution, in many cases by the magistrates.

In spite of its persecution of radicals, the magisterial Reformation was more moderate in its approach to other issues. Just as they did not reject the civil institutions of their day, the magisterial Reformers did not reject church tradition *in toto*. Calvin's extensive use of Augustine demonstrates both that he saw Augustine as a valuable guide to Scripture interpretation and that he was willing to criticize him when he deviated from Scripture's own teaching (see Lane, 1999). The magisterial Reformers believed that the Holy Spirit had worked within the church—but not in a way that rendered the church infallible. This work had resulted in valuable textual reflection on the Bible, with some previous interpreters demonstrating a greater fidelity to Scripture than others, so that consulting the texts of the church fathers and the medieval church could prove very illuminating. However, since these secondary texts were not inspired, they had always to be tested by their fidelity to sacred Scripture. Using Scripture as the church's *final* authority implies it is sufficient for Christian teaching, without validation of or supplementation by the Christian tradition. The radical Reformers, on the other hand, were wary of consulting any merely *human* sources of insight, believing they were largely corrupt, so they called into question any reliance on church tradition in interpretation, believing that "every individual had the right to interpret Scripture as he pleased, subject to the guidance of the Holy Spirit" (McGrath, 1988, p.144).

Biblical counseling advocates have made the phrase "the sufficiency of Scripture" the rallying cry of their movement. In doing so they are presumably making allusion to the debates of the Reformation era and suggesting that they offer a parallel to our era, since the Christian counseling community also faces the problem of relating Scripture to the texts of another body of literature, in the present case, the texts of modern psychology. As we noted in chapter three, similar to both groups of Reformers, the BCM is concerned that beliefs and assumptions contrary to the Scriptures are being imported into the church in our day, through the accommodation of Christian counseling and church practice to the ideologies of secular psychology. However, to my knowledge, no one in the BCM has carefully examined the original, Reformation use of the phrase "the sufficiency of Scripture" with reference to today's debate.

Upon such investigation, one notes there are a few important differences between the two textual conflicts that make a simple equation of the issues problematic. For one thing, in the sixteenth century, the questionable texts were themselves influenced by and based on Scripture, whereas, in the present, the questionable texts are mostly composed by secular researchers and theorists, which constitute a tradition that has had, obviously, very little influence from the Bible. At the same time, the Reformation debate was concerned with the formulation of Christian doctrine and morality, a task that most Christians would agree centers on Scripture, whereas the current controversy concerns the nature of human beings and the care of their souls, topics that can be investigated empirically, in ways that the doctrine of God cannot be. Scripture addresses the former topics, to be sure, but not exhaustively, and we have to ask whether it was God's intention for Scripture to be the *sole* source of information *for these topics.*

Consequently, the present textual controversy would seem to be more complicated. On the one hand, Christian psychologists today should be even more skeptical than the Reformers were of the extrabiblical body of literature in question, given modern psychology's secularity and general hostility to orthodox Christianity, and its lack of any relation to Scripture. On the other hand, there are good grounds to study that extrabiblical literature tirelessly, since well-done scientific research on humans—rightly interpreted—would presumably help Christians get even closer to God's understanding of human beings.

When we make a comparison between the groups in the Reformation era and our own, we find that the "Bible-only" position of Traditional Biblical Counseling bears a closer resemblance to the understanding of the *radical* Reformers than to the magisterial Reformers.[4] Pressing the analogy further, the strong integration, Christian psychology and progressive biblical counseling approaches have more in common with the magisterial Reformation, since they view the Bible as sufficient for counseling in certain key respects (to be discussed below), and see it as the final standard, by which other, relatively important texts are evaluated (analogous to church tradition). Let us examine some of the issues at stake in more detail.

Sufficiency and God's primary purposes for providing Scripture. Evangelicals, and the Reformation traditions from which they descend, have insisted that Scripture is sufficient for all that God intended to reveal. "The sufficiency of Scripture means that Scripture contained all the words of God he intended his people to have at each stage of redemptive history, and that it now contains all the words of God we need for salvation, for trusting him perfectly, and for obeying him perfectly" (Grudem, 1995, p. 127). Historically, the majority Protestant tradition has believed that the Bible was a reliable source of whatever it asserted, and therefore it was the sufficient and infallible source of all the information *necessary for salvation* (see Muller, 2003, Vol. 2; Rohls, 1998). As Ferguson (1988) wrote, sufficiency simply means that Scripture is "our guide to the way of salvation" (p. 61). The Belgic Confession put it like this:

> *The Sufficiency of the Holy Scriptures to Be the Only Rule of Faith*: We believe that these Holy Scriptures fully contain the will of God, and that whatsoever man ought to believe, unto salvation, is sufficiently taught therein. . . . The doctrine thereof is most perfect and complete in all respects. For since the whole manner of worship which God requires of us, is written in them at large, it is unlawful for any one, though an apostle, to teach otherwise than we are not taught in the Holy Scriptures. . . . Therefore we reject with all our hearts, whatsoever does not agree with this infallible rule. . . . (Article 7; see also the Westminster Confession, chap. 1).

The special sufficiency of Scripture for psychology and soul care. So, for what is Scripture sufficient, according to the magisterial Reformers? For the *first principles of Christianity*, that is, basic Christian doctrine regarding the nature of God, human nature, salvation and morality. Since counseling obviously concerns itself with human beings and salvation, and Christian soul care concerns itself in large measure with the human appropriation of divine salvation, this position leads to the conclusions that Christian soul care ought to be grounded in Scripture and Christians ought to reject any beliefs that would undermine biblical teaching regarding human beings and salvation. However, from this position, we cannot draw the conclusion that contemporary Christians are required by the Bible to reject psychological research and theory—that it is sufficient with reference to all scientific knowledge related to human beings and soul care.[5]

Salvation and ultimacy counseling. However, one can affirm that the Bible is sufficient for establishing the first principles of Christianity, and then argue that counseling deals with other matters, largely unrelated to God and salvation (e.g., early childhood trauma, personality disorders and automatic thinking), leaving Scripture with little influence in Christian counseling. Here is where the intuitions that lie at the base of the BCM position on sufficiency can be helpful. Fundamentally, the BCM understands that the Scriptures deal with all of life and so all of soul-healing. As Powlison (1997, 2000) has repeatedly suggested, the Scriptures are sufficient in the sense that their *scope* is comprehensive and covers everything that relates to Christian counseling.

To take this a step further, the Bible teaches that the triune God is the sovereign savior of the world and his salvation is ultimately the only means by which humanity can be genuinely healed from its core difficulties (1 Cor 1:18-30; Eph 1:3-23; Col 1:13-29; 1 Tim 2:3-6). Christian soul-healing, therefore, *in its entirety* is centrally related to God's work of salvation as revealed in Scripture (even when dealing with issues like early childhood trauma, personality disorders and automatic thinking that are not explicitly addressed in the Scriptures).

The importance of the BCM understanding of sufficiency here is underscored when we recognize that something analogous to the biblical notion of "salvation" is central to most secular counseling models, insofar as they assume some vision of wholeness, healing or adaptiveness towards which they help clients (Johnson & Sandage, 1999; Rieff, 1966; Roberts, 1987). We might call this focus in soul care "*ultimacy* counseling," since it deals with issues of the heart that are *inherently salvific,* involving the adjustment or reconfiguring of our ultimate allegiances, the quest for meaning, the realization of our potential and the flourishing of our nature in a virtuous and mature humanity, all matters that reflect the first principles of a community's edification framework. Consequently, the BCM is right to point out that a facile assumption of secular models of counseling risks the unwitting importation of false, alternative views of *salvation* into Christian counseling (in secular culture, a self-salvation) that provide a fundamentally different map for soul care. So, in *ultimacy counseling,* Scripture must be seen as the all-sufficient source of information regarding the ultimate, salvific issues of life that lie in the deepest regions of the heart—regardless of the client and the disorder—and that are the central, distinguishing features of Christian soul-healing (see Jones & Butman, 1991, pp. 56-58). The Scriptures offer a map sufficient for guiding humanity toward the maturity ideal known as Christlikeness.

But then what are we to say about information about human nature and soul care that is not found in the Bible—regarding things like early childhood trauma, personality disorders, and automatic thinking—knowledge that is valuable for soul care, but not *ultimate* and as central to the soul care process as is God's salvation? Would the existence of such *relatively* important information call into question the property of Scripture's sufficiency? The answer to this question depends on how one understands sufficiency. Given the *absolute* sufficiency doctrine of Traditional Biblical Counseling, it would seem so (Bookman, 1994b; Mack, 1997). But if sufficiency refers to matters of *salvation*, and we recognize that the scope of salvation is comprehensive of all of life, then we can conclude that the Bible is sufficient for ultimacy counseling—counseling *at the salvific core*—and *also* conclude that valid, extrabiblical knowledge that bears on soul care is not to be rejected. As Piper (2005) has written,

> The sufficiency of Scripture does not mean that the Scripture is all we need to live obediently. To be obedient in the sciences we need to read science and study nature. . . . In other words, the Bible does not tell us all we need to know in order to be obedient stewards of this world. The sufficiency of Scripture means we don't need any more special revelation. We don't need any more inspired, inerrant words. In the Bible God has given us, we have the perfect standard for judging all other knowledge. All other knowledge stands under the judgment of the Bible. (p. 4)

In light of the above considerations, in contrast to the absolute sufficiency position, perhaps we could give the position of the magisterial Reformation and the legacy of evangelicalism the unwieldy label *salvific-doctrinal sufficiency*.

Original divine authorial intent and the nonscientific form of Scripture. "It is of the utmost importance . . . that when Scripture is read its purpose should be kept in mind and no attempt made to draw final conclusions from it concerning matters about which it does not speak" (Woolley, 1946, p. 191). God authored the Bible using the everyday language and common-sense perspective of normal adults of that time *to equip them for every good work* (2 Tim 3:17; Jones & Butman, 1991, p. 41); it was not written to supply us with a complete science of human nature or its care. On the contrary, to the extent that it addresses psychological topics, it does so in the form of what has been called "folk psychology" or "lay psychology" (in contrast to a "scientific psychology").

A lay psychology consists of nontechnical discourse for understanding human beings—including a consideration of such things as thoughts, emotions, personalities, attributions, values, problems and treatment—communicated informally in families and subcultures, and indirectly in educational settings (like churches) not dedicated to the pursuit of psychological science (see Greenwood, 1991; Morton, 2002; Thomas, 2001). It is no disparagement of the Bible to recognize that the Bible contains a *divinely inspired, but largely incidental, set of intertextually related lay psychologies.*[6] Neither does the Bible present an advanced, highly organized model of economic behavior, linguistics, political theory or even philosophical theology (such as one finds in the works of Thomas Aquinas or Richard Swinburne), though its texts pertain to them all.

According to the sufficiency rhetoric of some, the Bible *does* provide a complete, detailed and final picture of all important psychological reality, and the *only* knowledge relevant to Christian counseling comes from the Bible. However, rather than this position being the *most* honoring of the Bible, it is in danger of not accepting its actual, inspired form. *A truly radical allegiance to the sufficiency of Scripture must vigorously respect the actual form of Scripture as it was given to us, discerning its legitimate scope of reference and not imposing on it an alien set of modern assumptions regarding its comprehensiveness.* God did not give the Bible to be a scientific or exhaustive treatment of anything, even of the nature of God. God could have inspired a theocentric, multivolume, scientific counseling textbook that covers a broad range of topics systematically (see Rosenthal, 1993 for a secular version). That would have been a great gift to the human race. But he did not choose to do that, and we must be content with and respect the form of the Scriptures that he actually gave us.

One issue here is genre. The Bible is composed of a variety of genres (e.g., law, narrative, poetry, proverbs, epistle; Bakhtin, 1986; Vanhoozer, 1998), but none of them even approximates that of scientific discourse. Scientific discourse is a descriptive genre that aims at the systematization of knowledge using a technical vocabulary to refer to phenomenal details, as well as generalizations about regularities (laws), and is composed of descriptive, univocal assertions, devoid of figures of speech (Kinneavy, 1971). Scientific texts are markedly different from the Bible. Intellectual integrity demands that such differences be taken into account in an analysis of sufficiency.

At the same time, we do not want to lose perspective here, for the lay psychologies of the Bible are ultimately of far greater importance than any scientific psychologies could ever be, because the Bible consists of psychologies of *wisdom*. God's communicative agenda in Scripture is *sapientia*, not *scientia* (Augustine, 1948, *On the Trinity* 12.14; Charry, 1997; Vanhoozer, 2005). A contemporary scientist seeks knowledge; the sage seeks wisdom. And the texts of the Bible convey wisdom about human nature—the deep things about human beings that we need to know to live well and become whole. Knowledge about human nature and scientific psychologies are good things—they should be sought—and the more knowledge we acquire about human beings, the better—after all, knowledge too comes from God, so our knowing it glorifies God. But wisdom about human beings is vastly more important, because it makes us better persons, something knowledge, in and of itself, can never do.

As the means for realizing God's intended sapiential agenda—for which the Bible *is* absolutely sufficient—it also provides a significant variety of divinely inspired, lay psychologies that contain *knowledge* of human beings of incomparable value. In the writings of the apostle Paul, in particular, we find perhaps the most thorough psychology in the Bible, one that addresses many of the effects of the Fall and redemption on human beings. However, just as with his insights into salvation (Gaffin, 1971), we do not find in Paul's writings a comprehensive exposition of his own lay understanding of Christian psychology, let alone the kind of absolutely comprehensive psychology that the omniscient God possesses (both wise and exhaustively comprehensive and detailed). The development of a full-orbed Christian psychology, just like a Christian theology (Gaffin, 1971), is a historical process.[7] Though begun in and beholden to Scripture, a Christian psychology will never be completed in this age but will be continually increasing as our understanding of humans through study of Scripture, Christian classics, empirical research and philosophical analysis continues to grow.

Because of its lay psychology form, reference is made to psychological constructs and dynamics at what might be called *midlevel conceptual and practical complexity and specificity.* The Bible gives us many *general* soul-care principles, goals and means. But it does not contain, on the one hand, higher-order *theoretical statements* regarding, for example, cognitive, emotional and volitional aspects of the soul, the structure of the personality or psychospiritual abnormality, or, on the other hand, lower-order detailed, step-wise treatment strategies for applying the gospel and remediating sin and biological and psychosocial damage. Such higher- and lower-order discourse is the fruit of scientific reflection and research.

For example, the Scripture says that sin comes out of the heart (Mt 15.19), but it nowhere describes the components that make up the heart, how the heart is related to the memory, emotion and reasoning subsystems, how original sin develops into specific sins, or how genetics and social experiences influence these processes. The Bible also tells us to cast our anxiety on Christ (1 Pet 5:7), but it does not spell out the precise cognitive, emotional and volitional steps for how to take anxiety to him from within our hearts and leave it with him. While the Bible is sufficient for salvation, doctrine and morality, the phenomena of Scripture itself force upon us the conclusion that it was not God's design to have the Bible answer *directly* all the concerns of psychologists or counselors for all places in all times, containing everything that would be of value to soul care in the future.[8]

Rather than stick to a well-intentioned but unnecessarily restrictive doctrine of sufficiency, let us take the Word of God we have been given and bring it into new realms unexplored in biblical times, guiding our understanding of psychological genetics, the formation of neural networks, emotion development, personality structures, attachment relationships and so on. Let us "unleash" the Word of God we have, suffuse its wisdom throughout the domain of soul care, and see what happens (Hauerwas, 1993; Johnson, 1992). The Scriptures are necessary for Christian counseling, but their wise teachings regarding soul-healing are general; from a scientific standpoint, they are relatively underdeveloped and unsystematized. The Scriptures themselves, then, contain an implicit call to "unfold" relevant scriptural teaching: developing, extending, elaborating and applying it to new topics, and to clinical conditions not dealt with explicitly in the Bible, informed by all valid sources of wisdom and knowledge.

Suppose there was a Nobel prize-winning engineering teacher at MIT who had been working on a new method of superconduction for a few years and had recently made a great breakthrough. In previous articles he had laid some of the foundations for his current work, and others had studied his efforts in this area with interest. He was also a good teacher and had a gifted group of students whom he had been training hard for two years, and he decided to give them a real challenge. For their senior group project they were assigned the task of discovering the same method of superconduction he had just discovered. While the students knew their teacher's general approach to such things, they did not know every detail of this particular line of theory and research. To make it harder, the teacher gave the class only a partial set of instructions and a list of only some of the materials they would need and left them to figure out the rest of the task on their own. At the same time, he told the class they were free to consult anyone and read any texts they wished to get help, but he knew he was the only one who really understood the breakthrough he had made. In fact, while other researchers were trying to build on his work, they were approaching superconduction using very different (and competing) paradigms, and the teacher knew that some of the guidance they would provide his students would be misleading to them as they worked within their own teacher's paradigm, and this he warned his class. To help them, some of the instructions that the teacher gave the students included criteria for how to distinguish those other researchers who were closer to his model from those who were far off as well as information on how to evaluate what the other researchers knew, that would help them solve this particular problem *his* way.

Such a challenging senior project! He could have made the task much easier by simply supplying all the relevant information and materials himself that they would need. Then the students could simply implement his instructions and solve the problem with relative ease. But this teacher knew he had equipped his students well, and he knew their potential, so he wanted to give them a problem that would bring out in them the fullest use of the training they had received and their skills in investigation, interpretation, resourcefulness and intelligence.

The reader gets the point. God could have made it much easier for Christian counselors too. But he apparently wants his children to use their God-given minds—in dependence on his Spirit and guided by his wise core instructions, and also making use of the knowledge of non-Christians that is corrupted in certain key ways (knowledge which he himself gave through creation grace)—to figure out how to build the best soul-care models the world has ever seen, to get as close as we can to the model that is in God's mind and heart. Why did God do it this way? Only God knows, but perhaps it was because the more difficult the challenge of a task, the greater the success, and the greater the success of God's students, the greater the honor that their good Teacher receives. A simpler task, though easier and safer, would give God less glory.

Sufficiency and a heliocentric planetary system. One more point needs to be raised related to sufficiency. In chapter two we noted another Reformation-era controversy that Christians in psychology can never afford to forget. Out of devotion to the Bible—thinking it mandated a geocentric model of the planets and the sun—some Christians (both Catholic and Protestant) severely criticized the Copernican theory that the earth was in a heliocentric planetary system. Eventually, the preponderance of extrabiblical evidence led Christian intellectuals to favor a heliocentric model. While naturalists and liberal Christians have tended to overreact to the implications of this episode in church history, it must serve as a reminder to Bible-loving Christians that Scripture cannot be approached in abstraction from the rest of God's work in creation. Christians simply cannot read their Bibles as if no other relevant information existed. There is an underlying harmony to all of God's works, flowing from the all-knowing, singular understanding of God. That centuries-old debate should forever caution Christians to question their assumptions about God's communicative intentions in Scripture.

Two facts, however, significantly distinguish the Copernican debate regarding astronomy and today's psychology/counseling debate. First, as we saw in chapter one, the Christian canon deals directly with psychological and soul-care issues (albeit at a lay level). Christians, therefore, cannot ignore the Bible's teachings on these matters when studying human beings and caring for their souls, without necessarily undermining their own system of thought and practice. Second, a science of human nature is itself necessarily constituted by a community's basic beliefs about human beings in a much more radical way than applies to a natural science (Taylor, 1985). One lesson from chapter four is that there will be substantial continuity between one's controlling worldview assumptions and one's observational beliefs, whether we recognize those underlying influences or not. To be true to their faith, Christian psychologists and counselors have to allow the Bible's first principles regarding human beings to shape their psychological theories, observations and practice, if their psychology is to apply well to the souls of Christians—whether members of other communities agree with it or not. For many reasons, the challenge of Christianly interpreting the secular psychology texts of today is much greater than in that former debate, but God appears to be calling his church in our day to become more sophisticated in our hermeneutics of texts than ever before.

We have spent a lot of time on this property of Scripture, because of the controversy concerning it within the Christian counseling community. We conclude with the following modest statement: the sufficiency of the Bible regarding psychology and soul care means that *the Bible is the Christian community's foundational psychology and soul care text, because it amply communicates enough about the nature of God, human beings and divine salvation that no other text is necessary for normal Christians to thrive psychospiritually.*

The Primacy of Scripture

The term *primacy* was *not* used in the Reformation debates with reference to Scripture. However it seems to have been implied in the notion of *sola*. *Sola scriptura* describes the practice of biblical authority in the church. *Sola scriptura* is the answer to the question "Where can we find the supreme norm by which to measure Christian deeds and Christian doctrine?" (Vanhoozer, 2005, p. 232). Perhaps the best translation today of the meaning behind *sola* in those Reformation debates is the term *primacy*, even more than *sufficiency*.

The term *primacy* has been used more recently to bring out more precisely Scripture's authority in our thought and life in relation to other sources of authority. Bloesch (1978), for example, argues that the Bible has a normative primacy over the church and its traditions, the conscience, miraculous signs and wonders, new revelation and over all cultural input, in the development of its theology. Scripture, he believes, has the "final word," when other sources of knowledge make competing claims. In contrast to an absolute understanding of sufficiency, the term *primacy* has the advantage of implying the existence and relative legitimacy of other texts and authorities, while also communicating that Scripture has the preeminent role to play in our understanding, in our case, of the soul-care agenda of the church. Ultimately, the notion of primacy reinforces that Scripture is authoritative, necessary and sufficient for salvation; but it goes a step further by clarifying the Bible's relation to all other authoritative forms of relevant knowledge—that of superiority. The Bible is the supreme text for Christian soul care, the text of texts, more important than any other.

Reference has repeatedly been made to Calvin's likening of Scripture to a pair of eyeglasses (1559/1960, 1.6.1). Let us read the text for ourselves and consider its relevance to primacy:

> Just as old or bleary-eyed men and those with weak vision, if you thrust before them a most beautiful volume, even if they recognize it to be some sort of writing, yet can scarcely construe two words, but with the aid of spectacles will begin

> to read distinctly; so Scripture, gathering up the otherwise confused knowledge of God in our minds, having dispersed our dullness, clearly shows us the true God. (Vol. 1, p.70)

This would seem to be a good metaphor to illustrate primacy. Scripture is not the object of our study; it is the means of our studying or seeing. The Bible has vision-enhancing power. Its textual priority means we see other things more clearly with its aid.

The special primacy of Scripture for psychology and soul care. Primacy conveys that the first principles of Scripture—and not the first principles of alien worldviews (naturalism, humanism or postmodernism)—must contribute the infrastructure of the disciplinary matrix and edification framework of Christian psychology and soul care, orienting our research and theory-building, and setting the church's counseling agenda. But, as suggested, primacy also has the advantage of implying that there are other texts that are relevant and of value for Christian psychology and soul care (including those from the Christian tradition and a good many more written by non-Christians), but of all the relevant texts, none compares to the Bible in importance for the formation of a complex, scientifically valid Christian framework. It is the Christian's semantic and axiological "touchstone." It alone provides an orienting meaning-system to which Christians are to return again and again to develop and enhance their grasp of the ultimate conceptual priorities, loves and goals most in keeping with reality and most formative for Christian well-being. God means for the Bible to draw us into a theocentric way of seeing and living; as we receive Scripture deeply, our thinking and loving is gradually transformed.

> Every interpretative endeavor of man presupposes the absolute interpretation of all things through Christ in Scripture. When man receives the revelation of God given him he must, from the outset, realize that his observational and conceptualizing endeavor is at every point subordinate to the teleology of Scripture. His "concepts" must from the outset "be seen to be limiting concepts" operating in subordination to the verbally revealed body of truth of Scripture. (Van Til, 1971, p. 243)

The divinely inspired texts of Scripture were intended by God to exist in a dialectical relationship with all other human discourse, with Scripture providing the ultimate, "framing" text through and within which they are to be interpreted.[9] "To practice *sola scriptura* is to treat Scripture alone as the 'norming norm' and tradition [or other psychology texts] as the 'normed norm'" (Vanhoozer, 2005, p. 234). We simply cannot properly understand any texts or objects apart from a Scripturally shaped disciplinary matrix.

So the property of primacy is of more than theoretical interest. The Holy Spirit works within us persuading us of Scripture's primacy, which becomes evident as our lives (personal and professional) come to be oriented more and more deeply by scriptural ways of thinking, appraising and living, drawing us into their circle of influence and convincing us of their preeminence over other beliefs, values and activities, whether bad or simply not as good. Scripture may not be an encyclopedia dealing exhaustively with all soul-care topics, but it is the supremely valuable prioritizing, regulating and goal-setting soul guide. It directs humans to seek, relish and love some things (God, his nature and his glory, salvation, justification, other humans), and avoid, reject and hate others (original sin and its various manifestations in thoughts, desires, patterns of love and hate, and behaviors). "The canonical Scriptures have *primal* and *final* authority because just these communicative acts and practices are the chosen media the Spirit uses to inform us of Christ, and to form Christ in us so that we may speak and act in our own situations to the glory of God" (Vanhoozer, 2005, p. 237).

In light of Scripture's primacy, Christian counselors need to spend more time focusing on the major themes of Scripture than on those of any other texts (Crabb, 1987), working hard to allow those themes to set the main agenda of their theory-building and counseling, each case and each session, as well as their own souls. Some form of prioritizing is inevitable for us, given our finite capabilities. We can only center our lives on a limited number of themes. Learning to center on the best, most important themes is a defining feature of wisdom (Vanhoozer, 2005). So to affirm the primacy of Scripture implies that the themes emphasized there will be accorded a special "weighting," drawing Christians to similarly emphasize and concentrate their activities around these scriptural themes, leading to a life (and a version of psychology and soul care) predominantly shaped by and oriented around the priorities of God.

This is especially important for soul care, since so many of life's difficulties relate in one way or another to one's priorities. All counseling is ultimately aesthetic (that is, concerned with virtuous beauty), so one of the main goals of Christian soul care is to help individuals receive and internalize God's value-system, virtues and loves. For example, it is natural (and understandable) to want to leave a marriage to a difficult person. Yet the Bible teaches that in most cases God is best glorified when individuals remain faithful to their covenant vows in spite of the personal cost. In a God-centered universe, God's glory is a greater value than a human's immediate happiness, and in the long run, these two agendas are coterminous. Therefore, irreconcilable differences cannot be considered grounds for divorce; they are grounds for glory. Within such a scripturally based values-context, Christian soul care helps believers to find the soul-transformation that lies beyond self-protection and the pursuit of personal pleasure.

Primacy is an important property of Scripture for our purposes, because it underscores that scriptural teachings need to provide the most important material in the Christian disciplinary matrix and the main pillars of its edification framework. At the same time it legitimizes the use of extrabiblical texts and counseling activities other than Bible teaching. The primacy of Scripture in relation to psychology and soul care means that *the Bible is the final, ultimate norm regarding human beings and their psychospiritual healing, so that it must set the agenda for Christian psychology and soul care.*

Scripture's Properties for Soul Care, According to Different Christian Approaches

We have looked at four properties of Scripture that bear on Christian psychology and soul care. Let us take a few moments to consider how the different approaches that Christians take to psychology (examined in chapters two and three) would presumably stand with regard to these four properties. We can dispense with the levels-of-explanation approach most quickly, since it holds that Scripture is not at all relevant to psychology, given that it defines psychology as solely an empirical science of human nature (as does the modern psychology it has embraced). So Scripture does not even have authority in psychology for this group. Most Christians are less comfortable with such a strict dichotomy between faith and psychological knowledge. Two positions, modern pastoral care and weak integration, would seem to hold that Scripture at least has some authority in psychology and soul care. Therefore, it may be consulted on certain topics, but that is not necessary, and the bulk of the writing of these two approaches is consumed with the findings of modern psychology, rather than biblical studies.

Post-liberal pastoral care takes the Bible more seriously than its liberal forebears. Its proponents would likely argue that Scripture is necessary for soul care and sufficient for salvation. However, there is some ambiguity regarding Scripture's primacy, at least among the authors tapped as representatives of this approach. Hunsinger (1995) seems to argue that Scripture and the human sciences are equally authoritative, whereas Purves basically neglects the human sciences. Neither position holds to the primacy of Scripture, but for opposite reasons. Anderson (1990, 2001), on the other hand, would seem to hold to the primacy of Scripture over other soul-care literature. Suffice to say that there does not seem to be a uniform position regarding the relation of the Bible to other texts among some current post-liberal (or neo-Barthian) models.

The biblical counseling movement upholds the authority and necessity of Scripture for psychology (that is, the study of human beings) and counseling, but the movement is divided on the nature of sufficiency. The Traditionalists affirm an absolute sufficiency position. Consequently, they would reject primacy, since they do not regard psychological research as truly relevant for their counseling. However, the progressives take a more complex view of the matter, more similar to the strong integration[10] and Christian psychology positions, than has often been appreciated. All three affirm the four properties of Scripture for soul care, and therefore are all committed to primacy, because, analogous to the position of the magisterial Reformation and its heirs, they hold that Scripture's sufficiency with regard to psychology and soul care refers to matters of Christian doctrine and salvation. See table 5.1 for a diagram that compares the different Christian approaches on these matters.

Beyond the four properties of Scripture we have examined, what distinguishes the Progressive biblical counseling, strong integration and Christian psychology approaches to psychology and soul care? Perhaps location. Each approach is guided by somewhat different aims, audiences and vocational context (Powlison, personal conversation, July 8, 2005). Progressive biblical counseling is taught in seminaries and Bible colleges, and is local and church-based, concerned with soul care in the congregation. Christian psychology is interested in the science of psychology and would be of greater interest to psychology teachers, researchers, practitioners and others dedicated to developing distinctively Christian versions of psychology and scientifically complex models of soul care. Strong integration has been largely guided by the demands and needs of professional Christian counselors and therapists, motivated by a strong desire to serve Christ and follow his Word in the culture at large. In

Table 5.1. A Comparison of the Understanding of Scripture of Different Christian Approaches

	Levels of Explan.	Modern Pastoral Care	Post-liberal Past. Care	Weak Integ.	Strong Integ.	Christian Psych.	Prog. Biblical Coun.	Trad. Biblical Coun.
Authority		X	X	X	X	X	X	X
Necessity			X		X	X	X	X
Sufficiency			Salvific-Doctrinal X		Salvific-Doctrinal X	Salvific-Doctrinal X	Salvific-Doctrinal X	Absolute X
Primacy			X?		X	X	X	

times past, such differences have led to some Christian culture wars. However, these different agendas need not be fundamentally opposed to each other, since all three can be pursued under the lordship of Christ. Perhaps now is the time for Christian pastors, theologians, counselors, psychologists and other interested parties to come together on these matters. As we center on Christ, we find ourselves standing closer to each other.

Conclusion

If Scripture has the properties that have been alleged here, then its importance and relevance to Christian psychology and soul care should be clear. These properties suggest that the Bible possesses a reorienting conceptual and aesthetic power which, when unleashed, creates new ways of seeing human beings, treating their problems and promoting their remediation. That is, to a large extent, what happened in the Reformation (as well as, interestingly enough, the Catholic renewal in the twentieth century called *Ressourcement*). This sort of revitalization of mind, heart, practice and relationship happens whenever Christians treat Scripture, more and more, as the primary text of their lives.

The next two chapters develop some of the implications of this one. Chapter six examines the hermeneutics of reading the Bible in order to formulate the first principles of Christian psychology and soul care, and chapter seven discusses how to read secular psychology texts when Scripture is primary.

Notes

[1]The fact that Scripture is God-breathed also legitimates human communication in general by dem-

onstrating that meaning can be conveyed through human language. If God can communicate meaningfully to humans through humans writing (or speaking) words, then humans can communicate meaningfully to humans through words also (Athanasius, 1954; Work, 2002).

[2]It should also be mentioned that all revelation from God provides this legitimizing function. The coming of the Son of God to earth was the ultimate sign from above that bestows meaning on all the rest of human speech and activity, including Scripture. Likewise, all theophanies (like the burning bush) and prophetic utterances and acts convey meaning that originates from outside of any human discursive system.

[3]Even the study of cognition, which most would consider a mechanistic phenomenon, is affected by worldview assumptions. Many contemporary leaders in cognitive psychology, for example, are evolutionary naturalists and therefore disparage the experience of free will as an illusion and deny the existence of a soul (Minsky, 1988; Pinker, 1999; Wegner, 2002). These beliefs affect how they view cognition within human life.

[4]To suggest that *sola* always means "(absolutely) alone" is to fail to attend to how the Reformers actually used the term (Vanhoozer, 2005, p. 232).

[5]To cite just one example, Richard Baxter (1656/1990), a latter-day Puritan pastor and representative of the Reformation, included in a sermon on melancholia a number of medicinal remedies, as well as numerous practical, soul-care recommendations not found explicitly in Scripture.

[6]I write "set" because of the different human authors of Scripture, and "incidental" because none of them were intending to write a psychology text. They addressed psychological topics incidentally, while seeking to accomplish other communicative purposes.

[7]The limitations of the actual form of Scripture create challenges for the biblical theologian as well as the counselor. Dunn (1998) points out that the scholar who desires to discern Paul's overall theology is not given a systematic presentation. Instead, Paul's letters provide textual *clues* that point toward what that theology might have been. The Pauline theologian must piece together Paul's theology from these epistolary clues. One could make a similar point regarding doctrines like the Trinity, the two natures of Christ, the atonement and the polity of the church. Orthodox trinitarian doctrine is based in Scripture but elaborates it in legitimate ways, ways that are suggested by Scripture but not entirely expounded there. In a comparable way, the Christian soul-care community needs to construct and test Christian theories of human nature and counseling based on the inspired offerings of the biblical canon and guided by the classics of the Christian tradition, but with the added challenge of discerning, capturing and utilizing the relevant truth in contemporary psychology. All this is a daunting task for even the most adventurous.

[8]Complicating the problem is the fact that the Scriptures are not just a revelation of *truths* regarding God, human beings and salvation. They consist, more fundamentally, of divine speech acts, revealing yes, but also encouraging, challenging, narrating and commanding (Vanhoozer, 1998, 2002, 2005; Wolterstorff, 1995). We also have to acknowledge that the various genres of Scripture do not lend themselves equally well to application to counseling needs. There are large portions of text made up of instructions regarding statutes, ceremonies and rites for the people of Israel, long narratives, worship songs, prophetic predictions and critiques of idolatry and immorality, and letters written to address various theological doctrines, ethical issues and ecclesiastical problems (Vanhoozer, 2005). Applying such a variety of literature to contemporary soul care in light of twenty-first-century opportunities and challenges is actually a monumental task and requires of the Christian community of pastors, biblical specialists, psychologists and counselors a great deal of prayer, hermeneutical reflection and humility.

[9]They are dialectically related because, while the Scriptures have primacy, since they offer us a divinely interpreted world, the Scriptures cannot be understood without a prior mundane discursive context

(prior both historically—Hebrew was spoken before it was used in the Old Testament—and ontogenetically—we conversed as children long before we read the Bible). A theocentric model of knowing and loving cannot be comprehended without both sets of human texts: one divinely inspired and the other the product of divine creation and providence.

[10]Contrary to most strong integration advocates, Farnsworth's (1985) model of embodied integration denies the primacy of Scripture. He argues that psychological and theological knowledge are equally flawed, so neither can be totally trusted, therefore neither can have primacy over the other. The Christian tradition has always recognized the finite and sinful conditions of human knowledge, but it need not lead to Farnworth's kind of skepticism, a skepticism that has far more in common with Kant than Augustine. It led in Farnsworth's case to an inability to appreciate that different authorities can have different degrees of reliability. Just as some research instruments are more reliable than others, and some persons are more reliable than others, so some written sources of knowledge are more reliable than others. The Bible is a one-hundred-percent uniformly reliable record of what God wished to communicate to humankind, whereas all other texts have the potential of being less reliable as a record of God's understanding of whatever they assert. Of course human knowledge is flawed in various ways, but that has nothing to do with Scripture's primacy. The cash value of Scripture's property of primacy is simply that the teachings of Scripture should be accorded greater weight in the formulation of our understanding of human nature and soul care than any other texts. That is all. Nonetheless this early attempt at ethical integration was noble and helpful for advocating the transcending of a purely intellectual approach to integration.

Another reason to affirm the primacy of Scripture over psychology texts is the fact that the Bible is already in linguistic form, whereas human nature is not. The aim of any science is to put into textual form a description of an object of study—in this case, individual human nature—and this leads to the possibility of error in the formulation of the description. Being a normative *text* makes the Bible a decided asset in descriptive formulation.

6

Interpreting the Bible for Christian Psychology and Soul Care

WHILE THE ENTIRE BIBLE WAS WRITTEN BY GOD with future Christians in mind (see 1 Cor 9:10), it was originally written *to* the people of Israel and *to* people and churches in the early days of the Christian church, often addressing specific problems of those days (e.g., what to do when one's ox gores someone or when one's Christian slave returns after having run away). The Scriptures come prepackaged, as it were, ordered and organized for specific communicative purposes at the time of their original composition. So we cannot expect clear, straightforward answers when we ask of it questions that were not being originally addressed. For example, the Bible does not provide us with a comprehensive discussion of divine attributes, moral problems, heresies or all the ways we can show love to someone. Rather, the finite, historically conditioned set of topics provided by God's written word are *illustrative*—given to exemplify how various issues should be approached so that the church could use those exemplars to help them think *Christocentrically* about novel problems that would arise later in its history.

Interpretive issues are no easier in psychology and soul care. Though Scripture teaches that it should be the Christian community's primary guide for soul healing, the form of Scripture itself must be allowed to affect how we put it to work in our soul care. For one thing, it was not written in the genre of scientific literature or psychotherapy treatment manuals. On the contrary, it consists of genres that at first glance might seem distant to soul-care concerns: rules, narratives, songs, obscure prophetic poetry and epistles that address a wide range of theological and ecclesial topics. At best (as we concluded in the previous chapter), the Bible presents a number of lay psychologies written at midlevel conceptual and practical complexity and specificity.

The question to be addressed in this chapter is: how are we to read the Bible so that it operates as our primary text in the formulation of Christian psychology and soul care, enabling us to develop *today* new psychological theories, research programs and soul-care treatments that go far beyond the explicit agenda of Scripture, while yet being constrained by its inspired soul-care agenda-setting framework? This is really a monumental hermeneutical task, far beyond what can be accomplished in one chapter, so we will only be able to touch on a few of the most relevant topics. We begin with a discussion of some directly hermeneutical concerns, followed by a consideration of some of the biblical soul-care themes that should form our spectacles for interpreting human beings and other psychology texts. Then, we shall finish up with a few thoughts about how the Bible might foster the development of a Christian psychology.

Issues in Biblical Hermeneutics for Psychology and Soul Care

There are four topics of some hermeneutical complexity that we shall consider with reference to soul care: the distinction between illocution and perlocution, the difference in the two Testaments, the unique genres in Scripture and the Bible's mission to interpret us.

Divine illocutionary and perlocutionary intent. We begin with a discussion of speech-act theory (Austin, 1962; Searle, 1970), which offers us some conceptual tools that can help us think about the use of Scripture for soul care. Speech-acts are acts that use language to accomplish things, for example to describe, motivate or express ourselves. Most statements, whether written or spoken, are a result of the intention of their speaker to communicate something. Consider, for example, Mary telling John, "The grass needs to be mowed." This statement has a meaning, but it is not immediately clear what it is. It may be a description of the length of the grass, or it may actually be a request to mow the grass. Mary's *intended* sense is termed the *illocutionary* meaning of the speech-act, and the issuing of that statement is called an illocutionary act.[1] However, the same statement can also be considered a perlocution, if it produces an *effect* in its hearer/reader. When a statement causes such an effect, it is also called a perlocutionary act. Speakers usually have desired effects they wish to be realized through their speech. These desired outcomes are termed "perlocutionary intentions" or the "perlocutionary trajectory" (Vanhoozer, 1998, p. 336) (though statements often have unintended consequences that must also be considered perlocutionary effects).

We must note, first, that the Bible claims for itself a "double-authorship", it is a product of "double-agency discourse" (Wolterstorff, 1995, 2001): God and the human author. This makes considerations of illocution and perlocution at least twice as complicated, since there is no reason to assume that the two authors of each biblical text had entirely the same illocutionary and perlocutionary intentions. On the contrary, it is necessary to conclude, as did the human authors of the New Testament regarding the Old, that the divine author's illocutionary and perlocutionary intentions could transcend those of the human author of Scripture (see Plantinga, 2003, p. 26). For example, Paul wrote that the narratives in Numbers were written "for our instruction, upon whom the ends of the ages have come" (1 Cor 10:11), even though Numbers was originally a portion of Israel's foundational covenantal documents and so was originally written to the Israelites. The utterances of Scripture, though written for immediate purposes by the human and divine authors to an audience millennia ago, were *also* written by the *divine* author to produce certain perlocutionary effects throughout the rest of this era. In other words, they were expressed for the purpose of making intellectual and aretegenic change in readers and hearers for centuries to come. God can surely have had more than one addressee in mind when he spoke the Scripture (Wolterstorff, 1995), but it is daunting to consider that the omniscient God intended all the legitimate uses of a passage by all of its hearers or readers down through the centuries!

For example, the psalmist reported,

> When my anxious thoughts multiply within me,
> Your consolations delight my soul. (Ps 94:19)

This is an illocution consisting simply of a description of the psalmist's experience and appreciation of God's goodness. It was perhaps originally written for public worship at the temple but then incorporated in the Psalter so that it would be used for worship continually within the Jewish covenant community, even after the temple's destruction. The human speech-act may not have been a perlocution; it is not a command or even a recommendation, but simply an expression of the psalmist's heart. But given God's authorship of it, we must conclude that his fuller understanding of his own consolations for us in Christ were included in *his* illocution, in a way that readers could have grasped only after Christ came and died and was raised on behalf of his people. Hence, God's illocutionary act was astoundingly more comprehensive than was the human author's. In addition, because of the revealed purposes of the Bible (e.g., 2 Tim 3:16-17), we can assume the divine author spoke this with perlocutionary intent likely absent in the human author's intention, leading us to infer that it is today supposed to encourage God's people to find release from their anxieties in Christ. Then it becomes a perlocutionary act afresh, every time someone understands its divine illocutionary meaning in the ongoing present and finds relief from her concerns by considering God's goodness in Christ. Thus:

> Since it performs an illocutionary act, Scripture is integrally related to its speaker; since it is thus an active address calling for a certain perlocutionary effect and imposing, like any other text, certain ethical constraints, it is integrally related to its addressees; since, as with all speech acts, the referential function and propositional content are inseparable aspects of an indivisible act, it is integrally related to its referents: God, humanity and the world. (Ward, 2002, p. 205)

One way of understanding the linkage between the Scriptures' complex illocutionary and perlocutionary functions—a way suggested by the overall reforming communicative agenda of Scripture—is to see the entirety of Scripture as constituting God's promises to realize his redemptive intentions in his people. The divine perlocutionary intent is realized exclusively through faith, which is the believing appropriation (or internalization) of the redemptive significance of the particular text. The more deeply this appropriation occurs, the greater the redemptive good experienced and the greater the perlocutionary effect of the statement. We might refer to this existential quality as "perlocutionary depth." The eternal goal of God's salvation is realized as the relevant divine illocutions of Scripture restructure the believer's character and life through the ever deepening appropriation of what are also Scripture's divine perlocutions, a goal that will be realized fully only in heaven.

The bottom line is that Scripture needs to be assimilated by counselors and counselees in such a way that its fullest soul-reforming potential is tapped. This requires reading individual passages, mindful of their original context and relation to the rest of Scripture, in order best to discern their perennial soul-care relevance. "And this happens . . . not in the timelessness of a general philosophical or scientific truth, but when its uniquely historical and at the same time unsurpassable timeliness gets through to me, provided I expose myself to being affected by it" (Balthasar, 1989a, pp. 30-31).

The soul-care significance of the two Testaments. The texts that compose the Christian Bible can be distinguished in a number of ways that have important implications for psychology and soul care. The most important distinction within the Bible is that between the Old and New Testaments. The Old Testament was written to and for *Israel,* the physical descendants of Abraham, Isaac and Jacob (along with others who converted), who are in a special covenantal relationship with him. The founding covenant documents that constitute the Torah include the obligations both parties (God and Israel) have toward each another, particularly the covenantal requirements imposed on the Israelites by God. This covenant was nonetheless preparatory, for it established a textual and social context for the coming of the Son of God into the world. Furthermore, because the emphasis of this covenant was on law and obedience, it stressed the importance to God of the conformity of his people to his character. This resulted in a heightening of the awareness of God's people regarding his holiness and his righteous standards, though this did not happen in large measure until the canon was near completion, after the judgment of God for their disobedience had fallen upon Israel and Judah. Only then, it seems, did the people of that covenant begin to grasp what it entailed.

"The Law was given through Moses; grace and truth were realized through Jesus Christ" (Jn 1:17). The New Testament begins with a fourfold portrayal of the Son, and the rest consists mostly of an exposition of the new covenant form of life of its human members, through numerous apostolic letters, the triune God himself having already fulfilled some of his own covenant obligations through the death of the Son. We are also told that many of the rest of his covenantal obligations (or promises) will be fulfilled through the Holy Spirit's work in believers.

The Testaments are interrelated in a number of important ways (Baker, 1991; Feinberg, 1988; Goldsworthy, 2000). First, the Old Testament contains "types" (persons, objects, institutions and events) that prefigure important persons and events in the New Testament, and promises, the fulfillments of which are described in the New Testament. There is also a profound continuity between the Testaments, for the Old Testament presents the origins of the human race, much about the nature of God and of humans, narratives of pre-Christian redemptive-history, and God's overall plan of redemption, all of which are assumed and reinterpreted in the New Testament in light of Christ.

However, there is also some discontinuity between the Testaments, since the new covenant documents supercede the authority of the old covenant documents, evidenced by the abolishing of a number of civil and ceremonial commands given to Israel. Furthermore, the New Testament expresses the spiritual and gracious nature of God's salvation more clearly than did the Old Testament. There also seems to be more promotion of the *fear* of the Lord in the Old Testament through an emphasis on God's majesty and holiness, whereas, building upon that foundation, the New Testament seeks to promote more the *love* of God. Of course, in any of these contrasts one can find evidence of the New Testament understandings anticipated in the Old Testament and emphases of the Old Testament resoundingly affirmed in the New. But the profound interdependence of the Testaments should not overshadow the fact of the new covenant's superiority over the old, including the supersession of the Old Testament by the New Testament, without disparaging the Old (see especially Romans, Galatians and Hebrews). While both Testaments together form the Christian canon, the New Testament is God's final written word to his people and so has preeminence of place.[2]

Christian preachers and other soul-care providers ought to keep such distinctions in mind when interpreting and applying the Old Testament. Everything in the Old Testament should be read in light of the New Testament—so that its implicit Christocentrism is made clear—and emphasis should be placed on the New Testament text, so its preeminence is grasped (Goldsworthy, 2000). Otherwise, there is the danger that an excessively law-oriented approach to Christianity will be fostered. The relation between the Testaments creates an example of intertextuality: the earlier canonical texts of the Old Testament arc to be read in the light of the later, *clearer* canonical texts of the New Testament. Fortunately, examples of just this kind of interpretation of the Old Testament can be found in the New Testament, so an initial schooling is provided. However, such a rereading is difficult to maintain across the Old Testament and requires training and practice.

As an example of this re-reading, let us consider a Christian approach to the Psalms. We notice at once their theocentrism. Whether declaring edifying truth through praise or manifesting remarkable emotional honesty before

God, they reveal the workings of a God-centered soul—so their value for Christian soul care is inestimable. However, the Psalms were written long before Christ's death and resurrection and Pentecost. Aside from a few confessions of sin, the Psalmists' approach to the life of faith is still more self-confident and less self-aware (e.g., "Vindicate me, O LORD, according to my righteousness and the integrity that is in me," Ps 7:8) than one finds in the New Testament (*after* humanity has crucified the Son of God). Knowing better their sinfulness, Christians now can only look to Christ for their vindication.

Because of the centrality of Christ to Christianity and the clarity of the gospel and its implications in the New Testament, it is in most cases desirable for Christians to spend proportionately more time in spiritual reading and meditation in the New Testament than in the Old Testament. Of course, the Old Testament ought not to be neglected, for its soul-care value is obvious (besides the Psalms, just consider Proverbs, Isaiah and Job), but Christians must learn to think and live Christocentrically, and this they learn best in the New Testament.

The soul-care significance of the different genres of the Bible. Another important interpretive distinction relevant for soul care concerns the particular genre of the text in question, a point raised earlier by Capps (1981). A genre is "a group of written texts marked by distinctive recurring characteristics which constitute a recognizable and coherent type of writing" (quoted in Cotterell & Turner, 1989, p. 99); it is a "species of literature" (Vanhoozer, 1998, p. 336) that projects a particular world in a particular way. Each genre has its own set of rules by which it is distinguished from others (though individual works may push the genre's boundaries). With these rules, genres function as "cognitive instruments" that uniquely shape the way the reader construes reality (Vanhoozer, 1998). Balthasar suggested that a genre is a "mode of seeing" (Vanhoozer, 2000, p. 84). The genre of a text provides the interpretive context for that text (that the present situation provides for oral discourse, Vanhoozer, 2000), and each genre is capable of articulating and mediating some aspects of reality better than others. The diverse canonical genres "serve to coordinate covenantal action" (Vanhoozer, 2005, p. 216), providing a range of different perspectives through which God's Word transforms us into godly covenantal members.

Vanhoozer (1998) suggests that an example of a particular genre is a "generic" illocutionary act that places the meaning of the text into a certain form, and so must affect its interpretation. However, we need to inquire into the *per-*

locutionary implications of genre. Since soul care based on God's Word is essentially a perlocutionary activity, it is worthwhile for us to examine the unique reformative features of the genres of the Bible.

Narrative. "A fundamental fact about the Scriptures is that they constitute a text with a developing story" (Lints, 1993, p. 262). Holding the entire canon together is a narrative—indeed, a metanarrative—of universal scope and significance. Beginning with the creation, the Bible records the history of God's interactions with particular human beings, up through the early days of the church, in order to reshape our souls. "A narrative displays an interpreted world" (Vanhoozer, 1998, p. 341), even a worldview. Consequently, the biblical metanarrative derived from the stories of the Bible presents the dramatic, trinicentric context for all human stories that enables us to make sense of ourselves in relation to God. This metanarrative is important for Christian soul care because it provides the primary means of constructing a *Christian* identity and developing Christians into holy images of God.

Then, the individual narratives found throughout the Bible offer descriptions of God's character and values (his loves and hates), as they show him wooing and blessing humans in grace, as well as punishing them for their sin, expressing himself in speech-acts and deeds, as the chief protagonist in the drama of history. Because likeness to God is the goal of human virtue and maturation, these stories are foundational for human development.

However, the narratives of the Bible also contain accounts of humans, who interact with God as well as each other. Some of the stories concern "heroes," individuals who exemplify social and moral norms, valiantly acting for good on behalf of the community or other specific people, and are held up implicitly as role models for the reader (Ryken, 1992). Such stories are supposed to stimulate the reader to realize the same attitudes and behaviors as the hero.[3] Epic stories are large-scale narratives, often centering on a hero, that deal with expansive, positive events in a people's history, like the exodus or David's rise to the throne and battles of conquest. In addition to the historical and human significance of the stories, read typologically such epics point ahead to the grand epic of Christ's redemptive mission and provide metaphoric power of relevance to one's own story of reformation into Christlikeness. Tragedy is the account of the downward movement of a heroic figure. Biblical tragedies, like those of King Saul, King Solomon and Samson, highlight the sinful choices of the protagonists that led to their downfall and are meant to persuade the reader to avoid doing likewise (Ryken, 1992).

Gospel. The most important narratives for the Christian are the four Gospels, since they present the life, death and resurrection of the Christian's supreme hero, Jesus Christ. Their value is beyond compare, since Christ is *the* image of God, the true human and the fulfillment of God's purposes for humanity. "The history of Jesus is thus the hermeneutical key to the biblical canon as a whole" (Vanhoozer, 2005, p. 223). We read of Christ to know who we are in him, and then how we are to live. As John of the Cross (1964) recommended to those seeking spiritual growth: "Let him have an habitual desire to imitate Christ in everything he does, conforming himself to his life; upon which life he must meditate so that he may know how to imitate it, and to behave in all things as Christ would behave" (p. 57). In addition, by telling of Christ's death and resurrection, the Gospels convey the stories that mediate the most important soul-care knowledge in the universe, for there we learn of our own death and resurrection in Christ (Rom 6:1-11; Gorman, 2001). Present-day Christians are "to make sense of *their* stories as Jesus did of his [for he read his life in light of the Old Testament], precisely by reading their own lives in light of the life of Jesus" (Vanhoozer, 2005, p. 222).

Law. A main goal of biblical religion is to increase the correspondence of the character of human beings to God's. The moral law in Scripture is fundamentally a verbal representation of God's character and consists of commands issued specifically to point toward and foster the realization of the human goal of likeness to God. In addition, the law also states the stipulations binding upon the covenant partners. This means that New Covenant members must be careful to fulfill the obligations of the New Covenant, and not those that pertain solely to God's covenant with Israel.

Though an emphasis on law is more predominant in the Old Testament than in the New (e.g., large sections of its founding texts, the Torah, consist of ceremonial and civil rules), texts of law that illustrate or express God's character pervade both Testaments. However, the moral law is clearly a two-edged sword for the believer, for an important part of its perlocutionary function is the promotion of an awareness of our sin. Paul's teaching in Galatians and Romans is extremely important for interpreting the moral law, because he understood that it could only be appropriated through Christ. Only after being justified by faith (Rom 5:1) and being given the gift of the righteousness of God (Rom 5:17) could believers view the law as a guide to righteousness. Otherwise, the law kills (Rom 7:11) by actually stirring up sinful desires (or self-righteousness), so hopeless is the human condition. Believers who have been spiritually abused may have difficulty reading the moral law without it activating perfectionism or excessive feelings of shame and guilt. Such people may need to spend more time on passages that deal with the gospel of grace, at least until they overcome more of the effects of their abuse.

Comprehensive soul care entails an articulation of ethical discourse, a realization lost on secular therapists for most of the twentieth century, but one being increasingly appreciated in our day (see Doherty, 1995; Fowers, 2000; Richardson, Fowers & Guignon, 1999). However, the Gospels teach us that great care must be taken by the soul-care provider when applying moral principles to the lives of others, because of the tendency humans have to add to biblical precepts their own traditions. Besides, God's design is to make us not moral robots but wise children who have been enabled to discern his will by the "gospelization" of his law. The most important fact for Christian soul care is the knowledge that the law is fulfilled in Christ.

Poetry. Large sections of the Bible consist of poetry, including the Psalms, Job, Song of Solomon and portions of the Prophets, and some poetic language (like figures of speech) can be found in nearly every book of the Bible (Klein, Blomberg & Hubbard, 1993). Poetry is more than a genre; it is a distinctive use of language, to be contrasted with prose. Poetry adheres to stricter rules of grammatical form (e.g., metrical patterns, alliteration and parallelism) and makes greater use of imagery and figures of speech, condensing meaning in the process. As a result, poetry often provides an intensified linguistic experience, more concentrated and often more profound than prose (Ryken, 1992).

Poetry taps into the human capacity to symbolize, form and activate semantic associations, and produce mental imagery, offering a richer, fuller and deeper encounter with meaning-content than might otherwise occur (and making use of more brain regions, in the process). Symbols, metaphors and mental images often add connotations to bare facts or propositions that can produce past memories, valuable emotions and unique insights and foster a deeper appropriation of truth. Research has found that such experiences can be a profitable means of soul-healing (Battino, 2002; Shorr, 1974; Shorr, Sobel, Robin & Connella, 1980), and the Bible is filled with such literary devices (see Ryken, Wilhoit & Longman, 1998). We might add that one of the benefits of internalizing biblical figurative language is that readers learn how to read their own lives figuratively. Being rejected by others is made more meaningful by "seeing it" as something else, for example, an identification with Christ and his purposes, rather than simply a tragic, painful tale, "signifying nothing."

Psalm. Besides having the kinds of poetic features noted above, the Psalms are singularly important for soul care because—of all the canonical texts—none deal so honestly and transparently with the vicissitudes of human life and the emotions that accompany it, and all within a theocentric framework of worship (Allender & Longman, 1990; Langley, 2002). A number of distinct subgenres have been identified within the Psalter, including psalms of praise, thanksgiving, celebration, lament and imprecation (Klein, Blomberg & Hubbard, 1993), each of which addresses a different aspect of psychospiritual well-being. For example, praise and thanksgiving psalms are meant to lift one's spirits by focusing attention on the good God and his blessings, the lament psalms exemplify the resolute pouring out of one's sorrows to God, and even the imprecation psalms demonstrate how to deal with the aggression of others (expressing one's anger to God and asking *him* to bring about justice as opposed to vengefully responding in kind and so escalating the aggression). Reading or assigning a psalm in soul care is a common pastoral practice because of the psalms' universal relevance to human life.

Wisdom literature. This genre is probably the most directly applicable to the practice and interests of soul care, and Proverbs, Job and Ecclesiastes are its primary canonical examples (and some psalms may be included in this genre, Murphy, 1996). Wisdom literature could be considered ancient "life coaching," since it offers practical guidance in how to live successfully before God and avoid patterns of behavior and thought that are both harmful to the self (Prov 6:32; 8:36) and contrary to God's ways (Prov 22:22-23; Eccles 12:13-14; Osborne, 1991). Ecclesiastes describes the journey of one who has failed in numerous attempts at finding satisfaction in life apart from God and has come to the conclusion that full satisfaction cannot be found "under the sun" but only in God. The book of Job addresses suffering—the perennial concern in soul care—in a God-centered way that also demonstrates spiritual development in the life of faith. At the same time it offers a portrait of poor soul care on the part of Job's friends (who anticipate the Pharisees).

Proverb. Proverbs constitute the genre most associated with the wisdom tradition. A proverb is "a brief statement of universally accepted truth formulated in such a way as to be memorable" (Osborne, 1991, p. 195). In the book of Proverbs there is a focus on individual success or failure, correlated with the virtue or vice one practices (Murphy, 1990). Many pearls of counseling wisdom are found in this book, like

> Pleasant words are a honeycomb,
> Sweet to the soul and healing to the bones. (Prov 16:24)

and

> Like one who takes off a garment on a cold day, or like vinegar on soda,
> Is he who sings songs to a troubled heart. (Prov 25:20)

Most relevant to our concerns is the fact that many, if not most, of its maxims are related to the well-being of the soul. The fool is a figure with many symptoms of psychopathology and the wise person is the epitome of psychospiritual excellence.

A common mistake made by Christians when reading or preaching from Proverbs is to assume unwittingly that the moral excellence it advocates is obtained by one's own efforts. By contrast, a Christocentric interpretation recognizes that the wise person described is fulfilled only in Christ—in whom are hid the treasures of wisdom and knowledge (Col 2:3)—whereas we are all the fool, by nature. Consequently, a New Testament use of the book of Proverbs for the purposes of soul care will seek to insure that it is recontextualized by the gospel of grace. Otherwise, reading Proverbs will tend to promote either self-righteousness or despair.

Prophetic literature. The prophetic corpus is large and there is much that could be commented upon. To narrow our focus, we will consider only a single set of themes common in prophetic literature: the restatement of the law and the consequences of current disobedience. We read there declarations of God's outrage at his people's continual resistance to his ways and the resultant pronouncement of curses upon them, as well as a corollary, ongoing call for repentance and the promise of coming redemption. This dialectical, alternating cursing-and-blessing message takes up most of the prophetic texts and indicates something of the complexity of God's views of things. On the one hand, in no uncertain terms, the repeated revelation of God's anger shows his holy opposition to those who disobey his Law and so deserve divine punishment. This message is given to heighten an awareness of human guilt and shame—important emotions that are supposed to correspond to God's values. Yet, on the other hand, his faithfulness to his wayward children is a sign of his enormous patience and forbearance, which should incite hope in the wayward repentant.

Surely much of the prophetic tone and message is difficult to read and receive (especially by those whose parents were excessively angry or harsh). However, the New Covenant believer reads it with the benefit of knowing the self-sacrificial way the triune God simultaneously fulfilled his judgment on sin and promise of salvation: through a uniting of both in God's own bearing of our well-deserved punishment in Christ. As a result, New Covenant believers can allow the New Testament's message of superabundant, overcoming grace in Christ to illuminate the message of God's anger and disappointment with the sin of God's people, to uncover personal ongoing resistance to God and to purify their soul and purge it of more of its remaining corruption. By itself, the prophetic message is deeply discouraging (Jeremiah's depression was warranted!), and people who are very discouraged—and especially if they are depressed—will likely not benefit much from it. However, as the grace of New Covenant salvation is increasingly appropriated, the believer will have greater capacity for the kind of self-reflection and sense of personal responsibility the prophetic message calls for, leading the believer gradually—ideally—to greater conformity to Christ.

Instruction. The way many Christians approach the Bible, one might assume it is primarily a textbook filled with doctrine, but explicit instruction does not make up as much of the Bible as we might think. Most of the instruction in the Bible is indirect, occurring incidentally through prayers to God (as in many of the psalms), prophetic declarations regarding God and narrative discourses that reveal characteristics of God and humans. There is little of the kind of formal instruction one finds in modern textbooks. We have already examined the book of Proverbs, which does consist largely of direct moral teaching, but since it uses the proverb format, it was treated as a distinct genre. The closest approximation to a genre of instruction besides the Proverbs is found in the Gospels and epistles of the New Testament.

Let us consider the Gospels first. The parables make up as much as a third of Jesus' overt teaching (Osborne, 1991). However, they are admittedly a difficult genre to interpret. As a matter of fact, Jesus factored that difficulty into his teaching, using parables to conceal as much as to reveal (Mt 13:10-17).

Nevertheless, Christ's parables are profound teaching tools, accessible to children and those untrained in formal thought, since they draw spiritual lessons from stories of everyday experiences, similar to allegory (Klein, Blomberg & Hubbard, 1993; Osborne, 1991). Perhaps the most significant aspect of his parabolic teaching is its value as an "encounter mechanism" that forces upon the hearer/reader a decision to choose for or against Christ and the kingdom he is describing (Osborne, 1991). Parables can be used in soul care to challenge some of the maladaptive preconceptions of Christians today and to foster a "re-framing" paradigm shift that can reorient them to think about their situation in more godly ways (Capps, 1981).

However, Christ also engaged in explicit instruction. Christians reckon his Sermon on the Mount (Mt 5—7) and upper-room discourse (Jn 14—16) to be the richest spiritual teaching ever recorded. Much of his teaching had direct soul-care application: the value of suffering (Mt 5.1-11), anxiety about physical needs (Mt 6:25-34), the obtaining of peace (Jn 14:27), encouragement to abide or dwell in Christ (Jn 15:1-7) and the help of the Spirit (Jn 14:26; 15:26; 16:7-16). These kinds of passages can be used directly in soul care, read in session or assigned for "soul-work" during the week.

Instruction in the epistles. But the mother lode of biblical teaching is found in the New Testament epistles, the apostolic letters written primarily to instruct the church in the significance and application of the gospel of Christ (though they also include some material one finds in a personal letter). Gospel instruction forms the backbone of the educational content of the Christian faith, and it has foundational value for soul care and psychospiritual development. The aretegenic material in the apostles' letters is so rich it defies a brief summarization, but it includes radiant doctrine about God (including his preeminent values), the significance of Christ's person and work, the nature of his salvation, moral instruction based in grace, as well as the fundamentals for building a new self-representation in Christ (Chamblin, 1993; Dunn, 1998; Ladd, 1974; Ridderbos, 1975; Schreiner, 2001). The personal nature of the epistles shows how the law and gospel are to permeate all of life: from the smallest details of one's day, through the mechanics of running a church, to the grand redemptive-historical narrative context of one's story. Christian soul-care providers help their counselees by encouraging them to meditate on the choicest epistolary passages dealing directly with soul-care issues (like Rom 5—8; Col 2—3; Eph 1—2; 4; 1 Pet 1—2; 1 John).

Apocalyptic literature. This genre is one of the least represented in the Bible (though there are a number of extracanonical examples), but it is a genre that many people, including non-Christians, are curious about. Biblical apocalyptic is found primarily in Daniel, Zechariah and especially the book of Revelation. According to Osborne (1991), it is a future-oriented text characterized by a description of the spiritual battle between God and his people on one side and Satan and the rest of God's enemies on the other; it conveys a pessimism towards the present age (which is the focus of divine judgment), the hope of divine deliverance for the followers of God and a theocentric outlook that assumes God is in control and will be victorious in the end. In addition, biblical apocalyptic makes much use of symbolism and figurative imagery, providing a literarily rich, suggestive tapestry for interpreting the realization of God's purposes in human history. Only a few examples of its soul-care value can be mentioned here.

To begin with, apocalyptic literature teaches that in the midst of the seemingly chaotic events of the contemporary world, God's will is being worked out and accomplished. This is revealed to encourage suffering believers, whose lives are being drawn into God's purposes, and this sometimes entails suffering. In spite of evidence to the contrary, the good God will succeed, and he will bring his people with him. In addition, the knowledge of divine judgment and vindication can be helpful for those recovering from abuse. Biblical apocalyptic also makes abundant reference to such soul-resonant symbols as water, fire, blood, robes and light, inviting the believer to be moved and changed by their imagery. Learning how to soak in such figurative language also equips the reader to see the divine symbolism that permeates all of life and that gives human activity some of its spiritual significance. Lastly, while it is easy to be distracted by interpretive puzzles in the text, the pervasive theocentrism of biblical apocalyptic (consider Rev 4—5) helps New Testament believers gain a wiser perspective on the world: they are in the midst of a profound battle for the souls of humankind, a battle that the holy, loving and sovereign God will win.

We should conclude this section on genre by noting that every genre has the same divine author. Divine authorship guarantees that, amidst the plurality of genres, there is an overarching set of redemptive purposes uniting their diversity into a single redemptive text intended to draw believers into conformity with God's Son.

The Biblical Text as Subversive Interpreter

One of the most forbidding aspects of the canon is its role as the unmasker of the human heart. "For the word of God is living and active and sharper than any two-edged sword, and piercing as far as the division of soul and spirit, of both joints and marrow, and able to judge the thoughts and intentions of the heart" (Heb 4:12). The author of Hebrews was referring specifically to the good news that has been preached to believers regarding Christ (Heb 4:2, 6, 14). However, since the Bible is the inspired record of that good news, it is by extension included within its scope. Consequently, the Bible is to be read in such a way that its light illumines reality, including the reality of the human heart, and such light sometimes causes pain, something humans are inherently disposed to avoid. As Søren Kierkegaard (1851/1990) opined, "If there were not so many illusions and self-deceptions, certainly everyone would admit as I do: I hardly dare to be alone with God's Word" (p. 32). The Bible poses a threat to our defenses. It is a surgical text; the master-text that uncovers the secret texts of our hearts.

Alas, the human heart is so deceitful, it is capable of rendering Scripture impotent. We can use the Bible in ways that inflate our narcissism and lead us to glorify ourselves. And God is willing to allow this. In fact, he speaks, at times, *in order to* harden the heart: "You will keep on hearing, but will not understand, and you will keep on seeing, but will not perceive; for the heart of this people has become dull, and with their ears they scarcely hear, and they have closed their eyes, lest they should see with their eyes and hear with their ears, and understand with their heart and turn again, and I should heal them" (Is 6.9; quoted in Mt 13:14-15). Ultimately, God will not be mocked. He is sovereign and rules over all things—overruling all things for his purposes and glory, even the abuse of his Scripture. Yet, we must say, reflecting the tenor of that word, that God delights in repentance and not in hardness of heart (Ezek 18:23, 32; 2 Pet 3:9).

So we are to understand that the Bible was given, at least in part, to unveil our hearts and reduce the hardness and breadth of its defensive structures (Johnson & Burroughs, 2000). Girard (1987) understands the Bible as the world's grand disclosive text, given by God to uncover the unconscious "scapegoat mechanism" that leads all communities to blame some individual or minority for their ills and then to do some form of violence to them in order to reduce the frustration of their unsatisfied desires. He believes that the Bible is the only text in the world that has revealed the existence of this mechanism. Though Girard's understanding of the cross has serious weakness, his biblically molded grasp of the scapegoat mechanism is dead-on (see Vanhoozer, 2004, for a constructive critique of Girard).

But the Scripture's subversive agenda is far more extensive than the fundamental issue Girard identified. It was given to disturb the peace and break open the opposition of the human heart to God and the Good by unveiling the unseen and unconscious autocentric dynamics that pervade human action, *even religious action in the name of God*, and lead to all human violence against others. The centrality of the figures of the Pharisees in the Gospel texts should alert Christians to this agenda. God's most ardent followers killed God's Son? How is this possible? Because of the radical deceitfulness of indwelling sin, it was necessary that God inspire a text, fixed for all time, calling to us from outside of ourselves, that would have as one of its primary perlocutionary agendas the subversion of pride and disclosure of our own hearts as we read.

The believer is to be the "text's convert" (Patterson, 1999, p. 54). God, through the Bible, teaches his child how to read.

> What the reader, as thus interpreted by the texts, has to learn about him or herself is that it is only the self as transformed through and by the reading of the texts which will be capable of reading the texts aright. So the reader, like any learner within a craft-tradition, encounters an apparent paradox at the outset, . . . it seems that only by learning what the texts have to teach can he or she come to read those texts aright, but also that only by reading them aright can he or she learn what the texts have to teach. (MacIntyre, 1990, p. 82)

Ultimately, one of the most important psychospiritual tasks facing the believer on the journey toward God is to become a reader who allows the Bible to interpret him or her through a hermeneutics of humility (Vanhoozer, 1998). These interpretive practices allow one to receive the message of Scripture profitably, that is, at the cost of one's self. In fact, there is no other way to read properly the biblical text than for it to lead first to the divestiture of one's self (Gal 2:20; Rom 6:6; Eph 4:23-25) and one's idols, and then to the resurrection of a new self in Christ (Col 3:9-10; Eph 4:23-25; 2 Cor 5:17). For all this, we clearly need God's help. So when we read, we must pray.

Dogmatic Schemes Relevant for Psychology and Soul Care

There is not room in this chapter to describe adequately the biblical material relevant for Christian soul care (that book, we hope, is forthcoming, Johnson & Langberg, 2009), but at least a few of its distinctives should be mentioned. These schemes provide some of the main means by which Christians should interpret human beings, as well as other psychology texts, and they form much of the unique soul-healing content of Christian soul care.

The redemptive-historical metanarrative and Christ. The Bible can be read as a metanarrative of human nature and history composed of four fundamental redemptive-historical events—which are also paradigmatic perspectives on the human condition—creation, fall, redemption and consummation (Boston, 1720/n.d.; Dooyeweerd, 1984; Plantinga, 2002; Spykman, 1992; Van Til, 1955; Walsh & Middleton, 1984; Woltiers, 1985). To properly understand human beings Christianly and comprehensively, it is necessary to view them "simultaneously" from the standpoint of these four archetypal events of history.

The human race was created good and in the image of God (Gen 1); so humans were made to be like God in a creaturely way. That goodness and that image, derived from and reflecting God's goodness and form, cannot be destroyed (Gen 9:6; Jas 3:9). So the created nature of human beings today (including their biological and psychological structures) is primordially good (Woltiers, 1985). No living human therefore should ultimately despair.

However, the human race became corrupted through their original disobedience (Gen 3:7-8). As a result, all humans are now born in "original sin" and move inevitably away from their Creator. This results in a spiritual uncleanness they cannot remove by themselves, an uncleanness that has alienated them from God. They are also in bondage to the devil (Eph 2:1-3). Human suffering is a consequence of this fall into sin (Gen 3:16-19), so previously unexperienced pain, hardship and brokenness were introduced into the human condition, and some of that suffering is realized, we know now, through genetic abnormalities or environmental insults. In this world the sins of others and societal and institutional oppression can profoundly contribute to physiological and psychological damage. The movement away from God known as original sin is shaped by this brokenness into personal sins (actions, whether behavioral or merely internal) and eventually into vices (character patterns) that are contrary to God's character and purposes, for all of which humans are held responsible by God. These actions and patterns in turn compound human brokenness. As a result of their sin, humans possess objective shame and guilt that make them worthy of eternal punishment.

God's rescue of human beings from their plight, prophesied and anticipated throughout the Old Testament era, was accomplished through the coming of the Son of God—in his life, death and resurrection—in which he took upon himself the shame and guilt of those whose sin he bore (Is 53; Jn 1:29; Rom 3:21-25; 2 Cor 5:21). Christ's life, death and resurrection provides the central, organizing recapitulation of the biblical metanarrative: his life fulfills the creation of image-bearers; his death was God's judgment for sin; and his resurrection was the beginning of human redemption and points ahead to the consummation. In Christ's story we discover the divine reframing of our story and the pattern for our life.

Those who believe in and receive the Son are given new lives and selves, are forgiven and have their uncleanness taken away, are made perfectly righteous in Christ and adopted into God's family, and are reconciled to the triune God (Jn 3:5-7; Rom 5:1; 8:16-17; Col 3:9-10; 2 Cor 5:19-21; 1 Jn 1:3). No psychotherapeutic intervention is more momentous and significant than Christ's work of redemption, and nothing is more important for Christian soul care than the forgiveness, freedom, righteousness and goodness that come to the believer through it. To know one's shame and guilt are taken away and replaced with God's goodness in Christ is the divinely ordained way into a new life of recovery. All humans are to be understood as created and sinful; believers in Christ are also to be viewed from the standpoint of redemption.

Finally, the human story ends in an astonishing climax of appraisal and consignment to one's eternal destiny. For believers, the consummation will be the everlasting, undeserved fulfillment of the redemption begun in this age; and for those who resisted the signs of God in their lives (Rom 1:20), it will mean the loss of whatever grace they enjoyed in this life, constituting an eternal separation from God and endless misery. The age to come has undeniable implications for soul care in this age. It places an immeasurable momentousness on human life and draws believers to encourage unbelievers to convert to Christ—in the light of eternity, evangelism is the most profound advocacy of a person's ultimate well-being imaginable. Christians learn to interpret their past and current experiences in the light of eternity, which casts a transforming hue on the former, making the suffering of this life easier to bear (2 Cor 4:17).

The covenants of grace. The concept of the covenant is also a pervasive theme in the Bible (Horton, 2002). God deals with people in terms of covenant, an agreement entered into by at least two parties. The biblical covenants are established by God with humans in order to provide a gracious, relational-volitional context within which they are to relate to each other, each fulfilling their covenantal commitments. The covenant is important psychospiritually, because it makes possible the development of human personhood in committed relationship with God. As noted above, the best and most important of these covenants is the New Covenant, an agreement offered by the triune God to any who believe in the Son of God, by whose death the covenant was ratified.

Christ, the primary focus of the Christian life. The Bible is mostly about the Lord Jesus Christ, the Son of God. He is the mediator between the triune God and humanity and has provided the only form of soul-healing sanctioned by God, through his life, death and resurrection. He is the way, the truth and the life, terms that point to his centrality in soul-healing. Genuine Christian soul care is *Christocentric* and attempts to take all treatment captive to Christ (see 2 Cor 10:5), so that God in Christ might receive the greatest glory. Christian soul care, then, is trialogical and always intrinsically involves at least three persons: the soul-care provider, the counselee and Christ. Prayer to Christ in Christian counseling would seem to be as natural as breathing.

Christian soul care attempts to draw the believer into greater communion with Christ, based on the believer's God-established union with Christ through faith in him. Christ is the source of true life (Jn 1:4; 5:21; 6:33; 8:12; 10:10; 11:25; 14:6), so a Christian's soul is healed as he or she abides in Christ (Jn 15:1-7), beholds him (2 Cor 3:18), knows his love (Eph 3:19) and lives in his name (Col 3:17). As a result, Christian soul care works at helping believers to realize and experience their unfathomable privileges in Christ through communion with him and the Father (1 Jn 1:3). This theme will be further explored in chapter twelve.

The fundamental priority of declarative salvation over reformative salvation. When individuals deeply believe the gospel, God performs certain declarative speech-acts with reference to them: he pronounces them to be justified, sanctified, adopted and beloved (Rom 3:22-24; 5:1; 8:16; 1 Cor 1:30; 6:11; Col 3:12). And God's performative speech does not return void. If he says they are righteous, then they are. Declarative salvation is the speech of heaven: believers are told they are now seated with Christ in the heavenlies (Eph 2:6) and blessed there with every spiritual blessing (Eph 1:3). Thenceforth, the Christian is to receive that word, more and more deeply, thoroughly and pervasively, so that it comes to transform his or her inner and outer life.

Modern counseling offers a secular substitute for the gospel of declarative salvation by attempting to assure people that they do not need to be saved since they are basically fine in themselves. Essentially it recommends a human-centered declaration of goodness. But this will not suffice for one who realizes that there are no grounds for one human to pronounce another clean, since deep down we all feel ourselves to be unclean.

The grace-law dynamic. According to the Puritan theologian John Owen (1954), God's Word summarily consists of the law and the gospel (p. 177). God's covenant entails obligations. A Christianity that produced no greater obedience or conformity to God would not be worthy of the holy God. The law is the description of God's character and purposes revealed for us, so that we might be more like God. However, because of sin, no human is capable of fulfilling the law of God perfectly (except Christ), and the law demands perfection. So the law reveals our sinful shortcomings and must condemn us, leading us to self-despair, unless . . . unless we become seduced into self-righteous self-deception (like the Pharisees), and identify ourselves with the law: the perennial religious "escape."

But the law, rightly (honestly) understood, only brings sinners into judgment. In that context alone can we hear God's declarative salvation sounding from above—the *gift* of righteousness, the *gift* of grace. Grace is God's unmerited favor toward us in Christ; it is the source of God's declarative salvation, and to grasp its meaning by faith is to obtain forgiveness, peace, contentment and the power to move toward God.

Maturation in Christian personhood and character formation is derived from the dialectical interplay of these two orders of meaning: law and grace. The law shows believers their sin and convicts them, and grace heals them of their guilt and shame and tells them of their perfection in Christ. Grace then encourages them to seek to become more like their loving Father, and the law then shows them what that likeness looks like. But the law will inevitably convict again, directing their attention more deeply into their hearts and its motives and self-deception, leading them again to Christ and the grace they need and have in him. On and on, deeper and deeper, higher and higher this spiraling process draws the believer, ever closer to Christ by the power of the Spirit. (Bonhoeffer, 1985, offers a helpful discussion of this dynamic.)

The already/not-yet tension. Believers also need to be reminded of the partial nature of their redemption in this age. God's declaration of perfect salvation is actually a verbal *precursor*, an eschatological harbinger of the complete salvation that is to come. In this age, the believer only experiences the "firstfruits" of salvation (Rom 8:23), the "pledge" of the Holy Spirit (2 Cor 1:22), resulting in the beginnings of the perfect transformation to come. Consequently, the believer's actual character in this age is always deficient, always compromised by what the Puritans called "remaining sin." There must be some spiritual likeness to God, or there has been no true change, but there is always more psychospiritual progress that can be made. This realization is very important, since a person's lack of perfection can itself be a major source of depression, anxiety and frustration. Apart from resting in their perfect salvation in Christ, believers are to be consoled by looking ahead to their completed perfection, that is to be revealed when Christ comes again (1 Jn 3:3).

The centrality of the triune God. Perhaps the one topic that most distinguishes a Christian worldview from all others is the place of the triune God in the system. According to Jonathan Edwards (1765/1998), the triune God—Father, Son and Holy Spirit—is infinitely the greatest being there is and all other things are by comparison insignificant. Consequently, the only fitting stance is to recognize God's supremacy and live in light of that realization. Having created humans to be virtuous, God made them also to be God-centered, to live out of a theocentric orientation, since any other way of living would be radically deficient, distorted, inappropriate and illegitimate. As a result, it must be intrinsically mentally healthy for humans to be theocentrically oriented. Christian soul care, then, will seek to enhance the capacity of others to center their lives on the triune God.

The love of God and neighbor. But how does one center oneself on God? It would not be enough to know objectively that God is the greatest being and yet not to care; to genuinely center oneself on God, one would also have to perceive his beauty. One's heart would have to be drawn out to this God; one would have to love and delight in this God with all one's heart, soul, mind and strength. According to the Bible, there is no more pressing responsibility and no greater privilege than the love of God (Deut 6:5; Mt 22:36-37). But there is a second responsibility (and privilege) related to it, the love of one's neighbor (Mt 22:39; see Kierkegaard, 1847/1946b; O'Donovan, 1986). The Bible teaches that these two commandments are indissolubly related (Jas 3:9;

1 Jn 2—4). Augustine (1997, p. 32) called them a "double love"; and O'Donovan (1986, chap. 11), "the double aspect of the moral life." Christianity, therefore, is fundamentally relational, and foundationally it seeks the glory (or happiness) of God and others. Since in a Christian framework, these directives go hand-in-hand, Christian soul care strives to realize both aspects. The psychospiritual implications of this dialectic have scarcely been explored.

Human fulfillment through conformity to Christ for the glory of God. This heading summarizes all the foregoing and succinctly states the Bible's main aretegenic theme. Human fulfillment, flourishing and true virtue are realized through becoming more like Christ, the perfect human being. God's glory is the end for which we were made, but a human being cannot glorify God any better than by becoming more like him. Growing desires to be like him that are realized in an increasingly Christlike life signify to the world the unsurpassable worth of God and contribute to God's glory. So, Christian soul care, above all else, seeks to foster Christlikeness.

Multiple Christian Psychologies

Finally, it must be conceded that this book has so far been somewhat misleading. It would terribly naïve to assume that there will ever be only one Christian psychology in this age. Many different interpretive approaches to the Bible have arisen within the Christian community—consider the diverse subgroups within the Roman Catholic and Eastern Orthodox communion (regional, ideological and institutional), as well as the slightly more obvious subtraditions that make up the Protestant communion—and it would be unworthy of a Christian psychology to downplay these differences. Rather than this being an argument against a Christian psychology (Jones, 1986), these differences will contribute to its richness and fruitfulness. Indeed, I write this as an evangelical Baptist descended from the magisterial Reformation, one who believes that total set of assumptions to be the most faithful to God's (with all due respect to my brothers and sisters). But a belief in the validity of those assumptions is obviously not shared by all members in good standing of the body of Christ. Moreover, the superiority of any subtradition can only be contended for; it cannot be legislated. It is only through dialogue with other Christian communities that the strengths of one's own community's distinctives can be tested and demonstrated (if they survive)—the worst that can happen is one's own subtradition is enriched. This is an inevitable and happy result of human finitude, which can only begin to approximate God's comprehensive understanding through the polyphony of multiple traditions (Bakhtin, 1981; Hart, 2003; Vanhoozer, 2005). As a result, we can gratefully recognize that in this age a Christian psychology will always be constituted by a number of viable Christian psychologies. So let us get to work, and let us work together.

In this chapter we have introduced the subject of how to interpret and use the Christian's primary text for Christian psychology and soul care. Having gotten our bearings, we might say, our next hermeneutical task is significantly more challenging.

Notes

[1]Though illocutions may also have multiple meanings (or "illocutionary points"), one of which is usually primary (Briggs, 2001).

[2]The position presented here has been termed a "new covenant" approach (Wells & Zaspel, 2002) or a "modified Lutheran" approach (Moo, 1993).

[3]In the interests of soul care, we must remember that some readers will tend to be discouraged by heroic narratives, for example, those whose self-representations are severely damaged and who have little faith.

7

Translating the Texts of Other Communities for Christian Soul Care

BY 1879 THE CHRISTIAN CHURCH HAD ACCUMULATED a wealth of religious literature on human beings and the care of their souls. This literature had been written over a period of thirty centuries and included the canonical Scriptures and much else—some of it intellectually rigorous and much of it good for the soul—a body of discourse that may be one of the greatest legacies of the church. However, in the short space of the past 125 years, a much more voluminous, extensive and scientifically rigorous literature on human beings and their psychological care has arisen, composed from within a modern disciplinary matrix. This latter literature has far eclipsed the former in value in the minds of most Western intellectuals (including some Christian counselors). And as has already been suggested, this succession in psychological literatures has contributed to an epistemological and soul-care crisis for the Christian community from which it has not yet recovered.

On the one hand, core aspects of modern psychology's disciplinary matrix are antithetical to some of the most important beliefs Christians hold that bear on human beings and their care. Without God in any of its theories, how helpful can modern soul care be to a theocentric Christian community? On the other hand, its comprehensive and sophisticated description of innumerable lesser psychological matters is astounding. Consider its contributions in neuropsychology, memory, intelligence, language, emotions, cognitive and social development, personality traits and what influences them, the *DSM-IV-TR,* biopsychosocial causes of psychopathology, models and strategies of psychotherapy, group influences and family dynamics, to name a very few. Though certainly not beyond criticism, modern psychology's accomplishments constitute genuine scientific advances and deserve to be incorporated into a comprehensive Christian understanding of human beings.

As we have repeatedly noted, Christians today differ considerably in how to respond to modern psychology and soul care. This chapter concerns how members of the Christian tradition—constituted by its God-centered and Bible-based orientation to human beings and their care—might best consider the discourse of the more recent tradition of modern psychology—a secular, empirical research-based orientation: two very different traditions with the same object of inquiry and treatment. According to MacIntyre (1984), a living intellectual tradition is "an historically extended, socially embodied argument, and an argument precisely in part about the goods which constitute that tradition" (p. 220). It is characterized by conflict, signified by internal debate about its own nature and values (its goods), interaction with the ideas of other living traditions *from the standpoint of its own tradition*, and its being taken seriously by those other traditions (MacIntyre, 1984, 1988, 1990). By the first of these standards, the Christian psychology and soul-care tradition is alive, but according to the last two, it has not been very well for quite some time.[1]

In the last two chapters we explored the role of Scripture as the primary text in the Christian psychology tradition. In this chapter we will consider how Christians can interpret the texts of the modern psychology tradition in such a way that the Christian tradition is itself strengthened and enriched, and not diluted or compromised. First, we shall reflect on the task of reading Christianly.

Christian Literacy: The Preparatory Task of Learning to Read

Reading is foundational to human life as we know it. Without it, there would be no philosophical traditions, no science and no technology. A complex religion also depends upon literacy, as a system of worship requires a common and fixed doctrine, stories and moral norms. As a result, "Religious learning involves reading. More than that, it is largely constituted by reading" (Griffith, 1999, p. 40). The following are some principles related to Christian reading that will guide the rest of the chapter.

Six guidelines for Christian reading.

1. The goal of Christian reading is conformity to Christ's mind, heart and life. This goal is the end of creatures made in God's image. When Christians read—even for the good of leisure—they should do so in a way that generally advances their conformity to Christ. Therefore, *what* and *how* they read has significance.
2. The Holy Spirit is the Christian's reading light. "In Your light we see light" (Ps 36:9). Fallen human beings need to read with divine assistance. Reading is necessarily dialogical (between author and reader); Christian reading is trialogical, for in addition to the human author, the Christian reading of a text is shared with and dependent upon the Holy Spirit.
3. The first task of wisdom is to find wisdom, but wisdom is needed to know where to look. Augustine (and Plato before him) recognized that growth in wisdom involves a paradox: How does one obtain enough wisdom to know how to get more? Augustine believed the first step is to recognize one's folly, and the second is to look for wise guides (MacIntyre, 1990). "He who walks with the wise grows wise, but a companion of fools suffers harm" (Prov 13:20 NIV). Therefore, the immature, especially, need to entrust their learning to wiser authorities. As one grows wiser oneself, one learns how to properly interpret discourse more wisely. By reading Christian "guides," the reader acquires the standards internal to Christianity by which to read well and gradually develops the ability to discern truth and error, superior texts and inferior (Stock, 1996). "On Augustine's views the powers of discrimination which are required to judge rightly in understanding secular literature can themselves become an expression of peculiarly Christian virtues" (MacIntyre, 1990, p. 83).
4. Texts need to be prioritized. Reading Christian texts, then, becomes a sort of literacy training ground for the Christian's general reading. The reader therefore needs a hierarchical scheme for categorizing texts (Griffith, 1999; MacIntyre, 1990; Stock, 1996).

   The canon. As has already been established, the Bible is the Christian's *arch-text*. "For the religious reader the [canon] is an object of overpowering delight and great beauty. It can never be discarded because it can never be exhausted. It can only be reread, with reverence and ecstasy" (Griffith, 1999, p. 42). Because the Bible alone is inspired and infallible, it is the *only* text that is deemed good for the soul without qualification. As Christian readers gradually become *biblicized*—so that they grasp more clearly the first principles of the faith (or a Christian worldview or metanarrative) and learn to distinguish them from those of alternative frameworks—they can turn to read other texts with more interpretive confidence, using the Bible, we might say, as their *reading glasses* (to adjust Calvin's metaphor a bit).

Classic texts of the Christian traditions. Reading one's canon leads naturally to exposition and composition (Griffith, 1999), producing a Christian literature that, first, has reflected upon the canon, and second, has reflected canonically upon the rest of reality. As a result, the Christian reader can get further schooling in Christian wisdom by reading noncanonical Christian writings, particularly the classics of the various Christian traditions: those that demonstrate unusual canonically guided insight and passion.

Of course, few in the West grow up in a Christianly pristine environment, exposed to undiluted canonical and classic Christian writings (and it is not clear that that is the best way to learn discernment anyway). As this process actually occurs in most cases, the first stirrings of Christian wisdom may be the *realization,* at some point (usually in early adulthood), of the aretegenic significance of the canon and the classics. Thereafter, "wisdom apprentices" learn to go back, again and again, to the canon and the classics, in light of new learning and exposure to novel ideas, in order to deepen their understanding of a Christian hermeneutic and further develop their reading skills.

Other quality texts. Next, Christians ought to read other texts of value, for informative, literary, scientific, pragmatic or leisure purposes, whether written by Christians or not. A holistic, theocentric Christian life (in contrast to a merely pietistic life) leads Christians into God's creation and human culture for the glory of God. This entails lots of reading on lots of topics, subject to personal interest and calling. Christians interested in psychology today must read quality psychology texts by non-Christians in order to become well informed about psychology, particularly since so many good psychology texts have been written over the past one hundred years outside the Christian traditions.

Inferior texts. The Christian reader also learns to recognize texts that are poor. They are not valuable, in any sense, so they are not worth reading.

Sadly, many such books can be found on the bookshelves of Christian bookstores and the self-help sections of their mainstream counterparts.

Bad texts. Christian readers also come to the recognition that some texts are actually bad for the soul: material that may be well-written in some sense and intellectually captivating, but ultimately seems likely to draw people away from the genuinely Good, True or Beautiful. Such assessments are especially important to discourage the immature or less mature from reading them while they are still being trained in the first principles of the faith. However, the church needs at least some Christians to read bad texts, first in order to respond to them, and second, to educate others regarding their contents. But such individuals are specially called to such tasks and out to be especially mature.

Banned texts. In some cases, religious traditions have developed an "index" of texts that are deemed irredeemably harmful (Griffith, 1999). Westerners are keenly aware of the potential for mischief and folly here. Indeed, in light of the Inquisition, Nazi Germany and twentieth-century religious fundamentalism, wise Christians have learned to be suspicious of often well-meaning but still overzealous "book burners." The noetic effects of sin show up here, as well. As a result, Christians should be very hesitant to consign works to such status, as a rule. At the same time, caution should not lead us to reject this category altogether, but to improve our judgment. Texts must not be banned without good warrant, but most Westerners would agree that some texts deserve such designation (pedophiliac magazines, at least), and mature Christians would likely consign more than modernists.

However, with regard to psychology texts specifically, it is hard to conceive of a work today that would warrant the label "banned" or even "bad" across the board. What scientific book written to describe some feature of human beings—regardless of its underlying worldview—could be legitimately considered by Christians to be *that* pernicious? Even evolutionary psychology research texts on mating behavior present information that ought to be of interest to the Christian scholarly community. Perhaps the issue here is actually developmental. Wisdom has some idea of developmental differences and does not wish to place stumbling blocks before the young (Mt 18:6) or the weak (1 Cor 8; Rom 14). So, for example, highly worldview-distorted psychology texts should probably not be assigned to most Christian high school students, because of the vulnerability of some of them. But publicly banning such works from general Christian readership, in our day, would simply create more interest—hardly the result the wise are seeking. On the other hand, there will be plenty of opportunities for the wise to advise the less mature to avoid some books, out of an informed determination that they simply are not good for their souls.

5. Noncanonical texts need to be read with a hermeneutics of both trust and suspicion. Christianity teaches that all humans are born with a sin-motive that distorts their minds and hearts (and therefore their discourse). Applying the antithesis principle to the reading of texts composed by non-Christians leads to a hermeneutics of suspicion (Ricoeur, 1965b), which in turn results in an attitude of *dissent* toward that which is discerned to be error, according to one's prior (Christian) understanding. In fact, the Reformation has taught us that this hermeneutic is even warranted when reading noncanonical *Christian* literature. Christians need always to ask when reading: What is distorted in this account, and what is being left out?

   Moreover, since Christian readers began their journey into wisdom with a recognition of their own folly, they maintain continually a hermeneutics of suspicion *toward their own tradition and understanding*, as well. Their accumulation of wisdom increases a grace-based self-criticism—not one that is falsely humble or hypercritical of oneself, but one that is increasingly discerning of one's limitations and probable blind spots, and that is truly humble and open to dialogue. This openness results from applying the creation grace principle to the reading of non-Christian texts, which also encourages a hermeneutic of trust—the expectation that reading invariably leads to greater understanding of some kind. This, in turn, results in an attitude of *consent* toward that which is true, good and beautiful, whatever the source. Discovering such goods brings glory to God, their ultimate source, particularly as they are appropriated into one's mind, heart and life, so that one is becoming more conformed to Christ.

   These two principles lead Christians to read the texts of other worldview communities *mindfully*—that is *dialectically* or *dialogically*—with core Christian understandings salient and prone to activation, but also open to learning from God and others, so that they are equipped to consent and dissent appropriately, as they read.

6. Reading non-Christian texts wisely increases wisdom. Only God's mind is comprehensive and exhaustive—our individual/communal understanding

is necessarily finite and fallen. So, in order to become more conformed to the mind, heart and life of God (at least in secondary matters), it is necessary for Christians to read other texts, including those written by non-Christians. At the very least, Christians can learn how non-Christians perceive them and think about spiritual matters (see Rainer, 2001) or even how their own religiousness can be self-serving (see Westphal, 1993). Reading thoughtful non-Christians can alert Christians to their own limitations, inconsistencies and blind spots, and to inadequacies in their own formulations. Moreover, if non-Christians have written texts that—according to Christian standards of rationality—appear to excel in describing certain aspects of reality (like human beings), Christians will increase in conformity to God's knowledge by reading those texts.

Though some texts are undeniably bad, it was never God's intention to protect humanity from bad texts. Consider God's permitting a serpent to question God's goodness. Adam and Eve tragically consented to that antithetic speech—but God turned that folly into a wondrous manifestation of his glory in redemption! Equally intriguing is the temptation of Christ, where he was exposed to discourse antithetical to God's Word—even the quotation of Scripture. Yet "he learned obedience from the things which he suffered," and was perfected through those sufferings (Heb 5:8-9). Our character, too, can be improved by such reading, and when non-Christians describe reality accurately, our knowledge will be increased as well. As a result, while everyone should not read everything—especially the immature—for those who are interested and called to do so, reading non-Christian texts can contribute to the glory of God. Having established that Christians should read such texts, we consider next what to do with them when we read.

The Task of Translation

It was suggested above that whether entirely aware of it or not, the Christian psychological community is in the midst of something of an epistemological and soul-care crisis, given the fact that the vast majority of the best psychology literature of the last 125 years has been composed by secularists who do psychology from within a decidedly different disciplinary matrix and edification framework. We are not dealing here with two different disciplines—psychology and theology—but with two different psychology communities,[2] each of which possesses a distinct psychological literature.

These literatures may be different enough from each other that we could liken them to two different languages. If that is so, the concept of integration may not be the best metaphor for the task facing the Christian soul-care community with reference to modern psychology literature, but *translation*. Such a proposal has been advanced by Alisdair MacIntyre (1988, 1990) with reference to similar problems in communication between the modern, postmodern and theistic moral philosophy communities. Translation depends on reading, but it is obviously more challenging, and according to MacIntyre (1988), it requires a number of special competencies: first, an "insider's" familiarity with the two language-systems with which one is working (so that they are both "first languages"), so that one can understand well what the *author* of the original text was trying to say *in his or her language*; second, the ability to recognize where translation is relatively easy, relatively difficult and even incommensurable, given the lack of comparable linguistic resources in the two languages; and third, the facility to render well the original text within the "receiving" language-system, given the communicative framework of *that* linguistic community.

At the same time, if the "integration" metaphor is too optimistic a label for the Christian's task in psychology, the term *translation* may imply too negative an assessment, since the worldview differences between Christians and secularists in psychology will have relatively lesser impact on their descriptions of many psychological topics (for example, discourse regarding lower-level phenomena—observables like neural firing, eye blinking, and behavior counts—and even many higher constructs, like visuospatial intelligence, hallucinations or extraversion). Because of the high degree of genuine commonality between Christians and modernists in a good deal of psychological discourse, perhaps their linguistic differences should be considered to be more on the order of distinct *dialects* than languages, since people who speak different dialects can usually understand each other to some extent. A dialect or idiom is a specific version of a language that may share many, but not all, of the linguistic features of another dialect of that language. But two moderately related dialects can still require translation, even when they share most of the same words, and, to extend the metaphor further, pronunciation may vary slightly across the entire vocabulary.

To be more specific to psychology, little translation will be needed (and perhaps simple integration will be enough) where the subdisciplines and specific focus are not much affected by worldview issues (neuropsychology and memory), whereas translation will be more necessary in areas which are more worldview-constituted (e.g., Christian discourse about the work of the Holy Spirit and secular discourse about the moral legitimacy of homosexuality, see chapter four for a discussion on worldview constituted beliefs). In the latter areas, the speech of one community may seem nearly unintelligible to the other, necessitating significant translation work before any appropriation should be attempted. Such decisions are decidedly of a hermeneutical nature.

With the above qualifications, the translation metaphor offers a different and possibly a more profitable way of conceiving of the Christian psychological community's interpretive task than does the modern understanding of integration. Integration seems to imply that the task is relatively unproblematic; the texts of modern psychology and Christian theology are all equally true; Christians simply need to read and put together the truth, like pieces of a puzzle. Translation, on the other hand, better conveys that there is a problem here; it suggests that the task begins with differences in communal interpretation, understanding and expression (including in some cases vocabulary) that must be taken seriously for genuine communication to occur—differences that arose in particular sociohistorical contexts. At the same time, we must avoid a kind of intellectual paranoia that sees differences where none actually exist.

Prerequisites for becoming a good translator. Just as in reading, Christian translators "begin" their task having been saturated with Scripture and the Christian traditions. "Begins" is in quotation marks because few contemporary Western Christians would be able to *initiate* their interpretation from within a Christian textual universe alone. From their youth, most Western Christians have read many kinds of texts from different worldview traditions, and if they are trained in the Western educational system, the main tradition they will have been exposed to is modernist. Consequently, most Christians know implicitly how to read in a modernist way, mindful of the goals of universality and neutrality regarding ultimate stances and ethical positions, and able to incorporate all texts within its "neutral" vista (see MacIntyre, 1984; Stout, 1981). Even Christians who work hard at canonical consistency have been exposed to modern reading norms and have undoubtedly been influenced by them. So, the notion of "beginning" translation with the canon and the traditions is a kind of Christian interpretive ideal that is never attainable. But this does not mean it is futile to aim at the ideal. In fact, we might say that this goal is an ongoing aspect of the working out of one's salvation and is nothing other than the renewal of the mind and heart from a way of life alienated from God to one increasingly conformed to and dependent upon the mind and heart of God.

At any rate, the first prerequisite for a Christian translator of modern psychology texts is a thorough knowledge of Christianity's own discourse of human nature. Obviously, this would be enhanced by the existence of a large, well-researched, scientifically sophisticated Christian psychology literature, integrally grounded in the Bible and the Christian traditions, but such does not currently exist. In the meantime, one's translation skills will be best cultivated by a thorough familiarity with the biblical canon and ideally at least some of the classic texts of the Christian traditions that bear on human nature. When translators become experienced and highly skilled readers of the corpus of their own tradition, it becomes what MacIntyre (1988) calls their "first language." However, as already intimated, we are using the metaphor "dialect" or "idiom," so we shall say that Christians need to become highly skilled readers of their own literature base, so that it is their *first dialect.*

The next prerequisite for becoming a Christian translator of modern psychology texts is a thorough knowledge of the idiom of human nature according to modern psychology. The challenge is to understand this second idiom *Christianly.* This task seems deceptively easier than it actually is for three reasons. First, as just acknowledged, Christians and non-Christians necessarily share much of the same vocabulary and understanding regarding human nature, inclining Christians to underestimate the degree of underlying conceptual divergence. Second, as we have seen, there are some subdisciplines and topics in psychology in which worldview beliefs make less of a substantive difference than others. Third, because modernist discourse was developed to be merely descriptive and to avoid reference to metaphysical and ethical issues that were deemed to be nonverifiable, modernist discourse tends not to make metaphysical or value claims that are explicitly non-Christian (e.g., "Turn from Christ!"). Rather, it poses a far subtler obstacle to Christian reconceptualization: the pervasive absence of ethical and theistic considerations. Sins of omission are always more difficult to identify than sins of commission.

Typically, naive Christian readers of a modern text understand less than they think they do, unaware of the mostly implicit, distorting worldview beliefs of its author. The modernist context of modern psychological discourse requires, then, that Christian translators become so proficient in the "second dialect" of the modern psychology tradition that they understand it as well as a first dialect (following MacIntyre, 1988, p. 374, we could call it a "*second* first dialect," but to avoid confusion, we will call it simply the *second* dialect, and we will call the "*first* first dialect," the person's "mother tongue" or "native tongue"). As a measure of such understanding, they should be able to pass as native modernist authors themselves. Otherwise, one could not be sure they were understanding the second dialect accurately. However, they must not become misled through reading the second dialect to read it as if it were their native tongue. Rather, they must interpret it *dialogically*—and not univocally—understanding as best as possible (1) what the modern author means, but (2) *from the standpoint of the native tongue*—with their own distinctive and relevant worldview beliefs always salient.

Let us pause here to note the difficulty that all this presents to those in the Christian psychological community. The vast majority of contemporary psychology graduate schools are modernist, and Christian counseling graduate schools originally had to be staffed by those trained in modernist institutions. (Here I should admit that I received my Ph.D. at Michigan State University.) As a result, most Christians in psychology actually become more proficient in the dialect of modern psychology than of the Christian. We have noted that Christian counseling programs typically require at least some coursework in Christian theology, recognizing that some familiarity with the dialect of the Christian tradition is valuable. However, much less time is typically spent working with the Christian dialect than the modernist, and for the most part comparatively little time is actually spent on closely comparing the two. As a result, at its best, the way Interdisciplinary Integration is often practiced amounts to a word-for-word translation, the only kind of translation of which the novice translator is capable.[3] This is a start, but far more helpful is the kind of sophisticated translation that people who know two dialects fluently (both as "first dialects") can do, so that they are able to translate either dialect into the other and back again, such that an experienced speaker/writer in either dialect would feel that either translation was essentially accurate. Such bilingualism is rare, and this has to change.

Traditional biblical counselors have their own translation predicament. To their credit they prize the Christian dialect of human nature and seek to be faithful to it. However, they typically refuse to become proficient in the dialect of the other traditions, and either ignore those texts or only read them to criticize them from the standpoint of the mother tongue (in a way that raises questions about their understanding of those texts). Essentially, they treat the psychology texts of other communities as if they were completely unintelligible and contained virtually no common vocabulary. An ignorance of the modern dialect and literature is, of course, considered a strength by some—it connotes a lack of contamination—but the other side of the coin is that it inevitably renders their evaluations of modern psychology suspect to those who know the dialect, since one cannot do interpretive justice to a body of texts one does not well understand.[4] As a result, their sometimes legitimate criticism of modern psychology goes largely unheeded by other Christian counselors.

In summary, an authentically Christian understanding of modern psychology texts requires first, proficiency in the Christian dialect, established by deep familiarity with the canon and the Christian traditions; then, second, fluency in the second dialect, but in such a way that the understanding of the native tongue is not compromised by the translator "forgetting" his or her first dialect through neglect—as sometimes happens when immigrant children eventually forget how to speak their native tongue. The Christian's native tongue must remain the "master-dialect" by continual, faithful reading of the canon and the Christian traditions, while becoming fluent in the new dialect. Once both of the proficiencies have been well-developed, and only then, should the work of Christian interpretation ideally begin.

Steps of translation of a text by another community. When translating a second dialect text into one's native dialect, five "steps" must be taken: comprehension, evaluation, translation, transposition and composition. We shall discuss each in turn.

Comprehension. The first step is *comprehension.* The second dialect text must be read in order to understand as best as possible the meaning of the text according to the author. This interpretive task alone is complicated, but (in spite of the claims of deconstructionists and other radical postmodernists) it is not in principle impossible. However, we will not attempt here to make that case.[5] The strengths of scientific discourse are that it includes a technical vocabulary that is supposed to be univocal in meaning and is ideally stripped of the ambiguities of figurative and everyday speech in order to aid in accurate description and optimal communication. So, with a certain amount of training, an adequate comprehension of modern psychological discourse by Christians for the purpose of translation should be attainable.

Evaluation. The second step is a reading for *evaluation*, a reading in light of one's native tongue, so that the text's meanings (including its connotations and assumptions) that conflict with those of the native tongue are rendered salient and these meanings can be separated from those which do not conflict. We noted above that reading noncanonical texts entails a hermeneutics of trust and suspicion. Humans generally speak and write in order to communicate something they want others to understand; in the genre of scientific discourse, scientists speak and write in order to describe something they have discerned in reality. Scientists publicize their findings in "reports," and their descriptive speech-acts are considered *assertions* (Searle, 1998). Consequently, the reader of scientific discourse ought to have the expectation that the author of the text is at least attempting to describe an actual state of affairs. This stance fosters a presumption that something of reality will be more or less accurately depicted in the report. These dynamics are part of a hermeneutics of trust. However, the skilled reader of scientific discourse also knows that errors can occur in scientific research and reasoning. Consequently, the text will also be read critically, aware of the canons of adjudication that presently exist for assessing the reliability and validity of the report, canons that themselves have changed (and usually have improved) over time. In addition, Christian readers, reading in light of their own canon's rationality (part of their disciplinary matrix), will note ways in which the discourse demonstrates the influences of modernism, distorting the description of the phenomenon being described.

Naturalism and some degree of reductionism necessarily truncate the reports of modernists, making it likely, depending on the topic, that their texts will leave out higher aspects of the phenomenon being researched (e.g., ethical and spiritual factors). For example, human agency and freedom are usually ignored or explained away in modern psychology texts, and reference to divine influence is downright impermissible (on the contrary, conversion is believed to be adequately explained by biological and psychosocial factors; see Beit-Hallahmi & Argyle, 1997). In addition, the metanarrative of evolution looms large in the disciplinary background of all modern psychological discourse (in evolutionary psychology, it is in the foreground), so its relative impact on the text should routinely be assessed. Depending upon the phenomenon under investigation, the description of human nature may be more or less compromised. Skilled Christian readers will be predisposed to identify the signs of such influences. This side of evaluation illustrates a hermeneutics of suspicion.

Translation proper. The third step consists of the actual *translation* of a second dialect text (or texts) into a text consisting of one's native tongue. MacIntyre (1988) suggests there are three ways translation between distinct linguistic communities may be done. The most direct kind of translation MacIntyre terms *linguistic innovation* (usually called *transliteration*), in which the terms/concepts of the second dialect that have no correlate in the native dialect are simply brought into the native dialect, as happens when Latin or French terms are used in English discourse. Still, in such cases, the Christian translator must take care to ensure that faulty connotations of the secular dialect system are not being "brought in" with the term (i.e., connotations that are incompatible with the native dialect's linguistic framework of meaning). The Christian psychology translator will have to make much use of this translation strategy because of the wealth of scientific terms developed within modern psychology that should be incorporated without much change into a Christian psychology, for example, terms like *frontal lobe, episodic memory* and *anorexia nervosa.* Such terms should be incorporated, because, upon careful reflection grounded in a Christian disciplinary matrix, (1) it is clear that such terms accurately label phenomena that actually exist, so that Christian psychological communities' conceptual resources are legitimately expanded with the incorporation of the new vocabulary, and (2) there are no obstacles to their being directly incorporated in a Christian disciplinary matrix.

Another type of translation strategy takes utterances from the second dialect that have terms in the first dialect which appear to have the same object and simply uses them interchangeably in translation. MacIntyre calls this *same-saying*. Examples of this type might include the use of the evangelical term *fellowship* for the modern psychology term *social support*, *agape-love* for *altruism*, or *trials* for *stressors*. (When trying to put longer utterances of modern discourse [like paragraphs] into Christian terms, we could call this strategy *paraphrasing*.) However, as one can see with these examples, the meaning of two terms from different language systems is rarely absolutely identical. There will often be slight differences in connotation that terms from the Christian discursive system offer that are absent in the modern.

This kind of translation is far more complex than transliteration and requires great care. Far too often, Christians have put equal signs between psychological terms and terms derived from the Christian tradition (e.g., self-actualization and sanctification, or negative self-esteem and sin). Christian translators must strive diligently to insure that they not overestimate equivalence, and that, when paraphrasing is deemed appropriate, the resulting Christian discourse approximately captures the valid, original (second idiom) meaning, and that the new Christian connotations, which replaced the modern connotations, constitute an improvement from a Christian interpretive standpoint.

The translation techniques mentioned so far are used when a second dialect text contributes clearly identifiable valid information that can and should be incorporated into the native idiom. Things get even more complicated when the worldview biases of the second dialect community are contaminating the descriptions, resulting in discourse that from the standpoint of the native dialect community contains falsehoods or at least false connotations. In such cases MacIntyre (1988) recommends *the use of interpretive glosses and explanations* that will permit the native reader of the final translation to understand the translated second dialect material *in light of the meaning-system of the native tongue.* In such cases the Christian translator should ask, How does the Christian discursive system alter, add to or subtract from this modern description? This strategy is necessary when working in areas where the conceptual differences between the two communities are sizeable. This would be the case when there are important features of reality that the secondary dialect text is describing that ought to be incorporated into the native dialect system, but where there are also simultaneously semantic incompatibilities (due to worldview differences) that cannot be obscured or ignored in translation without undermining the understanding of the native community.

An example of this kind of problem can be found in the modern body of research on attribution. Attributions are beliefs about what causes an event or an attribute. For example, when persons do well on an exam, they typically form an attribution about the success that serves to explain the occurrence, for example, they studied hard or they are just very smart. Attributions can be distinguished in a number of ways, but historically the most important way has been considered to be the dichotomous distinction: internal or external. Causal attributions for an action can be directed at something "inside" the person (ability, effort) or "outside" the person (luck, someone's assistance). In this scheme, from a secular standpoint, God must be interpreted as an external attribution, although usually God is not even considered (see Fiske & Taylor, 1984; Anderson, Krull & Weiner, 1996). However, the Christian is indwelt by the Holy Spirit and experiences assistance by God from within: "Work out your salvation with fear and trembling; for it is God who is at work in you, both to will and to work for His good pleasure" (Phil 2:12-13). To translate the secular literature on attribution accurately will require a fair amount of additional explanation to do justice to the Christian community's understanding of good action by Christians, and it warrants special research by Christians informed by our community's assumptions. Fortunately, this research has begun to be done, some of it, notably, by non-Christian theists (Pargament, 1997; Pargament, Kennell, Hathaway, Grevengoed, Newman & Jones, 1988; Ritzema, 1979; Ritzema & Young, 1983; Welton, Adkins, Ingle & Dixon, 1996).

Sometimes the translator will come upon secondary dialect material that so differs from the discursive practices and understanding of the native community that it is *incommensurable*. The native translator makes this assessment after concluding that the secondary dialect discourse is plainly inaccurate or at least seriously misleading, given the understanding of the native dialect community. At such points, the translator must make decisions about exactly how to communicate this incommensurability. When writing on similar topics competently addressed by modernists that are nonetheless incommensurable, the Christian scholar will usually be obligated to identify the similar but questionable terms/concepts and *critique* them within the native idiomatic discourse, while offering a *substitution* from the native idiom. Such communicative decisions are an inevitable part of every translator's task, crucially important for the Christian interpreter, because of concerns about the noetic effects of sin operative in modernity.

An example of this kind of terminological problem can be found in the human maturity-ideal process that Maslow (1954, 1968) labeled "self-actualization." Some Christians have engaged in same-saying in their translation (e.g., using sanctification [Timpe, 1999a] or comparing the fruit of the Spirit with the traits of self-actualization [McMinn, 1996]), whereas others have more wisely attempted to add glosses and explanations that show how a Christian understanding has similarities but is different (Watson, Milliron, Morris & Hood, 1995).

However, the judgment of incommensurability would seem warranted in this case. The human maturity-ideal process of Christianity is quite different from what Maslow meant by self-actualization. His understanding was radically individualistic (though not narcissistic), and even his choice of exemplars made it certain that orthodox Jews, Muslims or Christians could not be interpreted as self-actualized (1954, pp. 7, 221). The term *self-actualization* itself underscores its grounding in a humanistic discursive system where the Self is the ultimate value and source of meaning and power. By contrast, a Christian understanding of human maturity is intrinsically relational—humans are made in the image of God, and as Christians mature, they become increasingly conformed to the image of Christ, improvement which itself entails dependence on Christ. Moreover, God is the center of the universe for a Christian, so the highest motivational state for a Christian is the love of one's Creator and Redeemer.

While Christians will recognize some formal similarities between features of the human maturity-ideal process of both communities (e.g., in some of their traits and aspects of their peak experiences), at the end of the day, readers should accept Maslow's understanding of his term as definitive. Christians must be careful not to equate family resemblance with equivalence. Baboons and humans have many similarities, but the differences between them are still quite profound. Overlooking such disparities would not be tolerated in biological classification. This kind of oversight is especially problematic with psychological categories like a community's human maturity-ideal, because discourse on such topics is so dependent on socially constructed formulations that implicitly communicate fundamental worldview, ethical and spiritual commitments, and therefore may influence the naïve reader. In light of such considerations, it would seem that the term *self-actualization* is incommensurable with Christian speech and therefore fundamentally inappropriate as a label for Christian psychospiritual maturity (and therefore invalid even as a cross-community label for psychospiritual maturity). The term belongs in the modern dialect for *its* notion of the human maturity-ideal, and it is simply more accurate (and more scientific!) to leave it there. Christian psychologists already have available substitute terms within their Christian resources—like sanctification, Christiformity or conformity to the image of Christ—to use as scientific terminology for their distinctive human maturity-ideal process.

Christian translators of modern psychology texts, therefore, have four options: transliteration, same-saying (or paraphrasing), interpretive glosses and explanations, or critique and substitution. We might think of these four translation strategies as lying along a continuum of translatability, from word-for-word acceptance to rejection, as indicated by figure 7.1.

Transliteration	Paraphrase	With Explanation	Substitution
(Conceptual Integration)			

Figure 7.1. A continuum of translatability

Generally speaking, there would appear to be large regions of psychological discourse where the simpler translation strategies (transliteration and paraphrase) would more often be employed, for example neuropsychology, associative learning, memory, reasoning, linguistics, intelligence, emotion, personality traits and group processes. In contrast, the more complex translation procedures will tend to be used more consistently in areas of psychological discourse that are more worldview-dependent (development, motivation, personality, psychopathology, psychotherapy). But decisions regarding exactly which translation strategies to bring into play when working on a given topic can only be determined contextually, after reading carefully in that area and evaluating the material in question.

To the extent that we are either unaware of or downplay the subtle discursive implications derived from modern psychology worldview assumptions, Christians will be unable to read and translate such texts Christianly, and we will make less progress thinking for ourselves than we should. As the reader can see in figure 7.1, it is being suggested that the two terms on the left may be considered examples of conceptual integration. As we know, over the past fifty years, "integration" has generally referred to the *entire* paradigm of how to relate one's faith to psychology, a metaphor which seems to imply the mixing together of modern psychology concepts with Christian discourse across the whole discipline of psychology, without regard to context—that is, without differentiating more problematic areas from those that are less worldview dependent (though the worldview integration approach better addresses this concern than has interdisciplinary integration). Perhaps because integration has focused more on *concepts* than on discourse, integrationists have tended not to address the subtle linguistic complexities of communication between psychological communities that exist in antithetic worldview relationship to each other. In light of the above considerations, perhaps the scope of integration should be narrowed to the two procedures for appropriating knowledge from other worldview communities where the knowledge can pretty much be accepted "as is" and *integrated* with little or no linguistic modification. This would still mean that some amount of conceptual integration would be appropriate in much of contemporary psychology (which explains the popularity of the integration agenda for so many decades—in many areas it is valid).

Perhaps part of the difficulties that have attended the integration agenda has been that the term itself has simply been pressed to do too much labor. The term *translation* would seem a better candidate to refer broadly to the interpretive transfer of knowledge from other worldview communities to the Christian, because this metaphor brings with it connotations of a larger discursive/interpretive context. *Conceptual integration*, however, would seem to be a good label for the two simpler translation procedures. (Though it may be too complex to nuance this discussion any further, *integration* also has a meaning that would seem to make it a fit label for the *overall* goal of *Christianity* of bringing together all of one's knowing, loving and acting into a coherent, unified way of life under the lordship of Christ: the living of an *integrated* Christian life [which is the very different intuition that undergirds ethical integration].)

Transposition. After translation, the next task is *transposition* (or sublation). For the most part, the modern disciplinary matrix only allows for reference to biological and psychosocial dynamics. Therefore, when reading modern texts about various psychological features, it will usually be necessary for Christians to take this step in order to consider their ethical and spiritual implications. Transposition entails "taking up" the textual material dealing with biopsychosocial dynamics into a higher context of meaning—ethical or spiritual. For example, when summarizing a modern text on the physiology of religious experience, the Christian reader will need to address, as best as possible, the role of spiritual factors that can contribute to and influence brain activity. According to a Christian disciplinary matrix, without reference to higher factors, the lower factors are not properly or fully understood. Transposition will be discussed in much more detail in chapter eleven.

Composition. The fifth and final step involved in the Christian interpretation and translation of secular psychology discourse is *composition*, the production of a new Christian text. Christian composition derived from translation has two necessary components: first, it must be written in the Christian dialect, using all its available discursive/conceptual resources (particularly the canon and relevant Christian classics) as explicitly as possible, but second, it will demonstrate some degree of the *enrichment* of its discourse, as a result of its having incorporated material derived from the second dialect community. Both aspects of composition are essential for the formation of a rich and robust Christian psychology. In the composing of Christian psychological discourse, the resources of the canon and Christian traditions will be used without apology, even when it does not meet the discursive standards of the modern psychological community. Christians have a complex and thick vocabulary for describing some features of human beings—particularly ethical and spiritual dynamics—terms that are often entirely lacking within modern discourse. But there is no need to suppose that the discursive/conceptual resources of the canon and the Christian traditions developed in the past will forever be adequate for the ever-expanding scientific task of identifying the dazzling multitude of human characteristics that God created and knows. Human finitude requires the continual growth of an enhanced vocabulary and conceptual framework if humans are to increase in their conformity to God's understanding.

Though we have been arguing throughout for a community-based model of knowledge-construction, the fact is that words are not owned by communities. They can be wrested from their original contexts, taken captive for Christ (2 Cor 10:5) and render good service within a different discursive community. If the Christian community's understanding of human nature and its treatment is to become increasingly sophisticated and accurate (that is, more scientific), it must both remain true to its own defining canonical and classic resources, as well as augment those resources through dialogue with others who have developed a more sophisticated vocabulary and conceptual understanding of human nature. Skilled translation is necessary if the Christian community is ever to recover from its epistemological and soul-care crisis that has been created by the work of modern psychology. And it will be the better for it.

Difficulties in Translation, Part 1: Neutral Problems

We have already noted modernism's aim of value neutrality. Greatly complicating the Christian translator's task is the fact that modern systems of speech excel in description (above all, modern scientific literatures, which are in fact specialized descriptive systems), while simultaneously neutralizing "conceptions of truth and rationality and the historical context" (MacIntyre, 1988, p. 301) in the interests of a universal objectivity. One of the primary (though largely implicit) goals of modernism (which took a few centuries to realize) has been the development of a general, descriptive vocabulary sanitized of particularistic evaluative and moral judgments (see Clouser, 1991; MacIntyre, 1984). This "neutral" communicative ideal is maintained by most modernist intellectuals and throughout modern popular culture with reference to ethical issues (e.g., nothing is forbidden with regard to abortion, bioethics, sexual ethics) as well as religious belief (all faiths are equally legitimate), and ethical and religious neutrality has become a sacred ideology in the mental health field.

Stress and more. Let us consider a couple of examples of how this has worked. In earlier eras tragic events involving sorrow and suffering were termed *trials* (see the King James Version of 1 Pet 1:7; 4:12). Within their Christian context these terms connoted circumstances that were allowed by a benevolent Creator and Redeemer to be curative and formative; they were intended to produce a higher good by leading to improvements in one's character. Modern speech, especially within clinical contexts, has replaced such terms with the word *stressor*, a modification of the word *stress*. *Stress* is borrowed from the world of physics and refers to the natural forces exerted upon a physical structure that can weaken it. It is a fine metaphor, but scientific speech is supposed to be univocal, so it is not meant as a metaphor. Devoid of the religious and formative connotations of the earlier terminology that implied that evil events were meaningful, since they were permitted by God for good purposes, *stressor* signifies nothing more than a random event in a physical world determined by impersonal, stochastic laws. No higher purpose is implied with the word *stress;* humans must simply learn how to get along (how to cope) in spite of such capricious forces.

Replacing trials with the term *stressor*, therefore, involves some loss of meaningfulness for the Christian community. This does not mean Christians should never use it. However, since *stressor* lacks the theistic overtones of the earlier word, it may sometimes be desirable to refer explicitly to God's providence when using terms from the *stress* family in order to translate properly into the Christian idiom. And of course, the word *trial* is still available in the Christian vocabulary.

***The virtues and vices of the* Diagnostic and Statistical Manual.** Naturalistic, neutralizing sentiments are brought to fullest realization in the evolution of the *Diagnostic and Statistical Manual* classification schemes. On many levels, the development of the *Diagnostic and Statistical Manual of Mental Disorders* (revised 4th ed., American Psychiatric Association, 2000)—along with its international counterpart, the ICD-10—has to be considered a monumental scientific achievement. Those responsible employed the scientific tasks of description and categorization in the obscure and problematic realm of psychopathology, identifying over four hundred psychological disorders (including variants) over the course of one hundred years. This is not the place to debate the validity of all the classifications. No one doubts that there will continue to be improvements in our description of psychopathology—what science is not characterized by such debates? For our present purposes we will simply assume its overall empirical basis and scientific legitimacy. Instead let us reflect on one of its most puzzling, yet clearly defining features: the virtual lack of any ethical or spiritual evaluative language in a manual for identifying what is psychologically *abnormal* for human beings. Within the modern discursive system (where strong evaluative language has no corresponding ontological referent and so is chronically undermined and minimized), the identification of *abnormality* presents something of a challenge. In such a context, abnormality can be defined in terms of statistical infrequency, cultural norms, adaptiveness and personal distress. Christians should have no objection to these evaluative standards per se, but they are employed by modernity particularly because they imply no reference to moral or spiritual criteria (like immorality, vice or sin).

There is, of course, real utility for contemporary culture to develop a "universal" labeling system for psychological disorders that focuses on the empirically evident symptoms of such disorders and avoids any theoretically loaded terminology that would obscure the phenomenon being described. Nonetheless, a manual for the diagnosis of abnormality is necessarily as much about evaluation as it is about identification. So the paradoxical quality of this quintessentially modern text is striking: a text dedicated to evaluation that is devoid of overtly evaluative language.

Perhaps some readers may find this whole questioning of the *DSM-IV-TR* unintelligible, so contrary is it to current sensibilities and assumptions. But let us take a look at one of the clearest examples of evaluative cleansing, the lengthy *DSM-IV-TR* description of sexual sadism:

> The paraphilic focus of Sexual Sadism involves acts (real, not simulated) in

> which the individual derives sexual excitement from the psychological or physical suffering (including humiliation) of the victim. Some individuals with this Paraphilia are bothered by their sadistic fantasies, which may be invoked during sexual activity but not otherwise acted on; in such cases the sadistic fantasies usually involve having complete control over the victim, who is terrified by anticipation of the impending sadistic act. Others act on the sadistic sexual urges with a consenting partner (who may have Sexual Masochism) who willingly suffers pain or humiliation. Still others with Sexual Sadism act on their sadistic sexual urges with nonconsenting victims. In all of these cases, it is the suffering of the victim that is sexually arousing. Sadistic fantasies or acts may involve activities that indicate the dominance of the person over the victim (e.g., forcing the victim to crawl or keeping the victim in a cage). They may also involve restraint, blindfolding, paddling, spanking, whipping, pinching, beating, burning, electrical shocks, rape, cutting, stabbing, strangulation, torture, mutilation, or killing. Sadistic sexual fantasies are likely to have been present in childhood. The age at onset of sadistic activities is variable, but is commonly by early adulthood (sic). Sexual Sadism is usually chronic. When Sexual Sadism is practiced with nonconsenting partners, the activity is likely to be repeated until the person with Sexual Sadism is apprehended. Some individuals with Sexual Sadism may engage in sadistic acts for many years without a need to increase the potential for inflicting serious physical damage. Usually, however, the severity of the sadistic acts increases over time. When Sexual Sadism is severe, and especially when it is associated with Antisocial Personality Disorder, individuals with Sexual Sadism may seriously injure or kill their victims. (p. 573)

This disorder is obviously more freighted with moral significance than most in the *DSM.* But that is precisely why its description is worthy of attention, for it is such a masterful example of the highly sterilized language of modern science, absent of overt evaluative denotation regarding sexual sadism (though the reference to "victim" implies some covert evaluation). If we were not conditioned to such neutral descriptions in the literature, reading it would be almost chilling. One wonders, in fact, if the clinical language of the Manual at this point is almost guilty of the same lack of moral disapprobation that is a symptom of the syndrome being described.

Such questioning does not lead necessarily to the rejection of the entire DSM project. The scientific and social value of the descriptions and the categorization of psychological disorders would seem to be undeniable (even by the TBC, Asher & Asher, 2004). But that fact does not warrant a thoughtless appropriation of it, especially for Christians, since it is a text written in a different dialect than that used by the Christian community. Christians are aided in their critique by the biblical text, their canonical touchstone, which actually contains a fair amount of material on abnormality and has a host of terms that designate it, the foremost English translation of which is *sin*. The "sin" family (and its close semantic relations: ungodliness, evil, abomination, lawlessness and vice) denotes a disposition and set of ethical and spiritual motives, desires, thoughts and actions that are abnormal for human beings: this is not the way it's supposed to be (Plantinga, 1995). Most importantly, embedded in the biblical words for abnormality are connotations of accountability, responsibility, culpability and relationship to the Creator. At the same time, it would be misleading to assert that the biblical and modern languages for abnormality were either synonymous or antonymous. They are different, yet overlapping. Some forms of psychopathology may have no direct connection to sin (e.g., autism, head injury due to natural causes and Alzheimer's), whereas others are essentially ethicospiritual disorders, as defined biblically (e.g., adultery and idolatry).

However, a complex Christian understanding would lead us to expect that most forms of psychopathology probably include some combination of biopsychosocial damage *and* sin (since sin permeates human life and has led to damage to the body and soul and human relationships). Moreover, by any reckoning, the richness of description of the *DSM-IV-TR* is remarkable and its value for clinical work inestimable. It is a scientific text, and as such is far superior to the biblical text for the scientific task of the diagnosis of most mental disorders. Yet, from the Christian standpoint, since the biblical text reveals the Christian community's first principles, *it* addresses the *most important* kinds of abnormality, a dynamic that likely contributes to and influences many of the dynamic-structural disorders more neutrally described in the *DSM*.

The differences between the two dialects on this subject are substantial and formative, since the *DSM* descriptive scheme is a linguistic expression of modernity and is shaped by the same naturalistic and neopositivistic assumptions that undergird modernity (and its versions of psychiatry and psychology). As a result, from a Christian standpoint, the *DSM* text contributes to the undermining of ethical and spiritual diagnosis and remediation. By avoiding any ethicospiritual evaluative language for all adult psychopathology, one conveys the impression that individuals suffering (and enacting) such disorders bear no moral responsibility for resisting or overcoming it, an assumption intrinsic to naturalism. We must be careful here, since Christians have often mistakenly downplayed the deterministic influences on many disorders (and even sins). But, contrary to modern assumptions, sin-language is actually hope-giving. It implies that the human is not a mere automaton or organism, incapable of acting contrary to the disorder, but bears enough responsibility at least to seek help—help from others and ultimately from God—and a degree of culpability that is resolved on the cross of Christ. Sin-language pulls us into God's presence, and in Christ there is healing. So there is much at stake in the language-games of abnormality of these two communities. At some point in the future, the Christian community will have to develop its own DSM."[6]

Difficulties in Translation, Part 2: Worldviews in Conflict in Soul Care

Just as important as the language of abnormality is the language of soul care. Though they have plenty of features in common, the secular and Christian communities have significantly different ideals of what healthy, mature human beings are like, and those ideals provide the goals towards which their soul-care activity is directed. Consequently, translation is a major issue in soul care in the public square.

We have concentrated most of our attention in this chapter on the science of psychology, even though this is a book on soul care, in part because modern psychotherapy and counseling have, since their inception, regarded themselves as legitimated by their basis in scientific research. From Freud to Rogers to Beck, it has been clear that they sought to ground their soul-care assertions on some type of empirical research, whether psychodynamic, phenomenological or quasi-experimental. This assumption was essential to the received account of the transition from previous models of soul care, which were alleged to be steeped in superstition, ignorance and moralism (see e.g., Watson, 1925), to the new, "more objective" models that were based on a value-neutral and universal science (Slife, 2004). Modern soul care, so it was believed, is the unbiased application of the findings of objective research to people who are viewed throughout treatment without ethical or spiritual evaluations of any kind.

Consequently, modern soul care also found itself caught in a typically modern, paradoxical predicament. On the one hand, it originally had to operate as if values had been set aside, and the therapy was conducted without any suggestion of a moral judgment; the therapist was to view the client in terms of, to use Rogers's term, "unconditional positive regard." Yet, on the other hand, psychotherapy is permeated with values and evaluations from beginning to end: in diagnosis; uncovering and identifying of pathological or unhealthy patterns of thinking, acting or relating; and in the assumption of some therapeutic ideal that is the goal of the therapist's soul-care system (Richardson, Fowers & Guignon, 1999; Roberts, 1987).

"Unconditional positive regard" is itself a therapy value. And over time, some modernists (beginning with the humanists) began to admit that some values were an inevitable part of therapy. However, they continued to cultivate the appearance of value-neutrality by refusing to advise their clients regarding so-called private matters, like marriage and divorce, sexual behavior and religious beliefs. These they left up to their clients and instead attempted to affirm their clients' inclinations as long as they were not physically harmful to themselves or others (see e.g., Rogers, 1972, unconditional positive regard of extramarital affairs). Such a stance seems unobjectionable to its proponents, since the individual Self is implicitly posited as the ultimate authority regarding such allegedly subjective matters (Johnson & Sandage, 1999; Vitz, 1994). This allowed modern soul-care providers to maintain a sense of continuity with the modernist ideal of value-neutrality, and it allowed them to differentiate their stance from that traditionally espoused in the West (in ancient Greece and historic Judaism, Christianity and Islam).

Yet, upon continuing reflection and internal debate, it became rationally impossible to maintain the avowed modernist stance of value neutrality in therapy. Its practitioners have gradually come to acknowledge that contemporary soul care must deal with values. It is accepted now that soul-care providers have a set of values, some of which are necessary for good therapy (e.g., promoting psychological well-being is good), and clients have a set of values, which in most cases must be respected (except insofar as any modernist values are denied—e.g., causing physical harm to a child). According to research on practitioners, the modern therapist affirms a rather sparse list of generic, individualistic, universal values: self-awareness (Jensen & Bergin, 1988), self-direction in the face of barriers/limitations (Egan, 1990; Jensen & Bergin, 1988; Kelly, 1995), autonomy (Jensen & Bergin, 1988; Kelly, 1995; Mahalik, 1995) and self-confidence, effectiveness and adaptiveness (Howard, 1992; Jensen & Bergin, 1988). Still, this is extraordinarily telling. A modern "value-neutral" value-ideology is firmly in place, and it is assumed that therapists will, in the main, promote the goals and values of their individual clients, while helping them to become more effective in realizing them (apart from harm to self or others). Illustrative of this outlook are a couple of quotes from popular counseling textbooks from the late twentieth century: "Respect (in counseling) means prizing the individuality of clients, supporting each client in his or her search for self, and personalizing the helping process to the needs, capabilities, and resources of the client" (Egan, 1990, p. 65). "Counseling is a process whereby clients are challenged to honestly evaluate their values and then decide for themselves in what ways they will modify these values and their behavior" (Corey, 1991, p. 23). Because of the modernist desire for universality (which is latent in postmodernism), when spiritual or religious values are acknowledged to be a part of therapy, the kind of spirituality/religion that is discussed is a generic, universal kind of religion, unlike most of the actual religions of the world (see e.g., Richards & Bergin, 1997). Such individual values vary substantially from an orthodox Christian edification framework and are clearly not neural, something acknowledged by critics outside the Christian psychology community (e.g., Cushman, 1995; Rieff, 1966).

Ethicospiritual guidelines for Christian soul care. From a Christian psychology standpoint, what are Christian soul-care providers to do if they want to work outside a church context with counselees who have worldviews that differ from their own? It is impossible to address here all the complexities and challenges facing such counselors today, but a few words are in order. Christian psychology proponents ought to be open to working with all kinds of people; this is not just compatible with Christianity, it is mandated by it. However, they cannot counsel in ways that contradict their own worldview or edification framework. Consequently, they ought to do nothing in their soul care that would assist a person in moving in unethical or religious directions *that are contrary to Christianity.* Modernist and postmodernist systems tend to accept most counselees' ethical and spiritual values because they are skeptical about claims of ultimate truth, morality and religion. However, orthodox Christianity (along with orthodox versions of Hinduism, Judaism and Islam) simply has a different understanding of such ultimates, and it is unethical for orthodox Christians to help others become unethical or further removed from salvation in Christ. For the Christian counselor to do so would be to act without integrity.

Nonetheless, orthodox Christian counselors ought to work with any who want to work with them, regardless of their worldview. At the beginning of the first session, a Christian counselor should have the counselee read and sign an informed consent form that indicates the counselor's edification framework. If the counselee still wishes to work with the counselor, it is the counselor's responsibility both (1) to respect the counselee's ultimate beliefs and work in such a way that the counselee never feels pressured or coerced (what good counselor would want to do that?), and (2) to act consistently within a Christian edification framework. There is no reason why a Christian counselor could not work for months or years with non-Christians who wish to do so, so long as the counselor remains faithful to his or her covenantal allegiance to Christ.

Two issues are especially problematic for Christians working in a majority secularist mental health culture: evangelism and homosexuality. Evangelical Christians have been quite public about their willingness to share their faith in Christ and invite others to accept Christ for themselves. However, modernist and postmodernist edification frameworks forbid such activity, causing some confusion for Christians who work in most soul-care settings today. The irony here is that modernist and postmodernist soul care providers are free to draw their clients into their worldviews, but because modernism/postmodernism consist of language-systems avowedly devoid of ethical or spiritual commitments, they pass as neutral, and no one recognizes that evangelism of an extremely subtle sort occurs in every session. All mature, rational soul-care providers reject coercion, and all mature, rational soul care offers counsel regarding values, including ultimate values—soul care that deals with important issues cannot avoid dealing with ultimate values. There is certainly soul care that deals with what we might call non-ultimate therapeutic issues—training children how to deal with their learning disabilities, helping couples learn how to communicate better—but careful observation and reflection on one's soul care will disclose that ultimate concerns are always close at hand. American soul-care culture needs a radical rethinking of the issues truly at stake in soul care that will not prejudice the system against orthodox members of explicitly theistic soul-care systems.

Similarly, the ethics of homosexuality can scarcely be discussed in public anymore, such has been the success of modernism/postmodernism in removing its stigma and negative evaluation (this is particularly notable given its patent abnormality by evolutionary standards). Thoughtful Christians should have no desire to force people who are not Christians to accept specifically Christian sexual norms. At the same time it would be unethical for orthodox Christians to promote homosexual relationships and activity. Referral is always an option, but helping counselees become more effective in their immorality (as defined Christianly) lacks Christian integrity.

Modernist/postmodernist soul-care institutions will, of course, find such positions intolerable, so it would seem impossible for a Christian to counsel in a strictly modernist/postmodernist counseling center. However, I am hopeful that some postmodern institutions may have developed a sufficiently sophisticated critique of modernism to be able to grasp and even affirm the issues at stake for Christians here. Public mental-health institutions ought to be *pluralist* (rather than *secular*), where ideally the soul-care staff would proportionately represent the surrounding community, and each of the providers would offer soul care according to their own worldview—orthodox Christian, liberal Christian, orthodox Jewish, liberal Jewish, Muslim and yes, a few secularists as well—so that together they offer an array of worldview options that would truly meet the soul-care needs of their community. The intake form at a pluralist center would have a checklist indicating what kind of worldview the persons seeking help wanted in their counselor, including a box for "No Preference." Counselees who marked that box could then be distributed equally among the staff. Many Christian counselors would be able to work here effectively, and such centers ought especially to be sought by the Christian community in regions of the country where a significant number of orthodox Christians live. However, it would seem likely that many Christian counselors would still choose to work within local churches or in parachurch organizations, where those seeking help know they want counseling that is consistent with a Christian worldview. These issues deserve far more attention than they can be given here, but enough has probably been said to indicate the general direction a Christian psychology approach might take to these matters.

Summary of Translation Problems

The task of translation in psychopathology and soul care today is extremely daunting. It will likely require a few generations of hundreds of Christians dedicating much of their lives to the mastery of the two language systems and then working together to compose a single Christian discursive system of diagnostics and therapeutics that deals with biopsychosocial as well as ethicospiritual abnormality and treatment. The goal is the increasing approximation in Christian discourse of God's understanding (to the best of our communal ability)—guided by Scripture and classic Christian texts, and enriched by the careful integration of the unproblematic language of the modern psychological community and the translation of more problematic, but valid modern discourse.

Notes

[1]Thomas Aquinas became MacIntyre's hero, and he should be that of Christian psychologists too. Aquinas was an heir of the Augustinian moral and intellectual tradition—a centuries-old, decidedly Christian approach to reality that recognized the authority of Scripture and wise Augustinian teachers, whose guidance was needed to train less mature minds into the discernment of the Truth. Aquinas, however, lived at a time when an impressive body of classical literature was being reintroduced to Western civilization. One of the most important of these classical authors was Aristotle—who had a fundamentally different worldview but was undeniably a brilliant thinker and had developed many terms and procedures for understanding human reasoning and morality. We need not agree with Aquinas's entire system to see that for two reasons he is important for Christian psychologists today. First, he and we are situated in analogous periods of intellectual foment, caused by the existence of a remarkable intellectual tradition that differs in foundational ways from the Christian tradition. Second, he sought to reinterpret the Aristotelian corpus from a radically Christian standpoint in a way that greatly enriched the Christian tradition, giving it intellectual resources it did not already possess, by means of and without seriously compromising its own tremendous but very different intellectual resources (and that, in spite of Aristotle's serious intellectual limitations, from a Christian standpoint). Our challenge is very similar, except perhaps for the profound differences in the media of argument, since print and especially internet formats today make argument much faster, freer and more chaotic.

[2]Of course, there are actually many subcommunities that make up these two ultimate communities. Non-Christian communities can be subdivided into Muslim, Buddhist, Mormon and secular, to name a few, and the secular community can be further subdivided into naturalist, humanist and postmodern, and so on. Similarly, the Christian community is also composed of many subgroups. Augustine's point (and the biblical authors upon whom Augustine's Two Cities concept is based) is that humanity will ultimately consist of two groups of sinners—those who have finally rejected God and those who have availed themselves of God's rescue of them in Christ.

[3]An example of this kind of "translation" is demonstrated in chapter three of Carter and Narramore's (1979) integration classic, where theology subdisciplines are lined up next to psychology subdisciplines to show how they overlap in terms of their reference. The distortions of this attempt at showing points of convergence is obvious to anyone who is well read in both literatures.

[4]*The Christian's Guide to Psychological Terms* (Asher & Asher, 2004) is admittedly a step in the right direction.

[5]See Audi, 1998; Plantinga, 1993b, 2000, 2003; Thiselton, 1992; Vanhoozer, 1998, 2004, 2005; Ward, 2002; Watson, 1994; Wolterstorff, 1995; for strong defenses of this position.

[6]Mention should be made here of the first significant step taken in this direction by Yarhouse, Butman and McRay (2005). But they freely admit that their work is a Christian assessment of the DSM and not an alternative. And mention has already been made of the much more critical and less sophisticated assessment by TBC advocates (Asher & Asher, 2004). Of great importance is the new *Psychodynamic Diagnostic Manual* (PDM Task Force, 2006). By offering a substantial but compatible alternative to the *DSM,* the secular psychodynamic community may have done the Christian community a big favor and helped us to think outside of the *DSM*'s rigid restrictions.

Postscript

Composing a Body of Christian Psychology Literature: A Communal Project

IT SHOULD BE OBVIOUS BY NOW THAT THE PROJECT of a Christian psychology will never proceed far without the combined efforts of many people working on many different fronts. In order for a Christian psychology to be adequately realized, it will require the work of neuropsychologists; psychological researchers who specialize in all the subdisciplines of contemporary psychology and are deeply conversant with modern psychology and familiar with different research methods, including natural and human science approaches; biblical specialists, those who work directly with the text, as well as with Christian doctrine and its history; pastors and ministers; philosophers of epistemology, science, ethics and human nature; seminary and university professors; Christian counselors and psychotherapists of every stripe; and spiritual directors. Such a disparate group will be united in their fundamental agreement about the necessity of working within a Christian disciplinary matrix—rather than a modern one—and therefore will assume that the sources of knowledge for and scope of a Christian psychology are broader than what is acceptable to modern psychology.[1] What distinguishes the Christian psychology project from other related Christian paradigms is its major goal of producing a unique scientific body of Christian psychological discourse.

Allow me to summarize part two of this book: the overall aim of a Christian psychology is to understand individual human beings, as best as possible, the way God does, irrespective of the disciplinary assumptions of other communities. This intellectual freedom permits Christians to use whatever legitimate sources of psychological information are available, according to a Christian disciplinary matrix. Christian psychology will always be enriched when its proponents read the quality psychology texts of other communities, but it will only develop its own identity and a legitimate research program when its proponents deeply reprioritize and internalize Christianity's own canonical and classic texts—through which Christian psychologists learn how to become Christian "readers" of human nature and other texts. For any community, the originality of their own psychology is increased to the degree that the community possesses resources that are "its own" and relatively unavailable to (or at least underutilized by) other communities. Given the distinctiveness and richness of the Christian canon and other Christian classics, one might suppose the potential for a distinctive Christian psychology to be enormous. As a result of such freedom, it seems likely that unique Christian research hypotheses would be formulated and research programs would arise, and eventually relatively novel psychological theories would be developed that would contribute to a singular body of scientific literature known as Christian psychology.

What would happen if we were to look to the Bible to set the agenda for our community's psychology and soul care? Perhaps God would lead us down new paths, more scientific than our biblical and historical classics and decisively more Christian than modern psychological literature. Were we Christians in the field to immerse ourselves in biblical ways of envisioning human beings scientifically, we might be enabled to see human nature from such a different perspective that new research questions would open up that could significantly rechart the psychological map. Of course, Christian psychology would not be unrelated to other work in the field—after all, we all have the same human nature as the common object of our psychologies. However, such an immersion in our canonical texts could lead to new ways of thinking and practice that conform more to the mind and heart of God than anything that the secular academy or mental health establishment will ever produce.

And what of the Christian classics? As we saw in chapter two, the Bible has already influenced centuries of Christians who dealt with a variety of psychospiritual topics, including spiritual development, self-examination, union with Christ, the love of God, affect (or the affections), the passions, memory, desire, habit, intellect and reason, morality, the virtues and vices, the will, self-regulation, willpower, determinism due to natural causes and human freedom, motivation, hypocrisy (or self-deception), the unconscious, the causes and cure of melancholia (unipolar depression), spiritual development, guilt, imagination and love, many of which have also been studied by modern psychologists. Though it rarely achieved the level of sophistication and precision often demonstrated in twentieth- and twenty-first-century modern psychology, our psychological heritage shows how Christians have approached genuinely psychological topics from within their own framework. They also exemplify how Christians can think on their own, perhaps encouraging contemporary Christians to theorize and do research with greater independence from the intellectual powers-that-be that currently rule Western psychology.

As we have seen, the lay psychology we find in the Bible and the Christian tradition is not scientifically conceptualized and as comprehensive in conceptual focus as modern psychology, but it is *much deeper*. It is, to borrow the words of Søren Kierkegaard (1849/1980), a psychology of edification and awakening. In contrast to modern psychology's primarily *intellectual* and *descriptive* agenda to foster *knowledge*, the psychology of historic Christianity has been a project of *wisdom*, to foster *virtuous Christian character*. From the Christian standpoint, *sapientia* is far more important than *scientia*—but both are legitimate. So why not combine a wisdom agenda with a scientific agenda in one Christian psychology?[2] This would give us a psychology far deeper than mainstream modern psychology but also one that addresses a much broader range of psychological topics than anything yet developed within Christianity. Beginning with our own canonical and classical texts of wisdom about human beings, let us attempt a deep, scientifically sophisticated, virtue-promoting psychology that builds up souls as it investigates, describes and understands more of their features.[3] Such a psychology would bring glory to humanity's Maker and Redeemer.

At this point in time, a broad, deep and diverse set of Christian psychology research programs is largely a dream. But without such a dream, Christians will never challenge modern psychology's current hegemony. How might a Christian psychology look different from the modern psychology of today? In addition to modifying current psychological thought in various ways, it could make a variety of novel contributions in a number of areas, for example, neurological research that takes into account human and spiritual agency, theories of spiritual development, theocentric motivation theory that includes ethical and spiritual factors, attribution theory, the image of God and its development, original sin and its development, union with Christ, the impact of such union on Christian self-representations (e.g., the new self/old self duality), the indwelling Holy Spirit and its power and fruit, saving faith and its development, grace, the demonic, singularly Christian models of adult maturity and flourishing, a thorough reconceptualization of psychopathology that includes reference to ethical and spiritual abnormality, and therapeutic strategies and models that make use of Christian spiritual disciplines and redemptive resources that flow from the application of Christ's life, death and resurrection to the counselee.

Some good work has been done by Christians in some of these areas, but it was suggested earlier in the book that, contrary to anyone's intentions, the current paradigms may in different ways be inhibiting a more radical investment in the psychological resources of the Christian tradition. We will not really know of the viability of the project of Christian psychology until many hundreds of Christians have spent a number of decades seeking to realize it.

Up to this point, the best example of a Christian psychology research program of which I am aware has been the work of P. J. Watson. Over the past twenty-five years he has sought to document in different ways how all psychological research is conducted and articulated within a specific worldview framework, which he calls an *ideological surround* (discussed in chap. 4). Consequently, he (2005) has devised a number of research procedures (rational analysis, statistical controls for ideology, direct comparison of ideologies and empirical translation schemes) to analyze data in terms of ideological commitments, which he has used to examine commonalities and differences between modern and Christian worldviews as evident in subjects and researchers. Specifically, Watson and his colleagues found points of convergence between humanist and Christian understandings of self-esteem and of the rationality underlying mental health, and also evidence of an often subtle antireligious bias in a number of purportedly objective research instruments (the *Avoidance of Existential Concerns Scale* [Watson, Morris & Hood, 1988a], the *Personal Orientation Inventory* [Watson, Morris & Hood, 1989], the *Irrational Beliefs Test* [Watson, Morris & Hood, 1994; Watson, Milliron, Morris & Hood, 1994], and various measures of self-esteem and self-actualization [Watson, Morris & Hood, 1987]).

On the other hand, Watson has also attempted to validate empirically the existence of constructs unique to a Christian worldview. Around twenty years ago, over a series of studies, he and his colleagues examined empirical interrelations between Christian understandings of sin, grace and positive self-esteem (Watson, Hood, Morris & Hall, 1985; Watson, Morris & Hood, 1988a; Watson, Morris & Hood, 1988b; Watson, Morris & Hood, 1988c). More recently, he and his colleagues developed the *Healthy Sin Beliefs Scale* (Watson, Morris, Loy, Hamrick & Grizzle, in press), which was used in a study that found that certain Christian beliefs about sin (self-improvement, perfectionism avoidance, healthy humility and self-reflective functioning) were positively correlated with intrinsic religiosity and positive self-esteem, and negatively correlated with narcissism and depression. He (1998, 2002) has also taken the time to mine the work of the seminal but controversial Christian thinker Rene Girard for insights that would aid a Christian psychology. Most of this research and thinking was published in Christian journals of psychology.

At the same time, Watson's commitment to a Christian psychology led him to contribute to the field of psychology at large. Like many integrationists, Watson has published in mainstream journals dozens of articles that were not explicitly Christian but were nevertheless shaped by his Christian values and often motivated implicitly to advance a Christian psychology agenda within a scholarly, psychology context. Most of these articles addressed topics that had indirect relevance for the project of a Christian psychology, including research on narcissism, rational and irrational beliefs, and the psychology of religion. In addition, he has reviewed manuscripts for over twenty mainstream psychology journals; since 2001 he has been the executive editor of the *Journal of Psychology;* and for the past two years he has been the chair of his psychology department at a state university. And as an outworking of his Quaker commitment to peacemaking, he has been working together over the past decade with several Muslim psychologists of religion (e.g., Ghorbani, Bing, Watson, Davison & LeBreton, 2003; Ghorbani, Watson, Krauss, Bing & Davison, 2004).

To my knowledge, no one has developed such a thorough and self-consciously Christian psychology research program as Watson. For Christian psychology to become a legitimate scientific enterprise, God will have to raise up a community of such researchers who are able to contribute a great deal more work of this kind of depth and breadth in order to produce a viable body of distinct psychological literature.

Building a Christian psychology identity. The first and most important task facing us is the recultivation of our Christian identity as psychologists and soul-care providers. The massive accomplishments of modern psychology in the twentieth century likely contributed to an identity crisis (a common outcome of the minority experience). Part of the rationale behind the Christian psychology project is the need for institutional supports for Christian identity formation in the field, which would help encourage Christians to "come out of the closet." This is an underlying purpose served by existing Christian journals and books published by Christian publishing houses, but to the extent that the work being published is beholden to modern psychology, its value for Christian identity formation is correspondingly compromised.

The perpetuity of the Amish community demonstrates that isolation from other communities helps to preserve Christian identity. But the tradeoff is obviously enormous. If Christian psychologists and soul-care providers wish to engage the larger culture of which they are a part and even influence the field, the seclusion and isolation of the Christian psychology community is not a viable option. As many integrationists have recognized, it is necessary for Christians in psychology and soul care to find a middle way between capitulation to and isolation from modernity. The way to avoid these extremes is to maintain a twofold investment strategy. Our first calling needs to be to the church and the Christian community if our Christian identity is to be more fully established. This will be manifested in the priority with which we seek to publish in Christian publishing organs, interact with fellow Christians in psychology conferences and seek to minister to Christians in soul care and to influence non-Christians to consider the claims of Christ. However, our second calling is to the field of psychology at large. This second calling also needs to be rethought.

The transcommunity goal of a pluralist psychology. How outrageous is it to think that a Christian psychology could be a contributing force in the contemporary field of psychology? Postmodernism has helped many realize that the modern ideal of a generic, all-encompassing psychology to which all open-minded, rational parties can agree—one devoid of communal perspective—is an illusion. Everyone must read texts and study humans from some worldview perspective, whether naturalism, humanism, postmodernism, Marxism, Hinduism or Christianity. Consequently, there are good, Christian reasons and now good, postmodern reasons for Christians to also take the lead in helping move the *transcommunity field of psychology* toward a truly pluralistic stance, one that is not naïve about the discipline-constituting influence of worldview assumptions—as is modern psychology—but yet has what we might call the *broadest possible dialogical breadth.* There is great value in developing a communicative forum for human scientific discourse. In this forum participants who self-consciously operate from different disciplinary matrices can nevertheless strive to communicate with and learn from each other in ways that highlight commonalities in conception, without denying the worldview differences that exist. Such a project would ideally advance the development of each community's own understandings of human beings, while contributing to a vast, pluralistic field of psychology that would include all the world's psychologies, Christian and secular of course, but also Mormon, Jewish, Islamic, Hindu, Buddhist and so forth (something like this has already begun to occur in contemporary crosscultural psychology). According to philosophers of the natural sciences (like Kuhn and Lakatos), communal differences (of a theoretical sort) are common in the natural sciences (though downplayed by modernist ideology). However, since the human sciences are even more worldview constituted, not only should we expect them, we should relish them. Analogous to the value of multiple Christian traditions, the existence of different worldview communities will enable us to obtain a broader understanding of the nature of human beings, as well as the flexibility inherent in human nature as God created it. Think of the intellectual enrichment that would come to the field of psychology from such dialogue.

At the same time, difficult decisions will still have to be made regarding membership to this transcommunity, pluralist psychology. Transcommunal rational and ethical criteria will have to be used to exclude clearly bogus disciplinary matrices, for example, proastrology or pro-Nazi models—those that defy commonly recognized standards of rationality and morality. To some, this condition might seem contradictory to a pluralist psychology project, but historically the majority epistemological position of Christianity has never been relativism (or antirealism). A pluralist psychology as is being suggested here will surely have less stringent exclusionary criteria than does modernism, given the fact that most of the world's well-articulated worldviews posit assumptions that are not universally held. This need not be a problem for a pluralist psychology. Instead, pluralist exclusionary criteria would be restricted to issues like a lack of minimum moral integrity, intellectual competence, empirical support or philosophical sophistication.

Only a pluralist psychology deserves to be taught at the nation's public universities. Institutions that are committed to a particular worldview will be expected to teach psychology from that viewpoint (e.g., Christian, Jewish and Hindu colleges, as well as those private schools that continue to subscribe to modernist assumptions). However, *public* universities—those that are supposed to serve *all* the state's subcultures—should no longer be enforcing the monopoly that secularism currently enjoys in the human sciences of the West. The Christian community can take great encouragement in the recent willingness of the American Psychological Association to move in this direction by publishing such works as the *Handbook of Psychotherapy and Religious Diversity* (Richards & Bergin, 2000), *Judeo-Christian Perspectives on Psychology* (Miller & Delaney, 2005), and even a psychotherapy videotape on Christian counseling (McMinn, 2006)! The time would seem right for a new era in psychology, and Christian psychologists should be helping to lead the way.

Even so, from a Christian standpoint (also supported by Kuhn and Polanyi), a pluralistic psychology would by definition not be considered *the final psychology*. For one thing, finite human knowledge will never be complete. But more importantly, worldview beliefs are themselves a *necessary* means to obtain an accurate understanding of human beings, and there will always be significant worldview differences among psychologists in this age. Most importantly, our commitment to a pluralistic communication forum for psychology would in no way diminish the Christian community's belief in the superiority of its own worldview over all others—nor would we expect anything less from the proponents of other communities—one holds a worldview because it appears to be the best set of fundamental assumptions available. But Christians believe that only God's understanding of psychology is comprehensive, and while Christians would expect their psychology to be a closer approximation to God's than those of the other communities—because of the advantage given by their scriptural lenses—they also recognize that a growing approximation is a never-ending goal of increasing conformity to the mind and heart of God. So a final psychology will always evade even the Christian community, which therefore has to be committed to a continuous development of its own psychology, aiming at being the most comprehensive, but also being continually in dialogue with its own tradition as well as the psychological traditions of other communities.[4]

Conclusion

If Christian psychology is to form a vibrant, renewed psychological movement in the twenty-first century, it must face two immediate challenges. First, it will have to find itself. Christians in psychology will have to regain their self-respect and a respect for their own traditions and communities, so that their identity *as Christians* can more profoundly inform their disciplinary activity. But this goal is dependent on the second: we will find ourselves through reading—by a primary reinvestment in the canon and the Christian traditions, and secondarily a commitment to learn from all that is valid in modern/postmodern psychological terminology, theory and practice, understood in light of the canon. A creative and fruitful movement will arise from the interaction of these two activities.

An inspirational Marxist story. Twentieth-century Russian psychology contains an illustration of the possibility of developing a psychology out of a corpus of writings that is qualitatively different from mainstream American psychology.[5] Shortly after the October Revolution, a branch of Russian psychology began to develop an empirically based study of human beings that was rooted in the writings of Marx (Cole & Scribner, 1978; Zinchenko, 1982). Psychologists such as Vygotsky, Luria and Leonti'ev allowed the philosophy of Marx to permeate their thinking, so that their empirical and theoretical work became thoroughly Marxist (Levitin, 1982). Following Marx, they refused to follow a completely materialist line (like the Pavlovians) or an idealist line (like the Gestaltists) (Cole & Scribner, 1978); instead they incorporated both materialist and idealist approaches to human nature *dialectically* and attempted to take seriously the unique properties of physiological and psychological dynamics and their interactions. As a result of Marx's concern with praxis, they also studied human activity (rather than organismic behavior). Vygotsky, in particular, attempted to formulate a novel view of psychological development that was fundamentally social, believing, as a Marxist, that the social dimension has priority over the individual dimension (Vygotsky, 1978). They studied the best psychology of their day, but they studied it critically and translated it into their own idiom, striving for theoretical consistency and integrity, constrained by the writings of Marx (and secondarily, the writings of the Marxist tradition). At present, one can speak of a body of psychological knowledge that is rich, that is qualitatively different from American psychology (though in the past two decades, its influence has been felt here), and that is founded on Marx's writings.

Such an example demonstrates that a community of psychologists who share a worldview rooted in a particular set of writings can develop a unique body of knowledge and research program. Such a development was possible for the Russian psychologists because of their scientific integrity, the theoretical unity afforded by their disciplinary matrix and their relative independence from the rest of Western psychology. The task of the Christian community is made more difficult, because so many of us have studied and continue to work within a psychological paradigm that inhibits the development of a Christian psychology. However, were the Word of God to be let loose within our midst, a development analogous to what happened to Russian Marxist psychology might lie in our future.

The rest of the book seeks to develop the basic themes of a Christian edification framework that exemplifies the kind of canonical reading agenda that was described in part two. In part three we will consider how pervasive are the effects of the words of God in creation, in human development and in the Christian life.

Notes

[1]Interestingly, thirty years ago Gary Collins called for something along this line in *The Rebuilding of Psychology* (1977). It may be that the intellectual conditions for such a project are more conducive today to realization than they were in the 1970s.

[2]Such an agenda was suggested by Evans (1989) nearly twenty years ago.

[3]Such an orientation has not been entirely absent in modern psychology, e.g., in psychodynamic psychotherapy (to some extent), more clearly in humanistic and existential psychology, and more recently, especially in positive psychology, such issues have been raised. However, it has always been a minority perspective. The point here is that a Christian psychology is based on such an agenda.

[4]The Neo-Kuyperian, South African philosopher Hendrik Stoker (1973) suggested much the same, decades ago: "A Christian and a non-Christian pursuit of science (taken in a wide sense) differ in fundamental respects. Yet there is much agreement in the results of their respective pursuits. Moreover, God calls mankind to the pursuit of science. Notwithstanding the difference in principle, co-operation between a Christian and a non-Christian pursuit of science is, according to my view, unavoidable and a necessity. . . . Regarding the calling of a pursuit of science, Christians should not only reform science wherever and whenever it goes astray, but should primarily play their full part in forming science and should in both cases endeavor to convince non-Christian scientists of the truth of their presuppositions and scientific results based on these presuppositions, and to point out that they accordingly can 'better' understand and give 'better' explanations of the knowable than non-Christians on their presuppositions can do; and they should do all this to the honor and glory of God" (p. 49).

[5]I also presented this story in Johnson (1992).

PART III

"Let There Be Humans"

The Semiodiscursive Constitution of Human Beings

A CHRISTIAN DISCIPLINARY MATRIX FOR psychology begins with considerations of God. The triune God has spoken his creation into existence for the purpose of displaying his glory—the sum of all God's attributes, expressed through the prism of trinitarian activity. Humans, made in God's image, are special creatures, endowed with speech and emotions and made for relationship with God and one another. Through discourse and relationship—in dialogue—God causes individual humans to develop into "signs" of God. Each human is very complex, composed of four interactive "orders of discourse"—biological, psychosocial, ethical and spiritual—which in the mind of God together form a single, coherent "text" of a human being—a living text (a letter, 2 Cor 3:3) being written by the Spirit to experience and express God's glory.

8

The Ground of the Created Order

The Word of God

LET US REVIEW A NUMBER OF THE PREMISES that have been addressed thus far and upon which this book is based. First, the triune Creator of human beings has the definitive understanding of the soul and its improvement. Second, this understanding is made sufficiently available in the created order (including Scripture) that rational creatures like humans can reconstruct a finite but increasing approximation of God's understanding of individual human nature and its care. Third, psychology is the discipline that aims at the articulation and transcription of individual human nature and its care. Fourth, a Christian version of psychology will consist, in part, of texts authored by those who self-consciously aim at describing the triune God's understanding of individual human nature and its care.

To pursue a Christian psychology, another framework is needed than that assumed by modernity or religious dualism—a holistic model that seeks to do justice to all the relevant resources the Christian community has for the project. We shall begin this chapter by laying out how it appears that God constitutes the creation and redemption of human beings, and in the rest of the chapter we will discuss the semiodiscursive basis of creation and redemption. Some of this may seem unrelated to the alleged soul-care concerns of this book. However, the goal is to show the deep, underlying, meaningful unity of created reality and redeemed human life that makes possible a holistic Christian psychology.

The Internally Glorious Triune God, Hidden but Increasingly Manifested

God is infinitely glorious. But what does that mean? We cannot fully know, but we know enough to say that God is intrinsically, transcendently and infinitely majestic, good, holy, loving and happy. His glory is "the beauty of his manifold perfections" (Piper, 1996, p. 42). God's intrinsic beauty and worth is said to be God's *internal* glory, whereas the display of that glory to other beings is called God's *external* glory (Barth, 1957; Edwards, 1765/1998; Muller, 2003, Vol. 3, p. 547). Such is the nature of God's internal glory that it must be radiated or manifested outwardly, externally and temporally. God is personally committed "to display his infinite and awesome greatness and worth" (Piper, 1986, p. 42). The glory of God is fundamentally "revelatory" (Muller, 2003, Vol. 3, p. 541). Its excellence entails that it be displayed and shown forth. So a revelation or externalization of God's beauty is the manifestation of God's internal glory.

It was *fitting*, then, that God create a theater for his glory (Calvin, 1559/1960; Schreiner, 1991), a context within which his beauty could be displayed and then recognized by persons like himself in certain respects. These persons, made in his image, can become aware of God's beauty and love him the more they know him (Edwards, 1765/1998, p. 149), and then—because of their relative likeness to God—actually participate in and display that beauty in and among *themselves,* becoming *signs* of the glory of the triune God in their love of God and one another through the Holy Spirit. "God wills to glorify Himself. This means that He is not content to be what He is in Himself; He wills to manifest Himself as such. He wills to be revealed, known and acknowledged as what He is outside the circle of His own being. And for this purpose He has created us men and placed us in this world. In man God is to be glorified" (Barth, 1960, p. 183).

The hiddenness of God. Yet because of his infinity and invisibility, the glory of God can be fully appreciated only by himself (within the Trinity); the Christian tradition has always taught that God is fundamentally beyond the full comprehension of human beings (Ps 139:6; 145:3; Is 55:8-9; Rom 11:33-34; Bavinck, 1951; Frame, 1987).[1] As a result, he must reveal himself to humans, if they are to understand anything about him. Yet it would also seem obvious that God *could* reveal himself more fully than he has; for example, his glory is not directly accessible to our senses the way a material object is. (Atheists have used this as an argument against his existence, e.g., Schellenberg, 1993.) Summarizing a thought of Pascal, Wetsel (2003) wrote, "Any religion that did not proclaim God's hidden presence would contradict the whole of practical human experience" (p. 164).

There is no easy explanation here. Some have suggested that God's hiddenness makes faith more of a free choice (e.g., Murray, 2002). And maybe it is *fitting* that he is hidden. Perhaps his very majesty makes it appropriate that he *not* disclose himself in his creation too openly or too frequently, otherwise his uniqueness and transcendence would be compromised, something analogous to why we do not expect a visit from a king to the home of every commoner. Perhaps God's glory is being displayed in his apparent reticence to disclose himself. Though he is infinitely great, he is also infinitely humble (Varillon, 1983). He does not brag or boast. Though the Center of the universe, he does not have a narcissistic *need* to be the center of attention. Moreover, God's beauty would seem to be specially displayed through the course of its temporal unveiling. We like stories of a great treasure—hidden for a long time—that is suddenly discovered. And think of the joy in hide-and-seek; in the novelist who has something important to say but spends six hundred pages saying it with deliberation and poetic prowess; or in the planning of a surprise party for someone. The story of the gradual manifestation of the glory of God simply fosters the accumulation of greater joy in God and in all those who look for the increasing manifestation of his beauty. But whatever the reasons, it is obvious that God is keeping back the vast majority of his glory from the creation.

Nevertheless, the invisible, triune God has manifested himself in some ways, leaving *signs* of himself. As Pascal wrote, "Wishing to appear openly to those who seek Him with all their heart, and to remain hidden from those who shun Him with all their heart, God has moderated the way He might be known by giving signs, which can be seen by those who seek Him and not by those who do not. There is enough light for those whose only desire is to see, and enough darkness for those of a contrary disposition" (quoted by Wetsel, 2003, pp. 166-67).

So one can read the history of the human race as the story of the mostly hidden God's *gradual* manifestation to his image-bearers through *signs* of himself, embedded in the created order and also expressed in theophany, in Scripture, in the Son and in God's people. God's self-revelation through such signs permits him to remain largely hidden while manifesting his glory *in mea-*

sure. It appears that the infinite glory of the triune God is being parceled out *over time.*

The beginning of manifestation.

> In the beginning God created the heavens and the earth. The earth was formless and void, and darkness was over the surface of the deep, and the Spirit of God was moving over the surface of the waters. Then God said, "Let there be light"; and there was light. (Gen 1:1-3)

> In the beginning was the Word, and the Word was with God, and the Word was God. He was in the beginning with God. All things came into being through Him; and apart from Him nothing came into being that has come into being. In Him was life; and the life was the Light of men. (Jn 1:1-4)

Christians understand these two foundational passages to refer to the work of the triune God. This God, we learn in Scripture, is the supremely glorious Creator and Sustainer of the universe and the only Redeemer of humankind. The three persons of the Godhead manifested themselves in their creative, providential and redemptive activity, which is to be understood fundamentally as a set of speech-acts.

Like all things spoken, the Word of John 1:1 is the expression of a mind, here, the Father's mind. But the *Father's* Word is transcendently powerful; it accomplishes its meaning. It is a creating word, a realizing word. "By faith we understand that the worlds were prepared by the word of God" (Heb 11:3). God "gives life to the dead and calls into being that which does not exist" (Rom 4:17).

> For as the rain and the snow come down from heaven,
> And do not return there without watering the earth,
> And making it bear and sprout,
> And furnishing seed to the sower and bread to the eater;
> So shall My word be which goes forth from My mouth;
> It shall not return to Me empty,
> Without accomplishing what I desire,
> And without succeeding in the matter for which I sent it. (Is 55:10-11)

The image of a magician "casting a spell" and changing reality by his words is actually a good metaphor of God's speaking, which brings into being all other beings. God's Word is the actuating principle of the created order, both its origin and its sustenance. God "has spoken to us in His Son, whom He appointed heir of all things, through whom also He made the world, . . . and [the Son] upholds all things by the word of His power" (Heb 1:2-3). So God's word has brought to pass all the events of nature (Ps 147:15-18; 148:1-8), as well as human history and free human choices (Prov 21:1; Eph 1:11). So the universe is verbally ordered. There is a *semiodiscursive* structure to the creation, which derives from the creating, in-forming, providential word of God, the formative intelligence that orders all of created reality and is the reason for its intelligibility.

The Divine Modes of the Word of God

The purely divine mode: The eternal Son of God. Yet the phrase "word of God" is used in the Bible to denote a variety of entities. Upon close examination, it would appear that God's word has been and is expressed in a number of distinct forms or modes. These modes would seem to be analogous to the different modes of human meaning expression: body language, speech, writing and visual media (drawing, printing, radio, television and movies). But the most important mode of God's word is personal: Jesus Christ, the Son of God made flesh (Jn 1:1-13). God's speech is a function of his trinitarian nature, so the original form of God's word is itself divine: "the Word was God" (Jn 1:1; Vos, 1980b).

According to classical trinitarian theology, God the Father has spoken eternally in his Son and his Son is eternally a perfect likeness of the Father (Augustine, 1948; Bavinck, 1951; Olson & Hall, 2002). The Son resembles the Father exactly (Heb 1:3); he is the form *(morphē)* of God (Phil 2:6), possessing the same attributes as the Father, and the fellowship, glory and love that the Father and Son have shared eternally (Jn 17:5, 24) consist in a mutual delight in their differentiated similarity. According to the Christian tradition, the Son is everything the Father is, with two absolute exceptions: their relations to each other (called their *immanent relations*) and their roles with respect to creation and redemption (their *economic relations*). The Father is the Unbegotten Source, and the Son is eternally "generated" or begotten by the Father (LaCugna, 1991). They are the same in substance, essence or being, but distinguished by their relations to each other (in their subsistences or persons).

Edwards's understanding of the Trinity is illuminating at this point (Daniel, 1994; Holmes, 2001; Jenson, 1988; Pauw, 2001; see Edwards, 1971,

1994). Edwards (1989, 1765/1998) argued that the triune God is infinitely the greatest and most beautiful being there is, and part of God's greatness is the communication of that greatness. The triune nature of God is intrinsic to Edwards's account of God's greatness, because part of his greatness consists in the Trinity's loving, holy harmony, as well as in the differentiation of its individual members. God the Father "generates" the Son by communicating or speaking the Son (eternally); the Son is "God's own perfect idea of himself" (Edwards, 1994, p. 494), and the symmetry of their relationship is beautiful. Because of their virtuous love of perfection and their absolute similarity, the Father and Son love and enjoy each other perfectly. There is what Edwards called complete *consent* between Father and Son—a thorough, willing agreement with each other, infinite in scope. The Son knows the Father completely; that is, he knows his infinite significance infinitely and loves him absolutely, in a way corresponding to his significance.

It was also the Father's design that the Son be the verbal mediator between the Father and the creation (Vos, 1980b). He is the *Logos*, which is usually translated as "the Word," but could also be "the Proposition," "the Text," "the Discourse," "the Account" (Fries, 1978; Gundry, 2002) or as Hart (2003) suggests, "the true grammar of being" (p. 147). The Son should be understood to be "the ultimate meaning of the whole creation and as the revelation of the Father is inherent in it from the beginning"(Balthasar, 1989b, p. 246).

As the product of the Son's wisdom and power, the entire creation wondrously displays the glory of the triune God. However, the highest created manifestation of God's love would be the love of creatures for their Creator, so it is fitting that God formed conscious, rational beings, made in his image, who could consciously recognize God's greatness, wisdom and beauty, and love him on the basis of that knowledge. According to Edwards, the greater the reflection of God's glory, the greater the significance of the creature. So, a rock glorifies God, but an animal more than a rock, and a human more than an animal, and a mature, deeply aware adult more than a child, and a lover of God more than someone indifferent.

The divine-created mode of the Word of God: Jesus Christ. But only one person has truly loved God the way humans were supposed to. "God . . . in these last days *has spoken to us* in His Son," who is "the radiance of His glory and the exact representation of His nature" (Heb 1:1-3). "Representation" *(charaktēr)* means impression, and was the word used to refer to the stamp of a dignitary's head on a coin (Arndt & Gingrich, 1957). So the man Christ Jesus is a representation or a created "sign" of the Father. This is why, when one of his disciples, Philip, asked him to show them the Father, Jesus could say, "Have I been so long with you, and yet you have not come to know Me, Philip? He who has seen Me has seen the Father" (Jn 14:9).

In Jesus, the incarnate Son of God became "the glory as of the only begotten from the Father," who lived among us (Jn 1:14); he is the image of the invisible God (Col 1:15), in whom lives all the fullness of deity in bodily form (Col 2:9). "The image of God and son of God are thus twin concepts" (Kline, 1999, p. 23). Adam, the first image of God, is contrasted in the New Testament with the second Adam (Rom 5:12-21; 1 Cor 15:21-28, 45-57), the Archetype and head of a new race of image-bearers, the true fulfillment of humanity and of the image of God, crowned with glory and honor (Ps 8; Heb 2:6-9). Jesus, then, is what we might call the perfect, creaturely sign of God in the universe, one with the Father in purpose, love, goodness and holiness (Jn 10:30), while also being an earthly creature who was located at a point in time and space (though as the Son of God, he still mysteriously retained all the infinite qualities of God). Finitude entails such particularity.

In the life of Jesus the glory of God was specially articulated to humans (Balthasar, 1988-1998, 1989a). He was *the* Sign of God expressed on earth. His miracles, in particular, are said to be signs (Jn 2:11, *sēmeia;* Jn 6:2; 11:47) that indicate his preeminence as Lord and the "creative Word who can command and restore all the words of creation" (Hart, 2003, p. 328). But all of his actions were signs, from his outrage at the Pharisees and the moneychangers to the laying down of his life; all conveyed glory, beauty and meaning from God the Father. The cross and resurrection are arguably the most important signs in the universe. Christ underlined their semiotic nature: "An evil and adulterous generation craves for a sign; and yet no sign shall be given to it but the sign *[sēmeion]* of Jonah the prophet, for just as Jonah was three days and three nights in the belly of the sea monster, so will the Son of Man be three days and three nights in the heart of the earth" (Mt 12:39-40). Altogether, the incarnation, death and resurrection of the Word of God constitute the single greatest manifestation of God's glory in creation ever, best expressing the significance of God and providing the primary criterion by which to establish the relative significance of all else.

In His revelation, in Jesus Christ, the hidden God has indeed made Himself ap-

> prehensible. Not directly, but indirectly. Not to sight, but to faith. Not in His being, but in sign. . . . The Word was made flesh: this is the first, original and controlling sign of all signs. (Barth, 1957, p. 199)

As the God-human—the exact representation of God and the perfect human being—Jesus Christ is of the greatest importance in the definition of human being. He is the "real man" (Bonhoeffer, 1955, 1966; Barth, 1960), the true image of God and the form of humanity, after which all humans, made in God's image, were created, so he is also that toward which all humans are supposed to develop. He is "a real and appealing form of being, a way of dwelling among others, a kind of practice" (Hart, 2003, p. 147). He is the sign of God and the sign to God, the Way (Jn 14:6). As humans are conformed to his image (Rom 8:29; 2 Cor 3:18) and take on his likeness, they realize their created nature and become fulfilled. As a result, Christ's form is the fundamental form toward which all human development is moving. For Christians, there can be no psychology without reference to Jesus Christ.[2]

The Constitution of Creation by the Word of God

But let us return to the beginning and consider next the work of the Word of God. As we just noted, the divine Word of God brought the creation into existence, out of nothing. The Logos himself is the immediate, divine source of all else, and therefore is the source of all the meaningfulness found throughout the creation. As a function of God's Word, the creation demonstrates divine meaning, rationality and linguisticality (Wiker & Witt, 2006), but it is of only finite significance—like dust when compared with God himself—deriving whatever significance it has in relation to its Author. To better understand the creation, it is necessary to discuss its divinely authored purpose.

The doxological-semiotic purpose of the creation. Everywhere we turn in modern culture there are signs: along streets, on billboards and in buildings, communicating some message with words or symbols. But the term *sign* can be used far more broadly, to refer to anything that represents meaning: a track is a sign of an animal, a fever can be a sign of an illness, a gene is a sign that triggers the production of a protein in a cell, the word *rosebud* is a sign that represents a flower (or a sled), and a human represents God. Semiotics is the science of signs.[3]

Christians have long been interested in the notion of signs. Augustine (1997) discussed signs at some length and was the first Western thinker to recognize that certain marks in nature (like tracks) and words in language have a common semiotic function (p. xiii; see Deely, 1998). Augustine defined a sign as "a thing which of itself makes some other thing come to mind" (p. 30). But there was a special reason why he was interested in signs (he and many other Christians, e.g., Gregory of Nyssa; Bonaventure, 1978; Hugh of St. Victor; Nicholas of Cusa; Luther; Berkeley, 1929; Edwards, 1993; Hamann; Bavinck, 2004; Milbank, 1997; and Hart, 2003; see also Cameron, 1999; Daniel, 1994; Norris, 2001; Poythress, 2006). Secular semioticians are typically concerned only about what might be called the immanent or "proximate" scope of signs: their function as creaturely signs of other creatures (e.g., a word signifying an idea). Christians have given considerable thought to signs in order to bring out what might be called the "ultimate" scope of signs: their capacity to point to or refer to the God who transcends creation and who is the source of all signification (Nöth, 1990).[4] The entire creation consists of "images of divine things" (Edwards, 1994) and is therefore a grand "divine semiotics" (Daniel, 1994). As we saw above, because of human finitude, human understanding of God has to be mediated by signs of God ("for no man can see Me and live," Ex 33:20). Moreover, the noetic effects of sin so obscure the divine semiotics that God had to take extra measures to signify himself. According to Norris (2001), Augustine, for example, believed that

> God is obliged to communicate with signs, to make use of concrete terms to explain higher realities, to use objects which are manifest to the senses to describe invisible things, because the darkened understanding of sinful man cannot grasp truth directly. Humanity's fall from grace not only destroyed our immediate vision of God, but caused a fall into a universe of signs whereby God's word is veiled. God's labor to bring humanity back to its proper goal is one of accommodation, whereby he lowered himself through the Incarnation to a physical level where the Word could be seen and understood. The Word in flesh is the sign above all signs that is the basis for Augustine's understanding of both signs and relation. (p. 217)

In the twelfth century, Hugh of St. Victor wrote that "the whole sensible world is like a kind of book written by the finger of God—that is, created by divine power—and each particular creature is somewhat like a figure [a sign], not invented by human decision, but instituted by the divine will to manifest the invisible things of the wisdom of God" (quoted in McGrath, 1999a, p. 114). Edwards (1993) said of the created order: "I am not ashamed to own that

I believe that the whole universe, heaven and earth, air and seas, and the divine constitution and history of the holy Scriptures, be full of images of divine things, as full as a language is of words; and that the multitudes of those things that I have mentioned are but a very small part of what is really intended to be signified and typified by these things" (p. 152). So that "if we look on these shadows of divine things as the voice of God . . . we may, as it were, have God speaking to us" (p. 74).

So, according to some important leaders in the Christian tradition,[5] the entire creation is composed of signs of God, and its greatest value is found in its doxological significance. The hidden God has manifested himself to some extent in his creation, which is, as it were, a book, filled with words or signs, all of which convey something of the glory of their Author—some more, some less. This Christian semiotic understanding of the creation (Nöth, 1990) offers us a unifying way of understanding reality, one that is centered on God and that undermines many of the dualisms that have bedeviled Western thought (e.g., body-soul, subject-object, rational-empirical, cognition-emotion, psychology-theology), through the recognition that all human knowing is grounded in a hermeneutic of the signs of God, designed to lead us to God. We turn next to consider some of the major categories of God's semiotic creation.

The nature mode of creation. As mentioned above, the heavens and earth were created and are sustained by the word of God.

> [God] sends forth His command to the earth;
> His word runs very swiftly.
> He gives snow like wool;
> He scatters the frost like ashes.
> He casts forth His ice as fragments;
> Who can stand before His cold?
> He sends forth His word and melts them;
> He causes His wind to blow and the waters to flow. (Ps 147:15-18)

God's word is revealed to be the source of weather patterns that to us are hard to predict. We are also told that God's creation itself speaks:

> The heavens are telling of the glory of God;
> And their expanse is declaring the work of His hands.
> Day to day pours forth speech,

And night to night reveals knowledge.
There is no speech, nor are there words;
Their voice is not heard. (Ps 19:1-3)

This passage puts well the idea that though the heavens do not speak in human language, they possess a discursive nature and express their essential intelligibility. However, the utterances of the creation are mechanical, not personal. The speech of stars and trees is more like an echo or a recording than the voice of a person; it is the mechanical reproduction of Another's speech.

Even so, this mechanical "speech" provides evidence of God's "enstructuring" word throughout nature. Consider, for example, the concepts and laws of mathematics and logic ("Numbers, propositions, properties, states of affairs, and possible worlds . . . really are divine thoughts or concepts," Plantinga, 2000, p. 281); the symmetry (and beauty) of countless physical, chemical and biological forms (including those that appear to us chaotic, like fractal geometric patterns); the atomic structure of the elements and compounds, and the periodic table; the structure of DNA and the genetic code system; the physical structure and beauty of plants; the intricate intersystemic physiology of animals; the complexity of the ecosystems they inhabit; and beyond this earth, the organized regularities observed in the galaxies that fill the universe—to say nothing of the physical, chemical and biological laws that regulate them all. Regarding DNA, Carey (2003) suggests, "It is convenient to view the genome for any species as a book, with the genetic code as the language common to the books of all life-forms" (p. 35). The creation's vast meaningfulness is the expression of God's infinite, effusive understanding. Even individual natural events (like the falling to earth of a sparrow) are ordained by the will (or, shall we say, the word?) of God (Mt 10:29). The intelligent design movement seeks to identify evidence of this intelligible design, which is hard to account for adequately without a supreme intelligence who spoke it into being.

Human life and experience is entirely dependent on this network of created orderliness. Consider the influence of the human genetic code on specific psychological characteristics, the various biological processes of the human body, especially the endocrine and nervous systems, the structure of the human mind (including memory, emotion and motivation, and language and reasoning) and personality, human relationality, the sequence of human development and a moral sense (the law of God written into the brain, see Rom 2:12-14); all these are a function of the Son's formative speech in human nature that constitutes the formal foundation of human life.

So nature is filled with meaning. "*Meaning* is the *being* of all that has been *created* and the nature even of our selfhood. It has a *religious root* and a *divine origin*" (Dooyeweerd, 1984, Vol. 1, p. 4). And this enormous, natural framework of meaning "testifies" or "points to" its Origin (Stoker, 1973; Torrance, 1969). But the creation's meaning is semiodiscursive, so sentences, texts and mathematical formulas are required for humans to explicate the rationality embedded in natural objects. Augustine wrote that "language is a light in which creation is made visible" (Hart, 2003, p. 291). Elucidating this intelligibility is the task of science (McGrath, 2001; Torrance, 1969; Kuyper, 1998). Being created in God's image "bespeaks an ability imparted to man to unwrap the thoughts of God that lie embodied in creation" (Kuyper, p. 444). Textbooks and journal articles are simply human attempts to exegete the meaning of the texts that God has expressed in creation.

Yet, for all its complexity, nature does not possess narrative structure. It is cyclical or random, but not linear, the way a story is. God is telling a story in nature (consider the first five days of creation), but mere nature cannot comprehend it. Human life appears to be the only part of nature with a narrative sense.

The personal agency mode of creation. We have noted that the natural aspects of human life (e.g., the physical, chemical and physiological processes of the human body, and cognitive and emotional processes of the soul) are ordered by the word of God. We turn next to consider the role of God's word in individual human activity. This is a mysterious (and contentious) subject, but so important that we must take the risk of trying to describe the interrelation between human and divine activity. Superficially, it looks like humans do some things and God does other things. Yet, the Bible teaches that God works *all things* according to the counsel of his will (Eph 1:11), so we must not avoid the implications of this teaching, simply because it challenges our understanding (Johnson, 2002). A theocentric and biblical conception of human activity sees human creativity, imagination, initiative, decision and action as ongoing, temporal manifestations or realizations of God's will (or word).

Consider the following proverbs. "The king's heart is like channels of water in the hand of the LORD; / He turns it wherever He wishes" (Prov 21:1). If anyone is free, the king is. So if even the king's heart is turned wherever God wishes, then surely the hearts of ordinary people are providentially guided by

God. "It is the blessing of the LORD that makes rich" (Prov 10:22). Becoming rich is usually a process made up of days and months and years of human decisions and responsible activity, yet God blesses through such human effort. "Many plans are in a man's heart / But the counsel of the LORD will stand" (Prov 19:21). The terms "foreordain" (*proorizō;* Acts 4:28; Rom 8:29; Eph 1:5) and "predetermined plan" (*hōrismenē boulē;* Acts 2:23) are used in the Bible to refer to God's precreation, *articulable* script for future human history (sometimes called a "book": "In Your book were all written / The days that were ordained for me, / when as yet there was not one of them," Ps 139:16). Jeremiah makes most clear the divine *verbal* basis for human action:

> Who is there who speaks and it comes to pass,
> Unless the LORD has commanded it?
> Is it not from the mouth of the Most High
> That both good and ill go forth? (Lam 3:37-38)

These teachings reveal that God is purposefully involved in even the minutest details of human life, including the very decisions that constitute human history. Indeed, they are the outcomes of his speech-acts.

Though there have been dissenters to this view of God's providence in human life, Western Christian thinkers (both Catholic and Protestant) have generally affirmed it, referring to it as "concurrence" (Berkhof, 1939; Grenier, 1950; Muller, 1995) and, more recently, "double agency" (Horton, 2002). As in nature, God's involvement in human activity is linguistic. However, personal agency is distinctive, for the rest of creation expresses God's word mechanically, whereas mature humans are personal agents who themselves *act* with deliberation and therefore are responsible for their actions in a way that subhuman creatures are not. In the natural mode, God simply speaks and causes things to happen. But in the personal agency mode, God speaks *through* human activity, and humans are privileged to be willing (or unwitting) participants in the realization of his drama.

The capacity of personal agency is part of what it means to be made in the *imago Dei.* God has created humans to be able to act freely in a way analogous to God's freedom, but since humans are creatures, and sinful creatures to boot, human freedom is conditioned by contingent, finite and spiritual factors that limit but do not annul it. And the most important condition is that the free actions of humans are ultimately a function of God's verbal foreordination or decree. God is writing billions of stories, then, through the free actions of his image-bearers.

This doctrine of double agency should not be interpreted in a way that minimizes human involvement and undercuts human responsibility. A discrete human action should be understood as constituted both wholly by God *and* the individual personal agent. Yet, rightly understood, humans should see their participation with the Creator as pure gift and as entirely dependent on the contingent goodness of God, and so should give God all the glory, while living in thankfulness and gratitude (Mt 5:16; Jn 3:21; Eph 2:10). "God and man will never appear as equal partners. It is God who acts, on man, for man and then together with man; the involvement of man in the divine action is part of God's action, not a precondition of it" (Balthasar, 1988, p. 18).[6]

According to the Bible, then, the story line of an individual's actions are the result of a mysterious double authorship, the realization of an individual "subplot" in God's "world-play" through the decisions of the human actor/"co-playwright." As a result, all actions and experiences, including meaningful behavior, speech, memories, emotions and thoughts, express a two-fold degree of intelligibility and significance that transcend that of mere nature—they have meaning to the human agents who freely express them and they have meaning to God who ordained or allowed them. Even the discourse and texts that humans produce are themselves expressions, in some measure, of the word of God, not in an authoritative sense—as if God himself were speaking, as in Scripture—but in two secondary senses, as they consist of that which he ordained and to the extent they are meaningful.

This understanding of human life provides a theocentric justification for taking seriously human experience and memory. While actual history provides the standard to which our memories ought to conform, one's memories—*even when distorted*—contribute to the current constitution of one's story, and they cannot be absolutely discounted without rejecting what is ultimately, in some sense, a *part* of God's designation of history. Genuine objectivity (found in God's omniscience) includes an accurate comprehension of all aspects of reality, including the objective reality of human subjectivity. God knows our false perceptions and their place in our story.

Such a view of God's involvement in human life helps us understand how pervasive is God's sovereignty and his creation grace. *Every* good thing bestowed and *every* perfect gift comes from above, from the Father of lights (Jas

1:17), so this must include every human action, to the extent it is good. Only this kind of framework can make sense of Romans 8:28—that God works all things together for the good of his children (*all things*, including the actions of other people)—otherwise that verse offers little comfort. This model allows us to "read" the actions of others, even the evil actions of others, as part of a larger, meaningful plan that transcends the intentions of the human actors and grants a higher significance to all that happens, because it is part of a larger semio-discursive framework, God's drama: *"You meant evil against me, but God meant it for good"* (Gen 50:20). The stories and dramas of individual humans possess a significance greater than one's immediate experience, for they are plays within the ultimate play of God (Horton, 2002; Vanhoozer, 2005).

The ideal realization of human personal agency is seen when image-bearers act in conscious, deliberate dependence on God, responding to, reflecting and consenting to the word of God. This is the high point of human personhood and is exemplified by Jesus Christ, the perfect image. Unfortunately, human nature is vitiated by human sin, a condition of perverse distortion of the *imago Dei*. But sin is a special case of human activity that requires more careful consideration, which will be attempted below.

The sociocultural mode of creation. Closely related to the mode of personal agency, and interdependent with it, is the mode of social relations and culture. Individuals grow up within a network of face-to-face dialogical relations, within which they develop their identity; they form strong bonds to some people; and most of their life is spent conversing with and relating to others. And consider the importance of culture to the structure and quality of individual lives: material culture (like cars, hamburgers, shoes, dollar bills and computers) and immaterial culture (values, languages, styles, rules, laws, social institutions), types of relationships (physician-nurse, physician-patient), group relations (minority-majority relations; in-group/out-group), and virtue and vice (which are often related to others). An important task of individual development is the mastery of one's culture's social rules that regulate the conduct of its members, including manners, conventions, norms and laws. And then there are the existence and development of the social institutions of advanced cultures: government and politics, the economy, food production, the legal and penal systems, science, health care, mass media and entertainment, and religion and its gatherings and practices. The dynamics of social life are an enormous topic (studied in economics, history, linguistics, anthropology, social psychology and sociology), and individual human lives cannot be adequately understood apart from them.

Contrary to natural objects, which exist independently of humans, sociocultural objects (like rules and institutions) are constituted by human perception and understanding (Searle, 1995). Cultures are maintained through interpersonal relations and composed of *socially constructed objects,* realities that would not exist apart from their joint constitution by the members of a culture, mediated by discourse. For example, as a *natural* object, an American ten-dollar bill is composed of cotton and linen fibers, weighs a gram, is printed with green ink and so on. However, as a *social* object, a ten-dollar bill is a form of currency, established within American culture as "standing for" a relative economic value that can be exchanged for an amount of goods or services. Social reality is discourse-dependent; take away discourse and human culture would disappear (Searle, 1995). But discourse is not enough. Cultural background beliefs are necessary to perceive an American ten-dollar bill as anything more than a natural object (Searle, 1995). Things like dollar bills, a football game, a fashionable blouse, today's date, a marriage, the firing of a CEO and the selling of a car are social facts constituted by discourse-dependent conventions that entail certain socially shared beliefs and attitudes, and requiring rules to regulate their use or practice.

What is God's relation to such socially dependent phenomena? We are discussing them in this chapter, because social facts are also a part of the created order and therefore must be understood as existing according to God's will and dependent on his word. And there is also biblical warrant for this conclusion. To begin with, the divine establishment of the family—perhaps the most basic cultural institution—is spoken of in the first chapter of the Bible, where the creation of man and woman is described and we learn they were told to be fruitful and multiply (Gen 1:28). This implies at the very least that marriage and the nuclear family are normative cultural structures, encouraged by God's Word (Woltiers, 1985). We may conclude further, in light of other biblical teaching, that wherever these institutions flourish, God's creation grace is in evidence. But what about more complex cultural institutions? Consider the following passage in Isaiah:

> Does the farmer plow continually to plant seed?
>   Does he continually turn and harrow the ground?
> Does he not level its surface,

And sow dill and scatter cumin,
And plant wheat in rows,
Barley in its place and rye within its area?
For his God instructs and teaches him properly.
For dill is not threshed with a threshing sledge,
Nor is the cartwheel driven over cumin;
But dill is beaten out with a rod, and cumin with a club.
Grain for bread is crushed,
Indeed, he does not continue to thresh it forever.
Because the wheel of his cart and his horses eventually damage it,
He does not thresh it longer.
This also comes from the Lord of hosts,
Who has made his counsel wonderful and his wisdom great. (Is 28:24-29)

Knowledge about farming, as we know, is socially and discursively mediated. Up-and-coming farmers are instructed by other, more experienced farmers in the skills of their craft. Isaiah, however, says that this wisdom is ultimately a gift of God. And while the phrase "word of God" is not used in reference to this wisdom, the rest of the Bible's teaching on wisdom points to Christ and his word (Prov 8; Is 11:2; Jn 1:1-4; 1 Cor 1:30; Eph 1:17; Col 2:3).

Another important institution is addressed in Romans 13:1-2a, 6: "Every person is to be in subjection to the governing authorities. For there is no authority except from God, and those which exist are established by God. Therefore whoever resists authority has opposed the ordinance of God," for "rulers are servants of God" (see also 1 Pet 2:13-14). Human government is a social institution, sustained by the collective intentionality and activity (especially the speech-acts) of the members of a culture. Yet Paul indicates that it has been "established" by God (*hypo theou tetagmenai:* appointed, ordered or determined by God). It is his "ordinance" *(diatagē)* and so serves him and his purposes. The immaterial, socially constituted governmental structures that serve to regulate human conduct and administer justice (imperfectly, it must be said) concurrently exist according to the purposes of God. Though the term *word of God* is not used here either, attributing this establishment to the word of God is consonant with all we have seen regarding the word's function in the natural world, with Christ's role in the creation universally (in [Christ] *all things* hold together, Col 1:17; see Heb 1:3), and with the scope of what is suggested about God's involvement here (establishing, ordering). The divine ground of the social structures of culture is fundamentally no different than God's ordering of the weather. So, though the Bible does not give us a comprehensive discussion of *how* God maintains the social order, enough is said for us to conclude that he is directly involved in its existence and that it, along with the rest of the good creation, is ultimately dependent on his will (and word). We can safely conclude that social relations and culture, then, are also a mode of the creation that depends on the word of God.

The scope of the social mode can only be seen as enormous and dazzling in its complexity and divine glory. Cultures and their development are an important part of God's design for the human race and a function of his creation grace. Within his plan is the proliferation of human cultures and their evolution over the centuries, including the development of philosophy, science, technology and the arts, all of which are the outworking of God's cultural mandate to humankind: to have dominion over the rest of the creation, to be fruitful and multiply, and fill the earth and subdue it (Gen 1:26, 28; see Van Til, 1959; Woltiers, 1985). In fact, in God's plan, the Son's own incarnation was preceded by and related to the development of Hebrew culture, as well as Greek and Roman cultures. Indeed, without culture, there could have been no Bible like we have. The social mode of God's word is foundational to the realization of his plan to glorify himself in creation and redemption.

Kuyper (1898a, 1998; Bacote, 2005) was something of an early Christian sociologist, and he (1998) believed that cultural development was a function of humans being created in the *imago Dei*.

> God deposited an infinite number of nuclei for high human development in our nature and these nuclei cannot develop except through the social bond between people. . . . If it has pleased God to mirror the richness of his image in the social multiplicity and fullness of our race, . . . then . . . humanity will have to remain on earth for as long as it takes to unfold as fully and richly as necessary those nuclei of human potential. . . . God will take delight in high human development. He himself will bring it about and into view. Then he will seek in it his own glorification. The control and harnessing of nature by civilization, enlightenment, and progress, by science and art, by a variety of enterprises and industry will be entirely separate from the totally other development in holiness and integrity (in the Church); indeed, that *exterior* development may even clash openly with an *interior* development in holiness and become a temptation to the be-

> liever. Still, that exterior development . . . has to continue and be completed to bring the *work of God* in our race to full visible realization. (pp. 178-79)

Kuyper's exuberance might be lessened by twentieth-century holocausts and environmental degradation. Sin corrupts culture, as it does individual personal agency (which will be discussed below), so cultural progress is uneven and by no means inevitable. One example of this is the period of the Middle Ages, where it appears that well-meaning, heavenly-minded Christians were the glue that held European culture together, while simultaneously resisting its creative unfolding. Nonetheless, Kuyper's intuitions are sound—cultural complexity generally increases over time, due to the accumulation of knowledge—and flow from his recognition that all cultural good comes from above.

Kuyper (1898a) also came up with the principle of "sphere sovereignty," that cultural institutions are all beholden to their Creator, and that, therefore, each has its own relative autonomy from the other institutions and its own God-given normative structures. As a result, an institution cannot be made subservient to another institution or forced into another's form (e.g., a government should not be controlled by a religious organization and vice versa, and a university should not be run just like a business). This also suggests that social institutions have objective norms to which they must conform, if they are to thrive as they are intended by God (Woltiers, 1985). At the same time, this understanding can allow for a range of legitimate differences in the instantiations of an institution.

The church, psychology and the mental health profession. Before moving on, we should note in particular the cultural institutions most relevant to Christian psychology and soul care: the church, the science of psychology and the mental health profession. Perhaps the most important institution God has established is his church (Mt 16:18; Eph 2:15). Given its tasks to administer the Word of God and redemptive grace, the church has a central role to play in God's drama, and part of that role relates to the soul care it performs in our culture, through evangelism and biblical counseling (done by pastors and trained laypeople). But how are we to understand the science of psychology and the institution of the mental health profession, since they are currently dominated and controlled by secularists?

By creation grace mediated through his word, God has caused culture to develop in diverse ways and with increasing complexity, as his foreordained plan has unfolded. Therefore, we must conclude that the science of psychology and the mental health profession both ultimately belong to Christ. He is their Lord (Johnson, 1997a), and whatever truth, validity and value they possess is entirely dependent on his goodness. Admittedly these institutions are corrupted by human sin (as are all human institutions, even the church); but to the extent the science of psychology in its current form discovers anything of the intelligibility of human nature, and the current mental health profession helps humans resemble God in any way, they and our culture are the beneficiaries of God's expressed kindness. God is able to use for good even those who are opposed to his agenda (e.g., God used Assyria and Babylon to bring judgment on his people under the Old Covenant), but this does not mean that God *endorses* all that happens (any more than God was pleased with the evil that the Assyrians and Babylonians wrought; see, e.g., Habakkuk).

Psychological researchers study aspects of human nature in order to discern their implicit rationality and decode the text embedded in the phenomenon of interest. Then the researchers turn the findings into explicit texts that constitute—along with all the other theoretical and research publications in the field—the real intellectual capital of psychology: the body of its written discourse. Though produced by individual personal agents, all written texts are necessarily socially constructed (see Danziger [1990, 1998] for evidence of this in psychology). One's education and training, attendance at conferences and reading of other publications, and one's work as a counselor or counselee provide the discursive socializing experiences that make plausible and justify the practices of reading, researching, writing, teaching and counseling that one understands today as "psychology." Recent decades of work in psychology have yielded an enormous body of written texts that are currently considered "authoritative," and the institutions of psychological research and the mental health field as extant, including organizations like the American Psychological Association, define in our day the study and treatment of human beings. Yet because most of the participants of these institutions are committed to a secular and naturalistic evolutionary worldview—ultimately antithetical to God's understanding of things—their findings, writings and practices must be reinterpreted Christianly and in some cases translated into Christian discourse and practice by members of the church called to do so, if they are to be legitimately incorporated into Christian understanding and ways of life (discussed in chap. 7).

There is a corporate dimension to human likeness to Christ and an important part of image-bearing is the conforming of our corporate understanding to the mind of Christ. God takes pleasure in the church thinking about human beings the way he does; so the development of psychology, particularly a Christian psychology, brings increasing glory to God, the larger and more accurate the knowledge base.

The interdependence between the personal and sociocultural modes. Most of the activities and institutions that make up a culture are actually a product of the dynamic interaction between individual personal agents, their social relations and larger cultural forms. Fundamentally, there cannot be one without the others. The development of personal agency and the array of personal and vocational options that contemporary humans have available is made possible by familial, social and cultural support. Conversely, culture is itself "composed" of countless social actions of personal agents (like soothing a child, writing a policy or creating a new invention), which altogether provide the personal agentic infrastructure of a culture.

The term *creation grace* has been used here as a label for God's role in personal agency and sociocultural activity. Some view creation grace as something God makes available, that people are free to take advantage of or not, and that is certainly true. But the view assumed here (following particularly the Augustinian and Reformed traditions) goes further: God's giving of grace to humans commonly includes all the good in particular that humans realize *through their own actions*. This renders God the supreme author of the story of history; to deny this obscures some of the glory of his grace (I have already promised to discuss the role that sin plays in this history and God's rule over that sin).

The significance of sociocultural and individual activity is found in its relation to that which is ultimately significant. Through missions, cultures are to be introduced to the story of Christ. The sign of the cross casts a shadow on all human activity, social relations and cultural institutions, qualifies their value and reveals their ultimate meaning (or relative lack thereof). The kingdom of God moves into cultures through the gospel and transforms them as the stories of its individual members are drawn into God's redemptive-historical drama. Augustine's *City of God* was an attempt to describe this individual and culture-transforming movement in reference to Roman culture.

The effects of sin on the personal and sociocultural modes. Finally, while the good of individual and corporate human activity is constituted by God's words of creation grace, it is also seriously compromised by sin. The Christian tradition teaches that humankind is now natively opposed to God and his ways, because of *original sin*, "the innate depravity of the heart" (Edwards, 1834/1974, Vol. 2, p. 146). There is now in individual humans an uncreated disposition to resist God, a tendency exacerbated in community, resulting in a transcultural "world" that is opposed to God and his ways (Jn 1:10; 14:17, 30; 15:18-19; 17:14; see 1 Jn). Out of this sin comes the evil motives, thoughts and deeds that taint dialogue and damage human relationships (and development), and therefore that leads to the measurable disorder and damage one finds in human souls and in cultural institutions.

As a result, according to Christian teaching, personal and social activity is now corrupt. Evil and impurity "adhere to" and shape all human activity more or less; to the extent they do so, the activity cannot be understood as thoroughly expressing God's word (since it does not correspond to his character or will), and it is therefore correspondingly unintelligible. Sin is the only truly irrational aspect of reality; *ultimately* it makes no sense and defies explanation or understanding (Berkouwer, 1971).

God is devoid of sin himself and never tempts anyone to sin (Jas 1:13), but humans are strangely "free" to disobey God's word and to act autonomously from it—to the extent their hearts and lives do not correspond to God's design for human life—in marked contrast to the rest of the creation:

> Even the stork in the sky
> Knows her seasons;
> And the turtledove and the swift and the thrush
> Observe the time of their migration;
> But My people do not know
> The ordinance of the LORD. (Jer 8:7)

Consequently, God is to be recognized as the ultimate source or author of all the *good* in personal and sociocultural activity, while individual adults are the ultimate sources or authors of the evil of their hearts and activity (allowing also for Satanic and demonic influence), and that sin, in turn, is dialectically made more plausible and powerfully reinforced by fallen cultural institutions that oppress individuals in various ways. Nonetheless, Scripture also teaches that the evil of sin is—most mysteriously—*permitted* by the enstructuring word of God. Freely chosen sinful acts that are contrary to God's nature are paradoxically allowed by God (see Job 1—2; Gen 50:20), creating holes or breaches in the structures of the otherwise rational, created order that, in the end, provide opportunities to reveal more of the glory of God (see Jn 9:3; 11:4). This doxological intensification can be seen most profoundly in the crucifixion of Christ (Acts 2:23; 4:28). Because sin is a leech on God's goodness (Plantinga, 1995), there is no sinful human activity that is absolutely devoid of all good. Even the Holocaust demonstrated a tragically perverse efficiency made possible by a cunning diligence. So, even in the worst of human activity, to the extent that there is anything present that can be called good, the word of God is still being expressed, since there is no good thing that is not derived from God's actuating word.

This complex state of affairs poses an enormous hermeneutic predicament that has profound implications for human development and soul care. Humans who are created in God's image but born in sin are confronted in the world with *two* sets of signs, two sign systems that are antithetically opposed to each other. One set is ultimately and eschatologically true. It is the expression of the perfect understanding and will of God and is a reflection of his holy purposes, desires, understanding and affections, and it points toward the holy and loving God who has spoken the universe into existence and now calls humans to be his children in Christ. All truth, goodness and beauty participate in this massive, *God-sanctioned* sign system.

The other set of signs is ultimately and eschatologically false, but it nonetheless temporarily exists—by God's permission (giving it a *relative* comprehensibility). This sign system signifies all that is evil in the world, all that is contrary to God: meaninglessness, hatred, destruction, oppression and abuse. Consequently, it points away from God and would seem to call into question his existence and his good purposes and values. It has been with us almost since the beginning of human history—when the serpent began speaking: "Did God really say?" (Gen 3:1 NIV). Thereafter, all lies, myths and malevolent violence participate in another enormous, but false, God-*permitted* sign system. We might say that one of the most momentous tasks of life, then, is to interpret properly the signs (and texts) of the universe, discerning and developing a hermeneutic of trust toward the truth-bearing signs and a hermeneutic of suspicion toward the false, so that we can properly identify and distinguish them, dissenting from the false, but consenting to the true.

We must now return to the science of psychology and the mental health profession. The noetic-discursive effects of sin distort human understanding and therefore affect academic disciplines and professional practices, like psychology and soul care. As a result, the word of God that orders individual and sociocultural activities, like psychology and soul care, has been more or less garbled, a mixture of the two sign systems. A careful, critical reading of secular psychology texts reveals a marvelously rich rearticulation of the embedded rationality/discourse found in human nature, spoken into existence by God. However, that articulation is also somewhat distorted, to the extent that it deviates from God's holy design and purposes. Even more distorted are the affective effects of sin that disfigure human motives, values, goals and loves, leading to misplaced priorities and agendas in research and soul care. The dominant influences today in the mental health profession in the West are particularly compromised in this way, since they implicitly promote an autocentric value system. Of course, their practitioners are largely unaware of this underlying religious agenda, since they are convinced that they are open-minded and value-neutral. But it is precisely at this point that they are actually being most faithful to their self-deceived semiotics. So, there is a need for God to restore the human sciences and their professions to their God-intended design.

The Discursive Modes of the Word of God in Creation

We have been considering how the words of the Word of God are the primary enstructuring cause of the three facets of the creation: nature, personal agency, and sociocultural reality. We turn next to examine how God has expressed and continues to express himself in human discourse.

The mode of the covenantal/canonical writings: The Old and New Testaments. In part one we saw how important the Bible is to soul care. Risking some repetition, we need to reconsider the role of Scripture, but now in light of what we have learned in this chapter about the textuality of the rest of God's creation. To begin with, Scripture provides a fixed record of God's redemptive activity, including his speech-acts, which among other things communicates information about his nature, preferences and ideals, as well as his relation to sin and the human performance it shapes. We learn there that the triune God has authored a complex historical drama for his own glory that has as its central plot the deliverance of believers from their native, benighted opposition to God's purposes—through his own actions and discourse in Christ—and their journey into glory through their gradual reformation into the image of Christ until they are perfected in eternity. The Bible itself is of utmost importance in this story (Work, 2002) because it provides, first, a textual description of Christ, the very Word of God, most clearly in the Gospels, but really throughout the entire Bible (Goldsworthy, 2000); second, a sign-decoding book, a linguistically stable guide to the universe and to other human discourse, that permits God's followers to properly distinguish discourse and activity that lead away from and toward God; and third, the God-ordained means for realizing his redemptive purposes.

While all of creation has a semiodiscursive quality, because of the implicit meaning which God has established within it, the Bible is obviously unique; for it is the one *explicitly verbal* expression of God's mind and heart—written down for all generations. The Bible comes "prearticulated," in contrast to the meaning embedded within the rest of creation. We might say that nature and personal and sociocultural activity are all *implicit* or *embedded texts* that must be diligently studied (through research) in order to rearticulate their divinely constituted intelligibility and put it into writing, whereas the Bible is an *explicit text,* a *text proper,* that already expresses God's word directly in human language.

Also, it is the only set of human texts that are uniquely, divinely inspired (Crabb, 1981, 1987; Henry, 1958; Packer, 1980; Warfield, 1970b): "God-breathed" (2 Tim 3:16).[7] While God has ordained or permitted all human activity, including all text authorship, Scripture is not on the same plane as other texts. Divine inspiration makes the Bible God's Word in a robust sense. It is God's Word *simpliciter* (straightforwardly, utterly, without reserve), God's Word in a way that "marks it out" and sets it apart from all other texts.

One of the greatest challenges facing the church is figuring out something of God's intended relation between Scripture and the rest of the meaning embedded in creation. We have already noted that the Bible is our canonical "spectacles" (Calvin, 1559/1960), by which we are to interpret the meaning in the rest of the universe, that is, the embedded "discourse" in the created order as well as the actual discourse of the scientific texts of other communities (like those of modern psychology). In the Bible, among all the world's textuality, God "shares his heart," where he says what is important to him, where he makes specific promises about what he will do, and where he fixes in permanent form the specific discourse that is the means of human salvation and healing—the gospel of Christ. The texts of the Bible project a theocentric world—that is, a theocentric interpretation of the universe—which the reader can "walk into" through reading, in order to learn how to live in that kind of universe. Among the enormous number of human texts that have been written and the vast, immeasurable meaning in the universe, God has put a circle around one particular set of texts and said "Above all else, read this! *This* discourse is of greatest importance. Make it the core of your reading and receive it deeply into your minds, hearts, and lives to enable you to live well and to discern and understand rightly everything else I have expressed."

The mode of the gospel. There is another closely related mode of the word of God in creation that is especially relevant for soul care. We are told in the book of Acts that, years before the New Testament canon was completed, the word of God (or word of the Lord) was being proclaimed (Acts 13:5; 15:36; 17:13) and received (Acts 8:14; 11:1; 17:11), and was spreading and growing (Acts 6:7; 12:24; 19:20). It was called the "word of salvation," the "word of his grace" and the "word of the gospel" (Acts 13:26; 14:3; 15:7). In fact, the term *gospel* (*euangelion*, "good news") was used in the early church as a virtual synonym for the word of God concerning Christ that was verbally proclaimed (Acts 20:24; Rom 1:1-5; 1 Cor 15:1-8). This usage seems to suggest that the "word of God" can also be summarized as "the message of God's redemption in Christ," the core content of the gospel, which is the spoken means of Christian salvation (Rom 10:8-10; see Jensen, 2002). "God shines in [Christ], and then there is another glass wherein Christ is discovered, the glass of the gospel" (Sibbes, 1983, p. 246). This verbal summary of the core message of salvation, sometimes called the *kerygma* (Ladd, 1974, chap. 25), was expressed in speech, in contrast to the specific, far more elaborated canonical writings on the gospel of Christ that became the New Testament. One is written, the other is spoken, but both are the word of God expressed in human words. So when believers *speak* to others the truths of salvation, they are speaking the word of God, the gospel.

This usage is obviously important for Christian soul care, but let us explore why. Individual sentences (tokens) are concrete expressions of the truth found in propositions (Alston, 1996). For example, the proposition "Christ is the source of all truth" can be expressed in that sentence, as well as in "All truth comes from Christ," and "The only truth there is derives from Christ," and so on. A given proposition can be expressed in an enormous number of various sentence tokens. The verses of the Bible are important because they are the divinely inspired set of fixed sentence tokens that express many propositions about God, human beings and salvation that God wanted to serve as a canonical, linguistic standard of his salvific agenda. However, Christians are not simply to recite those verses over and over and over again. Their propositional content should be "put into our own words," as we restate the meaning that underlies the specific sentences of Scripture in new sentence tokens within new contexts and with new applications. If that is so, preaching and counseling today that summarize biblical narrative and teaching should also be regarded as a special form of the salvific word of God. Through faith in such words, one is saved (and being saved) and one's soul is being repaired.

The Constitution of the New Creation by the Word of God

The last word of God to be discussed is the word that is directly responsible for freeing humans from their enslaving autocentrism and creating new life in relationship with God. The minds of the unbelieving are darkened, we are told, and their hearts are blinded (2 Cor 4:4; Eph 4:17-18). So there is a need for a resurrecting and redefining word from God, a word that through Christ creates new hearts in God's image-bearers. "For God, who said, 'Light shall shine out of darkness,' is the One who has shone in our hearts to give the light of the knowledge of the glory of God in the face of Christ" (2 Cor 4:6). Directly analogous to God's words that constitute the creation, this word heralds and brings in the *new creation*. It is a distinct word of God, since it is intrinsically *reformative*, healing alienated sinners whose damaged knowing and loving capacities are being set right (in at least a preliminary way), and bringing them into a new kind of gradually growing freedom and joy in relation to God. And unlike Scripture, which, we have to admit, is inert on the page, *this* word—which uses Scripture and the gospel as its means—is a powerful word that brings about change: "Is not My word like fire?" declares Yahweh, "and like a hammer which shatters a rock?" (Jer 23:29).

The reparative word of God mysteriously issues forth by means of Scripture and the gospel of Christ, but it is made up of two distinguishable but indivisible parts: declarative and reformative, both of which are grounded in the believer's union with Christ. The reader will recall from chapter six that the declarative word of God comes from above and is what God says is true about the believer *in Christ* (regardless of the extent of its manifestation). The reformative word of God, in contrast, consists of the actual changes that occur to believers that result from God's declarative word. To understand these two parts better, we will need to digress to consider speech-acts again, but from the standpoint of salvation.

We also noted in chapter six that an illocution is a statement having a particular meaning intended by its author. Searle (1998) has identified five types of illocutions: assertives (statements that describe a state of affairs), directives (commands), expressives (statements that convey a person's experience or beliefs), commissives (statements that bind a person to a course of action, like a promise) and declaratives (statements that create a state of affairs in the utterance itself, e.g., "I now pronounce you husband and wife"). Declaratives are also called "performative utterances," in that they accomplish something in the successful performance of saying it.

At this point, a brief review is in order (Austin, 1962; Searle, 1970). It is possible to understand perfectly well someone's illocution, say to go outside and mow the grass, and yet not do it. Whenever a speech-act has an effect on someone, whatever the effect, the original illocution becomes (we might say, retroactively) a *perlocution*. It is now a speech-act that resulted in a change in the hearer/reader. We might add that the speaker's *intended* impact on the hearer is called the *perlocutionary intent*. Much of human action consists of speech-acts that are meant to influence others, and much human action, therefore, is to some extent a function of someone's perlocutions. The above distinctions are difficult, but they can help us better understand the verbal nature of salvation (Horton, 2002; Thiselton, 1992; Vanhoozer, 1998).

The declarative words of God in salvation consist of God's illocutionary pronouncements regarding believers, such as, they are justified (declared righteous and forgiven in Christ, Rom 3:24-26), adopted (declared to be a member of God's family, and having all the rights and privileges of a family member; Rom 8:17), definitively sanctified (set apart to God, a saint; 1 Cor 1:2) and beloved (Col 3:12). These statuses are, of course, announced in the Scriptures and preached in the gospel, and in those forms are offered to all; for example, an illocution issued in the form of a conditional declarative is: "if you confess with your mouth Jesus as Lord, and believe in your heart that God raised him from the dead, you shall be saved" (Rom 10:9). But the condition, then, must be met, in order for the declaration to be actually performed. God's definitive pronouncement of an individual's salvation is only made to those who believe (Acts 16:31; Rom 4:24; 1 Jn 1:9). There has to be an existential reality to true salvation—a personal consent to the announcement—without it the gospel consists of empty words. It would not be the communication of God's heart embraced by the believer resulting in communion (Lee, 2005); it would simply be God talking to himself, God's "wishful thinking." (This is essentially what liberal theology teaches by arguing that personal faith in Christ is not necessary for salvation.) On the contrary, hearing or reading the word of salvation offered, individuals must consent to it for it to be true for themselves. Then, *upon believing,* the gospel assertions become temporally realized declarations of God, that immediately bring about changes in the *meaning* of the individual believer.

As we have seen throughout this chapter, God's speech is the source of reality. In the present case, God speaks and brings about a new declared reality—the justifying, adopting word that applies a new network of meaning to the believer and bestows on him or her the "in-Christ" status of righteousness, moral perfection and membership in the divine family, so that believers now are truly good in Christ. Upon belief in Christ, these semiodiscursive realities are spoken and remain in heaven (Eph 2:6; Col 3:1-4). And what God says is, is. There is no higher court of appeal beyond his word. If God says a sinner is a saint and a child of God, then he or she is. It was Paul's great apostolic contribution to the church (rediscovered by the Reformers) to recognize and describe the discursive/performative basis of salvation, as summarized in his teaching on justification by faith.

But the second, *perlocutionary* part of the saving word brings about the actualization of God's declaration and includes processes like regeneration, conversion, sanctification and eventually glorification. Here, we might say, epistemology joins ontology, and a change actually occurs in the believer's being (cognitions, emotions, actions and relationships). "In the exercise of His will *He brought us forth* by the word of truth" (Jas 1:18, italics added). The believer is born again (Jn 3) and raised from the deadness of sin (Eph 2:1; Rom 6:5), and the old self gets crucified (Rom 6:6). There is the beginning of the new creation (2 Cor 5:17), and the believer begins to love God and others through a "new heart" (Ezek 36:26; 1 Jn 4:7-21). These changes are produced by the word of God made powerful by the Spirit, so that the illocutions announced in the Scripture or the gospel that proclaim this salvation become divine perlocutionary utterances as they make actual salvific changes in the mind, heart and life of the believer.

The Christian life consists of a dialogical interplay—mediated by faith—between these two parts of the one saving word of God. As the divine declarations are more deeply believed, the soul and life come to be more thoroughly reformed. With God's creation speech-acts—"Let there be light," for example—illocution and perlocution are one. Salvation can be understood as the bringing together *in human life and experience* of God's illocutions and perlocutions, just as they exist together in God's causal speech in the rest of the creation. Faith is the creaturely activity (itself a gift of God, Eph 2:8) that realizes the unity of these two parts of God's one word that must be distinguished in time. Further psychospiritual development entails the ongoing internalization and temporal realization of the divine declarations by the power of the Holy Spirit. That development consists of the same divine speech-acts becoming realized as perlocutions.

The logical priority of the declarative word must be grasped, since it is the illocutionary source of the perlocutionary effects that flow from it, by the Spirit (Vanhoozer, 2002, chap. 6). "For our gospel did not come to you in word only, but also in power and in the Holy Spirit and with conviction" (1 Thess 1:5). Sin is what renders the words of Scripture (God's illocutions) inert, so that their renewing meaning is not realized (their divine perlocutionary intent). The Bible is inevitably experienced by fallen humans as lifeless, when it is read *by itself,* apart from the Spirit, since by itself, it is no more able to give life than the law (Rom 7:6-13) or the letter (2 Cor 3:6). This is why Paul says the good and holy law is a ministry of condemnation through which sin kills us. Therefore, we have to distinguish between the word of God of Scripture and the gospel and the saving word of God expressed *through* Scripture and the gospel, or we risk mortifying Christianity by teaching Christians to be satisfied with an intellectual system and behavior code based on empty words and hollow rules, rather than based on the life of God in the soul of humans (Scougal, 1974), the God who raises people from the dead through his words ("Lazarus, come forth!" Jn 11:43). Christian soul care in all its forms (preaching, teaching, worship, counseling and fellowship) is involved in this perlocutionary and doxological drama.

The Manifold, Integral and Constituting Word of God

The Son of God/the Word of God has expressed himself in a number of ways. The creation is a function of his speech; he has spoken in human language in the discourse of the Bible and the gospel; and he speaks mysteriously through the Bible and the gospel in the recreation of the believer. All of this is derived from the one Word of God. In our attempts to understand aright all this meaning, therefore, we must not erect false barriers between the Word of God's various expressions. Instead, with Hart (2003), we could consider the entire creation to be one great poem. "It is as a kind of poetry that the discourse of being is revelatory, as endless sequences of beautiful turns of phrase, and the proper response to this language—the reply that properly grasps, interprets, and corresponds to the truth of creation—is doxology" (Hart, 2003, p. 292).

Our ultimate goal in psychology is to recognize the fundamental harmony of all the meaning pertaining to individual human beings in the mind and heart of the Father and expressed by the Word of God, his Son, and our goal practically in soul care is the realization of a profound harmony of God's expressions in the reformation of the created person (formed by the word of God communicated in nature, personal agency and culture) into greater likeness with Christ, through the scriptural gospel, made a saving word by the Holy Spirit. This knowing and this practice are kinds of worship.

The recognition of an underlying harmony of God's expressions in the created order is not new. The Belgic Confession, for example, refers to the "two books" of God's self-revelation (creation and Scripture):

> We know [God] by two means: First, by the creation, preservation, and government of the universe; which is before our eyes as a most elegant book, wherein all creatures, great and small, are as so many characters leading us to see clearly the invisible things of God, even his everlasting power and divinity, as the apostle Paul says. . . . Second, He makes Himself more clearly and fully known to us by His holy and divine Word, that is to say, as far as is necessary for us to know in this life, to His glory and our salvation." (Doctrinal Standards of the Christian Reformed Church, 1976, p. 70)

Thinking of John's *Logos* teaching, Spykman (1992) expands this to "God's three-fold Word" (p. 90): creation, Scripture and Christ. Barth (1936) too posited a threefold form of the word of God: preached, written and revealed (that is, experienced), and of course Jesus Christ, the Word of God central to his whole theology. And the Reformed doctrine of "effectual calling" recognizes the mode of God's speech that gives life to sinners (Murray, 1955). So this chapter's discussion is simply an attempt at a comprehensive model for understanding reality in terms of God's word.

The triune God has communicated something of his mind, heart and nature through these many forms of expressions, so that some of his beauty would be manifested, celebrated and reproduced. There is a pressing need in our day to realize the fundamental harmony of God's mind, heart and nature in the minds, hearts and lives of his children. One way to approach this project is to understand the universe to be pervaded by a kind of *intertextuality*, so the goals of the Christian psychologist and soul-care provider are themselves intertextual. Kristeva (1974) coined the term "intertextuality" to refer to the relation of a text and its interpretation to the linguistic background of the text and the reader. All writing, she said, involves a triad of writer, reader and the set of relevant texts that provide the context for the writing in question and its interpretation. A meaning of a text is rendered more intelligible by recognizing its interdependence with other related texts, the sum of which is greater and more meaningful than those individual texts by themselves. A set of texts necessarily forms a "symbolic network" that always stands in the semantic background of a particular text.

Kristeva was, of course, thinking of the interrelationship between sets of texts composed by humans. But given the semiodiscursive nature of the entire universe, Christians can extend the notion of intertextuality to refer to all of reality. The challenge of any science, but particularly a science of human beings, is to grasp as much of this intertextuality as possible (a set of relations only God knows exhaustively). The intertextual challenge before us is the composition of Christian psychology texts that describe the embedded text of human nature, by reading the scriptural text, relevant texts from the Christian tradition, and the scientific texts of modern psychology, and doing new research, all in order to understand most accurately human beings as God understands them and intends them to be.

Before concluding, let us consider a few encouraging analogies to the intertextual compositional task in which we are engaged. Imagine the difficulties facing the classical scholar who attempts to reconstruct an ancient text with only a few different text fragments, some of which overlap in content, but many of which do not. The final text that the scholar produces may not be an entirely accurate reconstruction of the original work, but that product is still better than the separate fragments by themselves alone, so the attempted reconstruction is a worthy venture. But, it must be pointed out, the goal is to reproduce the original, *single* text.

Detectives also engage in a sort of intertextual project. They write up a narrative (a single text) after examining a wide variety of evidence, including the testimony of different eyewitnesses and suspects, some of whom have different versions of what happened with varying degrees of detail. There are also different types of physical evidence that must be brought in (DNA evidence, marks on the rug, fingerprints, body wounds). All of this information is semiotic, and some of it is discourse. The detective must discern the single underlying story revealed by these various semiodiscursive media. Compared with such a task, Christian psychology would not seem impossible.

One more example. Both archaeology and paleontology work with various kinds of signs and texts: physical conditions (soil, rings of trees), marks that may have been made by humans (e.g., a rock that may have been a tool), definite human-made objects (pottery shards) and perhaps written materials using symbols that may need to be translated. These diverse sources of information must all be utilized in order to make sense of a single site and to compose a single text—a book or article—that reports the actual, original, single state of affairs as best as the archaeologist or paleontologist can discern it.

But the triune God wants more glory than will result from our merely writing texts that reproduce his understanding of human beings. He wants to reproduce his form in us fallen and broken image-bearers. Human lives, you see, are the site of God's intertextual project of salvation. There the Father weaves together all these various expressions, spoken by his Son and actualized by their Spirit, so that the words of the triune God compose increasingly theocentric personal agents, who are learning to love God supremely and others as themselves. In the next chapter, we will consider in more detail the nature of the soul's semiodiscursive composition.

Notes

[1]There are at least four reasons why God is beyond the complete grasp of humans. First, his infinite being outstrips the finite capacities of humans to comprehend him. "How unsearchable are His judgments and unfathomable His ways! For who has known the mind of the Lord?" (Rom 11:33-34). Second, humans are now sinful and alienated from God, and their capacity to perceive him is damaged and therefore even more limited. Third, persons have depth, and they must decide to disclose their inner being (their splendor) if it is to be known by someone else (contrary to impersonal beings). Since God is a person, it is necessary for him to reveal himself in order to be known. A fourth reason is that faith in God, as opposed to knowledge of the empirical world, entails a degree of divine hiddenness. Otherwise, our belief in God would be compelled, as it is when we see a material object, like a chair. These reasons do not entail that humans are incapable of knowing anything about him, but that humans can only know him partially and imperfectly, and that they are entirely dependent on his self-revelation to humans (see Barth, 1957, sec. 26; Bavinck, 2003; Frame, 1987, 2002; Howard-Snyder & Moser, 2002; Talbot, 2002; Balthasar, 1982, pp. 441-62).

[2]Scripture teaches us that Christ is the True Human—the very definition of human. Therefore, if Scripture is allowed the formative role it should have in the development of a Christian psychology (a science of human beings that approximates God's understanding as much as possible), Christology should be one of its subdisciplines, just as much as neuropsychology, associative learning or cognition. Christian theology (undertsood as the science of God) can have it as one of its subdisciplines too, but it belongs just as much to Christian psychology. In fact, so central is Christology to the project of a Christian psychology that it ought to exercise an orienting and organizing role, somewhat analogous to the role that associative learning did in modern psychology in the 1930s and 1940s, cognition did in the 1960s and 1970s, and neuropsychology may be doing today.

[3]A brief discussion of semiotic theory from a Christian standpoint can be found in appendix two.

[4]Stoker (1973) distinguished between a creature's ultimate meaning-moment (its significance in relation to God) and its proximate meaning-moment (its immanent significance, its unique meaning as a distinct being, a rose is a rose and not a horse).

[5]For those interested, a few more selections of such thinking: Luther believed that "God the Father initiated and executed the creation of all things through the Word; and now He continues to preserve His creation through the Word, and that forever and ever . . . hence as heaven, earth, sun, moon, stars, human beings, and all living things were created in the beginning through the Word, so they are wonderfully governed and preserved through that Word" (quoted in Zimmermann, 2004, p. 52). Abraham Kuyper (1998) put it this way: "God's thinking must be contained in all things. There is nothing in the whole creation that is not the expression, the embodiment, the revelation of a thought of God" (p. 443). And according to Danielou (1969): "Everything speaks to us of God because we live in a world that comes entirely from him. This universe of symbols is such that if our hearts were filled with God, we would see him in all things" (p. 5).

[6]The position we are presenting here is essentially that of Augustine, Aquinas, Luther, Calvin and Edwards. It is sometimes termed Augustinianism or Calvinism or the Reformed approach. This is not the place to debate the exegetical merits of this position; here we must simply assume it. However, for a discussion of this approach see Bavinck, 1956; Berkouwer, 1952b; Jewett, 1985; Thiessen, 2000.

[7]To explain its unique status, we must again make special use of the concept of double agency (Horton, 2002; Wolterstorff, 1995), in which a specific action (e.g., the writing of a letter) can have two personal agents as its cause, one of whom, in this case, is God. The difference between God-breathed double agency and double agency in divine providence over human affairs is that there is no mere divine *permission* in the writing of Scripture. Human activity in this age includes much that falls short of the holiness of God but that he nonetheless permits. But the Bible is the expression of the exact communicative intentions of God. To call the Bible inerrant, then, is to say that the texts of the original autographs, as penned by the human authors, say everything exactly as God wanted to say it, without qualification, and without any sin or error ("not the smallest letter or stroke shall pass from the Law until all is accomplished," Mt 5:18). This means that among all the world's texts, one set expresses precisely what God wanted to convey explicitly to the human race, and his divine authorship guarantees that it is a text free of the distorting influence of the noetic effects of sin.

9

From Signs to History

A Hermeneutic Analysis of Human Life

WE HAVE SEEN THAT THE ENTIRE CREATION IS embedded with meaning expressed by God. We sharpen our focus in this chapter to examine in more detail the meaning that uniquely constitutes human life. A mature human being is an intense concentration of divine semiodiscourse.

We need to begin this discussion, however, with a consideration of the relational context of human meaning. Western intellectual culture has been characterized by a one-dimensional understanding of human meaning, assuming that its construction is the project of the individual (perhaps with help from others). Many thinkers in ancient Greece and Rome, as well as in the modern West, have either implied or taught that the search for meaning was fundamentally a solitary quest, signified by the notion that self-understanding or self-realization was the chief concern of human life. This orientation seems to have reached its peak in the modern era (exemplified by Descartes's founding of his epistemological project in the individual's experience: *I think, therefore I am*). "Meaning-making," as it is called today (Kegan, 1982), is supposedly solely the task of the individual.

By contrast, the Scriptures posit a fundamentally relational orientation for human life (Anderson, 1982; Bonhoeffer, 1955; Barth, 1960; Grenz, 2001; Schwöbel & Gunton, 1991; Shults, 2003). Most basically, created reality originates from the triune Creator—who himself exists in interpersonal community—so that the creation is contingent and dependent. Human dependence on God is underscored, heightened and ennobled in the doctrine of the *imago*

Dei. Consequently, in the biblical worldview, God, not the self, is ultimate in human life, and human beings become meaningful only in relation to God. Augustine grasped this, the medieval church assumed it, and the Reformation worked out its theology within these parameters. Calvin (1559/1960), for example, discussed the relation between the knowledge of God and self as a prolegomenon to his theological system. With a few notable exceptions, Western Christianity, prior to the twentieth century, assumed there are *two* fundamental dimensions to human meaning: God and the individual—with God being infinitely supreme.

However, there is more to the relational universe of humans. Most importantly, as just mentioned, God is Trinity—Father, Son and Spirit are fundamentally *persons-in-relationship*—so that God's eternal relationality is basic to God's essence. Since the Trinity is the absolute foundation of Christian thought (Van Til, 1955), it points toward a reconsideration of human relationality. Upon reflection and observation, it can be seen that individual humans are actually fundamentally related to two communities: the Trinity and other humans (to whom individuals are related analogously to the Trinity). Both of these communal relationships have been heavily explored in the twentieth century, the former in the renewal of trinitarian theology over the past fifty years (Barth, 1957; Danielou, 1969; Schwöbel & Gunton, 1991; Thompson, 1994); the latter through psychological research and theorizing about the role of other humans in individual development (see Damon, 1998). Humans develop only in relation with other humans, and their growing understanding of themselves (and eventually of God) are influenced by those early relationships; in turn, one's relation with God is supposed to reshape one's relations with others and one's self-understanding. As a result of the "turn to relationality" (Shults, 2003) in twentieth-century thought, we realize now more than ever that adults' understandings of themselves, others and the triune God are reciprocal and interdependent.

At the same time, we must not overreact to individualism and embrace a radical social constructivism. Self and Other are ultimately co-equal in the Trinity and in humanity. The most advanced understanding of humanity's relational context is the recognition of the fundamental interdependence of persons-in-communion. The self-in-relation-to-God was a major accomplishment of Christianity. We must not go backwards in our understanding of relationality (a developmental insight lost on postmodernists, including those

Christians who overemphasize the social Trinity and human community, allowing the latter to swallow up the self). The individual person and love and respect for the Other and for God are all supposed to grow interactively. Dialogical communion of individual persons is the highest of realities.

The most comprehensive Christian model of the constitution of human meaning will assume that individual humans are essentially framed by two interpersonal-communal dimensions—that of the Trinity and that of other humans—so that individual meaningfulness is necessarily exocentric, rather than autocentric (Pannenberg, 1985). Meaning originates outside the individual—from others and ultimately from the triune God—and it is taken in, incorporated and internalized, in order for the individual to become increasingly meaningful. Meaning is fundamentally a gift from others. "Meaning-*making*" by the individual (what could also be called creativity) certainly occurs, but from the Christian standpoint, it begins in dependence and is maintained through dialogue (no poet writes without the hope of a reader), and it thrives in gratitude and love.

To round out the account, humans are embodied and exist within a fourth relational dimension—the *im*personal—which includes the nonliving and subhuman portions of creation (the mode called *Nature*), and this dimension provides the meaningful concrete context for human life lived within the other three dimensions. This model of the constitution of human meaning is represented in figure 9.1.

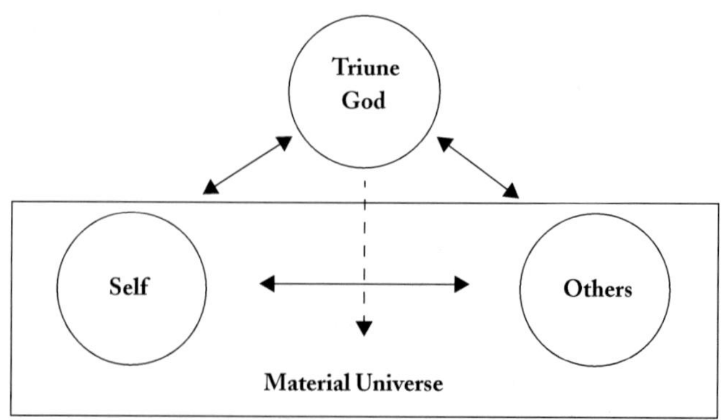

Figure 9.1. A four-dimensional relational model

In summary, the triune God established human life (and its meaning) through the Word of God who enlightens everyone (Jn 1:5, 9), so that individual humans—embodied and situated within a material universe—develop in relationship with two communal dimensions: the triune God and other humans. Divine meaning and likeness are constituted temporally in individual images of God, through dialogue and its internalization, which derives ultimately from the Word of God. In this chapter we look at the specific semiodiscursive phenomena that constitute individual human life and its development.

Hermeneutics and Psychology

So the task of this chapter is grand (if not grandiose): to describe the basic semiodiscursive meaning-structures and intertextuality of human life. In distinction from biblical hermeneutics (the interpretation of biblical texts), *general hermeneutics*, as developed by Gadamer (1975, 1976) and Ricoeur (1974, 1977, 1981a, 1984-1988), is concerned with interpretation per se, the activity involved whenever humans seek to understand anything. Interpretation is the act of meaning-comprehension. No communication occurs between human beings without interpretation; even self-understanding requires the interpretation of one's own thoughts and emotions (Taylor, 1985b). Accordingly, "human beings . . . are irreducibly hermeneutical" (Stiver, 2001, p. 50), and all of human life entails interpretation. Consequently, psychology—the science of individual human beings—is a study of human meaning: how it is stored, how humans process it, how it constrains and shapes human actions, how it gives shape to the soul, and how the soul develops accordingly. Modern psychology has not recognized how thoroughly hermeneutic is its calling, since it relies so heavily on neopositivist and natural-science assumptions in its work, and those in the natural sciences have tended not to recognize the hermeneutic foundations of their disciplines (for a critique see Jonas, 1966; Kuhn, 1962; Polanyi, 1958; Wright, 1971). In this chapter a Christian general hermeneutic is presented to provide a comprehensive framework for understanding the multifaceted complexity of human beings by construing individual humans as developing representations of meaning, who themselves are composed of representations of meaning.

As we noted in the previous chapter, semiotics is the science of signs, the discipline that explores all types of signs, and their functions and relations. It includes the study of symbols, communication, language, texts, media of all kinds, really anything having to do with the conveyance of meaning (see the

Encyclopedia of Semiotics, Bouissac, 1998a; and Sebeok, 1994). So semiotics has a broad relevance to psychology—far beyond how it has been traditionally conceived—and it should be seen as part of what constitutes a general hermeneutics. While a discussion of "signs," "meaning-structures" and "hermeneutics" may seem far removed from the care of souls, their integral relationship to Christian soul-care theory and practice will become clearer as the book progresses.

The Elements of Human Meaning

What are the basic formative ingredients that make possible the development of an individual, mature human being? Constrained by the soul-care agenda of this book, we will focus on six: a human body (with a normal brain), memory, discourse (and its corollary, conceptual thought, which includes reasoning), emotions, imagery and actions. The human body (including the brain) makes possible human life as we know it, providing the concrete site in which a human life is realized and by which (because of the brain) the building blocks of human experience and meaning are processed, experienced, stored in memory, and expressed. However, meaning is mediated to individuals through other humans, who themselves are members of some cultural community.

Words as signs. Words are the basic units of a language, and a language is a system of words and relations. Words are the most important types of signs, because when combined in various ways—in utterances—they have seemingly endless communicative potential. Language makes it possible to represent the meaningfulness of the world (including human culture) and communicate it to others. Without it, we could hardly process and store any kind of complex information beyond our immediate experience, and we could not pass it on or build upon it. Virtually all higher human thought and reasoning is carried out through language.[1] So the importance of language for human life cannot be overstated. One of the earliest tasks of the child is the mastery of the vocabulary of its family's language. Furthermore, since "language is the medium that is most directly and obviously amenable to intentional control" (Bucci, 1997, p. 177), it has tremendous value to adults, who can use language to adjust their understanding of the world and their life, so it is of special relevance to soul care.

Emotions as signs. The semiotics of emotions is more difficult to understand and has tended to be underappreciated, so we will examine them in more detail. An emotion is an intrinsically private, subjective aspect of human experience that signifies something. "A primary function of emotion is to provide information" (Clore, 1994, p. 103)—to oneself and also to others through words or body language—information regarding one's needs, goals and concerns (Greenberg & Paivio, 1997). But in contrast to the descriptive information conveyed by words, emotions provide *value* information, since they are "elicited by evaluations (appraisals) of events and situations" (Roseman & Smith, 2001, p. 3). Because emotions can be stored in memory, current emotions can also signify aspects of one's past, one's story.

In addition, the emotion system is motivational (Tomkins, 1962, 1963); emotions convey information that has the power to move people toward and away from things. Emotions may signify people's deepest drives, understandings and values, often with greater accuracy than their thoughts about such things. Emotions concentrate one's attention; signal one to approach or avoid; guide goal formation, planning and evaluation processes; and shape one's volition activity, including the initiation of one's choices, self-monitoring, task persistence and termination (Heckhausen, 1991). Jonathan Edwards agreed: "Affections," he said, "are very much the spring of men's actions" (1746/1959, p. 101). Bringing together the cognitive and motivational functions of emotion, the philosophers Nussbaum (2001) and Roberts (1988, 2003) define emotions as "judgments of value" and "concern-based construals," respectively. All this suggests that emotions are foundational to human meaning.

Types of emotion and their significance. Adult humans experience different types of emotion, including anger, interest-excitement, joy, distress, disgust, pride, fear, shame, guilt, anticipation, surprise and love (to name those which most emotion researchers/theorists agree on; Ekman, 1993; Epstein, 1984; Izard, 1977; Plutchik, 1994; Tomkins, 1962-1963).[2] Under normal circumstances, low-level positive emotion—a mild contentedness—appears to be the universal emotional default setting of human beings (Diener & Diener, 1996). In addition to a general set-point, human emotional experience appears to have two dimensions: (1) bivalence, that is, it is either good/pleasant or bad/unpleasant (Kahneman, 1999), a differentiation based on the activation of distinct neural systems (Davidson, 1992); and (2) arousal level, that is, it is characterized by a particular degree of arousal, from mild to intense. (These two dimensions form a circumplex model of emotion, Ekman, 1992; Russell, 1980.) Emotions of distress (sadness, anxiety, fear, anger, disgust, shock) are aroused in response to perceived loss, threat, mistreatment or disvalue, whereas pleasant emotions (joy, excitement, humor, surprise, wonder, anticipation) are activated in response to perceived benefit and novelty. But each emotion typically signifies a particular kind of evaluative meaning.[3] For example, sadness is often a sign of loss, fear a sign of the perception of possible harm, anger a sign of a frustration of one's desires or of a perception of injustice, and joy a sign of the fulfillment of some desire. Humans are born evaluators: for infants, crying expresses and indicates distress; in the absence of distress, there appears to be contentment. As we develop, our abilities to evaluate emotionally become increasingly complex and skilled.

The full range of emotional experience consists of a variety of affective experience, including such things as temperament, mood, motives, desires, attitudes, passions, values, loves and hates. In addition, because emotions can be stored in memory, they can influence future emotional dispositions so that one's current emotional capacities constitute a summation of one's emotion history, the aggregate of years of emotion experiences (Saarni, 2000; Shweder & Haidt, 2000). Most importantly, one's current motives, desires, attitudes, passions, values, loves and hates are the summative expression of one's basic, evaluative framework that has developed over one's life, and that lies at the base of all mature human activity—though it is not often well articulated. Well-developed religions and life-philosophies all posit an optimal set of loves (and hates) that are supposed to guide a person into and express a virtuous life (Taylor, 1989). Emotions, then, are very important elements of meaning.

The related and respective semiotic value of words and emotions. Compared to the tens of thousands of words in any given language, the few dozen emotions that form a culture's emotional repertoire are vastly inferior in their capacity to signify meaning. On the other hand, language by itself has its own limitations, since its representations are, compared to emotional signs, cold and empty of motivation and valuation (or what we might call "depth"). Think of the signifying capacity of a word processor. It can convey linguistic content, but not the passion of urgency, despair or awe (at least not directly, the way an emotion-system can). Words by themselves label and describe meaningful things, but emotions make possible a "warm" hierarchy of meaning that moves humans toward or pulls them away from things. Also, emotions can convey meaning that is inarticulable; some experiences, like intense joy or sublimity, are difficult to put into words (see Phil 4:7). Moreover, while language can accurately communicate one's beliefs, one's emotions signify the depth of one's evaluations and commitments regarding one's beliefs.

Language and emotion would both seem necessary to enable a fuller range of accurate representation of meaning than either of them alone would permit. Evaluative emotion, or *tone*, is always being conveyed in discourse through *intonation* (Bakhtin, 1986, p. 164). Words and emotions enrich each other; the fullness of linguistic expression and the color of emotional experience are both enhanced by their interaction. The importance of emotions has led many Christian thinkers to promote God-centered emotional experience (e.g., Augustine, Bernard, Luther, Edwards and Kierkegaard). As the Puritan Richard Sibbes (1961) put it, the affections are "the springs of all spiritual worship" (p. 101). This also explains why most counseling models address emotions in some fashion.[4]

Mental imagery as signs. Another type of sign foundational to human life is a mental image, an immaterial representation or "picture" of a concrete object or event, stored in visual memory or the creation of one's imagination (Ashcroft, 1994). According to Paivio (1990), humans have a special memory system assigned to the storage of concrete objects of vision (or audition) that uses a visual code (or auditory code), rather than, say, a semantic code, which stores linguistic meaning. These images can be manipulated in working memory, and episodic memory (the memory of personal events) often includes visual images. From infancy, human understanding of the world requires some sensory-based encoding and storage, and for sighted people, the most important type is visual imagery (think of its importance just for facial recognition of parents). However, as humans develop and master a language system, mental images can be invested with significance far beyond the meaning of a concrete object (e.g., blood signifying guilt, murder or forgiveness). As a result, mental images are a powerful tool for representing the physical world as well as the conceptual, and have also been the focus of a good deal of therapy.

Actions as signs. Human actions should also be understood as signs. All human actions are signs of something. A gesture, like pointing, has an obvious semiotic function, but even a child's reaching for a toy signifies a desire, as does an adult's application for a job. Most actions can be defined as "goal-directed, emotion-colored behaviors that are carried out in social and cultural contexts" (Skinner, 1999, p. 475). Consequently, human actions are especially packed with significance: they have identifiable propositional content and are the realization of motives, desires, plans, goals and intentions (Ricoeur, 1981b; Taylor, 1985d). Obviously, the most meaning-loaded type of human action is speech, which aims at the conveying of meaning to another. Much of human life consists of interpreting the meaning of the actions of others around us, and early experiences of the actions of others, especially those enacted with reference to ourselves, powerfully shape our personal development.

The catalyzing relation with others. A relational model recognizes that most of the meaning that fills individual adults was given to them from others—especially their *significant others,* who were the primary contributors of emotional, cognitive-linguistic, imagery and action signs that people have internalized. Humans, particularly young ones, are genetically programmed to look to others and accept their speech and body language—through which the children enter, intersubjectively, into their thoughts and affect, which the children, in turn, may store in memory. Others are sign-bearers and necessarily communicate cognitive-affective messages, such as love, rejection, enjoyment or boredom. Over time, significant others become signs themselves, signifying (and activating) by their presence delight, disgust, yearning or a sense of failure. Humans were created requiring the thinking, feeling and acting of others to provide the kinds of socially mediated, intersubjective "scaffolding" that eventually makes possible and shapes the development of their own thinking, feeling and acting (Rogoff, 1990; Vygotsky, 1978). Before we become individuals, we are social beings: persons-in-conversation (Harre, 1984).

As children grow up, they increasingly become creative sources of meaning to others in their own right. In fact, humans have *names*, signs of uniqueness that (in the case of humans) demonstrate their inviolable worth (in contrast, as a child David Pelzer [1995] was called "it" by his mother). One's relationships with others largely form the substance of one's life; one's greatest meaningfulness consists in the sum of one's relationships, and one's most laudable activities consist in the love of others. Others, then, become signs *of one's own life*. How do I treat them? Do I use them for my own desires or do I seek to strengthen them and better their lives? Their existence, as Levinas (1981) pointed out, stands as a summons to me to live outside myself and for their benefit. As such, they constitute a part of my calling. Others are person-constituting meaning-catalysts that provide the human context for individual development, and counseling turns this relational dimension of human life into a means of further soul improvement.

The material ground of human formation: signs and the body. The body plays a unique role in the communication of meaning. While we can imagine a bodiless existence where information is conveyed between people immediately, without words, telepathically, in this age interpersonal human communication occurs through the body. To pass on information, meaning must be expressed through gesture, facial expression, speech or writing, all of which require body movement. Just think of the meaning that a simple smile or a touch on the hand can convey. Human communication is always embodied. But of greatest importance to human life and communication is the material structure known as the brain, since it is the organ designed for sign processing and sign storage. The brain has its own sign systems, one using neurotransmitters and another the firing patterns of neural networks, which make possible *mental* semiotic activity: the processing and storage of immaterial signs.

The memory of signs. The storage of signs is foundational to all psychological development. Memory of words and their meanings (in explicit, semantic memory) and memory of emotions (in implicit memory), along with memory of personal events (in explicit, episodic memory), are essential to a full, mature human life, and these forms of memory are made possible (in this life) by the brain (Markowitsch, 2000). The brain stores—or *physically internalizes*—one's beliefs, and emotional and relational experiences (mediated through language, once those abilities develop), forming a knowledge base and a repository of memories and associations through which the self, others, the world and God will be interpreted. The experience and storage of signs are the basic *constituting forces* in human development; if optimal, they contribute to proper human maturation (by creation grace); if deficient, they deform the soul and inhibit healthy development. For example, a young child who is repeatedly physically abused by a drunken father will experience chronic emotions of anxiety and fear (which are signifying perceived danger to motivate the child to flee the harm, but unfortunately the child cannot escape), and these strong emotion-experiences will be stored (Markowitsch, 2000; Siegel, 1999). Much later, these emotion-memories may continue to shape the individual, perhaps causing symptoms of PTSD (e.g., nightmares or forms of dissociation) or contributing to a withdrawn personality disposition, in which anxiety is easily activated even when not called for, and the stored signs of past emotional trauma (usually without awareness of their origins) continue to be expressed (more or less) until resolved. "Memory is the way past events affect future function"

(Siegel, 1999, p. 24). Stored signs of past emotional trauma activated in the present bear testimony to the experiences of one's life and will not be remediated by ignoring them. The goal of Christian counseling is the provision of corrective semiodiscursive experiences that lead to a redemptive resignification that heals the soul through a better rewiring of the brain's neural circuits. We turn next to a consideration of larger, semiodiscursive structures that especially contribute to the constitution of human life.

The Actual Communication of Human Meaning

In the past, critics of semiotics have argued that it is of limited value because of its focus on the discrete semiotic units called "signs." However, semiotics has come to be understood as a metadiscipline that encompasses signification in general.[5] It now deals with larger units of meaning, including various forms of discourse like literature and cultural analysis. Today, the field of semiotics covers any kind of representation (Barthes, 1967; Greimas, 1990; Hodge & Kress, 1988; Nöth, 1990; see Bouissac, 1998a). Elemental human signs only exist within large-scale semiotic systems (culture, discourse and genre) and are expressed in specific forms (like a conversation or an essay for a class), and all the forms represent information. We shall examine next the nature of discourse.

Where the action is: The discourse of authors. The capacity for language enables humans to convey far more complex and nuanced meanings than animals. However, it is only through *discourse* that meaning is actually conveyed through specific utterances (or speech-acts) by an author (that is, a speaker or writer) for some communicative purpose (Ricoeur, 1974; Vanhoozer, 1998).[6]

Earlier, words were identified as the elements of linguistic meaning, but this was somewhat misleading, since the meaning of a word is only realized in utterances. Utterances are the actual elements of meaningful discourse (Bakhtin, 1986; Ricoeur, 1977) and are necessarily a fusion of language and emotion, concept and appraisal, a speech-act and its motive (Morson & Emerson, 1990). An utterance is a complete communicative act of any length—from a one-syllable word like "Help!" to a large novel. A text is considered a more-or-less lengthy utterance that conforms to stylistic and genre rules (Bakhtin, 1986; McHoul, 1998).

The two major categories of discourse are speech and writing.[7] Speech is more likely than writing to create emotional, intersubjective experiences (this is obviously the case in early childhood before children are literate, but the generalization holds throughout the life span). Spoken utterances are powerful means for communicating meaning. They include both the cognitive content (expressed with words) and the evaluative stance (experienced as emotion and expressed through intonation and body language). A *formative* speech-event occurs when the expression of meaning of others gets stored in one's memory. Such events are particularly influential in childhood as they are easily internalized by neural recording during this time of life, when the brain is especially sensitive to input. The darkest side of childhood development consists of the impact of the sin of others, which is mediated through malevolent discourse—and sometimes, aggressive behavior—for such experiences can also be stored and cumulatively shape the form of the child's soul and eventually its own expression of sin. Whatever their precise meaning, the utterances of others stored in memory form the foundational semiodiscursive infrastructure of the individual soul.

As we have already noted, Christianity is grounded in written discourse: first, in a set of canonical texts, the Bible, and second, in a subordinate set of texts: the sermons, creeds, treatises and devotional writings of Christians over the centuries. As we saw in chapters one and two, together these two bodies of literature provide Christians with what Edwards (1974) called the "doctrine of living to God in Christ" (Vol. 2, p. 158) that constitutes the discursive core of what Christians are to internalize in order to become well-formed persons. So discourse is basic to human and Christian life.

Intermediate meaning-structures. As the language capacities of children develop through dialogue with their caregivers and others, children internalize the meaning-elements they experience, so that they coalesce into larger, more stable "intermediate meaning-structures":[8] discrete beliefs and theories about themselves and their competences, others, the natural and sociocultural worlds, and God; attributions and explanatory styles; personal action constructs and dispositions; moods and states of mind; episodic memories, scripts, and narrative themes and tone; relationship structures and relational styles; value systems; and virtues and vices (see Mayer, 2005, for a helpful summary of many of these components). Composed of the elements of meaning that are realized through discourse, these intermediate meaning-structures are actually what get stored and form the infrastructure of the soul. Soul care sometimes works with simple signs (like a current feeling of anger), but most of the time it deals directly with these "midlevel" units of discursive meaning.

The form of authors. Discourse is authored by human beings through their communicative activity, their speech acts; humans are "producers of discourse" (Greimas, 1990, p. 13).[9] As we shall see, human beings are analogous to a text in the sense that they too are "*forms* of meaning." However, the meaning-full and unique form of a human being emerges (ultimately by virtue of God's creation grace) out of the individual's experience, derived from the individual's genetic and neurological conditions, dialogue with others, and the internalization and integration of that dialogue over time. The human form is a whole of acquired meaning—with special properties that emerge out of, transcend and therefore are greater than the properties of its constituent elemental and intermediate meaning-structures—and that form possesses a unique immaterial "shape" (see below). Human beings are special "sites" of meaning in two ways. First, they possess a special significance in their own right (established by God, the ultimate meaning-maker) as the *imago Dei;* and second, they become producers of meaning themselves, authors of discourse who live in dialogue with others—analogous to the Trinity. Discourse and human beings have an unusual interdependent and dialectical relation to each other.

The plural form of individual human beings. Human beings are, then, *forms of meaning*. The concept of form has been a perennial theme in the Western intellectual tradition, and it has typically meant figure, pattern, structure or whole; in German, the word is *gestalt.* Every object—the triune Creator as well as every creature he has made—has a particular form, a specific pattern of elements that together make it a whole entity. Every star has a certain form, every bird, every text and every soul. *Form* has, historically, been understood statically, as a structure frozen in time. However, this is clearly inadequate with regard to the form of persons, for which we need a dynamic notion. For example, the divine form of God is infinite power and activity, a Triunity of free agents who have existed in eternally active love and mutual glorification, the ultimate dynamic Form of virtuous personal agency (see Barth, 1957). By contrast, the human psychological form (laying aside the form of the body for the moment) would seem to be necessarily finite and temporal, and is therefore a changing, growing and developing structure, so it too, but for very different reasons, must be understood as a dynamic form. Fischer and Bidell (1998) define *psychological* form or structure as a dynamic system of organized components that changes over time.[10]

But the psychological form of a human being is complex. Philosophy, theology and psychology have come up with a number of ways to describe the psychological *whole* of an individual human being. We have already made repeated reference to one of those ways: *personal agent*. In addition to that term, we will examine three other useful labels for the psychological form of an individual human being: personality, self and character. Each of these terms refers to the *entire psychological structure* of a mature, individual human, viewed from a particular perspective. We will consider them as together constituting a human being—a *pluriform*, if you will—in order to grasp more of the complexity of human beings.[11]

Personality. Let us begin with the concept that has been the most well researched in the twentieth century. Personality, as it is most commonly understood, refers to the global set of the unique configuration of cognitive, emotional, behavioral and relational dispositions (called traits) that distinguishes one individual from others, for example, extraversion-introversion and achievement motivation, what has been called one's *dispositional signature* (McAdams & Pals, 2006). The study of this form has been termed the *idiographic* approach to personality (Allport, 1961; Winter & Barenbaum, 1999). Historically, it has involved no moral or evaluative considerations (see, for example, Pervin & John, 1999).[12]

Character. Character is also an idiographic topic, but it concerns the form of a human being from a distinctly ethicospiritual perspective. Largely neglected by modern psychology (until recently with the positive psychology movement; see Peterson & Seligman, 2004; Snyder & Lopez, 2002), it has been discussed more in Western philosophical literature, and it consists of the gestalt of one's unique cognitive, emotional, volitional and relational dispositions (called "virtues" or "vices" depending on where they are on the continuum) that distinguish one individual from others, construed in the light of some community's ethicospiritual discourse (see Hauerwas, 1974; MacIntyre, 1984; O'Donovan, 1986). Character is a way of viewing a human being "in his totality as a moral being" (O'Donovan, p. 205).

Such a focus has been of special interest within the Christian tradition (see 1 Cor 13; 2 Pet 1:5-8; Gregory the Great, 1950; Thomas Aquinas, 1945; Calvin, 1559/1960; Baxter, 1656/1990), so we would expect a Christian psychology to pursue the study of character avidly, recognizing it to be a psychological form constituted by many of the same biopsychosocial structures and processes as personality but interpreted from a different and higher global standpoint: the individual as an ethicospiritual being. The Christian community has long used evaluative language to label moral and spiritual dispositions (virtues and vices) that compose the form of a person's character and its objective beauty (or ugliness), words like *kind*, *grateful*, *malicious* or *stingy*.

Self. The term *self* is distinguished from *personality* and *character* by the extent to which the construct is intrinsically dependent on human knowledge. *Self* refers to a human being's own self-representations, including one's self-descriptions (beliefs about oneself), self-evaluations (feelings and judgments about oneself) and sense of identity (weighted commitment to certain self-representations, roles and values) (Harter, 1999; Westen & Heim, 2003). So the *self* is especially human-knower-dependent and consists solely in what individuals know and feel about themselves. The self is by definition self-constructed (though it originates out of the beliefs and evaluations of others; Harter, 1999). The self is important to human maturation, since the latter entails growth in one's accurate self-knowledge, self-understanding and sense of identity, as well as self-evaluation (all of which, for the Christian, are related to God).

Over the past forty years a large body of psychological research on the self has accrued (see Harter, 1999; Leary & Tangney, 2003). If persons know themselves well, their self coincides fairly well with their personality and character. However, the less accurate the person's self-knowledge, the greater variance there will be between them. Especially notable is the relation between self and character, for there is evidence that as healthy self-structures increase, so do virtues like authenticity and empathy (Harter, 1999; Tangney & Dearing, 2002).

Personal agent. The last human form we will discuss here is personal agent. Personal agency (or human agency) has been explored by contemporary philosophers (Audi, 1993; Bhaskar, 1998; Harre, 1984; Macmurray, 1957; Taylor, 1985a, 1989), as well as mainstream psychologists (see Bandura, 1989, 1999; sometimes by other names, see Deci & Ryan, 2002) and existential and humanistic psychologists (e.g., Bugental, 1965; Rogers, 1961), but its origins actually lie in Christian trinitarian discussions and subsequent Christian explorations (Schwöbel & Gunton, 1991; Ury, 2001). Mature personal agents are beings characterized by rational-linguistic ability; a high degree of self-awareness (compared to other earthly creatures); the capacity to form reasons, plans and intentions, and to act; responsibility (the awareness that they should be held accountable for their actions); and imagination (they can envision new, plausible possibilities in life). Healthy personal agents therefore should have the sense that they are actors (rather than just being acted upon by deterministic forces).[13] This form of human wholeness seems to emerge in mid to late adolescence and early adulthood (though there are clear precursors of personal agency evident in childhood and early adolescence). During this time one's individuated conscience starts to operate, when one begins to feel bad about something one has done, regardless of whether another knows about it. As actors who take (or should take) responsibility for themselves, personal agents sense a degree of freedom in and ownership for what they do. This is not a radical freedom (as existentialism taught) but a compatibilist freedom (or a "conditioned libertarian" freedom) that is shaped more or less by biological and psychosocial influences that come to be laid down in neural structures and so affect future action options (see Jeeves, Berry & Atkinson, 1984; Jones, 1997). Though younger children can know they have broken a rule and have disappointed their caregivers, only mature personal agents can grasp their fallenness and the personal culpability related to their wrongdoing. So personal agency would seem to be a prerequisite to becoming a mature Christian.

Personal agency also makes it possible to develop intimate, interpersonal relationships characterized by empathy, appropriate self-disclosure, a sense of dialogic communion and an "agapic" (or prosocial) orientation (Reis & Patrick, 1996), which requires a measure of psychological differentiation from others. Having the ability to act also means one can act upon oneself (and this has important implications for adult development and soul care). Personal agency entails a mature capacity for self-regulation. However, *Christian* personal agency is dipolar and includes the awareness that one is a co-actor—dependent upon God, according to his will and empowered for good by his indwelling Spirit (Phil 2:10-11; Johnson, 1997b).

Each of these four concepts—personality, character, self and personal agent—provides a way of viewing the form of the human. The *imago Dei* consists at least in part in this pluriform. Each form-type is composed of various intermediate meaning-structures (IMS), which in turn are made up of meaning elements. Some IMS fit only within one form (e.g., virtues compose character and not personality), but different forms may make use of the same IMS and elements (e.g., emotions are involved in all four), since the forms are essentially different ways of viewing the whole individual.

Form and splendor. Hans Urs von Balthasar wrote a masterful seven-volume work, *The Glory of the Lord: A Theological Aesthetics* (1982-1991), in which he argued that God's glory in the creation consists of the manifestation of his form. He also delineated a fundamental distinction between the form of an object and the splendor of its form (which he had found in Thomas Aquinas). According to Balthasar (1982), the form of something has a certain degree of beauty based on the configuration of its elements and their complexity, harmony and proportionality (consider the beauty of a horse or Michelangelo's *David;* Steck, 2001; Stump, 1995). The form of the triune God is the most beautiful of all forms, because God is infinitely the greatest being there is, particularly in that God consists of the most marvelous arrangement of ontological characteristics and moral virtues that can be. The form of a creature can be no more than a finite representation (or sign) of the beauty of its Creator, and its ultimate standard of comparison must always be that formal Archetype. But, following Thomas Aquinas, Balthasar went on to suggest that an object's *splendor* is the *depth dimension of its form* and refers to the form's inner radiance and luminescence, the form's genuine value, that lies, as it were, within it and that shines forth from it (see Scola, 1995; Steck, 2001). It is what we might call the density of its full significance. Consequently, the triune God possesses the greatest degree of splendor imaginable, because God has infinite depth and density of glory. Similarly, all creaturely splendor must be measured by the degree of its analogical depth resemblance to God.

Form, we might say, is the beauty evident on the surface, whereas splendor is the beauty within. Therefore only the omniscient God fully knows the splendor of something. Splendor is always something of a mystery to humans; it can be peered into but not fathomed (Balthasar, 1982). Also, while intelligence can identify form, it takes wisdom to perceive splendor. Grasping the form of a thing seems to be mostly a mental or cognitive enterprise, while grasping a thing's splendor is more an affective heart activity involving appraisal. But both form and splendor are involved and interrelated in an object's full beauty. Perhaps we could posit that something's complete beauty or glory is the multiplication of its form by its splendor.

To illustrate the difference between form and splendor, think of the crafting of a mannequin that has virtually the same physical form as a particular human being. The inherent meaningfulness of the real human being that it is modeled after far transcends the mannequin. The human has obvious depth that the mannequin lacks: the former is alive. As another illustration, consider two siblings who are taking care of their dying mother, one in order to guarantee a large inheritance, and the other out of loving devotion. The actions may have the same form, but their moral splendor is considerably different. Form and splendor are inseparable, since a thing's splendor is dependent on its form.

The importance of this distinction will become clearer in later chapters, but it is presented here because, although each of the four form-types has a distinct formal complexity, they can be distinguished better by their respective splendor.[14] One can rank them from least to most splendor—personality, self, personal agent, character—based on the depth each form seems intrinsically to possess. Such an interpretive determination allows one to prioritize which are more important in terms of the glory of God. With this examination of the four form-types behind us, we return to a consideration of discourse.

The human form of narrative/drama. We turn next to a consideration of narrative: discourse that describes the life of a personal agent, taking into its account the flow of time (temporality). Narratives are of great importance and interest to human beings (McAdams, 1993). Like all discourse, narratives are the results of the creative actions of an author. But narratives—fictional or historical—typically consist of a summary of the story line of a period of time in the life of one or more personal agents. The story line centers around a plot and includes an exploration of some of the agents' ideas, emotions, motives, projects and actions; the context in which they are situated (scene); and the actions of others and events to which they are exposed (Burke, 1945). The relational nature of human life also means that narratives largely consist of interactions and dialogue with others. Narratives, therefore, have a certain structure.

Narratives are made up of distinct units called episodes, which concern events and actions that occur in specific scenes. Events are occurrences that more or less disrupt the life of an agent (Propp, 1968) and obstacles to the agent's projects are especially important events. We have already discussed actions as a class of semiodiscursive elements. Here we note their function in narratives. Actions are events created by an agent (e.g., a baby crying). However, *personal* actions are actions of *personal* agents, and, as we have seen, they typically entail some degree of self-awareness, intentionality and responsibility, so in narratives they result in some freely determined change in the story's development (Audi, 1993; Davidson, 1980). Personal actions are of special note in narratives, heightening the interpreter's interest, since they are to some extent unpredictable (from the standpoint of the reader/hearer). One never knows for sure what personal agents will do until they do it. Though there is some predictability (due to their personality, self-understanding and character), personal agents in most narratives have some *creative capacity*, that is, they can act to some extent freely and are not fully constrained by the deterministic influences of their lives. But that relative freedom is also reflective of their moral character (or degree of virtuousness or viciousness). As a result, a story is a stage for the display of splendor. Challenges and barriers to one's projects create hurdles, the overcoming of which demonstrates the quality and depth of one's character.

A narrative is also a *form* of human being, analogous to the other form-types. This is because a narrative is also a gestalt of human meaning, as the organization of the meaningfulness of a human life *over time:* the *whole* story line of an agent's actions, relationships, significant events and accomplishments. "Life stories organize disparate experience into integrated wholes" (McAdams, 1999, p. 488), so that a mature adult's psychological well-being is signified by a coherent, well-developed personal narrative (McAdams & Pals, 2006; Siegel, 1998). The construction of a coherent narrative, therefore, is a desirable product of therapy.

A closely related type of discourse is a *drama*. Along with narratives, dramas provide a description of the story line of one or more personal agents and their relations. However, in contrast to mere narratives, dramas have *concrete* agents (actors), scripts, a director and the element of performance before an audience (Vanhoozer, 2005; Balthasar, 1988). The persons in dramas are embodied, that is, their bodily actions have been incorporated into the narrative. Scripts include rules for the drama's bodily action and a text of the dialogue between the agents and their interactions. A director is usually needed to realize the author's narrative in the here-and-now enactment, and dramas are written to be performed in the presence of others, on a stage or perhaps in front of a camera. What makes dramas more interesting, more compelling, and (often) more moving than mere narratives is the concrete presence of the persons and the actual enactment of the narrative "before one's eyes."

Before moving to the final section of the chapter, figure 9.2 is presented to provide a diagram of some of the categories of semiodiscursive phenomena that we have seen constitute a human life.

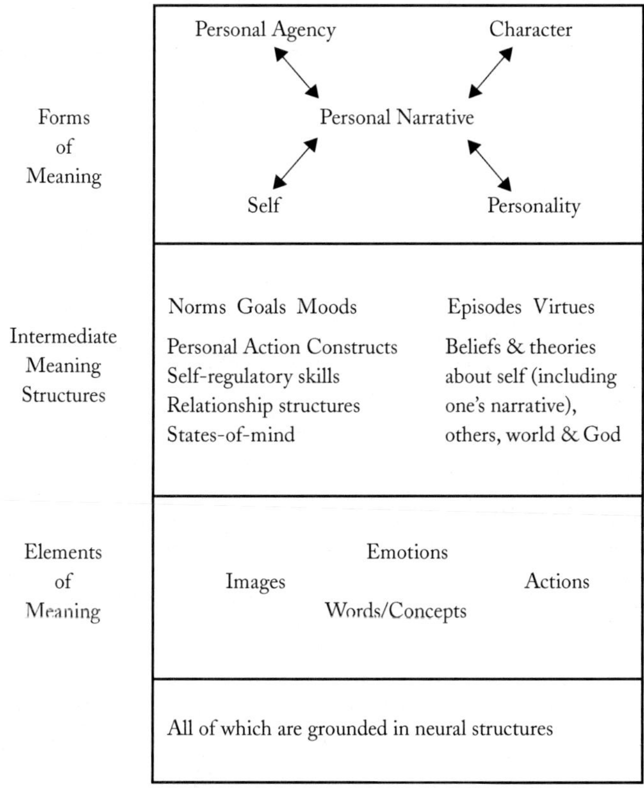

Figure 9.2. Psychological features of a human being stored in memory

The social form of dialogical communion. Because humans are necessarily relational, the form of individual human beings can only properly be understood in relation to others. As we have seen, individuals develop within a relational context of other humans and the triune God, with whom they are always engaged (whether aware of it or not). We just noted that most of the drama of human life is concerned with dialogue and interactions with people. So the formation of individual human beings is one goal of human meaning realization; dialogical communion is another.

Patterning human relations on the Trinity, the form of individual persons is only realized through relationship, dialogue and communion with others.

Perfect communion with others is a state of mutual understanding, consent and delight—something the Trinity has experienced forever. But in this life, humans at best experience limited and flawed communion because of their finitude, sin and relative immaturity, and only then to the extent that at least one person in the relationship enters into self-conscious, affirmative dialogue with the other. For the Christian, God is the perpetual, infinitely loving source and catalyst of the Christian's experience of this communion (a subject to be discussed in chap. 12). From that ground, Christians are to learn how to commune with one another—as well as those outside the faith—primarily through speech (including body language), in order to draw them into mutual dialogue and dialogue with God. The basis of such dialogue is agapé-love (or consent), which simultaneously affirms the other—where they are at—*and* seeks the other's further happiness in God. There are many aspects of this dialogical communion, including wisdom regarding where the other is at psychospiritually, empathy and compassion, respect, affirmation of their giftedness as primordially good, optimal self-other differentiation, desire for and actions aimed at the other's biopsychosocial and ethicospiritual improvement without judgmentalism or arrogance, and hope for the other in Christ. To the extent that humans fall short of this stance, their image-bearing of the Trinity is compromised.

The Beauty of History: The Designated Drama of the Triune God and His Image-Bearers

The textual record of the human race is filled with narratives and dramas, and there is no limit to the fictional narratives and dramas that could be composed. The last type of discourse we will examine is the narrative/drama called *history*, the essentially nonfiction "text" of the actual lives of human beings since the human race was created. What humans call history is truly *the* narrative, *the* drama: an unrepeatable, momentous, temporal unfolding of the generations of humanity up to the present consisting of the meaning of their lives. It is "the real story," and along with the rest of the created order, what we call "the real world."

History has all the features of narrative and drama, but it also possesses characteristics that make it unique. The Bible reveals some of these features. To begin there, we learn that history is the drama that God the Father authored from before the foundation of the world (a story sometimes called "the plan of God"; Ps 33:11; 139:16; Is 46:9-10; Eph 1:11). The Father is the ultimate author of the script of this drama (Horton, 2002), and the Holy Spirit, we might say, is the director, sovereignly bringing the Father's plan to realization through the human actors, including the Son of God (Vanhoozer, 2005; Spiegel, 2002, 2005).[15]

The deep doxological plot of history. As we noted previously, given the triune God's infinite greatness and virtue, it was fitting that his glory be manifested in a creation, within which it would be specially displayed in the incarnation of the Son of God. It was also fitting that his glory be manifested through his communion with created personal beings—images of God who could increasingly recognize and freely love God and magnify God's glory, knowingly participate in it and live in its light.

However, we noted above that hindrances to projects are what really bring out the splendor of one's character, and this agenda in and of itself did not offer any serious obstacles. So God composed an epic theodrama (Balthasar, 1988-1998; Vanhoozer, 2005) to allow a fuller display of the greatness of his divine beauty (Orr, 1904, pp. 280-81). First, God allowed a state of war against himself within the universe, wherein God himself would do battle with his created but fallen opponents, the devil and his demons (Boyd, 1997). Second, the image-bearers he created also turned away from him and became distorted images, all of which made his drama something of a horrible scandal (so far). Third, God's just character required that the guilt of those responsible had to be adequately addressed, but, fourth, the Father devised a way to overcome the evil and brokenness of his image-bearers, where his infinite love and righteousness (Jonathan Edwards would say, his *excellence*) could be simultaneously displayed. So the Father sent his own Son to take upon himself the punishment that his image-bearers deserved—while submitting himself to terrible abuse by those image-bearers—and through his death and resurrection, he destroyed the enmity that prevented communion between God and humans. This occurred, we are told, in "the fullness of the time" (Gal 4:4). So the triune God's work in Christ is the climax of God's doxological drama and therefore became the center of history. Now, through the Holy Spirit, God furthers his dramatic self-glorification by seeking and creating a new community of broken and sinful image-bearers who are being made increasingly capable of communion with the triune God by faith—in spite of their own remaining resistance to this project—and who then seek to bring the rest of the world back to God. God is a missional God (Wright, 2006). (One site of this engagement today is the field of psychology and soul care!) Christians are newly created, Paul wrote, "so that in the ages to come, [God] might show the surpassing riches of His grace in kindness toward us in Christ Jesus" (Eph 2:7).

The triune form of life* partially *manifested in history. "We can only begin to perceive something of His splendor and His glory insofar as His only Son, who dwells in the bosom of His Father and is hidden in His glory, reveals Him to us" (Danielou, 1969, p. 37). Throughout the Old and New Testament periods, God was gradually revealing more of himself to humans in various ways, but the Scriptures are best understood as the progressive written record of God's *incarnate* revelation (Bavinck, 2003; Balthasar, 1989a, 1991). Even so, it was a *veiled* revelation. Jesus Christ embodied the immaterial God (Col 2:9). When he came, he seemed quite unremarkable (Is 53). He looked pretty much like an ordinary man. His neighbors in Nazareth doubted his call (Jn 6:42), the religious leaders of his day were blind to his true greatness (Jn 9), he sought to minimize the publicity his miracles caused (Mk 1:44), and he used parables to conceal as much as to teach (Mt 13). His miracles were signs, to be sure (Jn 2:11; 4:54; 6:14), but not *proofs*—for signs can be wrongly interpreted (see Lk 11:15). And then, at the climax of his coming, the Son of God died—looking like a common criminal—a very curious event for the Lord of the universe to permit to happen to himself. Consequently, some have seen in the cross the most amazing act of divine hiddenness imaginable (Jüngel, 1983; Balthasar, 1989a), leading even Paul to say that the "word of the cross" is "foolishness" to some (1 Cor 1:18). Paul told us that "though [Christ] existed in the form *[morphē]* of God, [He] did not regard equality with God a thing to be grasped, but emptied Himself [and in the process, veiling himself], taking the form of a bond-servant" (Phil 2:6-7). Even his glorious resurrection was witnessed by comparatively few. Throughout his life, death and resurrection, God's glory was still fairly well hidden. All in all, redemptive history has been an account of the concealing of his glory as much as the revealing of it.

Nonetheless, Christ's first coming *was* a significant sign. Paul repeatedly referred to the manifestation of God's salvation in the revelation of Jesus Christ as a *mystery [mysterion]* now revealed (Ridderbos, 1975, Sec. 7, 8): "the revelation of the mystery which has been kept secret for long ages past, but now is manifested, and by the Scriptures of the prophets, according to the commandment of the eternal God, has been made known to all the nations, leading to obedience of faith" (Rom 16:25-26). Paul wrote that he was preaching "the word of God, that is, the mystery which has been hidden from the past ages and generations, but has now been manifested to His saints, to whom God willed to make known what is the riches of the glory of this mystery among the Gentiles, which is Christ in you, the hope of glory. We proclaim Him, . . . so that we may present every man complete in Christ" (Col 1:25-28; see also Jn 17:6, 26; Eph 1:9-10; 3:4-5; 1 Cor 2:7; 2 Tim 1:9-10). So God's glory in Christ, concealed for centuries, has now been revealed to the church and realized through his indwelling in believers, and through the church it is being manifested to the world.

Christ: The perfect pluriform. As the God-human, Christ is both the form of God (*en morphē theou*, Phil 2:6) and the form of a slave (*morphēn doulou,* Phil 2:7; which is also to say he is made the image of God [*eikōn tou theou,* Col 1:15] and the likeness of humanity [*en homoiōmati anthrōpōn,* Phil 2:7]). But in what does this God-human form consist? Form was defined above as pattern, figure, shape or whole structure. The form of Christ, then, is the "shape" or structure of his nature or being. This cannot refer primarily to his physical shape or body, since, we are told, he preexisted in the form of God, and God has no body (Jn 4:24). So it must refer chiefly to the structure of his *inner nature* or *personhood* (mediated by his human body in the incarnation).[16] This claim is supported and clarified by related teachings, for example, the image of God in the New Testament (which consists of righteousness, holiness of the truth, true knowledge and all the virtues mentioned in the context: Eph 4:22-24; Col 3:9-10) and the fundamental importance of imitating God (Mt 5:44-48; Eph 4:32; 5:1; 1 Pet 1:15-16; see Berkouwer, 1962; Calvin, 1559/1960). In these teachings Godlikeness is equated with *ethicospiritual* resemblance.

So, while the form of Christ has an ontological dimension, it must also consist in his ethicospiritual, characterological resemblance to God his Father, incarnated in his human body. However, the reader will recall that the form of human being was said to be pluriform, viewed from a total of five different perspectives, all of which help us to understand the definitive pattern of human meaning. Being the perfect form of a human being, Christ is a superlative personal agent, having a well-developed self and personality,[17] and a flawless, virtuous character, all demonstrated through his actions in the course of his story. Jesus Christ is the greatest single concentration of glory ever manifested by God in the creation, and his form and splendor provide the source and standard for the God-glorification of all other image-bearers.

Nietzsche, Sartre and Foucault were correct that human life has no ultimate significance without God. Genuine meaning in human life, we noted earlier, is exocentric. Here we learn another aspect of its exocentricity: it is incarnational (Zimmermann, 2004). It originates from outside the circle of sinful human discourse and "meaning making" and enters into that circle, transforming all discourse ever after. Those who resist this transformation are left with an empty shell of meaning, constructed out of nothing more than the dust of their own desires and wishes (a conclusion to which naturalistic evolutionary theory necessarily leads, see Baumeister, 1991).

The significance of God's history (and ours). With Christ as the lodestar for our journey into glory, history becomes momentous. In the light of Christ's life, every other human life is rendered significant, and this fact casts a degree of significance (or depth or splendor) upon every moment in each life. It also renders some events and actions relatively more important than others. An afternoon at the company picnic may possess less significance than an afternoon of explicitly Christian ministry in a Third-World urban neighborhood. The greater the relative significance of the actions of the personal agents, their context and even the agents themselves—in reference to Christ—the more momentous is the episode.

"To become a Christian is to be taken up into the drama of God's plan for creation" (Charry, 1997, p. 36). This means that each Christian's life story should be seen as a small part of the drama of God's history. Every bit of meaning, every thought and emotion, every goal and mood, every act and every pain all derive whatever meaningfulness they possess from God's doxological *telos* in Christ. Redeemed humans, therefore, have a pivotal role to play in the doxological drama. They are participants; they are actors expected to follow God's "script" (found in Scripture, Vanhoozer, 2005), in order best to participate in the outworking of God's glory. So, the free, loving response of God's children to his plan, as revealed in his word, is an essential component of that plan and *is* a manifestation of God's beauty.

The greatest human meaningfulness, therefore, is seen in derivative acts of *reception*, a covenantal reconstruction of meaning that involves consenting to God's doxological agenda and interpretation. When God lived as a human being, died and was raised, he immediately changed the sign systems, discourse and dramas of the Hebrew and Roman worlds into which he came, and the significance of his kingdom is still spiraling outward and providing the context within which all individual dramas are now to be interpreted. The Christian life entails an aesthetic hermeneutic based on the life, death and resurrection of Christ (Zimmermann, 2004).

The past. In contrast to fictional dramas, human history has an absolute inviolability. One side of its inviolability has to do with the past. There is what Heidegger (1962) called "thrownness," the fact that one finds oneself within a certain family, culture and time, having a specific body, genetic endowment and features, none of which one chose (though Christians understand who "threw" them there). In addition, the vast majority of events and actions in one's life are outside one's direct control (apart from one's own actions, and even here there is a degree of hindrance and resistance to one's volitions; see Ricoeur, 1966). And once events have happened, there is no way for them to be undone. In fact, as each moment passes, it is gone forever. Thus, it is all momentous (Edwards, 1834/1974, Vol. 2, pp. 233-36). Hypothetically, history could have gone differently than it did. There are an infinite number of possible worlds. One can envision some of those options in one's imagination (and sometimes feel emotions like regret). But there is only one actual world. It is the one possible world that God selected to realize. Its utter inviolability means that each individual's activity has a horizon of attainment, different for everyone but nonetheless necessarily finite. This designation therefore requires on the part of individual agents a submission or consent. So part of Christian maturation entails "coming to terms with" the past, including one's own actions.

The present. History is *the* drama being realized in the present. Mere dramas can be very engaging and moving. However, they are only portrayals of life. Real human beings are not mere characters in a story but personal agents who are living actual lives, whose being and actions have genuine significance; they are momentous and weighty, they have a bearing on others, and they possess greater to lesser degrees of glory. Their stories are to be images of Christ's story, *signs* of his glory, more or less. Herein lies the real differentiation in human significance.

Levinas (1981) brings out another feature of the present's momentousness: the face of other humans brings with it an obligation to care, challenge and love. Other humans awaken the personal agent to responsibility for the Other.

The Other's presence is ethically compelling and therefore also makes history momentous. However, human life is momentous more fundamentally because, according to the Bible, it is being performed in the present *coram Deo* (before God), before *his* face (Ford, 1999; see also Horton, 2002). Christianity teaches that history is ultimately a drama performed before the eyes of God: "For the eyes of the LORD move to and fro throughout the earth" (2 Chron 16:9). God sees everything (see Gen 6:12), including the innermost recesses of the heart (Jer 17:10; 20:12; Heb 4:13). Though this can be alarming for humans to consider, this is what gives each moment its final significance, for all humans will have to give an account of what they are doing today, "on the day when . . . God will judge the secrets of men through Christ Jesus" (Rom 2:16; see Rom 2:5-16; Acts 17:31; also Edwards, 1834/1974, Vol. 2, pp. 190-200). This, in turn, leads us to look ahead in our story.

The future. The fact that God's drama has not yet been completed may be the most momentous of history's unique features. God's plan, conceived before the world began, is being realized now, preeminently through the free actions of his image-bearers. This means that, while the future is not open to God (in the sense that he does not know what he will do or what will happen in the future), it *is* open to us. There are many possible futures from our standpoint. Part of being temporal/narrative creatures in history is that humans live toward the future: intending, planning, imagining (Ricoeur, 1984-1988; Venema, 2000). But Christians are to live toward *God's* future. The Bible tells Christians that they will be perfected (made like Christ) in eternity and dwell with God and each other in harmony and blessedness forever. This forward-looking orientation momentously alters the present.

Moreover, in a very different sense, in Christ, the future is now. As we saw in chapter six, there is an already–not-yet dynamic at work in human history (Ladd, 1974). Christ's salvation has not yet been fully realized in history, and it will not be until the end of history. In the "between times" Christians are to realize their own individual dramas eschatologically, in light of the end, to act and interact with others more and more, so as to realize the perfection of the end based on the perfection found now only in Christ (Heard, 1993). This happens as believers abide in Christ and do their best to follow his script so that their hearts and wills become gradually conformed to God's, more and more. As a result, their views of the future, their hopes, their plans, their intentions and even their imaginations come to be realized as God wishes.

Making Augustine more of a developmentalist than he actually was, we ought also to interpret each believer's story as a journey from the City of Humanity to the City of God, or as Bunyan put it, the Christian's pilgrimage from the City of Destruction to the Celestial City. (The drama might also be described, less poetically, as a sojourn from the City of Autocentrism to the City of Theocentrism.) The signs of God's word throughout the universe but especially in the Bible point us in the direction of God's future for us, and our travels move us ever closer to his ends: the manifestation of his glory and the increase of our happiness through participation in that glory. As suggested earlier, Christian pastors and counselors are trail guides on this Way, helping others to find their way by dying to this world's pseudo-significance and rising from the deadness of meaninglessness. In this way they will grow into the form of Christ, wherein is fullness of meaning. We make this journey together with other Christians—it is a caravan—as we travel, encouraging and challenging one another and seeking to bring others into our fellowship (through evangelism and missions).

Christian soul care helps counselees to accept the utterly momentous theo-drama within which they live. Their entire lives are only properly interpreted within the hermeneutical context of God's drama. Though somewhat hidden, the members of the Trinity are far and away the central characters, working on their project of glory and grace; but their history is becoming our history, since it is through the changing of our lives and our helping of others—in relation to Christ—that the manifestation of their glory is especially being realized.

The Hermeneutic Nature of Christian Child Rearing and Soul Care

To rephrase this chapter: children develop as they participate in dialogue with others and become, in turn, conversation partners themselves. They take in words "and these words are the words of other people, above all, the mother. Then these 'others' words' are processed dialogically into 'one's own/others' words' with the help of different 'others' words' (heard previously) and then in one's own words, so to speak (dropping the quotation marks), which are already creative in nature." (Bakhtin, 1986, p. 163). Childhood development should be seen as a kind of creational, foundation-building anticipation of the triune God's ontogenetic redemptive agenda of conformity to Christ. Analogous, perhaps, to the types in the Old Testament—persons, events, ceremonies and institutions that pointed ahead to Christ—children are supposed to be exposed to "types of Christ" in their lives—persons, events, ceremonies and institutions similarly pointing them to Christ. The *natural* semiodiscursive development of children was designed by God to prepare them for and issue them into the *spiritual* semiodiscursive development of the children of God. Humankind's main problem is the semiodiscursive distortions due to sin, directly and indirectly, that compromise individual development. Every person's form has greater or lesser significance in relation to his or her discursive context—which is ultimately the history of God's self-glorification. All this entails interpretation.

The care of souls, likewise, is hermeneutical. It is a type of conversation that draws counselees into something of an alternative discursive system than those they have known. It involves identifying their stories and the lies that they have internalized from their youth and any symptoms of psychospiritual disorder, and inferring and properly identifying the underlying conditions. It seeks to understand the counselees' story, as well as their current configuration of meaning (elements, intermediate structures, the pluriform), then providing wise interpretation of what is there, helping to undermine and remove that which is false and pathological, and fostering the internalization of more valid meaning, that is, that which corresponds better to the intentions in God's mind and heart through a fuller incorporation into God's history of redemption.

Notes

[1]Though human thought is logically independent of language (we can have a thought without being able to put it into words), most cognitive psychologists agree that human thought, especially the higher mental processes, is heavily language dependent. So for our purposes, we will treat words and concepts together.

[2]Theorists differ among themselves regarding what are the "basic emotions." Because emotions are subjective, it is difficult to achieve universal agreement about their features, but this is no reason to become a nonrealist and reject the possibility of attaining any knowledge on the subject. Human language is well equipped to communicate meaningfully and with accuracy about subjective experience. Emotion researchers posit anywhere from three to ten basic emotions—common to human beings across cultures—but most everyone agrees on anger, fear, sadness and happiness; see Plutchik, 1994, p. 58.

[3]Though there are exceptions. Some classes of emotional experience, like temperament and mood, are not intentional (though moods may be an aggregate of earlier intentional experiences). See below.

[4]"If affect is the fundamental motivational force in human nature, then affect needs to be central in our clinical theory and practice, in order to have a strong impact on changing patients' behavior" (McCullough, Kuhn, Andrews, Kaplan, Wolf & Hurley, 2003, p. 15).

[5]For those who are interested, there are a number of good reasons for seeing the broader semiodiscursive focus of this book as still fundamentally semiotic. For one thing, all texts make use of discrete signs, so anything having to do with words is fundamentally semiotic in nature. Moreover, though sentences are commonly distinguished from signs, since they are composed of word-signs and therefore express more than a single, atomic meaning (Ricoeur, 1977), Pierce argued that a sentence is actually a "compound sign," with the subject understood to be an index to the object it signifies and the predicate, an icon of the subject (Merrell, 1991, p. 66). If sentences are compound signs, then so are texts which are composed of sentences. A third reason to consider discourse a semiotic phenomenon is that larger units of meaning like texts, narratives and dramas (and their events and agents) often themselves function as discrete signs insofar as they express an identifiable theme (e.g., Shakespeare's *Romeo and Juliet* signifies "the tragic possibilities of human romance"; see also Vanhoozer, 1998, pp. 459ff.). A fourth reason is that some of the most meaning-filled types of discourse (e.g., poetry) make use of signs like metaphor that contribute to a text's persuasive power and beauty. As a result of such diverse considerations (and others), the field of semiotics has long understood all of culture, including all texts, to be fundamentally a semiotic reality (see, e.g., Barthes, 1967; Eco, 1976; Greimas, 1990, 1991; Kristeva, 1980; Nöth, 1990). Nevertheless, because of the broad range of meaning addressed herein (both signs and discourse) and the fact that most human meaning is linguistically based, the label "semiodiscursive" is being used throughout the book to label the complex focus of this model.

[6]Discourse can be composed in various forms for different purposes. Kinneavy (1971) distinguishes between expressive, persuasive, literary and reference types of discourse. Written discourse has been further broken down into fiction and nonfiction (the former labeling literature meant to describe imagined events), and into genre, as we saw in chapter six. A set of related texts, either by individuals or communities, forms a "body of literature" that permits other individuals to enter into a linguistically represented, projected "world" (the world "in front of the text," to use Ricoeur's terminology), even when separated from the author by time, distance and belief. Yet all discourse bears some analogy to the *actual* world of the author (to be distinguished from the projected "world"), so that, depending on the interpreter's aims (e.g., fiction or nonfiction) and competence, and to the extent the receiver accurately understands the discourse (e.g., its language of origin), the text provides the receiver with a linguistic bridge to both the communicator's projected *and* actual worlds. (Gadamer, 1975, referred to the interpretation of human discourse as a "fusion of the horizons" of author and interpreter, making communication of *truth* through language possible, though as Gadamer points out, receivers necessarily interpret from within their own horizon.) *Reference* or *scientific* discourse (consisting of descriptive speech acts) is composed of assertions and has as its express aim an accurate description of some feature of the actual world; that is its primary communicative function (Kinneavy, 1971). It is through attending to various types of reference discourse, for example, conversations with parents and friends, lectures by teachers and books by experts, that people form their beliefs about the world, their culture, themselves and ultimate reality, eventually developing rather involved theories about many such things (Case, 1998; Dweck, 2000; Flavell & Miller, 1998; Harter, 1999).

[7]Most would consider speech logically prior to writing (though Derrida, 1976, 1978, sharply disagreed), since writing would seem to be the fixation of speech into script (Ricoeur, 1981a). Writing has some advantages over speech. Written expression allows one's thoughts to become a fixed object and therefore can facilitate more thorough reflection, aiding in greater clarification through repeated rewriting. Moreover, whereas speech also communicates one's ideas to others, writing makes possible a "permanent" record of an individual's ideas, making it possible for others to more thoroughly understand that person's ideas and then build upon them. In fact, the development of culture can occur only when its speech can be transcribed, making possible business transactions, science, technology and, very likely, the development of formal reasoning (Olson, 1994). At the same time, speech has

the advantages of being less deliberate and expressed within an immediate interpersonal context, in many cases with knowledge of and response from the listener, in dialogue. Consequently, speech is usually more spontaneous, interactional and situation-specific (though online chatting provides a virtual union of writing and speech).

[8]Such structures have also been termed *personal action constructs* and *middle-level units* in personality (see McAdams & Pals, 2006).

[9]In appendix two the reader will find a brief discussion of secular semiotic theory, which tends to reject reference to personal agents. A Christian semiotic theory has no such ideological need to resist the recognition of the ontological status of personal agents.

[10]Though emphasizing the form of the individual human, we must always keep in mind that individual human beings are necessarily related to the material universe in this age, and always to other humans and the triune God.

[11]There are other concepts that would also help us understand the human form, for example, ego, but we will limit ourselves to these.

[12]Though the term *personality* is being used here, some interpretation/translation issues remain unresolved. To begin with, as suggested, modern personality theory assiduously avoided reference to moral considerations. The short explanation for this fact is that the neopositivist rules of discourse of the modern psychological community were developed precisely to avoid ethical considerations. Yet most personality traits described in modern psychology do have some moral significance. Take, for example, two of the "Big Five" personality traits, conscientiousness and agreeableness (McCrae & Costa, 1990). While there are strengths on both sides of each trait-continuum, the positive ends are clearly more socially desirable and share features in common with certain virtues (industriousness and perseverance, and kindness and gentleness, respectively).

At the same time, historically, idiographic personality study has restricted itself to traits that are relatively independent of moral content, going back to the four temperaments. There may be a valid intuition behind this reserve that undergirded modern personality psychology's aversion to moral considerations. But Christians cannot stop there. Moral traits (or virtues/vices) are form-features where one side of the trait-continuum is morally superior; these will be discussed next under the heading of *character*. But the Christian tradition has referred to something similar to idiographic personality traits but has called them *gifts* (Rom 12; 1 Cor 12; 14), language that conveys their origin in God's grace and underscores human dependence upon God.

[13]Unfortunately, human nature is so complex and terminology regarding the human form has changed over the centuries and differs between groups in the present, so it is hard to get universal agreement on one's terms. Søren Kierkegaard, for example, used the term *self* to refer to the same thing as that for which I am using *personal agent*, as does Harter's understanding of self-as-Subject. In this book, where I can, I attempt to follow the majority usage of contemporary psychologists and philosophers for the terms chosen, and I have tried to avoid an idiosyncratic use of terms. But some readers may fairly question the decisions that were made.

[14]All of the form-types have a distinguishing, complex form that has a certain beauty, but it does not seem possible to compare their degree of formal beauty (e.g., to say that the self has a more beautiful form than the personality), since they each seem to have a similar degree of compositional complexity (the self and the personality, for example, are each composed of a number of important features). However, each token (each individual example) of each form-type has its own respective degree of formal beauty (and glory), which can be lesser or greater (depending on measures of formal beauty); for example, more mature selves are more complex than less mature, and some personalities have a greater degree of harmoniousness than others.

Yet the form-types *can* be distinguished with respect to their splendor or depth. Human selves and personalities certainly have *some* splendor. They are, after all, more meaningful than a rock or a tree. But it would seem that they do not possess as much splendor as personal agents and characters, which both have an intrinsic ethical and spiritual significance. While even cats have a distinguishable temperament, personal agency is a capacity unique to fairly advanced beings (in the created realm, only humans, so far as we know). Acting, taking responsibility and loving for the sake of the other manifest a greater luminescence and depth than cats are capable of (as friendly as some of them may be). Personal agency is the basis of ethicospiritual freedom, wherein one is capable of choosing the Good, so the form of personal agency possesses more splendor than personality and the self. Character, however, is the form-type that most manifests splendor, since it has to do with the actual ethicospiritual significance of human action. We might say that personal agency greatly enhances one's potential for splendor, whereas character concerns the actual degree of the splendor-manifestation of which personal agents are capable, that has been woven into their current being. One may possess a relatively high level of personal agency (and so be highly reflective and responsible and so on), and yet be squandering it on frivolous and shallow pursuits because of a relatively warped or immature character. Personal agency is the means of character—indeed it creates character—and virtuous Christian character is the primary immanent goal of redemption and the Christian life. Consequently, character is the form-type that has the greater splendor.

It is an easy step from here to the realization that tokens of the form-types can differ in splendor, just like they can in form. Some people have greater capacity for personal agency, and some are more virtuous than others.

[15]As we saw in the previous chapter when we considered sin and human agency, the chief difficulty in this account arises from the seeming incompatibility of a history that is the working out of God's plan and the notion of human agency. In the Christian tradition this paradox has been called a mystery (Augustine, 1948; Aquinas, 1945; and Calvin, 1559/1960), and it resists a simple logical solution (Johnson, 2002). In contrast to all other creatures, adult humans, made in God's image, are able to act in novel and creative ways, transcending, to some extent, their genetic and environmental programming, and to realize their own freely owned projects, and yet all this human activity occurs "according to His purpose who works all things after the counsel of His will" (Eph 1:11). Since humans act freely and are not being coerced by God's plan, they are responsible for their actions.

[16]According to Braumann (1975, p. 703), one of the meanings of *form* in the New Testament is "essential character."

[17]Balthasar (1986) wrote that Christ had a "strong and distinctive personality, utterly unforgettable" (p. 171). See also Beck (1999).

10

Orders of Meaning

A Multilevel Analysis of Human Life

HUMAN LIFE IS PERVADED WITH MEANING, divinely endowed, ultimately the expression of the Word of God. The next two chapters seek to unpack some of the complex semiodiscursive essence of human life by analyzing it in terms of four interrelated levels of meaningfulness. But we begin with a story.

A Story of a Complex Soul

Ted is a forty-three-year-old married man, a father of four and an accountant. Lately he has been worrying constantly, with such intensity that he has had difficulty concentrating on tasks at work, focusing on what others are saying to him and sleeping for more than three hours a night. At times it feels as if his head is racing and his brain is on overdrive, and he gets an almost painful constriction in his chest. He has been feeling extremely self-conscious lately and experiences a vague but unyielding sense of impending doom. These symptoms began within a month after the arrival of a new supervisor, to whom he is accountable and whose work style is very demanding. The symptoms are beginning to compromise his ability to get along well with his family and his colleagues, and he recently has had some trouble completing projects at work.

A couple of months before the arrival of his new supervisor, Ted began to feel strongly attracted to a lonely, single, female coworker. They began to go out for dinner after work, which occurred a few times a month over the next three months, and which Ted hid from his wife. This coworker is now pressing him to spend more time with her. Ted is beginning to realize he bears some responsibility for fostering these desires, and he is feeling guilty and trapped. At the same time, Ted sees himself as a committed Christian who has taken his faith seriously since his conversion in high school. However, over the past year, he has felt increasingly disillusioned about his marriage and family life, and he admits that he has never experienced much intensity in his relationship with God. About six months ago, he felt so distant from God that he stopped spending any real time in prayer or Bible reading. He now admits he sometimes feels angry with God for how things have gone in his life.

Ted grew up an only child. His parents were both fundamentalist Christians who had extremely high, at times unrealistic, standards for Ted's behavior and performance in school (e.g., throughout high school, they challenged him to become a medical doctor, even though he was, at best, a B student). He describes his childhood as feeling like he was always "walking a tightrope," trying hard to keep his parents happy. In addition, he has a number of what might be called "high-strung" relatives, and his father recently told him that he had had a similar bout with anxiety in his mid thirties.

How are we to make sense of Ted's struggles? His physical symptoms suggest the activation of a physiological stress response, leading to something close to panic attacks, but how are those symptoms related to his genetics and his family upbringing? At the same time, it looks like he has sinned against his coworker and his wife, as well as God. In fact, it sounds as if he is avoiding God. But if there are biological and social influences on his anxiety, do those not undermine its ethical and spiritual sources? Is his anxiety a product or a cause of his hypocritical lifestyle? If the anxiety is simply a consequence of his recent ethicospiritual struggles, is there any value in acknowledging the biological and social influences on it? How can pastors, therapists and counselors best understand Ted's anxiety, when there are so many different dynamics at work?

The Complexity of Human Nature Is a (Word) Puzzle

Human beings have wrestled with such problems for millennia. Differences in understanding the ontology of human nature abound, from the radical dualism of gnosticism to the spiritual monism of Hinduism and the monistic reductionism of naturalism. Human nature presents a mysterious puzzle that would seem to confound human understanding (McGinn, 2000). Yet, for those charged with caring for and enhancing the well-being of people, there is an urgency to obtain the most accurate and comprehensive understanding of human nature possible. But can this puzzle ever be solved?

As suggested in previous chapters, Christians who hold to a realist epistemology generally make three assumptions regarding their knowing: (1) God understands all things, (2) finite, sinful humans have serious limits to their understanding, but (3) through careful consideration, humans can know certain things and their understanding can improve in its correspondence to God's. These assumptions help Christians to resist a sense of finality regarding their current understanding of complex subjects—like the composition of human beings—but they also encourage them to avoid a skepticism that would lead them to conclude that a better understanding is not possible. To orient us in our reflections below, we will briefly consider some models that understand humans to be composed of distinct levels of being or functioning.

The twentieth century notwithstanding, perhaps the most universally acknowledged feature of human nature has been a dualistic ontology. If decisions on such topics were reached democratically, the view that humans fundamentally have two "sides"—what we in the West call body and soul (or, more recently, the brain and the mind/cognition)—would be acclaimed the winner, such is the pervasive agreement among basic, ancient and most contemporary cultures (Johnson, 1998a). Virtually all preliterate religions assume that life forms possess an immaterial "power" (Frazer, 1922/1967; Riviere, 1987). Of most importance to Christians, the biblical authors usually distinguish the soul and its functions from the body (Gen 2:7; 35:18; Mt 10:28). The soul is credited with having feelings, thoughts and intentions (Ps 86:4; 139:14; Mt 26:38), and the soul appears able to exist, at least for a time, outside the body (Acts 2:27, 31; 2 Cor 5:8; Rev 6:9). So until recently, Christianity has been in broad support of some sort of duality (Hasker, 1999; Bavinck, 2004; Cooper, 2000).

Borrowing assumptions from the natural sciences, modernism has tried to stick to the "observable facts," so the notion of a soul had to be jettisoned, and the majority position among modernists in the twentieth-century West regarding the nature of human beings has been some version of materialistic monism: there is nothing to human nature other than matter. Consequently, during the first half of the century, psychological research focused on the body: either its physiology or its behavior. Later, however, the success of research on cognition demonstrated that the mind—and not just the brain—also had a kind of structure. Language systems, memory stores and semantic networks, for example, though immaterial, have an identifiable form, raising questions about the ontological status of these structures. Even so, most modern psychologists, influenced by positivism, resisted the implications of cognitive psychology that there is some kind of reality other than the material.

In spite of such peer pressure, Karl Popper and John Eccles (1977) and Eccles and Daniel Robinson (1984) have suggested that some kind of brain-mind dualism provides the best explanation of human experience and the available data. They use the term *worlds* and distinguish a *physical* world composed of physical and biological objects, a *subjective* world consisting in states of consciousness, and a *knowledge* world made up of cultural information and logical arguments, and they argue that these "worlds" interact in human life.

In defiance of strict materialism, phenomenology was a modern school of philosophy that also sought to take seriously the unique features of human experience, in particular, the nature of human consciousness (e.g., intentionality, temporality, intersubjectivity and the life-world; see Husserl, 1913/1961; Heidegger, 1927/1962; Merleau-Ponty, 1942/1963; Schutz, 1960/1967). Merleau-Ponty argued that there appear to be three "orders of significations" (pp. 132, 137) in the world: the physical, the vital (or biological) and the human, each of which has its own structure. The physical is characterized by material structure, the vital by order and purpose, and the human by consciousness. While he rejected the assumption that these orders are composed of higher or lower *substances* (like a soul versus a body), Merleau-Ponty believed they were related hierarchically, since the higher orders seem to transcend the complexity of the lower orders, while nonetheless are simultaneously grounded upon them. The lower orders are related to the higher as a part to the whole (p. 180), and higher orders involve a "retaking and a 'new' structuration of the preceding one" (p. 184). He thought that the lower orders ought not to be interpreted as being autonomous from the higher orders, since the latter integrate the former into a new level of signification. For example, when a couple eats together, the biological function of feeding is constituted a socially meaningful activity. This hierarchical understanding is very different from an approach that would see these orders as distinct parts that are mechanically put together in an organism; according to Merleau-Ponty, a mature human being is an integrated whole in which the lower features of its being are brought into a higher, more meaningful organization.

More recently, the analytic philosopher John Searle (1998) has argued that human consciousness has certain features that make it irreducible to merely physical or biological phenomena: unity, intentionality and subjective feeling, to name three. Yet Searle is no dualist; he has no use for the notion of a substantial soul. He believes instead that consciousness is simply a higher-order property of the brain, in the same way that liquidity is a higher-order property of a large group of H_2O molecules linked together at room temperature (p. 14). But he maintains that consciousness has a unique status, worthy of scientific study and distinguishable from the neurobiological dynamics upon which it is based.

Roy Bhaskar (1997, 1998; see Collier, 1994), a philosopher of the social sciences, similarly argues that human life and experience is best accounted for by reference to multiple, distinct "strata" that are organized in a hierarchy: molecular, biological, psychological and social. He thinks one must posit a hierarchy if and when certain strata (the higher) are rooted or grounded in and emerge out of the phenomena of another (the lower). Bhaskar's model permits one to explain the higher strata in terms of the lower, while still recognizing the existence of the unique features of the higher that are irreducible to the lower.

Based on the teachings of the Bible, the Christian tradition has tended to assume a fundamental body-soul duality (Cooper, 2000), though this issue is currently a focus of some debate (Green & Palmer, 2005). Moreover, Christians have always believed that the spiritual or divine dimension is a distinct source of activity and influence on the material and psychic worlds.

The Christian philosopher Søren Kierkegaard believed that humans exist in one of three "stages" or "spheres of existence," which he termed the aesthetic, the ethical and the religious (Kierkegaard, 1988).[1] Each, he said, is a fundamental life-orientation or motivational framework. To live according to the aesthetic sphere is to act according to one's own, immediate desires. Such an orientation characterizes human childhood, but adults can remain in this stage their whole lives. People in the ethical stage, in contrast, have recognized that proper human life entails the adherence to moral norms that often restrict the satisfaction of one's desires. The religious sphere is distinguished from the ethical by the awareness that one cannot fulfill the demands of the ethical sphere without help from God. Kierkegaard's stages or spheres are modes of human being that are articulable, related hierarchically (and developmentally [Evans, 1990]), and distinguished by different degrees of complexity and significance. We will explore much further his distinction between the ethical and the religious.

Influenced by Bhaskar as well as Polanyi (1966), the evangelical theologian Alister McGrath (2002) has recently argued that creation is a "multi-layered reality" composed of a hierarchy of strata. With Bhaskar, he acknowledges the basic distinctions between the natural and social levels of reality. However, as a theist, he regards the theological stratum as distinct from and undergirding the others, and as the most fundamental, since it concerns God, the Creator of all things.

Many other Christians could be cited in support of some kind of hierarchical model of human nature (e.g., Augustine, 1948; Thomas Aquinas, 1945; Calvin, 1559/1960; Kuyper, 1898b; Braine, 1992; Brown, Murphy & Malony, 1998; Dooyeweerd, 1960, 1984; Hasker, 1999; Von Hildebrand, 1990; Murphy & Ellis, 1996; Polkinghorne, 1988; Ricoeur, 1995; Scheler, 1928/1961; Taylor, 1985a, 1989; Van Inwagen, 1993). Virtually no one doubts that some kind of basic distinction must be made between the biological and the psychological or social. Even die-hard materialists acknowledge that the psychological must be accounted for, even if they label it "epiphenomenal" or self-refutingly suggest its properties are essentially identical to its neurological correlates (Hasker, 1999). So few would question making some distinction between mind and brain. It is more debatable to distinguish between major "strata" or "orders" within the psychological or immaterial side of human beings. Nevertheless, in light of the kinds of intuitions and reflections touched on above, there would appear to be four orders that together seem to provide the most adequate, simple and parsimonious framework for thinking about the complexity of human nature for soul care: the biological, the psychosocial, the ethical and the spiritual. It is hoped that by the end of this chapter, an adequate case for the existence of these four orders will have been made.

One must acknowledge that regardless of the orders one settles on, questions can always be raised about their actual reality. Positivism in particular (including the neopositivism that rules most of modern and postmodern psychology) only allows for a single type of empirically validated "reality," devoid of any metaphysical distinctions or value hierarchies; so modern and postmodern psychologists typically reject any notion of multiple strata. However, even among those who allow for the possibility of other strata, it will be hard to prove to everyone's satisfaction the validity of the set presented here.[2]

Nonetheless, we will assume that each of the orders treated in this model was established by God and constitutes a distinct meaning-system, with structures, processes and internal relations that can be identified and contrasted with those of the others. Each possesses an internal coherence—its own logic, vocabulary and grammar—and each provides a legitimate, meaningful perspective on human life and experience. Together they provide a fuller, more comprehensive picture of human nature than any of them does alone.[3]

Orders of Meaning

We have repeatedly referred to meaning, but we can go no further without defining it. Meaning is all that is conveyed through some means of communication.[4] Accordingly, the full meaning of a sign or utterance includes both its signification and its significance. Signification is that which is intended to be conveyed by the author (e.g., the description of the actual nature or form of something, like all that makes a dragonfly a dragonfly), whereas significance pertains to the actual import of what is conveyed, in relation to other considerations (e.g., the difference in value between a text dealing with the believer's union with Christ and one dealing with gardening). With regard to a science of human nature, signification has to do with knowledge, truth, form, information, description, the mind and knowing, whereas significance has to do with evaluation, beauty, splendor, import, depth, momentousness, appraisal, the heart and loving. In the modern era, signification was considered something objective and the focus of science (facts) and was separated from significance, which was considered fundamentally subjective, at best the focus of philosophy (like ethics or axiology) or religion. This tragic dichotomy led to a truncated (modern) psychology. A science of individual human nature is charged with elucidating the full meaning of human beings, and this must include both description and appraisal. This distinction is important for soul care because, as Edwards (1746/1959) recognized, humans were created with a system for comprehending both: the human intellect grasps signification (and knows information that often is true), whereas the human emotion-volition system grasps significance (and loves that which is beautiful). In order to help others correspond most fully to the Trinity's knowledge and love,[5] and so to become most whole, Christian soul-care providers must have some grasp of the signification and significance of the four orders below, insofar as they have relevance for the people with whom they work. We turn next to an examination of each order.

The Biological Order

There is something foundational about the biological order for human life. To put it bluntly: a compromised brain means a compromised life. The human physiological system would seem to undergird and make possible human life as we know it in this age.[6] So, we begin our consideration of the orders by examining the biological bases of human experience, thought, feeling and relationship. Constituted by God's word along with the rest of nature, the biological order encompasses the influence of genes, and the role of the nervous system—especially the brain—and the endocrine system in all higher psychological activity. Research on the biological order has exploded over the past few decades as imaging technologies (like fMRI and PET scans), event-related potential tools, animal studies and single-cell recording have revolutionized our understanding of regional brain function and its sequencing (Gazzaniga, 2000; Toga & Mazziotta, 2000), and large-scale behavior genetics studies have documented some of the specific contributions of heredity (along with the social environment) to many psychological variables (Bouchard, Lykken, McGue, Segal & Tellegen, 1990; Loehlin, 1992; Rowe, 1994).

Contemporary research is providing an expanding picture of the physiological conditions which make normal human thought, emotion, behavior, form and relationship patterns in this age possible, as well as those which impede their flourishing (though our understanding is far from complete). These conditions include such things as genetic determination and influence, prenatal development, neuronal and cerebral maturation, the impact of neurotransmitter production and reception, the consequences of neurological insult and the role of hormones on development and activity, as well as the influence of social experiences on the formation of neural circuits and other brain structures. We know something of how the biological domain is implicated in motor activity, associative learning, semantic and episodic (or narrative) memory (Gazzaniga, 2000), sexual desire and orientation, emotional experience (LeDoux, 1997), complex cognition and infant temperament (Clark & Watson, 1999; Rowe, 1997), as well as specific drives or motivation for food and water (Logue, 1993), safety, physical contact, pleasure (Kahneman, Diener & Schwarz, 1999), sex (Hyde, 1990), information (curiosity), affirmation and social interaction. These capacities and motives originate in and are shaped by genetic dispositions that come to be wired into the developing brain which, in turn, interprets body tissue states and incoming sensory stimuli and fosters certain kinds of activity and form patterns, that in turn bring about changes in the body and the environment.

The semiodiscursive nature of the biological order. The biological order is pervaded with information and has identifiable semiotic structure: genetic codes determine the development of brain structures and the assignment of neural function, related to the brain region (Smock, 1999); neurons fire according to a complex sequence of electrochemical events for the purpose of sending chemical signals; the transmission of different neurotransmitters and neuromodulators, as well as hormones and their functions, along with the organized firing of neurons in neural networks and pathways all transmit and process information according to the rules of their respective systems (Kosslyn & Koenig, 1992; Sebeok, 1994; Smock, 1999).

The brain is born with predispositions to seek out certain kinds of signs (like smiling faces) and respond in predetermined, communicative ways. Then, through experience, patterns of neuronal firings form neural networks, circuits and substrates that come to represent information in unique, neurological codes. And these processes function according to physical, chemical and biological laws. All this structure is evidence of an embedded semiodiscursiveness, a manifestation of the words of the Word of God. Though subverbal, it has an intrinsic intelligibility and so can be described using human symbol systems, like language and mathematics.

From what we can tell, all human experience in this age always has a measurable physiological correlate. Therefore, the biological order is uniquely foundational to human life as we know it. Most importantly, it provides the material *platform* for all higher psychological functioning. Consequently, when some of its structural features are damaged or functioning maladaptively, it affects the higher levels of human life.[7] The soul-care implications of each order will be explored in chapter fifteen.

The Psychosocial Order

This order is constituted by what was termed the personal agency and sociocultural modes of the creation (chap. 8). In ways far from well understood, the psychosocial order is grounded in and emerges out of the biological. It appears that, in this age, without the proper physiological platform, no psychosocial structures can be formed. By psychosocial order, we are referring to the immaterial dynamic structures that originate in social interaction but are gradually internalized within the individual human being, developing throughout life and giving definition and dynamic form to the embodied human. It is what in the Christian tradition has been called the spirit or soul of a human being, what modern philosophers have called "mind" (Rosenthal, 1991; Ryle, 1949), and what psychologists call "cognition."

This order is enormous and embraces all human psychological structures and processes within an individual, including sensations, perceptions, stimulus-response associations, motives, desires, emotions, imagination, defenses, various memory stores and all kinds of mental representations (e.g., images; concepts; schemas; episodes; social skills; knowledge of the world, self and others; and narratives), vocabulary, grammar rules, intelligences, personality traits and personal action constructs, as well as processes like encoding, storing, retrieving, problem solving, speaking, reasoning, planning and acting (Ashcroft, 1994; Mayer, 2005; Sternberg & Ben-Zeev, 2001).[8] As an example of mental structure, consider an "Abraham Lincoln" schema. Such a schema is composed of a number of nodes, individual pieces of information about him: his name, one or more images of him, knowledge about his presidency and leadership during the Civil War, the Emancipation Proclamation, his assassination and so forth. The "size" and complexity of such structures depend upon the amount of information that composes them. Piaget and other cognitive developmental researchers have documented how mental structures develop quantitatively and qualitatively, especially throughout childhood and, to a lesser extent, the rest of life. The mature human soul, then, consists of a complex immaterial dynamic structure. The study of this order has been the primary focus of modern psychology.

Why psychosocial? The term *psychosocial* is used for this order because psychological structures originally develop only within sociocultural relations through dialogue (Bakhtin, 1986; Harre, 1983; Rogoff, 1990; Vygotsky, 1978; Wertsch, 1991). The psychological structures of others mediated through dialogue provide a kind of discursive scaffolding (Bruner, 1983; Rogoff, 1990) that supplies the "raw material" for mental development and makes possible the next mental steps that individuals can take, until their soul structures develop well enough for them to think independently (and even then, most human thinking is still done with reference to others). Speaking with children while they are engaged in various cognitive tasks trains them how to attend, label, remember, solve problems, reason, plan and act (Rogoff, 1990, 2003; Wertsch, 1985).

The label *psychosocial* is also used to encompass the relational and systemic dynamics that contribute to the constitution of the psychological—for example, dyadic relations (especially those within the family) and family and group dynamics and influences, as well as broader, indirect social dynamics, including subcultural, cultural, technological and global influences.

The relation between the psychosocial and biological orders. Psychological structures of an individual, then, are made possible by both biological capacity and social facilitation. The evidence is irrefutable that the development of mind is dependent upon both the brain and one's early social experiences. If an individual human child has the prerequisite, properly functioning neurological equipment and the appropriate social support, psychosocial structures will emerge. Brain-imaging technologies have clearly demonstrated that the dynamic structures of the soul (e.g., reasoning) are directly correlated with corresponding structures and activity within the brain, such that, if a change occurs in the psychosocial order (e.g., reading activity), a corollary change occurs in the biological order.

Though the laws of psychosocial functioning are different from those of the biological order, the former order, in and of itself, similarly functions mechanistically or organismically, leading to a belief in what has been called "psychic determinism." Memories can themselves impact current emotional states that in turn can be influenced by a change in core beliefs. Cognitive therapy for depression, for example, is based on psychic determinism: changes in thinking will lead to changes in affect, and its success has been well documented.

However, the psychosocial order is clearly not a closed system, since it is mysteriously grounded in the biological order. At the same time, there is evidence that changes in psychosocial structure (e.g., belief or behavior change) can also lead to changes in neural activity and neurochemistry (e.g., Baxter, Schwartz, Bergman, Szuba, Guze, Mazziotta, Alazraki, Selin, Feng, Munford & Phelps, 1992; Brody, Saxena, Stoessel, Gillies, Fairbanks, Alborzian, Phelps, Huang, Wu, Ho, Ho, Au, Maidment & Baxter, 2001; Schwartz, Stoessel, Baxter, Martin & Phelps, 1996). Moreover, as we shall see, the psychosocial order can also be influenced "from above," by changes in higher orders of meaning.

The semiodiscursive nature of the psychosocial order. All human cognition is semiodiscursive, because the entire content of the psychosocial realm is encoded (or represented) in some form. Some cognition consists of procedural knowledge that resists verbalization (like physical skills), but even that can be captured by production rules (Anderson, 1983). Mental images represent visual objects (and even mental images can also be described). Cognitive psychology has determined that much of the mind consists of semantic and declarative knowledge—information that consists in symbols or propositions (e.g., one's knowledge of Abe Lincoln). So, in addition to the theological reasons examined in previous chapters and the social scaffolding reasons mentioned above, there is plenty of evidence that much of the psychosocial realm is a kind of discourse and that all of it is semiotic.

In addition, the grounding of the psychosocial sphere in the biological sphere involves a frankly mysterious, semiodiscursive "correlation," where the features of one order of discourse are mirrored by the features of another order. Put differently, information in one level's "language" corresponds isomorphically to information in the other level's "language." Psychosocial structures like mental images or emotions appear to be represented by neural firing patterns that constitute the biological storing and processing of the psychosocial information and experience. Artificial intelligence research has succeeded in mimicking this two-order correspondence by writing programs that enable computers to process information from real-world contexts and engage in processes like visual identification, navigation and problem solving. Visual code recognition by a computer scanner, for example, is made possible by the entering of lines of text of computer language to form a "discursive structure" known as a program. Taken altogether, this information helps to justify the inference that the psychosocial realm is a semiodiscursive order.

Limitations of the psychosocial order. Given the intent of modern psychologists to come up with a universally agreed upon science of individual human beings, it is understandable that they have been content with studying human beings solely in terms of the biological and psychosocial orders. However, important aspects of human nature are left out. Where, for example, is the human Subject? At its best, a focus on the psychosocial domain leaves us with nothing but empty structures and organismic, adaptive processes. There is much of interest here—attitudes and traits and group dynamics—but there is no person in the whole realm. By limiting itself to these two orders, mainstream, secular psychology can only produce a tragic and fundamentally distorted model of human nature (Van Leeuwen, 1982, 1985). The image of God simply cannot be adequately known apart from some consideration of God and the agentic and spiritual contexts of human life. To properly understand human nature in its fullness, it is necessary to go beyond the two lower strata, and make assumptions that cannot be universally agreed upon, some of which must be revealed by our Maker. So, research will be required that listens both to the human Subject to get "the view from within" (Varela & Shear, 1999) and to God through his inspired Word.

The Ethical Order

Because of the influence of positivism, human morality was not considered a valid topic of psychological study for most of the twentieth century. It is true that stages of moral reasoning and the socialization of moral norms were described in mainstream psychology in the latter half of the twentieth century, but psychologists typically did not permit themselves to countenance the actual validity of such things as moral awareness, human values, the sense of personal responsibility and the blameworthiness of an individual's actions. Yet such phenomena are fundamental to human life. Indeed, Christians have many reasons for believing that there is an ethical order of human life that transcends the natural orders of the merely biological and psychosocial. First, humans live universally within a moral framework (Taylor, 1989), which finds expression in the world's major religions and life-philosophies. Second, in spite of positivism's pervasive influence on modern psychology, humanist and existential psychologists like Rogers (1951, 1961), Maslow (1968), Frankl (1963) and May (1953) made a good case in the third quarter of the century that uniquely human values exist and must be assumed in psychology and counseling. However, the humanistic-existential psychology movement was unable to meet the empiricist epistemological requirements of modern psychology, so its influence waned (Seligman & Csikszentmihalyi, 2000). With the advent of the positive psychology movement (Aspinwall & Staudinger, 2003a; Chang & Sanna, 2003; Peterson & Seligman, 2004; Snyder & Lopez, 2002), moral virtues and agentic traits and dynamics are now being empirically investigated by mainstream, mostly secular psychology researchers.[9] The fundamental agreement of these diverse sources regarding the existence and importance of morality suggests that the ethical order is accessible to most humans. Moreover, ethical considerations are essential to soul care, since it is now widely agreed, even within mainstream psychology, that soul care entails the positing of some transempirical goals for therapy (e.g., the attainment of human well-being). Even so, Christians do not need secularists to validate the evidence from the Bible, Western jurisprudence and common sense that adult humans in general are ethical beings who are responsible for themselves.

Unique features of the ethical order. The ethical order is that "dimension" of the soul that concerns ethical reality. What follows is an outline of some of the main characteristics of this domain.

Personal agency. Because this topic was discussed in the previous chapter, only a summary of that material will be presented here. If human beings have normal neurological and physiological equipment, a "good-enough" physical and social environment, and facilitative psychosocial experiences, they will develop a sophisticated psychological system capable of speech and rationality, and eventually, *personal agency* will emerge. Full personal agency requires rational-linguistic abilities (especially the ability to reason, to some extent using formal logic) and a sufficient degree of self-awareness that makes possible self-evaluation. With these abilities humans can reflect on and assess their own inner life and behavior (Taylor, 1985b), form plans and intentions, and eventually choose to carry out a course of action. These abilities lead further to the assumption of personal responsibility for one's beliefs, attitudes and actions, what might be called the "ownership" of one's individuality (though this capacity is always negotiated in relation to others). Personal agents, then, are not simply the products of biological and social forces, but they *emerge* from their biopsychosocial developmental context to become individual moral agents who feel (and are) more or less responsible for themselves.

Conscience. The experiential sign and hallmark of the emergence of personal agency is the formation of a mature conscience. As Freud and many after him have recognized, preschool children develop some kind of "protoconscience." But this is basically no more than an awareness and internalization of the directives (and later the rules and expectations) of others. Related to the quality of earlier socialization/internalization of moral norms, in mid to late adolescence a deeper sense develops of the existence of genuine moral norms that transcend personal preferences and the standards of one's social environment, the violation of which results in guilt, independent of the presence of others (stage four in Kohlberg's model of moral reasoning development).

Moral awareness requires the proper development of the relevant biopsychosocial structures, which then become the platform for the module of the conscience. Contrary to most pre-twentieth-century Western thinkers, modern psychologists have been typically unwilling to ascribe modular status to the conscience (though that may be changing, e.g., see Thompson, 1998; and evolutionary psychologists are quite open to an "altruism module," Buss, 1999). Regardless, the existence of the mental structure of the conscience has long been assumed in Christianity (see Rom 9:1; 2 Cor 4:2; 1 Tim 1:5; Heb 10:22; Thomas Aquinas, 1945; Calvin, 1559/1960; Conn, 1981).

The conscience is best understood as a faculty or module responsible for the *perception* of the ethical order of meaning. It has both mental structure and neural regions dedicated to its realization (very likely in the prefrontal cortex, see Anderson, Bechara, Damasio, Tranel & Damasio, 2002) that, in conjunction with other capacities (like reasoning abilities and empathy), make possible the *perception* of the law of God (or "the Good") and its violation. When properly developed in the mature adult, the conscience enables one to perceive—behind a culture's rules and laws—a transcendent "oughtness" that most people sense comes "from above," that is, from beyond the construction of any individual or group (Taylor, 1989). As people learn to respond properly to its voice, they become more mature personal agents.

Relative freedom. The capacities of personal agency create the power known as psychological freedom, volition, free will or free agency (Taylor, 1985a; terms that have only recently begun to reenter the vocabulary of contemporary psychology). The fact that the acts of human agents are conditioned by biological and social factors cannot overturn or nullify the sense that humans have of being at least partially *agents* with a genuine degree of freedom, whose actions originate from their own decisions (Ricoeur, 1966; Taylor, 1989). This sense of freedom is related to a sense of responsibility for one's acts.

Creativity. Freedom to act is related to freedom to create. Based on prior training and experience (psychosocial prerequisites), personal agents are able to see new relationships, come up with new ideas, compose new music, write new stories and envision new possibilities. Use of one's capacity for novelty and invention bestows a special sense of competence (and in theists, gratitude) and is a notable feature of the image of God.

Love of neighbor and communality. The birth of ethical being entails the emergence and awareness of a host of new obligations to one's neighbor, a sense of duty to family, country and humanity, and standards that one be just in one's dealings with others and care for those less fortunate. In relation to others, a personal agent exists as a differentiated self, no longer psychologically embedded in one's immediate social environment. Consequently, personal agents are capable of becoming personally invested in and connecting meaningfully with others; they can empathize, suffer and rejoice with others, and act on the behalf of others, rather than in terms of mere self-interest or social rules. They are able to see, with Levinas, the obligation that the Other places upon the Self and to act accordingly. Because of their worldview, many modern psychologists could not perceive this order.

With regard to others, the ethical level is distinguished from the psychosocial in that, in the latter, humans approach each other as mere objects (e.g., objects of their desires or obstacles to them), whereas in the former humans are becoming relational Subjects who treat others reciprocally as Subjects too. This is more complex than what can be accomplished solely within the psychosocial realm and requires a degree and kind of intelligence, intentionality and empathy that transcends it. Such experiences are the basis of interpersonal or dialogical communion (Holquist, 1990; Hoffman, 2000; McAdams, 1993). Such communion involves a fundamental sense of equality and mutuality that transcends role differences without annulling them, a balance of power (Ricoeur, 1992) in which there is a "mutual recognition, mutual yielding/receiving, mutual delighting, mutual empowering" (Olthuis, 1997, p. 146), and a sense of communion that maintains a healthy sense of individual identity (what others have called "having appropriate boundaries," Cloud & Townsend, 2001). Something like this kind of mutuality in relationship is what Aristotle (trans. 1985) envisioned as the ideal of friendship; Christians call it the love of neighbor.

Capacity for virtue, vice and character. Another characteristic of mature personal agency is a capacity for virtuousness. From a Christian standpoint (and this was also the position of Aristotle, trans. 1985), virtue would seem to be an essential characteristic of mature personhood (Roberts, 1995). A truly mature person, then, is one who lives well, that is, ethically or virtuously. At the same time, being capable of virtue means personal agents are also capable of vice. Personal agents make choices that, because of sin, include evil choices, for which they are responsible. One's moral character is formed from one's choices.

This does not mean that less mature humans have *no* responsibility for their actions. Children and young teenagers—and even mildly and moderately mentally impaired people—should be held accountable by their society for their behavior, but commensurate with their abilities. A comprehensive assessment of responsibility must be based on an evaluation of one's capacities. Immature or compromised personal agents are incapable of acting fully at the ethical level. But "from everyone who has been given much, much will be required" (Lk 12:48).

Fostering a virtuous character is in part the responsibility of the community of one's upbringing. It requires being introduced to the community's ethical discourse—its language concerning the Good, speech about what "ought to be." Through dialogue about such matters, maturing persons come to sense that they should conform their lives to the Good, that they are free to do so (or not) and that doing so is intrinsically laudable (Taylor, 1989). So, mature personal agency is only realized in relation to one's community's set of articulable ethical standards. Given adequate capacities, a supportive social environment and their own resolve, personal agents may gradually become increasingly virtuous characters (defined according to their community).

Owning one's story and one's future. Two more dynamics of human life emerge as part of the ethical order. First, based on their advanced cognitive and reflective capacities, humans are able to own their own past narrative and drama and take responsibility for its future realization, a process Ricoeur called "emplotment." Mature persons at the ethical sphere realize they can write their own stories. Related to this, they are also able to take on themselves as a "project." That is, personal agents are able to see how they compare to their ideals and work toward improving themselves, a task Foucault (2005) identified as having classical roots, which he referred to as the "care of the self." The most productive soul care requires some such commitment.

The semiodiscursive nature of the ethical order. Like the lower orders, the ethical domain also possesses an intrinsic discursive quality. The main concern of the ethical order of discourse is good and evil. Wherever we find people evaluating themselves or others according to moral criteria (Rom 2:12-13), they are speaking the language of the ethical order. As we saw in chapter nine, personal agency is an articulable dynamic structure or form. The Christian recognizes the conscience to be an expression of the *law* of God written on the heart (Rom 2:12-15), and its corresponding emotions are ethical signs meant to lead to God. Moral rules, laws and principles are all linguistic expressions and form a kind of interconnected, discursive network of goods and norms (and their opposites) that together make up the ethical order. For those exposed to it, the Bible also shapes the ethical order; this is God's design, since the only infallible textual revelation of the law of God is in the Bible.

The Spiritual Order

There are many labels that could be given to this order. Some have preferred *religious* (e.g., Kierkegaard, 1992), but I have settled on the term *spiritual,* first because to most Westerners it denotes something beyond the natural, but more importantly, because the Christian version of this order is realized exclusively through the work of the Holy Spirit. Schweizer (1968) notes that the term *pneuma* ("spirit") in the New Testament refers to "the heavenly sphere or its substance." In this book, the spiritual stratum has to do with the "things above" (Col 3:2) or the realities in the "heavenly places" (Eph 1:3, 20; 2:6; 3:10; 6:12). Though all the orders belong to God, this one is especially "God's sphere" (Balthasar, 1982-1991, Vol. 1, p. 473), since it pertains directly to God and his activity. For the Christian, situated in this temporal creation, the spiritual order of discourse is also an eschatological reality, pointing toward that which lies above and beyond the creation, but which has entered into the present age, drawing the creation to its proper end on the basis of Christ's redemptive work (Dunn, 1998). The Holy Spirit is the ultimate agent of the Christian's new life. The entire salvation process begins in the Spirit (we are "born of the Spirit" [Jn 3:6]; see Gal 3:3), and believers are to live by the Spirit (Rom 8:5-14; Gal 5:16; see Tit 3:5-6). As Edwards (1746/1959) wrote, "'Spirit' as the word is used to signify the third person in the Trinity, is the substantive, of which is formed the adjective 'spiritual,' in the Holy Scriptures. Thus Christians are called spiritual persons, because they are born of the Spirit, and because of the indwelling and holy influences of the Spirit of God in them. And things are called spiritual as related to the Spirit of God" (p. 198). So for Christians, the spiritual sphere pertains to the order of the triune God's salvific discourse and activity, including all that the Spirit is accomplishing in this age to bring about the psychospiritual restoration of humanity in Christ, the perfection of which will only be found in the age to come. What are the distinctives of this order?

Unique features of the spiritual order. The spiritual order is that "region" of the soul concerned with the divine.

Ultimate significance. Because it deals with the most important meaning of all, the spiritual order is the most important order of discourse—it is the highest of the orders—but it is therefore also the furthest removed from the observable (or empirical). This helps to explain why it is the most disputed, and why such a great variety of plausible options can be found regarding it (for example, different religions and life-philosophies). Most of the world's religions make explicit reference to this sphere, and through a range of techniques, advocate types of experience that derive from the "Transcendent" and that go far beyond the more mundane concerns of sex, food and social relationships that constitute the biopsychosocial realms. Yet, from a Christian standpoint, even so-called secular religions or life-philosophies, like classical Buddhism, Marxism, humanism and naturalism, assume this realm. The absence of positive discourse regarding a "religious" order simply reveals that something in one of the three lower orders must have become ultimate (typically in the modern West, the Self) and that the awareness of the ultimate motive power driving their systems is latent and repressed. The spiritual realm deals with the individual's "ultimate concern" (Tillich, 1957a; Emmons, 1999), one's highest value (or hypergood, Taylor, 1989), or, from a theistic standpoint, one's deity (or, as in polytheism, multiple deities).

Consequently, the spiritual order is the arch-order of meaning. It offers a comprehensive, unsurpassable and central account that bestows a rationale on all of reality and human activity (Griffith, 1999), and provides the supreme context for all of human life. To have a purpose rooted in this order gives one a sense of significance greater than one's individual projects or even the ethical ideals held up by one's community. This is why this order is so powerful, at once the provider of life's meaning and also the justifier of any behavior done in the name of the Transcendent (including burning someone at the stake or terrorism).

Because it is the highest order of meaning, the spiritual is the "worldview" order. Within this "plane" lie one's ultimate, metaphysical beliefs regarding what kind of universe one lives in (e.g., naturalistic, monistic, theistic), the nature of humanity (e.g., cosmic accidents, organisms, images of God) and what kinds of beings there are in the universe (e.g., organisms, spirits, gods, God). Conversion experiences are a function of the spiritual order and are of major consequence, because a change in one's order of ultimacy affects everything else in one's life (that is, the lower orders of meaning). This is also where one's identity comes to be most centrally derived. People refer to this order when asked to describe themselves in terms of their deepest values: "I am a Marxist"; "I'm devoted to Krishna"; "I'm a vegan"; "I'm born again." So, this order is where one's fundamental assumptions can be found (whether conscious or not)—those that color all the rest of one's thinking, interpretations and conclusions. Clearly the spiritual order is important to soul care, a fact increasingly acknowledged in the past decade (Miller, 1999; Richards & Bergin, 1997).

Holiness and sin. For Christians, the spiritual order is concerned with holiness. The God of the Bible is said to be holy. Holiness is his chief attribute and distinguishes him from everything else (Harrison, 1988); it concerns God's separateness and distinctiveness—God is altogether other than everything else. So his holiness is his uniqueness, his superlative glory as the supreme and transcendent Creator and Redeemer of the universe, who exists as a Being before and beyond the creation. Everything in this order is related to holiness, and holiness provides its evaluative significance. And according to Christianity, that which is holy is of the greatest beauty and value.

But the spiritual order also addresses and describes the unholy and abominable, realities like sin and the devil and demons: all that is in opposition to God. Sin is the antithesis of holiness and only "shows up" in contrast to God's holiness. Consequently, it is only within the spiritual order that sin can be properly grasped. As a result, language describing sin should also be considered a part of the discourse of the spiritual order.

The discourse of eternity and grace. The language of the spiritual order has an unsurpassable and all-encompassing quality, because it is speech that pertains to the infinite and the eternal. In its fullness, the spiritual order consists of the never-ending expression of the boundless God. Consequently, finite humans cannot fully comprehend it. They can understand that which is revealed concerning the spiritual order, but at best, humans can grasp only a very small portion of this discourse; only one who is infinite could understand it fully. It is discourse that transcends and contains within itself all the meaning of the finite, temporal created order, so it puts into context the rest of the speech of creation, and it relativizes all other human discourse. This is especially important for Christian soul care.

In addition, Christianity's articulation of the spiritual order contains a unique, redemptive discursive core: the saving word of the gospel of grace. The framework for the spiritual order can still be called a law, but it is "the law of the Spirit of life" (Rom 8:2). In contrast to the divine discourse of law, obedience and judgment that characterizes the Christian *ethical* order, the lingua franca of the spiritual order is the discourse of reconciliation with God and redemption from sin and brokenness through Christ. God's manifold word of grace offered in the gospel—the declaration that the believing sinner is forgiven, adopted and drawn into the fellowship of the Trinity—is the heavenly word (Eph 1:3; 2:6), the eternal word, the word that transcends all other temporal words regarding an individual—that upon which believers are to "set [their] minds" (Col 3:2). Bonhoeffer (1955) refers to this as the "last word."

> There is no word of God that goes beyond His mercy. There is nothing that goes beyond a life which is justified before God. This word implies the complete breaking off of everything that precedes it, of everything that is before the last; it is therefore never the natural or necessary end of the way which has been pursued so far, but it is rather the total condemnation and invalidation of this way. It is God's own free word, which is the irreversible final word, and ultimate reality. Consequently it excludes any method of achieving it by a way of one's own. (p. 123)

As the final word, it is an eschatological word, uttered from the age to come into this age. It is the announcement in this era now of the word of Christ's final reconciliation, justification, adoption and purification of his people (Horton, 2002, 2005). Because it is ultimate, eschatological discourse, the spiritual order is the interpretive key for all the rest of the orders of meaning, prefiguring where humans are heading and preparing them for their destiny.

Union and communion with God. Most complex religions promote a sense of union with the Transcendent, whether the Brahman, Allah, the Tao or Christ. Such peak experiences provide a sense of peace, tranquility and union with Being that is deeply satisfying. Christians believe that humans are made in God's image and therefore made for union with the true and living God; so it is no surprise that spiritual experiences with counterfeit ultimates are psychologically fulfilling. But for the Christian, this need is only rightly met through union with Christ and the developing of a personal, living relationship with God. Conversion to Christ through faith in the gospel is the existential entrance into the spiritual order, according to Christianity. (Though, after conversion, Christians can regress to living in the ethical order for their ultimate significance, becoming what is called a *legalist*.)

In the spiritual order, everything is explicitly related to God. There, the Christian is never alone but is always *in Christ*. In this realm is the heart and height of Christian psychospiritual maturity: the love of God. Moreover, the human communion of the ethical order (love of neighbor) reaches its fulfillment here, in the fellowship of the church, based on their fellowship with God.

Sensus divinitatis. A specific, created structural capacity is probably required for participation in this realm, just as in the others (the biological: the brain; the psychosocial: the mind; and the ethical: the conscience). Calvin (1559/1960) referred to the psychic structure engaged with this sphere as the *sensus divinitatis.* Following Calvin, Plantinga (2000) believes that humans possess "a kind of faculty or a cognitive mechanism . . . which in a wide variety of circumstances produces in us beliefs about God" (p. 172). One could argue that it is through the proper functioning of such a module and its related structures (like relational capacities), along with its corresponding neural architecture (d'Aquili & Newberg, 1999), that the human is enabled to commune with and love God and experience God's love.

Unity of life. Emmons (1999) points out that religion seems to provide a sense of unity to one's life, offering a system of beliefs and morals that can bring together into one larger framework the various personal strivings that compose a person's life. He labels this the "coherence hypothesis" and has empirically validated some of its psychological benefits. For Christians, loving God and doing everything for his glory provide a framework for all human activity by making explicit the relation that all of life bears to God. This relation sanctifies the activity and reality that exist at lower levels of meaning (like painting or washing dishes) by bestowing upon them a higher and greater significance. This may be the most important psychological function of religion for it provides a way to see all the disparate aspects of one's life connected to one's highest aims. (The integrative unity of Christlikeness is discussed in chap. 17.)

Without the unity of life provided by an explicit engagement with the spiritual order (and to a lesser extent the ethical), an individual's life is "disintegrated, lacking a self" (Gouwens, 1996, p. 85). This lack is a chronic problem inherent to modern psychology. Having no explicit metaphysical commitments by which to orient itself, modern psychology consists of an enormous set of studies of various phenomena seemingly unrelated to each other, so modern psychologists have a diminished capacity for distinguishing the truly important findings from the insignificant. Based on modern psychology, modern soul care passes on this lack of metaphysical mooring and unwittingly contributes to the disunity of counselees by leaving them to be guided by whatever desires or values most move them at the time (within certain parameters). But this cannot contribute to a deep sense of integrity.

Theocentrism. The ultimate concern of Christianity is the triune God. So in this order God is talked about and experienced. He is undeniably central. Everything in the lower orders is a sign pointing to this God who is the final referent. The triune God is not a sign of anything else, pointing somewhere else. He therefore provides the transcendent ground for all meaning.

As believers are freed by redemption and move out of the egocentrism of their own biologically based and legitimate socialized motives (a function of creation), and also out of their sinful and self-righteous autocentrism—intensified by the "world"—they come increasingly to recognize what has been true all along but was vastly underappreciated and, because of sin, fundamentally rejected: the triune God is utterly glorious, the source and owner of everything good. As they self-consciously "dwell in" the spiritual order, believers realize more and more deeply that they belong to him, and he becomes supreme in their hearts and in all that they do, so that the glory of God is increasingly recognized as the fundamental agenda of human life.

The semiodiscursive nature of the spiritual order. The discourse of the spiritual order includes all that relates to God and his agenda, including other spiritual beings; spiritual processes of soul-transformation; eternal realities; God's plans, purposes and knowledge; descriptions of the fundamental opposition to God known as sin and the internal conflict against it that Christians experience. Words identify things and enable us to see them; Christians are enabled to see such spiritual things, if given the right language (with the help of the Spirit).

The Bible is an indispensable document that has primacy over all other texts, because it provides an inspired, fixed sample of the discourse of the spiritual order. As the source of the most accurate information available about the most important order of meaning, the Bible provides an essential semiodiscursive fountain, touchstone and base by which the rest of human discourse is transformed as it is brought up into the spiritual order (more about that in the next chapter).

Conclusion

We have seen that all the orders consist of semiodiscursive meaning, derived from the word of God. The way that God set things up, the relation of the orders to Christ is implicit in the lower three orders; only in the Christian spiritual order is the relation explicit. However, as has already been intimated (and will be explored further in the next chapter), the lower orders can only be properly understood within the context of the spiritual order. The implicit was designed to become explicit in the consciousness of God's image-bearers through faith.

All four orders are composed of their own structural features, dynamics and relations, and each therefore consists of its own semiodiscursive meaning system of internally related signs, propositions and texts. Each forms a coherent, relatively distinct system of signs and texts—meaning that operates according to its own laws and that has its own frame of reference. Because each order has its own intrinsic intelligibility, it cannot be reduced to the others. The "independent" quality of each order must be respected or some of its features will be overlooked and human nature will be misunderstood (and mistreated). Their semiodiscursive essence is a function of their being the product of the language of God. Our task in the next chapter is to examine how these orders of discourse are related to and interact with each other.

Notes

[1]Actually, Kierkegaard posits two religious stages: religiousness A (a kind of religious orientation characteristic of many religions) and religiousness B (the kind that characterizes true Christianity). For simplicity's sake and because here I am interested only in Christian development, we will only make reference to the latter.

[2]There are, of course, additional kinds of orders in human being that could be used. The Christian philosopher Dooyeweerd (1960), for example, asserted there were fifteen (cosmic modalities). As another example, consider the secular neuropsychologist Pennington (2002), who argues that there are four hierarchically related levels of analysis relevant to developmental neuropsychology: genetics (molecular and behavioral), neurobiology (the study of microscopic physiological activities and of brain region activity), neuropsychology (the study of the actual mental functions affected by neural deficits) and epidemiology (the study of behavioral symptoms, diagnosis and sociocultural factors). In the present book, three of Pennington's levels are subsumed by the biological.

Many readers sensitized to the role of the social domain in human functioning will wonder why the psychological and the social are not distinguished as distinct spheres in this model. They are distinct—as noted in chapter eight—and in a fuller, more complex model their distinguishing features would need to be treated more fully. However, for the purposes of understanding human development and soul care, it seems to me that the social and psychological are so interwoven and interdependent that it makes good sense to simplify the model a bit and combine them.

[3]Readers trained in philosophy or theology will know that the church has carried on a centuries-old debate regarding the ontological composition of human beings. Some thinkers hold to monism, the belief that humans are just one thing, either just physical (one version of which is nonreductive phys-

icalism; see Brown, Murphy & Malony, 1998) or just spiritual (see Berkeley, 1929; or Edwards, 1980). Others hold to the belief that humans are two things, body and soul, which is called a dichotomy or duality. One version of this view is termed *substance dualism,* and it has a long history of support in the church; see Moreland & Rae, 2000, for a current defense. Another version is emergent dualism; see Hasker, 1999. Still others hold that humans are three things (body, soul and spirit, called a trichotomy; see Delitzsch, 1966, for an example). While the perspectives mentioned above are all consistent with some of the distinctions between levels being made in this chapter, I will follow my advice in an earlier article (Johnson, 1998a) and sidestep most of the debate by pleading agnosticism regarding the actual ontological status of these levels and leave that to more able minds (and brains). As will become clear, the position here is compatible with a *soft* or *holistic* body-soul dualism, which, I think, can account for the differences we find between the biological domain and the other three. But the distinctives of the psychosocial, ethical and spiritual realms are all immaterial and would seem to be constituted in our experience through human discourse. Combined with the fact that, according to chapters eight and nine, *everything* is the expression of the Word of God, and so is created and sustained by divine language, I am content simply to call all of them "orders" (as well as spheres or levels or strata): orders of discourse, meaning, signification and significance. We will see that each of the orders has a semiodiscursive nature and its own unique features. Each is composed of meaning that can be elucidated and forms a discrete domain of signification and significance that is united with the others in the human person.

For those readers unconvinced that the immaterial orders have any status worth describing at all, it should be pointed out that the phenomena categorized under the psychosocial heading (e.g., mental representations) are things too, just not material things. They are conceptual or linguistic things. They have a discernable structure, but it is immaterial and abstract, more akin perhaps to a geometric object like a cube than to a material object like a die. Though it strikes materialists as implausible, grammar rules, mental images and memories are things, just as much as molecules, bears and stars (Bradley & Swartz, 1979; Loux, 1998; Moreland, 2001; Searle, 1998; Wolterstorff, 1970). For the Christian, there are simply no compelling reasons to reject the notion of immaterial things. God is not material, and since Christians believe *all things* are created and known by God, the mere fact that some created things are immaterial too (like cubes, grammar rules, moral norms, the soul and one's relatedness to God) does not render their description meaningless.

[4]In the twentieth century there has been enormous confusion about the nature of meaning, and modern evangelicalism has not been unaffected. For example, since Hirsch (1967) it has been common to distinguish between meaning and significance, where meaning is that which the author originally intended to communicate in a text (including its implications), and significance is any relationship that the meaning has to something else (a person, a later context and so on). It is impossible here to enter adequately into the debate surrounding this distinction (Cotterell & Turner, 1989; Thiselton, 1992; Vanhoozer, 1998, 2005), but something must be said, given the assumptions about meaning in this book.

Let me begin boldly by suggesting that Hirsch's stance is a function of the modernism that pervades his system. His understanding of meaning as simply the message the author intended to convey is (paradoxically) both objectivistic and subjectivistic (with the subject being the author and the object being the author's original communicative intentions expressed in the text). By overreacting to relativistic subjectivism (which admittedly is also a serious problem) and so distinguishing meaning from its relation to anything else, he erected an epistemological barrier between the object (the text) and the reader-subject as well as between the author-subject and reader-subject. At the same time, Hirsch's model simultaneously obfuscates the distinction between subject and object by locating the object within the subject, as if a text's full meaning was located solely within the conscious intentions of the author. So meaning, according to Hirsch, is ultimately a private affair, located within the modern Cartesian Subject (though admittedly expressed and now available in the text). To get at that meaning, one must do scientific investigation on the text through historical-grammatical interpretation to validate or determine the author's originally intended meaning.

In contrast, I would assert that meaning includes both signification (the content, which the author intended to convey) and significance (the value of what is being conveyed). There are many reasons for taking this tack. For one thing, some meaning has no conscious author, and so no intentions to describe. Communication among most animals, for example, occurs without communicative intentions. (Consider the dance of a bee that directs other bees to some flowers. That message signifies the location of some flowers and it has significance, in relation to the well-being of the hive.)

Hirsch's dichotomy aside, in the *Webster's New Collegiate Dictionary* (1974) meaning is defined as "the thing one intends to convey, esp. by language: *purport*," as well as "the thing that is conveyed, esp. by language: *import*." *Webster's* goes on to suggest that both signification and significance are involved in meaning. There, *signification* is defined as "an established meaning of a term, symbol or character with the implication that this meaning is uniquely the one called to mind by use of the term, symbol, or character in question," whereas *significance* refers to "a covert as distinct from the ostensible meaning of something."

But interpreters are interested in *covert* (or hidden) *meaning*, as well as the ostensible, for what if the full meaning is hidden even from the author's awareness? This happens all the time. Consider the unintended slander of another person. The speaker may only be aware of conveying the "objective facts of the matter," but is unwittingly communicating a negative evaluative judgment that puts the person in a bad light. The meaning of the utterance must be interpreted as including the unconscious negative evaluation.

Following *Webster's* and pre-Hirschian usage, let us bring significance back in to meaning. In the entry for *significance, Webster's* defines it as "something that is conveyed as a meaning often obscurely or indirectly" and "the quality of being important: *moment*." Such a definition leads to the conclusion that the significance of a text often transcends the author's understanding of that text. To explore one direction, an author may consider his discussion of the latest hairstyle of a famous actress to be very important. Yet a more sober evaluation might reckon the discussion to be of utter inconsequence. Significance is intrinsically a part of a text's meaning.

From a Christian standpoint, the worst thing that can be said about Hirsch's model is that being modernist, it is secular. It is a symptom of the influence of modernity on evangelical biblical interpretation that many who cite him did not seem to notice his modernist assumptions. But the Bible is an utterly unique book, since it has dual authorship (Horton, 2002; Vanhoozer, 2005). This literally changes everything in terms of our understanding of its meaning and significance, because one of the authors—God—is omniscient! I may not be aware of the relevant literature, but it seems to me that the implications of this point have yet to be fully worked out (if they ever can be! though few have made more progress in these areas than Vanhoozer, 1998, 2005), but they are far-reaching. To begin with, God's communicative intentions include the entire illocutionary trajectory of a text (e.g., its new meaning in the New Testament, see Hos 11:1 and Mt 2:15) (Vanhoozer, 1998), as well as all the perlocutionary effects that God intended that that verse's full meaning would produce throughout the entire history of its reading! Only God knows the full significance (or importance) of a text, but by the Holy Spirit, believers seek to understand and embrace both that which God intended to signify with that text and its importance in God's understanding.

To make things worse, the reader of this text will be aware that I am not merely speaking about discerning the meaning in linguistic texts. The point in section three of this book is that meaning is embedded throughout the creation. The task of understanding God's understanding of creation is of course daunting to say the least. An awareness of our finitude and God's infinity must lead us to humility in our conclusions but not to the despair of relativism. God is good and a good communicator. In faith, hope and love, we seek to understand his creation, with the help of his Scripture, in some small way that corresponds analogously to his understanding of its signification and relative significance.

Some readers will conclude that I have foolishly and necessarily opened up a hermeneutical Pandora's box that leads to communicative absurdity and incoherence. But nothing could be farther from my own communicative intentions. Arbitrary readings of a text—those that have no legitimate relation to it, that is, no relation that can be rationally supported—are false and should be rejected. Moreover, the author's communicative intentions are always of utmost concern when reading a text. Readers of a text are intrinsically seeking to discern an author's communicative intentions. Such a focus provides the "regulative principle for interpretation" (Vanhoozer, 1998, p. 260), even when the reader is also seeking to discern the covert meaning in the text and weigh its true significance. A hermeneutics of trust and suspicion ought always to be correlated in our reading, since we are reading humans who are finite and sinful. With regard to the Bible, divine inspiration precludes the distortions of the human sinfulness of the authors (just as Mary's original sin was not passed on to Jesus), but not the limitations of human finitude. God's omniscient understanding of the meaning of each biblical text necessarily transcends the understanding of its human author, and while the human author's communicative intentions provide the primary focus of interpretation, they cannot be presumed to exhaust God's communicative intentions. So, when reading the Bible, the entire canon becomes a secondary regulative principle (Vanhoozer, 1998), but we must go further and use the created order as a tertiary regulative principle, in order to do the best we can to discern God's communicative intentions in authoring a biblical text.

[5]According to Edwards (1746/2002), the communication of what is termed here *signification* may be the special responsibility of the Son of God, whereas the communication of what is called here *significance* may be the special responsibility of the Spirit of God.

[6]I say "in this age" to allow for a disembodied existence in the "intermediate period," between when people die and the final resurrection. See Cooper, 2000.

[7]Many materialists have tended to approach the study of the biological order as if it were a relatively closed system within an individual, such that its future state could theoretically be known solely based on a knowledge of its present state (and that of its environment), and the relevant physical, chemical and biological laws. However, quantum theory and chaos theory have qualified this stance, at least for some phenomena. Moreover, because the higher orders (that are realized out of the human biological order to which, in this life, they remain essentially united) are able to influence the biological order, an understanding of cause-effect relationships solely at the biological level can never be more than approximate (Pennington, 2002) and can never be absolutely determinative.

[8]Throughout this book, structure has tended to be the way the orders are described, because of its helpful "constitutional" connotations and the notion of form that unites this work, but all the orders actually involve process just as much as structure. There is a dynamic, temporal quality to the functioning of all the orders.

[9]This initiative was made plausible by a gradual but radical rethinking of positivist criteria (warranting the label *neopositivism*) that permits the use of consensual standards for truth rather than an absolute standard with which all interested parties must agree (Aspinwall & Staudinger, 2003). Though Christians should welcome this change, it must also be recognized that the standards of mainstream, secular psychology are still in their own way sectarian, since they continue to aim at a transcommunal universality that is fundamentally at odds with the notion of the intrinsic validity of any one community's moral vision, like the Christian or the Muslim or the Hindu.

11

Toward a Complex Model of Human Life

Semiodiscursive, Multilevel, Hierarchical and Holistic

HAVING EXAMINED THE MAIN CHARACTERISTICS of each of the major orders of discourse that compose human nature, our focus in this chapter is on how these orders are related to and influence each other. Our goal is the articulation of a complex, holistic model of human beings for Christian psychology and soul care. However, the first task facing us will be an assessment of some of the simpler, alternative models of human beings that have tended to inhibit the development of a more complex model.

Hindrances to a Complex Model

Two common intellectual paths are taken to reduce the complexity of human nature and simplify the task of understanding it and treating its problems. Strict naturalists like to argue that a human being is best understood as a product of natural laws and matter alone, arranged by evolutionary forces into the present form we find today. So, according to one such model (evolutionary psychology), human phenomena like altruism or romantic relationships should be seen as nothing more than adaptive patterns of behavior that increase reproductive success and species survival (e.g., Barkow, Cosmides & Tooby, 1992; Buss, 1999). Similarly, there are those in the psychiatric community who argue that severe psychological disorders are solely a function of genetic (mis)regulation and physiological processes (see Torrey, Taylor, Gottesman & Bowler, 1995). In contrast, in the first half of the twentieth century behaviorists and psychoanalysts commonly found the favored causal source for most psychological phenomena in the social environment.

Today, however, most secular psychologists recognize the importance of both of these sets of influences (biological and psychosocial) and seek the causes that shape human development in both nature and nurture, but their philosophical assumptions make it nearly impossible to see anything besides these two sets. As a result, the human subject (and its unique characteristics) and God (as well as any other supernatural influences) are left out of the equation. The attempt to explain higher-order phenomena in their entirety by exclusive reference to simpler, lower-level processes is labeled "explanatory reductionism" (or simply "reductionism"; Addis, 1995).

Levels According to the Levels-of-Explanation Model

Christians are necessarily deeply averse to reductionism, because they know that there is more to human beings than the biological and psychosocial orders. An approach for dealing with such issues favored by many Christian academic psychologists is the levels-of-explanation model. As mentioned in chapter three, it allows Christians to play according to the neopositivist rules of modern psychology while still believing in the existence of other "levels of explanation" that address supposedly nonpsychological phenomena like morality and spirituality. Those familiar with that model might wonder if the multilevel model presented in the previous chapter is basically the same. However, the similarity ends at the positing of multiple levels. Proponents of a levels-of-explanation approach were right to recognize the differences between strata, but historically they have permitted no genuine interaction among the different levels (see Myers, 1978), so that, for example, psychological information cannot be integrated with information from any other level (like biblical teaching), except perhaps in special Christian publications—outside the field of psychology—that explore the parallels between the levels (Jeeves, 1976, 1997; Myers, 1978; Myers & Jeeves, 1987). The assumption is that each level (or discipline) is methodologically autonomous from the others, leading to different understandings of human beings that are dissociated from each other and that are sometimes mutually inconsistent. This seems like an artificial and superficial solution created by contemporary social pressures that could cost Christians their intellectual coherence and some of their integrity.

The Seduction of Religious Dualism

However, there is an opposite extreme to which conservative Christians, in particular, are more likely to fall victim: religious dualism (Cooper, 1982; or sacred-secular dualism, Kok, 1998; or just "dualism," Walsh & Middleton, 1984; Wolters, 1985, pp. 53-56).[1] Religious dualists focus on the highest order of human life—the spiritual—and see it as *so* much more important than the other orders of the creation that the latter are neglected or seen as unworthy of serious attention, or, in the most extreme versions, are interpreted as being antithetical to the spiritual realm. In its purest forms, religious dualism ends up having nothing specifically Christian to say about nature or culture (the arts, technology and the sciences), because it values God and the spiritual order to the neglect or exclusion of the rest of God's creation.

Gnosticism was one of the first Christian heresies, and it was denounced by leaders in the early church for its religious dualism (beginning with Paul in Col 2:20-23 and 1 Tim 4:1-5; and John in 1 Jn 4:2-3). However, a tendency toward such thinking has been common throughout church history. "A regular feature in all gnostic systems is their disparagement of this world and all that belongs to it. Human beings essentially belong not to this world but to a higher realm" (Wilson, 2000, p. 230). Consequently, the gnostic impulse implicitly teaches that redemption is *from* the creation, rather than *of* the creation and *from sin*. Christian models of counseling that focus exclusively on God and sin and downplay reference to biological and psychosocial influences may have fallen under a gnostic spell.

Religious dualists typically fall into one of two general orientations: a creation-redemption dualism or a fall-redemption dualism. Creation-redemption dualism tends to minimize the impact of the Fall and its consequences in alienating God from human beings (demonstrating a weak doctrine of the antithesis). The incarnation is seen as significantly more important than the cross, and the penal substitutionary understanding of the atonement is usually rejected or disparaged. However, the spiritual realm (or the realm of grace) is seen as so much better than the natural that the relative value of the created order is paradoxically also undermined. This can show up in the implied vanity (or inferiority) of married life and physical pleasure (like sex), through the institutionalism of celibacy and the monastic life. By contrast, fall-redemption dualism tends to so emphasize the impact of the Fall that the creation is basically swallowed up by sin, so that the created order (and culture, and in some cases, technology and science—like the science of psychology) is perceived purely from the standpoint of the Fall. Without a robust doctrine of creation grace (because of an overemphasis on the antithesis), this form of dualism functionally pits God's grace in redemption against God's grace in creation, undermining their unity in God's purposes. The best protection against either form of religious dualism is the creation-fall-redemption model of reality (touched on in chap. 6), which makes it more likely that each "perspective" on human nature will be given its proper due.

At the turn of the last century, Abraham Kuyper recognized that religious dualism had a hold on many believers in Holland in his day:

> By taking this tack you run the danger of isolating Christ for yourself and you view life in and for the world as something that exists *alongside* your Christian religion, not controlled by it. Then the word "Christian" seems appropriate to you only when it concerns certain matters of faith or things directly connected with the faith . . . but all the remaining spheres of life fall for you *outside the Christ*. . . . This way of thinking results in your living in two distinct circles of thought: in the very circumscribed circle of your soul's salvation on the one hand, and in the spacious, life-encompassing sphere of the world on the other. (1998, p. 172)

Kuyper demonstrated that one of the intellectual benefits of holding a high view of God's sovereignty over nature and culture was that it undermined the plausibility of religious dualism. If God's lordship over his creation is properly understood, one will be less likely to live as if there were two independent realms in the creation (the sacred that is concerned with God and the secular or profane that has little or nothing to do with God). The entire creation belongs to God, and all of it must be seen, first and foremost, in relation to him. It is true that some facets of life are concerned with God directly and explicitly (e.g., religious practices like prayer), but because God owns the entire creation, everything in it is related to him—though that relation may seem, on the face of it, indirect and implicit (e.g., in nature and mathematics).

Religious dualism arises out of legitimate distinctions that become false when the contrast between two things is pushed to an unwarranted extreme (e.g., between religion and culture; the Bible and other texts; the Bible and the creation; body and soul; psychological research and biblical studies; counseling in the church by pastors and counseling by Christian professionals). If all the structures and processes of the creation are a function of the word of God, then *all* are important, even though some aspects are more important than others. This chapter and the last extend the semiodiscursive understanding of the creation, in order to try to do adequate justice to the underlying, meaningful unity of the various orders of human nature, while maintaining a recognition of the greater significance of the higher levels over the lower.

The strength of a modest religious dualism and the reasons why it proves so perennially popular are its God-centeredness and emphasis on the antithesis. As we have noted throughout, these themes are basic to true Christianity, for being a Christian requires absolute surrender to God's lordship and a life lived for God alone, in contrast to the world. Let us call this *simple theocentrism*. It is perhaps the first and foundational stage of the Christian life. Yet a more profoundly theocentric approach calls the believer to a more complicated position (like that of Jonathan Edwards, 1765/1998). Upon greater reflection and in light of Scripture, *all* the created aspects of human life are recognized as important *because they are made by God.* Therefore, *for God's glory* every aspect must be "given its due," corresponding to its particular significance in relation to God. Let us call this approach *complex theocentrism*. This more mature position continues to maintain an emphasis on the antithesis and the supremacy of the spiritual order over the others, but it also recognizes the relative importance of those others. God's glory is most manifested in Christ's redemption, but it is also displayed throughout the rest of his creation, even in its relatively inferior aspects. Contrary to religious dualism, a more thoroughgoing theocentrism understands that God is honored by an appropriate regard for all that he has done and made, including those created strata of lesser significance.

In contrast to the reductionisms and religious dualisms discussed above, the cultivation of a Christian holism is a matter of first importance for Christian psychology—a holism that strives to identify God's glory wherever it exists, by seeing the differential value of respective orders of human nature, while recognizing the intrinsic superiority of the highest strata.

Types of Relations Among the Orders

The bulk of this chapter concerns how the different orders of human nature are interrelated. Since humans function so seamlessly as whole beings, the interrelations between the orders must be profound and somewhat mysterious. Nevertheless, many lines of empirical evidence of inter-order relations have been identified (even if the researchers did not recognize the distinct orders). For example, neuropsychology research has documented numerous kinds of relations between the biological and psychosocial realms. Brain activity has been studied during performance on various kinds of psychological tasks using event-related potentials, fMRI, PET and SPECT scans that demonstrate that specific types of psychosocial mental activity only occur when certain regions of the brain are active. We have also found that when these neural regions are damaged, there is a corresponding loss of psychosocial function, which likewise demonstrates that some psychosocial capacities require specific properly functioning neural architecture.

Our growing understanding of the biological causes of psychopathology provides another kind of evidence. The biological correlates (genetic and biochemical) of many psychological disorders—like mood, anxiety, and schizophrenic and personality disorders—suggest that biological dynamics exert some causal influence on psychosocial phenomena in humans. Conversely, social neuroscience has helped us to understand better just how important the psychosocial realm is to the proper formation of the brain (Cacioppo, Berntson, Ernst & Ito, 2000). Particular kinds of relational experiences are necessary for the maturation and wiring of normal brain function, shaping the brain through the construction of neural networks and pathways between them. The field of health psychology, especially psychoneuroimmunology, provides more evidence of the interaction between the biological and psychosocial levels. There are also somatic disorders (like conversion disorder) that demonstrate the top-down influence of the psychosocial upon the biological, as does research that documents how belief change (through cognitive therapy) or behavior change (that regulates compulsive behavior) improves the biochemistry of the brain (see Baxter, Schwartz, Bergman, Szuba, Guze, Mazziotta, Alazraki, Selin, Feng, Munford & Phelps, 1992).

Then there is research on optimism, self-determination theory and various cognitive treatments of depression that have shown that changes in one's belief system (mental structures of the psychosocial order) impact people's interpretations of their actions and can help them take responsibility for themselves. Such findings reveal that the psychosocial sphere can influence the ethical. Cognitive dissonance theory has documented that choices one makes (for example, a decision to violate one's current moral code) can result in a rationalizing process that attempts to justify one's decision and actions to oneself (Myers, 2001), showing that an aberration in the ethical order can have an impact on the activities of the psychosocial. Seeking to confirm body-soul dualism empirically, Eccles and Robinson (1984) described research in which they asked subjects to perform certain activities and observed the *subsequent* activity in the brain.

Also, the fact that early childhood experiences with adults, especially parents, shape one's views of God demonstrates an important way that psychosocial dynamics can affect experience within the spiritual order (Kirkpatrick, 1992). On the other hand, religious conversions (a change in ultimate allegiance within the spiritual order) can sometimes produce profound changes in many psychosocial processes, including attitudes, feelings, behavior and identity (Miller & Baca, 2001; Paloutzian, Richardson & Rambo, 1999). Research that examines the biological correlates of religious experience (d'Aquili & Newberg, 1999; Azari, Nichel, Wunderlich, Niedeggen, Hefter & Tellman, 2001) seeks to identify interactions between the lowest and highest strata.

Ontological relations. So there is abundant evidence of interactive relationships among the orders, but how are we to understand them? We will first consider how the dynamics of the different orders affect each other in the actual development and experience of human beings. This will be followed by a discussion of how we ought to construe these relations.

Understanding inter-order change. It is very difficult to grasp how inter-order change occurs. It is relatively easy to understand changes *within* an order, such as a measurable decrease in memory storage on a task due to attentional distraction. In such cases, intra-order change occurs when information within an order is modified in some way or "conveyed" to a new location (e.g., from one mind to another). But how are we to understand changes in one order that appear to be related to changes in another?

Recall that from a semiodiscursive standpoint, all the strata deal with signs, that is, information represented in some code. In inter-order change, some of the information in code A belonging to order A is communicated or transferred to another order, resulting in changes in the information of code B in order B. So, ingesting a psychotropic drug results in a visual hallucination, or choosing to think about an event that happened earlier that day activates a specific neural network in the frontal lobes. In the case of brain/mind relations, there is an isomorphic relation between the biological order and the other, immaterial orders where changes in one side of the brain/mind divide result in or correspond to changes in the other. We might also call this inter-order change *translation*, regardless of the direction of change. Some kind of translation must take place when any processing in the three highest strata occurs, since all three depend on the brain. Without properly functioning, corresponding brain regions, humans do not experience the higher orders.

The inter-strata changes that occur among the three higher strata are subtler and more difficult to identify, since they are all immaterial. As an example, let us consider how the ethical order can affect the psychosocial. An example of information unique to the ethical order would be an affective response to a moral code violation in one's conscience (guilt feelings). A memory of an event (a psychosocial phenomenon) can be later altered by the activation of the conscience on account of a newly recognized moral code violation that occurred at that event (like criticizing someone—an alteration that is perhaps analogous to the way iron fillings on one side of a piece of paper are realigned by a magnet on the other). So ethical dynamics can reorganize and affectively color psychosocial phenomena by contributing their own novel information.

Information unique to the spiritual order has to do with God and heavenly realities. Similar to the influence of the ethical order on the psychosocial, the spiritual order conditions both of the immaterial orders "under it" by realigning their structural dynamics by reference to one's sense of ultimacy. Attitudes, memories, emotions and choices can, for example, be newly invested with spiritual meaning, and the conscience can be guided by the Holy Spirit's leading and reference to God's will.

To provide a specific example of this top-down influence, one's self-representations (a psychosocial phenomenon) can be significantly altered by the chronic activation of one's conscience, producing a pervasive sense of one's fallenness (involving both ethical and psychosocial orders), followed by one's conversion to Christ by the Spirit and the incorporation of the love of God through propositions of the spiritual order, like "God declares me righteous," into one's set of self-representations, resulting in a corresponding sense of peace (which would now be a function of the three highest orders). In addition, each inter-order translation at the higher levels is also accompanied by isomorphic changes in the brain.

Grounding relations and supervenient effects. With regard to these inter-order influences, three fundamental categories of interrelationship can be identified. Following Bhaskar (Collier, 2002), the most basic relation shall be called a "grounding relation," and it has been widely recognized by neuropsychologists and cognitive scientists regarding the relation of the brain to the mind. As we have seen, each of the higher strata is thoroughly dependent upon the conditions (structures and processes) provided by the lower strata upon which they "supervene" or are grounded (Collier, 1994, also calls this relation "rootedness"). The higher strata can only arise if the lower strata have properly developed and are properly functioning. So the dynamic structures of the lower strata make possible the quality of the higher-strata dynamic structures. In particular, the more deterministic levels of the biological and psychosocial orders provide the conditions within which humans can realize their potential to live as personal agents and images of God. In addition, this grounding relation has a developmental or temporal priority. The lower strata must develop sufficiently for the higher strata to develop properly. The requisite biological dynamic structures must be in place for the genetically programmed psychosocial potentials to actualize, and the latter, in turn, must have developed normally if optimal ethical dynamics are to be realized in adolescence and early adulthood; and then those ethical realities are a prerequisite for the actualization of desirable spiritual dynamics. Supervenient effects are the changes in a higher order that are *caused by* alterations in the phenomena of a lower order; for example, the release of female hormones that precedes a woman's menstruation can alter her mood. But one can recognize supervenient effects without having to assume that all higher-order phenomena are completely determined by them (Hasker, 1999).

One important additional consideration must be mentioned. In a Christian framework, the grounding relationships of the four orders are understood to come full circle, since all the orders are themselves grounded in the Son of God's providential support. We might call this a "transcendent grounding," since all the orders, even the biological, are contingent upon and ultimately based in God's transcendent sustenance (*according to* the spiritual order). This realization is extremely important, for without it (as in secularism), one is forced to conclude that the lower strata *cause* the higher. But from a Christian standpoint, this is not a comprehensive enough understanding. Rather, the proper development of the dynamic structures of the lower strata simply makes possible the emergence of those of the higher. God and his law (or character) exist whether or not any humans develop enough to recognize that fact. Most importantly, Christian teachings about grace tell us that the spiritual order cannot be perceived simply by the proper development of the lower orders (1 Cor 2; Eph 2:4-10). Nonetheless, the three lowest strata can still be said to ground the spiritual, if their proper functioning makes possible the module necessary for a proper grasping of the spiritual—the *sensus divinitatis*—even if that sense is still crippled by sin and unable to work adequately apart from God's grace.

Emergence relations and subvenient effects. As a result of grounding relations, the realization of the unique qualities that characterize the higher strata are made possible. This realization of novel dynamics that cannot be reduced to the features of the lower strata of discourse has been termed "emergence" (Archer, 1995; Bhaskar, 1998; Brown, Murphy & Malony, 1998; Hasker, 1999; Murphy & Ellis, 1996; Sellars, 1916; see also Popper & Eccles, 1977). The higher strata are composed of properties or dynamics that emerge from the properties or dynamics of the lower strata that ground them but cannot be reduced to those properties. For example, the properties of the psychosocial stratum emerge from the brain processes that produce them, but we cannot describe psychosocial processes adequately with biological discourse alone (like "Neurons in region 3A are firing"), without obscuring the novel features of the psychosocial reality that can only be captured with psychosocial discourse (like "I feel nauseous"). In the same way, the properties of personal agency, empathic relatedness and the conscience emerge from the psychosocial stratum in adolescence and early adulthood, and one's experiential awareness of God's forgiveness for sin, in turn, emerges from the ethical stratum (when accompanied by grace).[2]

Let us coin the term *subvenient effects* to refer to those changes in the lower strata that are a result of the emergent features of the higher strata that come to exert a "downward" causal influence ("top-down causation," Brown, 1998, p. 102), for example, an alteration in neural activation patterns initiated by a choice to engage in a novel course of action. Though not usually recognized by materialists, there are no good reasons to preclude the existence of subvenient effects, and in fact, there is abundant empirical evidence for them (see Eccles & Robinson, 1984, for an early argument in this direction). Every day humans think new thoughts, shake off moods and embark on new courses of action, and so demonstrate subvenience. The behavioral, cognitive and emotional changes due to salvation and Christian soul care are all the result of subvenient effects. Anecdotally, it is a common experience for Christians to meditate on scriptural truth and experience a modest change in their affect as a result (which we know at the biological level is due to an effect on the brain regions involved in emotion). Christians, more than naturalists, will see the value in directing more brain-scan research at subvenient relations.

The fact that both supervenient and subvenient effects occur demonstrates that none of the orders is a closed system. However, it must be admitted that their relations are not equilateral. Without the lower orders, the higher orders do not exist in this life—period—whereas there are definite limits to the influence of the higher orders upon the lower. One's language-processing abilities can be immediately and profoundly impaired by damage to certain regions in the left temporal lobe. At the same time, it is possible for normal adults to decide to resist the influence of a certain mood, grounded in a currently activated neural network, and through reframing, undermine the "hold" that that neural network currently has and successfully activate a different one. However, such subvenient influence on the biological order appears to be limited, and severe biological problems are usually not as quickly or completely overcome in this way (we always must leave open the possibility that God could intervene unilaterally, but this appears to be relatively rare in this age). The influence of the higher strata on the lower is subtler than the reverse (a "still, small voice"), and if the underlying structural dysfunction is resilient enough, the higher-order activity will be insufficient to remediate quickly the lower-level activity (e.g., persons with a severe personality disorder cannot by wishing immediately *will* the creation of more adaptive neural networks; such changes are very gradual).

Though much more research needs to be done to document subvenient relations, there is enough evidence for us to assume their existence. Christian soul-care providers ought to seek to promote subvenient effects on the biopsychosocial and ethical levels through the gospel and gospel-based counseling.

Epistemological relations. We have examined interactions among the orders of discourse with reference to the *actual nature of human beings* (a discussion in ontology: the study of the nature of things). We turn next to examine the orders with reference to *knowing human beings* (a discussion in epistemology: the study of knowing things). If it is true that humans actually consist of these four orders (an ontological claim), it is desirable for us to *understand* humans *in terms of those four orders*. This focus is an epistemological task that involves a very different set of considerations than the foregoing: the mental activities in which we must engage in order to grasp inter-order ontological relations properly. The importance of human knowing in this area is especially great, because, as we just saw, changes in our thinking can produce changes in other orders.

Transposition relations and orienting effects. Let us begin with the reminder that the fundamental ontological unity of the orders derives from their dependence on the triune God, who is therefore the center of all the orders (even though speech about him is *technically* considered discourse of the spiritual order). This means that all the orders are related directly to God and ultimately are interrelated in a hierarchy of meaning that extends from the highest order dealing with God to the lowest order, with each of the higher orders providing the context of the orders below them. Therefore, the spiritual order provides the most comprehensive discursive context for all the others.

Our problem is that being finite, rational creatures, it is difficult for us to do justice both to the truth that each order has its own distinguishing, irreducible features and to the truth that the orders exist in a hierarchy in which, to be properly understood, the lower strata must be subsumed into and interpreted in the context of the higher. Consequently, it is necessary for humans to engage in a temporal, intellectual process that "begins" with an understanding of the features of each order and then "brings them up," as it were, into the higher, more significant context, until all are subsumed within the spiritual order. We will use the term *transposition*[3] for this human mental activity that enables us to comprehend the orders in the way it appears God intends them to be understood. In transposition, in order to understand the lower order properly and more comprehensively, the knower interprets the dynamic structures of lower orders from within a higher order of meaning. From our finite standpoint, this appears to be a recontextualizing and resignifying of the dynamics of the lower order within a more important and more meaningful level of discourse, *though from God's standpoint, everything is already actually situated within its higher contexts.* In the Western tradition, something akin to this process has been termed "sublation."[4]

This process is a *hierarchical* transposition, by which the meaningfulness of the lower order is *redesignated,* so that the higher order gives the lower-order information a new depth and significance. There are only three possible "key changes" in the transpositions of this model, each shifting to a higher key: (1) when the biological is understood in terms of its psychosocial context; (2) when the psychosocial and its biological ground are grasped in terms of their ethical significance; and (3) when the biopsychosocioethical is read in light of its spiritual fulfillment.

This last key change, of course, is the most important. Even biological dynamics were created by God, are dependent upon God, point to God and so are to be read in relation to God. "Whether, then, you eat or drink or whatever you do, do all to the glory of God" (1 Cor 10:31). Because it is all God's handiwork, the entire creation is organically linked to the spiritual order, and it all has an intrinsic sacredness about it. We might say that transposition is an intellectual/faith procedure that enables *us* to see the ontological truth that "the world is charged with the grandeur of God" and that "there lives the dearest freshness deep down things" (Hopkins, 1953, p. 27).

Though transposition is a human mental activity, so that it seems to bestow new meaning on old, from a Christian standpoint it is simply the attempt of humans to reproduce something of the complexity of God's comprehensive understanding of human beings. So, rather than being a merely human construction, it actually consists of the unveiling to our minds of the divine archetypal knowledge-framework. As was suggested in chapter four, the goal of Christian psychological science is to understand human nature the way it really is, the way God understands it, and the goal of Christian therapy is to help human nature change in the way it is supposed to, the way God wants it to. This is a part of the teleological design built into the created order (O'Donovan, 1986). If the multiorder model of this book is correct, God has ordained that each order can realize its own, divinely established telos *only* by being reorganized within the higher-meaning orders—ultimately to the glory of God revealed in the spiritual order—which in turn *issues* in the fullest manifestation of the glory of God through the proper functioning of all the orders unto God. Humans were designed for transposition, so that epistemology would affect ontology through subvenient relations, so that whatever we do or think is subsumed self-consciously into the glory of God. Self-understanding within the spiritual order changes the self, and higher-order dynamics are supposed to become organizing principles that regulate and alter the lower-order realities.

The bottom line is that God's understanding of human nature is normative for us; conforming to it is a manifestation of his glory that furthers our well-being. However, because of human finitude and sin, the *actual* transpositional activity in which believers engage invariably falls short of God's understanding. Ongoing transposition of the orders requires active intentionality, shaped by Christian teaching and expressed in an ongoing and (ideally an increasing) internal surrender of ourselves to God and his understanding and appraisal of reality. Consequently, part of Christian soul care involves intentionally helping individuals transpose all of their life into the spiritual order.[5]

Differentiation and the Hierarchic Reintegration of the Orders

We must take a step back, at this point, to consider a necessary prerequisite to transposition: the prior, mental differentiation of one order from another. Orders cannot be transposed intentionally unless they have first become distinct in our minds (though it is not necessary that we be consciously aware of this process). One can only integrate things that are separate from each other. To illustrate, consider the genetically identical cells of the zygote. Before this mass can develop into a properly working body, its cells must differentiate into many distinctive types of cells, each of which has special functions. As differentiation proceeds, the same kinds of cells become integrated to work in a coordinated fashion, so that organs and body systems emerge, which themselves in turn integrate to work together at a higher level of organization and functioning than the original cells could have. Werner and Kaplan (1956) called this developmental process of differentiation and hierarchic integration the *orthogenic principle.*

Analogously, the mental activity of transposition can only occur where there has been some recognition (conscious or unconscious) of at least two orders. Without some prior mental differentiation of the orders, it is not possible to appreciate their unique features, let alone their interrelations. In such cases, the dynamics of discrete orders get blended together conceptually and the actual, more complex state of affairs is unable to be perceived. Reductionism and religious dualism are both failures to think orthogenically. So, transposition requires a prior differentiation and consists of a hierarchic reintegration.[6]

Summary

The unity of human nature is composed of four orders of meaning, among which is a complex interdependence. First, there is the supervenience of the higher strata on the lower by which the higher strata are grounded and their emergence made possible by the lower. In this age, supervenient relations appear necessary, and the lower strata exert a relatively strong formative influence on the higher. Second, there is a subvenient, teleological dependence of the lower strata on the higher, by which the lower strata become more meaningful and significant through their recontextualization within the discourse of the higher strata. Emergent relations lead to the development of more meaningful discursive contexts for the lower levels that gave them birth, offering a higher, more significant frame of reference that bestows on the lower levels a kind of purpose they could not have if they were the only meaning in the universe. However, emergent relations seem to exert a milder influence on the lower levels than the latter exert on the higher.

In order to understand human nature properly and do justice both to its multiorder complexity as well as its holistic unity, it is necessary for humans, first, to differentiate mentally the four orders by which humans are composed, and second, to transpose the lower orders into their higher discursive contexts. Only through the identification and then transposition of these orders is it possible for humans to approximate, in some small measure, the complexity of the divine understanding of human beings.[7]

The Rationality of Hierarchical and Contextual Relations

It has been assumed throughout this chapter and the last that the orders exist in a sort of hierarchy, but it was left till now to more fully make the case. To say that the orders are hierarchically related means that some orders are superior in certain respects to others. So why *should* we believe that humans are composed of orders that are hierarchically related? After all, modern psychology thoroughly rejects such ontological claims.

Justifications for the hierarchy. Modern psychology resists any such hierarchy because it is believed that such determinations cannot be made empirically. As a result, all knowledge is treated as equal, that is, no fact is considered more important than another. (For similar reasons, even the notion of human "nature" has been rendered suspect.)

But there are many lines of argument that point to such a hierarchy, and it seems important to discuss them, particularly because of the dominance of modern psychology in our day. One argument concerns the apparent emergence of some orders out of others. For evidence, consider that the orders alleged to be higher only exist when the orders alleged to be lower are functioning and have developed properly, and invariably the higher orders only develop after the lower ones have developed. Together this suggests that the higher orders may be a product of maturation and may signify that they have a kind of teleological preeminence. Admittedly, there is a paradox here, for the lower orders are necessary for the higher orders, rendering the "lower" orders of fundamental importance in another respect. But if one set of properties *emerges out of* another, that which emerged could be considered to be in some sense superior to that out of which it emerged, since the former would seem to be transcending its origins.

A related argument is that some orders appear to be more comprehensive than others. The higher levels possess within themselves both features of the lower orders of meaning which were "taken up" into the higher, as well as their own distinctive features, bringing to the lower order other, more complex considerations (e.g., ethical or spiritual). Put another way, the immaterial orders include within themselves the elements of the lower orders, as well as their own distinctive features. This would seem to make the higher orders more "all-encompassing."

Third, there would appear to be psychological benefits from bestowing on a "lower" order activity a "higher" order rationale than it would have if it were understood simply on its own terms (as is done in various forms of reductionism). For example, even a simple act like washing dishes becomes more rewarding when done for the sake of the other (in the ethical order) or the sake of God (in the spiritual). The levels also seem to be related hierarchically since the "higher" seem to go "deeper," phenomenologically or intuitively. They seem (to Christians at least) to lie more deeply at the core of our being. As the ancients, including Augustine, implied, an organism has a depth that an inanimate object does not. A rational organism is deeper in this way than a mere biological organism, and a mature ethical and spiritual being has greater "depth" than a young human child.

Skeptics will notice that all these arguments are circular, since they assume the very thing they are supposed to demonstrate, namely that the features of certain orders are better. This has always been a problem with assertions about values. As a result, we have to concede that these arguments are more suggestive than they are proofs.

Nonetheless, they are strengthened by a more empirical and less assumption-dependent line of argument. As noted above, in human life the lower-level activity of human beings is necessarily organized or oriented by higher-level dynamics, suggesting a greater importance of the organizing/orienting system (or order). Brain architecture, for example, is structured and organized by psychosocial activity (e.g., by perceptual, memory and cognitive processes), so that the latter would seem to be both more mature and superior, since it regulates the lower.

Altogether these arguments make a pretty good case for a hierarchy, but not an irrefutable one. But such is life. The legal system works with such ambiguity all the time. Quite often we have to hold to positions that are plausible and rational, but not indisputable. A rabid materialist (like Richard Dawkins or Daniel Dennett) would be completely unpersuaded by these reasons. And, of course, modern psychologists reject any ontological claims. Though we might wish it were not so, it appears that the most important things in life cannot be proven to the satisfaction of every thinking person, and we just have to live with that. Unfortunately, neopositivism rejects truths that cannot be universally agreed upon. Ironically, this limits the universality of neopositivism considerably. At any rate, the above reasons, at the very least, would seem to demonstrate that it is reasonable—even if unfashionable today—to believe that humans are best understood according to a multilevel, hierarchical framework.

Doxological reasons. But if the above set of arguments were not enough, the fact is that for most Christians the most powerful reasons in such matters are biblical. Only the Creator God knows perfectly what is truly important, so Christians in psychology are greatly aided by the inspired articulation in the Bible of God's understanding of significance. This argument too is circular, of course, but it is rational, deeply coherent and confirmed everywhere we look. The truth is that all value systems—whether evolutionary, utilitarian, deontological or revelational—are based in some circular reasoning (Frame, 1987). This is why there is so much disagreement about matters of religion, ethics and values (MacIntyre, 1984; Stout, 1988). One has to begin with some assumptions in order to get anywhere in human thought (see Audi, 1998; Alston, 1991, 1993; MacIntyre, 1990; Plantinga, 2000).

At any rate, according to the Bible, there *is* a hierarchy of values, and at the top is God himself and his glory. Consequently, the supreme goal of human life consists of the manifestation of the glory of God (Edwards, 1765/1998; Balthasar, 1982-1991), and the best way humans manifest God's glory is through resembling God's Son. So let us first consider the orders of discourse in terms of how they each relate to human Christlikeness.

We must begin by noting that the Bible teaches that humans are sinners and fall short of the glory of God (Rom 3:23), so their ability to glorify God and imitate him is severely compromised. As a result, our first consideration about the orders is to note that the discourse of the spiritual order contains the gospel of grace and effectively communicates the form of Christ to helpless sinners, and promotes conformity to Christ directly. Second, only the discourse of the spiritual order deals explicitly with God and his glory. Through it we learn of the triune God's redemptive agenda. So, according to doxological criteria, it would seem certain that the spiritual order is by far the most important. Through this discourse, God's glory shines the clearest, since here God's speech-acts in Christ refashion fallen image-bearers into his likeness.

Nonetheless, because the lower strata are created by God, they also must manifest something of his glory. As aspects of God's creation, the content and complexity of each stratum manifests God's knowledge and wisdom. For example, the proper functioning of the dynamic structure of the psychosocial and biological strata displays God's immense creativity and understanding, and so, in their own ways, they declare the glory of God. Just consider the brain.

All four orders manifest God's *beauty*—they simply lie on a continuum regarding the degree of explicitness, clarity or intensity of that manifestation. With the lower strata, the glory is arguably lesser in degree, since their articulation of the glory is less explicit. Similarly, the less clear the manifestation of Godlikeness, the lesser the glory. Therefore, living like Christ, according to the spiritual order, manifests the greatest glory. But the discourse of the lower strata also conveys some Godlikeness. The ethical stratum consists of the expression and human realization of God's moral character. To live virtuously, even if not Christianly, manifests more Godlikeness and hence more glory than to live viciously. To a lesser extent, the basic components of human nature of the psychosocial order are also features of the image of God, for example, reason, emotion, relationality, personality and the self. Consequently, human nature that is well formed according to psychosocial norms also resembles God, certainly more than animals and plants. And all human image-bearing is made possible by proper brain function—at least in this life.

Rephrasing the foregoing, each of the four orders of discourse consists of meaning. Each has its own codes and dynamic structures of signification, and so each expresses the wisdom of God. But what most distinguishes them is the greater significance or splendor displayed at the higher levels. There is beauty at each level, but the beauty of God manifested is greater at the higher levels, because it is signified more fully and clearly. The intrinsic rationality embedded in the lower strata is related to Christ, the Word of God, but that relation is implicit; the relation is only explicit in the spiritual order. As image-bearers of God transpose the lower strata into the spiritual, they render the relation to Christ of the lower strata explicit through faith and bring the created order to its doxological fulfillment in Christ. The hierarchical relationship of the four orders of discourse is represented in figure 11.1.

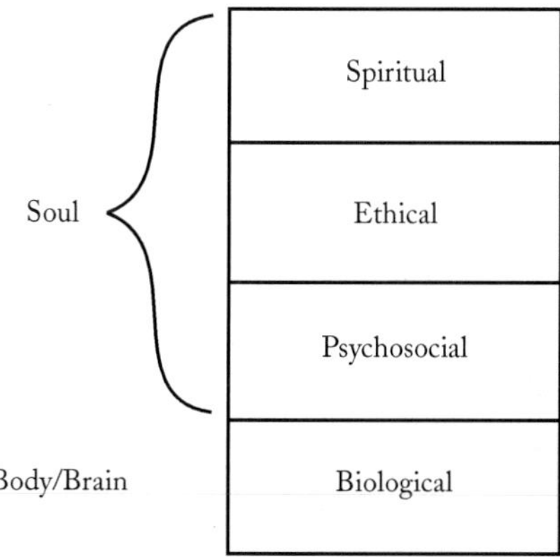

Figure 11.1.

There is, however, a danger of misrepresentation in figure 11.1, since it might seem to suggest that each order simply provides an autonomous perspective on human nature (like that assumed in the levels-of-explanation approach). Figure 11.2 (on p. 374) better illustrates how the lower strata are to be understood, as nested and contextualized within the higher, making clearer the holistic (and transpositional) nature of this model. Both diagrams are needed to represent the multilevel, hierarchical and holistic complexity of human nature.

Doxological Soul-Healing According to the Orders of Discourse

If human beings are best understood as being composed of multiple, hierarchically related orders, one should prioritize the loci of soul-care intervention accordingly.

Proper functioning at the lower levels always renders God a measure of glory, because those lower levels are also a function of God's discourse, and because brains and souls properly functioning at those levels are operating—to that extent at least—according to his design plan. But God's glory is greater in degree to the extent that his involvement is consciously recognized by humans and rendered explicit. All things being equal, the more overt the praise of God, the better:

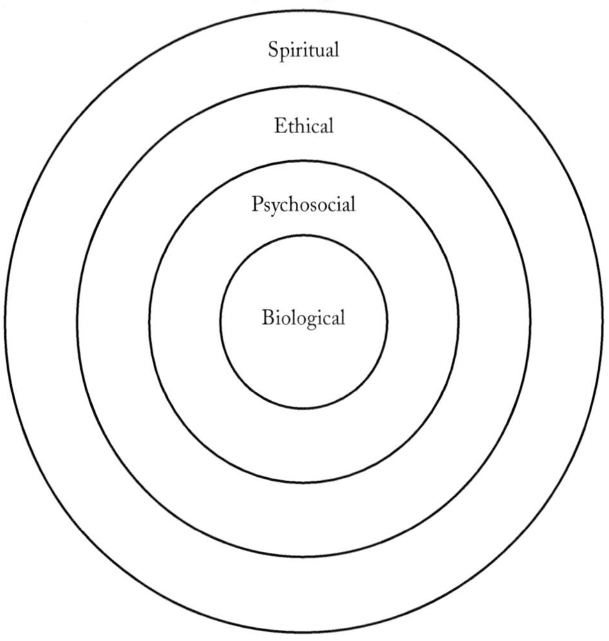

Figure 11.2.

> O magnify the LORD with me,
> And let us exalt His name together. (Ps 34:3)

Drawing one another into praise is the movement of the manifestation of God's glory. As a result of this doxological *telos,* proper functioning of brain and soul, *if achieved in God's name,* intensifies the luminescence of the divine glory they put forth. Here orienting relations come into play. Taking depression medication that improves brain function gives God some glory, since God is the ultimate source of all medical improvement, and because he designed brains to function properly. However, if the medication is taken *in God's name,* that is, with conscious and explicit gratitude to God (e.g., by thanking God for the creation grace that led to its use), God is given much greater glory, because the biological order is transposed into the spiritual by thanksgiving.

Taking this a step further: the remediation of depression through cognitive therapy—say working on irrational beliefs—gives God more glory than medication, because it treats humans as rational beings (made in his image), rather than just mere biological organisms whose souls can be fixed mechanically (with medication). But cognitive therapy gives God more glory when utilized with gratitude to God as the source of sound reason. And God gets considerably more glory when the unique Christian content of the spiritual order—the gospel of Jesus Christ—is incorporated into that cognitive therapy and brings relief to the depression.

Glorifying God while working with the lower orders. But if working at the spiritual order most manifests God's glory, should not Christians work exclusively within it? In fact, may it not even be illegitimate to intervene at the lower orders, for example, by resorting to biological or psychological remedies for what are ultimately spiritual problems (as traditional biblical counselors typically argue)? For example, does not taking medication for disorders that usually have some ethicospiritual dimensions—like depression or anxiety—lead to a dependence on something other than God as the solution? Similarly, does not the role of the therapist in relational therapies—as a healing attachment figure or transference object—lead to the therapist being idolized, so that the counselee comes to rely on the therapist for psychological support, rather than God? If so, are not Christian physicians or counselors promoting idolatry?

This is a genuine and valid concern, but fortunately, something analogous to this problem is alluded to—in principle—in Scripture.

> In later times some will fall away from the faith, paying attention to deceitful spirits and doctrines of demons, by means of the hypocrisy of liars seared in their own conscience as with a branding iron, men who forbid marriage and advocate abstaining from foods which God has created to be gratefully shared in by those who believe and know the truth. For everything created by God is good, and nothing is to be rejected if it is received with gratitude; for it is sanctified by means of the word of God and prayer. (1 Tim 4:1-5)

Paul was admittedly addressing a very different subject than we are, but a legitimate analogy can be drawn. Like food and marriage, medication for a biological problem (such as the improper production of a neurotransmitter) or the development of a healthy attachment bond to the therapist (to promote the repair of broken relational structures) is not intrinsically evil; both are related to damaged, created dynamics. On the contrary, *when used consciously and explicitly in dependence on God,* biological and psychosocial soul-care assistance is ultimately a gift of God. It is "created to be gratefully shared in by those who believe and know the truth." It is a good of creation grace and ought not to be *rejected, so long as it is received with gratitude, for it is sanctified by the word of God and prayer.* As a function of the word of God (Oden, 1989), creation-grace gifts are to be used, but only in a spirit of dependence, with a believing awareness that they come from God and an articulation of thanksgiving for God's goodness present in them. Put into this chapter's terminology, Paul was simply arguing for the transposition of food and marriage. The gifts of the creation are to be "brought up" into the spiritual order by faith. And if this is done, the gifts are *sanctified,* that is, they are themselves recognized as being holy and belonging ultimately to the spiritual order—as is everything that proceeds from the mouth of God, *rightly interpreted.*[8]

Explicitly Christian soul care for the glory of God. Both theoretically and practically, Christian soul care should be distinguished from other versions by a conscious and explicit fostering of the glory of the triune God. This occurs when Christian soul-care providers do all their work using explicitly Christian content and resources (making reference to Christ's life, death and resurrection in session, praying for help, and so on) in conscious dependence upon God. Such soul healing brings God the greatest glory, because it is itself an expression of the manifestation of his beauty, character and power in Christ.

Implicitly Christian soul care for the glory of God. But what if a Christian is not working in a Christian setting? Paul's teaching would seem to legitimate doing soul care at the lower levels alone, without *explicit* reference to Christ, so long as they do so (1) *consciously* and *implicitly* unto Christ (Tan, 1996), and (2) in ways that do not undermine God's ethicospiritual discourse and agenda. For example, Christian counselors ought to be free to work *implicitly* for the glory of God with people who have disorders that are fundamentally problems of the biopsychosocial orders, that is, those that are impacted relatively little by ethicospiritual dynamics—disorders like learning disabilities, Tourrette's syndrome, attachment disorders, social-skill deficits and even marriage communication problems—since the remediation of such difficulties is not *necessarily* tied to the gospel directly, but merely to a better reconfiguration of biopsychosocial dynamics. By inference from 1 Timothy 4, so long as such work is done consciously unto God—praying in Christ's name, grateful for God's creation grace—it is sanctified, set apart to God and no different from the faithful work of Christian plumbers, doctors and auto mechanics, who do their work unto the Lord (Col 3:17). Implicitly Christian work *does* bring glory to God, more glory than such work by those outside the faith (all things being equal—like the quality of the work) because God's glory is being consciously acknowledged inwardly, and this is a kind of manifestation. But the general direction of God's glory is to be manifested externally, so ideally the Christian should be characterized by a consistent movement toward explicitness and greater awareness. For example, when helping people with learning disabilities, it would be appropriate once in a while, and at the right moment, to thank God explicitly when there is success, just like an earnest Christian auto mechanic might do. This is not wild-eyed fundamentalism—it is natural, strategic and ethical for Christians to express such praise, so long as it is done with wise sensitivity regarding those with whom they work. If current rules for soul care in the public square do not permit such restrained transparency, then they need to be changed.[9]

At the same time, if we are not careful these concerns could lead to bondage. God does not *need* this acknowledgment, and Christians are not declared more righteous the more frequently they acknowledge God in their work. Christians engage in praise and gratitude primarily because God is deserving of it—it is fitting and true—and secondly because it is good for their souls and the souls of those with whom they work. Moreover, God is not some obsessive, thanksgiving bean counter, who throws a fit when people forget to praise or thank him. Such an understanding of God would contradict the effusiveness of his grace; God is filled with joy to overflowing. It is our hearts that God is after—that basic inclination in the depths of our hearts.

Soul care that falls short of the glory of God. On the other hand, the use of medication or psychosocial methods for soul care without any conscious or explicit connection to God (either by the physician or counselor or the counselee) essentially promotes a secular healing of the soul. Such soul healing is antithetical to God's design to manifest his glory in Christ, and so is fundamentally opposed to God's ethicospiritual purposes—whether we are aware of this fact or not (and we are usually not).

There are three types of soul care that are *necessarily* antithetical to a Christian agenda, since they are not even implicitly Christian. Most obvious is soul care done from an explicitly non-Christian ethicospiritual orientation, say secular, Buddhist or New Age. Far more common among Christians is soul care done at the lower orders, without conscious awareness of God, evidenced by a lack of prayerfulness or sense of dependence on God's creation grace. This kind of forgetfulness of God is a perennial problem for believers in all kinds of vocations, but it is particularly problematic in soul care, since God is the ultimate source of all genuine good in the soul (Ps 104:15; Acts 14:17).

But perhaps the most pernicious problem for Christian soul-care providers in the modern West is the temptation in public mental health settings to engage in secular practice that seeks to resolve psychological problems *at the spiritual level,* like meaninglessness, narcissism and idolatry (e.g., materialism, workaholism or other people), *but without Christ.* Working within the public mental health field today is admittedly complex because of secular rules that unfairly prohibit specifically theistic considerations. But dealing with spiritual problems apart from Christ is diametrically opposed to God's doxological design, because it *robs* God of the glory he seeks to reveal through Christ. Christians who practice soul care at the spiritual level as if God did not exist need to be helped to see the tragic incongruity of their Christian beliefs and their secular practice.

Reflections on a Case Study

Let us return to the story about Ted, with which we started our discussion of the four orders in the previous chapter, to see how a multilevel, hierarchical, holistic model might help us when working with a struggling individual. The reader will recall that Ted is a believer who was suffering from severe anxiety and guilt, which were compromising his ability to work and his relationships with others, and were likely related to biological factors and social influences from his family of origin, current stressors in his life, particularly his moral laxness with regard to a female coworker, and his poor relationship with God. How would a multilevel, hierarchical, holistic Christian counselor proceed?

Given the centrality of God and the supremacy of the spiritual order, we want always to begin explicitly with God, whenever we can. Ted desperately needs to discover in God a strong ultimate relationship that alone can fulfill his relational needs. Consequently, the counselor should pray with Ted and inquire consistently about his devotions and experience with God, perhaps spending some time teaching Ted how to discover more about God through reading the Bible and other spiritual books, and how to cultivate a more satisfying spiritual relationship with the true God.

Ted also has some additional ethicospiritual work to do, for he needs to repent of his sins to his coworker and wife and to God, confessing them and seeking forgiveness from both of them and God, and then following through with appropriate changes in his behavior. Unfortunately, Ted is likely experiencing a tragic but common relational Catch-22. The very mental structures necessary to form a healing relationship with God were probably somewhat corrupted by his poor relationship with his perfectionistic parents, so that now, when Ted looks up to heaven, he feels that God is chronically displeased with him. This feeling was recently exacerbated by his selfishness and poor judgment with regard to his coworker. There is no excuse for his sin—the ethicospiritual orders transcend the lower orders—but because of grounding relations, Ted would likely also benefit from some transposed psychosocial work—for example, the development of a healthy relationship, for a number of months (or even years?), with a wise and compassionate older Christian counselor who will model for him a concrete picture of God, resulting, by God's grace, in some healing of his internal relational structures. This, in turn, should facilitate the forming of a healthier bond with the infinitely loving and holy Father he has learned about in the Bible, through which Ted can experience a more thorough healing of the remaining damaged relational structures. His relations with God and others are interdependent and interrelated; progress in one dimension should lead to progress in the other. Over time, interactive improvements in both dimensions will serve to draw Ted more and more into communion with the triune God, the only inexhaustible source of relational goodness, love and grace.

Tragically, some people are so severely damaged biologically and psychosocially that they may have great difficulty benefiting from ethicospiritual discourse and praying to God, especially if they have been exposed to spiritual abuse. In such severe cases, working explicitly with spiritual discourse may be counterproductive, like forcing someone to exercise after surgery before they are really ready for it. On the other hand, depending on the problem, one may still be able to work minimally in the spiritual order (e.g., praying with the counselee) while concentrating on addressing lower-order damage first, for a time. Ted, for example, had problems with anxiety. If the anxiety was so severe that he could not function at work or home and could not engage in a meaningful relationship with God or others, it may be appropriate for Ted to see a physician and use some anti-anxiety medication for a while, until the physiological symptoms of anxiety are reduced and he is able to work profitably in the higher orders.

How long one should work primarily on lower-level dynamics will depend on the individual. Patience and wisdom are needed in such situations. But whenever it is done, the caregivers must maintain a holistic mindset to avoid drifting over time into an implicit secularism and giving the impression that the lower-level phenomena exist autonomously from God. The relative concentration on lower-level dynamics is done when wisdom demands it; and it is always an expedient activity, done for a time, *consciously for the ultimate glory of God.* Without a strong doxological orientation, indwelling sin will turn such concentration into a secularizing distortion that directly inhibits God's glory and compromises genuinely Christian soul healing.

Transposition is a continual act of faith, always envisioning lower-level realities in the light that descends from the spiritual order. Transposition is not optional for Christians—an extra religious flourish for those who wish to engage in it. It is part of taking every aspect of life captive to Christ, the surrendering of all of our lives into God's hands, the reckoning of ourselves to be dead to sin and alive to God. This needs to be worked on continuously or we *will* fall into idolatry.

The practical but weighty difficulty for Christian soul-care providers is that it may be necessary to work with troubled believers at the biological and psychosocial levels for some period of time before they are capable of working consciously at the ethicospiritual levels themselves, or at least before they can do so with consistency and thoroughness. So long as Christian counselors have made explicit their ethicospiritual orientation in their informed consent form, are themselves consistently conscious of the ultimate issues at stake and are (periodically) explicit in sessions regarding ethicospiritual matters, they are free to work at whatever levels wisdom dictates they should.

We also must recognize that it may be inevitable, given fallen developmental and psychopathological realities, that counselees will form unconscious dependencies for a time, on a medication or on a caring human being, *while the foundational, created biopsychosocial structural dynamics that provide the ground for the higher strata are being repaired.* Such dependencies may certainly become idolatrous, so the issue of idolatry has always to be addressed (as the progressive biblical counselors have reminded us). The tendency to idolize is a function of indwelling sin, which continuously threatens and warps the believer's God-centered direction of life, and the Christian soul-care provider must seek to minimize anything that would compromise God's supremacy.

But the solution to this perverse tension is not found in a religious dualism that tries to do an end run around the created order, bypassing the necessary repair of biopsychosocial damage and working solely (and gnostically) with the ethicospiritual alone. After the devastation left by Hurricane Katrina, some churches in Louisiana and Mississippi had to suspend most of their normal church activities while they worked to address more basic needs. Christian people-helpers have to learn how to work with and repair the damaged—but good—created structures of redeemed people *that are simultaneously fallen,* in order to work later with more directly redemptive resources.

Let us consider Ted's counseling experiences. His counselor was a kind, loving Christian, and Ted had never had a close relationship with anyone quite like this before. Though he was not aware of it at first, at times Ted did feel closer to his counselor than to God. At first, his broken, codependent and idolatrous relational patterns were simply being modified: in place of his fear of other people, he experienced an inordinate interest in what his counselor thought of him; both are a (correlated) function of idolatry. But Ted's counselor talked with him about these dynamics, and gradually, as Ted became more aware of this tendency—sometimes during therapy, sometimes in his devotions and at other times in other relationships—he was enabled to distinguish the motives derived from his sinfulness and those derived from his createdness and brokenness. So he gradually learned to repent more and more of the idolatry in this area and surrender up his unmet needs to God and yet still receive through his human relationships healing benefits to his biopsychosocial dynamic structures.

It may be that—in this present evil age, because of remaining corruption—our primordially good, created biological and psychosocial dynamic structures are remediated little by little, while at the same time we continue to corrupt them sinfully, *and only then* can we, and must we, learn to repent and relinquish them to God (through transposition). There is no absolute freedom from sinful corruption in this life, and the Christian therapist must not be intimidated by this fact into avoiding working with creational needs that are "necessarily" corrupt. The fact that believers are beings who are created-fallen-redeemed requires that repentance of sin *and* gratitude for God's goodness work coextensively, throughout the ongoing journey into Christlikeness. As believing counselees come to recognize their dependencies and idolatries for what they are, they need to be taught how to repent of the idolatry *while at the same time* receiving in gratitude the healing and strengthening of their good, created biopsychosocial dynamic structures. Because of its cognitive complexity, this will be one of the greatest challenges of Christian soul care.

It is not that different when working with unbelieving counselees. In fact, the same problem confronts the friendship evangelist who seeks to form good relationships with unbelievers in order to eventually lead them to Christ. The whole thrust of friendship evangelism is that gospel-conversion is seen as the end (or goal) of the relationship, but the gospel itself may not be spoken of for a while. Here is the problem: before an unbeliever is converted, all her good friendships are idolatrous. Should the Christian, therefore, not become a good friend? Some might think so, but such religious dualism is very shortsighted and ultimately contravenes God's purposes. Similarly, what are we to make of Christian parenting? All children have indwelling sin that disposes them to idolize loving, kind parents. Are parents to avoid getting too close to their children because of the risk of such idolization? Of course not. This religious dualism pits God's creational purposes against his redemptive purposes. God created parents to be extremely important images of God. The fact that sin can turn them into idols must not obscure the deeper, *earlier* truth that humans were created as images of God, intended by God to point them to God. The point here is that holistic Christian soul care—while always seeking to advance the glory of God—is willing to work at whatever discursive levels are deemed most useful to that end.

Rules of Intervention for Christian Soul-Care Providers

Four simple rules for soul care follow from the above considerations regarding the four orders of human nature.

Rule #1: Christian soul-care providers are free to work at all levels.

Rule #2: Christian soul-care providers should work at the highest levels possible.

Rule #3: Christian soul-care providers should work at the lowest level necessary.

Rule #4: Christian soul-care providers need to transpose lower level activity into the spiritual order.

Rule number 1 follows from the fact that all four orders are legitimate aspects of human nature as constituted by God. Benefit that comes from intervention at any level (so long as it does not detract from the significance and meaningfulness of higher levels) should be received with gratitude to God. Rule number 1 is an implication of the model being multilevel and holistic. Rule number 2 is derived from the hierarchical interrelationship of the orders. The higher strata really are more important than the lower, since they manifest more of God's glory, and because working on the higher levels provides a greater sense of significance and meaning. Observing rule number 2 insures that the model will not become reductionistic and secular. The existence of grounding relations leads to rule number 3. God created human beings in such a way that the flourishing of the higher strata depends to some extent on the proper functioning of the lower strata. Consequently, before one can work most successfully at the higher level, intervention at the lower levels will sometimes be required. Because of subvenient effects, intervention at the higher levels does lead to change at the lower levels, and such effects should be sought whenever possible. But there will be relatively less profit intervening at the higher levels than there might be if the lower levels are seriously compromised and unable to provide the necessary platform for productive activity at the higher levels. Taking seriously rule number 3 guarantees that the model will remain holistic, even though it is hierarchical, and keeps it from slipping into religious dualism. Rule number 4 helps make sure that all lower-level activity is done in the name of Christ. Decisions in Christian soul care, like major life decisions in general, are not simple, but they are to aim at a simple goal: the manifestation of the greatest possible glory of God.

Notes

[1]See Cooper, 1982, pp. 198-209 for a discussion of different types of dualisms, both good and bad. There are legitimate types of duality, for example, the absolute distinction between the self-sufficient Creator and his dependent creation (Van Til, 1955), the mysterious hylomorphism of body and soul, and the religious-ethical antithesis between sin and goodness (Cooper, 2000). However, the false religious dualisms noted here are faulty and sub-Christian for three distinct reasons: (1) they undermine the recognition of the holistic integrity of God's creation by suggesting that some aspects are radically better than others, when actually all of it is primordially good and capable of promoting the glory of God (apart from its contamination by sin), and so none of it is to be despised; (2) they can be taken to imply that the "nonreligious" aspects of culture or human life are functionally autonomous from God and have little to no relation to him; and (3) they can obscure the fact that even manifestly religious activities are sinfully corrupt in this life, apart from justification. As a result, many Christian thinkers have severely criticized religious dualisms (Cooper, 1995; Clouser, 1991; Lubac, 1969; Spykman, 1992; Walsh & Middleton, 1984; Milbank, 1990, 2005; Pearcey, 2004; Wolters, 1985).

[2]This model provides no argument against childhood conversion. God is the Lord of all the orders and can be perceived and received by children. However, it does suggest that many will be converted in mid to late adolescence, and those with childhood conversions should deepen in their faith at that time, a hypothesis, in fact, that is well documented.

[3]*Transposition* was first used in this sort of context in an essay by C. S. Lewis (1949), in which he suggested that the meaning available on the created order is actually a transposition *downward* from the divine order. He uses the incarnation as an example of transposition, where "the lower reality can be drawn into the higher and become part of it" (p. 19), in this case "humanity, still remaining itself, is not merely counted as, but veritably drawn into Deity." Another example he cites is the final resurrection (though why not also the resurrection of Christ?). Our experience of God *there,* he suggests, will be an "incredible flooding" of our current perceptions of God "with a meaning, a transvaluation, of which we have here not the faintest guess" (p. 20). This ontological transposition is comparable to what was called earlier a "transcendent grounding," and comports quite nicely with our epistemological transposition, which is a kind of believing response to God's "pulling us up into his order" through the resurrection of Christ.

However, the term *transposition* was also later used by Kristeva (1986) to refer to an aspect of intertextuality. In linguistic studies, as we have seen, intertextuality is the journey of a text, when it is used and read in later contexts, a gradual process that more or less alters the perceived meaning of a text over time. Kristeva (1986) adopted the term *transposition* to refer specifically to the transfer of a text from one sign system (or meaning system) to another (p. 111). When this occurs, the text occupies a different "place" of meaning, creating a new way by which it is understood, in relation to its new context. In using the musical term *transposition,* she was alluding to the change that occurs in a musical piece when a melodic passage is moved from one key to another. Kristeva's notion of a *temporal* transposition of texts is altered further here, since I am using the term to refer to the bringing up of the meaning of one order into a higher order. I know from personal experience how difficult musical transposition is and how much practice it takes to get good at it. The analogy holds there as well.

[4]For example, the "sublation" was used by Hegel *(Aufhebung)* to label the process by which ideas in earlier systems of thought are "raised up" and brought into a better, more complex system of thought (Froeb, 2006). And it was also used by Marx. "The idea of sublation is that the old idea or principle is not simply disproved and disposed of but is contained in the new higher principle that has replaced it" (*Encyclopedia of Marxism,* 2006).

There are also other models of thought that have attempted to describe the inter-order complexity of objects that exist in and are constituted by larger contexts of meaning. General systems theory (Bertalanffy, 1976) and structuralist theories, like Piaget's cognitive developmental theory and Saussure's semiotic theory, recognize that individual elements can only be properly understood when they are studied in terms of their relations to other elements and to the larger wholes they form together. In such models, by adding new elements to a system, the entire mix is reconfigured and all the elements are necessarily recontextualized. Such an understanding alone does justice to the radical reorganization of the lower levels that occurs when their meaning is redefined through their introduction into a higher order of discourse.

[5]In terms of ontogenetic (individual) maturation, the mental activity of transposition actually would seem to have an ontological, developmental basis. Through the course of human development, each order leads to the emergence of the next, which in turn comes to reorganize and restructure its grounding order(s). It begins with a large mass of neurons organizing into the shape of the brain in utero. During the first few years of life, that undifferentiated mass of neurons develops into a set of neural networks that make possible and condition social relations with important others. These networks continue to be modified through ongoing psychosocial experiences during childhood and ado-

lescence. This is a first order transposition, and it is largely passive, since the neurons are being ordered by psychosocial dynamics. Sometime during adolescence one's mental/social structures are incorporated into a larger ethical context, as the moral implications of these mental structures and social relationships are explored and assessed (changing their underlying neural networks). Then, at some later point, all the lower-level dynamics come to be marshaled for ultimate purposes, as the developing person forms explicit and implicit commitments and allegiances to realities having spiritual significance, altering how the lower strata are perceived. However, for most people these transpositions are typically relatively passive and unsystematic. People may see their ethical actions in light of their spiritual commitments, but they may not see their use of leisure time in the same way. What is being advocated *here* is the systematic realization of God's purposes, such that transposition becomes an active, deliberate, ongoing task in the Christian life, as we seek to surrender—self-consciously and intentionally—all of our lives to God in Christ. As suggested in endnote 2, transposition is our response of faith to Christ's work of redemption in which he enters the fallen creation so that he can take it up and resurrect it into a new creation. Our transposing faith is the first fruits of Christ's work of transposition.

[6]This could be alleged to be just old-fashioned integration, masked by different terminology. However, if it is, it is quite clearly not *interdisciplinary* integration. According to this model, all four levels belong to *psychology*—they all consist of discourse that pertains to human beings. The religious dualistic framework undergirding much conceptual integration resists the holistic orientation of this model (and so, paradoxically, resists integration). Nonetheless, integrationists so inclined may find the notion of hierarchic transposition offers a more comprehensive and holistic way of integrating specifically ethicospiritual discourse about human beings with biopsychosocial discourse than do some traditional integration models. Christian scholars and counselors need a model that intrinsically promotes the relation of all the orders to God, so that that relation becomes more and more explicit and self-conscious in our thinking and living.

[7]The relations between the ethical and spiritual orders are unusually close and very important, so a rather lengthy digression regarding their special relationship may be worthwhile. To begin with, most of the world's religions do not distinguish them sharply. In their texts, ethical and spiritual considerations are woven together rather seamlessly, since the moral laws they contain are believed to derive from the Ultimate. Likewise, in Christianity, the interdependence of the ethical and spiritual orders is assumed, since God is the source, end and chief exemplification of the Good. For the Christian, God and the Good are identical; God is Goodness Personified. As a result, a divine command theory of ethics is common among Christian ethicists (Adams, 1987; Hare, 2001; Mouw, 1990), and Christians who support a natural law theory of ethics similarly ground human ethical nature in God's design (e.g., Aquinas).

Christians understand that, when undistorted by human misunderstanding and sin, the ethical order is nothing other than God's law and flows from his character and will, and *so is entirely dependent upon the spiritual order.* Edwards, for example, believed that the human conscience reflects the law of God (1960, p. 68), and he showed that the exemplification of Christian virtue in the lives of believers has the glory of God as its end (1998, pp. 195-98).

So closely related are the ethical and spiritual orders in the Bible that the ethical is usually described with reference to God or his commands (see Ps 1; 19; 119; Rom 2:15). The book of Proverbs is largely a collection of ethical maxims, but the beginning of ethical wisdom, we are told, is the fear of Yahweh (Prov 9:10). We might say, then, that the ethical order has already been transposed into the spiritual by the Old Testament authors, resulting in an *ethicospiritual* framework for life.

However, a New Covenant approach to these matters constitutes an advance over the undifferentiated ethicospiritual understanding typical of the Old Covenant. In light of the cross, the awareness of God's demands leads to despair in one's ethical capacities: Not "God, I thank you that I am not like sinners," but "God, be merciful to me a sinner" (see Lk 18:11, 13). Believers are to grow in humility and self-understanding of their mixed motives, and seek help from above. Here is a differentiation between the ethical and the spiritual. But this ethical "law work" is not truly beneficial apart from the spiritual realization of God's forgiveness and our reconciliation with him in Christ, outside of our abilities, through grace, which gives us the courage to be self-aware. We see here differentiation and hierarchic integration (and resolution) in grace. *Then and only then* can the spiritual dynamic of grace be brought to its fulfillment through the believer's God-enabled keeping of the commands of God (Jn 15; Phil 2:12-13; 1 Jn 2). Altogether—Old and New Covenants—biblical revelation provides a "law-grace dynamic" (Bonhoeffer, 1985), by describing God's expectations in the moral law (especially emphasized in the Old Testament) and God's goodness toward us in Christ (especially emphasized in the New). Whereas themes like law, obedience, covenant obligations and stipulations, judgment for disobedience, and joyfully complying with God's law are especially underscored in the Old Testament—all of which contribute in one way or another to the formation of personal agency—themes like grace, forgiveness, humility, love, righteousness from above and supernatural power from the Holy Spirit are especially highlighted in the New Testament—all of which contribute to the reformation of New Covenant character.

Paul repeatedly made a redemptive-historical differentiation between the two orders. "We serve in newness of the Spirit [the new way of the Spirit, NIV] and not in oldness of the letter" (Rom 7:6). "The law of the Spirit of life in Christ Jesus has set you free from the law of sin and of death" (Rom 8:2). "But if you are led by the Spirit, you are not under the Law" (Gal 5:18). Paul wrote to the Corinthians that Christians are letters of Christ, "written not with ink but with the Spirit of the living God, not on tablets of stone but on tablets of human hearts" (2 Cor 3:3), servants of a new covenant, "not of the letter but of the Spirit; for the letter kills, but the Spirit gives life" (2 Cor 3:6). Comparing the Old Covenant system and the New Covenant system, Paul said: "If the ministry of condemnation has glory, much more does the ministry of righteousness abound in glory" (2 Cor 3:9). While this contrast should not be pushed too far, since the Old Covenant is based in faith and God's electing grace to Abraham and Israel (Rom 4:3; 9:4-18), and the New Covenant requires its members to keep Christ's commandments (Jn 15:10), the teaching of Paul in particular leads Christians to interpret the Old Covenant and its canonical documents as *primarily* concerned with (1) a divine establishment and articulation of the ethical order, and (2) the moral formation of the soul by obedience; and the New Covenant and its unique canonical documents (the New Testament) as *primarily* concerned with (1) the hierarchical reintegration of the ethical order into the spiritual, and (2) the renewal or reformation of the soul *in Christ* by grace. From its beginnings Christianity has taught that, through the course of redemptive-history, the ethical order was fulfilled and transcended in Christ, that is, in the spiritual order.

The ethical-to-spiritual transposition that is supposed to occur by faith through the grace that is in Christ is necessarily foundational to a mature understanding of the Christian life. Apart from the psychospiritual paradigm-shift that results from a deepening reception of grace, perhaps years after one's conversion (a "grace awakening," to use Swindoll's phrase [2003]), believers typically revert back to a focus on obedience and the law—though now the law includes Christian doctrine and distinctive behaviors—placing them, a second time, experientially, "under the law." On the other hand, "Are we to continue in sin so that grace may increase?" (Rom 6:1). Of course not. The ethical order is never done away with in the Christian scheme of things; it is simply transposed into a higher order, resulting in an obedience that "comes from above," from God's grace.

[8]The same theocentric, creational foundation underlies Paul's teaching about eating all foods (Rom 14), even food that has been sacrificed to idols (1 Cor 8), in spite of the opposition of those who are "weak in faith" (Rom 14:1). This teaching is remarkable, since one might think that if anything were

questionable and off-limits, it would be meat consecrated to a false god. But Paul says that "there is no such thing as an idol" (1 Cor 8:4), but that all things come from, go through and exist for the one true God (1 Cor 8:6); "nothing is unclean in itself" (Rom 14:14). By implication, those who are strong are free to eat, but only as they do so for the Lord, giving thanks to God (Rom 14:6), that is, strong believers must transpose their eating activity into the spiritual order. Nevertheless, whether one eats it or not does not make one better than another (1 Cor 8:8); all parties must refrain from using their knowledge to condemn the other. Paul goes even further by arguing that strong believers should not use their Christian liberty (1 Cor 8:9) in a way that disregards how it might harm the weaker believer. Perhaps the application of this to our concerns is that Christian counselors ought to hesitate to use lower-level interventions with fundamentalist counselees who have serious reservations about them, for their use might make them feel they were compromising their faith. This suggests that Christian counselors need to make such determinations in the first session and work patiently with people where they are at.

[9]Of course, this has to cut both ways. Christians have to be open to Muslims and Buddhists exercising such freedoms in the public square as well. But the main point here is that secularists are currently free to express their ultimate values without raising an eyebrow.

PART IV

The Communication of God's Glory in Christian Soul Care

THE PRECEDING SECTIONS OF THE BOOK were preparatory for this one. Here we will consider what is really at the heart of God's soul-healing, doxological agenda: the reformation of his people through the "taking in" of his glory, a process called *inwardness*, and the expression of that glory in Christlike lives, a process called outwardness. God designed the discourse of humans in dialogue to be a significant proximate means of these changes. We begin by examining the ways in which the triune God is personally involved in the reformation process.

12

The Trinitarian Ground and Goal of Christian Well-Being and Soul Care

Union and Communion with God

In chapters eight and nine, we considered the doxological agenda of the Trinity in the creation and redemption of human beings. In this chapter we probe more deeply into some of the specific activities of the Trinity in the redemption of human beings, particularly as that redemption is accomplished through Christian soul healing and maturation.

God's glory is specially manifested through conforming human beings to the image of the Son of God, but each member of the Trinity plays a distinct and direct role in the conformity process, and this chapter seeks to address the precise ways in which each one participates: the Father God is also the Father of believers, who are in union with the Son and his actions, and are indwelt by the Holy Spirit, who realizes their conformity to the Son. The celebration of these roles by believers and its healing effects is itself no small part of God's plan to glorify himself.

The Unity and Diversity of the Trinity in the Well-Being of Humans

As we have seen, the glory of the triune God is the ultimate end of creation and redemption, but that glory is uniquely expressed in the well-being of God's image-bearers, which is initiated, made possible and realized by means of the united actions of the triune God in salvation. The members of the Trinity are equal in divinity and authority and share all the same attributes (e.g., omniscience, omnipresence, omnipotence, holiness, righteousness, love and compassion), and they exist in perfect harmony, having the identical doxological agenda, committed to the same work and loving each other perfectly and absolutely. In addition, Father, Son and Spirit dwell in one another,[1] so that to know one (e.g., the Son) is to know them all (Jn 14:9-10). All three are wholly involved in creation and providence (Gen 1; Ps 104:30; Prov 8; Jn 1; Col 1:16), judgment (Jn 5:21, 27, 30, 45; 14:8-11) and redemption (Eph 1; 1 Pet 1:1, 2). "All the works of God . . . have one single Author, namely, God" (Bavinck, 2004, p. 319). Redemption is the primary concern of Christian soul care, so it is fitting that a chapter in this book be spent on the united doxological program of the Trinity in salvation.

At the same time, distinctions also have to be made between the Father, Son and Spirit regarding their eternal interrelations and their "economic roles" in salvation. With regard to their relations, the Father is the eternal source of the Son and the Spirit, the Son is generated by the Father, and the Spirit proceeds from both Father and Son (Bavinck, 2004). With regard to their works, the Father is in a special sense the Creator and Originator, the Son the Mediator and Redeemer, and the Spirit the immanent Agent of creation and re-creation (Bavinck, 1956, p. 151-56, 2004, p. 319, 2006, p. 570; Frame, 2002, p. 727). Concerning the history of redemption on earth, the Father planned, ordained and oversees it (Eph 1:3-6, 11; Heb 2:11; 1 Pet 1:2), the Son fulfills the Father's plan and accomplished and mediates redemption (Jn 5:37; Eph 1:7; Col 1:14-22; 1 Tim 2:5), and the Spirit completes the plan and applies and realizes redemption (Jn 16:14-15; Eph 1:13-14; 1 Pet 1:2) (Frame, 2002). Yet they are all one in purpose and love. Their glory is fully manifested in the display of both their unity and their diversity. The rest of the chapter examines some of the trinitarian complexity involved in redemption, while preserving the unified nature of their salvific mission, so that the Trinity's role as the ground of Christian well-being and soul care can be better appreciated and appropriated.

The Ultimate Father of the Believer

The Father's relationship with the believer exists within a remarkable web of interconnected relationships. First, there is the eternal relationship of the Father and the Son, which is foundational to the Christian's relationship with both of them. Second, observation and reflection on human development (from empirical research) show that an important part of the Father's plan was to form humans through a long process of maturation that entailed dependency upon (ideally) two human parents, both of whom are to be images of the Father, but one of whom constitutes a special paternal analogy ("from whom every family in heaven and on earth derives its name," Eph 3:15). Third, in the fullness of time, the Father and Son's relationship reached a new stage when the Son was incarnated in human form as Jesus Christ and became a human child, miraculously conceived in Mary through the Spirit (Lk 1:35). Raised by human parents, Jesus lived a life that exemplified the way all humans are supposed to relate to their human parents, as well as their Father in heaven. Finally, the Father's plan included his adoption of new children—once alienated prodigals but now increasingly loving sons and daughters, who are honored to be fellow heirs with their elder brother Jesus, so that now, the Father of the Lord Jesus Christ is also the Father of believers (after his resurrection, Jesus said to Mary Magdalene, "I ascend to My Father and your Father," Jn 20:17). This is an outline of God's rather complicated family narrative.[2]

When one begins with a theocentric orientation based on Scripture, a number of beliefs follow that have important developmental and clinical implications. First, everything in human life is meant to point to God and is properly fulfilled only in him. It was the Father's plan to create humans for a relationship of filial attachment, affection, submission and communion with himself, along with the Son and the Spirit. Positive experiences with parents—especially fathers—through the internalization of corresponding relational (psychosocial) structures, can pave the way for a loving, trusting and respectful relationship with the Father God. On the other hand, negative experiences with parents—especially fathers—form psychosocial structures that will likely hinder the ability to attach to and trust the Father God. However, such hindrances constitute conditions of potential glory that the triune God delights to surmount through relationship with himself (as well as through reception of the written Word, ecclesial practices and healthy relationships within the body of Christ). There are at least two special ways the believer's relationship with the Father is healing.

The bounty of the Father. As the Origin in a unique way, the Father is revealed to be the ultimate source of all goodness that one receives: all life and created goodness, including all gifts, personality strengths, psychosocial skills, and successes in life, all blessings and advantageous events, though mediated by the Son and constituted by the Spirit: "*Every* good thing bestowed and every perfect gift is from above, coming down from the Father of lights" (Jas 1:17). This goodness from the Father is supposed to testify to God's goodwill (Acts 14:17; Rom 2:4), but because, in a fallen world, undeserved evil also happens to us, there also seems to be support for the hypothesis that God is *against us*. Yet we are told that the Father delights in giving good: "If you then, being evil, know how to give good gifts to your children, how much more will your Father who is in heaven give what is good to those who ask him!" (Mt 7:11; see Mt 5:45; Jn 3:16). Guided in their interpretations of life by Scripture, believers learn to self-consciously consent to the Father's beneficence and reckon the undeserved evil to be *not* from the Father's maliciousness but from the devil (though admittedly *permitted* by God; see Job). Through this process, their souls get strengthened, a corrective of particular importance if they did not receive much affirmation or structure in childhood from their parents.

Even more important, the foundational salvific transactions and transformations that occur to Christians through faith are in a unique way related to the Father's ordaining activity. Election, the significance of the atonement, justification, adoption and glorification—indeed, all the blessings of salvation—are made possible by the Son and applied by the Spirit, but are in a special sense *established* by and for the Father (see, e.g., Is 53:10; Mt 26:39, 53-54; Jn 6:23, 37, 40, 44-45, 57, 65; 10:18, 29, 32, 36; 12:27; 13:3; 15:16; Rom 6:4; 1 Cor 1:3; Eph 1:2-5; 3:14; Phil 2:11; 4:20; Col 1:12; 3:15; 1 Pet 1:2). The salvific actions and speech-acts of the Father constitute the formal ground of Christian soul care. "This is the will of God, that he may always be eyed as benign, kind, tender, loving, and unchangeable therein, and that peculiarly as the Father, as the great foundation and spring of all gracious communications and fruits of love" (Owen, 1967, Vol. 2, p. 23). Jesus' best-loved parable is called "the prodigal son," but surely one of its themes is the *Father's* seeking, exuberant and joyful love manifested at the prodigal son's return. The Father's loving desire to forgive and redeem is always initiatory and necessarily precedes our response (1 Jn 4:10-14); he is "for us" (Rom 8:31-32). None of this should minimize the contributions of the Son and the Spirit in salvation—all three are working together for our good. But the children of the triune God are to recognize that all the gifts of creation and redemption originate in a unique sense *from the Father*, and as such are signs that the ultimate Paternal Reality in the universe is seeking to prosper and benefit their souls.

Communion with the Father. In addition, through their love relationship with the Father, believers are ideally to find their deepest security and sense of belonging. "In this is love, not that we loved God, but that He loved us and gave His Son as a propitiation for our sins" (1 Jn 4:10). The Christian's heavenly Father is the ideal father: kind, compassionate, genuinely desiring one's best yet perfectly just and righteous, who disciplines out of love for the improvement of his children (Heb 12:4-11). Consequently, the Father is the ultimate attachment figure (Clinton & Sibcy, 2002; Roberts, 1997).[3] Whatever the deficits of one's earthly parents, they are *infinitely* compensated for in this relationship; and whatever the strengths of one's earthly parents, they find their fulfillment in the ultimate Father. All believers—males and females—are said to be "brothers" of the first-born Son (Rom 8:29), fellow heirs with Christ (Rom 8:17), given the Spirit of adoption as "sons" by which they cry out, "Abba! Father!" (Rom 8:15). Knowing that the Father of Christ is one's own Father—in and through Christ and by the Spirit—is supposed to give one a sense of absolute belongingness: one has a resting place—a home—in the universe, in the familial-communal love of the triune God. With Christ (Heb 2:11), believers have the most powerful dad there is, one who is on their side and is protecting them from ultimate harm (Rom 8:28-39). And this greatest of filial relationships redemptively alters one's approach to all of one's other earthly relationships (especially with one's human parents—particularly one's father—as well as other authority figures).

The basis of the believer's relationship with the Father is union with Christ (to be discussed below). This union places believers "in the Beloved" (Eph 1:6), so that believers are themselves "holy and beloved" (Col 3:12), that is, loved by God in a way that corresponds analogically to the Father's love for his "beloved Son" with whom he is "well-pleased" (Mt 17:5; Lk 3:22). The Father also loves them perfectly and, together with Christ and through the Spirit, will come into believers and dwell with them (Jn 14:23).

> The Lord your God is in your midst,
> A victorious warrior
> He will exult over you with joy,
> He will be quiet in His love,
> He will rejoice over you with shouts of joy. (Zeph 3:17)

This Old Testament description of Israel is fulfilled in Christ and therefore applies to all those in Christ. So the Father's love for the believer is a love of complacency, delight and rest. In reference to the Zephaniah passage just quoted, Owen (1657/1965) wrote, "To rest with contentment is expressed by being [quiet]; that is, without repining, without complaint" (p. 25). The Father looks upon his children in Christ without criticism, without any negative emotion, but with pure approval and delight. This approbation provides a transcendent, affirmative basis for the construction of a Christian's new self-representation. For many reasons, then, the believer should seek to experience the closest imaginable communion with the Father, which in principle infinitely transcends the best love of human parents for their child. The more frequently and deeply believers experience that love, the greater their healing from the past and the deepening of their love of the Father, and the greater the glory of the triune God (see Wilson, 1998).

At the same time, we cannot allow the wondrous benefits of redemption to obscure the reality of the corruption of the created order, creating illusions about the kind of change we can expect in this age. Damaged psychosocial structures that are the result of poor parenting are not magically or automatically cured simply through our formal adoption by God. Poor parenting and its depressive consequences convince people (often unconsciously) that God is uninterested in them or even that he is their antagonist. It usually takes time and some thorough internal processing, grounded in redemptive faith, to undermine and overcome a sufficient portion of severe damage for fellowship with the Father to be experienced with some consistency. Without really understanding its developmental origins, Owen (1657/1965) points to the problem:

> Many dark and disturbing thoughts are apt to arise in [our relation to the Father]. Few can carry up their hearts and minds to this height by faith, as to rest their souls in the love of the Father; they live below it, in the troublesome region of hopes and fears, storms and clouds. All here is serene and quiet. But how to attain to this pitch they know not. (p. 23)

We understand better today how poor family experiences contribute to such alienation from the Father, combining with the indwelling resistance of sin with which all humans must deal. But the child of God participates in God's glory by gradually learning how to distrust her damaged and sinful attitudes toward the Father and to hope in her Father's greatness, seeking his help, relying on him, thanking him for his gifts and being healed by his endless, enthusiastic goodness toward us in Christ and by means of the Spirit.

The Believer's Union with Christ

We have seen that Christ's life, death and resurrection is the center of human history (Gal 4:4), by which he redeemed his people and procured for them a perfect, eschatological salvation, in which by faith they may live now. According to Paul, union with Christ is the means by which Christians share in Christ's work. He never seemed to tire of reminding his readers that Christians were "in Christ" and lived "with Christ" (Chamblin, 1993; Ridderbos, 1975; Smedes, 1983; Stewart, 1975). They died with him on the cross and were raised with him, their salvation exists in him, and now their entire lives are related to him (see Rom 6:1-11; Eph 1:1-14; 2:1-10; Col 3:1-17). According to Stewart, "Christ is the redeemed man's new environment. He has been lifted out of the cramping restrictions of his earthly lot into a totally different sphere, the sphere of Christ. He has been transplanted into a new soil and a new climate, and both soil and climate are Christ" (p. 157). The Christian's entire existence is saturated with Christ, so that "for me to live is Christ" (Phil 1:21). So significant is this theme in the New Testament that Murray (1955) concluded, "union with Christ is the central truth of the whole doctrine of salvation" (p. 170).

Divine illocutions and declarative union with Christ. We saw in chapter six that Christian salvation in this age consists of two components: declarative and reformative, with the former being foundational to the latter. Let us consider how these two aspects relate to union with Christ and how they are to be understood semiodiscursively. Of greatest importance to the Christian is the new set of meanings that are declared to be true about the Christian upon believing. After conversion Christians discover in the Bible that they are defined by God within a new language-game (Thiselton, 1980, pp. 415-21)—the sayings of the spiritual order—so that they are now pronounced righteous (Rom 5:1), holy (Col 3:12), saints (1 Cor 1:2), a new creation (2 Cor 5:17), children of God (Jn 1:12), fellow heirs with Christ (Rom 8:17) and so on, none of which described them before their conversion. These illocutionary meanings are bestowed on them by God, but they are characteristics of believers solely because they are united to Christ and therefore, as far as the Father is concerned, they share some of Christ's characteristics. Everything about the Christian has been re-signified, and now by faith believers are to re-cognize everything about themselves—their story and traits, and even their relations with the rest of reality. God's declarations entitle believers to form "dipolar" self-representations, by which they construe themselves as having now some of the characteristics that properly belong to the resurrected and ascended Christ (his righteousness, moral perfection and love have become theirs by divine prerogative).

Justification is an especially notable type of declarative salvation. All humans possess a tragic deficit of eternal significance, variously described by the terms *sinful, unclean, guilty* or *shameful.* These words denote a certain kind of meaning that applies to all humans: they are ethically and spiritually desecrated. The Bible teaches that the all-knowing Judge of the universe regards this as the case and so it must be true (and the human conscience universally confirms this assessment, more or less). Christ was the only person who has ever lived to whom those labels did not apply. But Christ, we are told, "became sin for us" (2 Cor 5:21). Since God is the ultimate Source of all meaning, he can reassign the meaninglessness of our sin and shame to Christ, who freely took upon himself our uncleanness and "saved his people from their sins" (Mt 1:21). By faith believers consent to this divine transcription of meaning through union with Christ and identify themselves with Christ on the cross, *realizing* that their sin's sinfulness or shamefulness has been removed from them. Union with Christ also entails a parallel transcription in the reassignment of Christ's perfect, eschatological righteousness to believers. By faith believers also consent to the gift of Christ's perfect righteousness and identify themselves with Christ in his resurrection, believing that they are accounted righteous (Rom 3:20-26).[4]

Divine perlocutions and reformative union with Christ. But Christian salvation is never merely declarative. "Union with Christ applies both to the objective work of salvation, our being forgiven, and to our personal transformation from sinners into saints" (Purves, 2004, p. 81). The divine illocutions of union with Christ become divine perlocutions through faith. Christian salvation is fundamentally semiodiscursive; the believer's Christian experience is a function of God's utterances: mediated by the Word and Son of the Father, through whom the Father's illocutions (meanings) become perlocutions (effects in us) by the Spirit (Vanhoozer, 2002). There is, therefore, a depth dimension to union with Christ. Merely to hear God's words is not enough (Jas 1:23-25); the declarative word of God is to enter deeply into one's being, changing both one's inner reality and one's outer way of life, and in this way reformative union with Christ is realized. "If you abide in Me, *and My words abide in you*, ask whatever you wish, and it shall be done for you" (Jn 15:7). The words (or the commandments of God; see Jn 15:7-13) take root and create life—analogous to the first creation of the living creatures (Gen 1:20-25)—as they change the believers' thinking, feeling and loving, and so their characters, decisions and stories. As in the beginning, when the Word of God spoke reality into existence, so now through his saving word, God speaks union with Christ into increasingly manifested reality.

Therefore, "union with Christ is the foundation of all our spiritual experience and all spiritual blessings" (Ferguson, 1981, p. 105). Those who are united to Christ come to participate in him: they become "partakers of the divine nature" (2 Pet 1:4). So Calvin (1559/1960) called union with Christ a "mystical union" (Vol. I, p. 737; see Tamburello, 1994): "As long as Christ remains outside of us, and we are separated from him, all that he has suffered and done for the salvation of the human race remains useless and of no value to us" (p. 537).

Once their eternal union with Christ (Eph 1:5) is actualized in the temporal sphere—historically—the elect experience movement toward God, a spiritual motivation able to overcome their resistance to God due to indwelling sin, the power of the Spirit of Christ drawing them inexorably toward a theocentric life and creating their willing participation (Phil 2:12-13). "Abide in Me and I in you," Christ commanded his disciples (Jn 15:4). This is at the core of the soul-healing process of salvation, "for apart from Me," he said, "you can do nothing" (Jn 15:5). It is Christ in the believer that is the hope of glory (Col 1:27), and Christ lives in the believer (Rom 8:10; Gal 2:20; Jn 14:23) through faith (Eph 3:17). This is the life of God in the human soul (Scougal, 1680/1976). Union with Christ entails a reformative fellowship with his sufferings as well as his resurrection (Phil 3:10; 2 Cor 4:10-11), so that "the history of Christ is reproduced *inwardly, but essentially*, in each one of His children" (Monod, 1962, p. 115; italics mine).

Entering into union with Christ experientially requires means and ends. In the next few chapters we will study the three means of dependent inwardness (self-examination, the deconstruction of barriers and the internalization of the signs of God). And union with Christ has two ends: its imminent end is its outward manifestation of Christlikeness, while its ultimate end is the glory of God. As the believer's union with Christ is actualized, the semiodiscursive features of Christ which were bestowed on the believer in the Father's salvific illocutionary speech-acts come to realization in the believer's changing form: increasing freedom to fulfill the norms of the New Covenant, because of a developing personal agency and a virtuous character that increasingly resembles Christ. God has designed to make us one with the Son (see Calvin, 1559/1960, Vol. I, p. 737), and this semiodiscursive unity is experientially realized as believers come actually to share more of Christ's features in their lives through faith.

Reformative union with Christ coincides with spiritual self-denial. Christian repentance and conversion entail (1) giving up an autocentric interpretive system in which the Self is one's preeminent value and (2) surrendering one's entire life to God in Christ, making possible one's re-signification by God in Christ. Through faith, then, the believer enters into the highest semiodiscursive order—the new creation—and in so doing transposes the rest of reality, including the biological, psychosocial and ethical orders—one's entire self—into a new system of meaning-relations. Though it occurs through faith, this recognition is a discovery and not a human construction, since everything is created by the Word of God and so exists pre-interpreted by God (Van Til, 1977). However, believers cannot "read" the rest of reality (including themselves) well, in the light of the spiritual order, until they gradually develop the requisite cognitive complexity to comprehend it and, most importantly, until their minds and hearts have been increasingly educated by the Holy Spirit (1 Cor 2:1-14; 2 Cor 4:6; Edwards, 1746/1959; Owen, 1954; Plantinga, 2000).

Communion with Christ. The highest privilege of union with Christ is the ongoing experience of Christ and his holy love in personal dialogical communion with him. Paul likens the believer's mysterious union with Christ to the marriage union of husband and wife (Eph 5:22-33). The best of Christian salvation is found in the believer's love relationship with Christ. By faith, prayer, the Lord's Supper and meditation on Scripture become the primary means of communing with Christ, a dialogue analogous to conversation and connection between humans in their close relationships. Through meditative prayer and worship, the believer personally connects with the person of Christ, speaking to him and hearing from him, and in this process, feeling Christ's affections toward the believer. Consider Samuel Rutherford's (1664/1984) thoughts on these matters: "I would seek no more to make me happy for evermore, but a thorough and clear sight of the beauty of Jesus, my Lord. Let my eyes enjoy His fairness, and stare Him for ever in the face, and I have all that can be wished" (p. 398). "I think it half a heaven to have my fill of the smell of His sweet breath, and to sleep in the arms of Christ my Lord, with His left hand under my head and His right hand embracing me" (p. 380).

Such expressions might make some uncomfortable, so affectionate they are. But in such experiences the Son of God changes the souls of his bride. The more emotionally vivid they are, the more likely these relational experiences with a perfect Lover will get stored in one's memory. As a result, new, healthier God-, self- and other-representations can be formed, and the pervasive gloom of a profoundly negative relational history can be gradually undermined and overturned. Christian soul care involves the promotion of experiential communion with Christ, so that the counselee's soul can be healed Christianly.

The topic of union with Christ is too important to leave only in the hands of theologians. Its relevance and potential for pastoring and professional Christian soul care to promote Christian maturation and the healing of internal damage of the believer are enormous. Union with Christ is thoroughly psychological in significance, for it concerns a Christian's self-understanding and self-evaluations, subjective experience and interpretation of reality, and it provides essential resources for the Christian healing of the soul. But it *is* thoroughly *theo*-logical as well. Christ is God, so union with Christ is union with God. The believer's union with Christ is one place where the integration of Christian theology (conceived strictly as the study of *God*) and Christian psychology is required. It has undeniable soul-care implications, since in that union God's being and happiness is joined to that of his people and their well-being forever.

The Life of the Holy Spirit in the Human Soul

We turn finally to the responsibilities of the third member of the Trinity in redemptive soul care and re-formation. Because the Spirit is the one who brings to fruition God's purposes, he has a profound and many-sided role to play. With regard to redemption, "the Holy Spirit is the bond by which Christ effectually unites us to himself" (Calvin, 1559/1960, Vol. I, p. 538). There is no reformative appropriation of declarative union with Christ apart from the Holy Spirit, and so no personal experience of union with Christ. For Paul, "to be 'in Christ' and to have the Spirit indwelling were two sides of the one coin" (Dunn, 1998, p. 414). The apostle wrote that "he who unites himself with the Lord is one with him in spirit" (1 Cor 6:17 NIV), just before reminding the Corinthians that they are a temple of the Holy Spirit "who is in you" (1 Cor 6:19). Surely the most profound benefit of salvation is the gift of the Holy Spirit: "The sum of all that Christ purchased is the Holy Ghost" (Edwards, 1994, p. 466). What is more wondrous in all the universe than that the infinitely glorious Holy Spirit indwells or "lives in" finite human beings (1 Cor 3:16; 6:19; Rom 8:9-11; 2 Tim 1:14)? This reality creates an utterly novel human experience: the life of God residing within the human soul as its home and possession. Having the Godhead dwelling within the believer through the Spirit provides the means for "a participation of God" (Edwards, 1746/1959, p. 203).

There is also an eschatological aspect of the Spirit's role in salvation, for the Spirit is a sign of the coming full redemption (Vos, 1980a). The Spirit is called a "down payment" or "first installment" of salvation (2 Cor 1:22). "The Spirit is the [down payment] of the process of transformation now under way in the believer, which will climax in the transformed resurrection" (Dunn, 1998, p. 421). This also teaches us that we must not expect that salvation will be perfectly realized in this age. Rather, we experience a preliminary and partial version of the perfect salvation that is to come.

In light of the Spirit's role in salvation, Coe (1999) argues that Christianity offers a *pneumadynamic* model of the human personality, psychopathology and psychotherapy. Christianity's experiential cornerstone is the indwelling of the Holy Spirit, in whom alone humans can find a sense of fulfillment that is truly satisfying. "Here we are found. God literally inhabits our spirit and makes a home in us. Now I am finally at home. I am in the Beloved, in Christ, and Christ is in me by God's Spirit" (Coe, p. 117). Coe points out that this is more than a relationship between persons; this is an actual union of persons—the persons of the Godhead with the persons of believers—established experientially through the Holy Spirit by faith.

There are at least four ways in which the indwelling Holy Spirit is the efficient ground of Christian soul care: in relationship, understanding, affection and power. We shall examine each in turn.

Spiritual relationship. The Holy Spirit provides the basis for healthy human relationships, both with God and with other humans. Love, *agapé,* is, after all, the fruit of the Spirit (Gal 5:23). "The whole of the Christian life . . . is characterized by what Paul calls the *koinōnia* (fellowship) of the Holy Spirit (2 Cor 13:14)" (Ferguson, 1996, p. 175). Humans were made for relationship, but the Holy Spirit promotes the fulfillment of this potentiality in Christ. Of first importance is the Spirit's role in bringing believers into the communion of love of the Trinity.

Fellowship with God. Before he died, Jesus said, "I will not leave you as orphans; I will come to you" (Jn 14:18). What did he mean? Having the Spirit is the same as having Christ himself (2 Cor 3:17; Eph 3:17); through the Spirit's coming Jesus himself comes to be with us. The Spirit is the personal, divine medium through which the fellowship of the Father and Son (1 Jn 1:3) enters into individuals and the church. The Spirit is a *paraklete*, a "helper" who is with believers always (Jn 14:16), who resides in them (Jn 14:17) and who ushers in communion with God: "In that day you shall know that I am in My Father, and you in Me, and I in you" (Jn 14:20). The indwelling Spirit makes Jesus present to us *within us* (Eph 3:17; 1 Jn 3:24; 4:13), and the corollary of their cohabitation in us is that the believer abides in them (Jn 15:1-7) by the Spirit (1 Jn 2:20, 24, 27).

We noted above that God the Father is also in a special sense the Father of believers, but it is the Spirit's work to bring about the subjective realization of their parent-child relationship. The Spirit is called "the Spirit of adoption" (Rom 8:15). He brings believers experientially into the family of God, bearing witness with the spirit of believers that they really are children of God (Rom 8:16), the one by whom *believers* cry out, "Abba! Father" (Rom 8:15), or (even more intimately) the one who *himself* calls out "Abba! Father!" within them (Gal 4:6).

In this union with the Beloved through the Spirit, we are enabled to enter experientially into the divine trinitarian love. Paul prayed that God

> would grant you, according to the riches of His glory, to be strengthened with power *through His Spirit* in the inner man, so that Christ may dwell in your hearts through faith; and that you, being rooted and grounded in love, may be able to comprehend with all the saints what is the breadth and length and height and depth, and to know the love of Christ which surpasses knowledge, that you may be filled up to all the fullness of God. (Eph 3:16-18, italics mine)

This prayer describes the kind of Christian experience with God that over time rewires the brain, creating relational memories stored with positive affect, fostering hope and reducing the proportion of negative affect stored in the system. Gradually, believers come to know and believe "the love which God has for us. God is love, and the one who abides in love abides in God, and God abides in him. By this, love is perfected with us" (1 Jn 4:16-17a). But this "perfection" is a developmental, incremental process, which goes on throughout this life, and may not even end in the life to come (Edwards, 1738/1969).

Communion with the Spirit. There are many benefits of perceiving by faith the presence of the indwelling Spirit. Given the profound distance there is between God's infinite and holy greatness and the believer's minute existence—a distance terribly increased and rendered absolute by human sin—it is an utterly extraordinary thing that God would have designed salvation to include the indwelling of the Holy Spirit. Truly, believers must have been reckoned righteous in Christ for God to permit his *Holy* Spirit to live in the human heart, out of which comes all that is evil (Mt 15:19). Think about this: a divine Person lives within the believer; an infinite Being resides inside each Christian. The human mind is incapable of grasping this with much success. But to the extent of one's capacities, it would seem to be deeply psychologically beneficial to meditate on this miracle of mercy. Within the believer, there is infinite wisdom, true emotional response to reality and the ability to live for God. Reflection on such a truth should also contribute to a profound humility and even silence at the thought. Such a gift is unspeakably good, and the believer is immediately encouraged in the believing of it. Regularly focusing on this reality during meditative prayer or worship should be expected to produce an experiential closeness to God that likely deliberately bears an archetypal, therapeutic analogy to the symbiotic attachment bond of the infant and its mother, as it brings the believing soul into the communion of the Trinity (Jn 14:16-20; 17:21, 23; 1 Jn 1:3).

Human fellowship. The indwelling of the Spirit also promotes healthy human relationships, for the Spirit brings individual believers into a community of love (1 Jn 1:1-3; Jn 13:34-35; 1 Cor 12—14). "For by one Spirit we were all baptized into one body, whether Jews or Greeks, whether slaves or free, and we were all made to drink of one Spirit" (1 Cor 12:13). Christ prayed to the Father regarding his people that "the glory which You have given Me I have given to them; that they may be one, just as We are one; I in them, and You in Me, that they may be perfected in unity, that the world may know that You sent Me, and loved them, even as You loved Me" (Jn 17:22-23). This human communal unity is produced by the Spirit (Eph 4:3, see also Eph 2:22). As Edwards taught, "Tis in our partaking of the Holy Ghost that we have communion with the Father and Son and with Christians: this is the common excellency and delight in which they all [are] united; this is the bond of perfectness, by which they are one in the Father and the Son" (Edwards, 1994, p. 448).

This "perfection" of Christ's body includes the granting of the gifts of the Spirit to individual members. "To each one is given the manifestation of the Spirit for the common good" (1 Cor 12:7). Each member is given a singular dignity by the Spirit's sovereign bestowal of a particular giftedness, so that everyone should have equal honor and significance (1 Cor 12:15-24), "that there should be no division in the body, but that the members should have the same care for one another. And if one member suffers, all the members suffer with it; if one member is honored, all the members rejoice with it" (1 Cor 12:25-26). One's ministry to other believers and the recognition of one's significance in the body should contribute to the building up of one's soul. As a result, "connecting" through good Christian relationships is a medium of the Divine Life, as well as a sign of that Life (Crabb, 1997, 1999).

Spiritual understanding. The believer's spiritual union with God is created and sustained by truth. Eternal life is to *know* the Father and the Son (Jn 17:3). In biblical Christianity, there is no dichotomy between relationship and truth, and an overemphasis on either one has to be regarded as heterodox.

The Holy Spirit is called the Spirit of truth (Jn 14:17; 15:26; 16:13; 1 Jn 4:6), the Spirit of wisdom and understanding (Is 11:2; see Eph 1:17), who will teach the disciples all things (Jn 14:26), guiding them into all truth (Jn 16:13) and bringing to remembrance all that Christ said (Jn 14:26). So genuine Christian understanding comes from the Spirit:

> For to us God revealed [the wisdom about Christ] through the Spirit; for the Spirit searches all things, even the depths of God. For who among men knows the thoughts of a man except the spirit of the man which is in him? Even so the thoughts of God no one knows except the Spirit of God. Now we have received, not the spirit of the world, but the Spirit who is from God, that we might know the things freely given to us by God, which things we also speak, not in words

> taught by human wisdom, but in those taught by the Spirit, combining spiritual thoughts with spiritual words. But a natural man does not accept the things of the Spirit of God; for they are foolishness to him, and he cannot understand them, because they are spiritually appraised. . . . For who has known the mind of the Lord, that he will instruct Him? But we have the mind of Christ. (1 Cor 2:10-14, 16)

According to Paul, *true* understanding occurs exclusively through the Holy Spirit, who gives us access to the mind of Christ. The Holy Spirit is "so united to the faculties of the soul that he becomes there a principle or spring of new nature and life," leading to a grasp of spiritual reality unattainable without him (Edwards, 1746/1959, p. 200). The Spirit produces a "new spiritual sense," using the normal, human reasoning faculties (p. 206).

Paul distinguished "words taught by human wisdom" (1 Cor 2:13; or the "persuasive words of wisdom," 1 Cor 2:4, "wisdom . . . of this age," 1 Cor 2:6), from those "taught by the Spirit," the kind of words he preached ("in demonstration of the Spirit and of power," 1 Cor 2:4). He had written earlier to the Thessalonians that "our gospel did not come to you in word only, but also in power and in the Holy Spirit and with full conviction" (1 Thess 1:5). He may have had a similar point in mind in 2 Corinthians 3, where he contrasted the mere "letter" of the old covenant with the Spirit in the new covenant. "The letter kills," he said, "but the Spirit gives life" (2 Cor 3:6). When Jews without the Holy Spirit read the old covenant, "a veil lies over their heart" (2 Cor 3:15), but the veil is taken away by the Spirit of the Lord (2 Cor 3:16-17). Of course, humans can make some intellectual sense of the words of Scripture, but reading without the Holy Spirit makes it impossible to understand *properly*—that is, spiritually—in a way that leads to true freedom. Without the Spirit's assistance, they stand as mere words (or letters), so they are necessarily misinterpreted in a fundamental way. Consequently, through the Holy Spirit, "there is a new inward perception or sensation of their minds, entirely different in its nature and kind, from anything that ever their minds were the subjects of before they were sanctified" (Edwards, 1746/1959, p. 205).

The Spirit alone makes the highest type of transposition possible. He frees believers to read the texts of lower orders of discourse in a new way—in Christ—in relation to Christ. This spiritual understanding is not limited to the interpretation of Scripture, but applies to all of reality, such that other persons, indeed all things, are interpreted in terms of the new creation (2 Cor

5:16-17; Gal 6:14), transforming believers by the renewing of their minds, enabling them to discern what the will of God is (Rom 12:2). This discernment entails nothing other than "an overcoming of the form of the fallen man, Adam, and conformation with the form of the new man, Christ" (Bonhoeffer, 1955, p. 38). Consequently, all signs and discourse and all the meaning they convey—concepts, symbols, texts, stories and history—are altered theocentrically by incorporation into the spiritual order of meaning. The human cognitive activity that the Spirit produces in humans that leads to God has traditionally been called *illumination* (Bonaventure, 1946; Calvin, 1559/1960; Ferguson, 1996; Muller, 2003, Vol. 2).

Inwardness and the Holy Spirit. The Holy Spirit's illumination is especially notable with regard to one's interior world. Paul underscored this point by repeatedly calling attention to the Spirit's presence *in the heart*. "The love of God has been poured out within our hearts through the Holy Spirit who was given to us" (Rom 5:5; see 2 Cor 1:22; Gal 4:6; Rom 2:29). In the New Testament the heart is considered to be the depth location in the soul, its central, orienting faculty (Dunn, 1998; Ladd, 1974). Moreover, the Spirit is directly associated with depth in the Scriptures. We read above that "the Spirit searches all things, even the depths of God" (1 Cor 2:10). Balthasar (1986) wrote that the Spirit is "absolute, free, divine subjectivity" (p. 75). We might say that the Holy Spirit is the infinite inwardness of God, given to us to reveal something of God's "inwardness" (what has been called God's internal glory or splendor) to humans.

Paul also identified the Spirit as the source of the deepest holy movements in the heart of believers: "The Spirit also helps our weakness; for we do not know how to pray as we should, but the Spirit Himself intercedes for us with groanings too deep for words and he who searches the hearts knows what the mind of the Spirit is, because he intercedes for the saints according to the will of God" (Rom 8:26). The Spirit would seem to lie "beneath" our consciousness and takes our inarticulate longings to the Father, shaping them according to his will (Schreiner, 1998). Perhaps Paul was mindful of Jesus' prophesy of the coming of the Spirit within those who would believe in Christ: "From his innermost being [*koilias*, belly, womb, heart] shall flow rivers of living water" (Jn 7:37). Arguing from Proverbs 20:27 ("The spirit of man is the lamp of the LORD, searching all the innermost parts of his being"), Edwards (1746/1959) wrote that the believer's accurate self-awareness would seem to be a product of the Spirit's communication of knowledge (p. 230).

The Holy Spirit is infinite and so lies deeper than anything else in our being. He knows everything, so he knows everything within us, what is conscious to us and what is unconscious. As a result, Christians ought to be open to letting the Spirit bring unconscious sin and unresolved issues into the light of one's consciousness. The indwelling Spirit provides the divine basis of Christian inwardness and self-awareness (to be discussed in coming chapters).

What is the inward significance of the Spirit's indwelling for soul care? It would seem likely that the indwelling Spirit meets some psychological needs. In the Garden of Eden, Adam and Eve appear to have had a relationship with God that seems analogous to the kind of relationship humans have with each other. But the New Testament believer's experience of the indwelling Spirit would seem to be in some respects a more intimate form of relationship. In any case, the Spirit's indwelling is a great aid in our healing—on the inside—from our sin and brokenness. The psychological benefits of the indwelling Spirit deserve study by Christian researchers.

Spiritual affections. Given that the Spirit resides in the heart of believers, it is no surprise that the Spirit is the author of spiritual affections. Jesus, we are told, was filled with joy through the Holy Spirit (Lk 10:21). Paul said that his conscience bore him witness "in the Holy Spirit" (Rom 9:1). The experience of worship (an emotionally charged experience) is from the Spirit of God (Phil 3:3). The kingdom of God, we are told, is "righteousness and peace and joy in the Holy Spirit (Rom 14:17; see also Rom 8:6; 15:13; 1 Thess 1:6), and "the fruit of the Spirit is love, joy, peace, patience, kindness, goodness, faithfulness, gentleness, self-control" (Gal 5:22-23), all of which have affective qualities. Of special importance to soul healing are joy and peace, which are essentially affective phenomena, and *agapé*-love (Rom 15:30; Gal 5:22; Col 1:8)—the most important affection of all (1 Cor 13; see Edwards, 1746/1959, pp. 106-8, 1969). The Spirit enables us to understand God's speech-acts/utterances in Scripture with the divine emotion with which they were conveyed.

We should conclude, then, with Edwards (1746/1959), that the Holy Spirit is the ultimate cause of all holy emotions: affections that correspond to ultimate truth and so move us closer to God in Christ and to conformity with Christ and his heart. The Spirit is the cause of virtuous emotions, and virtuous emotions are signs of the life of the Spirit (Jn 6:63; Rom 8:2, 6, 11; 2 Cor 3:6; Gal 6:8).

Edwards (1746/1959) was very impressed with the value of virtuous emotions, which he termed "religious affections." In his classic treatise of that name, he wrote that "true religion, in great part, consists in holy affections" (1746/1959, p. 95). He described in some detail the wide variety of emotions that make up true religion: the fear of God, hatred of sin and sorrow for one's own sin, a sense of God's beauty, desires for him, joy in God, gratitude and humility, to name a few of the twelve he identified (pp. 102-6).

Edwards believed that the Holy Spirit's work made possible a new set of spiritual affective experiences: a relishing, an enjoying, a rejoicing in things that before would not produce these emotions. In contrast to the intellect, which was concerned with understanding objects, the heart was the set of faculties concerned with movement toward or away from objects and included the appetites, the emotions, motivation and the will. According to Edwards, the heart produces a sense of value, beauty or glory and initiates action toward the beautiful and away from the ugly, so that, when enlightened by the Holy Spirit, the heart experiences a delight in God and his beauty, a consent to him and his ways, and a corresponding movement toward God and away from sin.

In addition to the more positive emotions of the Spirit, there is also at least one class of negative emotions produced by the Spirit, who "will convict the world concerning sin, and righteousness, and judgment" (Jn 16:8). The Greek word for "convict," *elenchō*, means "to bring to light or expose," and this exposure likely involves an activation of feelings of shame and guilt regarding one's own fallenness and wrongdoing (Jn 16:9; see Carson, 1991).[5] This can also be understood to be a spiritual activation of the created faculty known as the "conscience" (*syneidēsis*, Rom 2:15; Heb 10:22).[6] Spiritual conviction of sin can be very painful, but it can also lead us to Christ, greater honesty, and a deeper and more thorough appropriation of the healing grace of the gospel.

There is at least one more kind of emotion that could be a function of the Holy Spirit. When Christians feel negative emotions that do not correspond to God's will or character—frustration, jealousy, self-pity or self-absorbed anger—they are still significant signs of unresolved emotion schemes originating from one's past, calling to the Christian to take seriously something that needs to be healed and overcome; or signs of an irresponsible pattern of life; or signs of a lack of trust in God; or all of the above. Such signs can be repressed throughout one's life, till they "speak no more," but they should be counted a blessing of the Holy Spirit when the Christian is made aware enough to notice such signs and, even better, to understand their meaning as a call from God toward wholeness in Christ.

Some Christians have tragically concluded that these kinds of negative emotions are themselves simply sin (which they can be), rather than signs of sin (one's own sin or the sin of another against one); as a result, they simply reject them and deny them. But often this only succeeds in repressing such emotional dynamics, leaving them to poison the heart beneath the believer's awareness, where they can continue to secrete unbelief and alienation from others and contaminate the soul. But Christians should never flee from the signs of their own souls. Learning how to interpret these signs is invaluable for Christiformity, for, if left unresolved, they can serve as unconscious guides leading us away from God; but if properly interpreted and ameliorated, they can lead us closer to him.

Spiritual power. What exactly does the Spirit do within us to produce the redemptive changes that we have looked at thus far? We must not suppose that they come from the creation of a new psychological process or module. With reference to the intellect, Edwards (1746/1959), for example, says, "This new spiritual sense is not a new faculty of understanding, but it is a new foundation laid in the nature of the soul, for a new kind of exercises of the same faculty of understanding" (p. 206). Believers use the same created cognitive, affective and volitional faculties (or modules) that all humans share. Rather, these modules have been reoriented to the spiritual order, so they are used with different purposes for different ends, resulting in new affective experiences of love and hate, directed in different ways than they were before, which leads to new kinds of actions, that is, actions that correspond more to God's desires and character.

What does the Spirit do, then? The root meanings of the words for "Spirit" in both Hebrew *(ruach)* and Greek *(pneuma)* refer to "wind" and "breath," denoting movement, power and life (Dunn, 1998). Throughout the Old and New Testaments, the Spirit is the ultimate source of all that is in the created order. The Holy Spirit is the creating, providential and reconciling ultimate efficient cause of the creation and of redemption.

With regard to the Christian life, this means that the Spirit is the ultimate origin of the Godward activity of believers. "It is the Spirit who gives life" (Jn 6:63). "The law of the Spirit of life has set you free from the law of sin and death" (Rom 8:2). The Holy Spirit is "an abiding principle of action" in the believer (Edwards, 1746/1959, p. 202), "a principle of life" (Edwards, p. 200). Paul taught that "the gift of the Spirit provided the motivation and enabling power by which [Christians] were to live" (Dunn, 1998, p. 414). For the Christian, the Holy Spirit is the ultimate source of all good action.

Let us look again at Ephesians 3:16, where Paul prayed that God would grant his readers, "according to the riches of his glory, to be *strengthened with power through his Spirit in the inner man [or self];* so that Christ may dwell in your hearts through faith." This well describes a primary goal of Christian counseling: the strengthening with power of the inner self. But this empowerment comes from God's Spirit through our experiential knowledge of the love of God in Christ (Eph 3:17-19).

Having the Spirit within provides a unique attributional dynamic: I must change, but I change by the Spirit's enabling. As Christians mature, they learn how to act by increasingly relying on God's grace. In Philippians 2:13 we are told that God is the one who works *(energōn)* in us to will and to work *(energein)* for his good pleasure. The Greek words for *work* here share the same root as the English word for *energy.* God the Holy Spirit is the source of energy Christians need to fulfill God's will. Our thinking, emotions, desires, motives, loves and even our wills become unified and directed by the Spirit. This is how God changes us.

Holy Spirit empowerment makes humans free. "It was for freedom that Christ set us free" (Gal 5:1). Ultimately, on the basis of Christ's work, the Spirit has experientially redeemed believers and set them free to love and live for God. "Where the Spirit of the Lord is, there is liberty" (2 Cor 3:17). This is "the glorious freedom of the children of God" (Rom 8:21 NIV). Through the Spirit, believers are set free not only from sin and the power of the flesh (Rom 6:18; Gal 5:13, 17-23) but also from the oppressive domination of the law (Rom 7:6; Gal 3:2-5; 4:21-31) and Satan's control (Eph 2:1-3; Col 1:13). The capacity for personal agency is re-formed and realized *Christianly* through the work of the Holy Spirit, where its unique, divine basis is acknowledged by faith: "What do you have that you have not received?" (1 Cor 4:7). With a growing appropriation of the triune God's work on our behalf and within us, the believer is increasingly enabled to act righteously, resulting in the holiness of the Spirit (Rom 1:4; 6:19, 22; 2 Thess 2:13). "Holiness, which is as it were the beauty and sweetness of the divine nature, is . . . the proper nature of the Holy Spirit" (Edwards, 1746/1959, p. 201). The Holy Spirit is the one who makes Christians more holy, teaching them how to live more and more within the context of the spiritual order, and so for the glory of the triune God.[7]

The power of the Holy Spirit is unique. It is not the power of determinism that voids the significance and causal power of the brain, self-awareness and intentionality. Nor is it the power of coercion that would drive a person contrary to their nature or desires, or undermine their personal agency. That kind of causal influence is evident in the natural order and even in the psychosocial. But the ethical and spiritual orders require a different kind of power that releases from the disability of sin—a power that liberates one's created capacities and frees the personal agent to act according to the wisdom of God, liberating, not violating, the human will. As a result of Spirit-empowered freedom, believers are being gradually re-formed into more virtuous characters, characters that reflect the character of Jesus Christ. The power of the Spirit is most demonstrated in the actions of believers. By the Spirit, they put to death the deeds of the body (Rom 8:13) and no longer live the way they once did.

> Do not be deceived; neither fornicators, nor idolaters, nor adulterers, nor effeminate, nor homosexuals, nor thieves, nor the covetous, nor drunkards, nor revilers, nor swindlers, will inherit the kingdom of God. Such were some of you; but you were washed, but you were sanctified, but you were justified in the name of the Lord Jesus Christ and in the Spirit of our God. (1 Cor 6:9-11)

Paul understood that such change is dependent on the work of Christ and the Holy Spirit. So involved is the Spirit in this change that the ongoing, internal, ethicospiritual struggle that believers experience is said to be a conflict between the flesh (the remaining sin-resistance found within the body) and the Spirit (Gal 5:17); Paul here does not even mention the believer's necessary activity (to which he refers in passages like Phil 2:12-13). From the standpoint of God's involvement, the Holy Spirit makes the virtuous changes in the lives of those in whom he dwells. But at the human level, Spirit-indwelt people themselves act differently than they did, both positively (for different reasons they do good more frequently than they used to, and they perform deeds they did not used to do) and negatively (they do less frequently the evil they used to do, and they no longer do what they did).

Before concluding this section on the Spirit, we should note the interrelationship between the nature of the Scriptures and the motivating work of the Spirit. The Spirit inspired the Bible (e.g., Heb 3:7) and now inspires the speaking of the word: "And when they had prayed, the place where they had gathered together was shaken, and they were all filled with the Holy Spirit and began to speak the word of God with boldness" (Acts 4:31). The Word of God is the sword of the Spirit (Eph 6:17), that by which the Spirit's power enters deeply into the heart, illuminating and changing what is there (see Heb 4:12). So, Christian soul care sees the work of the Spirit and the work of Scripture as correlated and equally necessary for conformity to Christ.

Conclusion

The Father had a plan for fallen humanity that is being realized in the form of the drama of history. This plan involved the temporal revelation of the different members of the Trinity, for the sake of their unified glorification. "The goal of all history is being fulfilled in our being made anew into the image of Christ by the presence of his indwelling Spirit" (Coe, 1999, p. 116). The Trinity is the center of Christian soul healing and maturity—by means of the Word and Spirit, the triune God is bringing his rebellious image-bearers into his own glorious love and communion: the Father's paternal affection, union with the Son of God and his work, and the indwelling of the Holy Spirit. Through a communal dialogue with believers, the Father, Son and Spirit are drawing them into increasing conformity to the likeness of Christ through faith—so that individually and corporately they might manifest the greatest divine glory possible.

Notes

[1]See Jn 10:38; 14:10-11, 20; 17:21, 23; Rom 8:9. This has been called *circumincessio* (Western church) or *perichoresis* (Eastern church). See Frame (2002); LaCugna (1991).

[2]As many readers will know, Freud believed that faith in God is a faulty resolution of the oedipal complex (at least for males), based on a projection of childish wishes for an exalted Father-figure who supplements the inadequacies of the parents (especially the father) and then is fantasized to guarantee security in this life (Rizzuto, 1979). Christianity teaches that his anthropocentric interpretation could not have been more opposed to the actual state of affairs (Vitz, 1988). God the Father situated humans in a developmental setting that would prepare them, for good or for ill (ill because of distorted image-bearing), for relating to their Father in heaven.

Given the concerns of secular feminists with patriarchy, one would expect them to reject the Christian God, but liberal Christian feminists also reject trinitarian language for God. They question the adequacy of using a male appellation for any part of the Godhead. However, such a position takes too dim a view of Scripture. As the written Word of God, its vocabulary must be accorded more respect than that.

[3]This does not mean that we do not also have an attachment relationship with Christ and the Spirit.

All three are always involved in our communion with God (see Eph 3:14; 1 Thess 3:11). However, the Father is designated *our Father* (Mt 6:9; Phil 4:20) for reasons that need to be understood, explicated as clearly as possible, and utilized by God's children. The Father ought to be approached as Father (again, see Eph 3:14).

[4]Perhaps this meaning exchange can be considered analogous to the union of a pregnant mother and her unborn child, where chemicals called nutrients pass from the mother to the child, and other chemicals called waste pass from the child to the mother. In a similar way, union with Christ permits reciprocal transcriptions of information (or meaning) from Savior to saved and vice versa.

[5]Narramore (1984) distinguishes the conviction of the Holy Spirit from guilt feelings, calling the latter *our* response to the Spirit's conviction. However, it is hard to understand how the Spirit convicts individuals apart from the emotional signs of conviction of wrongdoing that we experience as shame and guilt.

[6]Some might argue that since the conscience is created, its activity is a natural phenomenon and should not be equated with the Spirit's work in redemption. However, as we have seen, the Spirit produces understanding as well as positive emotions. The conscience's activity, too, then, may be caused by the Holy Spirit (though of course it may not be; Christians must also learn to distinguish false guilt from true; here Narramore, 1984, has some very helpful things to say).

[7]"The Holy Spirit represents the holiness of God and is the member of the Trinity designated to produce that same holiness in the lives of the children of God" (Beck, 2002, p. 180).

13

The Call to Inwardness

Opening Up to the Glory of God

THE WEST HAS LONG BEEN CONCERNED WITH self-understanding and the care of the soul. A famous inscription on a temple at Delphi in ancient Greece exhorted, "Know yourself." Socrates, the exemplar of the Western philosophical tradition, considered his primary calling to be "to direct my enquiries . . . to myself" (Plato, trans. 1961, p. 478). Since his time, the quest to know oneself has been a prominent theme in Western thought (Taylor, 1989).

The search for self-understanding became a major agenda of the modern West in the late 1800s through the work of thinkers like Marx, Nietzsche and especially Freud. Freud, the father of modern psychotherapy, developed many theories and clinical practices aimed at helping people come to know themselves better in order to relieve their neurotic symptoms and cure their souls. Freud's influence was far-reaching, and it spawned a number of clinical models that sought to foster self-understanding, including classical psychoanalysis and object relations, existential and humanistic, and, less directly, cognitive psychotherapies. Though these models have their own distinctives, they all seek to promote self-awareness, but within what is fundamentally a secular and individualistic framework, in which the Self is, in an absolute sense, alone (see Cushman, 1995; Vitz, 1994).

In spite of its ancient origins and recent clinical developments, the topic of self-awareness was largely absent in the first sixty years of twentieth-century secular experimental psychology, which only recently began catching up with its Western heritage and developments in clinical psychology and psychiatry.

However, there is now an enormous literature on such topics as self-awareness (Carver, 2003; Ferrari & Sternberg, 1998a; Lewis & Brooks-Gunn, 1979), self-esteem (Crocker & Park, 2003), subjective well-being (Diener & Lucas, 1999), emotion awareness (Salovey, Bedell, Detweiler & Mayer, 2000; Tangney & Dearing, 2002), self-representations (Harter, 1999), self-theories (Dweck, 2000), and related mental and volitional skills (like self-management, self-control, self-monitoring, self-regulation, emotion regulation; e.g., see Bandura, 1986; Baumeister & Vohs, 2004; Salovey, Bedell, Detweiler & Mayer, 2000). Modern experimental psychology has made up for lost time.

The West, then, has long manifested a serious interest in self-understanding. However, as we noted at the beginning of chapter nine, secular Western thought maintained a truncated and distorted understanding of human beings—whether a one-dimensional perspective (the individual human) or, more recently, a two-dimensional (the individual and others)—whereas a Christian worldview assumes a three-dimensional personal framework (the triune God, others and the self) for understanding the individual (situated in a material creation). Christianity has had a decisive impact on Western thought. What role did it play in the West's interest in the self and in self-awareness? It will likely surprise both secularists and fundamentalists to discover that much of this interest is a *direct* result of Christianity's influence. An overview of this legacy takes up this chapter.

The Bible's Call to Inwardness

Going back to its canonical inception, the Judeo-Christian tradition has been interested in exploring and improving the "inside" of human beings for the glory of the triune God, a journey that is sometimes called "inwardness" or "interiority." This agenda developed in the Scriptures independent of and in contrast to the Greek quest for self-knowledge, for its orientation was theocentric.

The Torah and inwardness. As far back as the Torah, the Scriptures advocate a faith concerned with seeking, loving, serving and obeying God with *all* of one's heart and soul (Deut 4:29; 6:5; 10:12; 30:2), a qualification which inevitably raised the question, how much of my heart is loving God? Loving one's neighbor *as oneself* (Lev 19:18) similarly invited questions regarding the quality and degree of one's neighbor-love, in comparison with one's self-love. A significant degree of self-awareness is required to fulfill these fundamental commands of biblical revelation, but within a relational context of God and others.

Descriptions were given in the Torah of people who "hardened their hearts" (e.g., Ex 8:15; 9:34), and with reference to the wilderness wanderings, God tested the Israelites specifically "to know what was in your heart, whether you would keep His commandments or not" (Deut 8:2). Through such texts, subsequent readers were instructed to reflect on their own heart-religion. As a remedy for their partial love, God said he would perform spiritual heart surgery on his people and "circumcise your heart and the heart of your descendents, to love the Lord your God with all your heart and soul" (Deut 30:6). The first books of the Bible show that God is keenly interested in his people's inner life. Readers of these texts were not to read passively; their perlocutionary intent, at least in part, was to promote the reader's self-understanding.

Old Testament narratives and inwardness. From another vantage point in the canon, consider how remarkably unvarnished and revealing are the stories of the Old Testament in their portrayal of the moral complexity of the heroes of the Israelite people. What was the intended dialogical effect on one's self-understanding of reading of Abraham's lying, the deceitfulness of Jacob and the envy of Joseph's brothers; Moses' anger and the Israelites' complaining in the wilderness; the Israelites' chronic apostasy throughout; the carnal immaturity of Samson; and the fall of Saul, the first king of Israel? Consider David, the warrior-king "after [God's] own heart" (1 Sam 13:14), who yet committed adultery and covered it up with murder. God must have intended readers to conclude from these narratives that, even when given the oracles of God (Rom 3:2), humans are so inwardly compromised that they are utterly unable to benefit from that word in their own power.

The Psalms and inwardness. Consider, further, the honest transparency of the Psalms, often containing emotion-loaded expressions of the deepest concerns of their authors and modeling an inner dialogue of soul-searching in the presence of God (Allender & Longman, 1990).

> Why are you in despair, O my soul?
> And why have you become disturbed within me?
> Hope in God, for I shall again praise Him
> For the help of His presence
> O my God, my soul is in despair within me. . . .
> Deep calls to deep at the sound of Your waterfalls;
> All Your breakers and Your waves have rolled over me. (Ps 42:5-7)

> Out of the depths I have cried to You, O LORD. (Ps 130:1)

The psalmist was very aware of the different states of his soul.

An important support for self-understanding was the realization that the omniscient God knows the human soul fully, so he can be relied upon to guide humans in self-awareness.

> Examine me, O LORD, and try me;
> Test my mind and my heart (Ps 26:2),

and

> Search me, O God, and know my heart;
> Try me and know my anxious thoughts;
> And see if there be any hurtful way [lit. "way of pain"] in me. (Ps 139:23-24)

In contrast to the Greek philosophers, the Hebrews understood that God was a dialogue partner in the process of their self-understanding.

Wisdom and inwardness. And what of the wisdom literature?

> The purposes of a man's heart are deep waters,
> but a man of understanding draws them out. (Prov 20:5 NIV)

and

> The spirit of man is the lamp of the LORD,
> Searching all the innermost parts of his being. (Prov 20:27)

Repeatedly the reader is told to question his or her own understanding of things:

> Trust in the LORD with all your heart
> And do not lean on your own understanding. (Prov 3:5)

> The way of a fool is right in his own eyes,
> But a wise man is he who listens to counsel. (Prov 12:15)

> All the ways of a man are clean in his own sight,
> But the LORD weighs the motive. (Prov 16:2)

The sage railed against self-deception and advocated a self-critical questioning of one's motives and unconscious agenda. Job's friends show that a highly moralistic understanding of religion and knowledge of many religious truths (taught in the Torah) does not guarantee that one is speaking for God, and Job himself shows that extreme suffering can bring unconscious indwelling sin to the surface of an otherwise blameless, upright and God-fearing man (Job 1:1). The Wisdom texts were intended by God to unsettle the complacent Old Covenant (and New Covenant) reader and provoke self-reflection.

The Prophets and inwardness. The books of the prophets go further in exposing the reader's inner corruption. Jeremiah wrote in seeming despair, "The heart is deceitful above all things and desperately wicked. Who can know it?" (Jer 17:9 KJV). Even the worship of God can be corrupt:

> This people draw near with their words
> And honor Me with their lip service,
> But they remove their hearts far from Me
> And their reverence for Me consists of tradition learned by rote. (Is 29:13)

The prophets taught their readers to beware of religious self-deception and to understand that a tragic gap can exist between one's conscious self-understanding and one's inner reality.

But these texts also show that the resources of the Old Covenant were not adequate to overcome these problems. The prophets looked ahead to an age when God's law would be written supernaturally on the hearts of God's people (Jer 31:33); indeed, they would be given a completely new heart and have God's Spirit within them (Ezek 36:26-27). As a result, it was said, they would come to loathe themselves for their iniquities and abominations (Ezek 36:31), self-knowledge that would also lead them to know God more intimately, on the basis of divine forgiveness (Jer 31:33-34).

The Gospels and inwardness. Nothing in the Old Testament, however, can compare to the self-awareness promoted in the Gospels. Christ came, Simeon said, "for a sign to be opposed . . . to the end that thoughts from many hearts may be revealed" (Lk 2:34-35). Shaped by and intensifying some of the Old Testament themes we have just examined, Christ's teaching was characterized by a radical challenge to examine one's heart and motives. "When you pray, you are not to be as the hypocrites; for they love to stand and pray in the synagogues and on the street corners so that they may be seen by men" (Mt 6:5). Yet Christ's hearers were not to judge others but to focus only on the logs in their own eyes (Mt 7:1-5). Charry (1997) suggests that the Sermon on the Mount is based on a "norm of . . . rigorous self-criticism" (p. 66) and argues that Matthew challenged "his audience to internalize Jesus' teachings" (p. 80). But these themes pervade the Gospels: "You Pharisees clean the outside of the cup and of the platter; but inside of you, you are full of robbery and wickedness" (Lk 11:39). "How can you believe, when you receive glory from one another and you do not seek the glory that is from the one and only God?" (Jn 5:44). Many Gospel passages seem to pose the underlying question: "You *think* you know what your motives are, but what are they *really?*" Christ came to enlighten people (Jn 1:9; 8:28). To what? The knowledge of God and also the knowledge of themselves. In Christ, God spoke "out of his own depths, and speaking as a man, he discloses at the same time, the depths of man" (Balthasar, 1989a, pp. 9-10).

Most astounding and disturbing is the subtext of the central conflict in the Gospels, that between the Jewish religious leaders and Christ. Part of the subversive dynamic of the Gospel texts is the ease with which readers can identify with the good guys (Christ and the disciples) and distance themselves from the bad guys (the scribes and Pharisees). "Those stupid hypocrites!" But that is precisely the perlocutionary intent of these texts: to expose the New Testament believer's judgmentalism, for we are too much like them. The Pharisees were zealous followers of the true God, who killed him when he came to visit them "disguised" in human flesh. *This* is the end of religion. Nothing religious can be taken for granted after God's followers crucify his Son in the name of God. Admittedly, this theme is not spelled out too plainly. Given the nature of self-deception, the more explicit the teaching about it, the more, paradoxically, it gets masked and turned into a new Pharisaic standard. So the text must conceal, even as it reveals. Self-deception must be undermined from within, for self-knowledge never results from a forced confession.

John's Gospel offers an explanation of the murder of God's Son: "He came to His own, and those who were His own did not receive Him" (Jn 1:11), for "men loved darkness rather than the Light, for their deeds were evil. For everyone who does evil hates the Light, and does not come to the Light for fear that his deeds should be exposed" (Jn 3:19-20), even the most religious of people!

God intended that reading the Gospel texts over and over again would lead his future followers to go further and deeper, and question their own superficial self-awareness and expose their own remaining autocentric hypocrisy and self-righteousness.

Apostolic inwardness. The entire New Testament was written in light of the most astonishing episode of self-deception in human history. The cross is the great, cosmic unmasking of human defensiveness, pretense and hostility to God—beginning with the people of God. On the eve of the crucifixion, Peter, the rock of the early church, had professed his absolute fidelity to Christ shortly before denying him three times. He came to know himself better that night, and he wept bitterly. Surely his newfound self-insight was foundational to his formation into the first apostolic leader of the first local church (Jn 21:15-18). Paul, the other great apostle of the early church, had been a "blameless" Pharisee (Phil 3:4-6) and a dedicated persecutor of the church (and the Christ) he later came to serve, and God chose *him* to write some of the most important texts of the New Covenant canon. Profoundly aware of his past (1 Tim 1:15), he taught of our universal falling short of God's glory (Rom 3:23), our lack of *truly* seeking God (Rom 3:11), and our native deadness in sins (Eph 2:1), and he announced that God now offers a perfect righteousness to those who will simply receive it (Acts 13:38). Harkening back to the Torah, but now in light of all that had passed in redemptive history, Paul advocated for a *new* religion of the heart: "But he is a Jew who is one *inwardly;* and circumcision is that which is *of the heart, by the Spirit,* not by the letter" (Rom 2:29, italics mine).

There are many other strands of evidence that Paul was committed to inwardness. He distinguished between the "the inner self" (*ho esō anthrōpos;* Rom 7:22; Eph 3:16) and "the outer self" (*ho exō anthrōpos;* the visible body; 2 Cor 4:16)—phrases not used in the Old Testament—indicating an awareness of a phenomenological duality between one's interiority and one's body and behavior. Paul suggested that the Corinthian Christians use the observance of the Lord's Supper as a time for self-examination of their motives (1 Cor 11:28). And he must have been fairly aware of his own soul, since he made repeated reference to his own internal, psychospiritual struggles, as well as those of Christians in general (e.g., Rom 7:7-25; 2 Cor 1:8-10; 2:1-4, 13; 4:8-11; Gal 5:17). The basis of his self-awareness and great humility was likely his deep understanding that he had been declared perfectly righteous in Christ, enabling him to be more honest about himself and his weaknesses than almost any other biblical author (except perhaps the psalmist). The chief of sinners was also the chief writing apostle to the church, and in that capacity he modeled an interiorizing orientation that was grounded on the objective work of Christ.

Scriptural Metaphors for the Bible's Role in Inwardness

We turn next to focus on some metaphors found in the Bible, which aptly convey the Bible's disclosive power to show readers themselves (Capps, 1990a) and bring healing and maturity. Metaphors provide pictures that can illuminate a feature of something by putting it in a different light. We observe first that the Word of God is referred to in the Bible as an "assessment instrument" of the human heart and life. Kierkegaard (1851/1990) based his book on the Bible's role in self-examination on James 1:22-23:

> Prove yourselves doers of the word, and not merely hearers who delude themselves. For if any one is a hearer of the word and not a doer, he is like a man who looks at his natural face in a mirror; for once he has looked at himself and gone away, he has immediately forgotten what kind of person he was. But one who looks intently at the perfect law, the law of liberty, and abides by it, not having become a forgetful hearer but an effectual doer, this man shall be blessed in what he does.

Here the apostle James likens the Word of God to a mirror. It shows humans beings what they look like, ethically and spiritually. Looking into this mirror reveals one's createdness and limitations, sins and hypocrisy (as well as one's identity in Christ), so that gazing by faith at oneself in the mirror of God's Word and consenting to what it says about us—God's "law of liberty" (a wonderful, paradoxical label)—produces changes in our self-representations and self-evaluations, and eventually our actions and story.

Another diagnostic metaphor is the word of God as sword:

> For the word of God is living and active and sharper than any two-edged sword, and piercing as far as the division of soul and spirit, of both joints and marrow, and able to judge the thoughts and intentions of the heart. And there is no creature hidden from His sight, but all things are open and laid bare to the eyes of Him with whom we have to do. (Heb 4:12-13)

In its larger context, the opening "for" of this passage indicates that the word referred to is the word spoken to the Israelites in their wilderness wanderings, and likely also to the Scripture cited earlier in the passage, but it may also refer more broadly "to God's warnings to his people throughout OT and NT times" (Ellingworth, 1993, p. 260; see also Hughes, 1977; Lane, 1991). The passage warns that reading the Bible and hearing the gospel properly are dangerous activities. This sword (*of the Spirit*, according to Paul in Eph 6:17) is alive and active (powerful, *energēs*) and cuts more deeply (piercing, *diiknoumenos*) into human nature than anything imaginable, dividing things indivisible and exposing and assessing the inner workings of the human heart. This passage personalizes or divinizes the word of God—giving it the omniscient eyes of God—suggesting that in Christ the triune God opens up and lays bare the soul as the word does its exploratory work in the consciousness of the reader/hearer, drawing believers into a self-awareness that corresponds more to God's awareness of the soul. Commenting on this passage, Calvin (1979) argued that God wishes himself to "touch all our inmost thoughts and feelings, and so there is no part of our soul which ought not to be roused" by his word (p. 100). It goes deep. Perhaps we could extend the metaphor further today by comparing the word of God to a scalpel, a surgical instrument that brings some pain, but for good purposes, eventually correcting the malady (e.g., removing the "cancer growth" of a sinful stronghold or defense mechanism).

But the word of God is not merely diagnostic; it also brings health and well-being. It is often likened to food. "Man does not live by bread alone, but man lives by everything that proceeds out of the mouth of the LORD" (Deut 8:3; see Mt 4:4; Lk 4:4). Food for the body is a symbol of a deeper kind of *soul*-nourishment. Jesus called himself "the bread of life" (Jn 6:35, 48), saying that those who believed on him would not hunger or thirst (Jn 6:35). He was teaching that truths about his person and work can feed and strengthen the soul.

Bread and wine are especially symbolic of his New Covenant salvation (Mt 26:26-28), and Jesus told his followers, "He who eats My flesh and drinks My blood has eternal life" (Jn 6:54). The physical acts of eating bread and drinking wine, and swallowing them in the Lord's Supper, are embodied symbols of taking in the gospel truth of Jesus' death on the cross and the realizing of our union with him (Carson, 1991); they signify the bringing of spiritual health, strength and vigor to the one who deeply believes the gospel. It is Christ's body and blood that are *true* food and drink (Jn 6:55), that is, *for our souls*. By deeply believing in Christ's accomplishment on the Cross "for oneself," we are experiencing our union with him (Jn 6:56). The gospel is to permeate our inner being and become part of us and fuel our lives in Christ. Such meditations ought to accompany our taking of the Lord's Supper.

The prophet Jeremiah was called by God to preach difficult words to his generation. He also used eating as a metaphor to describe his experience:

> Your words were found and I ate them.
> And Your words became for me a joy and the delight of my heart;
> For I have been called by Your name. (Jer 15:16)

Jeremiah internalized God's words, and they produced joy and delight. This pictures the kind of soul healing the word of God is supposed to produce.

Picking up on this scriptural theme, Roberts (1997) states that humans are "verbivores." He writes: "Whoever feeds on the word of God lives; whoever does not take this word into himself, ruminate upon it, swallow it and digest it into his very psyche starves himself as truly as he would if he quit eating physical food" (p. 81). We become what we eat; the words we take into our being shape the kind of people we become. So the word of God is essential to Christian maturation.[1]

There is one more biblical metaphor for the word of God to consider. "Your word is a lamp to my feet, and a light to my path" (Ps 119:105). God's word shows the path we are to walk by describing for us human conduct that conforms to God's will. As we consent to it and let it guide our actions, we will not stumble so often and will see how we are supposed to live, becoming increasingly virtuous. However, given Scripture's inwardness agenda, let us extend this metaphor, for the Word of God is also a light *within*, revealing that which is contrary to God's ways and pointing toward internal activities that lead to life. This extension is important since godly action (which was likely the concern of the psalmist) is dependent on the quality of one's interior life. Internal and external activity are interrelated.

The metaphors we have examined bring out in different ways the inwardness-promoting dynamic of Scripture: it helps us to look within, it reveals our internal reality, it shows us our sin, and, when it enters deeply into our being, it fosters spiritual life. These themes will be explored in the coming chapters.

Much more could be said from the Bible, but we have seen enough to conclude that the inspired texts of Scripture call their readers to look within with God's help, challenging them objectively from without to reject their indwelling sin and self-deception so they can draw nearer to God. Let us see how the church has responded to this call.

Inwardness in the Christian Tradition

As we noted above, the pagan sages of the ancient West advocated self-understanding, and their influence was undoubtedly a goad to the church. However, it was primarily God's written word that was the catalyst for the church's growing interior focus. Classical Christian inwardness was not radically subjective, for it has always been anchored outside the self in God and his word.

Many in the early church extolled inwardness, but arguably the most important was Augustine, and he pursued it with unusual rigor (see Cary, 1999; Taylor, 1989, chap. 7). Certainly influenced by the pagan agenda to "know yourself," Augustine taught that Christian salvation similarly entailed a search within: "Do not go outward; return within yourself. In the inward man dwells truth" (*On True Religion* 34.72).[2] But for the most part he took the search in a very different direction: "O sinners, return to your own heart and abide in Him that made you" (Augustine, 1942, p. 60). Augustine believed that humans needed, first, to transcend the material world by descending into themselves and there find evidence of God's handiwork in the immaterial soul, and then, through the intellect, to ascend to the transcendent God who is recognized as the only source of the light and wisdom found within (1942, p. 71; also Cary, 1999). We must also remember that Augustine (1997) believed that the Bible was the necessary guide for interpreting one's interior world.

Augustine's inward agenda was grandly illustrated in his *Confessions*, where he engaged in a searching examination of the story of his life, including his thoughts, feelings and motives. Written as a prayer, his self-examining narrative showed how Christian inwardness really has God as its end.

> Where have you not walked with me, O Truth, teaching me both what to shun and what to seek, when I set before you such things as I have been able to see here below and begged your counsel? With my bodily senses I surveyed the external world as best I could, and considered the life my body has from me and the senses themselves. From that I turned inwards to the depths of my memory, like so many vast rooms filled so wonderfully with things beyond number: and I considered and stood awe-stricken: for no one of these could I discern without you, and I found that no one of these was you. . . . Nor in all these things that my mind traverses in search of you, do I find any sure place for my mind save in you, in whom all that is scattered in me is brought into one, so that nothing of me may depart from you. (Augustine, 1942, p. 206)

Augustine's inward orientation is not beyond criticism. Ancient influences, particularly Neoplatonism, shaped his articulation. Plato sought truth within because he believed that only through one's reason could one access *Nous*—or Mind—the ultimate source of understanding, and this assumption was foundational to the Neoplatonic search within. In contrast, the Bible underscores the importance of *hearing*. By listening to others, particularly to the God who speaks in Scripture and in creation, humans grow in wisdom. In fact, the Bible gives the direction to "set your mind on *the things above*" (Col 3:2), to God in Christ. So biblical inwardness is grounded in objectivity. Augustine certainly recognized this, but his own articulations were undoubtedly influenced by the somewhat more subjectivist intellectual trends of his day. Nonetheless, his contributions to Christian interiority were seminal. To be fair, he was moving away from Neoplatonism throughout his life and toward an increasingly God-centered system (Van Til, 1959). In contrast to Neoplatonism, Augustine's life of self-examination through the reading of Scripture *coram Deo* (before God) gave his approach to inwardness a distinctly Christian cast (Stock, 1996). Building on Augustine's insights, our model will make more clear the grounding of Christian inwardness in sources outside the self: in the triune God whose proper abode is heaven (Eph 1:20; Heb 1:3; which of course was Augustine's foundation), his declarative salvation to us in Christ, the Bible's inspired record of these matters, and other humans who are signs to us of God and so also can mediate to us God's truth.

Augustine's approach left a lasting impression on the Latin Church (Driscoll, 1993), and the influence of his interior agenda can be seen in Gregory the Great (1950), Bernard (1983), Anselm, Bonaventure (1978), Julian of Norwich (1977; Abbott, 1999, chap. 5), Thomas à Kempis (1864), Ignatius (1964), Francis de Sales (1609/1949), and Pascal (1941), among many others. Thomas à Kempis's (1864) *The Imitation of Christ* is a classic of interiority that has often been republished by Protestants, as well as Catholics. He wrote:

> The inward Christian prefers the care of himself before all other cares. And he that diligently attends unto himself, can easily keep silence concerning others. You will never be thus inwardly religious unless you pass over other men's matters with silence, and look especially to yourself. If you attend wholly unto God and yourself, you will be but little moved with whatsoever you see abroad. Where are you when you are not with yourself? And when you have run over all, what have you then profited, if you have neglected yourself? If you desire peace of mind and true unity of purpose, you must still put all things behind you, and look only upon yourself. (pp. 89-90)

Perhaps the highpoint of Catholic interiority was reached in the works of Teresa of Ávila and John of the Cross. Teresa's (1961) *Interior Castle* is a description of the journey into the inner rooms of the soul on the way to more intimate union with God. John of the Cross (1964), the more rigorous thinker, explored the inward journey to God with a more systematic bent in *Ascent of Mt. Carmel* and *Dark Night of the Soul*. Both Teresa and John argued that the soul contained many hindrances to union with God (though sometimes confusing creation and sin), which had to be removed before one could experience God in greater fullness. Consequently, they encouraged an exhaustive self-examination to root out all desires for anything other than God. Their influence can be seen in the twentieth century in the works of von Hildebrand, Merton, Balthasar, Nouwen, Keating and Groeschel.

Reformational inwardness. Though the medieval Catholic tradition has been criticized by Protestants for its tendencies toward traditionalism, asceticism and the subjectivism of some of the mystics (Corduan, 1991; Horton, 1996), its interiority was in pursuit of the triune God, and Scripture was avowedly its authoritative guide (see, e.g., Richard of St. Victor, 1979, pp. 138-39). Nevertheless, the Reformers raised legitimate questions about the interiority of some of those who had preceded them. The soul is a mysterious thing, and its darkness is compounded by sin's deceptiveness. Consequently, the early Reformers and their followers tied their self-understanding more closely to the textual objectivity of Scripture (Beeke, 2004; Horton, 1996). Moreover, the Reformation rediscovery of Paul's doctrine of justification by faith reestablished that doctrine as the only sound basis upon which the Christian can engage in the convicting work of self-examination.

Nonetheless, the Reformers were still heirs of the Middle Ages. They were influenced by Augustine as well as by the interiority of the Roman Catholic tradition that followed him. While Luther's conversion was aided by a study of the apostle Paul's writings, his own journey to Christ as an Augustinian monk involved a far more introspective journey than Paul took. Not en route to Damascus (or Rome), Luther was led to Christ by the law's crushing exposure of his interior sin. Along with Augustine and the bulk of the medieval tradition, Luther, Zwingli and Calvin associated the knowledge of God with the knowledge of the self. Calvin (1559/1960), for example, opened his *Institutes of the Christian Religion* by declaring that the knowledge of God and self *together* constituted true and sound wisdom, and he says (somewhat surprisingly) that he could not tell which had the priority, given their profound correlation. But in contrast to Augustine, his knowledge of self was somewhat darker and especially focused on its fallenness (rather than it being a pathway to God). This emphasis was symptomatic of the age but was also, to a large extent, a reflection of the radical doctrine of sin in Scripture, and it certainly contributed to the recovery of Paul's teachings on justification by faith and made them especially encouraging. As Charry (1997) writes, according to Calvin, "Proper self-knowledge produces self-displeasure, the first step toward deconstruction of the self in preparation for the reconstruction of a new self. This basic dynamic of deconstruction and reconstruction re-enacts on a psychological plane the *exitus-reditus* pattern that the Christian story itself follows" (p. 215).

Puritan inwardness. The Puritan movement in England was especially indebted to Calvin's theocentric, existential and scriptural system, and the Puritan corpus evidences the most profound commitment to inwardness and spiritual development in the English language. Puritan leaders like Rutherford, Owen, Flavel, Sibbes, Bunyan and Baxter all assumed the value of a Bible-based interiority and encouraged it throughout their writings, believing that, following Calvin, an understanding of the fallen self was necessary to appreciate one's need for a Savior. As Owen (1967) suggested, "Until men know themselves better, they will care very little to know Christ at all" (Vol. 5, p. 21). *The Holy War* is John Bunyan's (1682/1977) less well-known allegory of a city called "Mansoul," inhabited by various "citizens" before and after conversion (like conscience, reason and the passions), and it was written to help believers understand their internal dynamics.

Throughout the *Christian Directory*, Richard Baxter's (2002) massive guide to practical theology, he encouraged his readers to inspect their souls and weigh its thoughts, motives and desires in light of God's Word. He (2000) also wrote a lengthy essay on the subject of inwardness titled "The Mischiefs of Self-Ignorance and Benefits of Self-Acquaintance," where he gave many reasons for Christians to become more self-aware. For example, he says the self-ignorant cannot be Christian, cannot pray or give thanks adequately; they cannot know how to conduct themselves well; they cannot understand and apply the Bible; and they cannot help themselves or others to grow in knowing God. Reminiscent of Augustine, he said, "The principal glass for the beholding of God is the reasonable soul beholding itself"

(p. 824). He concluded the first section of the essay with some urgent appeals:

> Come home you wandering, self-neglecting souls; lose not yourselves in a wilderness or tumult of impertinent, vain, distracting things; your work is nearer you: the country that you should first survey and travel is within you. . . . Let the eyes of fools be in the corners of the earth! Leave it to men beside themselves, to live as [outside] themselves, and to be still from home, and waste that time in other business that was given them to prepare for life eternal. . . . Some men admire the heights of mountains, . . . and they pass by themselves without admiration. The compendium of all that you study [outside] you is near you, even within you, yourself being the epitome of the world. If either necessity or duty, nature or grace, reason or faith, internal inducements, external repulses, or eternal attractives and motives might determine of the subject of your studies and contemplations, you would call home your lost, distracted thoughts, and employ them more on yourselves and God. (pp. 825-26)

Puritan inwardness extended and radicalized Reformation inwardness. With Luther and Calvin, the Puritans promoted the normalization of growth in the knowledge of self before God, but because of some latent "hyper-Calvinism," some became consumed with identifying the internal evidences of election, genuine conversion and the fruit of the Spirit (e.g., Thomas Shepherd, 1991). Believing that spiritual change could only come from God, the inward focus tended to consist of a simple, bivalent assessment: Is the fruit within bad or good? If the fruit was bad, one had to grieve for one's sins, attend the means of grace (preaching and Bible reading), and seek and wait for the Holy Spirit to bring the good fruit; and if the fruit was good, then one had proof that one was elect, and so the primary motive for interiority was taken away. Puritan interiority would have been improved by four refinements: (1) a more charitable focus on the inward fruit of a Christian's life (which one can always find deficient, because of remaining sin) and a greater focus on Christ the Redeemer and justification by faith; (2) a greater appreciation for the gradual nature of spiritual growth and the dependent role of the believer in that process; (3) a consideration of the internal dynamics of *creation* structures, and not just a dualistic focus on the Fall and redemption; and (4) a biblical radicalization of inwardness that would lead Christians to continue to subject their own appropriation of Christianity to critique.

Kierkegaard and the radicalization of inwardness. In Søren Kierkegaard, Protestantism's interior agenda seems to have reached its own kind of zenith. A provocateur to his age (and ours), he stressed the value of subjectivity to an extreme. However, he must be interpreted in light of his era, for he was reacting against an equally excessive Christian moralism, objectivism and Hegelian rationalism. With this in mind, his understanding of inwardness stands as one of the greatest legacies in the Christian tradition.

Kierkegaard's (1849/1980) depth-understanding of the noetic effects of sin may be more radical than that of anyone else in the Christian tradition up to that time. He believed that being a fallen human entails an often unconscious sense—which he called *despair*—that we fall far short of that for which we were created. Since the despair is painful, humans seek to avoid awareness of it as much as possible, purposely but unconsciously perpetuating their self-deception. This refusal to come to terms with the true state of one's soul constitutes the essence of sin, which Kierkegaard termed "the sickness unto death." With Augustine and Calvin, he believed that the knowledge of God was directly correlated with the knowledge of self. Benefiting from a few more centuries of Christian reflection, Kierkegaard recognized further that the construction of the Christian's self was a reflexive *project*, an interactive, developmental process involving both forms of knowledge: "The more conception of God, the more self; the more self, the more conception of God" (p. 129).

For Kierkegaard, inwardness is a central aspect of Christian faith and maturation. But faith, for Kierkegaard, is not so much an act—and certainly not mental assent to some propositions—as it is a way of living consciously before God that defines the self: "Faith is: that the self in being itself and in willing to be itself is grounded transparently in God" (p. 132). Faith is accepting all that one is before God. For the Christian, this means being open to all that one is—as sinner and forgiven—in his presence (p. 185). This constitutes the highest form of self-awareness and alone permits a nondespairing, that is, a joyful, knowledge of God and oneself.

Of special interest for our purposes is his book on how to read the Bible, called *For Self-Examination* (1851/1990), that we noted above was based on James 1:22-25. Kierkegaard believed that the value of reading Scripture for our well-being was inestimable, yet he also confessed that he wanted desperately to avoid it, since it so profoundly convicted him of his shortcomings, so that "I hardly dare to be alone with God's Word" (p. 32). And he chided those who would study the Bible merely "objectively"—with many commentaries and language helps—only to lose sight of God and themselves in all of the merely intellectual analysis.[3] In fact, he alleged that Christians paradoxically (and unconsciously) sometimes engage in such activity in order to defend themselves against the very Word of God they study! This is because Christians who are without much self-awareness can be deceived by a mental familiarity with the Bible into thinking that they are being conformed to God's Word.

Analogous to Luther's rediscovery of Pauline justification, Kierkegaard's interior agenda was a profound restatement of the subversive agenda of the Gospels and an exposé of the remaining hypocrisy in the heart of every Christian. Going beyond the Puritans in self-criticism, his model amounts to a seismic shift in Christian self-understanding. *Even one's accurate Christian beliefs and moral behavior may be used for sinful, autocentric purposes.* Reading the Bible should call into question one's idolatrous self-understanding—including one's self-righteousness *as a Christian*—and should arouse a "restlessness oriented toward inward deepening" (p. 20). The result of such reading should be the fuller reception of the Word of God into one's soul, leading to its greater conformity to the Christ of Scripture.

Reservations about inwardness and a defense. Before moving on, two groups of readers may be troubled by the focus on subjectivity advanced in this chapter, and it would be good to anticipate and address some of their concerns. Some Christians are deeply suspicious of subjectivity in general, believing that any promotion of it leads to individualistic, self-absorbed "navel-gazing" and inevitably undermines a focus on objective truth (e.g., see Ganz, 1993). No doubt some forms of subjectivism betray such an orientation. As Taylor (1989) has ably demonstrated, modern and Enlightenment thought fundamentally distorted the originally Christian interest in interiority (for further criticism of modernist individualism and subjectivity, see also Bellah et al., 1985; Cushman, 1995; Johnson & Sandage, 1999; Lasch, 1979; MacIntyre, 1984; Stout, 1981; Vitz, 1994). Whereas the inwardness practiced within the Christian tradition focused primarily on God and sin (hardly the fruit of narcissism), the modern West perversely turned the inwardness agenda of Christianity into self-exploration and self-expression for their own sakes, manifesting modernity's underlying motives of autocentrism that were increasingly replacing the influence of Christian theocentrism in the culture (see Vitz, 1994). When God was removed from the West's self-understanding dynamics, its inwardness agenda was necessarily corrupted, and it became antagonistic to its theistic origins. Maturity came to be defined as having rejected the faith of one's childhood and embracing a barely disguised form of narcissism (see Lasch, 1979; Taylor, 1989—though creation grace has restrained this orientation to some extent, tempering it so that modern Westerners are not living nearly as selfishly as they could be). The supremacy of God in Christianity had helped to keep subjectivity and inwardness within their proper bounds, but with God out of the picture, they became idolized and ultimate (in a series of modified initiatives: romanticism, pragmatism, existentialism, therapeutic humanism, 60s hedonism, consumerism and materialism, and now "post"-modernism).

However, pointing to a misuse of something does not constitute an argument against it. Subjectivity is a legitimate, irreducible part of the created order (see Frame, 1987, for a defense of this dimension, which he called "the existential perspective"), and its created purpose is realized—and its exploration legitimized—in pursuit of the glory of God. As in other important matters, the City of God promotes a *different version* of inwardness than the City of Humanity (Van Til, 1969, p. 135)—a *theistic* and *relational* inwardness. This emphasis will hopefully address the concerns of another group of likely skeptics of inwardness: Christian relationalists or communitarians who would tie it to the excesses of an extreme Western individualism.

A Christian interiority is not autonomous, but is ectypally grounded in the triune God's archetypal knowledge. Human inwardness should be an image of divine inwardness in two ways. First, God is absolute subjectivity (i.e., he knows himself exhaustively and comprehensively), so Christians should seek to know themselves as God knows himself. Second, being omniscient, God has a complete and objective knowledge of each human being, including our internal world, so Christians should know themselves as God knows them. In both ways, humans image God in their self-understanding. Of course, because of their finitude, human self-understanding will never be more than analogically like God's. But human subjectivity, self-awareness and self-understanding are important aspects of image-bearing.

There are also doxological grounds to pursue Christian inwardness. Interiority is worthwhile, if for no other reason than that it is within one's inner self that one relishes and worships God, so that the improvement of one's inner capacities can contribute directly to the manifestation of God's glory. Taking Calvin a step further, conformity to Christ's image is mysteriously correlated to the deepest internalization of God's objective character and to the greatest self-awareness and self-understanding. A proper concern with the subjective is due to an interest in the *quality* of the "interior response of redeemed man 'to the praise of the glory of his grace'" (Balthasar, 1990, p. 21). Theocentric interiority enhances the monitoring and increasing of the quality of our praise of God. Only by looking within can one discern and dismantle one's internal barriers to God and his word, which is the mortification of the old self (Col 3:1-11; Eph 4:22-28). Furthermore, inwardness facilitates the internalizing of God's word and the construction of one's new self in Christ. Simply put: in order to re-form the soul (through union with Christ), one must understand one's soul.

A dialogical model of human nature and soul care recognizes that inwardness is fundamentally social. According to Vygotsky (1978), higher mental functions (like self-awareness) are first inter-psychological before they become intra-psychological and able to be utilized on one's own. The fact is that individuals are drawn toward or away from inwardness, depending on their social and educational experiences. Moreover, adults are assisted in their interior journey through dialogue with wise and loving guides—pastors, counselors or spiritual directors—who have made the journey themselves (with *their* guides) and have developed some expertise in working with others. Inwardness and communion with others are not antagonistic to each other; on the contrary, they increase reciprocally.

Critics have legitimate suspicions about modern subjectivism, but not all interest in subjectivity is dangerous. *Inwardness is ultimately valid if it is theocentric, Bible-based and dialogical.* A God-centered approach recognizes that the true ground of the soul lies outside the self, and it leads the soul to look to God for its salvation, wisdom, self-understanding and healing. It also supports a reliance on others in the journey. A theocentric, scriptural-relational orientation actually protects Christians from the dissipating effects of individualism, narcissism and self-absorption. Christian inwardness is, paradoxically, an "opening out to what is beyond" (Hart, 2003, p. 32), and it seeks to take that which is beyond—ultimately the objective knowledge of God in Christ as revealed in the Scriptures—into the subjective depths of the soul.

Toward God's *Comprehensive* Understanding of One's Self

Historically, Christian inwardness was primarily focused on the most important interior matters: God, sin and matters of conscience (ethical issues), and not the kinds of developmental or family-of-origin issues that have constituted much of the focus in modern soul care. Christian inwardness today must be careful to maintain and strengthen the biblical emphasis. There are good doxological and therapeutic reasons why God's soul-care guidebook directs our attention to ethical and spiritual matters, which we will examine in chapter fifteen. However, as was discussed in chapter eleven, a *complex* theocentrism will also take with due seriousness the created internal dynamics of the soul and their damage—*out of respect for God's ordaining word which structures human life.* The Creator's omniscient understanding of the soul includes many aspects that he chose not to include in the Bible (e.g., neuropsychology and human development). Such aspects should not be despised simply because they are not in the Bible. A *theocentric* image-bearing orientation aims at reproducing in us as much of the mind and heart of God as possible.

Consequently, Christian inwardness should be guided by the biblical emphasis on God and sin, but also open to exploring, when worthwhile, other internal created dynamics (some of which are damaged by the Fall), things like significant shifts in one's emotional arousal level, the impact of past abuse on one's current perceptions, the content of one's stream of self-talk, painful flashbacks from one's story, fearful attitudes one has around authority figures, or affect-laden states of mind/brain that characterize one's daily experiences. A regard for the primacy of Scripture must constrain our soul care priorities; so, generally speaking, the therapeutic focus of Christians ought to be directed primarily toward identifying and overcoming personal sin. But one cannot neatly and cleanly separate one's sin from the rest of one's internal world. Moreover, our omniscient Creator-Redeemer loves us and knows and cares about our *entire* internal world, including our created structures and their damages, and he perfectly understands their subordinate importance within the hierarchy of the orders of human life. As a result, growth in one's self-awareness about such matters has a relative value and is rendered even more worthwhile if it enables believers to better glorify God.

In fact, the Bible on a few occasions even points us in this direction. It teaches, for example, that the actions of parents can have a profound impact on children. "Train a child in the way he should go, and when he is old he will not turn from it" (Prov 22:6 NIV; see also Prov 22:15; 23:13; Eph 6:4). And Christ's words on this score are deeply troubling to any self-aware parent: "Whoever *causes* one of these little ones who believe in Me *to stumble* [*skandalizō*, to cause to fall, to sin], it would be better for him to have a heavy millstone hung around his neck, and to be drowned in the depth of the sea" (Mt 18:6, italics mine). Just as it took the church centuries to appreciate the significance of Paul's teaching on justification, it has taken many centuries to begin to grasp the implications of such biblical teachings on family life in the kingdom of God.

Some secularists, it is true, have suggested that biopsychosocial factors minimize human responsibility and have redefined wrongdoing accordingly (as has been done with homosexuality), leading conservative critics to criticize the "victim mentality" and blame-shifting that typically follows from reductionistic assumptions, which itself can undermine one's ability to take responsibility for oneself. But Christians must correct, not overreact to, the excesses of secular psychology (which have also been resisted by more balanced secularists; see Martin, Sugarman & Thompson, 2003; Peterson & Seligman, 2004; Damon, 1988). The opposite extreme is no more intellectually honest if it compromises the Christian community's understanding of created biological and psychosocial influences on human development and how best to promote redemptive soul-healing. Such knowledge does not nullify God's Word in Scripture regarding himself and human nature and salvation; it simply improves our understanding of the entire context into which God's Word is being introduced. All these dynamics belong to God. Believers must claim them for God, reinterpret them biblically and redemptive-historically, and, where appropriate, translate them into Christian psychological theories, so that the understanding of the Christian community will become increasingly more sophisticated and will increasingly correspond more completely to God's *comprehensive* understanding.

Three Aspects of Inwardness

Inwardness encompasses many different topics. With a soul-care agenda in mind, we will concentrate on inwardness under three headings: self-examination, the identification and deconstruction of barriers, and the internalization of the signs of God. As will become clear, these three aspects are not mutually exclusive or independent of each other. On the contrary, they are reciprocally interdependent and entail one other: as one aspect develops, it promotes the growth of the others. This interdependence is illustrated in figure 13.1.

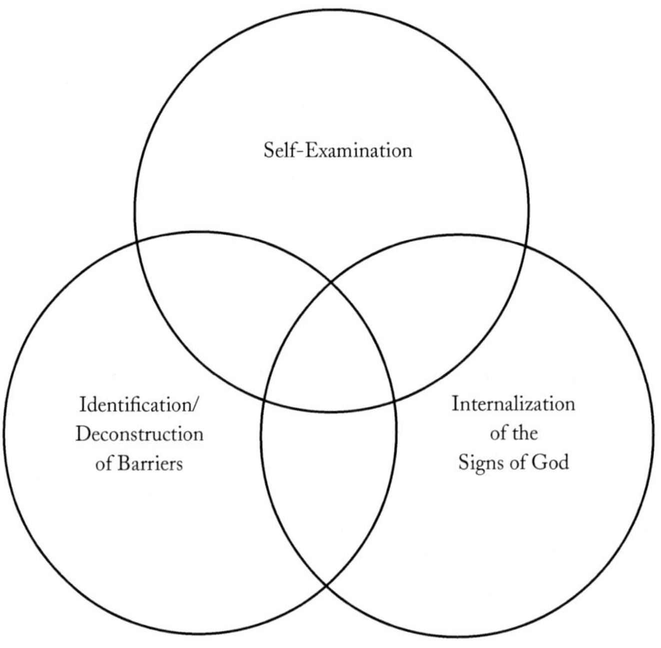

Figure 13.1. Aspects of inwardness

The next three chapters will examine these three aspects of inwardness.

Notes

[1]According to Roberts, the human self is by nature in-formed by words. We are changed "by virtue of the stories, the categories, the metaphors and explanation in terms of which we construe ourselves, we can become spiritual Marxians by thinking of ourselves in Marxian terms, spiritual Jungians if we construe ourselves in Jungian terms, and so forth" (p. 81).

[2]This perspective, admittedly, sounds strange to most modern ears (maybe especially evangelicals). Influenced by Plato, the classical mind was trained to view the external world with some disdain—since it is changeable and perishable—and to see the internal realm as more important and valid, since through reason one has access to Reason and imperishable Ideas. Augustine, along with most of the church fathers, adopted a Christian version of this attitude, believing that in moving inward, one turns away from the distractions of created things, which can become idols and are essentially unworthy of love. Modern Christians might argue that turning inward is simply a different movement toward created things. The Christian should not turn within, they might say, but to God. But according to Augustine, in the turn within, one actually finds two very valuable kinds of Christian understanding: the wisdom that comes from a knowledge of oneself (regarding one's finitude, corruption and self-

deception), and most importantly, but perhaps surprisingly, one finds the true God, the source and ground of the soul (importantly, God is never identified with the soul!), and—here is where his Christian teachings especially distinguish him from his non-Christian influences—the former knowledge leads the soul to recognize its need of and absolute dependence upon God.

[3]Though Kierkegaard (1851/1990) was not opposed to scriptural scholarship (see p. 28).

14

Inwardness, Part 1

Self-Examination

WE SAW IN THE LAST CHAPTER THAT INWARDNESS has long been promoted within the Judeo-Christian tradition. Self-examination has historically been the primary focus of this orientation. This is understandable, since self-examination is the logical first step in the movement inward. One must first observe and evaluate what is going on within before one can intentionally make any changes there.

The task of self-examination is mentioned explicitly a few times in the Bible. The author of Lamentations wrote, "Why should any living mortal, or any man, offer complaint in view of his sins? Let us examine and probe our ways, and let us return to the Lord" (Lam 3:39-40). Paul told Christians to assess the quality of their life: "Let each one examine his own work, and then he will have reason for boasting in regard to himself alone, and not in regard to another. For each one shall bear his own load" (Gal 6:4-5). He also encouraged the Corinthians to inspect their motives before taking the Lord's Supper, so they could make sure to take it with the proper frame of mind: "Let a man examine himself, and so let him eat of the bread and drink of the cup. For he who eats and drinks, eats and drinks judgment to himself, if he does not judge the body rightly. For this reason many among you are weak and sick, and a number sleep. But if we judged ourselves rightly, we should not be judged" (1 Cor 11:28-31). And Paul later advocated self-examination to determine the reality of one's salvation, "Test yourselves to see if you are in the faith; examine yourselves! Or do you not recognize this about yourselves, that Jesus Christ is in you—unless you fail the test?" (2 Cor 13:5). Perhaps this activity contributed to what may be a development in his own self-awareness over the course of his life. Toward the beginning of his writing ministry he humbly referred to himself as "the least of the apostles" (1 Cor 15:9), but later as "the very least of all saints" (Eph 5:8) and toward the end of his life as "the chief of sinners" (1 Tim 1:15).

Some General Considerations Regarding Self-Examination

Self-examination is a biblical mandate. But before developing a Christian approach to the subject, we will conduct a critical survey of some of the research that has been done in this area, mostly by secularists. We will begin with a comparison between three closely related terms.

The relation between self-examination, self-awareness and transparency. Self-examination has two prerequisites: self-awareness and transparency. Self-awareness has been termed "self-focused attention" (Carver, 2003). Most basically, self-awareness is the consciousness that one exists, but it really includes an awareness of any aspect of oneself. So self-awareness is a cognitive state concerned with self-knowledge (Carver, 2003; Ferrari & Sternberg, 1998a; Lewis & Brooks-Gunn, 1979; Stern, 1985). But self-awareness is a graduated variable; it exists in degrees. Transparency (as understood by Kierkegaard, 1849/1946b, p. 132) is a certain kind of *high-quality* self-awareness. Higher primate adults and two-year-old humans have a degree of self-awareness, but transparency is a trait of which only adult humans are capable. It is a conscious, deliberate *openness* that entails some measure of self-acceptance—for Christians, self-acceptance in Christ. Therefore, transparency has ethical and spiritual implications lacking in primate self-awareness. Transparency is a virtuous state of mind: a "psychological mindedness," an openness to one's inward gaze and a willingness to engage in self-examination.

Self-examination, in contrast, is a task, an intentional, internal activity of the soul. Whereas transparency is a *quality* of a personal agent—the capacity or readiness to be self-aware—self-examination is a *function* of the personal agent, an *action* in which a personal agent engages (see Carver, 2003; Harter, 1999). So, self-awareness, transparency and self-examination are interrelated. In order to engage in self-examination, one must already be a certain kind of person—one who has some degree of self-awareness known as transparency, and the greater the transparency, the more willing one will be to engage in self-examination. Honest self-examination leads to greater self-awareness and ideally more transparency, and so the spiral goes. Christian soul care promotes self-examination to enhance self-awareness and transparency, in order to become more authentic, that is, more like Christ.

The value of self-examination to soul care and healing. One does not find the term *self-examination* in modern psychological literature. However, there is a family of related concepts that overlap with it (e.g., self-awareness). Of particular interest is research regarding the value of this family of concepts to soul care. In a review of fifty years of process-outcome research on psychotherapy and counseling, Orlinsky, Ronnestad and Willutzki (2004) examined what they called *participant self-relatedness*, which they define as "the reflexive aspect of the individual's experience while engaging in activities and relationships, an aspect that is recognized more clearly in terms such as self-awareness, self-control, and self-esteem" (p. 319). By "self-awareness," they mean the client's experience and reaction to varying levels of internal arousal, and their perception and construal of their own moods, desires and intentions; and they define "positive self-relatedness," as "openness, centeredness, and psychological mindedness"[1] (p. 319; see also Clarkin & Levy, 2004). The authors note that such variables are positively correlated with healthy soul-care outcomes. They also cite literature that found moderate to strong positive therapy outcomes for some interventions that promote self-examination (questioning, reflection/feedback, interpretation), as well as moderate to equivocal positive outcomes for other related interventions (addressing "patient" affect, evocative exploration and "patient" self-exploration). Clarkin and Levy (2004) note the generally positive benefits to therapy of client ego strength (which they define as "personality assets that enable an individual to tolerate and overcome his or her anxieties and to acquire new, more adequate defenses," p. 207). Some degree of ego strength is very likely a component of what in this book is termed *transparency.*

In research on the general characteristics of effective psychotherapy and counseling over time, Prochaska and Norcross (1994) and Prochaska (1995) found that some activities that promote what we are calling self-examination (and transparency) lead to better therapeutic outcomes, including *consciousness raising* (offering observations, confrontations and interpretations) and *self-reevaluation* (promoting self-awareness and reflection upon one's affect, cognition, relationships and values). Furthermore, they note that these features are most evident in the earlier stages of therapeutic change, those they label *precontemplation* (when the person is unaware of any problems), *contemplation* (when the person is aware a problem exists but does not yet do anything about it) and *preparation* (when the person forms an intention to change and some effort is directed at getting ready to change). Working on a different research agenda, Pennebaker (1997) and Niederhoffer and Pennebaker (2002) have reported that expressing one's emotions due to trauma is related to improved immune function and positive behavioral effects (like higher grades and increased job offers). They speculate that this may be due to the benefits of releasing inhibited thoughts and feelings, organizing one's thoughts, finding meaning in the trauma and building on one's social networks through sharing.

So research on secular soul care has found that greater self-awareness, particularly in the early stages of change, enhances the therapy prognosis. We cannot, of course, simplistically generalize these findings to Christian soul-care outcomes directly, because of the significant differences in the two edification frameworks. To give just one example, one might suppose that the resources of the gospel would make Christians more willing and able to engage in self-exploration than secular therapy that relies on self-forgiveness. Unfortunately, very little research has been done on explicitly Christian therapy, let alone outcome studies on specific components. Until such work is done, the best we can do is study research on secular therapy, and unless there are good reasons to believe that variables relating to the Christian faith would substantially alter the results, consider that research to provide evidence that is likely to be more or less analogous to conditions within the Christian community. In the present case the extant research would seem to offer empirical support for the value of self-examination in Christian soul care.

The problem of rumination. Mention should also be made of "private self-consciousness," that is, the tendency individuals have to reflect on internal aspects of the self (Leary, 2002). Private self-consciousness can be found in two forms: *reflective* self-consciousness, which is motivated by curiosity, and *ruminative* self-consciousness, which is motivated by negative feeling-states. The former would seem to be a highly desirable trait for people in counseling, but the latter form (which could also be called self-preoccupation) is seriously debilitating. Ruminative self-consciousness is a "'neurotic' form of self-awareness that involves unnecessarily dwelling on past or future events or self-evaluations" (Leary, 2002, p. 137). It is related to increased negative affect, like sadness (as in depression), and fear or worry (as in anxiety). Such preoccupation gets in the way of healthy relationships—for example, individuals engaged in rumination are so focused on themselves that they are hampered in their ability to listen to and empathize with others. Furthermore, rumination disrupts human action, because it reduces one's available mental resources (Leary, 2002).

This research documents the common-sense observation that self-examination can be excessive and counterproductive. It should also remind Christians of the dangers of focusing on sin, the law and obedience in a way that compromises soul healing—something to which Paul alluded (Rom 7; 2 Cor 3) and was a common problem in the Puritan era. "We ought to abstain from too much feeding our thoughts upon our corruptions in case of discouragement, which at other times is very necessary" (Sibbes, 1973, p. 150). One's awareness of one's sin can be used by the devil (the "Accuser") to overwhelm one's capacity to process it—particularly if one has not grasped the gospel at a depth that corresponds to one's experienced shame. In such cases, the soul-care provider should direct the counselees' attention to their "positive" gifts from God—especially God's declarative salvation, as well as creation gifts. And persons who do not respond well to such counsel may be helped with medication that undermines obsessive ideation.

The development of self-examination. There is abundant evidence that the capacity to examine one's inner world is a function of brain development. It is now well documented that self-awareness occurs in the frontal cortex (Banfield, Wyland, MacRae, Munte & Heatherton, 2004; Carver, 2003; Craik, Moroz, Moscovitch, Stuss, Winocur, Tulving & Kapur, 2002; Kihlstrom, Beer & Klein, 2003; Ochsner & Gross, 2004; Siegel, 1999). The fundamental reason such awareness is uncommon until early adulthood is because the requisite brain regions have not reached their fullest maturation until then.

Metacognition, emotion regulation and action regulation all entail the ability to reflect on one's internal world (cognition, emotion and volition, respectively), a capacity that develops throughout childhood, adolescence and into adulthood (Ferrari & Sternberg, 1998b; Moshman, 1998). As with all higher-order thinking, people with lower intelligence have difficulties engaging in such self-reflection. As a result, if one has below average intelligence, self-examination will be correspondingly hindered, and in some cases, it never develops at all. Therefore, soul-care providers must be mindful of the cognitive capacities of those with whom they work, particularly if there are other signs of limited intelligence. This may help explain why people of higher intelligence in general seem to benefit more from psychotherapy.

At the same time, none of this should be interpreted as undermining the work of the Holy Spirit in Christian self-examination. Every good thing—including healthy self-awareness—is a gift of God, and self-awareness that leads to greater communion with the triune God is strictly a fruit of redemption. However, though he does not have to, God typically works by means of the created capacities of his creatures, so it is appropriate for us to recognize the relative limitations of and seek to foster those capacities.

Specifically Christian Considerations Regarding Self-Examination.

We turn next to examine some of the distinctives of a Christian model of self-examination.

God, others and self-examination. We have already noted that the three-dimensional, dialogical-personal universe assumed in a Christian worldview leads to a different understanding of self-knowledge (Calvin, 1559/1960). Christian self-examination is done *before God* and with reference to Christ. It is God-centered and therefore involves a sort of prayerful self-awareness. "Only by being before God can one totally come to oneself in the transparency of soberness" (Kierkegaard, 1875/1990, p. 106). And Christians ought not to examine themselves apart from Christ and his work of redemption; this is really what makes Christian self-examination possible (see more on this below).

However, Christian self-examination is also necessarily social. To begin with, it is aided by the expertise of others. "A plan in the heart of a man is like deep water, but a man of understanding draws it out" (Prov 20:5). When working with a wise soul-care provider, through questions, directions, teaching and support, the individual is being "scaffolded" or apprenticed in self-examination (see Rogoff, 1990, on the social facilitation of psychological activities). Moreover, our openness with images of God is also a sign of our openness with God. "Confess your sins to one another, and pray for one another so that you may be healed" (Jas 5:16). People ought not to share indiscriminately, but they are deceiving themselves if they think they are being honest with God when they are unwilling to share their secrets with a trustworthy friend or spiritual guide. Journeys are always improved when traveling with a friend.

Dialogue with another provides a mirror for the soul. That is because individual humans are fundamentally co-beings—self-other constellations (Holquist, 1990). In dialogue humans are neither submerged in nor autonomous from others but are interactively moving toward interpersonal communion. As a result, according to Bakhtin (1981), self-understanding is inevitably furthered through dialogue. At the very least, the other sees things about myself that I cannot see, things which can be shared in conversation (Holquist, 1990; Morson & Emerson, 1990). Even the facial expressions of the other—anxiety, hurt or anger—tell me something about myself (particularly as it activates my own similar feelings). But even more profoundly, the individual experiences him or herself uniquely in dialogue and in the presence of others, so that the individual engaged in self-examination will generally want to be listening inwardly, when conversing with others. Such an understanding is not, of course, exclusively Christian. But genuine dialogue is a model of trinitarian communion.

Self-examination through the lense of redemptive-historical analysis. We noted in the previous chapter that sin and the fruit of redemption have tended to be the primary concerns of inwardness in the Christian tradition. These interests sharply distinguish Christian self-awareness from modern and are a proper reflection of the Bible's orienteering influence. As the Word of God is received, it promotes in healthy, holy Christians a growing awareness of their own fallenness (see Berkouwer, 1952a). Furthermore, the Holy Spirit came to *convict* the world of sin, righteousness and judgment (Jn 16:5-7). Being indwelt by the Holy Spirit, Christians should be the *most* convicted. One would not expect modernity to advance such an agenda, and Christian counselors who are uncomfortable with focusing on sin in their soul-work ought to question whether they are reflecting more the values of modernity or of Christianity.

Looking for sin. Scripture pervasively directs the Christian's attention to the evidence without and within the insidious influence of indwelling sin. A major divine perlocutionary agenda of Scripture appears to be the believers' identification of their own sin and its effects. The biblical narratives report various kinds of sins through the context of someone's story, often demonstrating the divine displeasure against sin (e.g., Gen 6:6-7) and the punishing consequences for the individual or community (e.g., Gen 19:23-29) to underscore the seriousness of the sin. The Torah provides a detailed covenantal-legal framework for identifying sins (e.g., in Lev) (as well as ritual uncleanness). The book of Proverbs is filled with brief descriptions of problematic patterns of vice and their outcomes, and the prophets denounce various categories of sin and indict humans as hopelessly sinful (e.g., Jer 13:23). The Gospel narratives offer a novel and more complex approach to sin (though anticipated in the Old Testament) by emphasizing the sinfulness of the sins of the heart and showing (through the actions of the scribes and Pharisees) that religious hypocrisy is the worst kind of sin. Many classes of sins are also highlighted in the apostolic epistles (Rom 1:28-31; Gal 5:19-21; 2 Tim 3:2-5), but perhaps the most important theme on this subject is the primarily Pauline notion that sins are the expression of *sin* (Rom 7:8-17, called indwelling or remaining sin by the Puritans) or the flesh (Gal 5:17-21), an underlying condition of spiritual death (Eph 2:1) and resistance to God (Rom 8:7).

In light of this teaching, Christians are to be characterized by *watchfulness*. "Above all else, guard your heart, for it is the wellspring of life" (Prov 4:23). "Be of sober spirit, be on the alert. Your adversary, the devil, prowls about like a roaring lion, seeking someone to devour" (1 Pet 5:8). "Brothers, if someone is caught in a sin, you who are spiritual should restore him gently. But watch yourself, or you may also be tempted" (Gal 6:1; see also 1 Tim 4:16).

Scripture trains readers to engage in self-examination primarily to identify sin. Christians are called to a never-ending search for evidence of its influence. Sins are important ultimately because they are signs of sin. The easiest to recognize are one's sinful deeds, but the general thrust of Scripture moves the reader inward, so one is also drawn to discriminate one's sinful thoughts. Of special importance is the degree to which one agentically perseveres in such thoughts. However, because emotions signify one's values, they are particularly informative regarding one's remaining sin. For example, Christians ought to listen to their hearts for emotions that are contrary to what Christ would feel (e.g., a cherishing of some desired sin or sorrow at another's success), or a lack of emotion where it should be present (e.g., no compassion for someone who is suffering). According to Owen (1967, Vol. 6, pp. 188-202), the strength of one's indwelling sin can wax and wane, and he believed that Christians should be able to distinguish periods of spiritual carelessness from vigor based on the felt liveliness of sin in its resistance to God's purposes.

The self-deceptive quality of sin makes it particularly difficult to identify (Jer 17:9; Rom 7:11). "Everyone who does evil hates the light" (Jn 3:20), including Christians, to some extent, because of remaining sin. Given sin's tendency to hide itself, Christians can never conclude that they are free of self-deception. Consequently, sometimes evidence of its influence must be sought indirectly. For example, a weakening of one's interest in devotions and worship is often a valid sign of spiritual declension. "What a man is in secret, in these private duties, that he is in the eyes of God and no more" (Owen, 1967, Vol. 6, p. 300).

Perhaps the most important preventative to sin is to be on guard for *temptation.* "Each one is tempted when he is carried away and enticed by his own lust. Then when lust has conceived, it gives birth to sin; and when sin is accomplished, it brings forth death" (Jas 1:14). This suggests that temptation includes a state of soul *prior* to actually sinning: a subjective arousal of one's indwelling sin alone is not itself sin. The key to avoiding sin, then, is to be aware of when temptation is occuring and to resist it. One of the most thorough treatments of this subject is Thomas Brooks's (1980, Vol. 1) *Precious Remedies for Satan's Devices,* which includes hundreds of Christian therapeutic strategies (remedies) for identifying and resisting temptation. Vigilance regarding the identification of sin is fostered by a sense of its vileness (Owen, 1967, Vol. 6, p. 227; Venning, 1965) combined with a humility for one's sinfulness and peculiar vulnerabilities, awareness that can lead to depression in some but can be kept in check by a greater sense of one's adoption and righteousness in Christ.

Sin and redemption. As important as the hunt for sin is, there are good, biblical reasons to question whether the traditional exclusive concentration upon sin in self-examination was reflective enough of a redemptive-historical model of human nature derived from Scripture. The prophets have an important role to play in the canon, but the whole counsel of God cannot be reduced to their emphases. The New Testament, for example, reveals that Christ and his redemption are more important than sin. He overruled sin through the cross (Rom 5:20; Col 1:20; 2:14), and the believer's self-examination ought to reflect that priority. At the very least, this means that believers should spend far more time overall meditating on the redemptive work of Christ on their behalf than on their sin. Reflecting such sentiments, the Scottish pastor Robert Murray McCheyne reportedly told his parishioners that Christians should look upon Christ a hundred times for every one time they looked upon their sin.

The fact is, one cannot properly understand sin apart from redemption, and *in the light of grace.* This is the case, first, because our own sin cannot properly be identified on its own terms, irrespective of Christ, but only from the standpoint of the cross. Only there can one's sin be recognized as the scandal it is, and only then, in the light of God's forgiveness, can one dare to look on it (relationally) with a deep sense of one's culpability (Barth, 1956; Bonhoeffer, 1955). Second, a repentant believer's sin has already been nailed to the cross, so faith requires that it not be viewed "abstracted" from the cross. To view such sin "on its own" would be to view it as an unbeliever. And third, because of union with Christ, the believer now shares in Christ's holiness and righteousness (Purves, 2004). Reflecting this sensibility, Bunyan (1977) argued that believers should only pray with a conscience self-consciously cleansed by the blood of Christ. "The scripture calls upon us to take heed that we neglect not thus to prepare ourselves" in this way for worship (Vol. 2, p. 659). Bunyan advocated an *evangelical* or *gospel* form of self-examination, so that both sin and redemption were factored into the believer's self-awareness.

Consider the apostle Paul. Though he was extremely negative in his own self-assessment (calling himself a "wretched man," Rom 7:24, and "the foremost" of sinners, 1 Tim 1:15), he did not advocate dwelling on one's failings. Rather, "whatever is true, whatever is honorable, whatever is right, whatever is pure, whatever is lovely, whatever is of good repute, if there is any excellence and if anything worthy of praise, let your mind dwell on these things" (Phil 4:8). Throughout his writings, his own negative self-appraisal (as a sinner before God) was more than compensated for by the pervasive extent to which his new status in Christ permeated his self-understanding. "Where sin increased, grace abounded all the more" (Rom 5:20). Perhaps the apostle Paul is placed before us in the New Testament as the archetypal, postresurrection sinner-believer, even in the weight of redemption over sin in his self-understanding.

And what about creation? The Bible refers explicitly to sin and redemption far more than to creation. But that does not mean that the creation is unimportant or that it is unrelated to the believer's self-examination. The creation, after all, opens the Bible and provides the primordial backdrop to the rest of the biblical narrative. And the creation belongs to the Creator, so it must be honored as such. Moreover, sin does not destroy the human creation. Consequently, Christians are entitled and perhaps obligated to take some interest in creaturely aspects of themselves, including those that are relevant to soul care, like brain physiology, human development, relationships, cognitive and emotional structures, and so on. Christian self-examination—shaped by a redemptive-historical model—ought to do justice to the created aspects of one's interior world.

We have already noted Paul's teaching that created goodness is sanctified (or transposed) by the word of God and prayer and is to be received by God's people with gratitude (1 Tim 4:1-4). What does this mean for self-examination? To begin with, Christians ought to recognize and rejoice in their own created internal dynamics with gratitude. Theocentric, affirmative self-awareness promotes gratitude and can be an aspect of worship, which is also encouraging to the soul. And without much personal recognition of God's created goodness toward oneself, it is difficult to comprehend God's goodness toward oneself in the gospel. Helping believers, through self-examination, to consent *in Christ* to the good created gifts with which God has differentially endowed them is a foundational Christian soul-care strategy. Non-Christians also ought to be encouraged to see God's kindness as evidence of his interest in them, meant to lead them to repentance (Rom 2:4).

And what about when the creation is broken? Christians ought to focus more on redemption than on sin and also consider regularly their created goodness. Yet Christiformity entails that self-examination be directed at what is wrong and deficient, and not just what is already right and good. In addition to sin, attention must also be paid to broken or damaged *creational dynamic structures*, aspects of the individual within the biological and psychosocial spheres that have been corrupted by the Fall. Consequently, to facilitate the most comprehensive soul healing possible, Christian self-examination should also take into account things like traumatic memories, faulty reasoning processes and false beliefs, defense mechanisms, inappropriate affect, inaccurate self- and other-representations, the reactions of others and so on.

To be most reflective of God's understanding and most productive, Christian self-examination is conducted within a redemptive-historical framework. Only a model with these multiple perspectives can provide the comprehensive framework for self-examination we need: one that can do justice to the complexity of the Christian's behavior and interior world.

Self-examination and the role of appraisal. Though the point has not been made yet, self-examination involves more than a cognitive process of learning that leads to self-knowledge. It also necessarily involves *self-appraisal*. According to a redemptive-historical model, judgments must be made regarding the goodness or badness of what one finds within. As Sibbes (1973) suggests, "Let us sift our actions, and our passions, and see what is flesh in them, and what is spirit, and so separate the precious from the vile" (p. 165). When one examines oneself, many different phenomena are uncovered that must be discriminated and contrasted. As we just noted, by far the most important distinction is the differentiation between, on the one hand, those structural dynamics that are a function of God's work in creation and redemption—which are good and so are manifestations of God's glory—and, on the other hand, those structural dynamics which are a function of sin (indwelling and personal), as well as those that are damaged—which compromise or inhibit the manifestation of God's glory.

Then, further discriminations must be made within these two basic categories of pure goods from God and bad aspects of oneself. Within the former, Christians ought to discriminate between created and redeemed structural dynamics, because while both are good, the fruits of redemption are more important, because they are effected directly by Christ's life, death and resurrection, which manifest God's glory more than anything else, including the creation.

The second category is more complex. Sin has to be reckoned a pure evil (Chisholm, 1986), individual humans are held responsible by God for their sin, and it must be handled in a distinctive way (confession and repentance). Damaged creational structural dynamics, in contrast, are a mixed evil, since they themselves are creations of God (e.g., impaired reasoning abilities or distorted emotional responses), and unless the damage results from one's personal sin, individual humans are not held responsible for it. The structures themselves are a kind of "weakness" (see 2 Cor 12:9-10), not sin, and so must be handled differently (acceptance, perhaps boasting in them, but also remediating them to the extent one can) (Johnson, 1987). A diagram of these four categories can be found in figure 14.1.

	Good, Desirable	Bad, Undesirable
Structural Features	Creational	Damaged Creational
Directional Dynamics	Redemptive	Sinful

Figure 14.1. Internal structural dynamics

Blurring the lines between these four categories is a common dilemma in everyday Christian experience, but it can lead to serious problems in one's self-understanding and in attempts to bring about healing. For example, one can judge something sinful that is actually creational (like marital sexual expression), or one can assess something that is actually sinful to be redemptive (like hatred for gay people).

In summary, self-examination has both a cognitive and an evaluative component. It involves self-awareness and leads to greater self-knowledge, but it also entails appraisal. Self-examination involves distinguishing creational and redemptive structural dynamics within (which are to be received with thanksgiving and gratitude, and fostered and increased), as well as fallen structural dynamics that are a function either of indwelling or personal sin (which are to be confessed, repented of and resisted) or damaged creational structures (which are to be accepted before they can be remediated as much as possible). All require some kind of reception or ownership.

Specific Psychological Foci for Self-Examination

We turn next to consider some of the psychological dynamic structures to which self-examination can be directed within the redemptive-historical framework presented above. Because modern psychology has conducted a tremendous amount of research into related topics, a careful interpretation of that literature can enable the development of a contemporary Christian understanding of one's internal "world" that is more comprehensive than that of earlier advocates of self-examination in the Christian tradition. Our discussion here will be limited to some of the types of internal phenomena most relevant to Christian maturation and soul care.

Awareness of God. The most important focus for self-examination is one's awareness of God. As the psalmist and the author of Job noted, and as the great saints down through the ages have attested, this sense ebbs and flows, even in the experience of mature believers. The Reformed tradition in the seventeenth century called times of God's felt absence "spiritual desertion" (Lewis, 1975; Voetius & Hoornbeeck, 2003). Though God is always present ontologically and covenantally to believers, they do not always experience his presence. Having the felt sense of his presence is a source of great consolation to believers and a fundamental means of Christian soul healing. However, it cannot be the basis of their faith. In fact, his perceived absence weans believers from looking primarily to their emotions for solace to look to Christ and his word. There is one thing worse than his perceived absence: not noticing when he is absent.

In addition, as a result of prior experiences of other humans and God, people have formed a "God-image," a mental representation of God that may not correspond accurately to the God of the Bible, especially if they were exposed to grossly distorted image-bearers earlier in life. Becoming aware of the distortions in one's "God-image" is instrumental to reconstructing it according to scriptural revelation (and godly Christians).

Awareness of self-regulation. Mature humans are able to regulate their internal world—their thoughts, feelings and actions. Here we discuss the examination of one's self-regulation.

Metacognition. Metacognition encompasses an awareness of one's mental system and its processing. One aspect of metacognition is knowing what one knows. Some forms of psychopathology (like depression or anxiety) are related to a deficient understanding of reality. There are countless beliefs which people hold that contribute to their internal struggles. Christians are hampered by an inadequate grasp of relevant scriptural truths, for example, regarding God's nature, Christ's work, the gospel and the benefits of union with Christ. Thinking that one's current understanding is accurate or sufficient when it is not can therefore be an impediment to appropriating the remedy one needs. Self-examination can therefore be directed to one's knowledge base and its validity.

Of special importance is one's set of self-representations and self-evaluations (affectively charged self-representations; see Harter, 1999), including how they may differ from or correspond to reality (i.e., God's view of things). Areas to focus on here include an exploration of one's thinking and feelings about oneself (e.g., presence of logical contradictions in one's beliefs, faulty arguments or poor evidence, like "I never do anything right"), self-beliefs (including false beliefs like family myths, inaccurate self-perceptions and attributions), levels of self-esteem and orientation to future events (e.g., optimistic or pessimistic, including the tendency to ignore God in either case). Specifically Christian self-examination in this area also includes the development of a complex redemptive-historical self, with a highly differentiated creation-fall-redemption self-conception.

Attention can also be directed to one's ongoing internal dialogue (Cozolino, 2001). Humans are always engaging in self-talk that is typically habitual and serves to maintain current values and tendencies. Therapy usually requires examining the ongoing conversations one is having with oneself.

Emotion awareness. "Self-knowledge and the individual's inner life are characterized most saliently by emotional experiences" (Salovey, Bedell, Detweiler & Mayer, 2000). As we have noted, emotions are signs of subjective reality, particularly one's perceptions of values, significance and love, an indicator of aspects of one's story and one's current heart-orientation. Self-examination must be especially attuned to emotion signs of ethical and spiritual brokenness and alienation, like shame and guilt.

Alexithymia is a constellation of symptoms that includes the inability to identify feelings, limited imaginal processes and a cognitive style focused on the environment (Taylor & Bagby, 2000), and it hampers therapy (Parker, 2000). Working with people with alexithymia involves helping them mentally represent and verbalize their emotions and emotion-states more successfully. While alexithymia may be an unusually severe deficit, mere *affect phobia* is ubiquitous (McCullough, Kuhn, Andrews, Kaplan, Wolf & Hurley, 2003), so worthwhile Christian soul care will usually involve helping others to explore their emotions.

Awareness of action regulation. Closely related to one's self-representations are the cognitive-volitional dynamics that shape human action, referred to as action regulation processes. These include such activities as self-monitoring; management of internal conflict between competing goals, desires, strivings or motives; self-punishment or self-reward; sense or awareness of the Holy Spirit's action enablement; resource allocation; cognitive reappraisal; the boosting of self-regulatory strength (or willpower) through reflection and meditation on spiritual truth; defensive activity; strategy activation, or the absence of any of the above (see Baumeister & Vohs, 2004, and Heckhausen & Dweck, 1998, for secular discussions of these kind of phenomena).

Action regulation is of great importance to psychospiritual growth, since it is involved in changing one's internal world. Action regulation involves something like the following sequence: (1) examining some current aspect of the self; (2) comparing it to some standard—whether a personal, social or divine standard; (3) if a discrepancy is found between the standard and the present state, taking action to bring about a desired change (there may, of course, be different and multiple actions taken, depending on the goal); (4) making additional comparisons of the present state to the standard until the desired state is achieved (Carver & Scheier, 1981; Carver, 2003; Duval & Wicklund, 1972; Leary, 2002; Miller, Pribram & Galanter, 1960). The internalization of self-regulation skills will be discussed in chapter sixteen.

Awareness of one's interpretations of one's past and present. One can also focus on how one's internal dynamics are related to one's story and one's earlier relationships. In addition, one can reflect on one's memories of significant events and one's actions in the past, and examine one's past interpretations of those events and actions, and how those interpretations square with God's perceptions of them, as best as one can now discern. In the same way, one can reflect on one's interpretations of one's current life-space (including thoughts, goals, relationships, vocation and events in one's life) and assess whether they correspond to God's understanding of the same.

The problem of self-deception. As mentioned above, a profound hindrance to self-examination is the tendency humans have to engage in self-deception (what Freud called "defense mechanisms"; see discussion in Johnson & Burroughs, 2000; McCullough, Kuhn, Andrews, Kaplan, Wolf & Hurley, 2003; Vaillant, 1992). It is a truism in the counseling field that among people who come in for counseling (to say nothing of those who avoid therapy but could benefit from it), many are characterized by a degree of resistance to self-examination and gaining insight into their underlying dynamics (Egan, 2002; Fromm-Reichmann, 1960; Clarkin & Levy, 2004; Schneider, 1998). As we have already noted, the Scriptures taught long ago that the human heart is prone to self-deception (Jer 17:9). Because of sin and the created desires to be perfect and avoid pain, humans resist self-knowledge that might put them in a bad light and cause painful feelings of embarrassment, guilt or shame. This is particularly the case if in childhood they were exposed to environments that chronically activated such feelings. Since this general tendency is so pervasive among humans, soul-care providers must factor its existence into their ongoing dealings with those they seek to help, and they must learn how to work with this dynamic, rather than against it, to be of the most help. Timing is everything in soul care, and it is usually the case that such resistance is more easily addressed after some degree of trust has been formed between counselor and counselee. A large proportion of a person's soul struggles are usually being maintained by unconscious defensive activity (McCullough, Kuhn, Andrews, Kaplan, Wolf & Hurley, 2003), so that as one's defenses are softened and transparency grows, the individual is able to work much more effectively on internal and relational conflict. Not only do the defenses hinder self-examination, they are usually a part of the psychopathology that Christian soul care seeks to deconstruct. As the Christian soul is healed, Christians learn how to rely more and more on God to be the "defense of [their] life" (Ps 27:1).

An example of therapeutic self-examination. Let us consider an example of Christian counseling that promoted self-examination. As we come across illustrations of self-examination topics that we have discussed, they will be identified in parentheses. Joan came to me for counseling with a serious concern. She told me that she was a Christian who had been reasonably happily married for twenty-five years and had two grown children. She also indicated that she had been working in the same department with a person of the opposite sex for the past three years on a series of projects. They had always gotten along well, but over the previous few months, he had begun paying her special interest (e.g., sending her e-mail love notes and chatting with her during breaks and lunch times), and she had been shocked at her response. She began to weep with me and admitted to having strong feelings of attraction toward this man and thinking about him throughout her workday. And sometimes, when she was at home, she indulged in sexual fantasies that she afterward regretted. She stated that she really did not want to become involved with this man. She had come in for counseling because she wanted to overcome her feelings for him and figure out how best to deal with the situation.

We should note first that it was Joan's self-awareness that led her to come in for counseling. She was aware of her unwanted emotions of attraction and desire, which she recognized were inappropriate and sinful (an example of self-appraisal, based on redemptive-historical self-analysis). She knew that these desires were fallen and had to be resisted, rather than cultivated.

What did her feelings signify? First, that she was a sinner. Such an awareness is actually a good thing; it is a fresh reminder that we are *still* sinners, and sometimes Christians forget this (through self-deception). The strength of her current desires may also have been a sign that she had been too distant from God as of late, and her covenant commitment to God had been unconsciously wavering. She needed to confess this gradual pulling away and what amounted to her idolatry of this other man (God awareness).

At the same time, by her own admission, she realized in a new way that she had been less happy in her marriage than she had been aware (emotion awareness). Over the past few years, her husband had taken on new responsibilities and had been spending more time at work than was probably appropriate. As a result, the two of them had been slowly drifting apart and had lost the intimacy that had characterized the earlier years of their marriage. Humans are created with needs for intimate communion with God and with others. Consequently, her desires for this other man were mixed, from a redemptive-historical standpoint. Underlying her sinful desires for this coworker were good, created desires that flowed from neglected needs that had been activated in these circumstances, indicating that her husband had been neglecting her and that she had been doing nothing about it (and may even point back to deficits in her family of origin). Her good, created desires for interpersonal communion, combined with her indwelling sin, resulted in a sinful misdirection of those good desires. These are not excuses; there are no excuses for sin. But becoming aware of these good, created desires that were supposed to be directed to God and her spouse, that were being thwarted for various reasons, helped her to understand her previously obscure internal dynamics, which in turn helped her to overcome the fallen direction those desires had taken and encouraged her to more vigorously redirect them to her spouse and especially to her God (all this involved some fairly complex redemptive-historical self-analysis).

At the same time, Joan had been experiencing a contrary set of emotions—desires to resist this temptation—that were a function of her good, created conscience, coupled with the Holy Spirit's power, motivating her to resist and overturn her sin. This arrested the sinful direction she had been toying with. Her self-examination also recognized God's goodness from creation and redemption working within her (self-appraisal), and part of her soul-work involved strengthening these realizations. Also, as she worked out her repentance, she needed to receive Christ's cleansing forgiveness and learn afresh how to rest in the gospel of his grace.

Joan was a dedicated counselee and engaged in ongoing, intentional self-reflection, promoted by her journaling, and she became aware of how some of her past actions had subtly communicated to her coworker that she was open to being pursued. In fact, she realized that her earlier unwillingness to clearly confront his behavior must have contributed to his pursuit (awareness of self-deception; action regulation awareness). She also came to appreciate that ever since her kids had left home, she had been feeling lonely and neglected by her very busy husband, and even somewhat angry about her situation (awareness of self-representations and self-evaluations; interpretations of her story; emotion awareness). And she realized that when she was daydreaming about this man, she was not managing her thought life but was passively allowing her sinful desires to "take over her mind" (awareness of a lack of proper metacognition and action regulation).

This is not the place to talk about the content of her therapy. We note here just that the wisdom she gained through her self-examination contributed significantly to her repentance and recovery. To fully understand almost any serious soul struggle or type of psychopathology will usually require examining various facets of one's inner life and evaluating them from the standpoint of the three perspectives of the redemptive-historical metanarrative.

Conclusion

Dialogue is central to the work of self-examination: "Why are you downcast, O my soul?" (Ps 42:5). While a primitive self-awareness is possible, even for the great apes (Povinelli & Prince, 1998), complex self-understanding requires the power and capacity to articulate that internal phenomena to oneself. Language gives us tools for identifying, and also for objectifying, that which is within, helping us to clarify and specify what we sense darkly and intuitively. One reason soul care helps individuals grow is because the provider asks questions, puts into new words, clarifies and in other ways assists the counselee in articulating internal structural dynamics that were previously unacknowledged. Prayerful self-examination with Scripture promotes soul-searching dialogue with the triune God.

If the Christian tradition is correct, self-examination goes hand-in-hand with coming to know God and experience him more fully. And if research over the past one hundred years is correct—and if we are properly interpreting it—our relations and experiences of others are profoundly interrelated with our experience of God and our ability to self-examine. A significant part of Christlikeness includes growth in all three interpersonal dimensions. In the next chapter, we consider barriers: barriers to self-examination, to the signs of God and to God's glory, and introduce the subject of how to dismantle those barriers.

Notes

[1]Psychological mindedness is a client trait, long recognized as helpful in therapy, that has been defined as "the patient's desire to learn the possible meanings and causes of his internal and external experiences as well as the patient's ability to look inwards to psychical factors rather than only outwards to environmental factors . . . [and] to potentially conceptualize the relationships between thoughts, feelings, and actions" (Silver, 1983, p. 516).

15

Inwardness, Part 2

The Identification and Deconstruction of Barriers

HUMANS WERE CREATED FOR FULFILLMENT IN the triune God and a flourishing human life in community in God's will. However, for many Christians, such fulfillment seems hard to come by, and change is often slow. In this chapter we want to discuss the second aspect of inwardness: identifying and removing different types of blockage to a fulfilling life in God.

Humans are sinners who have grown up in a fallen world. As a result, everyone has barriers to activities needed to fulfill our being and calling, barriers to (1) communion with the triune God (addressed in chap. 12), (2) self-examination (chap. 14), (3) the internalization of the signs of God's Word (chap. 16) and (4) a greater participation in and manifestation of God's glory in their lives (chap. 17). In order to express the glory of God better, it is necessary to recognize and repair some of these internal hindrances. In *The Soul's Journey into God*, Bonaventure (1978) advocated getting "the mirror of our soul . . . cleaned and polished" (p. 56). In this chapter, we focus on "cleaning and polishing the mirror" so that we might best reflect more of God's form and splendor.

By contemporary, mainstream standards in psychology and psychiatry, this chapter is controversial, for it offers a *Christian* way of conceptualizing psychopathology. Mainstream attempts at classification of psychopathology are based on strictly naturalistic criteria, such as personal distress, disability in functioning, statistical abnormality, cultural deviance or potential of harm (American Psychiatric Association, 2000). These criteria all have their place, but there are two other considerations of importance to Christians that alter the discussion of psychopathology. First, a Christian orientation will be doxological; it will be guided by considerations of God's glory. From this standpoint, psychopathology is any internal barrier to a person's manifestation of God's glory, and its severity is to be evaluated by this criterion. Second, the Word of God has been posited in this book as the formal cause of the structures of the creation, especially human nature. It follows from this that, from a Christian standpoint, psychopathology ought to be defined as any psychospiritual aberration from the form of the Christ of the canon. This way of thinking draws our attention to barriers that inhibit the reception of the signs of God, particularly his words, as factors that also constitute and are evidence of psychopathology.

People outside the Christian community would not be expected to accept this approach to psychopathology, but for Christians a number of advantages follow. First, it *orients diagnosis and treatment processes away from the self and toward God*, and away from modern autocentric and anthropocentric models toward theocentric models. Second, it is widely acknowledged that the modern functional orientation to diagnosis focuses on publicly verifiable criteria (and there are definite strengths in such an approach—not least of which is the wide agreement on symptomotology that it permits, irrespective of theoretical or religious orientation). But this strength is also its weakness, since such a model cannot do justice to the uniquely human, cultural and spiritual features of psychopathology (a concern illustrated in part by the recent publication of the *Psychodynamic Diagnostic Manual,* PDM Task Force, 2006). A doxological and canonical approach offers a better framework because it *defines abnormality in terms of meaningfulness* (or lack thereof). Third, in contrast to diagnosis that flows from modern individualism, this way of seeing *underscores the relational and dialogical nature of human being*, particularly the nature of humans as fundamentally related to the triune God and to other humans. Fourth, an emphasis on the word of God with reference to psychopathology *highlights the semiodiscursive quality of all psychospiritual disorders and of their remediation.* This helps unify our study of human nature, psychopathology and therapy, and has practical implications that will be explored in the final chapters. And finally, this approach *offers a holistic model of soul care* that can do better justice to all the orders that constitute human beings, in contrast to reductionist models that view psychopathology as strictly biological in nature or, at best, biopsychosocial.

Yet there is no attempt here to develop a classification system that would rival those already in use. Such a project lies far beyond the scope of this chapter and is so daunting that one gets faint at the prospect. But that project too is essential for the Christian soul-care community, if it is to move beyond the naturalistic models of abnormality that currently exercise a monopoly on diagnosis in the West and have captivated much of the Christian thinking on these matters over the past fifty years, and move toward a way of reconceiving psychopathology in ways that comport better with a Christian worldview (a project pushed forward recently by Yarhouse, Butman & McRay, 2005).

The first step in undoing psychopathology is a proper diagnosis. Consequently, the first part of this chapter is essentially an extension of self-examination—what we might call *negative evaluation:* the identification of psychopathological conditions that constitute barriers to conformity to Christ. The second step in undoing psychopathology is actions aimed at its amelioration. In the second part of the chapter we will spend some time considering the deconstruction of those barriers.

Barriers According to the Orders of Discourse

This is a book about signs, particularly the signs of the triune God. However, one of the oldest notions of a sign comes from medicine, where it was applied to the physical symptoms that indicated the existence of an underlying disease (Sebeok, 1994). Physical symptoms are signs of something wrong with the body. The field of psychopathology—the subdiscipline of psychology concerned with disorders of the soul—is likewise concerned with symptoms, and since the founding of modern psychology, a great deal of energy has been spent developing a diagnostic system for identifying psychological (or psychiatric) disorders based on the presence of signs of dysfunction. While many involved in diagnosis and treatment complain about the DSM system (see, e.g., Kihlstrom, 2002; Malik & Beutler, 2002; PDM Task Force, 2006), few doubt that there are identifiable symptoms of psychopathology and, further, that those symptoms are signs of underlying conditions of psychological damage and disorder. In keeping with the multilevel model of human beings presented in chapters ten and eleven, however, we will organize our discussion of psychopathological barriers according to those levels. However, in contrast to the order in which we examined the levels in those chapters—according to their developmental unfolding (from lower to higher)—in this chapter we will consider the levels in order of their psychopathological significance (from higher to lower).

Symptoms of opposition in the spiritual order. It will surprise some to consider just how important psychopathology is in the Bible—it is discussed as early as the third chapter of Genesis. There we learn that the first man and woman became ashamed and hid from God because they were naked, and their distress and desire to hide was a direct result of human disobedience. The Bible identifies shame as the first affective consequence of the fall (Gen 3:7-8), and a sense of shame (or uncleanness) signifies that something is wrong at the core of human beings. Shame is activated when humans feel there is something wrong with them (Tangney & Dearing, 2002), and it will be assumed here that shame is the emotion-sign of spiritual disorder. There are many implications of this account, but surely one of the most important is that humans have been psychologically disordered since this point and have been hiding from God, themselves and one another ever since.

The Bible is an amazingly honest book, all the more remarkable because, though its main theme is the manifestation of God's glory, its major secondary theme would seem to be the persistent resistance of human beings to participate in that glory and fulfill their calling as responsive images of God. Humans now, the Bible makes clear, are born with a strong disposition of opposition to God and his ways. Post-Fall human existence is marked by a usually unconscious defiance of God (Kierkegaard, 1849/1980, p. 93), an implicit unwillingness to truly rest in God and God's will.

We find in the Bible, in fact, a vocabulary of psychopathology. *Sin* is the abnormality word of the discourse of the spiritual order—the order that concerns *ultimacy*—as a result, sin pertains to psychopathology that has reference to ultimacy, that is, to God. Sin is the fundamental movement away from God, the primordial opposition to his nature and ways, the usually unconscious denial of his glory and his supremacy over all things. Given how important God is and is supposed to be to us, sin is the most serious type of psychopathology there is: the worst kind of insanity, the kind to which other, lesser forms of insanity are meant to be analogies. That the human creature opposes the Creator, mostly unconsciously, is its greatest, most tragic psychological abnormality, and the kind with the most serious human consequences, since, unless remedied, it results in everlasting suffering in the age to come. All this, of course, differs considerably from modern notions of psychopathology, where severity has been defined in terms of the devastation of their effects on one's adaptive functioning in this life—another legitimate, but infinitely lesser, criterion, it must be said.

The ultimate criterion is our inner opposition to God's supremacy over all things. Sin is an appalling type of concealment that directly obscures the glory of God (Balthasar, 1982, p. 584). "Sin is contrary to, and set against the glory of God, and all that should or would give glory to him, or has any tendency to do so" (Venning, 1669/1965, p. 35). It essentially denies God's beauty, greatness and worth, and the legitimacy of his authority and supremacy. Because God is gloriously, infinitely meaningful and is supposed to be the center of significance in our lives, the perpetuation of this void by adults is reprehensible. Human sinfulness is an abominable breach in the meaningful fabric of the universe, the active increasing of a kind of mysterious black hole in the evaluative center of human life, the heart—and the human resistance to this teaching is evidence of its truth.

And this form of psychopathology permeates human life. Humans, the Bible says, are conceived in sin and brought forth in iniquity (Ps 51:6). All humans are by nature children of wrath (Eph 2:1) and have fallen short of God's glory (Rom 6:23). There are none who are unaffected by this rebellious void in human beings (Rom 3:10-18), and no region of human nature unaffected.

So humans are born with a psychopathological condition that the Bible calls "sin"—known as "original sin" or "indwelling sin" in the Christian tradition. Out of this alienating void comes truly novel actions—actions that are not a loving response to the word of God but that are "original" in the sense that they are independent of God, that is, they are contrary to his revealed design. These actions are called *sins*, and sins are signs of humanity's inner opposition to God's will known as sin.

The symptom of idolatry. What do humans do about that breach in the spiritual order? They must find something to fill it. They set up "idols in their hearts" (Ezek 14:3; Powlison, 1995a). Idolatry is the putting of anything besides the true God in the place of ultimacy; it is "the first and fundamental sin" (Jenson, 1997, p. 60). As we saw in chapter ten, that which is ultimate in one's life gives a transcendent and unifying sense of purpose, meaning and significance. The idol is that which competes with God in the human heart for supremacy, so it constitutes the clearest symptom of spiritual psychopathology.

There are at least three types of idolatry. *Primitive* idolatry is evident when some aspect of the creation or some product of human activity is made ultimate and is explicitly worshiped, for example, an animal, the sun, a statue or any false construction of God. These idols are easily identified and serve as obvious signs that the worshipers are not followers of the true (and invisible) God. As Berkhof (1979) noted, when the worship of Christ thoroughly permeates a culture, such idols no longer make sense, so they disappear. However, a second kind of idolatry, a "*secular* idolatry," arises from the ashes of the first. We might call it the *latent* worship of anything that is not God. In Christian and post-Christian cultures, in the absence of any legitimate, explicitly religious objects of ultimacy besides for the true God, humans are led by their despair, informally and largely unconsciously, but irresistibly, to a secularized idolatry that renders ultimate some part of nature or human culture, for example, physical beauty, other persons, a car or a stereo, an ideology, or even virtuous activity. The New Testament points in this direction with its identification of greed with idolatry (Col 3:5). Surely the most important idol (particularly in the modern West) is the Self (see Ezek 28:2[1]). This would support the notion that pride is the archetypal sin at the base of all sin (e.g., Barth, 1956), or that original sin is essentially narcissism (L. Conver, personal conversation, September 22, 2004).[2]

A third type of idolatry could be called "*Christian* idolatry." This is seen where elements of the Christian faith come to be taken as ultimate. This is the most difficult form of idolatry for Christians to recognize, because it clings to the trappings of Christian subculture and, in the worst cases, to the very means of grace that foster one's relationship with God. Nonetheless, these means can become unconsciously identified with the Self and subservient to its narcissistic agenda and so take on an idolatrous significance in relation to God. Here, religious activity (e.g., church-going, praying, personal devotions, evangelism), the Bible, Christian doctrine, pride in one's denomination or branch of Christianity, a gift of the Spirit, the type of Christian counseling we do and even the fact of one's salvation can be unconsciously abstracted from God and become paradoxical sources of self-aggrandizement and self-satisfaction. They can make believers feel superior to others and so become, at least in part, the unconscious focus of one's ultimate reliance, paradoxically dissociated from the very God to whom they are supposedly related. "We [can] make an idol of truth itself, for truth apart from charity is not God, but His image and idol, which we must neither love nor worship" (Pascal, 1941, p. 191, no. 581).

It may be hard to believe that otherwise noble means of grace can be so perverted, but nothing demonstrates the power and pervasive influence of the despair of sin—in even the Christian heart—more clearly than Christian idolatry. "Watch out and beware of the leaven of the Pharisees and Sadducees" (Mt 16:6). There is *no* safe haven in this age, even in the church, where human beings can assume that sin is not a danger. On the contrary, Satan will come as an angel of light (2 Cor 11:14) and attempt to turn the best blessings of God against God and ourselves, if it were possible. The search for and destruction of idols is an ongoing task in the Christian journey.

Are there psychological benefits to Christian teaching on sin? Before moving on to psychopathology in the other orders, something should be said about the therapeutic value of the Christian doctrine of sin. Perhaps one of the best evidences of God's greatness is that he can take that which defies his meaningfulness and seeks to undermine all meaning—and render it meaningful. The Word of God became sin (2 Cor 5:21), by which he mysteriously gave sin a kind of meaning. Through the cross, sin becomes "that which is overcome" and past sins are newly defined as "forgiven sins," as their threat to God's glory is overcome and surpassed by that glory (Rom 5:20). God's nature (his power and compassion) is uniquely magnified *precisely* in the face of that which sought to defy it. This is sovereignty par excellence, a novel manifestation of God's beauty. Only a hardened sinner would see in the signs of this beauty an excuse by which he might continue in sin. (Even hell, as the divine, holy response to unrelenting, unrepentant opposition to God, insures that God's glory cannot be ultimately undermined.)

But are there benefits for humans that we could say derive from sin? We must be careful here, for positive answers to this question cannot legitimatize our sin (Rom 6:1-2). But God is *so* good that he can turn our evil into his good to us. For one thing, sin is the great "equalizer." Though some have comparatively more soul damage than others (e.g., those who suffer from schizophrenia), *all* humans fall short of God's glory and deserve hell, so no one is ultimately worse than any other *before God,* for this is the worst form of psychotherapy. Second, coming to terms with our sin through the cross must produce greater depth and humility. In fact, third, only a counseling model that takes human sin as seriously as Christianity does can adequately help people who are overwhelmed with their genuine guilt and shame. They *know* how bad they are and are not helped when others who, in seeking to help, minimize it.

And fourth, our sin rightly handled drives us closer to God and to others. For these reasons, Christian counselors must not overreact to the obsessive focus on sin of fundamentalism and conclude that reference to sin in Christian soul care is counterproductive to human well-being.

But are there psychological costs to Christian teaching on sin? At the same time, Christians must concede that the Christian doctrine of sin has been tragically misused by Christians and sometimes done untold damage. Children have been abused, spouses have been mistreated, and parishioners have been browbeaten by Christians, supposedly to root out sin. It is hard to fathom the horror of hatefully terrorizing a child through continual shaming and beating in order to rid that child of sin—the parent's sin craftily masking itself through projections in the fight against the child's sin. As we realize now, such treatment hurts and damages people and spreads, rather than diminishes, sin (something Jesus may have been alluding to in his reference to those who place stumbling blocks before children, Lk 17:1-2). In fact, severely troubled people are often haunted by excessive and unwarranted shame and guilt they internalized from others (Tangney & Dearing, 2002)—and they often project that *again* onto others. As a result, many have concluded—even some Christian counselors—that the fault is the Christian teaching, and so have abolished sin terminology from their soul care. But rather than run to the opposite, secular extreme, Christian soul-care providers need to learn how to exemplify the *right* handling of sin—gentle and humble, healing and upbuilding; not seeing it where it does not exist, but addressing it in love where it does, and challenging it wisely and appropriately. "Neither do I condemn you," Jesus said. And then, "Go your way. From now on sin no more" (Jn 8:10).

The devil and the demonic. In considering psychopathology within the spiritual order, mention must also be made of the devil and demons who exert a destructive spiritual influence on the human race (Eph 2:1-3), and even on Christians. Demon possession is an awful form of psychopathology that can distort the *imago Dei* almost beyond recognition. Modernism cannot discern such conditions, but they have been well documented by missionaries in the Third World. Exorcism is a soul-care activity that prayerfully uses the name of Christ to free persons held captive to such unholy power. But all humans are affected by the prince of this world, so prayer and guidance regarding this antithetical influence is an important part of routine Christian soul care. While some Christians see a demon everywhere (and terrible harm has also been done by Christians in this area), Christian counselors need spiritual discernment and must be prepared to address the demonic themselves or refer to a wiser, more experienced exorcist when necessary (Amorth, 1999; Bufford, 1988; Montgomery, 1976; Nevius, 1892; Powlison, 1995b).

Resistance in the ethical order. As we noted in chapter ten, there is a close relationship between the spiritual and the ethical orders. This is very evident when considering psychopathology, because disunion with God is reflected in disunion with others and with oneself (Bonhoeffer, 1955). Here we consider the evil that is the *evidence* of indwelling sin. Because of orienting effects (see chap. 11), the psychopathology of the ethical order is properly interpreted as flowing from the psychopathology of the spiritual order.

We also noted before that the emergence of this order is signified by the ripening of a mature conscience, which arises in mid to late adolescence, demonstrating the arisal of personal agency and mature human responsibility. And we saw that the ethical order is grounded on the development of the underlying dynamic structures of the biopsychosocial orders, but its meaningfulness concerns norms that lie beyond the self and that transcend one's biopsychosocial desires, that is, the Law of God or the Good. So it will be suggested that the disorder of this sphere consists of the evil actions of personal agents generally against their neighbor. As a result, the pathological symptoms of this order include a vast array of wrongdoing, usually against others and always against God's will. I am referring here to *sins,* including malevolent violence and abuse (unjustly causing another being pain); inappropriate coercion; hatred, envy and malice; prejudice, judgmentalism and strife; and sexual immorality of all kinds (premarital, extramarital and homosexual); basically the violation of norms, rules and laws that are reflections of the Good, for Christians, the Law of God. Part of God's ethicospiritual agenda in inspiring the Bible was to provide a textual standard by which humans could identify his definitive understanding of the Good.

Focus on the pathology of the ethical order tends to be directed toward evil behaviors, perhaps because they are the easiest to identify. However, evil activity can also be internal (like the fostering of feelings of hatred, resentment or envy). But whether internal or behavioral, if they are practiced over time, they become vices—evil patterns that come to be woven into one's brain and contribute to the formation of evil character. So sins, vices and an evil character are all signs of an inner resistance to the Good—to God's law—an ethical corruption of the soul. Guilt is the emotion-sign of abnormality here, a self-conscious negative emotion that signifies the *doing* of wrong (in contrast to shame, which is a feeling of wrong *being* [Tangney & Dearing, 2002], that according to this model corresponds more to sin in the spiritual order). Evil, wickedness and vice (and their related terms and subcategories) constitute the abnormality terminology of the ethical order of discourse and provide a way of describing the psychopathology of personal agents who resist the Good of God.

The key point here, however, is that personal evil is the accomplishment of personal agents: those who have a sufficiently well-developed human nature that they can be legitimately held accountable for their actions and therefore are capable of wrongdoing. So all normal adults (i.e., those not severely mentally impaired) are indicted in the ethical sphere, just as they are in the spiritual. But whereas all humans are equally sinful by nature—they all fall short of God's glory—there is wide variation between humans regarding their personal evil. It is plain to all that some people are more wicked than others and practice more evil than others.[3]

The symptom of malevolent violence. As suggested above, sins are signs of sin. Sins are important, for they are concrete expressions of one's inner opposition to and alienation from God. The apostle Paul composed lists of sins in a few of his epistles (Rom 1:28-31; 1 Cor 6:9-10; Gal 5:19-21; 2 Tim 3:2-5) to increase awareness of them. But we will focus on only one class of sins here. Perhaps the archetypal evil against humans is malevolent violence, which consists of destructive physical acts that have the intent of harming someone, for example, murder, rape or assault. Violent actions can cause people physical pain, and visible signs like bruises, bumps and lacerations. A lesser category, but in some cases more painful, is psychological or emotional aggression: statements or body language that cause *emotional* pain. An even lesser category of harm—but still damaging—is neglect, in which individuals responsible for caring for others (e.g., children) do not give them adequate care (including nutrition, safety, supervision and guidance, or affection).

The account of the Fall in Genesis 3 is about spiritual psychopathology, whereas the account of Cain and Abel in Genesis 4 helps us understand ethical psychopathology and its relation to the spiritual. In the first place it is clear from the narrative that the murder of Abel was a function of Cain's disturbed relation to and views of God (which we are to understand are somehow derived from and the consequence of the primordial sin of their parents). Second, the aggression was due to Cain's envy and bitterness regarding God's preferential treatment of Abel (which some would say was due to Abel's better understanding of the negative consequences of sin and the offering of a blood sacrifice, as opposed to the less judicially significant offering of the giving back to God of some of his gifts).[4] So Cain slew his brother Abel, cutting short his life, an act which symbolized humanity's disordered ethical nature. Where malevolent violence is found, the *imago Dei* has become falsified. In contrast to the mutually affirming harmony of the Trinity, the aggressive human signifies that there is something deeply wrong in the human heart, and that wrong flows from human autonomy from God.

The relation of the fallen self to the Good. But the ethical is concerned not just with evil but also with knowledge of good (Gen 2—3) that resulted from the primordial disobedience. This knowledge of good and evil is a kind of false ethical pride and suggests that the psychopathology of the ethical order includes (1) some understanding of the word of God (whether Scripture or the law of God written on the heart) and (2) a usurpation of God's goodness, resulting in confidence in *oneself* as the author of one's good, as well as an autonomous arbiter of what is good and evil (Bonhoeffer, 1955). So, because of sin, the ethical order *itself* is now vitiated by a falseness, rendering human understandings of goodness and the Good autocentric and fundamentally flawed.

With help from Kierkegaard, we will reckon that underlying the pathological symptoms of ethical disorder (the practice of wrongdoing)—at the very core of the pathology of this order—are two very different construals of the Good *in relation to oneself:* an "earlier" stage, that one is good in relation to the Good (a distortion of reality for fallen humans and a fruit of sin's self-deception), and a potentially "later" stage, the realization that one has fallen short of the Good (a prerequisite to a Christian passage into the spiritual order).

The earlier thinking begins in adolescence, when the ideal or false self begins to be constructed (Harter, 1999) and where an image of oneself as good, competent and superior is maintained in consciousness and used as a somewhat fictional source of consolation. The ideal or false self is shaped by the internal law of God and social influences, but is created and sustained by the distorting and self-aggrandizing effects of indwelling sin. The earlier thinking is also the primary source of religious dualism: looking merely at the surface or behavior of human beings, it believes some people are basically good (me and those like me), and some others are basically bad (like serial killers and terrorists), so it falls short of the later insight, that all humans are sinful and corrupt. This superficial ethical orientation can be maintained throughout adulthood by defensive activity geared toward protecting one's ideal self and is illustrated, for our benefit, in the Gospels by the Pharisee.

Signs of "the gap." The problem for maturing humans is that one's sense of the Good inevitably leads to the recognition that one has transgressed the boundaries of the Good. Paradoxically, while unity in one's self is being forged through personal agency, one's increasing self-awareness enables one to recognize internal conflicts of many kinds, including conflicts between one's desires and the Good. As one acts on one's desires, a gap arises between one's sense of the Good (and one's ideal self) and the reality of one's actions (see Hare, 2002). To avoid the conclusion that one is a sinner, one's sense of well-being becomes increasingly dependent upon sin-fed, narcissistic illusions, because of the created need to preserve one's identification with the Good.

Normal adults do not develop without *some* awareness of the gap. Depending on one's earlier development, including the models to which one was exposed, there will be more or less evidence that one is not identical with the Good. In early ethical thinking, people fairly easily discount such evidence by considering it minor aberrations from an otherwise good person (after all, "nobody's perfect"). A sense of guilt (that one has *done* wrong) may be experienced; but the doing of wrong does not necessarily lead to the conclusion that one *is* wrong (which would lead to a sense of shame and uncleanness), so one can return to the idealism of the false self and buoy one's spirits with illusions of one's basic goodness. However, if the evidence that one falls short of the Good is too great to be dismissed, one is cast into the opposite predicament, despair in one's inabilities to conform to the Good. As a result, one comes to feel a more mature sense of shame (than is possible in childhood).[5] Bonhoeffer (1955) wrote that shame in particular is a sign of one's disunion, of one's resistance to God, the Good and others.

Before the Fall, God created humans with an emotion system that would permit the valid experiences of guilt and shame in response to "the gap," which was to develop later. But such complex emotions are largely socially constructed in the course of one's development, so experiencing them can be distorted. Both can be activated excessively or not often enough in childhood. If activated too much, humans can come to experience "false guilt" (Tournier,

1965; Narramore, 1984) and "false shame," both of which are based not on God's view of things but on a distorted self-understanding, related to damaging social experiences. False shame, in particular, can be especially debilitating (see Tangney & Dearing, 2002, regarding the effects of shame in general). Adult depression, for example, is quite often characterized by an excessive, overwhelming sense of one's constitutional ethicospiritual inability.

Conviction: The self-awareness of fault. The intrinsic quandary of the ethical order is its utter insufficiency to provide a basis for psychospiritual well-being, without self-deception, for there is always more one could do and be. By listening to the signs of "the gap" (one's valid guilt and shame), humans can come to a deeper, more fundamental self-awareness than the self-righteousness of early ethical thinking—like that expressed by Paul in Romans 7:24: "Wretched man that I am!" This awareness (understood ethically) is a function of the conscience (schooled in some way by the Law), as well as (understood spiritually) the convicting work of the Holy Spirit (Jn 16:8).

The Christian journey of inwardness leads to the mature ethicospiritual sense of a *fault* in the nucleus of one's being (Ricoeur, 1965a)—a core contamination—the awareness of which is the dawning of the spiritual understanding of psychopathology. One's sense of shame is seen to be fundamentally valid (even if it is false to some extent). Though this is a painful realization that leads to despair, from the Christian standpoint it is a necessary stage in one's developmental journey into psychospiritual maturity (or more accurately, a place to which one returns again and again as one spirals into greater wholeness). This "conviction of sin" contains a sense of self-helplessness that provides the needed impetus to reject the narcissistic and autocentric orientation endemic to human nature in order to seek a salvation that comes from above. Unfortunately, some tragic individuals remain stuck in this despair and never recover by entering into the spiritual order of grace.[6]

Symptoms of obstacles in the psychosocial order. We turn next to consider the kinds of psychopathology evident within the psychosocial order of discourse. The variety of psychosocial damage possible is enormous and has been widely explored over the past 150 years, leading to the DSM series, in which syndromes of symptoms have been identified to aid in the diagnosis of psychopathology. The Christian and secular communities can obtain much agreement regarding this order's psychopathology because the identification of psychosocial damage is less worldview-dependent than the recognition of ethical and spiritual disorders. But a Christian approach to these kinds of damage is still distinguished from a secular approach by its interpretation of them as obstacles to God's doxological and therapeutic purposes. Rather than attempt an exhaustive list of psychosocial obstacles, the following is merely a sampling.

Psychosomatic symptoms. Somatoform disorders consist of physical problems that appear to have psychogenic causes and can involve pain, paralysis, gastrointestinal problems, hypochondriasis and sensory impairment with no known physical cause. The physical symptoms of these disorders are actually signs of an underlying *psychosocial* disorder. Because of their somatic nature, however, they can constitute a distracting signal, directing attention away from the actual psychosocial causal dynamics.

Cognitive and behavioral symptoms. Behavioral dysfunction includes such things as inappropriate learned reinforcers, a deficient behavioral repertoire, behavioral excess, hyperarousal in response to certain stimuli, maladaptive conditioning (e.g., in children who are reinforced for tantrums), impulse control problems and addictions (which can be considered "the abuse of reinforcers," Fowles, 1993). Cognitive processing damage includes any impairment in attention, memory, reasoning, language reception or expression, or sequential processing of information. False beliefs also belong to this order and include inaccurate beliefs about others, reality, the future, God and oneself (though false beliefs of different kinds can admittedly arise from very different causes). The presence of hallucinations, delusions and obsessions, dissociation between systems of belief or aspects of the self (including subselves), and defenses are examples of psychosocial disorder.

Emotional symptoms. An important class of affective-motivational abnormalities is inappropriate affect, which encompasses excessive emotionality (like a pervasively sad mood, overwhelming guilt or shame, extreme euphoria or chronic irritability); exaggerated emotion, like self-dramatization; diminished emotionality (like dull or blunted affect, or lack of guilt or shame when it should be present); and extreme emotional lability (like mood swings). Human motivation can also be disordered, by having invalid motives and goals (e.g., for sex with children), excessive strength of a motive (achievement motivation that transcends affiliation motivation), or lack of motivation, purpose or enjoyment of life. Absence of emotion may also signify a lack of psychospiritual wholeness, due to defensive activity, affect phobia (McCullough et al., 2003) or emotional numbing (Litz, 1992).

Volitional symptoms. Many individuals suffer from volitional dysfunction, which includes indecision, lack of exertion, impulsivity and impairment in action regulation (including self-monitoring, planfulness, goal setting and goal maintenance). Such conditions can be found in childhood, before mature personal agency has developed and so before they contribute to full-blown ethical or spiritual outcomes. While they obviously affect personal agency, they should not be conflated with it, since they would seem to be dynamic structures, better understood as psychosocial factors that later may mitigate personal agency and its proper formation.

Relational symptoms. Mental representations of self and others are based on repeated experiences with others, especially the earliest experiences, and they form an "internal working model" or a general "self-other constellation" that is activated in social interactions. Benjamin (2003) argues that current relationships are shaped by past internalizations of early relationships that formed a mental template made up of rules like "Be like him or her," "Act as if he or she is still there and in control," and "Treat yourself as he or she treated you." Our early emotions are mediated by caretakers, so that our emotional life is originally shared intersubjectively (Stern, 1985). As a result, self/other-representations can be formed with specific negative emotion schemes attached to them. Relational damage includes attachment disorders (tendencies toward ambivalent or avoidant attachments with others), lack of empathy, low tolerance for interpersonal conflict, codependence, sexual problems and social phobia, as well as systemic distortions, for example, enmeshed or disengaged family relations, exposure as children to unhealthy power relations and the assignment of the role of scapegoat. Such barriers compromise the ability to internalize the form of healthy image-bearing. Critical and abusive experiences with others in our early years can distort our *present* perceptions of others, which may be relatively inflexible—so that we are unable to perceive and respond to differences between people—and which may promote distrust, aggression, servility or chronic neediness, thereby directly inhibiting our ability to love them and to receive their understandings, their joy and love of us, and their healthy and virtuous character, even influencing our experiences with God.

Form symptoms. Damage to the self constitutes a fundamental dilemma, since it lies at the core of the individual and inhibits self-awareness and so easily obstructs communal dialogue. Chronically low self-esteem, distorted self-representations, defense mechanisms, dissociative disorders like DID or depersonalization, weak or rigid ego boundaries, egocentrism, extreme childhood shame, and gender identity disorders all compromise the integrity of the self.

One's narrative is another important aspect of the pluriform. We know through research that experiences of trauma and abuse can seriously debilitate one's narrative sense and personal memories (Siegel, 1999). Such experiences also contribute to feelings of self-disgust and self-hatred, fear of and anger toward others, and distrust of God. The cost to the adult of severe abuse in childhood is enormous.

Especially pervasive psychosocial damage is evident in personality disorders. These are patterns of experience and behavior that compromise overall functioning and are relatively inflexible, stable, cross-situational and of long duration. They consist of a constellation of particular symptoms in cognition, affect, volition and social relations. Such deficits seem to be woven into the structure of one's personality and profoundly affect later development of personal agency and character. Because of the degree and pervasiveness of the damage, personality disorders are particularly resistant to change.

Much can go wrong with the primordially good, created dynamic structures of the soul. We must note that the greater the psychosocial damage, the more the capacity of individuals to image God directly is hindered. So, while sin and evil are more important forms of psychopathology—since they are a function of opposition and resistance to the manifestation of God's glory—psychosocial damage is significant, because its obstacles inhibit a human's capacity to most fully resemble God. Moreover, scriptural teaching leads us to infer that God is especially committed to those who have psychological damage and desirous of improving their well-being (Mt 9:11-13; 11:19; 18:6; Lk 6:20; 1 Cor 1:26-28; 2 Cor 4:7; Jas 2:5).

Symptoms of determinants in the biological order. Since humans are embodied, human life is, in a fundamental sense, a biological reality. One of the consequences of the Fall into sin is that physical suffering and biological limitations are a basic facet of human experience. With regard to psychopathological conditions, humans can have an array of what are called here *determinants,* biological features of humans that exercise some causal influence on their experience. The term *determinant* is used advisedly. It is not meant to suggest that these influences *completely* determine psychological variables (though in extreme cases they do; for example, severe brain damage severely limits intelligence). But human embodiment needs to be taken seriously, and it necessarily influences human experience. The bodily quality of human life creates certain constraints that condition every human life (and story), and direct it toward a specific range of possible developmental pathways—narrowed by particular social experiences and choices.

Genetic determinants. Genetics are a biological a priori that make possible a certain quality of human life. Humans are born with genetic predispositions that determine foundational psychosocial possibilities related to intelligence, personality and physical appearance. An infant genetically disposed toward introversion, for example, is more likely to feel a degree of behavioral inhibition that will influence social relations, that could lead to experiences of social rejection, which in turn could lead to greater withdrawal (Kagan, 1998; Rothbart, Posner & Hershey, 1995). Biological limitations in the ability to store information will directly inhibit one's ability to internalize knowledge, including the Word of God. For example, depending on their extensiveness, brain abnormalities, like those seen in autism and mental retardation, will limit internalization, more or less profoundly. Genetic variance related to personality, intelligence, physique and physical appearance can differentially alter many aspects of one's developmental trajectory. In addition, some humans possess a genetic vulnerability or risk that, if activated under a certain set of circumstances (e.g., chronic, aversive social experiences, Cacioppo, Berntson, Sheridan & McClintock, 2002), will express itself in the development of a severely debilitating psychopathological condition such as schizophrenia.

Neural determinants. While the interactions of biological and psychosocial influences are not entirely understood, it is clear that maladaptive events, especially poor relational experiences, can detrimentally "sculpt" the brain. For example, animal studies have found that high levels of stress result in damage to the hippocampus, an important part of the limbic system responsible for memory storage (Sapolsky et al., 1990). When rats are repeatedly exposed to uncontrollable shock, their brains become hypersensitive to stressful experiences in the future (Petty, Chae, Kramer, Jordan & Wilson, 1994).

Early parent-child interactions have been found to influence the production of various hormones and neurotransmitters that, in turn, aid in the formation of the orbitofrontal cortex, a part of the brain known to be important for future social functioning (Cozolino, 2002). Maladaptive social experiences (like poor attachment) in the first few years of life lead to the construction of neural networks that easily activate negative emotion centers in the limbic system, which create the experience of anxiety, fear or anger when faced with stimuli that resemble those present in the earlier experiences (Siegel, 1999).

There is also reason to believe that the formation of stress reactivity, self- and other-understanding, and relational structures occurs during sensitive periods, when brain regions dedicated to these processes are developing and are especially susceptible to formative influences (Siegel, 1999). For the most part, these sensitive periods occur during the first five years of life.

Another category of biological barriers consists of chronic problems with neural transmission, as a result of under- or overproduction of neurotransmitters or excessively low or high numbers of postsynaptic neurotransmitter receptors, leading to the under- or overactivation of certain neural pathways, creating psychopathological symptoms like hallucinations (in schizophrenia—too much dopamine/too many receptor sites) or sad affect (in major depression—too little serotonin/too few receptor sites).

Because of the role of the brain in grounding all higher-order functioning, problems here are experienced throughout the system. And similar to what was said about psychosocial obstacles, disorder at the biological level necessarily affects the capacity of humans in this life to image God and reflect his will. Moreover, Christ's ministry made clear God's concern and desire toward those with biological problems (Mt 4:24; 8:16-17; 14:14; Lk 5:15; Jn 9).

Interactive Relations Between the Barriers of Different Orders

A semiodiscursive, multiorder model of human beings may be especially useful for understanding psychopathology because of its assumption that all orders consist of some form of information representation and transfer, including transfer between orders (that is, the orders are interactive; though admittedly, the mechanisms of brain-mind transfer are still quite mysterious). Each order has its own signs to interpret: genes, neurotransmitters and neural firing patterns; discourse, emotions, memories and others; God's law and the conscience (and its emotional dynamics); and spiritual experiences with God (and their emotional dynamics); and the notion (or metaphor) of semiodiscursive translation is one way to talk about how disorder in any of these spheres can affect the others.

The interaction of biological and psychosocial dynamics in the development of psychopathology is well documented, if not well explained (see, e.g.,

Cacioppo, Berntson, Adolphs, Carter, Davidson, McClintock, McEwen, Meaney, Schacter, Sternberg, Suomi & Taylor, 2002; Faraone, Tsuang & Tsuang, 1999; Fowles, 1993; Ingram & Price, 2001; Pennington, 2002; Si egel, 1999). We do not understand very well how psychological structures like thoughts and emotion-states influence neural structures and processes (or vice versa), but we do know that such causal effects occur. For example, rejection by an attachment object (at the psychosocial level) can trigger the release of stress hormones (at the biological)—that in turn may alter levels of neurotransmitter production—and the rejection may also lead to the development of neural networks that store the sad experience in long-term memory (Carter, 2002; Francis & Meaney, 2002; Siegel, 1999). In addition, biopsychosocial barriers will affect structural dynamics "further up:" one's choices, the development of personal agency and conscience formation (at the ethical level), as well as one's religious beliefs, perceptions of God (one's God-image), and the quality of felt opposition to God and his ways (at the spiritual). For example, poor human relational experiences in childhood can profoundly affect one's later ability to perceive and relate to God (Spero, 1992; Vitz, 1999), and inhibit the positive therapeutic impact that one's personal relationship with God is designed to have. Conversely, higher-order pathological dynamics can directly affect lower-level barriers. For example, sinful choices will repeatedly activate unhealthy/non-Christian thoughts, beliefs and desires that will come to be more permanently laid down in the neural structures of one's brain through reactivation, habit formation and the potentiation of those neural structures, which makes them more likely to be activated in the future. The existence of such inter-order interactions confirms the holistic hypothesis that all the orders of discourse are implicated in psychopathology.

The place of sin within an interactive, multiorder system. The biblical counseling movement has taught us to see sin as the most notable kind of psychopathology. Because of sin's preeminence, it is desirable to understand its pervasive, interactive role within the entire multiorder system and its relation to the other orders, with reference to psychopathology.

To begin with, the Bible teaches that the general havoc in the creation pertaining to human life is related indirectly to sin. The curses upon human life in Genesis 3 are a synecdoche that signifies a tragic disruption in the natural order bearing on human life, which brings humans pain and sorrow. We should infer from this that the biological and psychosocial damage of humans is part of the symbolic fallout from the primordial sin (Dembski, 2006). However, sin's damaging effects on the biopsychosocial orders can also be direct, when due, for example, to the evil acts of parents or other caregivers directed against the developing child (whether abuse or neglect). As a result, sin's disordering functions should be understood to permeate human being, from the highest to the lowest levels, so that the meaninglessness of sin is evidenced directly in a person's unbelieving dispositions and evil decisions, and indirectly in damaged mental, emotional and relational patterns, and dysfunctional neural networks and neurotransmitter processing.

From another standpoint: human sin would appear to require the platform of the lower levels of human beings. Brains, the proper development of a mind and the capacities of personal agency are necessary for the activity of sin in its fullest manifestation. But this would seem to suggest that damage within the lower orders affects sin's expression. An implication of the grounding/temporal priority of the biological and psychosocial is that the specific sins persons struggle with, whether the sins of the serial adulterer or the practical atheism of the otherwise upstanding and church-going bank president, are indeed influenced (but not caused) by the biological and psychosocial influences (grounding effects) to which they have been exposed. If so, it would seem to be the case that some of these lower-order factors condition ethicospiritual responsibility—without annulling it.

For example, high levels of testosterone are related to higher levels of aggression (a reality of the biopsychosocial orders); yet malevolent violence is an expression of sin and is blameworthy (a conclusion according to the ethicospiritual orders). So, while adults with elevated levels of testosterone may have a biological predisposition toward aggressive behavior, this lower-order variant can only be adequately interpreted within its higher-order contexts. Such adults are therefore still ethically and spiritually responsible to deal with their aggressive predispositions in socially and divinely sanctioned ways (by playing football, for example, and not by getting into fights). If they commit acts of evil, other humans must hold them responsible for those deeds and regard them as reprehensible and criminal, and treat the perpetrators as the ethicospiritual beings they are. Yet a *comprehensive* human understanding of such problems—one that corresponds in some measure to God's understanding—cannot be gained by *ignoring* the lower-level influences and focusing *only* on their ethicospiritual blameworthiness. The lower-level dynamics constitute *extenuating circumstances*—without their necessarily being *exculpating influences.* We can safely assume that the omniscient, just God is able to take into account the lower-level grounding effects, as well as their ethicospiritual desert.

Conversely, those who are freer than others from such lower-level conditions and yet do the same deeds would seem to be more responsible and therefore, from the divine standpoint, will be held more accountable. The Bible supports such a conclusion: "From everyone who has been given much, much will be required; and to whom they entrusted much, of him they will ask all the more" (Lk 12:48).

No one can deny that those with biopsychosocial damage are worse off, in some sense, than those without it; for example, such damage may involve more emotional pain. In addition, it seems to be the case that indwelling sin is more able to break out in obvious ways among people with high levels of biopsychosocial damage. But the New Testament also implies that such people are not more despicable because of their biologically and socially shaped damage. On the contrary, God chose the weak, the despised, the base and the foolish of this world, "so that no man may boast before God" (1 Cor 1:29). Christ said, "Blessed are the poor in spirit" (Mt 5:3), and "It is not those who are healthy who need a physician, but those who are sick; I did not come to call the righteous, but sinners" (Mk 2:17).

The foregoing can be summarized in three points: (1) sin is the worst form of psychopathology, and it permeates all forms of human life, including those who are functioning well in the biopsychosocial realms and those who are not; (2) the underlying presence of sin is symbolized in biopsychosocial damage (as in schizophrenia), whereas sin's pervasive presence tends to be masked in the absence of such damage; and (3) the meaninglessness deriving from sin indirectly and directly contributes to the disorder of the lower orders, and the lower orders' lack of coherent meaningfulness, in turn, conditions and shapes the empty and futile expression of sin in a human life. So, a Christian understanding of sin proves to be of great value in developing a holistic and integrative Christian understanding of psychopathology that respects both human responsibility and how it can be compromised.

A multiorder case study. Let us consider again the complex case of Ted, from chapter eight, since it demonstrates well how these orders interact in psychopathology. You may remember that he was a middle-aged accountant, married with four children. He worried constantly and had difficulty sleeping and concentrating on tasks at work. His head felt like it was racing, and he was getting an almost painful constriction in his chest. These symptoms began shortly after getting a new, hard-driving supervisor. Ted himself was an only child, and his parents were both fundamentalist Christians with very high performance standards for Ted. As a child he had felt that he was always "walking a tightrope," trying hard to keep his parents happy. These would constitute the major biopsychosocial symptoms of Ted's condition. Ted's anxiety was also likely related to his strong romantic feelings for a lonely, single coworker. This coworker appeared to be getting serious about him, and he realized he was in large part responsible for her feelings and so felt guilty and trapped. At the same time, he was a committed Christian who for years had been reasonably faithful but recently had grown disillusioned about his life and his relationship with God. As a result, he had stopped spending much time with God. He admitted that he sometimes felt angry with God for how things had gone in his life. These would be the major ethicospiritual symptoms of psychopathology in his life.

Underlying biopsychosocial factors (genetic and social) undoubtedly contributed to his current ethicospiritual predicament, without absolving him of his responsibility. In addition, his ethicospiritual problems, in turn, were compounding his biopsychosocial symptoms (e.g., the stress due to his dalliance was leading to the activation of his sympathetic nervous system, resulting in symptoms of panic). So his current anxious state of mind would seem to be a multifactorial function of biological vulnerability, psychosocial stressors and ethical and spiritual guilt, exacerbated by the current spiritual vacuum in his life. Minimizing the problems of any order distorts our understanding of the full state of affairs in Ted's case.

The Nature of Gospel Deconstruction: How Union with Christ Undermines the Barriers to Glory

According to Augustine (1997), the Christian is on a journey. "Our minds must be purified. . . . Let us consider this process of cleansing as a trek, or a voyage, to our homeland; though progress towards the one who is ever present is not made through space, but through integrity of purpose and character" (p. 13). We turn next to consider the activities involved in the purgation side of the soul's journey, that is, the deconstruction of its specific multiorder barriers to Christiformity and greater Christlikeness. We begin by noting that the way progress is made is through the believer's union with Christ.

We have seen repeatedly that the believer's entire existence has been redefined according to the declarative word of God. Everything about the believer—everything biological, psychosocial, ethical and spiritual—is now related redemptively to God; having been mystically joined to Christ's life, death and resurrection, the believer has entered into communion with the triune God (1 Jn 1:3). Christ has created an analogous passageway by which we can follow him, a healing path through the cross and beyond, a *via dolorosa* by which all that is of the "old" is being crucified more and more and the created self—now in the beloved (Eph 1:6)—is being redeemed, empowered and made a new creation—a new self, a dipolar self—more and more fully throughout this life. Where does this gospel healing begin?

It was suggested in chapter eleven that Christian soul-care providers should seek to work at the highest levels possible (Intervention Rule 2). As a result, we will also organize this section by beginning with the highest levels and working our way down. As the reader may recall, we do so primarily because healing at the higher, more explicitly theocentric levels leads to God getting greater, more explicit glory. But there are also some practical benefits from following this rule, since genuine success at the higher levels will affect all the levels below, and such activity unifies the soul in Christ and contributes to an increasing integration of previously diverse and conflicting psychospiritual dynamics. So there is real therapeutic value in a holistic, hierarchical model of soul care that deals with first things first.

The role of articulation in gospel deconstruction. Before we begin our descent, however, another word must be said about words. A semiodiscursive model of soul care and psychopathology maintains that psychosocial obstacles, ethical resistance and spiritual opposition can be overturned, at least in part, through being personally articulated by means of the discourse of the spiritual order. Personal sin and evil need to be confessed to God, and it appears that psychosocial damage (for example, defensive structures, dissociation and chronic negative emotions) and memories of its causal events (for example, past abuse and suffering) need to be verbalized and/or symbolized in order for humans to be released from the bondage and pain that has been "locked up" in the semiodiscursive structures stored in memory and the brain (Bucci, 1997; Cozolino, 2001; Greenberg & Paivio, 1997). Formerly dissociated neural networks can be integrated through discourse, and previously internalized false signs or meaning structures can be, to some extent, similarly decoupled from the soul, a release that is successful corresponding to the depth of the verbalization.

Minimally, to be effective and Christian, this articulation must be done self-consciously, with God, through the gospel. A Christian model of this process involves a rearticulation of these dynamics in relation to the cross and the resurrection of Christ. It is a gospel retelling of one's story according to the story of Christ. But usually, because of prior false internalization, this verbalization is also facilitated through human dialogue—by interacting with a wise human guide, like a mature pastor or a trained counselor. If the individual is ready, such dialogue can create insights, when responding to questions, having one's strongholds provoked into activation or simply walking together with a spiritual friend into new territory or regions of the soul long neglected or forgotten. Such dialogue challenges c ounselees to bring out into the open their latent psychospiritual dynamic structures through explication, and this seems to lead to their undoing.

The barriers to Christiformity in the upper three levels are constituted primarily in discourse. Perhaps given the implicit semiodiscursive nature of the created order (including human nature) and the way human development occurs through dialogue, the created damage and vices derived from earlier development and personal action need to be put into discourse in order to detach the stored abnormality (e.g., false beliefs, excessive negative emotions or sinful dispositions) from the good, created structures with which it has been associated. Similarly, because of the dramatic/historical quality of human life, individuals must process and "work through" the distortions of their story if that story is to be fundamentally reframed and more fully integrated in light of and into God's redemptive-history. This may require the reactivation of painful memories and distorted beliefs, the surrender of them to God and the replacement of the original, excessive negative emotions that were bound to those memories with more valid, healthy emotions that better reflect God's transcendent, normative appraisal of the event, *without denying anything relevant, including the pain, the horrible significance of the events or the original emotions themselves!* And this rearticulation can change the brain's neural wiring.

If the releasing verbalization is sufficiently deep, so that the faulty structures are unloosed (and theoretically, depth can always be increased), the next step is to receive the most relevant signs of God, like the words of God in

Scripture so that the dynamic structures of the soul come to reflect more of the form of Christ (but more about this in the next chapter).

In the very dismantling of the fallen and damaged structures of one's soul, the form of Christ is being actualized, specifically, the form of his death. Through confession and repentance, as well as the intentional surrender and relinquishment of psychosocial damage in Christ, believers experientially unite by faith with Christ's death on the cross to sin, the old aeon and its pain. In this way Christians die and are buried (Rom 6:1-11), "carrying about in the body the dying of Jesus" (2 Cor 4:10). The Catholic tradition has called this process *purgation* (Groeschel, 1993; Tanquery, 1930; Underhill, 1990).

Treating Opposition in the Spiritual Order: Christian Soul Care as Gospel Renewal and Repentance-Promotion

It is all too common for Christians to seek to attack sin directly. Thinking that sin is like any other problem, it is assumed it simply needs to be exposed, addressed and done away with. However, sin is unlike any problem in the creation, and it is impossible for sinners—even redeemed sinners—to confront sin head-on like that. Such an approach, Paul was inspired to reveal, leads to death (Rom 7:5; 2 Cor 3:7). Only in Christ and through the gospel of Christ can Christians make any headway in their treatment of sin. This point cannot be emphasized enough. And because sin is the fundamental form of human psychopathology and contaminates everything all humans do, and because the spiritual order transcends the others, a gospel therapeutic treatment of sin guides the entire Christian orientation to the other forms of psychopathology all the way down the line.

What is a gospel therapeutic approach to sin? On the cross, Christ became sin on our behalf (2 Cor 5:21). As suggested in chapter fourteen, before one can deal effectively with one's sin, one must look upon it first in Christ on the cross (Barth, 1956; Bonhoeffer, 1955, 1966). There our sin is revealed to be the unfathomable horror it is and, simultaneously, God's love for humans is displayed, sin is overthrown, and its destructive power nullified. The gospel alone can melt the heart, soften the defenses and draw the soul to make real headway in overcoming sin. The gospel, we might say, is the leaden suit which enables us to handle sin with its deadly effects. Without it, direct contact with sin inevitably kills us, through despair or self-righteous self-deception. But in order to understand how to use the gospel remedy, let us take a few steps back.

As already mentioned, beginning in late adolescence or early adulthood, an awareness of being unable to fulfill one's ethical ideals can develop, and a sense of fundamental despair, shame and guilt can grow (in contrast to the psychosocial awareness of having broken social rules that even preschoolers are aware of). There are many ways that this sense of fault can be handled (as we see in the world's religions and in modern psychotherapy). But given its perceived transcendent quality, the most satisfying response psychologically is one that takes it seriously. And no meaning-system takes human shame and guilt more seriously than Christianity, since these emotions are fundamentally signs of sin.

The prerequisite of the highest type of soul-healing intervention is an awareness of sin. This is more than an awareness of mere wrongdoing (an experience of the ethical order). Rather, sin awareness is a sense of uncleanness *before God*, in relation to God. As humans grow in a recognition of their shame before God and experience a degree of despair in themselves, a sense of the radical nature of their predicament also grows, leading them to see the necessity of a complete resignation of themselves and a fundamental rejection of their reliance on their own ruined capacities (Owen, 1965, Vol. 2). Because shame is the self-conscious negative emotion that signifies a sense of badness of *being*, the Christian recovery process entails the cultivation of genuine shame as a catalyst that continually moves us back to the cross.

Consent through gospel repentance and self-denial. Kierkegaard taught that "repentance and remorse belong to the eternal in a man" (1847/1938, p. 41), and the Puritans recognized that the gospel provided the only real relief from the "work of the law" that convinces persons of their evil and sinfulness before God. The psychopathology of sin is resolvable only through a repentance that accords with the Christian gospel of the spiritual order. At the core of Christian recovery is a repentance that centers on the cross and resurrection of Christ and relies on the transcendent action of God's grace in Christ.

Repentance is a key part of the response to the gospel invitation into the spiritual order (Mt 3:2; Mk 1:15; Acts 2:38), and it involves a radical change of mind and heart toward sin and one's entire autocentric orientation. "Psychology shows repentance to be profound, personal, and all-pervasive. The change wrought in repentance is so deep and radical as to affect the whole spiritual nature and involve the entire personality, including the intellect, the emotions, and the will" (DeMent & Smith, 1988, Vol. 4, p. 136). Through the gospel, humans are enabled by the Holy Spirit to repent, by which they take responsibility—as personal agents in Christ—for their opposition and resistance to God. The first step in repentance is *confession,* in which one acknowledges in so many words that one is hopelessly sinful and one takes ownership for one's sin before God but in Christ.

There are no halfway measures in the sphere of ultimacy. In an ongoing way, the believer needs to break through self-consciously one's existence "in the flesh" (Rom 8:1-11) by faith—letting go of the control of one's life and all false sources of ultimacy. "Repent and turn away from your idols" (Ezek 14:6). The necessary corollary to the love of God is the hatred of all that is opposed to him.

Another way to understand repentance is Christ's concept of self-denial (e.g., Mt 16:24), used to underscore the radical nature of the transition into the spiritual order as a kind of self-renunciation. Using our multiorder framework, self-denial can be understood as a renunciation (and death) of the self of the three lower orders insofar as they are corrupted by sin. Full repentance/self-denial requires the recognition of (1) the ultimate vanity of the lower orders of life (since their meaning is transcended by a fuller spiritual meaning in the triune God), and (2) the fallenness and corruption of those orders. But repentance is always paired with faith (Colquhoun, 1826/1965)—faith in another, higher, eternal order, that of the "above things" (Col 3:4). Repentance is just the side of this basic action that faces one's spiritual pathology. This single activity of "faith-and-repentance" results in a fundamental *decentering* of the self and a *recentering* in the triune God. It is the radical resignation of a personal agent, that is, a resigning, reconfiguring or rewriting of the soul along gospel lines.

This transposition to the spiritual order is affective and volitional because it is a resigning at the core of one's identity. It is a losing of oneself in Christ's death in order to find oneself in Christ's resurrection (Mt 10:39 and Rom 6:1-6), a dying to one's old self and to this world (Gal 2:20; 6:14; Col 3:1-11), and it involves a hating of all of one's closest relationships (Mt 10:37; Lk 14:26), indeed, a hating of oneself (Lk 14:26; Jn 12:25)! This is what Pascal had in mind when he wrote that "the true and only virtue is . . . to hate ourselves" (quoted in Rogers, 1998, p. 3). Though the command to hate oneself in order to follow Christ can be grossly misinterpreted, it makes perfect sense if it is understood as a relinquishment of the biopsychosocial and ethical Self who lives autonomously in relation to God. We are to hate *that* self—the *old* self—in order to discover (and affirm) our created/new self in Christ and in the spiritual order: a *resurrected* biopsychsocioethical self, defined according to the gospel.

The puzzling language of self-denial makes sense *only* as a description of an action of *ultimacy in Christ*, necessary for participation in the spiritual order. *If attempted at the lower levels, it leads to a destruction of the self*—a hatred of the created self. It is only from within the standpoint of the spiritual order and its description of fallenness and sin that self-denial emerges as a legitimate, life-giving activity. Admittedly, the self's denial of itself is a paradox; words to describe it are strained to the breaking point. But it is through this paradoxical language that the new self emerges and grows into the spiritual order. Repentance/self-denial consists of an internal, conscious, absolute rejection of idolatry and the life of independence apart from God—thoroughly corrupted by sin and ultimately powerless—and a resolute seeking of God alone as the one who is able to rescue, heal and renew the self. This psychospiritual "passing from death to life" provides an ongoing metaphoric death/resurrection cycle that believers are to practice experientially, day after day (Rom 6:1-11)—for, contrary to some understandings of Christian perfectionism, this process is never complete and finished in this life.

Primary and secondary repentance. Two kinds of repentance/self-denial can be distinguished. *Primary* repentance will be called "mortification" (Rom 8:13 and Col 3:5 KJV), and it is an active, direct and aggressive disavowal of all of one's contaminated life, which is now brought to the cross. It is a kind of spiritual suicide that constitutes a radical, gospel-dependent break with what used to hold one in bondage. Such a disavowal alone makes possible a substantial change in the direction and pattern of one's life. Getting free from an addiction often requires something analogous to this kind of ruthless action, but primary repentance is foundational to the entire Christian life.

Secondary repentance is derived from primary repentance. However, it goes deeper into the heart and is developmentally more advanced, a result of the believer learning the "faith skill" of letting God take sin away through the cross. Many related terms have been used in the Christian tradition for this process, including "detachment" (John of the Cross, 1964; Tanquerey, 1930, p. 564), "resignation" (Thomas à Kempis, 1864, p. 203), "self-resignation" (Owen, 1965, Vol. 2, p. 58), "surrender" (Caussade, 1986; Smith, 1952, p. 37; von Hildebrand, 2001, pp. 481-500), "dependence," "yieldedness" (Rom 6:16-19; Roberts, 2001), "letting go," "abiding" (Jn 15:1-5; Murray, 1985), "resting," "active receptivity" (Balthasar, quoted in Steck, 2001, p. 22) and "relinquishment." In certain respects, it is the absolute opposite of bodily action, where one seeks to change the environment *directly* by physically moving one's body. In contrast, secondary repentance is a kind of *indirect* volitional activity, since it *necessarily* and *intrinsically* entails dependence upon God. Perhaps it could be called an "active passivity" or "passive activity," since it still involves a vigorous application of one's will and emotions that is paradoxically "reversed." To put it most simply: secondary repentance enables one to change one's internal environment spiritually *by God through faith.*[7] If primary repentance does not mature into secondary repentance, the heart will not get the deeper healing and growth it needs.

This gospel-based repentance/self-denial dynamic should be understood as an ongoing way of life and not a once-and-for-all event that only occurs at conversion or at some subsequent point. Christ taught his disciples to take up their cross *daily* (Lk 9:23). In his classic on repentance, Colquhoun (1826/1965) points out that *evangelical* repentance is "an abiding principle, a lasting disposition of soul, a gracious principle lying deep in the heart, disposing a man at all times to mourn for and turn from sin" (p. 27).

As we move on to consider how to undermine barriers in the lower orders, we want to see everything with reference to the spiritual order. For one thing, genuine changes "above" (in the upper levels) have effects that cascade down throughout the rest of the soul system. But distinctively *Christian* soul-healing entails that all the specific changes in the lower orders are self-consciously *transposed into* the spiritual order. In effect, the rest of the chapter is simply the fleshing out of the *ultimate* repentance discussed above, but in the ethical, psychosocial and biological spheres. At the same time, the changes within the lower orders *are* lower-level phenomena, and the dynamics of each order have their own irreducible nature and unique features, which must be taken seriously on their own terms.

Treating Resistance in the Ethical Order: Christian Soul Care as Gospel Humility-Promotion

The goal of deconstruction within the ethical order is the repentance of one's evil. Specific sins of thought, word and deed—sins of commission and omission—and, even more important, habitual patterns of life contrary to God's will—called vices—need to be identified, confessed, mortified and surrendered. By God's grace, one learns to "change one's mind" toward, on the one hand, one's evil thoughts and beliefs, desires and feelings, images and actions, and gradually, more and more fully, relinquish them. We are to learn to dissent to evil from the heart—not in a hypocritical mental opposition that unconsciously affirms our self-righteousness, but through a heartfelt coming to terms with and rejection of the behavior, thoughts, delights and choices of one's old self/flesh/indwelling sin.

In addition, ethical repentance must include (ironically) the surrender of one's *morality*. Most humans typically see the call of the ethical sphere as simply the rejection of that which is evil and the affirmation of the Good. But as we saw earlier in the chapter, Christianity teaches that one's entire ethical existence is fallen (there is none righteous, not one, Rom 3:10; all fall short of the glory of God, Rom 3:23). In Christ, Paul considered his former *blameless* life as a Pharisee to be rubbish (Phil 3:7-8).

One useful tool for the deconstruction of the ethical order is the growing, experiential realization of one's pervasive fallenness, manifested in growing feelings of genuine guilt for one's evil actions, *now* before God but moving toward resolution in Christ. The cultivation of negative, self-conscious emotions is surely a painful path of growth; it too is a kind of death and part of Christian self-denial, involving a surrender of one's evil as well as one's good. In addition, there should be a gradually increasing, overall antipathy toward evil itself, including the evil of hypocrisy and self-righteousness.

Deconstruction in the ethical realm is painful because it involves the death of the autonomous Self: both the good and the evil of the old self. But Christian deconstruction within the ethical order paradoxically leads to a strengthening of the new self. As Kierkegaard implied, the new self is realized through choices, and ethical deconstruction entails repeatedly choosing God's ways and resisting, in grace, the resistance of the autonomous Self.

One of the most important outcomes of deconstruction in the ethical order is a theocentric and life-affirming humility that comes from consenting to the Good wherever it is found (including in oneself), and simultaneously realizing one's insufficiency in oneself to conform to the Good. One's consent to the Good itself undermines the barriers of one's practice of evil, and the humility it produces undermines the ever-threatening barriers of self-righteousness. All of this occurs through transposition; it is a gospel repentance of the ethical order, performed in the Spirit in loving dependence on Christ.[8]

Treating Obstacles in the Psychosocial Order: Christian Soul Care as Gospel Healing of Soul Damage

We begin by recalling that the obstacles of damaged psychosocial structures are *not* themselves sin. They are a portion of the good created order, but parts that have been disfigured, and as such they are *signs* of sin, symbols of the harm and destructiveness of sin, but not themselves moral and spiritual evil. However, since their damage constitutes obstacles to the manifestation of the glory of God, their healing is a good and desirable thing. How does Christian soul care promote psychosocial healing?

> Arise, cry out in the night,
> as the watches of the night begin;
> pour out your heart like water
> in the presence of the Lord. (Lam 2:19 NIV)

Combined with self-examination and empathic dialogue with those who image God fairly well, Christians seeking psychosocial healing need to "pour out their hearts" before the Lord. Through these processes they become increasingly able to recognize and undermine the maladaptive and dysfunctional created dynamic structures of their souls in light of the grace dispersed by the Christian reconfiguration that is occurring "from above," including such dynamics as painful memories of trauma; false beliefs about oneself, others and reality; poor relational structures, inappropriate feelings, desires and motives that do not correspond to reality; crippling mental imagery; and behavior patterns that are the result of poor socialization. All these phenomena have ethical and spiritual significance, for they are sites where sin can easily "break through." The spring of indwelling sin is in the heart, but it seeps through these cracks of the soul, signifying the deformity of sin symbolically and providing a medium for its expression. But as a part of the created order, psychosocial damage also has a "givenness" that is a result of its having been internalized/stored earlier in one's development. Often, significant change at the ethicospiritual levels will lead to some indirect, corollary changes in the structures of one's soul, but it is usually the case that special effort will have to be directed toward the deconstruction of specific, damaged psychosocial structures which will have to be intentionally addressed one by one.

Their direct undoing requires that their false meanings be articulated and released, by which they are objectified, deconstructed and disbelieved, through various modalities of therapy (depending on the specific damage). This Christian "disidentification" (Walsh & Shapiro, 2006) requires opening up one's soul to the light of God's healing gaze, knowing that, because of union with Christ, God perfectly accepts the believer. Consequently, the believer is freed to "come to terms with" damaged soul structures without fear. Memories of past events, thoughts and feelings have to be acknowledged first, in order to be dismantled, if the person is to be released from their emotional power. The acknowledgment is analogous to confession, though we are here dealing with damage, not one's own sin or evil. Humans do not bear responsibility for damage caused by biological or social influence. But as personal agents and believers, they are responsible to seek recovery. And for healing of the damage to occur, it has to be recognized and owned as a part of one's (fallen) self, but then objectified and relinquished. This will require, for example, disbelieving one's former beliefs, seeing the *ultimate* invalidity of one's emotional responses (though they may have been appropriate in one's childhood) and objectifying one's memories or painful images without repressing them (Jones, 2003). This consists of a self-conscious process of detachment that nullifies, to some extent, the negative emotional power of the damaged structures and so renders those structures more easily managed and modified, and also less likely to be reactivated in the same ways in the future so that they are less likely to be maintained.

Christian deconstruction of psychosocial damage flows from the gospel. "By his wounds we are healed" (Is 53:5 NIV). "Cast your anxiety on [Christ]," we are told, "for he cares for you" (1 Pet 5:7 NIV). By faith and union with Christ, Christ's death on the cross can reach into the deepest parts of the soul. The power of God unleashed at the cross is infinite and able to undermine *all* the effects of the Fall—including damage to psychosocial structures—a healing that begins now through faith but will be fully accomplished only in the age to come. In addition, even supposedly neutral behavioral and cognitive strategies (like systematic desensitization or the use of logic to demonstrate the irrationality of a belief) ought to be utilized with gratitude to God and sanctified by the word of God and prayer (see 1 Tim 4:4-5). The same Christ is the source of *all* wisdom and knowledge, so he should also get the glory from such creation-grace strategies.

It is true that the deconstruction of psychosocial dynamic structures can be done with or without reference to Christ. But if it is done without any self-conscious reference to Christ, it would seem not to be *Christian*. For the sake of God's glory, Christian soul-care providers ought to help believers transpose psychosocial interventions and their effects into the spiritual order, tracing their origins in the providence and redemption of the triune God, seeing everything in relation to the death and resurrection of Christ. All of the old age—sin, evil and the damage to the creation—is passing away, as the new creation is being realized. The Christian use of every legitimate therapeutic modality differs from that of secularists mainly in that, as the author of Lamentations suggested above, Christians pour out their hearts *in the presence of the Lord.*

Treating Determinants in the Biological Order: Christian Soul Care as Gospel Mechanics

Gospel redefinition of believers frees them to receive all good gifts from God through Christ to whom *all things* have been subjected (Eph 1:22), including medical technology. Multiorder Christian soul care, we recall, seeks to work at the highest levels possible but the lowest levels necessary. Successfully dealing with ethicospiritual and psychosocial problems should produce some beneficial biological effects, including such things as reduced activation of faulty neural networks and enhanced neurotransmitter processing. However, sometimes, because of relatively severe biological damage, higher-level work is not enough. So there will be times when medication will have to be used to deconstruct temporarily some of the symptoms of those disorders (e.g., depression, anxiety, psychosis, OCD; see Welch, 2005; Vernick, 2005; Winter, 1986). As the Puritan Richard Baxter (1981) wrote about the use of physical agents (like medicine, soups and exercise) for melancholia (the term in his day for depression), "The soul and body are wonderfully co-partners in their diseases and cure; and if we know not how it doeth it, yet when experience telleth us that it doeth it, we have reason to use such means" (p. 287). When advisable, Baxter said, Christian soul-care providers should avail themselves of the help of physicians.

Drug treatment and other forms of biological intervention are necessitated when semiodiscursive adjustments at the higher orders are ineffective. Lower-order interventions ought not to be despised by Christians. Biological remediation too is a gift of God and should be received with gratitude, sanctified as it is by the word of God and prayer (1 Tim 4:1-6; that is, when transposed into the spiritual order). Sometimes it is necessary to make temporary, neurochemical changes in the brain so that more enduring changes (new neural networks, higher-order beliefs) can be attained. Nonetheless, the limitations of biological intervention must also be acknowledged, since an exclusive reliance on the use of medications only deals with the biological symptoms and does not lead to long-term structural changes either at the neuronal level or the higher spheres. Consequently, only using medication will undermine the fostering of construction at the higher levels, resulting in a depersonalizing and despiritualizing of the individual. Medical treatment alone does not deconstruct damage; it simply improves the mechanics as long as it is being administered. When mood is altered *solely* biochemically, and no efforts are made to facilitate the growth of new neural networks through the fostering of healthier, higher-order structures (e.g., more adaptive reasoning patterns, the replacement of false beliefs about God through loving relationships and so on), and no appeal is made to the individual to take some responsibility for soul change by choosing better ways of acting (in dependence upon Christ and his word), the counselee's brain and soul have not been lastingly changed. Even worse, only taking medication can reinforce a passive external attribution style that hampers recovery: "The medication changes me; it is not God and not I."

Contrary to modernism, Christianity views humans as more than mechanisms or organisms and requires that Christians treat them as more. So the temporary, semiotic changes made at the biochemical level through medication must be placed within the larger *discursive* contexts of the higher orders. Only in this way can a comprehensive, holistic and more seamless "text" of the counselee's life be woven, a text that best reflects the one Word and mind and heart of God. It should therefore always be assumed that biological interventions will only be used in conjunction with higher-order therapeutic work, and only for as long as necessary, to help the counselee develop theocentric higher-order structures that can generate and maintain the desirable biological conditions on their own (e.g., enhanced neurotransmitter production; new neural networks), ideally without medication. However, such is the damage to the body derived from the Fall that the brain cannot always be repaired with higher-order discourse, so that some individuals may have to use psychotropic medication for their entire life.

Ted's multilevel soul deconstruction. To understand better what holistic, hierarchical, Christian deconstruction looks like, let us consider briefly the help that Ted received (the fellow with generalized anxiety disorder, whom we have repeatedly considered). Soon after beginning counseling, Ted was placed on anti-anxiety medication in order to reduce the intense biological symptoms of anxiety that he was experiencing, enough so that his soul-work could be productive. As a result, his thinking slowed down, he was more focused, and with the training and encouragement of his counselor, he began engaging in a realistic regimen of Bible meditation and prayer. His counselor also immediately helped him to face his unconscious idolatry of his coworker, which had led to his ethical shortsightedness with her. Ted responded well and took responsibility for his mishandling of the situation and misleading of her. He talked with her, confessed his poor judgment and expressed his regret, and they agreed not to socialize after work. Fortunately, their emotional affair had not proceeded too far, and their relationship basically returned to its previous collegiality.

Ted's counselor also trained him how to use a number of Christian cognitive-behavioral strategies to undermine the anxiety arousal he continued to experience periodically: for example, he used relaxation strategies before his devotions and regularly thought about how his union with Christ protected him from ultimate rejection and failure, and this helped him to objectify his feelings that got activated when his boss pressured him to work harder. After a couple of months, he was taken off the medication, as he learned how to manage his anxiety without it. Most of the counseling over the next nine months was spent helping Ted to properly evaluate his misperceptions of God and relinquish them, to take responsibility for the cultivation of his relationship with God and to begin to foster a more satisfying, theocentric orientation in his life. He gradually began to question and let go of many of the false, unconscious attitudes and beliefs about God, his family, his supervisor and himself that he had developed over the previous years, including distortions he came to realize he had internalized in childhood. He also got reinvested in his local church.

Toward the end of that year of counseling, Ted came to recognize that he had been deeply encouraged by his counselor's patience and high ethicospiritual standards, as well as his growing insistence that God was pursuing Ted for good, and this all went a long way toward helping him make the difficult decisions he had to make, especially in the early months of treatment. His counselor had been a sign of God's love and holiness. By the time treatment was terminated, Ted had embarked on a renewed and improved journey toward God, fostered by the deconstruction of a variety of barriers at many levels.

In the next chapter we consider the third step of inwardness: the internalization of the form of the Word of God.

Notes

[1]"Your heart is lifted up and you have said, 'I am a god, I sit in the seat of gods, in the heart of the seas'; yet you are a man and not God, although you make your heart like the heart of God." But most in the West today are probably best understood as polytheists, having multiple idols that are invested with various degrees of ultimate meaningfulness, with the Self standing as the supreme god in the pantheon.

[2]Over the past twenty years, the progressive wing of biblical counseling has done Christian counseling a valuable service by showing how idolatry is the fundamental soul-problem of human life (Powlison, 1988, 1995a, 2003, 2005; Tripp, 2002; Vernick, 2005; Welch, 1997b, 2005; see also Fitzpatrick, 1999). They have taught that idolatry of some aspect of the creation underlies many of the psychological struggles that people have and is often manifested powerfully in the lives of those who come for counseling.

[3]Another distinguishing feature of the psychopathology of the ethical would seem to be that it concerns maltreatment of some part of the created order—especially humans (others, as well as the self)—whereas the spiritual concerns God directly.

[4]I admit that this is speculation and cannot be deduced from Genesis 2. However, it is an inference commonly drawn in the Christian tradition.

[5]Mature shame and guilt are to be distinguished from their childhood antecedents—see Erikson (1963)—since their mature forms are more cognitively complex and take into account one's growing attainment of personal agency and responsibility.

[6]Taking our cue from Paul, who suggested that the law was a schoolmaster that leads to Christ (Gal 3:23-24), Christians might construe the Old Testament revelation as the Word of God given to intensify the experience of the ethical sphere and to draw people to greater ethical self-awareness through conviction of sin, and then on to the cross. The Puritans well understood that this "work of the law" (Owen, 1967, Vol. 5, p. 82) was a necessary prerequisite to saving faith. Without it, one did not properly experience one's desperate condition. However, the Puritans had their own limitations, for many seemed not to have a healthy balance between law and grace, and used the law in a heavy-handed way that led to much discouragement and, in turn, to some of the misunderstandings found in contemporary views of the Puritans. Nevertheless, we can see today that, without understanding fully what they were doing, they were promoting the development of personal agency in their emphasis on the law.

[7]Some of the monastics recognized the passive/active nature of this process. And Keswick teaching also used this language. Unfortunately, the insights of Keswick teaching were often combined with a simplistic developmental scheme that viewed spiritual change as a sudden event that catapulted the believer into a state of inner peace and relative freedom from spiritual struggle. By contrast, the Reformed tradition has maintained that growth in grace is gradual and is realized through small changes of gracious, dipolar activity that accumulate over time. On the other hand, the traditional Reformed approach may not have sufficiently appreciated the unique surrender-like quality of this process in its emphasis on the active obedience of the believer in sanctification. A postformal synthesis of these understandings may be necessary to best capture the actual nature of this paradoxical process.

[8]If I understand it correctly, this is an application of a Lutheran approach to sanctification (see Forde, 1988; Bayer, 2003).

16

Inwardness, Part 3

The Constitutive Internalization of Signs of Glory

IN THE PREVIOUS CHAPTER WE EXAMINED the second aspect of inwardness: the deconstruction of barriers to glory. However, we neglected to address a serious conundrum (alluded to in chap. 13). The barriers can only be removed as the resources needed for their dismantling are internalized, and the barriers themselves prevent that necessary internalization! This fact is one reason why adult soul healing begins so slowly. How does the project of inwardness really get off the ground? It is really necessary to work on all three interior tasks at the same time (self-examination, deconstruction of barriers and the internalization of the signs of God's glory). So the actual developmental trajectory is a complex, reciprocal interaction of all these facets. For the sake of simplicity, the facets are being discussed, somewhat misleadingly, in a linear fashion. In this chapter we conclude our discussion of inwardness on the internalization of the media of the form and splendor of God.

In chapter nine we considered the enormously rich, semiodiscursive context within which humans live, move and have their being, all of it a function of the Word of God, Jesus Christ. This context provides the formative meaning-structure that gives individual human beings their particular "substance." In this chapter, we will examine the *reparative* process, whereby adults internalize meaning or glory (derived from the Word of God) in order to heal and build up the form of their soul into greater conformity to Christ. The goal is the reconstitution of our subjectivity according to God's word in Christ (Zimmermann, 2004, p. 283).

Internalization, Construction and Consent

We have already seen that this internalization is promoted in the Bible. One of the biblical metaphors for the word of God was food, especially bread (chap. 14; Jer 15:16; and Deut 8:3; Mt 4:4). In addition, the relevance of internalization to human development and soul care has been recognized by a remarkable breadth of contemporary, secular psychological schools of thought. Since its first formulations, behavioral theory was based on the fact that animal behavior can be conditioned through the connection or pairing of stimuli from the environment with the behavior. Information from the external world gets "taken in" and "associated" with the organism's behavior. Analogous processes have been described throughout other areas in contemporary psychology. Cognitive psychology studies *mental representations* of reality stored in the mind (Ashcroft, 1994; Mandler, 1998; Paivio, 1990). Piaget (1954) identified *object permanence*, an early accomplishment of infant cognition, in which a representation of an object in the physical world is deposited in memory. Object relations, self and attachment theories refer to the formation of *self-* and *other-representations* or *internal working models*, respectively, as inevitable internalizations of one's relational world (Bowlby, 1969/1982; Kohut, 1977; Stern, 1985; Tyson & Tyson, 1990). Social cognitive theorists have documented the internalization of self-representations, norms and types of motivation (Bandura, 1986; Deci & Ryan, 1985; Dweck, 2000; Grusec & Kuczynski, 1997; Harter, 1999; Kochanska & Aksan, 1995; Kochanska, Murray, Jacques, Koenig & Vandegeest, 1996; Ryan & Deci, 2000). And the early Soviet developmentalist Vygotsky (1978), along with the modifications of his more recent intellectual heirs (e.g., Harre, 1984; Rogoff, 1990; Wertsch, 1985, 1998), understood cognitive development to consist of the internalization of interpersonal discourse into the intrapersonal structures of the mind.[1] Given their theoretical diversity, the broad similarity in these formulations is remarkable and leads to the conclusion that internalization is a fundamental construct in human development and common to different types of psychological development.

At the same time, the notion of internalization could be misleading, for it may seem to imply a merely passive reception of information from without. Yet, aside from low-level stimulus-response associations, internalization does not happen without the active enlistment of the human person in the process. So most forms of internalization should be understood as involving *construction* by the individual. This point is especially important in soul care with adults. Given that mature humans are personal agents and that barriers to further maturation have already been sown in childhood, adults must themselves be actively involved in the internalization process. The Holy Spirit does not magically create conformity to Christ, irrespective of the person's involvement, but typically uses means and works through human activity. This is a part of God's design in redemption: to make *images of God*, who are co-agents who rely upon God through faith that God uses to bring about change. However, in stark contrast to the anthropocentric constructivisms of modernists (like Piaget or many cognitive scientists) and postmodernist versions (that consider the self purely a *social* construction), a Christian approach understands that this internalization is done (1) by consent, (2) in dependence upon the Holy Spirit and (3) with a recognition that the internalization aims at meaning derived ultimately from God.

Pistis, "faith," is the biblical word that labels the human activity that receives God's word through which humans are saved (Rom 1:16; 5:1; Eph 2:8). In the Greek New Testament, the noun for "faith" and verb for "believe" both have *pist-* as their root. Evangelicals have long acknowledged that faith is important for initiation into salvation. But it is also by faith that salvific truths become more deeply ingressed and psychospiritually reformative. "We do not regard the promises of mercy that God offers as true only outside ourselves, but not at all in us; rather . . . we make them ours by *inwardly embracing them*" (Calvin, 1559/1960, p. 561, emphasis mine). Deeply believing God's saving word brings it into our experience affectively and more fully releases the power of its speech-acts to heal. In this chapter, however, we will be working from an even broader claim: faith is the fundamental means of Christian maturation, through which the Form of the Word of God is internalized and comes to constitute the Christian soul.

Throughout this book the term *consent* has been used as a synonym for *faith.* To consent is to believe a proposition "with feeling" (with sentiment). Consent, then, is to believe something *from the heart.* As the biblical writers understood, even demons believe (Jas 2:19); thus biblical faith must be deeper than that. Consequently, we will follow Jonathan Edwards (1980, 1989) in using *consent* as a label for the deepest affirmation of God's word, in order to distinguish that activity from mere mental assent (a-sent, without sentiment; Anderson, 1980; Niebuhr, 2005). Edwards believed that the Trinity was characterized by fundamental consent to one another and that humans were created to be analogues of the Trinity, consenting wholeheartedly to the triune God and his word, and then characterized by consent to one another. Consent, for our purposes, is the psychological activity by which the meaning or glory of God in its various forms is internalized by believers. As human personal agents consent to and receive the word of God, it changes them and comes to constitute their form. Through consenting to the relevant signs of God, believers personally take on more of the form of God and so become increasingly conformed to the image of Christ, the true image of God. This Christian approach to internalization could be termed *covenantal constructivism* (Johnson, 1996).

Building upon God's good creation. Before we discuss the major media of the form of God to be internalized in soul care, we must consider the creational foundation upon which subsequent internalization is built. We do not internalize in a vacuum. In chapter fourteen, self-examination was said to involve self-awareness and self-appraisal. Christians on the way to God must become well acquainted with themselves before God and learn to appraise and distinguish that within which is damaged and/or sinful (and therefore needing to be deconstructed) as well as *that within which is good and based in God's providential or saving word.* That which is being internalized in the present is necessarily planted in the soil of God's *prior* work of soul formation. Within every adult, no matter how damaged or sinful, there is some good, created infrastructure—a result of earlier, healthy proper development—that provides the foundation upon which future internalization is based: happy memories, reasoning abilities, positive personality traits, social skills, a strong conscience, musical ability and so on. These competencies are gifts of God's creation grace, and an important part of the task of Christian soul care involves assisting counselees to recognize these gifts. As we have often noted, such things are sanctified by the word of God and prayer and are to be received with thanksgiving (1 Tim 4:4-6). Consent to God through gratitude for these providential gifts is a virtue that provides a theocentric, relational foundation for one's personhood. In fact, "One becomes a 'person,' one might say, analogous to the divine persons, only insofar as one is the determinate recipient of a gift; one is a person always in the evocation of a response" (Hart, 2003, p. 263). Further internalization, then, builds upon and strengthens the good, created structures of the soul, which are fundamentally God's gifts.

Major Kinds of Internalization Relevant for Soul Care

In chapter eight, we saw that there are a number of ways the Word of God has been expressed in creation. The words of God that create and hold together nature, personal agency and culture constitute human beings. If they have been exposed to Christian discourse, they are also shaped by Scripture and the gospel, and if they have been divinely converted, by God's salvific calling. In chapter nine, the semiodiscursive substance and context of human life was analyzed, and we examined its elements and forms, and the texts and contexts that give that form shape, particularly its narrative/dramatic/historical context. The signs of God involved in the construction of human beings is so rich, complex and diverse, it would seem advisable to try to simplify things as much as possible without distortion. So we will recategorize the breadth of human meaning that God has expressed into four major categories that seem the most relevant to soul care. The following four categories of media of internalization are arguably the most important in the work of helping people become more Christlike: Scripture, others, God's will and dipolar self-regulation skills. The interrelation between these four loci in Christian soul care is diagrammed in figure 16.1. We turn next to a discussion of each of these four categories in turn.

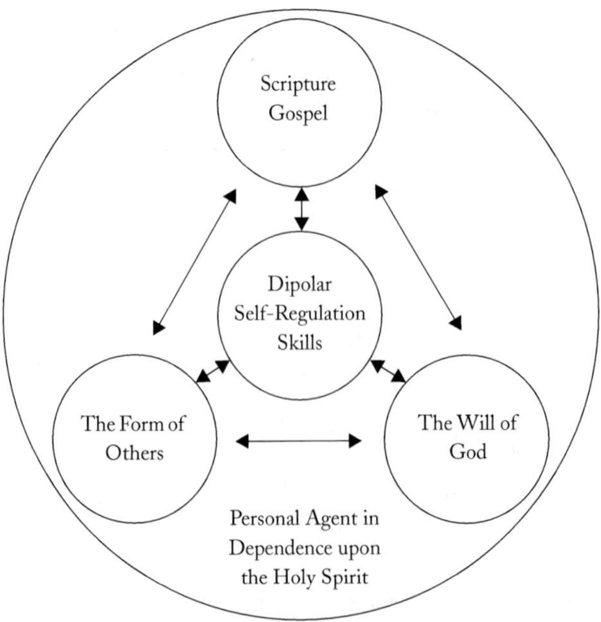

Figure 16.1 The different loci of the signs of God to be internalized

The Internalization of Scripture and the Gospel

Throughout this book, we have reflected on the unique value of Scripture and the gospel to the Christian community and to Christian maturation, and we have repeatedly affirmed the epistemological primacy of Scripture over all other texts and all the rest of the meaning of creation. As a result, we begin with Scripture, since the Bible should be in some sense the guide of all the other kinds of internalization that we will consider.

In this chapter we will explore the "taking in" of Scripture and the gospel in ways that give life: "the words that I have spoken to you are spirit and are life" (Jn 6:63). James put it like this: "receive the word implanted, which is able to save your souls" (Jas 1:21). What does it mean to receive the implanted word? It is not enough to affirm its propositional content or focus on obedience to its commands. As we have seen, there are many different kinds of texts and genres in the Bible, all of which are to be received in accordance with their divinely authored meaning: narratives, wisdom literature, law, psalms of praise, teaching, apocalyptic and promise. The internalization of Scripture entails properly receiving it all. Adapting Vanhoozer (2002, 2005) for our purposes, we might say receiving the word implanted is to understand rightly the various divine speech acts (or illocutions) of the Bible and appropriate them deeply in the heart (consent), so that their divine perlocutionary intent is realized fittingly in the manifestation of one's life.

By receiving God's illocutions/perlocutions in Scripture and the gospel into our being, God's form comes to be experientially realized in us. And through this process, we gain special access to the Son of God. "Every word of scripture goes directly, vertically, to the depths of God, i.e., to that deep center of fullness and unity where all the externally disparate words and aspects converge. And he, the Son of the Father is this fullness. He alone is the Bread of Life for which our souls hunger; we need not go any further, looking for any other bread, for its spiritual satisfaction would be illusory. He suffices" (Balthasar, 1986, p. 130). We take in Scripture and the gospel to take in Christ, the Bread of Life.[2] So how do Christians internalize the Scriptures and the gospel?

Cognitive internalization (from remembering to wisdom). The first step of the internalization of Scripture is cognitive. Without mental processing, there can be no deeper processing. As we have already considered, according to Edwards (1746/1959), notional understanding occurs "wherein the mind only beholds things in the exercise of a speculative faculty" (p. 272), what he called the "intellect," engaged in understanding concepts and facts. Edwards was referring to the set of processes psychologists now call cognition, which includes implicit and explicit memory systems, language, mental representation (including propositions and images), narrativity, and rationality or reasoning (including problem solving), what has sometimes been termed the "cold" system of the mind. We might also call this the "information processing system." School-based learning utilizes such processes.

Memorization and recall. The simplest type of cognitive learning is the memorization or storage of specific facts in long-term memory, whether an image of a shepherd, a Bible verse or a definition of justification.[3] The storage of such information is foundational to higher forms of cognitive processing, which all must rely on one's knowledge base for their operations. However, the limitation of this type of cognitive learning is seen in the fact that one may store such information (e.g., Bible verses) without understanding the material. As a result, this form of cognitive internalization of Christian truth is considered rudimentary and does very little, in and of itself, to reform the soul.

Comprehension/understanding. More important is the understanding of the meaning and significance of biblical information. This includes such processes as grasping concepts, putting ideas into one's own words, reading and interpreting discourse, and drawing new inferences, activities which are categorized as "reasoning." Then, in addition to comprehending information, one's understanding of the material must be stored in long-term memory for enduring structural change to occur. This "midlevel" cognitive internalization is at the heart of the educational enterprise and is involved in almost all forms of contemporary soul care (except perhaps strictly behavioral treatment), but it is obviously basic to the internalization of Scripture.

Higher-order processing beyond comprehension: Elaboration. There are many uses to which an understanding of biblical truth can be put. *Analysis* breaks down a set of information into its component parts and relations. We can analyze a text, for example, in order to trace its argument, relate one truth to another or construct a systematic treatment of a doctrine. *Synthesis* gathers and constructs comprehended information into a logically related system and can craft it into a coherent text. Both these uses require inductive and deductive reasoning, and sometimes problem-solving skills are involved when conceptual or practical difficulties are uncovered in the process of understanding.

In a classic article on memory, Craik and Lockhart (1972) argued that the more deeply information is processed (e.g., semantic elaboration is deeper than visual pattern recognition), the more likely the information is stored and later recalled, an insight with a good deal of empirical support (Haberlandt, 1999). This suggests that the more fully one engages the meaning of the text or truth, the better will be the storage and recall (and so the greater the internalization). Also, the more one engages the material in a variety of contexts, the more likely transfer of knowledge (or skill) to similar but new domains or contexts will be fostered. This general principle is also supported by the fact that expertise is associated with greater recall (Kimball & Holyoak, 2000). All this suggests that the more fully one elaborates information, the better the internalization (Craik & Tulving, 1975).

Wisdom and discernment. We turn finally to intellectual virtues. Significantly, the deepest, most important sort of reflection, wisdom, has long been encouraged in the Judeo-Christian tradition. Biblical wisdom makes use of the above processes but does so in the context of everyday life, with special reference to moral and spiritual issues. According to two secular psychologists, wisdom is "expert knowledge involving good judgment and advice in the domain [of the] fundamental pragmatics of life" (Baltes & Smith, 1990, p. 95). This is helpful but falls short of a Christian definition, since the Judeo-Christian tradition is theocentric: the fear of Yahweh is the beginning of wisdom (Prov 1:9). There is no Christian wisdom apart from a deep consenting to God as one's Creator, Lord and Judge. Discernment is a closely related intellectual virtue in the Christian tradition, grounded in one's knowledge of God's law that leads to right acting (Pieper, 1966; Vanhoozer, 2005). Both wisdom and discernment are a function of the deepest cognitive internalization of the Scripture and the gospel that issues in the capacity to reflect on life in light of the triune God and his agenda in a way that disposes one to act virtuously.

Promoting the cognitive internalization of Scripture and the gospel. It is well known that rehearsal of information is strongly related to its retention and retrieval. Consequently, the more one thinks about a passage or doctrine, the greater the likelihood that its meaning will be stored. Also, the more individuals think about conceptual material, the better they will remember and understand it. So soul-care providers should foster ongoing reflection on relevant Christian passages and teachings and their relation to one's life and one's relationships (this could be called Christian cognitive therapy or psychoeducation).

Repetition is important, but not as important as depth of processing (Craik & Lockhart, 1972; Craik & Tulving, 1975). Hearing, reading and studying Bible passages and books that explore relevant Christian doctrine (e.g., God's attributes, one's identity in Christ), so that they are well understood and retained and can be utilized in the future, is necessary for any deeper appropriation of Scripture and the gospel. Counselors should assign homework, like reading, journaling and appropriate worksheets, so that counselees can reflect on and elaborate the meaningfulness of biblical information in multiple, everyday contexts, in order to facilitate the storage of biblical information as deeply as possible and its transfer to similar but new settings, relationships and activities. Application to oneself is a distinct cognitive activity that ties salvific truth into one's self-representations; from there it can be brought to bear on one's intentions, goals and plans. Self-talk (as illustrated in Ps 42), or "telling yourself the truth" (Backus & Chapian, 2000) is usually necessary to foster such elaboration with reference to the self. Basically, whatever cognitive activity one does with reference to scriptural or gospel truth—however one elaborates the truth—fosters internalization.

Carditive internalization of the affections (from feeling to loving). The commonsense distinction between head and heart is virtually a truism in everyday discourse, and it is based on a valid, experiential distinction between cognition and emotion that expresses an awareness of a depth dimension to the soul. We turn next to consider an internalization of Scripture and the gospel that is greater than the merely cognitive. Edwards (1746/1959) contrasted *notional* understanding of Christian truth with what he called *spiritual* understanding. He believed that the latter was distinguished by the engagement of the "religious affections," and he located such understanding in the heart or the will. It "consists in the sensations of a new spiritual sense" that is moved by "the supreme beauty and excellency of divine things" and results in a love of these things, most importantly, the love of God (p. 271).

For Edwards, the *heart* (*kardia*, Gk.) referred to an "organ" of the soul responsible for a wide variety of human experience, including appetites, desires, feelings, emotions, motives, loves (and hates) and the will—the origin of action that inclines the individual to move toward or away from something. His distinction between mind and heart should not be exaggerated. He recognized that both lay at the center of the human being, overlapped considerably and properly influenced the other.[4] Today we understand even better the complex interrelation between cognition and emotion (Johnson-Laird & Oatley, 2000), as well as cognition and motivation (Gollwitzer & Bargh, 1996; Heckhausen, 1991; Kuhl, 1985). Indeed, today we would also make a greater distinction between emotion, motivation and volition (choice activity), as will be seen below. Nevertheless, there is real value in the overarching distinction between head and heart or cognitive and carditive. *Cognitive* refers to psychological activity that processes the *nature* of an object (understanding what kind of an object it is), while *carditive* will refer to psychological activity that processes the *worth* of an object (understanding whether it is good and to be sought, or bad and to be avoided).[5] Carditive activity involves appraisal. As mentioned in chapter nine, the common denominator of all emotion is its bivalent quality: it signifies something positive or negative. So the heart directs the individual toward or away from something.[6]

Carditive internalization for Christians involves the activation and storing of values that are supposed to correspond to God's values—his preferences, loves and hates. Since these values are most clearly revealed in Scripture and the gospel, carditive internalization begins with the processing of biblical/gospel discourse in such a way that one's affections are engaged and these experiences are retained in memory.

Examples of affective internalization. How can this be promoted? Through reflecting deeply on topics like God's beauty, Christ's suffering on the cross or the believer's union with Christ in a way that leads to a sense of love, worship, shame or joy. One of God's perlocutionary intentions when he inspired the Scriptures was that it would engender in the reader/hearer an intersubjective experience (with the indwelling Holy Spirit) in which the believer shares for a time the feelings that God has toward some theme, event or person. This joint emotional experience with God from the standpoint of our activity is one aspect of what is called faith or consent. As a result of many such experiences, the brain gets "rewired" axiologically (in terms of one's values).

One of the best ways to promote the internalization of godly emotion is Bible meditation and prayer (Tan, 1996). "By study we seek the truth in books or in some other source outside our own minds. In meditation we strive to absorb what we have already taken in" (Merton, 1960, p. 53). "One who really meditates does not merely think, he also loves, and by his love—or at least by his sympathetic intuition into the reality upon which he reflects—he enters into that reality and knows it so to speak from within, by a kind of identification" (Merton, p. 52). We might call meditation on Scripture and the gospel (and related Christian books that promote psychospiritual development) *therapeutic reading* (reading that promotes the soul's healing).

Many believe that the affections are outside of one's control (in contrast with cognition). But this is a misleading exaggeration. It would be more accurate to say that emotions are *less* controllable than cognition, for they can be guided and regulated. For example, it is possible to train one's attention to focus on thoughts that are more likely to promote the emergence of peace. This kind of emotional experience has to be fostered and relished, or it will not happen; there is often internal resistance to emotional experience of many kinds, especially godly emotion. There is a paradox here. One must pray to receive godly emotions, but one ought not be merely passive and simply wait for God to magically change one's emotions. God wants humans to seek him, to reach out for him and to receive him. "Abide in me," after all, is an imperative (Jn 15:4).

What feelings should be promoted? Of greatest importance is the religious affection of love (Edwards, 1738/1969, 1746/1959), particularly the love of God. Also valuable is conviction of sin through the godly sculpting of the conscience. "Christians . . . have the book of God to rectify the inward book of conscience" (Sibbes, 1862-1864/1981, Vol. 3, p. 213). One of the most important objects for affective internalization is the death and resurrection of Christ. The believer has been united to Christ in his death and resurrection (Rom 6:1-11); however, this central, redemptive-historical event has to be more deeply internalized for it to realize Christ's transforming intentions. One must take it into the center of one's being in order to "reckon" oneself "dead to sin, but alive to God in Christ Jesus" (Rom 6:11).

A positive, applied example of Christian emotion internalization is the activation of appropriate emotions in light of a fresh godly experience (like feeling joy upon seeing something of God's beauty), which forms new neural patterns (memories) and forges desirable neural pathways between reflection regions and emotion regions. One can also replace an inappropriate feeling (after one has properly worked through it in deconstruction) by a feeling that corresponds more to God's preferences. For example, after negative emotions surrounding an event are decoupled from the memory, it is desirable to associate other, healthier emotions with these events, emotions that conform more fully to God's comprehensive appraisal of the event (e.g., contentment rather than despair, in light of Rom 8:28). Secular theorists working in this area have called this kind of procedure "counter-conditioning" (Prochaska & Norcross, 2006) and "emotion restructuring" (Greenberg & Paivio, 1997, pp. 120-29).

Optimal emotional arousal. As is well known, the relation of emotional arousal to productive activity is a U-shaped curve. Too little emotion is unmotivating, and too much emotion is overwhelming and disabling; so it is for Christiformic internalization of affect. Generally speaking, for optimal effects, Christians should cultivate midlevel arousal of emotions that are a relatively accurate reflection of God's feelings (as best as we can discern from Scripture) about a troubling issue or person. Up to a point, higher arousal increases the likelihood that the emotion experience will be stored in long-term memory and the more likely it will be rehearsed, further insuring its maintenance in long-term memory (Hyde & Jenkins, 1973). Also, the more frequently similar experiences occur and the longer they occur, the deeper (and more extensive and pervasive) their influence, which in turn increases the probability that that emotion will be aroused in the future in similar contexts.

An important part of the distinctive therapeutic agenda of Christianity entails the ingression of God's character and salvific truths. Christians need to attend particularly to *God's loves* so that their affective life more and more reflects God's. Consequently, affective meditation on the Scriptures/gospel (and books based on them) can increase the degree of emotional investment one has in God and his ways and can change the structure of the brain and the experience of the soul accordingly. Singing hymns and listening to creative, deep and theologically solid Christian music can also enhance carditive internalization.[7]

Carditive internalization of the will (from intending to practicing). As noted above, Edwards located both emotions and the will in the heart, thus emphasizing their commonality and close relationship: they are both "directional" in nature and thoroughly interdependent, and together they define the depth of the soul. For these reasons, everyday discourse, in the West at least, likewise locates both the affections and the will in the heart. On the other hand, other Christian thinkers (like Aquinas) and most psychologists today are inclined to make a greater distinction between the emotions and the will, emphasizing their differences in structure, process and role within, and suggesting they are distinct modules. As a result of these combined considerations, the affections and the will will both be categorized as carditive, but each will be examined separately. The phenomena and dynamics described in this section have also been labeled *conative* (Little, 1999) and *volitional* (Gollwitzer, 1996).

Regarding internalization, the will is being treated as "deeper" than the emotions, because phenomenologically the emotions seem more ephemeral than the will, and because volitional phenomena have to do with one's predispositions to act, which seem to lie more at the defining core of one's character—the most important form of the soul—than emotions. Here we will consider the role of Scripture/gospel internalization in the development of the internal conditions necessary to foster the practice of virtue.

Christ referred to the semiodiscursive basis of this process: "If anyone loves Me, he will *keep My word*. . . . He who does not love Me does not *keep My words*" (Jn 14:23-24; see also Jn 8:51-52, 55; 15:20; 17:6; 1 Jn 2:5; Rev 3:8). The New Testament term for "keep" *(tēreō)* means also to observe or to fulfill (Arndt & Gingrich, 1957). To keep one's own word is to fulfill what one has committed oneself to. To keep God's word is to accomplish his will or obey him. Paul similarly encouraged the Philippians to "hold fast" the word of life (Phil 2:16; *epechō*). These phrases refer to the kind of internalization of Scripture and the gospel that affects human plans, goals and intentions to act. It renders some courses of action plausible and even probable, and others unsatisfactory, unworthy of investment and, with reference to some actions, even sinful. Because one can believe God's word superficially (Jas 2), "keeping it" or "holding it fast" is more important than merely believing it is true and evidences deeper internalization.[8]

In order to engage in any human actions, certain intellectual, affective and dispositional structures have to be in place. To begin with, human action has to be mentally represented before it can be implemented; it requires the assumption of a set of goods, and plans and goals to attain those goods (Gollwitzer, 1996; Kruglanski, 1996), all of which leads to the formation of personal action constructs (Little, 1999; see also Cantor, 1990; Emmons, 1986; Little, 1999)—affectively charged dispositions toward certain types of activity, that guide one's actions.

How does Scripture/gospel internalization affect one's action dispositions? It provides inspired information regarding God's understanding of goods and some of the means for realizing those goods. For example, in Scripture God reveals himself to be the highest good of humanity and promotes prayer, Christian fellowship and exposure to God's word as means to become increasingly centered on him, while also commanding certain kinds of actions that bring him glory. Such discourse is supposed to shape the believer's action priorities and possibilities. As Scripture is internalized, certain action possibilities make more sense; and new plans, goals and personal action constructs are formed that are the means by which new patterns of action are implemented and eventually routinized. Believers must receive Scripture in such ways in order to change their action dispositions for the better. To promote volitional internalization, meditative prayer is again recommended. Meditation on the goods of Scripture and the use of guided imagery and mental rehearsal to envision the implementation of God's Word through future grace foster the development of tendencies toward godly action. But the most important way to improve one's dispositions toward virtue is to act often in the desired ways; by this means one's character gets reformed. Everyone knows this is easier said than done. So some preparation (like using meditation to cultivate the right kinds of desires and motives) will help.

The Word of God in Scripture and the gospel provide the primary semio-discursive material for the internal reformation of Christian believers, by presenting a description of God's design for human life, the form of Christ. The obvious limitation of the Bible is that it is only a set of texts on paper. The proper, God-ordained development of human life requires more, for example, interaction and dialogue with other persons, God and images of God.

The Internalization of the Form of Others

We have often mentioned the importance of others in human development. Here we focus on the *reparative* effects of knowing God and working with skilled soul-care providers on the seeking believer. As we saw in chapter nine, individual humans are situated within a four-dimensional relational framework. Humans are made for relationship with God and other humans who are signs of God. Before getting to know God, other humans are the primary personal form with which children engage. Through dialogue and other activities, early discourse-shaped experiences with other humans catalyze emotional experiences, create images and model actions, much of which is stored in memory, and so they have a remarkable, long-term effect on the developing child. Though the degree of impact of relationship on the individual lessens after childhood, human relationships are basic to human life across the life span. *And this is the way God intended it to be.* Humans are made in the *imago Dei*, so they are supposed to be communal signs of the triune God on earth, and human nature was evidently created by God to be shaped by those who resemble God. "The other is not . . . *originally* an idol of thought, but an icon in which the infinite is pleased uniquely to disclose itself" (Hart, 2003, p. 144). Consequently, images of God provide a unique kind of sign of the Word of God. We have seen that Christ, the Word of God, is the archetypal image of God (Grenz, 2001; Horton, 2005; Kline, 1999), the ultimate pattern of the human form. Other humans are to be understood as ectypes or replicas of that Image/Word—more or less resembling the Archetype. As the Word perfectly resembles the Father (Jn 14:7-9), other humans more or less resemble the Word. So God has ordained human life in such a way that the forms of humans themselves are a concentrated medium of the meaningful Form of God, more or less. "There is the sweet sight of God in the face of a friend" (Sibbes, 1973, p. 192).

In the Christian framework, relationship and truth are absolutely interrelated and interdependent. After all, Christ himself is the Truth (Jn 14:6). Nevertheless, this relational kind of internalization is obviously quite different from the storage of textual speech-acts in the Bible or expressed in the gospel. Consider how different experientially is the quality of a human relationship from factual information about the relationship, between coming to know someone personally, through an engaging conversation, and the kind of information one reads off an intake form at a mental health clinic. It is necessary to understand how the relational locus of internalization helps believers become more like God.

Modern theories of "taking others in." The psychoanalytic tradition has studied the nature of the internalization of others since Freud and has even used the term *internalization* to describe the process (Hamilton, 1988). The Rogerian tradition (and subsequent research, e.g., Beutler et al., 2003) has documented empirically the healing benefits of being in a therapeutic relationship with someone who is healthier than oneself. Currently there are many models of therapy that see human relationship as central to the healing process, including social-cognitive, interpersonal, attachment and object relations therapies, and self psychology.

Social-cognitive approaches to the self recognize that children incorporate aspects of others into their selves (Leary, 2002). Perhaps the simplest form of other-internalization studied by the social cognitive approach is imitation or modeling, which consists of copying behavior (Bandura, 1986). Though most influential in childhood, the impact of modeling continues throughout life.

Object relations (OR) theory explains how our past relationships with others shape our current self- and other-representations. OR therapists found that time spent with the therapist can modify the counselee's internal social representations in healthier ways, based on the healthier relational style of the therapist. Attachment theory is closely related to OR theory and similarly suggests that the *working models* of adults (their internal construction of close relationships) can be changed for the better when they experience positive attachment experiences with healthier adults (Fonagy, 2002). Counselors facilitate this process when they provide an atmosphere of safety and security, by offering a consistent, predictable environment in which the counselee feels affirmed, trusted and loved (Slade, 1999).

Kohut (1971, 1977, 1984), the founder of self psychology, coined a term for the social construction of the self in therapy: *transmuting internalization.* Through the formation of an empathic bond in therapy, the counselee's past relational structures get activated, leading to perceptions/hopes that the therapist will be able to meet the counselee's relational needs (through merging or mirroring[9]). By affirming and understanding the counselee, the therapist does meet some of the counselee's relational needs, but because no human can meet all the needs of another, the counselee experiences some frustration. The therapist then provides an explanation of the counselee's experiences to help the counselee develop internal structures (e.g., more positive self-representations) that will address the counselee's needs more realistically, leading to the development of a new, healthier self and relations with others. Voluminous research on modern psychotherapy has found the therapeutic alliance (and related therapist traits) to be one of the most significant variables positively affecting therapy (Orlinsky, Ronnestad & Willutzki, 2004).

These theories and research assume a modern, autocentric and evolutionary disciplinary matrix, so they have no doctrine of sin and no appreciation for the theocentric purposes of human relationality. Nonetheless, they would seem to provide relatively accurate models of a genuine creational dynamic: how an ongoing, supportive relationship between a more damaged adult and a healthier adult can significantly alter the former's self- and other-representations, making him or her more realistic, less defensive and more loving. What is not always fully appreciated in these theories is the role of communal dialogue in these processes. It is *in* the verbal interaction that occurs through strategic discourse (communicating hope, probing and raising questions, offering encouragements and challenging assumptions)—through the give-and-take of loving, purpose-driven conversation—that the individual engages with another and is moved toward maturation. Christians see in these relational, dialogical dynamics creation-grace processes that are ordained by the triune God. However, they may also be fruits of redemptive grace: when both persons are in Christ and indwelt by the Holy Spirit, and the exemplary person signifies fairly well the triune God's character, so that the beneficiary is drawn closer to the triune God experientially and ideally becomes a little more like the triune God inwardly. Within the skillful, supportive context of the therapeutic alliance, an intersubjective medium is created through which the internalization of the discourse (e.g., beliefs) and appraisal (e.g., affirmation or consent)—that is, the *imago Dei* form—of the therapist occurs.

The development of* imago Dei *internalization. Thus far, probably no group has reflected on the process of other-internalization more than the psychoanalytic school and its heirs. According to N. Hamilton (1990), "Internalization refers to any mechanism for including something new within the person" (p. 68). He suggests there are three types of interpersonal internalization: incorporation, introjection and identification. Incorporation is the most primitive type of internalization and consists of a fantasy of ingesting or merging. "Incorporation implies a psychological 'eating' prior to the development of clear self-other boundaries. The object is taken in and disappears inside the non-differentiated self-other matrix" (Hamilton, 1990, p. 68). In adults with severe psychopathology, like psychosis, there may be incorporation fantasies, in which the self and the Other merge and become one. In less damaged but still hurting people, for example, those merely lacking a well-developed sense of self, a yearning for this kind of experience may still be voiced in counseling (or in marriage), for example, when a counselee (or spouse) says to her counselor (or marriage partner), "I feel like I just can't get close enough to you," or "I wish I could take you into my tummy," and this may be symbolized in dreams of being pregnant and carrying the person inside. But there are more modest and legitimate kinds of incorporation in counseling, for example, the taking in of the counselor's interest, appropriate affection and words of affirmation, encouragement and challenge.

Introjection is not as primitive as incorporation, since it is revealed by the presence of a stable mental structure left behind in the individual: an internal object that resembles the person to whom one has formed a strong emotional bond (either positive or negative); however, the internal object is still felt to be relatively distinct from the self. For example, through the course of many interactions, a counselee lacking sufficient self-structure to manage well her internal world may form an *introject* of the counselor, so that later in the week when experiencing a conflict with a coworker, the counselee can almost hear the counselor giving internal advice on how to handle this, almost as if he were standing there and talking to her, yet she knows he is not. The existence of introjects constitutes a necessary middle stage in the internalization of healthier self-structure.

Identification is the most mature and deepest form of other-internalization and involves an alteration in one's self-representation, so that it resembles the Other. This is a necessary and desirable aspect of normal development. Children with authoritative parents by early adulthood typically come to identify significantly with their parents and share many of their opinions, attitudes and interactional style. This can also occur in therapy when the therapist's beliefs, affects or strategies—some of which may have been formerly experienced introjectively—are more fully appropriated by the counselee as his or her own. For example, identification is evident when counselees are tempted to despair but instead speak encouraging words to themselves—like the counselor has done in the past, perhaps, but now the self-talk has a felt sense of being the counselee's own personal convictions. They have become the *counselee's* beliefs. "The internalization of new experience and the building of new internal objects occurs throughout life. It is fundamental to the process through which the self develops cohesion and vitality, maintains its sense of self, and grows in complexity over time" (Scharff & Scharff, 1998, p. 223).

Christian reflections. A Christian translation of this literature has to make reference to the creational and theocentric dynamics involved. For adult Christians in dependence upon the Holy Spirit the adult internalization of the human Other is a good and desirable process, an important means of taking into oneself the form or image of God to the extent that the other resembles God. The curative value of such relationships depends on the extent to which the caregiver is, in fact, conformed to the image of Christ; conversely, this process is compromised the more the counselor departs from that image. This makes it extremely important that pastors, counselors and other soul-care providers are relatively psychospiritually mature themselves, and it places some limits on who should be providing care and when. For example, it may be that some people are suffering too much from their own relational damage to be very effective in this way. There is wisdom in the recognition that some people who want to help others may need more healing themselves before they can be of much help. On the other hand, the more mature the counselor, the more he or she will have the resources to handle severe relational deficits in counselees and promote healthy transmuting internalization.

Christian soul-care providers, however, need to transpose the affirming/mirroring experience theocentrically by keeping the following considerations in mind. First, the relational quality for which Christian therapists are to aim is resemblance to the archetypal mutual affection that the members of the Trinity have for each other. Second, the ectypal counselor-counselee dialogue is itself related to God, so that the counselee understands that the counselor's objective is to image God faithfully through affirmation of the counselee, the raising of questions, counselor transparency and the establishing of emotional intimacy, the teaching of Christian truth, and the challenging of blind spots and sin. The goal is to maintain an awareness of the tridimensional personal context of human life (in this setting: God-counselor-counselee). When this happens, a beneficial, distinctly Christian (trialogical) therapeutic alliance is formed.

What exactly is being "brought in" in *imago Dei* internalization? Just as the Bible is a representation of some of the mind of God, so humans are semiodiscursive images of God, that is, representations of the form of God. A key aspect of conformity to Christ's image involves dialoguing with people who are more psychospiritually mature than we are so that we can engage conversationally with their form, grasp more of its rationale and beauty, learn how to consent to their healthy features and their views of us, and receive their love and holiness, with the result that we gradually come to resemble something of their form. Consent necessarily takes in that to which it consents.

Others as idols. Powlison (2004, chap. 10) has raised some legitimate concerns about relying too much on the relationship between counselor and counselee, believing that it may promote idolatry (see also Almy, 2000; Tripp, 2002). Any aspect of the creation can become an idol (Rom 1:23), especially humans made in God's image—particularly *caring* humans, who can become ultimate, often unconsciously, in a person's heart. However, in seeking to avoid that danger, Christian and biblical counselors must be careful to avoid religious dualism and pit God's creation against God. He created image-bearers—signs or icons of God (Col 1:15) that are supposed to resemble him—and he evidently ordained that they would legitimately have a profound influence upon each other. In ultimate dependence upon God and his salvation, Christians should make use of every legitimate, creational resource available to help people become more whole and more conformed to the image of Christ, so long as we alert people to their respective spiritual dangers. Otherwise we may develop a soul-care model that aims at theocentrism but unwittingly works contrary to God's actual design for glorifying himself—in this case, through human relationships—and so undermines what God wants to accomplish through *us*. As signs of God, Christian caregivers are supposed to be a relational bridge between the God that they are seeking to image in their lives and those with whom they work.

There is an inevitable tension, in a fallen world with fallen hearts, between a proper, God-centered use of his creation and a continual temptation toward idolatry of that creation. This is not accidental. God did not make the way to himself in this age superficially easy. In order to promote a healthy, God-centered counseling relationship, the counselor ought to discuss the dangers of idolatry with their counselees and assist them in turning over to God their natural created desires for relationship, but desires that are now necessarily corrupt and prone to idolize. The reader will recognize this is simply an example of repentance (a kind of deconstruction discussed in the previous chapter), in this case a putting to death or letting go of fallen desires for idolatrous relationship that get activated through transference feelings for the counselor. Good relationships with wise, loving therapists will challenge us to learn how to distinguish false, idolatrous desires from healthy created desires for relationship, as well as how to receive the healthy love of the therapist *in and through Christ*, as coming from Christ and leading the counselee to him.

The Internalization of a Healing, Deepening Relationship with the God of Scripture

As important as human relationships were designed by God to be, the triune personhood of God is to be the center of Christian relational healing. However, because of the hiddenness of God in this age, we have no access to the actual, concrete form of God such as the world had in Jesus Christ, when he lived on earth. Now, our experience of him is structured by the Bible and the gospel in the context of the church, and actualized by the Holy Spirit, who bears witness of Christ (Jn 15:26). God's form—revealed in Christ, described in the Bible, and communicated through the Holy Spirit—is the ultimate Archetype in relation to which the individual believer and the church as a whole is to become conformed. Consequently, Christian soul healing needs to promote repeated *experiences* of the actual, immaterial Form of God, mediated by Scripture.

Meditative prayer: The dialogical means of experiencing the triune God. Meditative prayer—communal dialogue with God—is the fundamental way human persons are to relate to the divine Persons. Meditative prayer is the closest actual approximation to trinitarian communion human beings can have. By engaging in conversational interaction with God that receives and is guided by his spoken word in Scripture and the gospel and responds to him in prayer, humans enter into the eternal pattern of love and communication of the Trinity.

Recognizing an interior dimension to prayer, the Catholic tradition has distinguished kinds of prayer according to their depth (Danielou, 1996; Tanquerey, 1930). Mental prayer is understood to be the first stage, where one expresses conscious thoughts to God using one's cognitive capacities. It consists of verbal declarations of praise and thanks, confession of sin, affirmations of belief and petitions, based on Bible study and a growing understanding and internalization of the Christian faith (Tanquerey, 1930).

Affective prayer, as the term indicates, engages the emotions and is the product of the meaning of God having been more deeply ingressed into the soul. As Christians come to know their God better through increasingly beneficial meditation upon Christian truth and greater self-awareness, they inevitably develop more sophisticated feelings of love, awe and gratitude toward him—as well as personal conviction—and express their feelings to him through prayer. Because this prayer engages the affections, it is deeper, more profound and more inward than mere intellectual declarations and so indicates a greater internalization and enjoyment of one's relationship with God. Tanquerey suggested that affective prayer is fostered by intentionally seeking to love God and by meditating on him and his works. The basis of affective prayer, then, is found in the affective appropriation of scriptural truth through worship and meditation. In the course of this kind of meditative prayer, in which our cognitive and affective capacities are both engaged with God—communicating to him and he to us—we draw closer to the Form of God.

The Catholic tradition has also identified a more advanced type of prayer, the deepest of all, called contemplative prayer (Tanquerey, 1930). As the soul becomes more focused upon God, it becomes better able to center itself on God alone. Whereas mental and affective prayer may cover a range of topics at prayer, contemplative prayer is characterized by a simple, calm focus upon a single object—God himself—from "the inmost depth of the soul" (Tanquerey, p. 651). "Happy is the soul that hears the Lord speaking within her, and receives from His mouth the word of comfort" (Thomas à Kempis, 1864, p. 121). Though the soul is very still in contemplation, it simultaneously involves "activity in the highest degree" (von Hildebrand, 1990, p. 120), for it seeks a manifestation of the Object's splendor from out of its "transcendent depths."[10] No experience in life is more prone to change us into God's likeness than deep, meditative prayer.

Protestants have tended to be skeptical about such activities (Corduan, 1991; Horton, 1996). Some have been concerned about mysticism in general, believing that it leads to irrationality and an "emptying of the mind," and the fact is that some of its proponents have carelessly recommended devotional practices that deliberately avoid the use of words or symbols and that therefore bear more resemblance to the practice of Eastern religions than Christianity (for a critique of this, see Corduan, 1991). As the reader might suspect, this author has similar reservations about any model that intentionally minimizes cognitive content. Without Christian experience being normalized by truth, there is no way to know what deity one is worshiping or what religion one is practicing.[11]

But Catholic thought in general does not promote devotional practices that are devoid of Christian truth (see early Merton, 1951; Tanquerey, 1930).[12] Moreover, while Protestants have felt that advocates of extreme forms of Christian mysticism[13] are incautious, if not reckless, in their advocacy of "darkness" over the light of Scripture, they freely admit that the human mind cannot be expected to comprehend all of God (Bavinck, 2004; Calvin, 1559/1960; Hodge, 1995; Frame, 1987, 2002).[14] His peace "surpasses all comprehension" (Phil 4:7), his love "surpasses knowledge" (Eph 3:19), his judgments are unsearchable and his ways unfathomable (Rom 11:33). Prayer with him would be expected to lead, at times, to experiences of his transcendence and infinite greatness. Such experiences should be sought, not repudiated; otherwise, we will find ourselves conversing with a finite "god" that our little minds can handle. But orthodox Christian meditative prayer—though it can be overwhelmed by God's infinity—does not leave truth behind. One can only love what one knows. Rather, such prayer is simply an intense, deep form of prayer, based on truth and open to an infinite God.

Forging neural pathways between one's God-image and one's* Imago Dei *internalizations. As a result of experiences of God in meditative prayer and scriptural teaching, humans form a mental representation of God (one's God-image; see Howe, 1995). However, it would seem necessary and inevitable that earlier experiences with people made in God's image interact with one's God-image (Spero, 1992). What is the relation between one's other-representations and one's God-image? Individuals who have experienced relatively healthy relationships with relatively healthy others and have formed fairly healthy introjects of them, because of the resemblance of those healthy others to God, are more likely to possess internalized structures that can rather readily be used as cognitive and carditive means to connect with the form of God revealed in Christ and Scripture, and communicated through the Holy Spirit. On the other hand, this process is made more difficult if one's introjects are quite at variance with the triune God's character. Because of their structural defects, such individuals will have a greater need to form *new* cognitive and carditive structures (grounded in the formation of new neural networks and pathways), derived largely from Scripture and meditative prayer, and derivatively through relationships with healthier Christians, in order to be able to connect better and more deeply with God. Ideally, there is supposed to be a continual mutually reinforcing interaction between one's experiences of God and of those who resemble God.

The Internalization of the Will of God

A little reflection reveals that the created order is composed of a plethora of patterns, known as norms, laws, rules or principles. The physical universe operates according to what have been called "laws" (McGrath, 2001). Regularities are no less important to the social universe (Searle, 1995; Miller & Prentice, 1996)—though the term *laws* has a specific, legal connotation within the social world. Perhaps as a result, social regularities have tended to be called norms, rules or principles.

Christians understand that God could have created a universe with different norms than those in *this* universe. Though he could not mandate immoral norms (or he would contradict his own goodness), he could have established any number of physical laws differently than he did (e.g., absolute zero could have been calibrated differently, human reproduction could have been asexual, or humans could have been telepathic). As we saw in chapter eight, the Bible teaches that cultural structures are also an imperfect expression of God's will (e.g., Rom 14:1-12), and the extant variety of cultural norms demonstrates more of the breadth of God's creativity than the uniformity of natural laws does.

Submission to God's will expressed in submission to cultural norms. Researchers have discovered that an important part of early childhood cognitive development is the recognition of lawful regularities that exist in the creation (see Piaget, 1954). In subsequent years, children also come to form representations of their social world as well, which they learn about through discourse and socialization. These norms include a wide variety of phenomena, for example, the existence of others; family rules for appropriate behavior, manners and other social conventions (like fashion); rules for economic transactions; standards of excellence; social stereotypes; gender norms; scripts for how to conduct oneself in specific social settings; appropriate expectations, duties and obligations in various contexts; social roles; laws of the government; beliefs regarding the Good; and moral and spiritual norms (Durkin, 1995; Miller & Prentice, 1996; Searle, 1995).

Since such social phenomena are a function of the word of God, it is appropriate to consider how their being internalized contributes to God's glory and optimal human well-being. We find in the book of Proverbs and through our own observation of human lives that people who do not conform to such norms have problems in living. People who experience the physical world in ways contrary to established norms (e.g., who hear voices no one else hears) or those who chronically violate social norms (e.g., by showing up to work significantly late) have serious difficulties in living and their problems with "normativeness" are considered by most people to be a sign of dysfunction, if not psychopathology. Sin, in fact, *is* lawlessness *(anomia)* or normlessness (1 Jn 3:4), and sin's destructiveness in human life is manifested, or at least symbolized, wherever such chaos is found. Generally speaking, as believers internalize and conform to the kinds of social norms identified above, they are submitting to God's will, becoming more mature and responsible, and contributing to their psychospiritual well-being. This glorifies God. Consequently, their being internalized deserves to be a focus of Christian soul care.

Submission to one's particular calling/mission. But there are some types of norms that are not universal but are specific to oneself (O'Donovan, 1986). Perhaps foremost is the need to consent to aspects of one's life. For example, to become more mature one must come to accept those who are a part of one's story: family members, those with whom one works, one's neighbors and the members of one's church. Consenting to their existence *before God* means accepting their characteristics, gifts, roles (e.g., the degree of authority they have over oneself), weaknesses and foibles, and even sins, as part of God's plan for oneself. For various reasons, this consent can be difficult. But such individuals are, in a significant sense, part of God's will for the believer, who has to learn how to receive them before God from the heart in order to grow. The norm to forgive others for their sins against us fits here.

Closely related to the foregoing are the obligations we have to specific others. For example, being married to someone imposes a requirement to have a special regard for that person, different from the regard one has to all people in general and to any other person in particular. Additional obligations include appropriate and reasonable care for one's property, other family members besides one's spouse, church members, neighbors, coworkers and other citizens. In addition, Christians would seem to have some special responsibility toward those in one's life or community who are especially disenfranchised, for example, the homeless, the mentally ill, orphans, minorities and so forth (Jas 1:27; 2:5). "I inherit from the past of my family, my city, my tribe, my nation, a variety of debts, inheritances, rightful expectations and obligations. These constitute the given of my life, my moral starting point. This is in part what gives my life its own moral particularity" (MacIntyre, 1984, p. 220).

Along a different but comparable vein, each individual has his or her own strengths and weaknesses that he or she must come to accept, including such things as body shape, physiognomy, physical limitations, gender, level of intelligence, personality and various competencies (or lack thereof). Kierkegaard (1849/1980, p. 82) argued that a mature Christian faith is exemplified in a willingness to accept oneself entirely, including one's limitations and one's possibilities, self-consciously before God.

A final class of personal norms to be accepted is one's relative station in life, including one's *location* in the world (geographical, economic and historical). Each person is here and not there, now and not then. Internalizing God's will similarly entails coming to terms with one's suffering, as well as the blessings that one has experienced and currently possesses, and learning how to do the best by them. We have been exposed to and currently experience certain events and conditions, some unpleasant and others enjoyable. Each person must *own* their story. All this is our own personal reality, ultimately established by God (see the book of Job, Rom 8:28; Eph 1:11; Jas 4:13-15); we are called to consent to it, and in therapy people often need to work through the barriers we have to such consent, establishing in the process a cohesive sense of one's identity and where one has come from *before God.*

These conditions together could be termed one's *calling* or one's *mission* from God (Vanhoozer, 2005), and therefore are a function of the word of God. However, sometimes one's individual calling comes into conflict with one's social norms. For example, if societal authorities require everyone to deny God, Christians are called to "obey God rather than men" (Acts 5:29). Sometimes Christians will be culturally marginalized for the sake of the kingdom, even to the point of martyrdom. Scripturally taught discernment is required to recognize which aspects of God's will have precedence in a given situation. Christian soul care involves training counselees to discern for themselves what precisely is God's mission for them in various contexts, since God's glory is specially manifested in consenting to his will, particularly when we have to deny ourselves (and our standing in the community) to follow him (Mt 10:32; 16:24). But wisdom is needed to distinguish the call of martyrdom from mere rashness and folly.

Strong and weak consent to one's calling/mission. This would be a good place to make a contrast between strong and weak consent. Christians are to respond to that which is good with *strong* consent—a wholehearted acceptance of the goodness that is from God. However, evil in the world cannot be approached in the same way. Evil is contrary to God's nature, so it must be resisted. To it, Christians must *dissent.* Yet, it is also—mysteriously—part of God's will that humans be exposed to evil. So one must "come to terms with it," and this "coming to terms" will be called *weak* consent. For example, if Tom is in a car accident, and his face is so disfigured that it can never be restored to its previous state, he must consent to this providence, even while knowing that the disfigurement itself is evil and not something in itself that God enjoys. Grief is fully compatible with weak consent. So, some kind of consent is necessary, when faced with any providential event, whether good or evil.

Similarly, not all social norms and personal callings must be accepted happily. Some laws are unjust from God's standpoint and should be changed (e.g., Jim Crow laws); some attitudes of parents are sinful (chronic derogatory criticism); some limitations can be improved upon with effort and practice (e.g., reading disabilities). In fact, *part of God's general calling upon Christians in this age is the overturning of evil in all its forms, whether physical, psychosocial, ethical or spiritual.* So, we must qualify the above discussion with the *normative* understanding that (1) some norms are relative and should only be accepted provisionally, and (2) some norms are simply evil and should be wholly resisted. Wisdom, again, is required to distinguish norms that are to be accepted from those that are to be questioned, adjusted or rejected from the standpoint of a higher norm. Therefore, the internalization of God's will in such cases cannot be entirely established a priori. It depends on a host of factors that have to be understood and evaluated in time, so that the very internalization of God's will contributes to the development of prudence and patience.[15]

In light of all that we have considered, the well-being of Christians is fostered as they discern and consent to God's will for their lives. This consent is a function of their psychospiritual maturity and has a depth dimension, so that the particulars of God's will can be embraced more or less wholeheartedly. Resistance to such norms is frequently a contributing factor to psychopathology. Consider, for example, a woman who is five foot seven inches tall, weighs one hundred pounds and believes she is fat, a young man who believes his family's myth that he is "good for nothing," a father who never calls his eldest daughter to find out how she is doing, or a worker who uses company time to play video games. Such beliefs and practices are unhealthy, pathological and more or less sinful, since they do not conform to the holy and wholesome will and word of God. Christian soul care at times consists of educating counselees about norms that they either do not know or do not adequately understand, and of skillfully wooing them to come to terms with those norms that they are obliged to accept, for their own peace of mind, to enable them to be most effective in their social world and to live more for the glory of God.

The development of will-of-God internalization. A group of secular researchers has documented a developmental trajectory for the internalization of social norms that would seem relevant to our discussion (Deci & Ryan, 1985; Grolnick, Deci & Ryan, 1997; Ryan & Deci, 2000, 2003). They argue that children have a natural propensity to internalize the norms and values to which they are exposed and make them their own. They also note that this process of internalization can be forestalled and impeded, depending on the adequacy of the socializing environment. Their work describes a developmental continuum of the internalization of norms. The most primitive appropriation of norms they call *external;* in this the person conforms to a norm solely because of environmental contingencies, like rewards or punishments. The perceived locus of causality (deCharms, 1968) is exclusively external to the person, evidenced in the abandonment of the norm in the absence of the contingency. Consequently, very little internalization has occurred; whatever has is limited to information regarding contingencies. This kind is typical of young children, and even the behavior of animals is regulated by such "norms." This is exemplified in a child who memorizes a Bible verse merely so he can get a star on his chart.

The next type of norm-internalization is *introjected*, in which the person accepts a norm but without personally owning it. The external contingencies have been affectively appropriated, so that one is motivated by one's emotions, including negative emotions (e.g., shame and guilt) and positive (feelings of superior performance and desire for social praise). The norm in question has been "brought in," so to speak, but not very far. The primary focus is still environmental, for example, social approval. As a result, the person experiences a fair amount of inner conflict between personal desires and concerns about social evaluation. This category is illustrated in sporadic attendance at church, mostly out of guilt.

The third orientation they term *identified*, where the person values a norm personally (identifies with it), but it operates as an isolated phenomenon, without connection to other norms and values. Identifying with a norm means it is internalized enough to be recognized as important. As a result, conformity produces some personal enjoyment and sense of accomplishment, without concern about others. Nonetheless, the norm is dissociated from other norms, so that it is not integrated within a system of other norms, resulting in inconsistencies in norm compliance. For example, a minister may have a genuine, personal commitment to the Christian faith and yet emotionally abuse his children at home. More advanced, then, is the stage of *integrated.* This occurs when norms are deeply appropriated into a coherent, hierarchical set of values that shapes one's overall identity. As a result, there is coherence in one's value system, indicating that the person's norms are embraced by the entire self. This leads to a high degree of satisfaction in norm adherence.

Even so, all the previous approaches treat norms *instrumentally*, that is, as a means to some other end. The final stage, according to these researchers, is *intrinsic* norm-internalization, evident when norms are followed because of an enjoyment in the normed activity itself. Such internalization results in the greatest sense of satisfaction and productivity, because the norm itself is its own end. Consider, for example, people who engage in devotions because they are intrinsically enjoyable and beneficial.

A Christian translation of self-determination theory. On the surface, most of this theory seems unobjectionable from a Christian standpoint. But the Christian interpreter will recognize some aspects that diverge significantly from a Christian understanding. We should begin by noting that its authors have aptly termed their model *self-determination theory* (Ryan & Deci, 2000). A Christian understanding of norms is fundamentally relational, since legitimate norms are viewed as the will of God. Without God in the model, self-determination theory can only describe norm development as a movement from social dependence to autonomy (though admittedly, its notion of mature autonomy includes a positive role for *human* relationship, see Ryan & Deci, 2003). From a Christian disciplinary matrix, however, this theory's thoroughgoing autocentrism compromises its generalizability to the Christian community. Its proponents' extensive secular research program (based in a humanistic worldview, see Ryan & Deci, 2000) convincingly demonstrates that the theory accurately describes the major features of the development of norm-internalization among secular subjects. Nevertheless, the Christian translator can deduce from this research several broad, community-generic insights: that deeper norm-internalization involves a more thorough, pervasive integration of norms, a greater sense of responsibility and personal investment, and a greater sense of well-being. Interpreted Christianly, then, this research suggests there is therapeutic value for all communities in helping counselees more deeply internalize valid norms. But since a Christian worldview assumes valid norms are from *God*, the development of norm-internalization has to be rearticulated along theocentric lines.

Let us examine a few such considerations. First, each stage of will-of-God internalization can be understood in relation to God, the ultimate norm-giver. Even extrinsic motivation is used by God to change behavior (for example, the Bible teaches that God punishes unrepentant sinners). In humanistic theory the Self is the ultimate norm-giver; in Christianity all norms are subject to God and all norm adherence is fundamentally a spiritual and relational reality. Second, contrasts between intrinsic and extrinsic models dissolve in Christian maturation with respect to God. As Christians mature, they enter more deeply into a sense of dependency on God for everything, which itself empowers their activity (Phil 2:12). Secular approaches to human beings can never do justice to Christian motivational and normative dynamics, because they have no way to take into account *God* working *within* the individual. Lastly, as Bernard of Clairvaux suggested centuries ago, intrinsic motivation for Christians is itself a complex, multistage affair. According to the Christian tradition, the love of God is supposed to be an intrinsic end (it is enjoyable in itself), which nonetheless has God and his glory as its extrinsic end. Bernard's (1983) stages of the love of God suggest that one can love God in a lesser way—for the enjoyment one derives from the relationship (a quasi-autocentric but intrinsic love of God)—or for the beauty that lies within God (a simple theocentric but intrinsic love of God), or, in the highest episodes of spiritual delight in God, one can love God is such a way that one's good, created self-interest is taken up into God's purposes (a complex theocentric but clearly intrinsic love of God). Self-determination theory could never document such Christian complexity, but it *is* a good *secular* theory. So it should challenge Christians to translate the theory into our own idiom and spur us on to do our own research on the norm-internalization of Christian subjects from within a Christian worldview.

In the meantime, we must be content with translation. Applying the stages of norm-internalization to Christian soul care suggests that counselees will benefit from submitting more and more deeply to God's will as revealed in the norms and callings to which they are to consent. Practically, this means counselors may need to identify their counselees' lack of consent to God's will, help them recognize that lack as a problem, foster motivation for change and train them in the means of grace that facilitate deeper Christian norm-internalization.[16]

The Internalization of Dipolar Self-Regulation Skills

Finally, we examine an aspect of internalization closely related to the taking in of the godly form of human beings: the taking in of the internal activities and skills of more mature others that all humans need in order to regulate, monitor, adjust and complete their own actions. Psychospiritual maturation leads to and necessitates the development of a host of processes and skills that *regulate* the mature human soul. In contemporary psychology they are termed *self-control* and *self-regulation processes* (Bandura, 1986; Kopp, 1982; Vohs & Baumeister, 2004),[17] but we will call them *skills of dipolar self-regulation*. Like norms, they are discursively based, but whereas norms are divinely and sometimes socially established obligations for one's life, self-regulation skills are the processes or procedures one uses to organize and regulate one's actions—whether internal or external. They are called *dipolar* in order to underscore the dependence of the individual on the grace of God and to distinguish a Christian understanding of such skills from their secular construal.

Is it appropriate to consider such dynamics an aspect of the Form of God? In response, we should note that God sovereignly controls himself. "I AM WHO I AM" (Ex 3:14). "God is finally and ultimately self-determinative" (Van Til, 1955, p. 77). This is demonstrated throughout Scripture, where God regulates his own emotions and actions, being long-suffering, for example, and holding back his anger and delaying judgment for the sake of those he is seeking to save. To cite one case, we are told that God "put up with" or "bore with" *(etropophorēsen)* the Israelites in the wilderness for forty years (Acts 13:18). Finite humans are not born with such skills. In order to become a mature image-bearer, human beings must *develop* such skills through the course of their lives, in interaction with other, more mature humans. Having biologically based desires, as complex animals do, further compromised by sin, requires a developmental process, by which we learn how to reflect on our thoughts, delay gratification, modulate emotions, and decide when to act and when to stop, as a central part of becoming mature beings. David modeled self-regulation when he addressed himself, "Why are you in despair, O my soul? And why have you become disturbed within me? Hope in God" (Ps 42:5). All the good intentions to imitate Christ will do us no good if there is not adequate dipolar self-regulatory *infrastructure* to see those intentions through to their realization. This is a missing piece in most Christian sanctification literature.

The social facilitation of self-regulation skills and structure. The *activities* we are focusing on in this section are all enacted *within*. Even external behavior requires internal activities like monitoring and terminating. As suggested above, internalization involves a degree of personal construction, in which the individual takes in structures and activities that were first social. In childhood, individual activity is often controlled and regulated by others, primarily through speech (e.g., "Look over there" to guide a child's attention). Depending on our developmental capacity, through watching others and interacting with them, the activities of others come to be co-opted by ourselves. At first, we learn to engage in them only with others present, when they guide us and help us to stay on task, monitor our progress, look for important features of the task environment and indicate when we have satisfactorily finished the task. But over time, these socially facilitated skills are internalized, so that we are enabled to engage in them *on our own*, without their assistance (Gauvain, 2001; Rogoff, 1990; Vygotsky, 1978; Wertsch, 1985, 1998). The social support of the individual's activities has been termed scaffolding and guided participation (Gauvain, 2001; Rogoff, 1990), and the goal of such support is the relatively independent activity of the individual, who has internally constructed (1) the mediated cognitive structures to which he or she has been exposed through discourse, and (2) the self-regulating activities in which he or she has participated in relationship with others.

Soul care consists of scaffolding opportunities for the task of psychospiritual maturation. For example, through the course of remembering a painful event in his life, a counselee may begin to experience extreme sadness and anxiety, and start to feel overwhelmed. Once some measure of empathic attunement has been attained (i.e., joining together intersubjectively with the counselee), the counselor can provide scaffolding of the counselee's emotions by talking to him, perhaps affirming him by articulating what the counselor empathetically understands is occurring, and by gradually "soothing" the counselee, telling him, for example, that it is okay to feel sadness in light of such an event, that God is very present and concerned, and that anxious feelings can be reduced by challenging them (without repression). Through the use of such strategies, the counselor is socially mediating self-regulation structures that, ideally, the counselee will eventually internalize and come to practice on his own in relation to God. So, though self-regulation soul-care skills are internal, they usually originate in one's social world.

The internal structures that make possible self-regulation are sometimes called the *executive*, a mental module distinguished by the self-regulatory functions it performs. Self-regulation skills develop throughout childhood and adolescence, at least in part because the frontal regions of the brain (Aman, Roberts & Pennington, 1998; Banfield, Wyland, MacRae, Münte & Heatherton, 2004; Goldberg, 2002; Zelazo, Muller, Frye & Overton, 2004) and the anterior cingulate (Davis, Bruce & Gunnar, 2002)—the regions dedicated to self-regulation—are some of the last regions of the brain to develop, ripening in late childhood and adolescence, and so in most individuals are not really capable of becoming well developed until late adolescence or early adulthood. Various types of psychopathology can be a result of underregulation of the self (contributing to such outcomes as impulsive behavior, aggression, excessive emotional expression and rumination) or overregulation (leading to outcomes like hypervigilance, extreme introversion, affect phobia and dissociation) (Bradley, 2000). Both compromise godly image-bearing and are worthy of the focus of soul care.

Types of dipolar self-regulation skills. Self-regulation skills are required to process, monitor, interpret, modify and enact human life and experience, and they can be categorized according to the depth of their focus: metacognition, emotion regulation and action regulation (Carver, 2003; Larsen & Prizmic, 2004).

Metacognition. This set of skills involves the awareness and monitoring of one's cognitive activities, knowledge regarding cognitive tasks, including one's past performances and overall competence, and strategic knowledge of when to use specific knowledge or procedures (Ferrari & Sternberg, 1998b). It also includes metamemory, an analogous set of skills directed at one's memory (Metcalfe, 2000). Internalizing these skills is important for psychospiritual maturity, since they are involved in the monitoring and regulating of one's thoughts and so are necessary for self-examination and transparency and the repair of faulty thinking. Moreover, our thoughts guide our actions, so change in action is always precipitated by metacognitive activity. Many forms of psychopathology involve poor metacognitive skills, including many personality disorders, depression and anxiety. Recovery from abuse may require specific metamemory abilities, for example, an awareness of one's memory limitations and how to push to activate long-avoided memories. Cognitive therapy is, in large measure, the training of counselees in metacognitive skills. Christian soul care should model metacognitive skills by reflecting accurate content of the counselee's speech; using probing questions, helping counselees identify their false beliefs about God, self, others and the world; developing with the counselee rational and Christ-centered strategies for self-analysis; and advocating acceptance of one's identity in Christ.

Emotion regulation. Even more important for psychospiritual maturation are the skills known as emotion regulation (Bradley, 2000). As we have noted, emotions are signs of the concerns that direct one's activity, and they vary in terms of hedonic valence (positive or negative), as well as intensity or level of arousal (Larsen & Prizmic, 2004). Infants lack the capacity to regulate their own emotions and desires, so they "almost exclusively rely on parents for the regulation of emotion" (Calkins, 2004, p. 325). Childhood is usually marked by an increasing ability to control and guide one's emotional experience (Schore, 1999).

In recent years, psychologists have come to recognize that an important aspect of human maturity is the development of emotional intelligence (Bar-On & Parker, 2000; Epstein, 1998; Salovey, Bedell, Detweiler & Mayer, 2000). This is a set of competencies that includes "the ability to perceive emotions, access and generate emotion to assist thought, understand and reason about emotion, and reflectively regulate emotions to promote emotional and intellectual growth. All involve the ability to consciously process emotional information" (Lane, 2000, p. 171). Emotion regulation comprises the ability to be aware of and open to feelings (both positive and negative); to monitor and reflect on emotions; to engage, prolong, objectify and process an emotion state; and to manage one's own emotions (Mayer & Salovey, 1997).

Various forms of psychopathology are correlated with a limited ability to regulate one's emotions, obviously the mood and anxiety disorders, but also schizophrenia, eating disorders, borderline levels of functioning and some personality disorders, like histrionic and obsessive-compulsive (Bradley, 2000; PDM Task Force, 2006; Schore, 2003). Excessive guilt or shame, as well as vices like lust, hatred and apathy also evidence a lack of emotion regulation. Development of these skills is especially important for survivors of severe emotional or physical abuse, since they did not typically receive much scaffolding of their emotions, and their experiences left them with an internal legacy of intense negative emotion-states and emotion memories that—depending on their defensive structure—may continue to be activated in the present.

Psychospiritual maturity requires the ability to experience and modulate one's current emotions effectively, so that they do not become debilitating and yet their meaning can be recognized and worked through so that they can properly guide one's actions (McCullough et al., 2003). As the Puritan pastor Richard Sibbes (1961) put it many centuries ago, "Grief . . . must . . . be *bounded and guided*" (p. 100). Though the following is an oversimplification, part of human flourishing consists of being able to diminish negative feelings appropriately (without repression) and to facilitate the appropriate activation of positive feelings. For example, becoming Christlike necessitates fostering the love of God and neighbor and the hatred of sin, while deactivating vicious patterns of emotional attitudes, like bitterness and hypercriticism. Christian soul care, then, should provide scaffolding for emotion regulation abilities through empathic listening, promoting emotion awareness, soothing the counselee when overwhelmed; affirming the feelings of one's created self in Christ and their appropriate expression to God, self and others; helping counselees identify defensive patterns and unhealthy, inappropriate or sinful feelings and encouraging their relinquishing of them to the cross of Christ, and encouraging feelings of love of neighbor and love, awe and gratitude to God.

Action regulation. Actions are shaped by thinking and emotion, but they require their own type of regulation. Action involves such processes as the forming of action dispositions, evaluating action options, selecting goals and forming and maintaining an intention. Once one acts, the processes include modulating effort, screening out distractions, monitoring and assessing performance, testing to see if a goal is achieved and deciding when to stop (Heckhausen, 1991; Johnson, 1997b). The necessity of action regulation for a mature Christian life should also be self-evident. Christlikeness requires the formation of dispositions toward and the performance of certain kinds of virtuous actions, and a corollary disposition away from and decreasing frequency of certain kinds of vicious actions. Reflection must be directed, then, at goals, intentions, effort and perseverance, as well as the reasons and feelings undergirding action performance.

Certain forms of psychopathology involve deficits in action regulation, including addictive behavior, impulse control, aggression, schizophrenia, indecision or chronic inactivity, and hyperactivity or excessive activity, and some personality disorders, like antisocial, histrionic and obsessive-compulsive. Cognitive-behavioral, problem- and solution-focused, and reality-based therapies all seek to foster action regulation. However, most kinds of therapists provide scaffolding for action regulation by contributing verbal assessments of counselee behavior, seeking to stay focused on the task at hand (even when the counselee jumps to another topic) and exploring the counselee's action regulation in session.

Christian soul care facilitates godly action regulation by promoting awareness of triggers of inappropriate or sinful behavior and increases in arousal, reflecting on the counselee's explicit and implicit goals (including secondary gains), talking through future scenarios and appropriate action options, role-playing and then discussing the internal dynamics that the counselee was experiencing, and the assigning of homework, including rehearsal of actions in vivo and journaling afterward that promotes reflection on action regulation issues.

Summary. An increase in self-regulation skills in these three areas (cognition, emotion and volition) is essential to Christian maturation. What separates Christian and secular soul care here is the dipolar nature of Christian self-regulation. Christians realize that all good action is ultimately a gift of God, and Christian maturation entails developing a dipolar mindset that rests on God in one's actions, including internal actions that promote the strengthening of the soul. So good Christian soul care will seek to promote the recognition of its dipolar nature.

Comparing Depth of Internalization Across Media

Conformity to the form of Christ entails the internalization of the signs of that form, and the direct experience of that form in worship and prayerful meditation.[18] As defined in this book, good internalization takes in the four types (or five, depending on how one counts) more thoroughly and more deeply (or ingressively) throughout the soul, leading to its manifestation in life.

Martin (1996), a secular psychotherapist, has suggested that internalization is important to all forms of counseling and therapy, and he applies Harre's (1984) four-stage internalization model of human development to the process of therapy, suggesting that therapy promotes deeper levels of the internalization of relevant conceptual and linguistic forms (which we recognize as a gift of the Word of God). Martin defines the first step—*appropriation*—as the initial internalization of new, healthier psychological structures (including such things as beliefs, strategies, practices, narrative material, values and symbols). Such cognitive internalization is foundational to the present model, but given Christianity's interest in the heart, it would be advisable to add a carditive substage to Harre's model to underscore the internalization of concerns, desires, loves and hates, and values underlying the merely cognitive.

Harre's second stage—*transformation*—is the *use* of the internalized psychological structures "to organize an individual's ongoing experiences" (Martin, 1996, p. 20). According to Martin, this stage leads counselees to actually *do* something different *internally:* to view themselves and their world in a new way—and it sounds like it might correspond to what was termed here a volitional level of carditive internalization. The third stage—*publication*—is the expression of new meaning-structures in the public, social sphere of life, through action, including speech. The final stage of Harre's theory—*conventionalization*—occurs when these meaning-structures become incorporated more broadly and accepted into the routine life of one's community.[19] Both of the social levels of Harre's model of *internalization* indicate that genuine internalization inevitably manifests itself in public discourse and activity. We shall explore such manifestation in the next chapter.

In this chapter, various kinds and degrees of internalization have been documented in Christian thought and in contemporary thought and research, suggesting that each locus can be internalized along a continuum from the more superficial to the deeper and more pervasive. Dipolar self-regulation skill internalization is somewhat unique, because these processes simply operate on other internal dynamics, which themselves vary according to their level of depth—from cognition to emotion to volition. Figure 16.2 provides a visual comparison with Harre's model of human development and shows the depthward movement of internalization across all the kinds, demonstrating the breadth and scope of this model.

The appropriation of the signs of God according to these types consists of two basic levels: cognitive and carditive. The first step for adult internalization is cognitive, and the focus is on truth and reality. Without some degree of understanding, the Word of God cannot lead to any deeper, lasting change in the person.

But mental understanding must arouse affect if the signs of glory are to substantially improve the form of one's soul, so deeper appropriation first involves the activation of emotions in light of the these signs of God. If these signs do not lead to the activation of the appropriate emotions, genuine movement toward God and greater maturation will never happen. The cultivation of proper emotional responses to reality fosters and evidences its further internalization.

Volition is also shaped by the internalization of signs of God's form. Harre refers to this degree of internalization as *transformation* (though he eschews any notion of a will, see 1984). This even deeper consent to God's signs predisposes Christians to act in ways that correspond to God's form, dispositions that will tend to be manifested in outward action.

<table>
<tr><th>Harre's Model</th><th>Scripture/ Gospel-Internalization</th><th>Experience with God</th><th>Imago Dei Internalization</th><th>Norm Internalization</th><th>Dipolar Self-Regulation Skills</th></tr>
<tr><td rowspan="5">Appropriation</td><td>Cognitive: Memorization</td><td rowspan="3">Mental Prayer</td><td rowspan="3">Reflection Regarding Others</td><td rowspan="3">Reflection Regarding Norms</td><td rowspan="3">Metacognition</td></tr>
<tr><td>Cognitive: Comprehension</td></tr>
<tr><td>Cognitive: Elaboration</td></tr>
<tr><td rowspan="2">Carditive Internalization: Emotion</td><td rowspan="2">Affective Prayer</td><td>Incorporation</td><td>External</td><td rowspan="2">Emotion Regulation</td></tr>
<tr><td>Introjection</td><td>Introjected</td></tr>
<tr><td rowspan="3"></td><td rowspan="3">Carditive Internalization: Volition</td><td rowspan="3">Contemplative Prayer</td><td rowspan="3">Identification</td><td>Identified</td><td rowspan="3">Action Regulation</td></tr>
<tr><td>Integrated</td></tr>
<tr><td>Intrinsic</td></tr>
<tr><td>Publication</td><td colspan="5">Personal Manifestation</td></tr>
<tr><td>Conventionali-zation</td><td colspan="5">Communal Manifestation</td></tr>
</table>

Figure 16.2 Loci of internalization

A Summary of the Internalization of the Signs of Glory

The purpose of figure 16.2 is to illustrate the broad unity that exists in the internalization of these kinds. Why such a focus on deepening internalization? Because Christianity is interested in glory or beauty, and a being's total glory is the splendor (or depth) of its form. If the form of Christ is to be most fully reproduced in the believer's form, it is necessary that something of Christ's depth be likewise exemplified. The Son of God is infinitely deep—so great is his beauty—so that absolute conformity is necessarily out of the question. But the deeper the glory of God goes into the human soul and the more elaborate the form it constructs, the greater the density of glory that form possesses. We turn, in the next chapter, to the outward expression of the internal glory, termed *manifestation*.

Notes

[1]A major focus of cognitive psychology has been the study of *representations* stored in human memory (Ashcroft, 1994; Mandler, 1998; Paivio, 1990). Explicit memory (or declarative memory), by definition, is information that can be verbalized, and there are two kinds. *Semantic* memory (memory for general knowledge about the world) forms representations, but does so through language. For example, one can refer to a tree and its unique features by using language to represent it in descriptive (or assertive) sentences. More complex states of affairs can also be verbally represented through discourse. Memory of personal experience is called *episodic* memory, and it too can be verbalized. For example, one can describe events from one's past. Visual imagery can be stored in either episodic or semantic memory (Ashcroft, 1994). These "pictures" are visual representations of aspects of the world. Concepts of concrete objects can also be visually represented. For example, most sighted people can easily form a mental image of a tree, not necessarily a specific tree, but a generic one. That image is a mental representation of what a "tree-in-general" looks like. Mature human memory is filled with millions of representations of aspects of the natural, social and spiritual realms, and of personal experience, and allows us to store information about the world external to ourselves, as well as information about ourselves, *inside ourselves* (Perner, 2000). Knowledge is representation (Mandler, 1998), so knowledge about anything involves internalization.

To describe memory as a set of representations about the world does not mean that human memory is infallible. On the contrary, laboratory research has found human memory is easily led astray and can frequently misrepresent one's past and knowledge about facts. Nonetheless, the fact remains, human memory is realist in design and intention (Plantinga, 1993b), and, depending on the event, in everyday life it is more accurate than it is faulty (consider the notable differences between a normal adult's memory and one with dementia; see also Metcalfe, 2000). The point of this discussion is simply that human memory is designed to store or internalize information about or experienced in the world.

But the human mind does more than remember. From the standpoint of cognitive psychology, the human brain/mind is considered to be an information-processing machine, a living, carbon-based computer. Like a computer, it takes in information (called input, e.g., a set of three words) and encodes it (forms an internal representation of it), some of which may be stored (or internalized or saved), performs internal operations on the representations (e.g., compares their meanings) and then produces results of that processing (called output, e.g., decides which two are most similar). This orientation recognizes that the human brain/mind uses "bottom up" processes that relatively passively take in information and also "top-down" processes that organize the information conceptually and actively work on it, constructing human knowledge that is shaped by sociocultural assumptions. The human brain/mind, for example, automatically forms concepts based on an organizing of objects according to similar features, with the more abstract concepts being largely provided and conditioned by culture. Concept formation is a result of a more complex type of internalization than mere memory, and propositions and schemas are even more complex forms of knowledge representation that deal with states-of-affairs in the world (Sternberg & Ben-Zeev, 2001). Language is a particularly important type of representation, since linguistic symbols can be used to represent extremely complicated states of affairs. Human maturation requires the internalization of some language system, since it is the primary means for humans to internalize other complex aspects of reality.

From a different vantage point, Piaget and the cognitive-developmental approach he advanced came to similar conclusions. Piaget recognized that the human mind was formed through its interactions and engagement with its environment. In its quest for understanding, the human mind uses two formative processes: accommodation, in which the mind adapts itself to the form of the world to which it is exposed (an internalization process), and assimilation, in which the mind adapts the form of the world to the mind's current understanding (a constructive process). In addition to documenting *object permanence* (Piaget, 1954), he also documented the changes that occur in the minds of children as they encounter the perceived regularities of the world, including space, causality and time, gradually resulting in the development of a formal logical system for deducing similarities, differences and relations among concrete and abstract objects. The embodied human mind, according to Piaget, both takes in form from the world and imposes form upon it. Piaget was a modernist, and his approach to genetic epistemology was profoundly shaped by Kant. So, officially Piaget was agnostic about the extent to which human knowledge was valid. But his Kantianism did not prevent him from recognizing that the world shapes the mind of the child.

The importance of internalization has also been recognized from another quarter in object relations, self psychology and attachment theories. We will hold off most of the discussion of this perspective until the appropriate section below, but all three approaches believe early childhood relations get internalized and in the process have a profound impact on the formation of the self as well as future social relations. Object- and self-psychology theories claim that within the first two years of life, children are forming self- and other-representations based on their ongoing experience of their self-in-relation-to-other constellations. Happy, soothing and satisfying experiences with others, as well as those that are distressing, neglectful and conflictual, are stored in memory and result in self-representations and other-representations that will be reactivated in future activities and relationships (Tyson & Tyson, 1990). Similarly, Bowlby posited the existence of an "internal working model" that is formed through early attachment experiences with primary caregivers (Thompson, 1998). He asserted that this internal working model guided future attachment relations throughout life. With different emphases, each theory suggests that others are "taken in" to the developing child and come to affect such things as the children's sense of agency, experience of emotion, ways of thinking, conscience formation and gender identity, as well as their ability to relate to others (Stern, 1985; Tyson & Tyson, 1990).

A relatively recent social cognitive approach to personality and motivation, termed self-determination theory (Deci & Ryan, 1985; Ryan & Deci, 2000), also highlights the important role played by the internalization of social factors in individual development. Its proponents argue that one's personality and self-development are closely related to one's social experiences and social roles and the extent to which one comes to deeply identify with the projects of significant others, so that even one's adult goals and life activities are related to the earlier internalization of one's social world.

Other social cognitive models of human development have focused on the importance of parental socialization and the corresponding quality of child internalization for understanding the child's appropriation of norms, values and rules that is necessary for healthy, adaptive human functioning. Grusec and Kuczynski (1997), Kochanska and Aksan (1995), and Kochanska, Murray, Jacques, Koenig and Vandegeet (1996) report that such factors as parental affect and control, and parenting strategies are mediating variables that affect the child's developing emotion awareness, sensitivity to standards and their violations, compliance, self-control and self-regulation, and goal formation (though they point out that parent-child effects are always bidirectional). Christians have biblical warrant for expecting such effects.

The final model to be mentioned in this context is that of Vygotsky and the more recent social constructivist school that has been influenced in large part by him. The early twentieth-century Marxist developmental psychologist came up with an approach to individual human maturation of cognitive, affective and personality structures that sees them as grounded in one's social experiences (Rogoff, 1990; Vygotsky, 1978; Wertsch, 1985, 1998). Vygotsky recognized that individual development begins with the social regulation of children's mental and emotional processes and that children only gradually become able to regulate their own capacities as the healthy social scaffolding they experienced is internalized and comes to constitute their own cognitive and emotional functions.

> It is necessary that everything internal in higher forms was external, that is, for others it was what it now is for oneself. Any higher mental function necessarily goes through an external stage in its development because it is initially a social function. This is the center of the whole problem of internal and external behavior. . . . Any higher mental function was external because it was social at some point before becoming an internal, truly mental function. (Vygotsky, quoted in Wertsch, 1985, p. 62)

Vygotsky was also influenced by semiotics and gave considerable attention to the role that signs play in human development. For example, he noted similarities between tools and signs. Both are used by humans to act upon reality: the tool brings about changes in external, material reality and the sign brings about changes in internal, mental reality. The sign "is a means of internal activity aimed at mastering oneself; the sign is *internally* oriented" (Vygotsky, 1978, p. 55). Vygostsky understood that language was uniquely foundational for individual human development. Language is an objective entity (it can be empirically studied), and yet it exists subjectively, or rather intersubjectively, and makes it possible to communicate meaning. It provides the means necessary to bridge two persons' subjectivities and pass meaning from one person to another, again bringing external reality into the individual. Through language (one's culturally mediated sign system), the *inter*mental becomes the *intra*mental (Goldhaber, 2000). Discourse is the social means for organizing and constructing the individual's mind, and it becomes the individual's means for thinking on his or her own. As a result, the individual's internal, mental reality is formed through the internalization of semiodiscursive structures within the larger social context within which one develops.

The compatibility of these theoretical approaches, especially a Vygotskian orientation, with a Christian semiodiscursive model would seem relatively unobjectionable. Through its emphasis on memorization, learning and catechization, Christianity has always promoted internalization. Our understanding of the processes of internalization is not itself very worldview dependent, but it still needs to be recontextualized within a Christian worldview framework that recognizes the ethicospiritual orders and the divine-human relational dimension.

[2]The Puritan theologian John Owen recognized that "holiness is the implanting, writing, and realizing of the gospel in our souls" (Owen, 1954, p. 221). And by "the gospel" Owen meant "the truth which is according to godliness" that the gospel "ingenerates."

[3]One way to categorize different levels of cognitive processing is Bloom's (1956) classic hierarchical taxonomy of cognitive educational objectives: knowledge (or memorization), comprehension, application, analysis, synthesis and evaluation (ordered from simple to complex). Its enduring presence in educational literature throughout the past half century is probably due to its intuitive appeal and experiential validity, but it cannot be regarded as an ontologically valid hierarchical scheme because the hierarchy flows from conceptually based judgments that are hard to substantiate empirically (e.g., it would seem impossible to be sure that the cognitive complexity of each of the four highest categories are accurately ordered, e.g., is application or analysis necessarily always more cognitively complex than evaluation?). Nevertheless, its hierarchical format corresponds well (inversely) with the notion of inwardness, and we are using a similar but simpler hierarchy in this section.

[4]He also believed that "there is the nature of instruction" (p. 272) in spiritual understanding, since it creates a kind of experiential knowledge that can be gained, stored and made use of in the future.

[5]Edwards grounded such a dichotomy in the Trinity (cognitive understanding is a sign or representation of the Son's representation of the Father's *knowledge* and carditive understanding is a sign or representation of the Spirit's representation of the Father's and Son's *love*) (Danaher, 2004). Also, in this book the term *carditive* instead of Edwards's term *spiritual* will be used to denote emotional and volitional activity, because Edwards's term might suggest that the Holy Spirit is not involved in cognitive processing or that any activity of the heart and will is necessarily from the Holy Spirit, and also because the term *spiritual* is used for the highest order of discourse.

[6]We might note that Edwards is not the only one to have made a fundamental distinction between "head" and "heart." More recently Epstein (1990, 1994) has tried to distinguish two parallel systems of information processing in human beings: a cognitive and an experiential. Similarly, Bucci (1997) differentiates the subsymbolic and nonverbal symbolic information processing levels (which are affect-driven and largely unconscious) from the verbal-symbolic level (which is conscious and a function of deliberation). Ironically, we also now understand that this fundamental distinction is *all in the head:* it is actually a difference in brain region activation. One way that carditive activity is *deeper* than cognitive is that it engages the affective regions of the brain and nervous system dedicated to the experience of emotion, desire, motivation and volition (the limbic system—particularly, the amygdala and the hippocampus—the frontal and prefrontal cortices, especially within the right hemisphere, as well as some elements of the peripheral nervous system within the chest and stomach), whereas mere cognitive activity is located solely within the neocortex. Since most of the neural architecture responsible for emotion is embedded more centrally within the brain system, beneath the cerebral cortex, emotion experience is literally *deeper* within the brain than mere cognition. But apart from physical location, the activation of the emotion-centers of the brain *feels* deeper phenomenologically, more at the "core" (or heart) of the individual. As a result, the type of activation and storage done with the emotion and volition modules can be considered *depth* internalization. So, the commonsense distinction between head and heart is grounded in identifiable neural and nervous system structures.

[7]A number of contemporary artists write and perform Christian music with a soul-moving agenda, including Sara Groves, Jars of Clay, Caedmon's Call, Derek Webb and Switchfoot. And good worship music can help counselees focus on God and reap carditive benefits.

[8]Carditive internalization is also intimated in the link that Jesus (and John) taught between love and obedience. "If you keep My commandments, you will abide in My love; just as I have kept My Father's com-

mandments, and abide in His love" (Jn 15:10). "This is My commandment, that you love one another, just as I have loved you" (Jn 15:12, also Jn 15:19). Through the believer's keeping of Christ's commandments, the love of God in the heart spreads into action dispositions that conform to God's will.

[9]In order for the soul-care process to lead to greater well-being for the counselee, there must be a certain kind of intersubjectivity, one that consists of affirmation and empathy from the therapist. Kohut (1977) referred to this task as "mirroring."

[10]Different Catholic authors have speculated about this stage of prayer being composed of a variety of substages (including the Dark Night of the Soul and so on), but there is no universal agreement about such matters.

[11]Christian advocates of centering prayer must take this concern more seriously. For example, to recommend prayer without words or images early on in the Christian life, to relatively immature believers, is simply irresponsible spiritual direction, particularly in a cultural spirituality context where Eastern religions are more highly valued than Western. It is more than a coincidence that many proponents of centering prayer are religious pluralists. The historic, orthodox position of the church down through the ages is that the highest Christian experience is grounded in the deepest internalization of Christian truth.

[12]"Faith is not based on experience, which is always limited and discouraging, but on the promise; in other words, faith means to believe in things that we have not experienced. It means to set out, at God's word, for an unexplored country, for the inheritance that God has promised us: participation in his life" (Danielou, 1996, p. 34).

[13]This approach to Christian spirituality has been labeled the *apophatic way* or the *via negativa*, in contrast to the *kataphatic way* or the *via positiva*. The former approach emphasizes God's dissimilarity to the creation and his ineffable and incomprehensible nature, and promotes the experience of God beyond the sensible, the verbal and the rational. The latter approach emphasizes that God can be understood analogically through created things and is grasped through language (like Scripture), and promotes the experience of God through truth (Egan, 1993a, 1993b). The Reformation was intrinsically a kataphatic revival, and all models of spirituality based in Reformational thought will be tied to scriptural and related analogical modes of understanding God. Our experience of God must be guided by his signs, though his fullness necessarily transcends the capacities of those signs to bear the infinite freight of his glorious significance.

[14]Some of whom could warrant the title *mystic* themselves, like Calvin (1559/1960, Vol. 1, p. 737; see Tamburello, 1994) and Edwards (1746/1959).

[15]Depending on the norms in question, Christian psychospiritual maturity also depends on the extent to which one *deeply* consents to them. Some norms do not warrant deep appropriation (e.g., investment in the latest fashions), whereas other norms require a high-level commitment (e.g., one's marriage vows or acceptance of an unchangeable physical handicap).

[16]Our focus on internalization may seem to undermine the roles of creativity and personal agency in human activity. However, it is understood that the internalization of God's will and word actually makes it possible for creativity and personal agency to emerge in the course of proper human development. This will be touched on in the following chapter.

[17]Some regard self-control and self-regulation as synonyms (e.g., Vohs & Baumeister, 2004), whereas others (e.g., Kopp, 1982) regard self-control as the simpler process of the two, focused on behavior (delay of gratification, Mischel, Shoda & Rodriguez, 1989) and therefore a developmental precursor to self-regulation, which is focused on cognition and affect. While Kopp is right to distinguish the two, we will use the term *self-regulation* to refer to both types of skills.

[18]Some readers will have noticed the profound interdependence and interrelation of these types of internalization. For one thing, maturation in one type helps to foster the others. Let us consider, for

example, the effects of Scripture-internalization on the others. It seems likely that deeper internalization of the gospel would reduce one's anxiety, shame and guilt, and therefore make it easier to receive love from others as well as criticism, and presumably help one to regulate one's thoughts, emotions and actions. In addition, Scripture explicitly promotes the internalization of many social and personal norms. The Bible also advocates associating with godly persons for the benefits that brings ("He who walks with the wise grows wise, but a companion of fools suffers harm," Prov 13:20 NIV) and challenges less mature persons to imitate more mature (1 Cor 4:16; Heb 6:12; 13:7). Finally, Scripture encourages some self-regulation skills directly, like self-control (Prov 10:19)—calling it a fruit of the Spirit (Gal 5:23)—and others indirectly, for example, patience requires emotion and action regulation. The possibility that Scripture-internalization promotes the other Form-internalizations deserves empirical attention.

What about the relation between other types of internalization? It is well known that social support reduces anxiety and stress. So it may be that healthy relationships with others—especially with the triune God—would also help people become more self-reflective and honest in their Bible reading. One would also expect that people with well-developed self-regulation skills would be good at reflecting on their emotional reactions to others, their acceptance of them, the extent to which they feel connected to them, and empathizing with them, thus facilitating their relationships with them.

We know that the quality and characteristics of early relationships are highly influential on the child's internalization of moral rules. For example, the internalizing of psychosocial norms is highly dependent on one's relationships with others, especially early childhood relationships (Grusec & Kuczynski, 1997). Researchers have found that certain child-rearing strategies (e.g., use of power assertion and induction—read: interactions with the relational styles of others) contribute to or inhibit the internalization of social norms. Kochanska (1991, 1993, 1995), for example, uncovered two pathways for the internalization of morality: with temperamentally more fearful toddlers, gentle discipline was helpful; for more assertive toddlers, greater security of attachment. Just as one's self- and other-representations are affected by the quality of our early relationships, so our norm-representations are affected by such things as security of attachment and the emotional tone of interactions. For example, deeper internalization of maternal norms has been found to be positively related to mutual positive affect (Kochanska & Askan, 1995). So, assuming normal neural function, proper internalization of others contributes to norm-internalization. On the other hand, maladaptive socialization leads to gaps in such internalization.

Research has also found that problems with attachment in early childhood are related to difficulties in childhood self-regulation (Calkins, 2004); and people with poor adult attachment have difficulty reflecting on their thoughts, whereas healthy adult attachment is related to good metacognitive self-monitoring (Slade, 1999; Vondra, Shaw, Swearingen, Cohen & Owens, 2001). In addition, difficulties with self-regulation are related to problems with later social behavior (Campbell, Pierce, March, Ewing & Szumowski, 1994), suggesting an interrelation between those two loci. It is also worth noting that self-control and self-regulation are often practiced in reference to social norms and expectations (Bandura, 1986; Miller & Prentice, 1996; Tesser & Martin, 1996). Developmental research has documented that norm-internalization and self-regulation skill internalization occur in similar sequences and at similar ages, so their correlation would also seem to be established, though the study of their developmental interrelation has not, to my knowledge, been well documented.

In summary, these different kinds of internalization would seem to be deeply interrelated and in significant ways interdependent. The reformation of godly personal agency and character in adulthood occurs through consenting to the word of God throughout the deepest levels of the soul: preeminently, to Scripture through meditative prayer, but also to the form of godly others in the

Christian community—in relationship with respected and loved role models who themselves are Scripture-saturated—and especially to the form of God itself in communion; to God's will for one's life with respect to the norms of human life and one's personal calling; and to the internal self-regulating infrastructure of God and others, which enables people to manage their inner life and outward actions most effectively and virtuously. So, it would seem beneficial in Christian soul care to promote the interrelated and interdependent internalizations.

[19]This would be evidenced in Christian soul care when segments of the church at large accept certain ways of thinking and acting regarding certain soul problems—an illustration of this is the labeling of psychospiritual difficulties as *strongholds* that require spiritual power to overcome them, a term that has been used in some Christian circles since at least the 1990s.

17

The Call to Outwardness

The Manifestation of Christlikeness

INWARDNESS CAN NEVER BE THE ULTIMATE end of Christian soul care. Guided by its doxological orientation, the ultimate goal of Christian inwardness lies outside the self and in God. Furthermore, just as God did not keep his glory to himself, so he intends his glory in us to be *manifested*. "Where glory is there must be manifestation" (Sibbes, 1983, p. 240). Rightly understood, "subjectivity is as much a public existence as it is a private one. Subjectivity is thus more than mere inwardness: it is 'outwardness.' The person who retreats from extrinsic subjectivity into the secrecy of inner life actually moves away from true subjectivity and tends to become impersonal and 'mere' object" (Anderson, 1982, p. 62). Inwardness and outwardness are interrelated, even interdependent. Like breathing in and breathing out, the internalization of glory leads necessarily to its externalization in the lives of God's people, by means of the Spirit's power.

When Jesus was told that his mother and brothers were waiting outside for him, he responded by saying, "My mother and my brothers are those who hear the word of God *and do it*" (Lk 8:21). The word cannot just be internalized; it must be lived!

> Every good tree bears good fruit, but the bad tree bears bad fruit. A good tree cannot produce bad fruit, nor can a bad tree produce good fruit. Every tree that does not bear good fruit is cut down and thrown into the fire. So then, you will know them by their fruits. Not every one who says to me "Lord, Lord," will en-

ter the kingdom of heaven, but *he who does the will of My Father who is in heaven.* (Mt 7:17-21)

I am the vine, you are the branches; he who abides in Me, and I in him, he bears much fruit; for apart from Me you can do nothing. If anyone does not abide in Me, he is thrown away as a branch, and dries up; and they gather them, and cast them into the fire and they are burned. If *you abide in Me*, and *My words abide in you,* ask whatever you wish, and it will be done for you. *My Father is glorified by this, that you bear much fruit, and so prove to be My disciples.* (Jn 15:5-8)[1]

The children of God are "manifested" by doing righteousness and loving their siblings (1 Jn 3:10). If there is no evident manifestation of the internalized word, the New Testament is clear: it has not been savingly internalized.

We could summarize this entire book as follows: *the primary goal of divine salvation is the manifestation of the triune God's glory through the historical reformation of broken sinners, as they learn how to consent increasingly to the word and ways of God and their lives become an increasing analogy to the life of Christ* (Horton, 2002, 2005; Vanhoozer, 2005). This is the metanarrative theme that gives inwardness its rationale, focus and persuasive power.

We have already noted that Martin (1996), in his description of (secular) counseling change, argues that internalization is an important outcome of skillful counseling. Influenced by Harre (1984), Martin labeled the stage following internalization "publication" (p. 20), the public expression of what he considers the "products of internalized transformational activity." In this chapter we will look at a Christian understanding of this stage of the counseling process, which we will call "outwardness" or "manifestation."

Believers and Christlikeness

For obvious reasons, the life, death and resurrection of Christ manifested God's glory more clearly that any other aspect of creation, but it also made possible the continuing manifestation of his glory in the healing and edifying of his people. In the resurrection the Son was called "the beginning, the firstborn from the dead" (Col 1:18; see Rom 8:29). Through the resurrection Christ initiated the new creation and began a new race of humanity. Now "if anyone is in Christ, he is a new creature; the old things passed away; behold, new things have come" (2 Cor 5:17). Since believers have been raised with Christ (Eph 2:6; Col 3:1-4) and have become a part of the new creation themselves (Gal 6:15), they too participate in and foster new creation glory. God has declared believers to be new selves (Eph 4:22-24; Col 3:9-10), so that, insofar as their new selves are realized in this age, they signify that a new era has dawned, a time in which God is receiving more of the glory due his name, from a growing proportion of his image-bearers on earth.

As we saw in chapter twelve, this happens only through the indwelling Holy Spirit. After Christ ascended into heaven, the Father and the Son sent the Spirit of life (Rom 8:2) to earth (beginning at Pentecost; Jn 7:39; Acts 2) and brought in the dispensation of the revelation and manifestation of the Holy Spirit (concluding the verbal revelation of the Son with the closing of the canon, Bavinck, 2003, pp. 382-83). "The Spirit gives life" (2 Cor 3:6), so that the new creation life of Christians comes to play a pivotal role in the current manifestation of the glory of God. During the present dispensation of the Spirit, "objective revelation passes into subjective appropriation" (Bavinck, 2003, p. 383), by the Spirit, through the Christian's faith. If the Son is *especially* the form of God, the Spirit is especially the splendor of God—the depth of God—which no one knows except the Spirit (1 Cor 2:10-11). And the Spirit has been given to believers so that some of that splendor would be further manifested.

> The purpose of revelation is not Christ; Christ is the center and the means; the purpose is that God will again dwell in his creatures and reveal his glory in the cosmos: *theos ta panta en pasin* (1 Cor 15:28). In a sense this, too, is an incarnation of God. And to achieve this purpose the word of revelation passes into Scripture. Hence Scripture, too, is a means and an instrument, not a goal. It is the product of God's incarnation in Christ and in a sense its continuation, the way by which Christ makes his home in the church, the preparation of the way to the full indwelling of God. But in his indwelling, accordingly, it has its *telos*, its end and goal. (Bavinck, 2003, p. 380)

Each believer's life now provides a unique, ontogenetic narrative setting for God's ongoing revelation of himself to the world. The triune God has manifested himself through signs of himself (most preeminently Christ)—recorded in the signs of Scripture—and humans are sign-ingestors (or *verbivores* as Roberts [1997] memorably put it), which—as the signs are internalized—re-form the dynamic structures of the soul more and more into the likeness of God in Christ, so that, more and more, believers become signs of God themselves, through their own speech and other actions during the course of their life history and interactions with others. Sign internalization precedes sign manifestation. In the church "by means of Scripture God himself now bears revelation into the world and realizes its content in the life and thought of humankind" (Bavinck, 2003, p. 383). By walking in the Spirit, the Christian "becomes a sign, entirely, an inflection and reflection at a distance of the divine glory, a deferral of God's presence that is simultaneously a real embrace of his infinity, an impression of God that is also another emphasis, another expression" (Hart, 2003, p. 202).

But the believer's life is only a sign of God. Even here, the glory manifested is only a trace. The believer's new life "is *hidden* with Christ in God" (Col 3:4). Believers are indwelt by the Holy Spirit (1 Cor 6:19; Rom 8:9), but no one can see this Spirit. Just to suggest that one is a child of God, specially indwelt by God, would seem to most of those outside the faith to be audacious in the extreme (1 Cor 1:27-29). Indeed, centuries have gone by, Christ still has followers, and yet the most charitable observer must acknowledge that the participants in the new creation are not so different from the rest of humanity as we might expect (especially when compared with other highly moral subcultures, like the Mormons or orthodox Islam). Throughout the rest of this age, God's glory continues to be partially concealed and partially revealed.

How Maturing Believers Most Manifest God's Glory

As Vanhoozer (1998, 2005) has taught us (and Wolterstorff, 1995, before him), God's speech was more than revelation; it was action. God's speech-acts have informed us about God, it is true, but they also had perlocutionary intentions. God's speech-acts were intended to turn us into those who look like the Son of God. As the signs of God's glory become more deeply internalized (from Scripture, others, God's will and dipolar self-regulation), believers increasingly manifest the glory of God themselves: *inwardly* as their internal world reflects the inner world of God (their form and splendor), and *outwardly, in performance,* as their speech and other actions in their stories (especially in their relationships with others) display in history the life, death and resurrection of Christ. The rest of this chapter concerns some of the most important features of this agenda.

The Doxological Goal of Human Development

The *telos* of God's redemptive agenda for humans is *Christlikeness*. Humans glorify God best by resembling the Son of Man. Humans are created in the *imago Dei,* but they are fallen, and they need to be re-created in the *imago Christi,* the image of Christ, *the* image of God. The new creation is found *in Christ* (2 Cor 5:17), and believers are "created in Christ Jesus for good works . . . that we would walk in them" (Eph 2:10). So Christians have been newly created to be good like Christ.

Christ himself gave his disciples a *new* commandment: "that you love one another, even as I have loved you" (Jn 13:34). And this archetypal directive is echoed in many ways throughout the New Testament: "Walk in love, just as Christ also loved you" (Eph 5:2). Believers are to have the same attitudes as Christ (Phil 2:5); they are not to please themselves but their neighbors, "for even Christ did not please Himself" (Rom 15:3). Christians should be generous with poor believers, because "though [Christ] was rich, yet for your sake He became poor" (2 Cor 8:9). Specific applications are made to husbands, who are to love their wives as Christ loved the church (Eph 5:25), and to servants, who are to suffer patiently under injustice, since Christ left an example of such patience for us to follow: *"for you have been called for this purpose"* (1 Pet 2:21).

This telic analogy is related repeatedly to the *form* of Christ. God, we are told, has predestined Christians "to become conformed *[symmorphous]* to the image of His Son" (Rom 8:29); "beholding as in a mirror the glory of the Lord, [they] are being transformed *[metamorphoumetha]* into the same image from glory to glory" (2 Cor 3:18). Paul prayed "that I may know [Christ], and the power of His resurrection and the fellowship of His sufferings, being conformed *[symmorphizomenos]* to His death" (Phil 3:10), and that Christ may be formed (*morphōthē*) in others (Gal 4:19).[2] These passages all use verb forms with the same root—*morphē* or "form"—and make clear that Christ is the archetype, model or *telos* of the Christian life. They have also led some Christians to call the process of Christian maturation *Christiformity*—a term with a long history in the church (see Hughes, 1984), and one that aptly labels what is to be the primary aim of Christian soul care. We turn next to consider ways in which the believer's form can resemble the form of Christ.

The Pluriform and Christlikeness

Before we examine the necessarily historical quality of the manifestation of Christlikeness, we will consider how it is expressed in the four psychological form-types we examined earlier (personality, self, personal agency and character). We saw in chapter nine how Christ was the perfect human pluriform. In the case of other humans, however, the human pluriform is fallen, so each of the form-types is corrupt in ways peculiar to itself, and each may be more or less damaged in individuals. The personality and self may be somewhat broken or even fractured; personal agency may have been compromised by abuse or neglect and will be compromised by some degree of self-deception, and the character will be more or less autocentric and possibly wicked. So how is Christlikeness exemplified in the form-types?

To begin with, becoming a personal agent is a main divine objective of human development, and next to character, personal agency is the most important form-type. So, Christians glorify Christ by becoming more self-aware, reflective, relatively free, responsible, creative and internally unified. The internalization of the media of the Word of God awakens Christian personal agency and brings it to full maturity, and only mature personal agents can engage in inwardness, admit their weaknesses, thank God for their strengths, deeply confess their responsibility for their sin and therefore deeply seek the divine cure for their sinfulness and brokenness. Through the quality of such activities the glory and beauty of God are powerfully displayed.

Christ did nothing apart from the Father (see Jn 5:30-44; 12:44-50), so Christlikeness in personal agency involves wholehearted, dipolar dependence on God in one's actions. And while Christ did not have sin, his life in sinful believers would presumably instigate increasing efforts at repentance and renewal. This is an important reason why personal agency is such a central focus of Christian soul care. Christlikeness entails *being one's own project:* being the kind of personal agent who actively seeks to become more like Christ in dependence on him. So, the more personal agency one has, the more of God's glory the Christian is able to manifest.

From the standpoint of Christianity, character is the most important form-type, because it has the most potential to manifest splendor or depth of form. Christlikeness is mainly an issue of virtuous action (not just behavior) and character (not just nice personality traits). With character, we find enormous differences in the degree of glory individual Christians manifest, but the more virtuous one's character, the greater the glory of God displayed through it, because the greater its internal splendor, the greater the resemblance of the ectypal sign to the archetypal Form.

In contrast, a Christian's *personality* would not seem to contribute very much to Christlikeness, at least directly, except insofar as particular personality traits might overlap with one's character (as in conscientiousness). Individual differences in personality simply provide the unique creational context for one's Christlikeness. For example, presumably, extroverts and introverts can glorify God equally well. Perhaps God's design for glory through one's personality is not so much by its alteration through redemption as by its *intensification*. Lewis (1952, pp. 187-88) believed that the uniqueness of each personality is enhanced by conformity to Christ, so that each Christian becomes more fully himself or herself. As believers become more like Christ, they become more freed by redemption to pursue their own giftedness, created interests, motivations and creativity: their individual *differences* (see Hart, 2003). The splendor of the glory of God shines uniquely through each human personality (like the light through a stained glass window, the different colored pieces perhaps symbolizing different traits), so the glory of God dignifies and fulfills each unique personality, whatever its form (though the splendor displayed would seem to be essentially the same for all personalities). If so, then *communal* personality differences may especially contribute to Christlikeness in the world. The great personality diversity represented in the church displays something of the personality breadth of the infinite Son of God, concentrated in Jesus Christ, but then dispersed through the individual personality differences of the members of Christ's body, bringing about a range of the manifestation of some of God's beauty (Beck, 1999).

With regard to the *self,* Christlikeness would seem to consist in a well-developed, complex and accurate self, one composed of truthful self-knowledge—and lots of it—valid self-evaluations and a strong sense of identity. Christ's self-assessment would have mirrored his Father's assessment of him (see Jn 5:30-38; 8:50-55; 12:44-50), so Christlikeness in the self entails the Christian's consent to God's knowledge and evaluations of him or her, as best as can be discerned. Because the self consists of self-representations, of all the form-types, it would seem to be the easiest to make more Christlike, since it can be the most quickly changed by the simple acceptance of scriptural teachings regarding the believer's status in Christ (though, we must add, the *deeper* the change—regarding core self-beliefs for example—the slower the change). Then, the deeper and more fully integrated these speech-acts of God become with the rest of one's self-representations, the more the self manifests God's glory. There are at least two reasons for that. First, the believer is more like God in the way God thinks and appraises the believer. And second, these self-beliefs will contribute to a sense of contented wholeness in Christ (justified, saint, beloved), which would likely promote internal harmony, transparency, self-understanding and the development of godly character. So, the form of the self can contribute substantially to the believer's Christlikeness.

Christlikeness Manifested Historically

Well-formed Christian souls in community may be the best display of God's glory in the creation. But to refer merely to the formal structures of Christlikeness apart from their historical embodiment, as we have just done, is quite abstract and therefore can be misleading. The eternal form of God is infinite and dynamic. Finite, temporal creatures can only exemplify that form *over time* or historically. Christlikeness is actually a dramatic accomplishment, displayed in embodied godly actions, engaged in particular settings of one's life, usually in relation to others, in the coauthoring (with God) of an increasingly coherent narrative of a life-in-Christ, turning believers gradually into incarnational signs of God. Christlikeness consists in *performance,* the etymology of which means "to carry the *form* through *(per)*" (Vanhoozer, 2005, p. 253). The believer's story is supposed to exemplify more and more clearly a recapitulation of Christ's life, death and resurrection. In Christ's story we discover the divine reframing of our story and the pattern for our life. "The translation of the narrative of Christ into practice must proceed as an imaginative reappropriation of that narrative, a correspondence by way of variation, and requires a feeling for—and capacity to 'perform'—the shape of Christ's life" (Hart, 2003, p. 339).

So when Christians do such things as consent to God's created goodness in them, turn the other cheek to their enemies, bear the sins and sorrows of their neighbors, submit to unjust authorities or receive their resurrection to newness of life out of the deadness of their sin, the allegory of their lives bears a resemblance, more or less, to the story of Christ. Through the indwelling Spirit of Christ in believers, kenosis, incarnation, crucifixion and resurrection happen again and again, so that some of the beauty of the Word is being further expressed through their lives.

In addition, the true greatness of an individual's story should be measured by the depth of character displayed. If Christ is the ideal form of the Christian, the Spirit is the Christian's splendor, from whom comes the *intensive* beauty of the individual believer: his or her peculiar depth. The Spirit alone makes it possible for believers to live in more consistently Godward ways over the course of months and years, and this dipolar agency molds their characters into a more beautiful, unique form, one that has a singular, increasingly wondrous depth. Christians, therefore, can also be distinguished by the *density* of the glory in their daily lives. The more deeply the glory of God is ingressed, the truer the person's substance and the weightier her bearing. One of the synonyms Kierkegaard used to describe this concentration was "earnestness." An earnest life points inward (to the person's splendor), but especially upward (to the infinitely deep God and to the realities in "the heavenlies"). Like nothing else in the creation, hearty, vigorous, mature believers glorify God, because they signify the God who is infinitely deep and infinitely weighty. But given the dramatic/historical nature of human life, the density of the glory of one's life has to be lived outwardly before God and others in embodied actions in the dynamic, dialogical and interpersonal flow of history, and exemplified in a thousand ways, a few of the most important of which are discussed below.

The love of God. Edwards (1989) believed that God created humans precisely because his glory is so wonderful that it warranted the recognition of conscious beings beside himself. God did not *need* that recognition, but it was fitting and desirable that his creation would contain some beings who would be able to comprehend something of his beauty and express it. "Intelligent beings are created to be the consciousness of the universe, that they may perceive what God is and does. This can be nothing else but to perceive the excellency of what he is and does" (Edwards, 1994, p. 252). Edwards also taught that human happiness follows from such perceptions, consisting in knowing (with the mind) and loving and rejoicing in (with the heart) this God and his glory.

> The manifestation of God's glory to created understandings, and their seeing and knowing it, is not distinct from an emanation or communication of God's fullness, but clearly implied in it. Again, the communication of God's virtue or holiness is principally in communicating the love of himself. . . . And thus we see how, not only the creature's seeing and knowing God's excellence, but also supremely esteeming and loving him, belongs to the communication of God's fullness. And the communication of God's joy and happiness consists chiefly in communicating to the creature that happiness and joy, which consists in rejoicing in God and in his glorious excellency; for in such joy God's own happiness does principally consist. And in these things, namely, in knowing God's excel-

> lency, loving God for it, and rejoicing in it; and in the exercise and expression of these, consists God's honor and praise: so that these are clearly implied in that glory of God, which consists in the emanation of his internal glory. (1989, pp. 528-29)

This complex passage suggests that there is a profound interrelation between consciousness, understanding, love and joy. The greater the consciousness of God's glory, the greater the understanding of it, the greater the love of it, and the greater that glory will be experienced and manifested.

Scripture is important in this process, because it provides the primary cognitive means for the human participation in his glory. "Since both head and heart, the whole person in being and consciousness, must be renewed, revelation in this dispensation is continued jointly in Scripture and the church" (Bavinck, 2003, p. 384), as believers individually and communally receive and believe the Scripture more and more in the depths of their being. And the greater the depth of its internalization, the greater the capacity one has for knowing, fearing, loving and enjoying God, all of which display his glory. And we have access to none of these emotions apart from the Spirit.

At the base of the believer's affective repertoire of glory is the fear of God. Fearing God is the fundamental affective response of humans to the glory of God—the beginning of wisdom (Prov 1:9), we are told—without it, the contingent and sinful image of God is not properly related to its great Source. The fear of God is foundational to all other affective responses to God, including adoration, love and delight, giving them the appropriate tone. As close as believers are to their God, their status as dependent, sinful creatures remains basic to the relation.

At the affective heights is the doctrinally based love of God, because knowing God truly cannot but produce fear, admiration, consent, desire and awe in persons with the psychological equipment for appreciating virtuous beauty. Intense, positive affections of love, delight and joy toward him especially signify his worth and beauty, and such appraisal leads to worship. In public worship and meditative prayer, the believer communes with the triune God and participates in and experiences God's communal love, receiving and giving back to God some of his splendor—the deeper the love of the believer, the greater the density of the glory.

Necessary internal correlates of Christlikeness. Because the splendor of one's heart and character is a measure of the glory that personal agents express, there are certain characteristics of the heart that are necessarily related to the quality of their glory-manifestation. We will look at three such virtues.

Holiness of heart. Holiness is God's absolute ethicospiritual purity, his truest splendor and his defining communicable virtue. Believers have been set apart for God and by faith have entered into the spiritual order—the order of holiness (see chap. 10), so they are holy ones (1 Cor 1:1), called to be holy (1 Pet 1:16). Consequently, the indwelling Spirit of holiness (Rom 1:4) fuels in their hearts a desire for spiritual cleanliness that seeks freedom from sinfulness and the deeds of the flesh: "Let us purify ourselves from everything that contaminates body and spirit, perfecting holiness out of reverence for God" (2 Cor 7:1 NIV). Christlikeness is holiness—a prime sign of Christian well-being—and this divine desire feeds all other Christian virtues.

Authenticity of heart. We have assumed throughout this book a model of human beings as existing in three interpersonal dimensions: the individual's development is tied necessarily to one's relationship to God and to others. As a result of greater inwardness, one's growing sense of self-acceptance in Christ promotes the ability to recognize one's weaknesses, failings and sins, and encourages transparency: the "opening up" of the soul to the gaze of God, self and others. Over time, this should foster the growth of the virtue of authenticity, with the result that some will be able to sense that the believer is being more *real,* like there is less in the Christian's demeanor than there used to be of the duplicity, gamesmanship and manipulation that so often mar human relationships.

Authenticity has sometimes been promoted by humanists for self-serving purposes—"Be true to yourself, no matter what"—so it has been criticized by some as an intrinsically self-centered concern. But one can articulate a higher ethic of authenticity (see Taylor, 1991); and a theocentric articulation will guard against narcissistic excesses. Like the cleaning of a dirty window, through the Christiformic process of increasing transparency, the internalized beauty and goodness of God is better able to shine out of the individual, rendering her more true to herself and to God, and manifesting more of her splendor. "The purity and clarity with which the word of God presents itself in the world is in direct proportion to the transparency and purity of the medium of faith that receives it and from which it creates its own form" (Balthasar, 1989a, p. 539). Transparency is interrelated with purity of heart.

Unity and purity of heart. The triune God is almighty and does whatever he wishes. His sense of purpose and resolve are infinite. There is no hesitance, no weakness of will, no indecision on God's part and no inner conflict that compromises his intentions. His heart is pure, simple and intense. For humans to become more like him entails the development of a purer and more resolute heart. "The Gospel intends us to attain to true simplicity, [which is] the sense of an inward unity of life" (von Hildebrand, 2001, p. 71). Kierkegaard suggested that purity of heart is to will one thing (1847/1938; Connell, 1985). Bonhoeffer (1955) similarly argued that believers should become less conflicted as they become increasingly conformed to the single will of God. This occurs as believers—negatively—deconstruct their soul's damage and undermine their remaining sin, and—positively—internalize the signs of God and become increasingly centered on the triune God. Gradually, the maturing Christian comes to act with a greater sense of purpose and resolve, with less inner conflict, allowing for a fuller presence of character and awareness of what is at stake and what is most needful in the moment. Depth of character is lacking in people whose lives are distracted from the reality and depth of things, and consumed with self-protection and the pursuit of their own self-gratifying—and fragmenting—agenda.

This virtue also entails an increasing sense of narrative unity as Christians come to interpret the events and actions of their life with growing coherence and purposefulness and an integral stability to the self (MacIntyre, 1984; Taylor, 1989): "My life was not a waste. There were reasons that things went the way they did. Now I am being incorporated into the story of God's redemption and the spread of his kingdom, and God has been preparing me all along for my current life of worship, love, and ministry." The "quest" of Christiformity strengthens this narrative unifying of the self.

Part of the increasing narrative unity occurs as the painful memories and affective residue of trauma and poor past relationships that make up the narratives of some believers are resolved in Christ (see Benner, 1990; Langberg, 1997; Payne, 1995; Seamands, 1981, 1985; Smith, 2003). The severe negative emotions that were automatically stored with those memories and experiences (the anxiety, fear, sorrow and anger) must be decoupled from the memories themselves—through the cross and resurrection—in order for healthier, more positive affect (like a sense of resolution) to coexist with those memories. Very gradually, as God's more comprehensive views and feelings about such things are internalized, the pervasive negative mood that often attends those who have experienced trauma, neglect and abuse is replaced by a growing sense of hope, trust and significance—as well as a more authentic capacity to forgive and love the perpetrators. There is a reciprocal relationship between one's Christian narrative and this emotional healing process: as the healing increases, the narrative becomes more integrated and unified, and as the latter happens, the person's construal of the suffering changes, and so further healing is fostered.

The internal unity and wholeness of Christian maturity results in a more properly functioning soul-system: emotions and cognition working in harmony and accurately reflecting the true state of affairs; action properly regulated by emotions, values and reason; loves and hates corresponding to their objects according to their actual ethicospiritual value, defined according to God's work in Christ. An outcome of this unification is a type of wisdom that Vanhoozer (2005) calls "perspective." This is the ability to know what really matters in light of God's theodrama. "Having perspective enables us to make wise judgments about what is truly good and fitting in a given situation, given what God has done in Jesus Christ" (p. 335). As the souls of believers become increasingly shaped by doxological considerations, more and more of the disparate aspects of one's life and thinking find their meaning in God. A growing discernment results that recognizes the greater relative value of some truths and actions over others (spiritual beauty is more important than physical beauty; helping my neighbor with her roof is more important than watching television) (see von Hildebrand, 1990, on recollection).

The reciprocity of humility and gratitude. Along with love, humility and gratitude are fundamental components of the distinctive virtue set of Christianity (see Augustine, 1950, p. 310)—virtues that were out of place in ancient Greece or Rome and are largely foreign to the modern era of self-actualization. Humility is an inevitable consequence of Christian authenticity. As they grow in grace and self-awareness, believers become more aware of their weaknesses and sins (Berkouwer, 1952a; Calvin, 1559/1960). According to Edwards (1959, 1974) humility is a basic sign of true Christianity: "When therefore we see love in persons attended with a sense of their own littleness, vileness, weakness, and utter insufficiency; and so with self-diffidence, self-emptiness, self-renunciation, and poverty of spirit; these are the manifest tokens of the Spirit of God" (1974, Vol. 2, p. 268). Consequently, Christian humility points to God as the ultimate source of whatever good there is in the individual: "Let him who boasts, boast in the Lord" (1 Cor 1:31); "What do you have that you did not receive?" (1 Cor 4:7); "Let your light shine before men in such a way that they may see your good works, and glorify your Father who is in heaven" (Mt 5:16).

The humility of believers is especially appropriate, because the triune God—in spite of being infinitely great—is infinitely humble; in fact, his paradoxical humility is a part of his superlative magnificence. The Son and the Holy Spirit both exemplify this trait with reference to the Father. The Son was sent by the Father and obeyed him (Jn 7:18; 15:10; 16:5, 28; 17:4), he wondrously came as a baby, he glorified the Father (Jn 17:4), and he did nothing "out of himself" (Jn 5:19; 12:49). The Spirit points to the Father and Son, both of whom sent him (Jn 14:26; 15:26), the Spirit glorifies the Son and also does nothing "out of himself" (Jn 16:13-14). If two members of the Trinity display such humility, how much more fitting is it that mere creatures are genuinely humble!

There is, also, a kind of false, servile humility to which Christians are tempted that looks God-centered on the surface but actually undermines the manifestation of God's glory because it is unable to appreciate and affirm God's goodness within oneself (whether by creation grace or redemptive grace). For example, in response to praise, some Christians say, "Oh no. I didn't do anything good. I'm just a sinner. It's all from God." There is some truth in these statements, but to other Christians they feel somehow illegitimate and excessive. It is actually an immature distortion of God-centeredness (paradoxically promoted by the hidden autocentrism of remaining sin) that praises God outwardly while denying in the heart the actual, doxological state of affairs: *God's goodness in the believer.* A theocentric, dipolar humility is able to deeply rejoice in God's goodness evident in oneself through creation and redemption, while *simultaneously* acknowledging that all one's good is ultimately from God.

Gratitude is reciprocal to being a humble beneficiary of God's goodness. As believers become more conscious of their absolute dependence on God, they become more attuned to recognizing every physical or spiritual benefit they enjoy as a specific act of God's love. All humans are immersed in such grace continuously; believers are simply being awakened to the enormity of their indebtedness to the infinite God who loves to share. The psalms of thanksgiving are a portrayal of the form of Christ in the articulation of believers who seem characterized by an eager accounting of God's exuberant goodwill toward them, expressed in grateful singing.

Maturation and the development of glory-capacity. There is also a special significance to the process of being healed in Christ. As Christians overcome their internal barriers to God's glory, their overall *capacity* to glorify God correspondingly increases. There would seem to be, then, a developmental dimension to the manifestation of God's glory throughout adulthood. Consequently, Christians in their fifties and sixties ought to have greater ability to participate in and manifest the glory of God than they did in their twenties and thirties. This growth in doxological capacity is what is supposed to make aging noble and worthwhile—rather than something shameful, as it is in modern Western culture—and it also makes one's early adult years important as preparatory and foundational for further glory-expression "down the road."

Cruciformity. Though the Son of God always existed in the form of God, he "emptied Himself, taking the form of a bond-servant, and being made in the likeness of men. Being found in appearance as a man, He humbled Himself by becoming obedient to the point of death, even death on a cross" (Phil 2:7-8). Christ's form, therefore, includes *kenōsis*, the emptying of oneself or denying oneself for God and others. A significant theme of Christ's teaching was the requirement that his disciples take up their cross as part of following him (Mt 10:38; Mk 8:34; Lk 9:23; 14:27). This theme later became a central motif in Paul's understanding of the Christian life. According to him, conformity to Christ necessarily involves sharing in the fellowship of his sufferings (Phil 3:10). Gorman (2001) labels the Pauline use of this theme "cruciformity." Paul taught that Christians have been joined to Christ's crucifixion mystically (Rom 6:1-6; Gal 2:20; 6:14), and their entire orientation to themselves, to each other, to those outside the faith and to the world in general has been fundamentally altered. The lives of believers are rendered meaningful precisely in their symbolic resonance with and portrayal of Christ's death. In this world, old relationships and meanings have been done away with, and one's new-creation life (2 Cor 5:14-17; Gal 6:14-15) now consists of sacrificial service for Christ and his body. Through such identification, believers become "living metaphors" of Christ, signs testifying of Christ's death on behalf of the world, and so they specially manifest his glory.

Glory and the jar of clay principle. Human weakness is particularly revelatory of God's power and goodness. Paul wrote:

> We have this treasure [the light of the knowledge of the glory of God in the face of Christ, mentioned in 3:18 and 4:4-6] in earthen vessels, so that the surpassing greatness of the power may be of God and not from ourselves; we are afflicted in every way, but not crushed, perplexed, but not despairing; persecuted, but not forsaken; struck down, but not destroyed; always carrying about in the body the dying of Jesus, that the life of Jesus also may be manifested in our body. For we who live are constantly being delivered over to death for Jesus' sake, so that the life of Jesus also may be manifested in our mortal flesh. (2 Cor 4:7-11)

The paradoxical implications of this passage for Christian soul care are far-reaching, for it turns the value of natural competence on its head and suggests that the greater one's limitations, the greater the potential for glory (and eternal reward). God seems to enjoy taking such "jars of clay" and making them "heroes" in order to manifest his redemptive power (think of the stories of Abraham and Sarah, Gideon, and David and Goliath). It would seem to follow, then, that the *worse* a believer's biopsychosocial damage and even ethical problems, and the *more* barriers a believer has for accomplishing much in this world, the greater the overall glory-potential in that person's Godward story. This renders an extraordinary degree of significance to the sufferings one has endured, for the power of Christ and the resurrection life can be marvelously displayed in the midst of pain, limitation and affliction through the healing, overcoming and undoing of such evils in the name of Christ, at least in some measure, in this life.

A related implication would seem to be that the *further* one travels down the road of psychospiritual maturity, the greater the glory of that story. When persons enter their twenties, they are largely the recipients of a particular "endowment" or "inheritance" of meaning—more or less—that they have internalized, and the specific forms of some souls at that point are notably damaged. The more progress made by such "jars of clay," that is, the further they travel to conformity with Christ, the more God's greatness is displayed in their lives. This is true even though at the end of their life, their form may still in some sense be less whole than that of others who entered their twenties fairly well formed—given their advantaged background and family life—and who do not make anything near the same amount of progress, in an absolute sense, that the more damaged individuals did.

Because of creation and redemptive grace, some parents were skilled at fostering their children's healthy formation, whereas other parents were ill equipped for such training. However, it seems that God receives a special kind of glory from those raised by the latter, since God "personally," we might say, and more directly can build their souls and teach them the skills of life "from scratch" through the Holy Spirit and the gospel. There is a paradox here, because for many reasons it is, of course, *best* for people to grow up in healthy Christian families, primarily because they will be far more likely to become Christians themselves and will be better equipped to live sacrificially for others as they mature, and such activity greatly glorifies God. But the soul-healing effects of salvation make *more explicit* God's involvement in soul-improvement than does God's creation grace to children, mediated through created structures like their families (after all, non-Christians can raise relatively psychologically healthy persons without Christ's help); so God gets greater glory. Weaknesses that God can use to specially glorify himself make possible a kind of cruciformity that is being overcome in the resurrection-life.

This too is about beauty. Perhaps one way to assess the splendor of a Christian's life is as a function of the degree of Christ's form that has been internalized multiplied by the degree of suffering one has endured. In a special way, Christian beauty is manifested in holy, loving saints who have suffered much.

Interpreting the signs of God's hiddenness. We could say that suffering, pain and abuse are signs of God's hiddenness or apparent absence. They are also, according to the interpretive guide of the Bible, signs that the human race has fallen into a state of alienation from God. Satan is currently the ruler of this world (Eph 2:2; 1 Jn 5:19), in a limited but real sense, and his reign results in suffering for those made in his God's image. But, of course, God is not actually absent. He is the omnipresent Lord of the universe, and the history of redemption is the theodrama of his reclamation project, in which he gradually reasserts his rule and slowly manifests his light in the context of a world of darkness. Now Christ is sowing seed (Mt 13:37), announcing the end of Satan's reign (Jn 12:31) and disclosing the light of the gospel of his glory, and encouraging his image-bearers to sell all they have to buy a field or a pearl of great value (Mt 13:44-46), a value that is not yet fully manifest.

The sufferings of a terrible life are not minimized by their transposition into God's theodrama; they are transfigured. There is a special resplendence in the light God shines through lives that are being healed from the darkness of bondage and brokenness. There is a special kind of delight that occurs when someone discovers some gold coins, hidden up in a dusty attic, in an old cigar box. The hidden, elusive God delights to reveal his glory in such ways, in the most unlikely and unexpected places. God seems to want to demonstrate the beauty of his goodness and holiness in broken, damaged and sinful persons through their recovery and reformation into the Son's crucified and resurrected likeness. By working with people with such paradoxical, doxological potential, Christian soul care itself attains its greatest significance.

The love of neighbor. We have seen that the glory of the triune God is most clearly manifested in the love of God. But in the Christian scheme, the love of others (the love of the ethical order) is necessarily correlated with the love of God (of the spiritual order). First, because in loving other humans, we are imitating God's love of them (and so participating in it; 1 Jn 4:7), and second, because we are representing or signifying the love of the members of the Trinity for one another. Christians are called to love others, in various concrete ways, precisely because it is the concrete manifestation of the love of God (Mt 5:45-48; Jn 13:35; Eph 4:25-32; 5:2, 25).

The love of family and friends. Love of family and friends signifies the love of God. God is our Father and friend, so family love and friendship picture God's love. However, such love is strongly genetically programmed into the human form. Virtually all humans (and even the higher mammals) care for their biological relatives, and the love of friends is enjoyable and generally reciprocal, so neither counts that much for glory (Mt 5:46). Such love is a function of creation grace, which makes possible relatively healthy biopsychosocial development, regardless of redemption, and can be easily explained by the motive of self-interest.

Nonetheless, some know little of such love, so disordered was their story. Moreover, family and friends are still sinners. Consequently they present a challenge for our genetically wired motives to love. Friends can turn away; family members can become alienated. Because of sin, even the love of family and friends needs redemptive assistance that enables people to forgive those who have sinned against them, and Christians are charged with cultivating more loving families and friendships that challenge one another to find Christ and pursue Christlikeness.

Marital love. Though grounded in biological motives to reproduce and have sex, marriage provides a special context for the manifestation of glory. In a way that is analogous to God's eternal love for his people, marriage is based in a lifelong covenant commitment to a sinner. The biological motives are strong enough to ensure people will enter into marriage. However, they are not necessarily strong enough to keep self-centered sinners together. Consequently marriage becomes a symbol of God's covenantal faithfulness to his people, who sin against him time and again. The main difference, of course, is that both spouses are self-absorbed sinners. As a result, Christian marriage requires the gospel at its center to make it work. When it is working according to its design, both spouses are growing in conformity to Christ.

The love of spiritual brothers and sisters: communal manifestation. The glory of God is intrinsically dispersive. "Infinite sharing is the law of God's inner life" (Merton, 1955, p. 3). So the manifestation of God's glory entails the fostering of truth, beauty and goodness in *others.* Of special significance is the love that only the body of Christ can manifest (i.e., the church universal, as well as local assemblies of God's people; both display God's glory uniquely). To begin with, the body of Christ provides a special analogy of the Trinity. Each church is one body composed of many parts, members or persons. As the three members of the Trinity love, affirm, consent to and glorify one another, so the members of the body of Christ are supposed to love, affirm, consent to and glorify each other in Christ. In addition, the Holy Spirit who Edwards (1994) wrote is the "act of love between the Father and the Son, infinitely loving and delighting in each other" (p. 260) is also necessarily the source of the love of believers to one another. Through the reciprocal signs of the love of believers, the world beholds indirectly the manifestation of the triune love of God (Jn 13:35-36; 17:20-26).

The problem, again, is that churches are composed of sinners. So church members and leaders can be insensitive, irritating, resentful and self-seeking. As a result, the local church and the church universal provide profound opportunities to display Christ's love to his people in concrete form. "The Church's being is constituted in self-giving agency" (Patterson, 1999, p. 144). As believers grow in loving one another—more and more relating without self-promotion or coercion—they speak a "non-violent semiosis" (Milbank, 1997; Hart, 2003) that presents a relational rationale, which contrasts starkly with the ways of a self-seeking world.

Moreover, believers need each other. They benefit from dialogue that enlightens and challenges, from seeing exemplary models of Christlikeness before them (including the modeling of confession and humility), and from internalizing their godly desires and actions (Girard, 1996, pp. 62-64). The example of Others provide previously unimagined options for us. Without them, we would not as easily conceive of the possibilities available to us in the gospel.

As the church becomes increasingly adept at fostering the kinds of inner and outer change that are God's design, the attitudes, theories and strategies that foster such activity will become a part of the church's collective mindset and communal conversation, a stage Martin (1994, p. 20; following Harre, 1984) called "conventionalization." For various reasons, the twentieth-century church did not make such soul-change a high priority, a neglect evinced in the relative lack of love that characterizes many contemporary churches. Christian pastors, teachers and soul-care providers are needed today to help the church and its local expressions better realize communal conformity to the image of Christ.

The love of the stranger, the poor and the enemy. As much as loving family, marital and church relations can manifest glory, they can all be explained by biopsychosocial factors, that is, by self-interest. Consequently, they manifest less glory than the types of love that are harder to explain with such factors. For example,

> Love your enemies and pray for those who persecute you, so that you may be sons of your Father who is in heaven; for He causes His sun to rise on the evil and the good, and sends rain on the righteous and the unrighteous. For if you love those who love you, what reward do you have? Do not even the tax collectors do the same? If you greet only your brothers, what more are you doing than others? Do not even the Gentiles do the same? Therefore you are to be perfect, as your heavenly Father is perfect. (Mt 5:44-48)

Jesus is referring specifically to the love of enemies, but we might paraphrase the passage this way: the more difficult the person is to love, the more the love of that person resembles the love of the Father. Jesus seems to place a higher premium on *difficult* love (Carson, 2000), because it is a better sign of God's agape love than is mere friendship or family love. In addition to the love of enemies, difficult love includes the love of strangers and those who are different, the unpleasant and those who make us uncomfortable, and the disadvantaged (including Third-World poor, minorities, prisoners, the homeless, the elderly, the mentally ill and victims of adultery and divorce), as well as every kind of sinner (like wife-beaters, drug addicts, abortionists, selfish billionaires and pedophiles).

Broken sinners need the long-term, committed love of members of God's body to help undo the effects of the Fall and to draw them to Christ. When Christians take into their homes prostitutes and their children, alcoholics or gay men dying of AIDS, the Spirit of the Christ of the gospels is being re-signified, not in empty words but in manifest action.

What about self-love? Where does self-love fit into Christlikeness? Did Christ love himself? This is a complex topic. Contrary to the thinking of many secular therapists (and some Christians), in the Christian scheme of things, humans do not *first* need to love themselves before they can love others (Fromm, 2000). Love of self *by itself*—abstracted from relationship—is not healthy or mature from a Christian perspective. Self-love can only properly be understood within the three personal dimensions of human life (God-others-self), and in terms of the redemptive-historical metanarrative (creation, Fall and redemption).

Self-love *is* a primordial, created motive, intrinsic to all humans (something like it is even found in animals), but sin has rendered it intrinsically pathological (see 2 Tim 3:2). Created self-love has been exaggerated by sin and turned into narcissism. But through the Spirit—in redemption—as the love of self is transposed beyond the legitimate, created, but egocentric self-love of the child, and as the narcissistic self-love of the sinner is increasingly put to death in Christ, created self-love learns how to embrace God as the best fulfillment of its desires.[3] Created self-love finds its redemptive realization in the love of God, others and self, according to their worth. Loving God, others and self are interdependent, reciprocal and irreducible to each other, so that, from a Christian standpoint, one cannot have one without some degree of the others. This comprehensive *consent* to self, others and God is a sign of the self-fulfilling and communal love of the three persons of the Trinity, each of whom loves himself infinitely in their infinite love of one another and of all that bears their resemblance.

The verbal communication of glory to others. Edwards used the word *communication* to refer to any kind of transfer of glory. However, in keeping with modern usage and Christian understanding, the term in this book refers to the transfer of glory through *discourse.* Communication can occur, of course, through facial expressions and embodied actions, but discourse is basic to uniquely human communication of any kind, and glory is powerfully expressed through words.

The simple, verbal confession of the triune God to others is a basic kind of verbal glory.

> My soul will make its boast in the LORD;
> The humble will hear it and rejoice.
> O magnify the LORD with me,
> And let us exalt His name together. (Ps 34:2-3)

The *publication* of God's glory must not be limited to the "automatic" declarations of the heavens (or the earth); it must also be articulated by the only earthly creatures who can speak.

> There is also creaturely testimony to His eternal Word, not everywhere, but where His eternal Word has chosen, called and created for Himself witnesses: a testimony by the word of the prophets and apostles of this Word; by the visible existence of His people, His Church; by the Gospel which is delivered and to be heard in it; by the sacraments in which this Gospel has also a physically visible and apprehensible form; and finally, by the existence of us who believe this testimony. (Barth, 1957, p. 199)

Parenting, teaching, sharing with another, Bible-study discussions in small groups, witnessing, preaching and counseling are all forms of dialogue where humans communicate glory *directly*, through explicit reference to the reality of the objects of Christian discourse: the triune God, the work of Christ, the nature of salvation and God's involvement in one's life. Testimony is a "constitutive dimension of selfhood" (Ford, 1999, p. 83)—we become a certain kind of self, based on that to which we testify—and prophetic witness is a constitutive dimension of the *imago Dei* (Horton, 2005).

Apologetics, evangelism and missions (discourse that has as its aim the conversion of others to Christ) are tremendous goods from the standpoint of the kingdom, not because persons in hell will not glorify God—their judgment manifests the holiness and righteousness of God—but because saved sinners in heaven will give God greater glory. Evangelism and missions are especially fervent forms of verbal glory, since they proclaim God's supremacy through love of the other and self-denial. They engage with those outside the faith out of concern for their greatest well-being while risking personal rejection (in extreme cases, martyrdom), because challenging other people's worldviews often makes them uncomfortable. Evangelism and missions seek to add new voices to the worship of God (Piper, 1993), so the manifestation of God's glory is quantitatively increased through conversion. Though evangelism and missions can certainly be done for self-serving and pathological reasons, in principle they are signs of psychospiritual well-being; God-loving people who love their neighbors will share Christ with them.

It follows then that Christian counselors should look for opportunities to share Christ with colleagues and counselees who are not Christians. This must be done fittingly, but it should not be prohibited in therapy simply because secular canons of therapy forbid it. The fact is that secular therapists are free to share their secular forms of meaning-making all the time. Secularism has the perverse advantage of having its evangelistic intentions well concealed—even from its proponents. Orthodox Christian counselors (as well as other orthodox theists) should be given the same trust and latitude as secular counselors.

The role of imagination and discernment in manifestation. Growing in Christlikeness leads Christians to envision their future accordingly. As redeemed personal agents, they need not assume they must simply repeat their past or deterministically play out their biological or psychosocial "program." Redemption makes it possible to break out of one's psychosocial *repetition* and act increasingly freely in Christ. Believers can begin to envision new possibilities for themselves, encouraged and regulated by the written Word of God and its story, and modeled by godly others. This redemptive freedom glorifies God as Christians act in ways contrary to that which natural-science models of human development would predict. Christians are enabled to see their future selves (Markus & Nurius, 1986) acting in novel ways—developing new emotional responses to life, new motivations, new thoughts and new actions—the utilization of their Scripture-shaped imagination being a necessary step prior to the realization of the Word of God in their actual activity (see Patterson, 1999, pp. 88-92).

For the Christian, the revelation of the law of God is not merely a standard for Christian conduct; it is first and foremost a revelation of God's love for the believer in Christ—and all that comes with that love (declarative salvation)—secondarily, it is a description of the kind of person the believer is becoming—the "first-fruits" now, in this age, and perfectly in the age to come. With imagination grounded in a realistic faith in future grace (Piper, 1995), believers can write new plot developments into their story; they can see holy potential for themselves in Christ and are enabled to take small, novel steps toward Christlikeness that would not make sense if they had nothing more than their previous history and their own resources to go on. "All the expectations of God are future expectations. All the possibilities of faith and love are future possibilities. And all the power that touches me with help to live in love is future power. My hope for future goodness and future glory is future grace" (Piper, p. 65). As believers internalize the Word of God in mind and heart, and imagine themselves in its light, they will come to *realize* that Word, just as a basketball player uses his imagination to visualize the making of future baskets. "Imagination . . . is thus the medium through which God acts to reveal to us the true story of both God's and our own lives" (Patterson, 1999, p. 89).

God has closed the canon of Scripture as a written text, but "the canon remains open in the sense that it invites the church's ongoing understanding and participation" (Vanhoozer, 2005, p. 237). Our imagination is not *limited* by Scripture; it is *set free* by Scripture to advance the glory of God as far as possible through Christiformic change in our lives. Of course, only God knows what is realistically possible for a particular individual, at a certain point in time—given earlier parts of their story—but Scripture provides the divinely authorized guidebook to this pattern of change and contains other stories that illustrate its realization (as well as its opposite). By faith Christians receive the gift of perfect, verbal righteousness in Christ, and by faith Christians are to imagine taking the next steps in fulfilling that *calling*—not so far out that it produces either chronic disappointment or self-deception, but far enough to move beyond one's past.

And where does that imagination lead? Vanhoozer (2005) suggests that human actions should be characterized by "fittingness." Knowing what actions are *fitting* requires the virtue of discernment (or *phronēsis*). "What is 'fit' is what rightly finds its place in the 'whole'" (Vanhoozer, p. 256), and the "whole" includes Scripture and the current situation. Godly actions "fit" to the degree they correspond to the telic ideal of human life presented in Scripture, and they address well the exigencies of the contemporary scenario (including such things as one's personal limitations, the participation of others, environmental affordances, cultural agendas and so forth). "This I pray, that your love may abound still more and more in real knowledge and all discernment, so that you may approve the things that are excellent" (Phil 1:9-10). A bold, godly, phronetic creativity envisions fitting ways to act that uniquely and best glorify God in particular settings, and that therefore are especially excellent or beautiful, that is, they fit harmoniously into God's word and purposes.

Scripture wires the believer's poetic imagination for metaphorical fulfillment. "The church's fitting contemporary performance stands in a metaphorical relation to its canonical script" (Vanhoozer, p. 261). It is not a slavish repetition of Scripture—that is useless and really impossible, because we do not live in that identical context—but our performance should bear a strong resemblance to its teachings, particularly to the life of Christ (see Eph 5:23-32; 1 Pet 2:18-25). Being Christlike means living metaphorically: "an action is good only if it agrees with (God's) theo-drama" (Vanhoozer, 2005, p. 329). And the more it agrees, the more glory it manifests.

There should also be, according to Wells (2004) and Vanhoozer (2005), an improvisatory quality to Christian action. He is not referring to "unscripted" or "random acts of kindness," but to a spontaneity grounded in God's loving freedom in Christ. Wisdom (or *phronesis*) trained by Scripture guides mature Christian action in grace, so that it tends to flow more from the free and holy love of God in the heart than from calculated duty and a set of fixed rules for all situations.

Faith expressed through a Scripture-based imagination provides the bridge between the word internalized and the word displayed in the embodied lives of God's people. A virtuous Christian imagination is consenting to what God has done in Christ on one's own behalf, concretized in a vision of new steps in the love of God and neighbor. Christian soul-care providers help those with whom they work by pointing to realistic futures of increasing grace and glory, by verbally describing what they see is possible in the next few steps.

Anti-Christlikeness: The Problem of Hypocrisy

Before we are finished, mention must be made of the imitation of the imitation of Christ. Jesus Christ was far harder on the Pharisees than he was on prostitutes and alcoholics. Why? One way of explaining it is to say that hypocrisy constitutes an abominable pseudo-manifestation of the glory of God. It has the appearance (or form) of theocentrism but no substance (or splendor). It may sound strange to say it (given this model's semiodiscursive emphasis), but *all* there is in hypocrisy is words—empty words—words without passion. The truest human signs of glory come out of the heart. This fact makes it tragically possible for the *appearance* of religion—whether in word or deed—without inner reality. This is the result of a deadly, internal dissociation of human life from its explicit, trinitarian, ethicospiritual context, a fissure that is the product of sin, that turns the person into either a religious zombie, on the one hand, or a religious actor, on the other, faking emotions that ought to be there but are not.

In hypocrisy, a semiodiscursive model truly falls apart, because the signs and discourse are empty; they are deceptive; they lack weight or bearing. The professed doctrines and behaviors appear to signify certain things, but upon closer examination they signify nothing. There is the barest of internalization—mere mental assent—so the words and concepts are superficial and hollow, because they do not flow from the heart and from an ingressed depth of personal agency and character.

The sort of "word play" that affirms religious concepts without love bothers God a great deal. The canonical Gospels make this unequivocally clear. The blindness of the Pharisees provides such a stark contrast to the Light of the world, who came to unveil the quality of the glory-seeking of the human heart. "I do not receive glory from men; but I know you, that you do not have the love of God in yourselves. . . . How can you believe, when you receive glory from one another and you do not seek the glory that is from the one and only God?" (Jn 5:41-42, 44). "He who speaks from himself seeks his own glory; but He who is seeking the glory of the One who sent Him, He is true, and there is no unrighteousness in Him" (Jn 7:18). The Gospels teach us that we are all hypocrites, of whom I am chief. Christ alone loved his Father with his whole heart and his neighbor as himself—Christ is the only true believer—and our hope for genuineness is only derived from his light and life.

So Christians must always beware of having the "form *[morphōsin]* of godliness," but not the power (which comes from the Spirit [2 Tim 3:5; 1 Thess 1:5] and is experienced sporadically in this age). Such form, empty of divine splendor, is what led to the greatest semiodiscursive contradiction of all time: God's covenant people killed him when he came to earth. The death of Christ serves as the ultimate sign of judgment on *all* religion—to the extent that it originates from ourselves.[4] The cross alone is able to unmask our religious hypocrisy and open up our hearts to their own tendency toward Christian duplicity. As the sign of the cross is more and more properly understood, standing at the center of the Christian's semiodiscursive landscape, the Christian's self-righteous self-understanding is more and more undermined. Now, the word of the cross is to bring about continually an unveiling of our own religious self-deception, working its way ever deeper into our hearts. Paradoxically, theological liberalism (with its deliberately empty assent, an "enlightened" appreciation for the symbols of the faith, but not the substance) and fundamentalism (with its unwittingly empty assent, evidenced by an obsessive focus on inerrant doctrine and sexual ethics) end up having more in common at the core than one might think. In very different ways, both manifest an attraction to superficial, self-serving substitutes for union and communion with Christ and a deepening appropriation of his cross and resurrection.

Hypocrisy is a black hole to glory. Astronomers cannot see black holes, because they draw everything into themselves, even light. But one can see their *effects,* as they gradually destroy what is within their influence. Nothing is more spiritually devastating to a child than to grow up in a home that has a great deal of Christian hypocrisy. Tragically, the dissociation of discourse and heart is internalized in the formation of that child. In homes saturated with such hypocrisy, Christianity, though often talked about, signifies nothing, and it leads the child to confusion and deadness, usually anger and possibly depression, and often a rejection of God. Nevertheless, "with God all things are possible" (Mt 19:26). The light of God's glory is such that it can shine out of black holes, overcome their effects and resurrect them, and turn them into stars.

Full Disclosure

Though God has revealed himself in Scripture and reveals himself throughout the creation, his greatness is sufficiently veiled that some sinners reason themselves to atheism and agnosticism. But someday the manifestation of the glory of God will be fully disclosed. With reference to the Pharisees and their hypocrisy, Christ taught, "There is nothing covered up that will not be revealed, and hidden that will not be known. Accordingly, whatever you have said in the dark shall be heard in the light, and what you have whispered in the inner rooms shall be proclaimed upon the housetops" (Lk 12:2-3). At the end of the age, everything will be opened up and all will be made known. Christ's second coming will be very different from his first. He came, then, as a human baby, an arrival revealed to only a few shepherds and sages. But when he comes again, "every eye will see Him, even those who pierced Him; and all the tribes of the earth will mourn over Him" (Rev 1:7). No longer hidden, the scope of his manifestation will be cosmic, and no one will be in the dark.

The individual Christian will share in that manifestation. "For you have died and your life is hidden with Christ in God. When Christ, who is our life, is revealed, then you also will be revealed with Him in glory" (Col 3:4). This is supposed to give the Christian an added measure of contentment in this age, knowing that in the end, all puzzles will be resolved and every person will know the true nature of reality. Tears will be wiped away (Rev 21:4), at least in part because God's doxological purposes regarding the particulars of one's story will be more fully explained and God's people will have a better understanding of their significance in redemptive history. The manifestation of any glory in this age is an eschatological anticipation (and sign) of the full disclosure that is to come. Consequently, the maturing Christian now looks ahead, to the end of God's story, trusting that the troubles and turmoil of his or her own story will be made more meaningful in the final transposing speech of God to his children. We look ahead to the time when the "momentary, light affliction" of our present life will be seen to have produced for us "an eternal weight of glory far beyond all comparison" (2 Cor 4:17).

Most importantly, all the good of the creation and of redemption will redound to the glory of the triune Creator of the universe and Redeemer of his followers: "To Him who sits on the throne, and to the Lamb, be blessing and honor and glory and dominion forever and ever" (Rev 5:13). While believers will share in that glory, in *that* day God alone will be seen as the ultimate source of all the good that any image of God experienced or produced. In that age, our eternal well-being will be forever sweetly united to his eternal joy in the open manifestation of himself and his beauty to his bride (a beauty already being given to his bride eschatologically; Eph 5:27). There we will experience the fullness of psychospiritual well-being that necessarily exceeded our limitations in this age. In the meantime, we live as signs, dependent on signs, all of which point us to that great end.

Notes

[1]At the same time, we must be careful not to circumscribe the work of God by assuming we can always recognize it. Because of divine hiddenness and the mysteriousness of his ways in this age, it is likely that he is working in many converts some time before the signs of his work are evident. This must be insisted on, even in the face of such important soul-care movements as that of the Puritans, who seemed obsessed with correctly diagnosing the state of the human soul in such a way as to burden the consciences of God's people and likely underestimate the grace of God. The fact that our age has the opposite problem must not move us to an overreaction.

[2]Another related passage is Romans 12:2, where Paul encouraged believers to "be transformed [*metamorphousthe*] by the renewal of your mind." See also Colossians 3:10: Christians "have put on the new self who is being renewed to a true knowledge according to the image of the One who created him."

[3]See Edwards (1989) in *Charity and Its Fruit*, for an excellent theocentric discussion of self-love; see also Piper (1996) and O'Donovan (1980).

[4]The Puritans focused a great deal on hypocrisy. However, they viewed it statically—either one was a hypocrite or one was not—so it was usually discussed in terms of the unregenerate. This limitation in their own self-awareness stunted their ability to recognize this very deadly remnant of indwelling sin in believers and led many sincere believers who sensed their relative hypocrisy to doubt their salvation.

18

Promoting Christiformity Through the Therapeutic Delivery of Signs of Glory

CHRISTIAN SOUL CARE SEEKS TO PROMOTE Christiformity by fostering inwardness—particularly the internalization of the constituting word of God—and outwardness, the manifestation of God's glory in human life. The final chapter of this book is an attempt to describe the most important *modalities* to be used in the pursuit of these goals. A modality is a *God-established means or pathway by which Christian soul care is facilitated.* We will explore a number of them to see how they might assist in the delivery of the signs of glory—the word and will of God, the form of others, and dipolar self-regulation—and promote Christiformity.

From Models to Schools to Modalities

Contemporary psychotherapy and counseling is made up of a large number of therapeutic models, perhaps as many as two hundred (Garfield & Bergin, 1994). Depending on how one looks at it, the current state of Western soul care is either hopelessly fragmented or richly diverse. What is the cause of this therapeutic multiplicity? Some biblical counselors have suggested it is due to gross confusion in modern soul care and to the impossibility of making scientific claims in this area, arguing that the diversity proves their invalidity (e.g., see Almy, 2000; Ganz, 1993). Since the psychologists cannot even agree among themselves, how can we possibly take modern soul care seriously and think it has any value? There is a point here. It is obvious that modern soul care—particularly in pop psychology—has been characterized by a proliferation of "new and improved" therapy models that are often little more than modestly altered versions of previous models.

But there are also good reasons to view this multiplicity in a more positive light. For one thing, therapy with humans is highly idiographic, inevitably shaped to some extent by the individual counselee's needs (see Yalom, 2002) and even more by the individual counselor's or theorist's dispositions. It is therefore not surprising that many approaches have developed. One might suppose that any thoughtful counselor could come up with a somewhat distinct model of therapy (shaped by his or her own gifts, training and experience). More importantly, God's infinite understanding presumably possesses an unlimited variety in treatment approaches (grounded in his purposes and character), so using the number of extant models as itself an argument against them would seem to be a red herring, from a theocentric standpoint. In addition, surely some of the diversity of counseling approaches is a reflection of the extreme complexity of human nature. Nevertheless, it is still very likely that the roughly two hundred models of modern soul care can be categorized in various ways.

Schools of psychotherapy. To a large extent, these many models can be fairly easily grouped into a much smaller number of therapy families—different "schools of psychotherapy"—that are defined by a distinctive therapeutic focus, and in some cases, shaped by a particular worldview. In the twentieth century, modern psychotherapy has looked something like a game of "family feud," with proponents of one family fighting against another, object relations theorists against orthodox Freudians, cognitive-behavioral therapists criticizing psychodynamic therapists, and systems counselors arguing against the individualism of the other therapies, and so on.

Some of this contentiousness is likely due to the identity needs of some to become members of *the* school that is better than all the others. The Reformed theologian Abraham Kuyper (1898b) explained the existence of certain scientific "schools of thought" as a function of the diversity and complexity of the creation, *combined* with the need of the fallen mind to obtain an ultimate sense of meaning and a comprehensive view of reality apart from God—that is, to find in a school the intellectual key that unlocks all the secrets of knowledge. Ideally, Kuyper argued, Christians have no need for such an ultimate, comprehensive *creation-based* framework of meaning, since they are in a fulfilling relationship with the transcendent Creator of the creation's diversity and complexity. Therefore, Christians do not have to take sides regarding a certain model of counseling and join a particular school. They are in Christ's school; they are *his* disciples and find their meaning in *him*. Consequently, Christians should not feel constrained to study psychotherapy in terms of a "schools" approach: psychoanalysis, Jungian therapy, Gestalt therapy and so forth. This has the single advantage of documenting the historical context of their development into modern schools. However, it may also create conceptual and evaluative confusion in our students by seeming to imply that each school has equal merit, by obscuring the *actual* contributions of the different schools (their focus on specific created modalities, see below), and by downplaying the modern or postmodern worldview assumptions embedded within the edification frameworks of their models. The last point is especially important, if we are to develop thoroughly Christian models of soul care. It is often very difficult to tease out the worldview assumptions of these schools, since they are not usually discussed explicitly in the primary sources (and often even the secondary sources, though Jones & Butman [1991] is a terrific exception).

Moving to modalities. Instead, the value of the *best* "schools" of therapy can be better appreciated by Christians if their contributions are interpreted as the result of their having identified particular, irreducible and justifiable intervention pathways for soul care, called a *modality*. Legitimate counseling modalities are those that address some significant dynamic structural feature (or set of features) of human nature, interpreted from the standpoints of the Christian ground-motive (creation, fall, redemption, consummation).

It must be admitted that much of our current understanding of these modalities developed out of modern and postmodern psychology, a realization that always entails for Christians a hermeneutic of suspicion regarding the subtle but pervasive effects of secularization and autocentrism on the psychological discourse.[1] But whereas these issues have serious implications in some areas—like the content of therapy discourse—there is no compelling reason to conclude that these effects would render the identification of the modalities themselves specious. The utility of working in the modalities identified in the twentieth century has been well documented empirically. If there *are* God-established modalities for soul care, then those means or pathways for therapy are a part of the created order (corrupted by the Fall), and they should be identifiable and usable, regardless of the worldview of the researchers/practitioners.

The Christian worldview would not lead us to suppose that redemption would create new modalities—any more than it creates new faculties (Edwards, 1746/1959)—rather, redemption works within and through the fallen created order, so we would expect that the unique resources of Christian salvation would be mediated through the same modalities that all soul-care systems must use. One might even argue that if therapy works with a secular use of these modalities, their use by Christians should prove empirically to be more efficacious, given the additional redemptive resources that Christianity possesses (e.g., the Holy Spirit, divine forgiveness and so on). Most importantly, if the modalities themselves are ordained by God, there should be good biblical and doctrinal reasons that legitimate them, and ideally some evidence that they have long been in use in the Christian soul-care tradition.

The main problem that Christians will have with the secular literature on the modalities is not the modalities themselves but *how secularists* use them. All modern and most postmodern psychologies are secular, and they all promote autocentrism (moderns and postmoderns differ in the degree of social construction recognized). This leads most of them to concentrate on aspects of the psychosocial order (and to a lesser extent, the biological). A few models deal with the ethical and spiritual orders (for example, existential-humanistic, New Age and Eastern therapies, see Wilbur, 2000), but because of its secularism and positivism, *mainstream* psychological thought has been fundamentally incapable of positing a system of holistic, hierarchical orders that can comprehensively map human complexity (with the exception of positive psychology). On the contrary, secular, mainstream therapeutic assumptions have tended to lead away from seeing humans as whole persons and working with *all* relevant aspects. Because modern and most postmodern psychology rejects metaphysical discourse, they have very limited semiodiscursive resources to enable the articulation of an overarching, holistic framework for understanding human beings in all their complexity. As a result, modern/postmodern research tends to be piecemeal and fragmented. The most holistic models in mainstream psychotherapy tend to be the result of a pragmatic eclecticism that uses easily documented, differential treatment of specific disorders, paradoxically trying to heal the soul's conflicts by dealing with only some of its parts. It should not be supposed that the following model is final and comprehensive. Undoubtedly there are legitimate modalities that have been left out (e.g., solution-focused therapy). What follows is simply one metasystem of how some of the most important created soul-care modalities can be integrated into a holistic Christian model of soul care in order to best deliver Christian therapeutic resources and foster their internalization and manifestation to the greatest effect.

A Metasystem of Modalities

Over the past thirty years, however, a number of secular therapists and therapy researchers have recognized that the complexity of human nature and its problems require the development of some type of metasystem that incorporates more than one modality. Beginning with its first edition (Bergin & Garfield, 1971; now in its 5th ed., Lambert, 2004), the *Handbook of Psychotherapy and Behavior Change* has assumed an openness to diverse, empirically validated therapy perspectives. Lazarus (1989) has recommended a *multimodal* approach to therapy, where one may intervene at the sensory, cognitive, imaginal, affective, behavioral, interpersonal and biological modalities, depending on the clinical problem. Beutler and Clarkin (1990) and Beutler and Harwood (2000) have advocated a *systematic eclecticism* that makes use of whatever strategies have been found to work well with specific disorders and types of persons, based on competent research. Concerned about the atheoretical implications of the term *eclecticism,* Norcross and Goldfried (1992, 2005) have promoted the concept of "integration" as a label for the combining of a variety of modalities in clinical practice that strives for a high degree of theoretical coherence. And Prochaska (1979, 1995) has developed a *transtheoretical* model of therapy based on the identification of common features of various therapy models that promote healthy change across a series of common stages. All of these efforts at clinical holism are laudable and are an expression of what most experienced soul-care providers know: that comprehensive soul care must embrace multiple modalities. Most of these metasystemic models are in part a response to therapy research that has found that different types of therapy work better with some people than others and on some problems better than others (Beutler, Malik, Alimohamed, Harwood, Talebi, Noble & Wong, 2003; Clarkin & Levy, 2004).

In this chapter a holistic edification framework will be laid out as the final chapter of this proposal. I prefer the terms "holistic" or "metasystemic" over any of the other available terms (especially eclectic), in order to underscore both the underlying unity in the mind of God of all the diverse aspects and orders of discourse of a human being—the kinds of expressions of the word of

God and the therapy modalities—as well as the unity provided by the goal of human development in the form of Christ. Implicit in such a metasystem is a basic norm: that providers should strive to do all soul care within an overarching, coherent edification framework, if they are to avoid mechanistic and fragmented (and fragmenting) soul-care practice. It is hoped that the edification framework presented in this book takes seriously the fundamental unity provided by a Christian orientation, as well as does justice to the complexity of human nature and the diversity of legitimate therapeutic options available for Christian soul care.

At any rate, given the complexity of human nature and the different perspectives by which one can approach it, no one metasystem of modalities will be entirely satisfactory to everyone and every community. Different soul-care providers and communities will differ in terms of how to organize the available knowledge and how to weight the different modalities. In addition, the Christian community will have to do a lot more of its own research on distinctively Christian soul care in order to become more confident regarding the doxological and reformative value of particular soul-care theories, principles and strategies, including the respective value and weight of the different modalities, than is possible at this stage. Nevertheless, the following diagram in figure 18.1 represents the modalities for therapy that seem to me to be irreducible and that best correspond to the distinctive features of created human nature and that therefore provide the most helpful intervention pathways for Christian soul care, given our current understanding.

Our journey in this chapter will consist of an examination of each modality, along with some of the empirical support for its existence, followed by a discussion of specifically Christian uses of the modality. Before we embark, one more point must be made. Soul work within a particular modality utilizes specific strategies. Depending on what level of discourse they are addressing, strategies also differ in terms of their worldview dependence. Some strategies are relatively worldview independent, for example, those that operate at the lower levels of human nature (the biological and psychosocial)—on mechanistic, organismic or logical aspects of human nature that are fairly universal across cultures. Medication, behavioral technologies and the development of a therapeutic alliance are good examples of relatively worldview independent strategies. A strategy such as systematic desensitization with a phobia can be

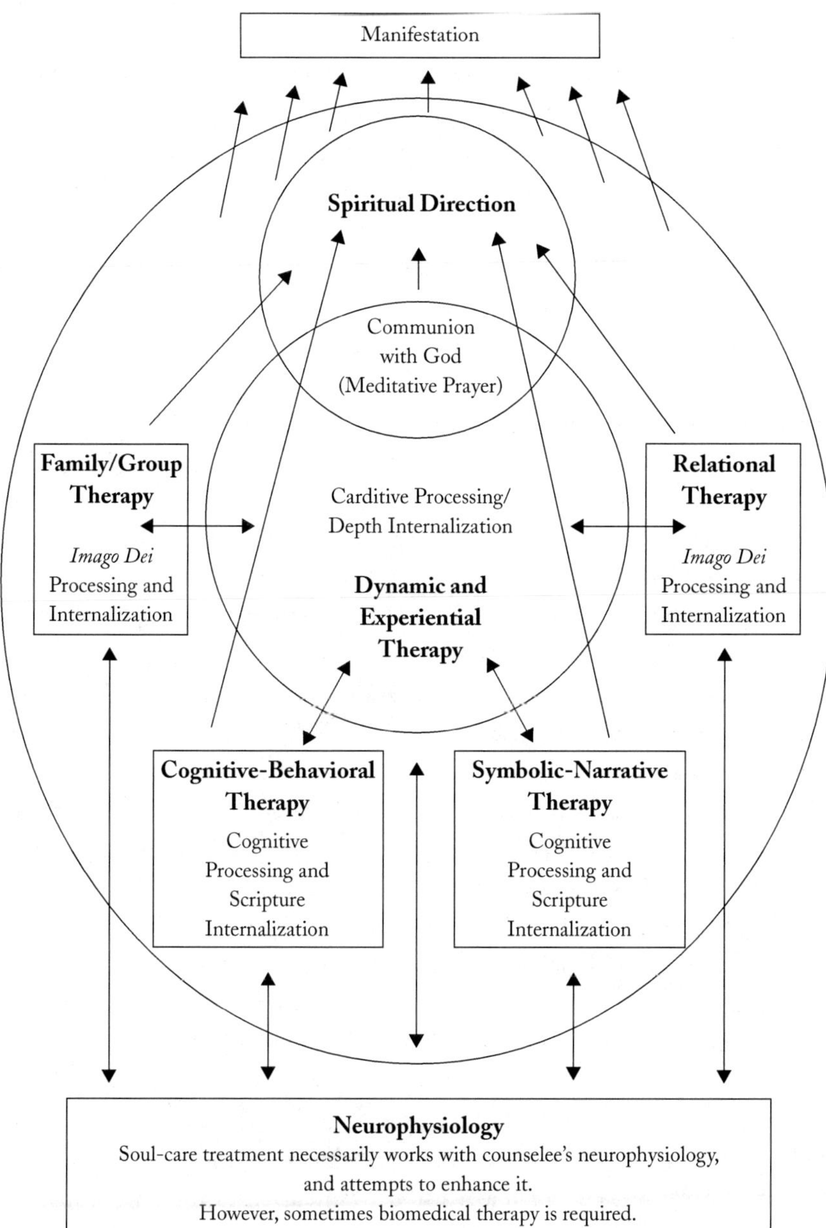

Figure 18.1. Redemptive soul care via created modalities

utilized by members of most worldview communities without too much controversy. However, I say "relatively" worldview dependent, because all soul change necessarily entails at least implicit reference to one's worldview and ultimate values, since everyone must take a position regarding whether God is or is not the ultimate source of such change.

Other strategies are moderately worldview dependent. That means that (1) they operate more directly at the higher orders (psychosocial, ethical and spiritual), (2) they involve more discursive content, and therefore (3) one's worldview assumptions must alter the strategy to some extent, but nonetheless (4) the strategy has features that are generic enough that it can be used by members of different worldview communities. For example, all soul care consists of dialogue, but the counselor's psychoeducational discourse will differ depending on the worldview of the counselor and counselee. Lastly, there are some strategies that are highly worldview dependent. Here we are talking about those that only make sense within a particular edification framework, because they operate largely at the ethical and spiritual orders, where worldview differences are most pronounced. Prayer and Scripture meditation are examples of therapeutic interventions that are highly worldview dependent.

The biomedical modality. As a result of the wealth of research on brain function accumulated over the past fifteen years, we understand better than ever before just how dependent the soul is on the brain. Every therapeutic intervention must activate some neurological substrate for the experience to be processed, and then the information must be sent to the hippocampus and other relevant neural regions that are related to the particular object of attention (whether interpersonal, conceptual or autobiographical, and so forth), so that the experience can be stored in memory, meaning *internalized* (Cozolino, 2002). This is essential for long-term therapeutic change to occur. Thus the soul-care provider should have some understanding of the role of neurological activity in therapy and be mindful of it during sessions.

In addition, as suggested earlier in the book, it is justifiable to work with people directly within the biological order to aid their souls. Drug therapy involves the introduction of biochemical information into the body that alters brain activity in ways that can assist in the remediation of important psychological functions (which in turn should make more possible the internalization and manifestation of the glory of God). However, biomedical therapy is a temporal, mechanistic process, like the running of a software program. For example, the benefits of medication are available only while it is active in the system. It cannot make positive permanent changes in the brain (on the contrary, the only structural changes produced by medication are negative, e.g., shown in drug tolerance). Moreover, a reliance on biomedical interventions can reduce a sense of responsibility for one's recovery as a result of attributing the change to the medication and not to one's own activities (in dependence on God). Consequently, Christians will be wary of an over-reliance on this modality, ultimately out of concern to best advance the glory of God and human well-being.

Medication, however, can create temporary conditions that enable healthy structural change through the introduction of more valid beliefs, new memories and the release of negative emotions that can result from higher-order interventions. Therefore, biomedical therapy should not be seen as antagonistic to a redemptive therapeutics. Just as in the use of medication for other physical problems, medication can be responsibly used in an overall theocentric model of soul care, in order to restore a basic level of brain activity and functioning necessary for doing higher-order soul work.

The cognitive and behavioral modalities. The first psychotherapeutic modalities to be discussed are the cognitive and behavioral. For a number of reasons, work with behavior and cognition has frequently been grouped together as if they formed a single therapeutic modality: first, since both can be similarly understood from a mechanistic standpoint; second, because both can utilize therapeutic exposure to information (whether environmental stimuli or knowledge); and third, since many life problems involve both behavior and cognition. Nevertheless, they would seem to be distinct enough to necessitate separate discussions.

The behavioral modality. Behavior is the manifestation of form, so Christianity is certainly concerned with human behavior. However, modern psychology came to define behavior quite narrowly, as the observable activity of organisms shaped by associations with environmental stimuli, so this approach to behavior focuses on a rather restricted, but still notable, domain of human functioning.

Stimuli can be attractive or aversive, motivating activity toward or away from objects (or objectives) in the environment. Attractive stimuli are called reinforcers; organisms act in ways to obtain them. Aversive stimuli are called punishers, and organisms act to avoid them. Associations between stimuli and behavioral responses (S-R units) come to be internalized, leading to patterns of behavior based on the predicted presence of the stimuli. With regard to therapy, these "internalized predictions" provide an implicit (preverbal) set of organizing motives and perceptions that can draw people toward some objects and away from others, a noncognitive, motivational orientation to the universe that underlies all cognitive-discursive activity. But the organismic basis of stimulus-response associations—which was its original focus—has led behavioral therapy traditionally to work with biological motives and relatively low-level psychosocial motives (like affiliation and praise) (though that is changing, see below).

Behavioral therapy seeks to extinguish associations between emotions/behaviors and stimuli that are deemed maladaptive, and it structures opportunities for the learning of more helpful associations (e.g., in systematic desensitization, which involves response substitution: training a person to replace one affective response [e.g., fear] to a stimulus [spiders] with another response [calmness]). Besides helping persons develop a more adaptive repertoire of behaviors, behavioral therapy also has cognitive implications, since histories of reward/punishment contingencies can alter the *perception* of stimuli. In addition, more recently, behavioral analysis has tried to take into account discourse in its models, since words can shape behavior through verbal control, rules and derived stimulus relations, and can communicate rewarding or aversive significance (Hayes, Follette & Follette, 1995). Among the major therapeutic strategies used in behavioral therapy are behavior practicing, role-playing, systematic desensitization, exposure in vivo and relaxation therapy.

A Christian appropriation of the behavior modality. Since behavior therapy focuses on mere behavior and its learned associations, and Christian soul care might be supposed to deal solely with higher-order phenomena shaped by Christian discourse, some might question whether the idea of Christian behavior therapy is even meaningful. However, the relatively simple process of stimulus-response learning is God-created, developmentally foundational to human life and influential throughout the life span. Any process *that* ubiquitous in human life should be of interest to Christian psychology.

Christian behavior therapy can be conceived of as shaping human behavior into patterns that best approximate elements of the form of Christ. And now, with contemporary behavior models recognizing the stimulus value of discourse, a Christian approach to behavior therapy would seem to have plenty to work with. As Bufford (1981) pointed out, biblical motivational stimuli encompass the most basic (avoiding of harm to self; Prov 6:32) to the most lofty (fellowship with God; 1 Jn 1:3). A number of Christians, in fact, have advocated the use of behavioral principles in counseling (e.g., see Adams, 1973; Bufford, 1981; Gallagher, 2000; Jeeves, 1976; McMinn & Campbell, 2007).[2] But a comprehensive account of Christian maturity recognizes that a behavioral approach alone cannot address the depth dimension of mature human behavior or contribute substantively to a mature form of human life, since it only works on lower-level dynamics like discrete behaviors shaped by environmental factors. As a result, it cannot contribute directly to the reformation of personal agency and virtuous character.

But any time Christian caregivers seek to introduce new behaviors or alter or extinguish old behaviors, some use is made of behavioral principles. Working with many childhood problems, people with conditions like mental impairment or low intelligence, and indigent counselees, schizophrenia and certain types of bipolar disorder, physical addictions, eating disorders, anxiety disorders, many sexual disorders, communication problems and interpersonal conflict often necessitate the use of reinforcement and punishment to modify behavior in healthier directions. Because behavior therapy typically works at preverbal and noncognitive levels, it can sometimes work extremely well with problems that originated or are maintained at such levels (like phobias), and help to bring about some degree of Christiformic change.

In addition, viewed from a behavioral standpoint, Christians advocate many soul-care activities that may start out as or that amount to behavioral interventions, such as the spiritual disciplines (including prayer, Bible reading, fasting, church attendance and fellowship), meeting with other Christians as accountability partners, engaging in leadership opportunities in church contexts and practicing social skills or good deeds within the Christian community or in outreach. A behavioral analysis of such activities would recognize that at least a part of their effectiveness results from the pairing of these behaviors with reinforcing outcomes (like joy in God, a sense of competence, affiliation) and/or with the avoidance of some aversive stimuli (like loneliness).[3]

So Christian soul care that deals specifically with the behavior modality is legitimate and worthwhile. People working there simply must always be engaging in transposition, mindful of the need to augment behavioral efforts with the use of other modalities that are better able to draw counselees beyond a merely biopsychosocial orientation into the motivational schemes of the ethicospiritual orders of Christianity. The fact is that human behavior itself is only identifiable within a complex, social, semiodiscursive system. Without language, humans would not have the cognitive capacity to distinguish discrete behaviors for the purposes of isolating and shaping them (Taylor, 1964). As behaviorists themselves are now recognizing, a traditional behavioral orientation requires higher-order discourse within which to make sense of its therapeutic goals and aims.

The cognitive modality. If even behavioral therapy requires discourse, they all do. Counseling simply cannot occur without some conversation between the participants. But traditional cognitive therapy (CT) focuses primarily on discourse. However, CT has tended to look past the discursive quality of the interaction and examine the propositions present in the counselee's beliefs, and memories, images and reasoning. Many psychopathological problems are derived from or related to faulty thinking and false beliefs. Traditional CT seeks to repair distortions in the psychosocial order of the counselee by directly addressing reasoning processes and beliefs to foster more effective living. Oftentimes the attitudes and beliefs that underlie a counselee's counterproductive actions have not been articulated and examined. The cognitive therapist trains counselees to analyze their core beliefs, automatic thoughts and reasoning processes and to internalize more life-enhancing beliefs and reasoning procedures (Beck, 1995).

The strongly rational-discursive nature of this modality is obvious. CT operates fundamentally within the psychosocial order with concepts, propositions and belief systems to alter the counselee's understanding of self, others, the future and the world. The value of cognition in soul healing in general cannot be overstated, since, regardless of one's worldview, most change within *all* the higher spheres (psychosocial, ethical and spiritual) is primarily mediated by discourse and thought. However, its primary concentration on beliefs (i.e., propositions) and rationality tends to result in a relative neglect of the emotions and of relationships (except indirectly), as well as other therapeutically relevant mental representations, like symbols and narrative. As a result, counseling exclusively limited to the cognitive modality can be relatively superficial and may limit deeper, carditive healing and internalization of greater significance.

Extant secular soul-care models that work primarily within the cognitive modality have been termed cognitive therapy (Beck, 1976; Beck, 1995), rational-emotive therapy (Ellis, 1962; or more recently, rational-emotive-behavior therapy; Ellis, 1998), cognitive-behavior modification (Meichenbaum, 1977), problem-solving therapy (D'Zurilla & Nezu, 1999), schema therapy (Young, Klosko & Weishaar, 2003) and psychoeducation (Beck & Emery [1985] acknowledge that "cognitive therapy is based on an educational model," p. 186). The efficacy of many cognitive strategies in secular therapy has been widely demonstrated, including the identification of maladaptive automatic thoughts; guided self-dialogue; reframing; the challenging of beliefs and reasoning; covert modeling (using one's imagination); the modification of current imagery (Beck & Emery, 1985) and the creation of healthier imagery; reflection on what happened in a recent social interaction; homework between sessions, like practicing mental or social skills; the mental modification of behavioral explanations (Seligman & Buchanan, 1994) and intermediate and core beliefs (Beck, 1995); journaling; and the use of bibliotherapy (the reading of therapeutically relevant books), to name just a few.

A Christian appropriation of the cognitive modality. If all soul-care systems have a significant cognitive component, Christian soul care would seem to have a special commitment to CT. Since its inception, Christian salvation has entailed belief change through words and concepts, through conversation, preaching, teaching and writing. God's inspiration of Scripture itself profoundly demonstrates that a cognitive approach to soul healing is part of God's redemptive design (Crabb, 1977, 1987; Work, 2002), and the entire Christian tradition has been devoted to promoting the renewing of the mind by cognitive conformity to its primary soul-care text. It is through the questioning of present faulty beliefs and patterns of thought, and replacement with more accurate beliefs and patterns, that cognitive internalization of Scripture, the gospel and Christian doctrine occur.

So it ought to surprise no one that many Christian counseling authors have favored the cognitive modality (see Anderson, 1997; Anderson, Zuehlke & Zuehlke, 2000; Backus & Chapian, 2000; Capps, 1990b; early Crabb, 1975, 1977; McGee, 1990; McMinn, 1991; McMinn & Campbell, 2007; Nielsen, Johnson & Ellis, 2001; Propst, 1992; Tan, 1987a) and traditional biblical counseling is rightly labeled cognitive-behavioral (see Adams, 1973, 1979; Mack, 1979, 1994c, 1994d; the same can be said about many progressive biblical counselors, but the latter have sought to break out of this mold, see e.g., Powlison, 2005; Tripp, 2002; Lane & Tripp, 2006a, 2006b; and Welch, 2004a). Examples of specifically Christian cognitive strategies can be found throughout Christian counseling literature, as well as more general Christian literature aimed at promoting Christian maturity, including such activities as listening and learning in Christian educational settings (like Bible studies and Sunday school), learning doctrine, processing a sermon, reading and memorizing Scripture, reading Christian literature that questions false religious beliefs and promotes accurate Christian beliefs, listening to one's negative thoughts about self ("I'm a failure") or others and labeling it "old self" and then substituting Christian propositions or evaluations ("God says I've been forgiven"), fostering one's identity in Christ (for example, through believing I am justified) and reframing a depressing event in light of eternity.

Distinctively Christian CT discourse typically concerns ethicospiritual realities. However, there is a large realm of what we might call *common* CT discourse that concerns general psychosocial dynamics and strategies, which Christians and non-Christians can all make use of, for example, working on a realistic daily schedule, practicing communication skills or developing a sound logical argument that concludes "I'm not a miserable failure if I don't finish a project on time." Christians and non-Christians share so much in common (e.g., common environments, logical ability and cognitive equipment; see Van Til, 1972), it is only to be expected that they will share many of the same understandings of reality and standards for rationality, and seek to promote some of the same rationally based soul-care ideals. Christian psychology does not require that *everything* Christian counselors say has to be explicitly Christian, no more than discourse at a church business meeting (if the roof is leaking, we have to talk about the roof). Let us call such strategies "pluralist," since they can be used by therapists from different worldview communities.

But analogous to what was suggested in the behavior modality section, adult cognition is always situated within some ethicospiritual context, whether we are aware of it or not. As a result, it is an illusion to think that even common CT can be engaged in independently of the participants' worldviews. There is no truly neutral part of the universe (Clouser, 1991); to believe otherwise is simply evidence of secular reasoning. Christianity obligates its followers to take every thought captive to the obedience of Christ (2 Cor 10:5), and so to actively transpose all beliefs and reasoning into a Christian ethicospiritual context. Part of soul healing involves relating more of one's memories, beliefs and problem solving to the triune God's agenda, whether or not they contain explicitly Christian content. Christians become more unified and integrated through this ultimate reframing. So Christian CT can still be Christian, even when working with common psychosocial cognitive dynamics, as it discerningly seeks to draw counselees into God's universe of discourse.

The relational modality. As we have touched on repeatedly throughout this book, humans exist in a three-dimensional personal context. Early social experiences sculpt the developing nervous systems of children (Cacioppo et al., 2002; Siegel, 1999), as well as the formation of their self-representations and their perception of others (Stern, 1985; Thompson, 1998), forming an "internal working model" of human relationships. These mental representations form relational templates for future interactions. If these representations were formed through relationships with mentally healthy, loving persons, the child will grow up able to relate relatively realistically to others and to enter empathically into relationship with them. However, when exposed to less than desirable responsiveness, empathy and engagement in early childhood, individuals will grow up having dysfunctional other-perceptions ("Others cannot be trusted"), more or less serious structural deficits in their self-representation ("I'm worthless"), and maladaptive attitudes regarding relationships themselves ("Relationships always hurt" or "I *have* to get married!"). Fixed to these maladaptive mental representations are emotion schemes that were also formed in earlier relational contexts through the "affect-bearing" discourse and actions of significant others, which are easily activated in current relationships that bear some similarity to the earlier ones.

As we saw in chapter nine, others are themselves signs. They can signify goodness, acceptance, security, trustworthiness and stability, and they can also signify pain, fear, insecurity, chaos and despair—and all the breadth in between. So, while our experience of others is always meaningful, much of what is stored from our other-experiences is preverbal, and the activation of memory traces of others has become automatized, so that much of their current significance and motivational power are unconscious. Soul care within the relational modality aims at the re-formation of internal representations of self and other, so that they become healthier and more accurate than those formed in childhood. These new internal representations are forged through healthy relationships in adulthood, for example through wise, loving conversations between counselor and counselee.

Some of the value of relational therapy is due to the opportunity it affords to explore one's relational and emotional history in a safe relational context (grounded in the therapeutic alliance) and to activate some of one's relational-emotional representations with reference to the therapist (an activity called *transference* by psychodynamic therapists), in order to help the counselee adjust more realistically to the limitations of actual human relationships (Henry, Strupp, Schact & Gaston, 1994). As the meaningfulness of one's affect-laden experiences is articulated, greater self-understanding results, along with greater control over one's current experiences with others. In contrast with the cognitive-behavioral approaches, relational therapies are less concerned with homework and the development of specific strategies to be practiced outside session, and are more interested with the re-formative quality of the therapeutic relationship itself through counselee transference, therapist empathy and the counselee's projective identification with the counselor's constructive perceptions of the counselee.

Because of its longevity (going back to Freud) and the demonstrated clinical value of relational approaches (Henry, Strupp, Schact & Gaston, 1994), many models of relational soul care have evolved, including classical psychoanalysis, notable aspects of Carl Rogers's approach (1951, 1961), interpersonal therapy (Klerman & Weissman, 1993; Sullivan, 1953; Benjamin, 2003), supportive-expressive therapy (Luborsky, 1984), supportive therapy (Rockland, 1989), object relations therapy (Fairbairn, 1952; Kernberg, 1976), self psychology (Kohut, 1971, 1977), relational psychotherapy (De Young, 2003; Magnavita, 1999), imago relationship therapy (Hendrix, 1993, 2001), therapy grounded in attachment theory (Holmes, 1996; Levy, 2000; Sperling & Berman, 1994) and reparative therapy (Nicolosi, 1997).

A Christian appropriation of the relational modality. Just as cognitive-behavioral therapy is used by many kinds of therapists, Christianity cannot lay unique claim to relational therapy. Nevertheless, Christianity would seem to have a worldview in which working within the relational modality is especially fitting. We have seen that Christianity is an intrinsically relational system of thought and life. For God's sake, then, Christian counselors are drawn to work to undo the damage of growing up with severely distorted image-bearers. Loving others through soul care to draw them to God and into the form of God is a great way to love God. The church, rightly understood, is to be a community of increasingly reciprocal love—manifesting the love of the Trinity—that brings redemptive healing to its members through their relationships. The development of a healthy human relationship with a mature, loving soul caregiver can be a catalyst for a breakthrough in one's relationship with God, as one experiences—perhaps for the first time—a concrete, healing exemplification of God's love and holiness (see Stanley, 2001). Christian soul-care providers are incarnational representatives of Christ (Jones & Butman, 1991; Langberg, 1997). Christianity provides a rich metadisciplinary context for understanding human relational development and therapy; Christians can argue, the best (Anderson, 1982; Balswick, King & Reimer, 2005; Joy, 1997; Shults, 2003; Shults & Sandage, 2006). As Jones, Butman and Mangis (1991) note, a relational approach "holds much promise as a possible foundation for future elaboration of a thoroughly Christian understanding of human personality" (p. 115). Because of such considerations, many Christian counselors have emphasized a relational approach (see Capps, 1993; Crabb's "biblical community" period, 1997, 1999; Kirwin, 1984; Lake, 1966; Langberg, 1997; McMinn & Campbell, 2007; Meissner, 1987, 1991; Sorenson, 2004; Tripp, 2002; Lane & Tripp, 2006b; Sphar & Smith, 2003; Wilson, 1998; and it would seem to be the favored modality at Rosemead School of Psychology).

We noted in chapter sixteen that some Christians have wisely warned of the dangers of working with the relational modality, since it can make *human* relationships the primary focus of therapy, rather than God, and so unwittingly promote dependency on humans, rather than God (see Almy, 2000; Powlison, 2004, chap. 10; Tripp, 2002). This caution must always be kept in mind when doing relational therapy, and while working with transference issues, efforts may sometimes need to be directed at helping the counselee repent of what have become idolatrous attitudes toward the counselor. However, properly understood, transference experiences are qualitatively different in the tridimensional relational framework of Christianity (God-others-self) (Louf, 2002). Rather than being relationally neutral and merely helping persons accept the limited relationship possible with the therapist (and with all humans), in the sorrow of transference, the therapist can point persons to the unlimited love they have with their Father, in union with Christ, and with the indwelling Holy Spirit.

This discussion again demonstrates the necessity of transposition in Christian soul care. Christian relational therapists must naturally, but regularly, bring their conversations regarding psychosocial dynamics into the higher contexts of Christian ethicospiritual discourse. Theocentric relational therapy will always leave the counselee with the impression that the most important therapeutic relationship one has is with the triune God.

Family and group modalities. The most influential relationships humans have with other humans are with their families. In addition, group work—where a group of persons get together to help each other psychologically—can create a marvelous context for relational growth. As a result, the family and a therapy group both provide a special kind of relational modality for soul care, and a set of therapies has arisen around each one. The influence of relational therapies on family-systems and group therapies has been enormous (Dies, 1995; Kaslow & Celano, 1995), so one would expect there to be significant overlap in their focus and treatment goals. But the family and group approaches are distinguished from relational approaches, because, whereas relational therapy tends to focus on past relational history and the current relationship between the therapist and counselee (where past and present come together in transference), both family and group therapies, in different ways, tend to focus more on one's *current relational context* as the pathway of soul cure, making adjustments in it that hopefully lead to changes in one's internal (cognitive, emotional and relational) representations. Family therapies do this by promoting changes in one's current family or couple relationships (mindful of past family history), and group therapies, by introducing individuals to a new, more supportive, therapeutic social environment.

In addition, what most distinguishes family and group therapies from relational therapies is the theoretical assumption that human individuals are best understood, not as isolated individuals with internal conflicts, but as individuals-in-relation-with-others. Such an approach views the primary unit of therapeutic interest as social, so that the counselee's internal dynamics are generally viewed in terms of the individual's functioning within the group or family and in relation to them. Supported by general systems theory (Bertalanffy, 1976), the individual's psychological system is understood to be a function of the larger social system of which it is a part. Current distress and healing are understood to be related to unresolved issues from one's family of origin, but one's present social context is considered therapeutically more important, whether that context is one's current family or the members of one's therapy group.

The family modality. Family therapy seeks to help the members of the family renegotiate power and love relations, communication and affect patterns in ways that contribute to the well-being of all the members of the group. There are many models of family theory, including structural (Minuchin, 1974), intergenerational-contextual (Boszormenyi-Nagy & Spark, 1973), systemic (the Milan group) and multigenerational (Bowen, 1978). Depending on the model, family therapists focus on such things as rules that maintain the family's homeostasis, boundaries, alignments, assigned roles of family members, degree of differentiation and enmeshment of family members, and family myths, and they typically help family members better understand the pathological features of the past form of their system (in some cases mapping out the family relations in a genogram), and encourage them to view family members more positively and learn new, more productive ways of relating and conceiving of oneself and others.

The group modality. Group therapy seeks to create a new, healing social system in which members feel supported and where they learn how to become more transparent and to articulate their significant issues, while simultaneously training them *in vivo* how to relate to others in healthier ways (Burn, 2004; Yalom, 1975). Group therapies fall along a continuum from groups that assist individuals to resolve internal conflicts or personal relational issues to groups that focus on the group itself and its processes, for the purpose of aiding the group members' maturation. Issue-oriented groups provide low-cost, proven ways of benefiting individuals, that revolve around specific therapeutic issues of concern, such as grief, substance abuse, sexual addiction or coping with a health issue.

Groups are helpful, because they create a social context for self-examination, deconstruction of barriers and internalization. Group dynamics and activities like in-group/out-group, conflict exploration and resolution, group homogeneity, leadership and power relations, and roles and relational style (withdrawn, supportive, peacemaker and so on) provide unique opportunities for experiencing and reflecting on one's remaining relational limitations and struggles.

In contrast to relational therapies, which emphasize the curative role of the therapist and relationship with him or her, family and group models place the therapeutic focus on a larger social unit, with the result that (when the family is the modality) family members are challenged to relate to one another in novel and healthier ways that come to be mutually reinforcing as the new experiences are stored in memory, and (when the group is the modality) group members ideally form a loving but challenging set of motivating guides toward psychospiritual well-being, who communicate truth and create new memories of positive social experiences.

A Christian appropriation of the family and group modalities. As the creator of human nature, God designed families and groups to have the kinds of dynamics that empirical research has documented exist. For this reason alone, Christians ought to take seriously the psychosocial dynamics of families and groups. These are identifiable by non-Christians and Christians, and both communities will have in common many of the same kinds of family and group relationships (as they do neural networks and types of cognitions). However, as with the relational modality in general, Christian soul care would seem especially open to working specifically with the family and group modalities, given scriptural teaching on the importance of the family and the calling of believers to be mutually supportive of one another. Because the family and group are two kinds of social modalities, the same justifications and cautions discussed above regarding relational therapy apply here. There are, however, at least a few uniquely Christian ways to consider these modalities.

One wonders, for example, what is the impact on a family system when God is recognized to be a member of that family—the ultimate Father who is perfectly loving and holy—immediately becoming the most important family member (but who is unfortunately also invisible, rather than concrete!). Obviously, it is hard to imagine how this transposition can occur in an experientially moving way for every family member at the same time. Nonetheless, according to systems theory, when a new element is brought in, it changes the system. Though children will likely derive little direct benefit from such reflections (because of their inability to think abstractly), these kinds of considerations could conceivably reconfigure the adults' and maybe the adolescents' perceptions of themselves and their family, altering the entire emotional atmosphere of the family. For example, there are no black sheep in God's family, and as the most important member of the family, God's opinions transcend everyone else's, so much so that the negative evaluations of family members are nullified and transformed.

Groups provide a marvelous laboratory to work with ethical dynamics. How group members treat one another, tardiness, commitment, use of time and issues of justice and care can all be explored for the purposes of self-examination and reformation. But *Christian* groups ought also to be distinguished by Christian spiritual discourse. In addition to praying together for God's help, the effects of Christ's death and resurrection can be discussed in relation to particular problems, and how salvation addresses the therapeutic issues upon which the group is working.

Christians can also work to help their own churches become healthier social systems—a metaphorical family—than what is available in the world and in many literal families (Crabb, 1999; Hibbs, 1991). Over the past few decades, many churches have become part of a religious "group revolution," organizing small groups for Bible study, prayer, fellowship and outreach, and in so doing offering a degree of connection and accountability unavailable in traditional churches and to many non-Christians. Some larger churches also provide issue-oriented groups that help Christians deal with specific issues within a Christian context. And in a secondary way, the entire functioning of a local church can be seen to have group therapy implications. If it is functioning properly, the local church becomes a place where healthy power-relations and community can be experienced. Church leaders can exemplify a servant-leadership model that can be reparative for those who have been in abusive families (or abusive churches). Christian fellowship in any form—meals after church, adult Bible classes, hospitality in homes, lay counseling, mentoring and other close supportive church relationships (to say nothing of formal counseling in the church)—can create social experiences that are healthier than what one has experienced in the past and therefore hold the possibility of gradually altering one's relational orientation for the better within a Christian discursive context. The tragedy of so many churches is that they fall so far short of their possibilities in Christ to be a model of the triune God.

Symbolic and narrative/dramatic modalities. We move next into a discussion of two modalities that have not been given as much attention in the field as the others we have examined so far (though that has been changing in recent years), but ones that are nonetheless very valuable types of delivery of the signs of God, and ones that are easily defensible from the standpoint of Scripture. Symbolic and narrative approaches are linked together here because of some commonalities between them. To begin with, the human ability to understand both symbol and story is made possible through discourse. The first function of language, we might say, is the provision of names for things. In order to master their language, children first must learn labels that stand for objects. But, as Piaget noted, children in the preschool years very easily engage in "concrete symbolization," where objects "stand for" other objects (like "This rock is a dinosaur bone") and people "stand for" other people (like "Johnny will be the Daddy and Mary is the Mommy"). Later, adolescents learn to engage in abstract symbolization, where words themselves "stand for" objects other than their common reference, as in a metaphor. Only at that point can poetry be appreciated. Experience and facility with language make it possible for words or images to be invested with surplus meaning beyond their typical usage. Discourse is also used to link together a series of happenings into an episode of one's life forming a "story," an ability that likewise begins in the preschool years; but later, in adolescence, stories themselves can function as symbols, referring to something meaningful beyond themselves, for example, redemption, domination or love.

The two modalities also both have a relation to literature. Narratives and drama are types of literature, and symbolism pervades great works of literature. Furthermore, while it is unclear what the connection is, if any, narrative and symbols like metaphors both appear to be processed in the right hemisphere (Banich, 1997, p. 457). Though dependent upon left-hemisphere language processing, metaphoric and narrative mental activities seem to involve unique neural structures in the right hemisphere that make possible the organization of elements into a meaningful whole or gestalt. Moreover, both stories and symbols can also elicit strong emotion activity. Stories and symbols can be embedded with personal meanings regarding one's deepest concerns, particularly the events of one's own story. But certain types of emotional processing are also known to occur within the right hemisphere, including the interpretation of emotion meaning and facial expressions, the ability to express emotions and the experience of emotion (Banich, 1997, p. 428). So there may be neurological reasons why symbols and stories can specially activate emotion, at times when rational processing cannot. Regardless of the physiological reasons, therapeutic experience shows that soul care that works with symbol and narrative have a singular role to play in assisting emotional processing.

The symbolic modality. In common usage, a symbol is "something that stands for or suggests something else by reason of relationship, association, convention, or accidental resemblance" (*Webster's New Collegiate Dictionary,* 1974, p. 1180) (a symbol is a sign). The human mind is highly disposed to recognize similarities or analogies between different objects. Preschool children enjoy symbolic play and can understand many types of symbols (Deloache, Miller & Pierroutsakos, 1998). Through relationships, experiences and cultural teachings, individuals internalize various symbols that contribute to their self-understanding and interpretation of the world, which come to reinforce their prior experience and also express it, as they are found in thoughts, daydreams and dreams. In addition, symbols can express one's deep longings, goals, needs and loves, including desires for difference and change.

Symbols can also have positive or negative associations. The experience of individuals who have been traumatized may be pervaded with negative symbols that express and add to their distress and pain. For example, a pregnant woman who was repeatedly physically abused as a child might have recurring images or dreams of her child dying in her womb, symbolizing the sense she has of her own brokenness, felt destiny to fail and psychospiritual deadness. Psychological symbols are found throughout literature, art and cinema, which helps to explain why humans enjoy and sometimes resonate so deeply with such works.

Freud (1938) believed symbol was basic to human life (though he mostly focused on sexual symbolism), demonstrated by his investigations of dreams and things like slips of the tongue. Jung (1968) saw a broader significance in symbols and, perhaps more than any other figure in modern psychotherapy, sought to treat the soul by analyzing and interpreting the symbols of his counselees—and of humans in general—by understanding the underlying meaning of dreams, as well as the stories and myths of various cultures. More recently, Battino (2002), Carlsen (1996), Grove and Panzer (1989), Pearce (1996) and Tompkins and Lawley (2000) demonstrate different ways in which metaphors can be used therapeutically.

A Christian appropriation of the symbolic modality. But God was the first symbolizer. He set up his creation so that it was pervaded by symbols (Edwards, 1993), and his Scriptures are filled with distinctive symbols, many of which have directly therapeutic significance (such as the cross, shepherd, lamb, blood, rock, shield, father, light and darkness, and wine and bread, and so on; see Ryken, Wilhoit & Longman, 1998, for a treasure chest of scriptural symbols). Of special significance are *types,* which are persons, events, objects or institutions in the Old Testament that symbolize something of Christ's person or work or Christian salvation. The Bible contains a plethora of therapeutically powerful symbols to assist God's people in the internalizing of God's salvation. In his spiritual allegories *Pilgrim's Progress* and *The Holy War* Bunyan made great use of such symbolism for redemptive therapeutic purposes. Symbols can be invested with intense emotional meaning and so can touch the soul in ways that propositions cannot; both pathways "into" the soul are legitimated by God's use of both prose and poetry in Scripture. Christian therapists can make use of scriptural symbols in beneficial ways through dream analysis, discussion of symbols in stories and movies, and guided imagery in session, and the training of counselees to engage in this work on their own. A number of Christian counselors have attempted Christian use of symbolic material in therapy, including Kelsey (1982, 1986), Sanford (1987, 1989), Manning (2002) and Payne (1995).[4]

As we have seen, Vanhoozer (2005) argues that God intends for Christians to use their imagination to help them recognize the metaphoric similarities of their life and God's theodrama (climaxed in Christ's life, death and resurrection), so they derive significance from the similarity and seek to conform their life to its symbolic, archetypal referents. Scripture encourages such symbolic reframing. Christians are to love their enemies as their Father does (Mt 5:44-45), to imitate Christ when they suffer (Acts 5:41; 9:16; 1 Thess 1:6-7; 1 Pet 4:12-19) and to view their employment, authority and marriage relations metaphorically (1 Pet 2:18-21; Eph 5:22-33). The realization that one is symbolically representing the meaning of a higher, transcendent order goes a long way to help one endure suffering or abuse. This modality can also be used by Christian counselors to expose negative symbols that exercise unconscious influence on their counselee's experience.

The narrative/dramatic modality. A common problem that one finds in much current, secular therapy is that it tends to be atomistic. For example, a counselor may apply specific strategies to various symptoms of counselees without regard to an overarching or unifying context that guides the therapy and grounds it in a higher set of purposes or meaning. One exception to this generalization is the development of secular narrative therapy, which has sought to make more explicit the larger, meaningful contexts of human life. As we examined in chapter nine, narrativity is a fundamental feature of human nature (having its own neurological architecture, Banich, 1997; Cozolino, 2002; Siegel, 1999), and normal humans form their own more or less well-developed life story or drama. However, painful events, particularly when the pain is chronic, can infuse one's narrative with hopelessness or anxiety regarding the future, which in turn can inhibit one's sense of personal agency. Narrative therapy works with counselees' stories to help them relinquish harmful narrative themes and interpretations of events, invest constructive meaning into their own stories and develop a more realistic but optimistic vision for the future. "The organization and coherence provided by narratives offer the opportunity for teaching, repairing, updating, and creating new stories. The new story can then serve as blueprint for new behavior" (Cozolino, 2002, p. 166). As Ricoeur (1988) has noted, one's personal identity can be *refigured* through internalizing the narratives one reads (or hears) and then enacts in practice, in relationship to others. He (1984-1988; Venema, 2000) coined the term *emplotment* for the process of taking in narrative materials so that one's one own identity and narrative are altered.

Though only recently identified as a distinct modality, elements of narrative therapy have been used since the inception of modern psychotherapy. Because of his explorations into the stories and dreams of his counselees, Freud can be regarded as the first modern narrative psychologist (Schafer, 1992; Spence, 1982). However, he did not seem to grasp the constructive power of narrative and so did not advocate the use of narrative itself as a therapeutic strategy. Following Freud, psychoanalytic, Adlerian, Jungian and relational models likewise could be considered quasi-narrative therapies because of their investigation of earlier life experiences, dreams and stories. Some family-systems therapists help families to assess the scripts that have been given to family members and to rewrite those scripts (see Atwood, 1996). And Milton Erickson promoted the use of stories in his therapy (see Freedman & Combs, 1996, pp. 9-12; Pearce, 1996, chap. 2). Cognitive therapy advocates the narrative strategy of picturing more adaptive future events through mental imagery and rehearsal. Really, all therapists work in the narrative modality when they listen to their counselees' stories and foster hope in the therapeutic process, thereby altering the counselees' views of their future.

Some therapists, however, make narrative or drama considerations central to their work (Anderson, 1997; Brown & Augusta-Scott, 2006; Diamond, 2002; Eron & Lund, 1996; Freedman & Combs, 1996; Monk, Winslade, Crocket & Epston, 1997; White & Epston, 1990; White, 2007). Typical narrative strategies include helping counselees reinterpret their tragic story in a different light, engage in worthwhile projects that give their lives more significance, read meaningful fiction or nonfiction stories to encourage and challenge themselves, envision a better future than what one might expect given their past and use guided imagery to rehearse the envisioned future. Drama techniques can also be worthwhile, for example, role-playing, cinematherapy (watching and processing movies for the purpose of psychological insight) and psychodrama (acting out or portraying symbolically internal psychological dynamics or significant relationships in one's life; see Moreno, 1977).

A Christian appropriation of the narrative/dramatic modality. Unfortunately, most secular narrative therapy is currently grounded in a relativistic postmodernism, so its proponents resist the notion of absolute truth and a metanarrative (see, e.g., McKenzie & Monk, 1997). As a result, narratives are cut loose from their correspondence to the actual historical state of affairs (God's history). The tragic effects of such poor philosophy may not be obvious at first, but the therapeutic counterproductivity of this stance will become increasingly evident as counselors attempt to help their counselees come to terms with the real world. Regardless, narrative and relativism are not necessarily linked. Christians can prove this by proposing narrative and dramatic approaches to therapy that take objective truth seriously, similar to what Horton (2002, 2005) and Vanhoozer (2005) have done in their narrative approaches to evangelical theology.[5]

Christians can hardly avoid doing soul care within the narrative/dramatic modality, given Christianity's grounding in the metanarrative that constitutes the redemptive-historical structure of Scripture. Of special importance, of course, is the theodramatic climax of history: the life, death, resurrection and ascension of Christ. But from Genesis to Revelation, narrative and drama are foundational to biblical revelation. Scripture portrays salvation as an incorporation into God's redemptive history (Rom 1:1-6; Gal 1:4; 4:4-5; Col 1:13).

Augustine (1942) understood the narrative implications of scriptural revelation and recognized the doxological benefits of a detailed reconstruction of one's story in light of the gospel. Such a project gives believers a deeply satisfying sense that their lives have a transcendent meaningfulness. As we have noted repeatedly, each person's story makes a contribution to the overall story that God is writing in history. In addition, Scripture reveals that human lives are situated within an epic war between God and the forces of evil. To fight against those forces internally (against the "flesh," Gal 5:17-19) and externally (the world and the devil and his demons) adds a cosmic dimension to the significance of one's activities. Christian counselees should also be helped to see their lives as a redemptive analogy of Christ's life, death and resurrection (Vanhoozer, 2005). Other Christian therapeutic narrative themes include a soul-building motif ("By God's help, my character and life are improving") and an eschatological motif ("In the final chapter of my story, I will be perfect and dwell in everlasting happiness"). Such considerations lighten the burdens of one's present experiences and put them into a broader perspective.

Sermons often contain stories that promote internalization of truth, and stories can be read for psychospiritual benefit. Biographies of the saints have long been popular. Bunyan's *Pilgrim's Progress* and *The Holy War*, Tolkien's *Lord of the Rings* and the works of Milton, C. S. Lewis, Walker Percy and others can be read for soul healing and edification. Today, movies can be viewed for Christian soul-care purposes. For example, *The Matrix* can be reinterpreted as an allegory of Christian conversion, and *The Passion of Christ* gave many Christian viewers a profound sense of identification with Christ. Christians who have made explicit use of narrative in their soul-care writings include Allender (2005), Eldridge (2000), C. Lee (2004), D. Lee (1993), Payne (1995), Tripp (2002), Vitz (1992a, 1992b) and Welch (2004a).[6]

If one of the primary goals of Christian soul care is to foster the deepest possible internalization of the Word of God, soul care using the symbolic and narrative/dramatic modalities would seem essential. Both foster right-brain internalization of the Word of God (in coordination with the left brain, more linguistically based, internalization). Given that symbols, narratives and dramas seem especially to facilitate emotional processing, soul care using these modalities offers great potential to promote deeper, carditive internalization.

Experiential and dynamic modalities. All the modalities we have examined address carditive dynamics in some measure, even cognitive therapy (when focusing on *core* beliefs). However, some modalities especially attend to the dynamics of the heart, and they are of special interest to Christian soul care.

The dynamic modality. Soul care within the dynamic modality in modern psychotherapy also originated with Freud and was further developed by the varied movements that he influenced, including classical psychoanalysis; Jungian, Adlerian and Neo-Freudian (Horney, Fromm, Sullivan) therapy; the ego psychologists, object-relations therapy and self psychology; and even the existentialist and humanist approaches. Dynamic soul care is focused on one's unconscious and internal conflict, obscured by defense mechanisms/defensive activity that inhibits awareness. In the dynamic point of view, "the patient is seen as being motivated to keep an idea and its associated affect out of awareness. This defensive effort arises because the idea and its associated affect are considered by the person to be incompatible with the dominant mass of ideas making up the ego" (Wolitzky, 1995, p. 15). Humans are characterized by many conflicting motives, ideas and agendas, and these conflicts often involve negative emotions. To avoid these emotions, psychological structures evolve that keep the pain from awareness and inhibit their activation (called defenses). As a result, people's conscious awareness and understanding regarding their motivation often differ in some measure from their actual motivation, and they experience some resistance to having these inconsistencies exposed. The focus on unconscious conflicts and defenses led some to call work in the dynamic modality "depth psychology."[7]

What is the unconscious? Though there is sharp disagreement today about the construct validity of the notion of an unconscious, research has amply documented that many internal activities occur automatically, without the individual's conscious initiation or awareness (Hassin, Uleman & Bargh, 2004). Rather than thinking of the unconscious as a single module, it is probably more accurate to consider it a label for a family of interrelated substructures, processes and activities that are simply beneath conscious awareness. However, some of those dynamic substructures, called defense mechanisms or defensive activity, seem to work at inhibiting "full, conscious awareness of some reality for the purpose of self-protection" (Johnson & Burroughs, 2000, p. 175). Soul care of any kind usually involves helping counselees recognize and relinquish some of their defenses (McCullough et al., 2003).[8]

A Christian appropriation of the dynamic modality. We have noted repeatedly that Christianity is a religion of the heart. Consider that the first effects of the primordial sin involved hiding and blameshifting (Gen 3:10, 12), self-deception is reckoned a serious character flaw (Prov 1:18, 32; 6:32; 9:8; 12:15; Gal 6:3; Jas 1:26; 1 Jn 1:8), humans "hold back" or "hold down" the truth in unrighteousness (Rom 1:18; *katechontōn;* usually translated "suppress," but according to dynamic terminology, it should be translated as "repress"), and we saw in the last chapter the problem of hypocrisy. Given the Bible's assessment of the human condition, salvation must address the depth problems of the human heart, if humans are to be rescued in this life. Søren Kierkegaard (1849/1980) should perhaps also be mentioned as the first Christian dynamic psychologist, who explored the pervasive self-deceptive tendencies of sinful humanity before Freud was even born (1851/1990; see Evans, 1990).

As we noted before, Christians cry out for help to their omniscient God.

> Search me, O God, and know my heart;
> Try me and know my anxious thoughts;
> And see if there be any hurtful way in me
> And lead me in the everlasting way. (Ps 139:23-24)

Christian soul care trains counselees to shine the healing light of the gospel into the conflicts of their hearts. In Christ, the Lord becomes "the defense of [the believer's] life" (Ps 27:1), so other defenses can be surrendered. The gospel of justification by faith is God's primary means for overcoming self-condemnation due to shame and guilt, so that increasingly the inner conflicts that characterize fallen humanity are resolved in the peace of Christ (Col 3:15), leading to ever greater transparency before God, self and others.

Moreover, a number of defenses are specifically ethicospiritual in nature. For example, religious orientations can serve unconscious, oppositional purposes. All false religions involve a distortion of general revelation, and their universal advocacy of good works enhances a bogus confidence in one's ethical competence. Idolatry is a defensive strategy regarding ultimacy. Atheism and agnosticism are forms of denial and rationalization that help one to evade feelings of accountability to one's Creator. Pantheism is an extremely radical form of grandiose narcissism that conflates the self with God; whereas religions that posit the Ultimate as having a "dark side" (like Taoism, Hinduism and Star Wars!) or flawed deities (e.g., the myths of ancient Greece and Rome) reduce the sense of uncleanness and shame common to humanity by bringing God down to our level and serve to minimize the scandal of human transgressions.

However, religious defenses can also be seen in Christians who have a spirit of arrogance or pride associated with their Christian position, understanding or works. Even worse, Christians can perpetrate "spiritual abuse" and domineer over parishioners or wives or children, giving the abuser unconscious secondary gains, such as feelings of superiority and the gratification of desires for power and control. Christian depth soul care is necessary because Christianity (just like the Judaism of the Pharisees) can be perversely subverted for autocentric purposes, purposes that feed sin rather than kill it. Only the light of God's law and gospel, shining ever more deeply, can penetrate the remaining darkness in the Christian heart (Heb 4:12).

The Bible lays adult responsibility for self-deception and the seeking of help on the individual (Jas 1:22). Uncovering and relinquishing the defenses is a Christian's ethicospiritual responsibility. However, this biblical emphasis on personal responsibility—necessary for recovery—is compatible with a recognition of the psychosocial influences that shaped (and still shape) one's current defensive structures, particularly in response to childhood emotional, physical and sexual abuse. Therefore, knowing that the Christian is motivated by a gracious imperative to walk increasingly in the light, a Christian soul-care use of the dynamic modality will be balanced by a patient sensitivity to the degree of defensiveness, vulnerability and woundedness of the counselee (Johnson & Burroughs, 2000). Productive work with the defenses can never be rushed. It takes time to internalize the gospel and learn how to rely on the Holy Spirit in this process. The Holy Spirit, after all, resides in the innermost parts of the believer (Rom 8; 1 Cor 2). Such realizations led Coe (1999) to term Christian soul care *pneumadynamic*—rather than psychodynamic—since it requires the enlightening work of the indwelling Holy Spirit.

Some modalities are more useful for promoting the internalization of the glory of God (like cognitive and narrative). Dynamic work, in contrast, is necessary for the preparatory work of self-examination and the deconstruction of barriers. The value of Christian dynamic soul care should be obvious. Narramore (1984) (and the Rosemead School of Psychology) may have done as much as any to promote a Christian use of the dynamic modality. But such is the sovereignty of God's Spirit that the progressive wing of the biblical counseling movement also developed a dynamic orientation (more theocentric but less complex in self-awareness) with their focus on the idols of the heart (Powlison, 2004; Welch, 1997b) and heart examination (Tripp, 2002; Welch, 2004a). Rosemead and Westminster are, after all, on the same team.

The experiential/emotion-focused modality. While its overall orientation is significantly different from dynamic therapy, experiential (or emotion-focused) therapy also addresses the human heart. It is a relatively recent addition to contemporary research and thinking about therapy modalities (see Epstein, 1994; Gendlin, 1996; Greenberg & Paivio, 1997; Greenberg, Watson & Lietaer, 1998; Mahrer, 1983), but it has already acquired an impressive empirical record of benefiting counselees (Elliott, Greenberg & Lietaer, 2004). Current secular, experience-oriented therapies focus on the subjectivity of counselees to help them grow in self-understanding, through listening to and articulating their emotional experience, in order to further their ability to take responsibility for themselves, become more honest and regulate their emotions better (Greenberg & Van Balen, 1998).[9] As we noted in chapter nine, "feelings are vital signals that need to be attended to" (McCullough et al., 2003, p. 175). Work in the experiential modality involves the activation and regulation of the emotion regions of the brain (Cozolino, 2002; Greenberg & Paivio, 1997) and is what gives experiential therapy its sense of depth.

Persons who experience repeated negative emotions in childhood may form negative emotion schemes that cumulatively lead in later life to pervasive or recurrent activation of negative moods or states of mind that can severely compromise their functioning and are associated with many serious psychopathological conditions. Research has found that, in general, the articulation of these episodes permits their fuller integration into the survivor's understanding, which makes possible greater emotion regulation, that in turn leads to healthier management of negative emotion activation in the future (Cozolino, 2002; Greenberg & Paivio, 1997). Until this disconnection occurs to some extent, the individual remains "embedded" in the earlier negative emotional evaluation derived from past experiences, and their original significance and interpretation go unquestioned and continue to influence functioning.

However, experiential therapy focuses *primarily* on *present* emotional experience, believing that one's current emotional experience is usually a good guide to what is deeply important to the individual. On the other hand, defensive activity can cause emotion dissociation (recently termed *affect phobia*, McCullough et al., 2003). As a result, people can lose touch with their created emotion-system. In such cases, counselors will need to use dynamic therapy, along with experiential, to help counselees surrender their defenses, so that their emotion-system can function the way it was designed to by God.

In addition to encouraging the experiencing of emotion and the articulation of one's current emotions, experiential therapy uses techniques such as reowning one's emotions (Greenberg & Paivio, 1997), focusing (Gendlin, 1996), the empty-chair and the two-chair techniques (Greenberg, Elliott & Lietaer, 1994), guided imagery (Shorr, Sobel, Robin & Connella, 1980) and role-play in order to promote greater emotional awareness, processing and regulation.

A Christian appropriation of the experiential/emotion-focused modality. The origins of experiential therapy in the humanistic psychology movement should alert Christians to the fact that its secular versions will be severely compromised with autocentric and anthropocentric assumptions (see Jones & Butman, 1991; Roberts, 1993; Vitz, 1994).[10] Further complicating a Christian appropriation of this modality is the fact that some Christians are highly suspicious of emotions and subjectivity. It is hoped that, by now, soul care with the emotions has received a sound Christian justification in this book, so there will be no attempt here to make that case. Given the importance of the emotions in a Christian model of healthy human functioning (see Edwards, 1746/1959; Allender & Longman, 1990), it is essential that the Christian soul-care community refamiliarize itself with this modality—while avoiding an overemphasis on subjectivity (unrelated to the Word of God)—in order to foster greater healing of the human heart and its affections. As Edwards himself suggested, "such means are to be desired, as have much of a tendency to move the affections. Such books, and such a way of preaching the Word, and administration of ordinances, and such a way of worshipping God in prayer, and singing praises, is much to be desired, as has a tendency deeply to affect the hearts of those who attend these means" (Edwards, 1746/1959, p. 121). In that spirit, Christian soul-care providers will seek to do whatever fosters, in the long run, the realization, expression and communication of godly emotions.

Unfortunately, Edwards's high Calvinism inclined him to so emphasize the spiritual origin of such emotions that he did not spend equal time considering the human role in their cultivation. He seemed to teach that people either have godly emotions (if they are true Christians) or they do not (if they are not), so he offered little counsel for how believers could nurture such emotions—in dipolar dependence upon God—particularly when their emotion-systems have been damaged, as a result of the Fall and being raised by sinners. Consequently, this model can be considered an elaboration on and extension of Edwards's understanding of the religious affections, in which theocentric soul-care providers are free to work directly with the emotions of one's counselees in order to deconstruct faulty emotional schemes and themes and foster healthier ones. Since emotions are signs (of one's story, one's present perceptions and one's values and ultimate commitments), their messages signify something of the original reality. The reader will recall that past emotions can be stored in memory, so while one's current emotions may not correspond to current reality very well, they are keys to what remains unresolved by God in the person's past. Christian experiential therapy works with emotions, because they provide invaluable symptoms of what remains to be deconstructed and redeemed, so that healthier emotion patterns can be subsequently fostered by the signs of God, so that they increasingly signify the heart of Christ.

The two-chair technique can be used to allow Christian counselees to give a more objective voice to the inner conflict between the old self (flesh) and the new self (Spirit), which is often shrouded in subjective fog, so that the emotions and attitudes of the old self can be better identified, weakened and surrendered, and the new-self orientation can be validated and strengthened. Much of the content of Christian cognitive and symbolic-narrative therapy can be used experientially, but with the goal to take in the speech-acts, narratives and symbols of Scripture more deeply—by the Holy Spirit—so that they engage the emotion centers of the brain and strengthen the Christian's character.

Of greatest importance is emotional experience centered on God through private and public worship. Christian counselors should regularly encourage (and monitor) the ongoing prayer, meditation and worship activity of their counselees. Reading of the Bible and devotional books to promote the affective experience of truth should be encouraged. Christians are changed through savoring and delighting in God's beliefs, attitudes, feelings, values and loves (Piper, 1996). Other God-focused experiential strategies include regular, deep reflection on the indwelling of the Holy Spirit and getting outdoors to take "creation walks" that allow God to speak to the soul through the glory of his physical and animate creation.

Many Christian soul-care writers have advocated different types of what could be called experiential therapy, including Baxter (1656/1990) and Sibbes (1961), and, more recently, the healing prayer movement (see Richardson, 2005; Allender & Longman, 1990; Payne, 1991, 1994, 1995; Seamans, 1981, 1985; Smith's [1996, 2003] "theophostic" model. But as one might expect (and its critics are fond of pointing out), Christian soul care with the emotions needs much more critique, research and refinement. Of special importance is a better understanding of the role of Scripture in the healing of the emotions.

Spiritual warfare. Before moving on, special mention should be made of the Christian experiential strategy of exorcism. Often neglected in our day because of ignorance, inexperience, fear or unbelief, the examples in the New Testament, the experiences of missionaries in the Third World and some contemporary Western manifestations make clear that some humans live under the control or influence of demonic beings (Amorth, 1999; Anderson, 1990; Bufford, 1988; Lawless, 2002; Montgomery, 1976; Nevius, 1892; Powlison, 1995b). Somehow these beings are able to alter the experience of human beings, in some cases taking control over their consciousness, behavior and language faculties. Faith, prayer and fasting have been used to deliver people from such bondage, leading some Christians to specialize in this type of soul work. However, much more investigation is needed on this form of therapy by responsible and sympathetic researchers.

The spiritual direction modality. With this modality, we come to one that has been used, in one form or another, throughout the history of the Christian tradition. Usually, in contrast to psychotherapy and counseling, spiritual direction is done with people who tend not to have significant psychospiritual struggles but who want to grow deeper in their personal relationship with God. For those who have attained a relatively high degree of godly *form*—perhaps because they grew up in a "good-enough" family and/or they have received significant healing in Christ in adulthood—there is still the potential for growth in splendor. Given a relatively well-developed capacity for God, the soul can always become *larger* (metaphorically speaking), so that the individual can better love and glorify God. Perhaps because of a growing dissatisfaction with a lack of spiritual focus in Christian counseling, a number of Christian counselors have been increasingly drawn to this modality (Benner, 1988, 2003, 2004a; Crabb, 2003, 2006; Moon, 2004; Moon & Benner, 2004; Wilson, 1998).

To prevent any readers from drawing a false inference, it must be stated clearly that advocating this modality does not in any way imply that the other modalities are not to be used for spiritual purposes. Such a conclusion follows from religious dualism (see chap. 11),[11] but it is incompatible with the model of Christian holism developed in this book. Theocentric soul care will use explicit Christian spiritual discourse in *all* the modalities to promote Christlikeness. Rather, spiritual direction is that form of soul care to be used with people who are relatively free of damage but want to grow deeper in their character and in their relationship with God. There is, then, a profound continuity between Christian psychotherapy, counseling and spiritual direction, since a theocentric, holistic understanding of life undergirds them all. Moon and Benner (2004) aptly suggest that psychotherapy seeks to make people "normal," whereas spiritual direction seeks to make people "abnormal" or rather "above normal" in terms of their ethicospiritual maturity.

Benner (2004a) defines spiritual direction as "a prayer process in which a person seeking help in cultivating a deeper personal relationship with God meets with another for prayer and conversation that is focused on increasing awareness of God in the midst of life experiences and facilitating surrender to God's will" (p. 94). Spiritual direction is a valuable form of Christian soul care because, first, finite human beings can never exhaust God's infinite being and so their relationship can always grow; second, spiritual development proceeds according to its own norms, and these are not self-evident and easily discovered; third, the human heart is deceitful, particularly regarding spiritual matters; and fourth, consequently, one can benefit from the wisdom and experiences of spiritual guides who have made more progress than oneself (Chan, 1998; Guibert, 1953; Tanquerey, 1930).

Spiritual direction consists of descriptions of what to expect on one's spiritual journey and the pitfalls of spiritual progress, given human sin and self-deception; advanced training in the relevant spiritual disciplines, including self-examination, lectio divina (spiritual reading), prayer and meditation; lessons in interpreting the spiritual significance of all of life; and the self-disclosure of director and directee to assist in the overcoming of remaining sin (Benner, 2002; Chan, 1998; Tanquerey, 1930). Through such guidance, relatively mature Christians may be enabled to become unusually conformed to the image of Christ.

The character modality. As we have often noted, the major goal of Christiformity is Christlike character, so character is the most important form of a human being that emerges from human development (chaps. 9 and 17). Because modern psychology has, until recently, eschewed considerations of character, most of the work on character has been done by philosophers working in the virtues tradition (see Kreeft, 1992; Kruschwitz & Roberts, 1987; MacIntyre, 1984; Sherman, 1989; Sommers & Sommers, 1989). To review, character, within this framework, is an ethicospiritual form of a human being that develops over time and, while influenced by genetics and upbringing, is primarily a result of one's personal agency and one's own actions, aimed at either evil or good, in the context of one's story and one's community. Though character actually lies on a continuum, it is usually described dichotomously—as either virtuous or vicious—and as composed of corresponding traits—virtues or vices, respectively.

Over the past decade or so, an increasing number of psychologists and counselors have begun considering character (Chang & Sanna, 2003; Doherty, 1995; Fowers, 2000; Keyes & Haidt, 2003; Peterson & Seligman, 2004; Richardson, Fowers & Guignon, 1999; Snyder & Lopez, 2002). This was long overdue. As Cushman (1995) noted, it is impossible for psychotherapy to avoid considerations of ethics and morality, since it must assume certain values and goals toward which it seeks to move people, and he argues that modern psychotherapy is no exception. This newer approach posits an ethics advocacy agenda for the counselor—she should point counselees to virtuous patterns of action—as well as an ethics education agenda—she should also teach about the virtues and how to inculcate them into one's life so that they shape one's character. "We learn how to be virtuous by receiving guidance and encouragement from others who know more about virtue" (Fowers, p. 115).

How, then, does one do character therapy? At the risk of oversimplification, secular character-therapy would seem to be something of a "just do it" (or a "just practice it") approach to soul care. Since Aristotle, virtues ethicists have advocated disciplined practice of the virtues, modeled after the character of others more virtuous. And it appears to be possible for reasonably competent and mature individuals to make progress in certain (non-Christian) forms of virtuousness (though it must be acknowledged that this orientation, by itself, would seem to have limited value for working with people whose capacities are severely compromised).

Character therapy is distinguished from mere behavior therapy, because the former appeals to humans as personal agents who are capable of acting with some freedom according to virtuous reasons, whereas the latter treats humans as organisms who are simply motivated by environmental patterns of reinforcement and punishment.[12] This focus on action is extremely important, because soul care can tend to concentrate excessively on internal dynamics and change, and neglect consideration of the actual embodied, interpersonal, dramatic quality of human life. As we have noted, significant internal change leads to its manifestation in outward action. Character therapy is interested in both inwardness and outwardness, because a virtuous life consists of an authentic character manifested in moral relationships with others.

A return to figure 18.1 will show that all the other therapy modalities ought to be utilized to contribute to the improvement of human character and so should be considered as constituents of character therapy. It would seem appropriate to regard character therapy as the overarching and unifying ethicospiritual framework for all of the modalities.

A Christian appropriation of the character modality. It should be obvious that this modality is the most important in the chapter. After all, the Christian faith was intended by God, above all else, to be *aretegenic* (Charry, 1997), that is, virtue-engendering. But what distinguishes *Christian* character therapy? As we have seen, a Christian understanding of character has many unique features, the most important of which are that Jesus Christ is the primary archetype and exemplar of Christian character, and conformity to his character is the primary ethicospiritual goal of Christian maturation. There are, however, a few more notable distinctives.

To begin with, in contrast to naturalistic and humanistic assumptions that human nature is either morally neutral or positively good, a Christian model of Christian character assumes an internal ethicospiritual dualism (creation/redemption and sin) that entails a vigorous, ongoing struggle against the flesh (as well as the world and the devil) *in addition* to the mere resistance to change that non-Christians also experience. Moreover, Christianity teaches that "virtue has no being outside the plenitude of God's goodness" (Hart, 2003, p. 196). The necessary practicing of the Christian virtues, then, only occurs through the grace of God. Consequently, Christians believe the attainment of any virtue is still compromised by sin and can only be *properly* realized through a dipolar, dependent, active participation in the Holy Spirit's virtuous grace that rests on Christ's work. It is the realization of Christ's virtue in his people. Basically, Christian character is seen where the form of Christ and the splendor of the Holy Spirit come together in the manifestation of a deep and well-formed ethicospiritual beauty.

Conclusion

In concluding the chapter (and the book), it would be good to summarize its major underlying assumption: the different modalities of Christian soul care are unified by a radically theocentric agenda.[13] The use of these modalities is Christian to the extent that it aims at the glory of God as its highest end, by fostering the counselee's analogical performance of Christ's life, death and resurrection through a deepening and manifesting faith in Christ (Vanhoozer, 2005). We concede one may use all of these modalities without *any* reference to God or Christ—as secular therapists do (and some Christians). But God's glory is at stake in the therapy of our day, and his truth, goodness, beauty and power are best displayed when his role in our soul healing is consciously acknowledged, made explicit and relied on, and when his Scripture is given the primary role in guiding the development of distinctly Christian psychological research, theory building and soul-care practice. To the extent our faith is explicit and authentic in our work, we manifest our own conformity to Christ. As we, and those with whom we work, more and more come to flourish in communion with the triune God and with the rest of the church, we together become better signs of the Divine Life. Such is our common calling, so that Christian soul care, properly conceived, has a significant role to play in the end for which God created the world.

Notes

[1]Perhaps if Christians had been active in Christian psychology throughout the twentieth century, some of the modalities would have been first identified by Christian psychologists. But the fact that they were first identified by modern psychologists does not nullify their validity.

[2]Many Christian counseling authors will be cited in this chapter who exemplify work in the different modalities. It will be obvious to the reader that these authors differ among themselves and sometimes from the author of this book in a variety of ways. Their being cited is not an endorsement of everything they have written, but it is done (1) to underscore that there is a deeper solidarity among orthodox Christian counselors found in our common union in Christ, (2) to identify *Christian* users of specific modalities, and (3) to familiarize the reader with these authors' contributions to the field. It is hoped that orthodox contributors to soul care who were not mentioned will not feel slighted but will attribute their being overlooked to the limitations of the author. On the other hand, the contributions of the modern pastoral care movement will be noticeable by their relative absence. This is due to my assessment, stated earlier, that the theologies that undergird their soul care betray a greater allegiance to modernism or postmodernism than to the Christian faith—though I would like to be proven wrong.

[3]However, such activities—considered merely as behaviors, apart from any inward deepening—are relatively unfruitful and can even become hindrances to further psychospiritual growth, since the behaviors themselves have only the form of godliness but no power (or splendor). On the other hand, such activities are not irrelevant to the Christian life, since Christian psychospiritual maturation entails the inculcation of such behavioral patterns, when they are combined by faith with a reliance on the Holy Spirit of power, so that they come to be characterized by increasing depth, as the individual develops.

[4]Unfortunately, of these authors, only Payne has been sufficiently critical of Jung and his worldview. As is characteristic of weak integrationists, the others seem to embrace many of Jung's concepts without concern for their original anti-Christian context. Jung was raised in a dysfunctional Christian home and spent his life developing an alternative religious system for moderns. On the other hand, Jung's use of symbolism regrettably continues to make some Christians uncomfortable with *any* Christian soul care that works with the symbolic modality.

[5]Many twentieth-century Christian theologians and philosophers have articulated a narrative approach to Christian thought, including H. Richard Niebuhr, Hans Frei, Stanley Hauerwas, Paul Ricoeur and Alasdair MacIntyre. Most of these theorists share a postmodern interest in narrative and are reacting against modernist commitments to propositions and theory, but they are not equally skeptical of truth claims. Regardless, the profoundly narrative quality of biblical revelation should make a narrative approach to counseling of compelling interest to Christians.

[6]Some might question the value of examining one's story, believing such an exploration shifts responsibility and blame to others or to painful events in one's past (see, e.g. Adams, 1973), and certainly one can interpret such things in ways that undermine personal agency, but this is not a necessity. Understanding how one's actions are in fact influenced by certain social factors can actually help the individual to objectify the internal forces maintaining those actions, thus rendering them more capable of being regulated and dismantled, and so increasing one's personal agency. In addition, after one has been a Christian for a time, one's personal agency can be further bolstered by celebrating one's emerging capacities to image Christ when considered in the light of one's earlier difficult experiences. Since, as we have seen, a major goal of Christian soul care is to foster personal agency in dependence on God, a narrative perspective can foster both personal agency and God's glory.

[7]Many dynamic therapists also work in the relational modality. So for the sake of simplicity, some might favor consolidating them into one modality of interest—the dynamic-relational. They are being distinguished in this model because each would seem to offer a focus that constitutes a distinct and meaningful pathway for intervention, and there would seem to be special benefit in specifically addressing one's intrapsychic dynamics—that is, the defenses and unconscious conflicts—apart from the important, even dominant, role that social relationships often play in those defenses and conflicts.

[8]The therapist's interpretations regarding unconscious dynamics and defenses has traditionally been considered the curative agent in dynamic therapy. The therapist's expert help was thought necessary because, given the relatively unconscious nature of the defenses, counselees are unaware of their existence. However, throughout the twentieth century, dynamic therapy became increasingly cognizant of the therapeutic counterproductivity of having the counselor be seen as the source of all wisdom. Consequently, the trend in recent years has been to train counselees to become adept at doing their own self-examination. The real therapeutic instrument may actually have been the dialogue with the skilled therapist, who trained counselees how to engage in such dialogue internally by asking searching questions, modeling hypothesis-making, and scaffolding the analysis and processing of defenses and emotions. The Christian recognizes that God's help is essential for such activity if it is to deal profitably with issues of ultimacy.

[9]Even cognitive therapists recognize the necessity of working with emotions (e.g., see Beck & Emery, 1985; Beck, 1995); it has just not been their primary focus. And Epstein (1994) has developed what he calls a cognitive-experiential theory that attempts to do justice to two distinct systems operating within human beings—a cognitive and an experiential—each of which can operate somewhat independently of the other (a model suggestively analogous to Edwards's distinction between notional and spiritual understanding).

[10]As an example, perhaps of unconditional positive regard, Greenberg and Paivio (1997) cite with apparent approval a counselee who left a difficult marriage simply after exploring negative emotions about the marriage.

[11]Chan (1998), for example, sharply distinguishes between *psychological* soul care and *spiritual* soul care.

[12]However, human choice and learned associations obviously work together and become mutually reinforcing, and over time lead to a relatively more fixed and habitual pattern of behaving/acting that

produces one's character. Repeated choices of more virtuous actions result in that pattern of actions eventually becoming intrinsically rewarding.

[13]With a therapeutic metasystem like the one proposed in this chapter, it would have been desirable to articulate how the different modalities overlap and impact each other. Unfortunately, this book is already too long, so we will have to leave that for another time.

Epilogue

WE COME TO THE END OF WHAT HAS BEEN A long trip. Let us take a few moments to consider the goals of our trip and review some of the highlights. A primary objective was to describe some of the major contours of a contemporary Christian edification framework, and a secondary aim was to advance discussion regarding what a Christian disciplinary matrix for the science of psychology might look like. A tertiary and largely implicit purpose was to provoke a fresh consideration of explicit Christian activity in the public square—both in mainstream psychology and in public mental health—something largely forbidden according to the standards of modern scientific discourse and soul care.

Perhaps the most daunting aspect of the book was its reliance on semiotic theory—in particular a *Christian* semiotic theory. The organic reasons for this theoretical alliance are hopefully clearer now than they were at the beginning. The major rationale for utilizing a semiotic model is that God created human beings for the purpose of signifying his glory. The main features of this doxological agenda can be seen in figure E.1.

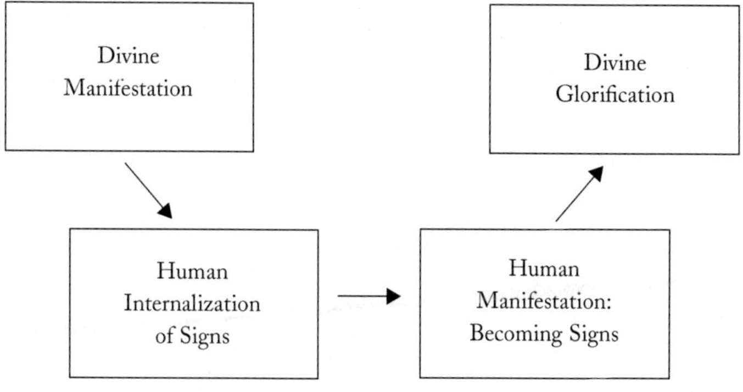

Figure E.1. A general model of a doxological semiotics

God—infinitely glorious but largely hidden—has spoken, and his words manifest his glory. He has done many things with words. The entire creation is a set of signs, composed of meaning, needing to be interpreted and elucidated. He has spoken the first principles of life and psychology in human language through the prophets and apostles. And "in these last days he has spoken to us in his Son" (Heb 1:2)—Jesus Christ, the true definition of human being, and the Alpha and Omega of Christian psychology. God designed humans to be singular signs of God—more commonly called images of God—who find their happiness as they more closely resemble God in dramatic form and splendor. But this journey of manifestation is not easy. To begin with, humans are finite, so maturation is necessary but slow, dependent as it is on gradual biological processes and formative social influences. Moreover, the human fall into sin has substantially compromised this creational process. According to Christian teaching, humans are born with a disposition away from God, and to complicate matters further—according to observation, common sense and now massive research—humans are also characterized by differential damage to the biological and psychosocial dynamic structures that compose their body/soul. As a result, image-bearing is neither simple nor painless to realize in this life. But such is our divine calling. And part of our recovery is the recognition that a more fulfilling and satisfying calling does not exist.

At the center of his project of self-glorification in this creation, the triune God established himself as the way in which humans would be restored to their calling and enabled to make progress in it by means of the life, death and resurrection of the Son of God, and by the Holy Spirit's application of Christ's work to the minds, hearts and lives of those who consent to it. With this in mind, Christian soul care is concerned with helping others to examine themselves, to deconstruct their internal barriers to this project and to take into themselves the glory or meaning of God by all the relevant means by which God's form is expressed—Scripture and the gospel, relationship both with those who resemble him and with the triune God himself, submission to God's will in all its complexity, and dipolar self-regulation. As Christians become re-formed by God's life, Word, will, likeness and regulatory capacity, their lives—together and in the world—look more like God's triune life. This communal resemblance brings joy to God and to us.

That is the essence of this book. There are, however, two serious limitations to the project laid out here that should be acknowledged. First, so much of what has been stated has not been empirically substantiated, particularly according to a Christian disciplinary matrix. Not all Christian assertions can be empirically substantiated, at least not in the modern sense of empirical—consider the existence of God. But the Christian psychology community cannot neglect documenting its theories to the fullest extent possible. It is a part of human joy to be curious and to discover more of the mysterious particulars of God's creation. And in a science-driven culture like ours, research is in a real sense a part of our evangelistic calling. Consequently, the book could have been called "a proposed research program." Much of it ought to be considered a set of research hypotheses that require empirical validation. Given a hypothetico-deductive model of science, hypotheses must come before research, so there is a place for outlining a research program. But the fact is that the contemporary project of a Christian psychology will require hundreds of research studies if it is ever to be realized and taken seriously.

Second, a book of this scope is commensurately weakened by a lack of knowledge of details and subdisciplines outside the author's competence. Such is surely true in this case. Its limitations point to the need to train up students to be psychological specialists of various kinds who also have significant metadisciplinary competence in biblical studies, philosophy or both, working together on projects with others similarly but differentially skilled. The development of a Christian psychology will not proceed far without an influx of young scholars and researchers who have caught its vision.

Finally, we note again that the book is subtitled "A Christian Psychology *Proposal.*" But what exactly was being proposed? That the never-finished Christian psychology project provides the model most likely to resolve the epistemological and soul-care crisis facing the evangelical church in our day regarding how to understand individual human beings and remediate their psychospiritual problems. At the same time, none of its conversation partners should be seen as its enemies but as its friends. Christian psychologists are trying to listen to and learn from their friends, and one has responded to them in this book, which itself is a very small step in the dialogue/trialogue of human history that has been initiated by the triune God. *Respondez s'il vous plaît.*

Appendix 1

A Biblical Coherence Theory of Truth in Counseling

ANOTHER ISSUE THAT COULD BE RAISED concerns the underlying philosophical stance of the biblical counseling movement (BCM). Since the BCM is largely a movement of seminary professors, pastors and laypersons, not much energy has been spent working on the movement's philosophical framework. However, philosophical assumptions are present in every system of thought and practice, whether articulated or not, and it is possible to cull some of those assumptions in the BCM.

As we noted above, the founding of the BCM can be traced back to Jay Adams, and Adams was influenced by and in deep agreement with the thinking of Cornelius Van Til (see Adams, 1970, p. xxi; Powlison, 1996a, p. 7), a strongly conservative, Reformed presuppositional apologetics professor at Westminster Theological Seminary from 1932 to 1971 (where Adams taught from 1963-1983, and where much of the intellectual leadership of the BCM was trained: e.g., Mack, Hindson, Tripp, Welch and Powlison). A presuppositional method like Van Til's is transcendental (Frame, 1995), that is, it begins with certain a priori truths (in Van Til's case, derived from the Bible) that provide the conceptual foundation for all the rest of one's thinking. As an apologetic method it suggests one should address a person's fundamental assumptions rather than beginning with certain self-evident truths derived from logic or experience (like the order of the world) or with historical evidences for the Christian faith. Van Til's overall contributions to Christian thought are enormous and have unfortunately had less of an impact than they should have had, partly because of his strong presuppositionalism and partly because of his highly critical approach to the views of others (unnecessarily reinforced by his presuppositionalism).

Van Til was most influenced by the thought of Reformed theological giants like Calvin, Kuyper, Bavinck and Warfield. However, he studied with idealist philosophers while getting his Ph.D. at Princeton, and he continued to use its terminology and some of its conceptual framework throughout his life, though always from within a thoroughly Reformed theological system (Frame, 1995; McConnell, 2005; Stoker, 1973). Though there are many forms of idealism, the ontological idealism to which Van Til was exposed (Frame, 1995) maintains that reality is actually based in ideas and is in some way dependent on Mind and/or minds (Rescher, 1995). For the most part, the modern version developed out of Kantianism in the early 1800s, by means of Hegel. According to the ontological idealist orientation current in the late 1800s and early 1900s, reality is best conceived of as a single, harmonious, rational system. "Philosophical truth was thought to be a unity" (Acton, 1967, Vol. 4, p. 116). Therefore, in epistemology, such idealists tended to favor a "coherence theory of truth" or a "coherentist theory of knowledge," both of which maintain that the ultimate test of the truthfulness of a concept or theory (or its justification) is the extent to which it is logically consistent with all of one's other concepts (Audi, 1998; Lehrer, 1992; White, 1970). New concepts are accepted as true only after being assessed for their coherence with "what is already accepted or believed, i.e., a particular system of presuppositions on which a worldview has been erected" (Young, 1954, p. 57). This, of course, differs significantly from a more empirical approach to reality, which places greater premium on examining objects in order to form knowledge about them (an approach labeled the "correspondence theory of truth," especially common among scientists. This latter approach maintains that beliefs are true, if they correspond to the way the world is).

Van Til avowedly rejected modern idealism as a philosophical system, since it departed in significant ways from orthodox Christianity (McConnell, 2005; Van Til, 1977). However, he appears to have retained something approximating its epistemological stance—a coherence theory of truth—though modified in a significant way. Van Til's model of knowledge began with God's understanding of reality as the ultimate coherent system and criterion of truth, so he saw the goal of human understanding as analogical: to think in a way that corresponds to God's thought (though finite creatures can never know what exactly God knows) (an assumption that also pervades the present work). However, since humans are now sinful and fundamentally opposed to God, their knowledge system is intrinsically corrupt. The Bible, therefore, is of prime importance, because there God has infallibly revealed the way He thinks—his system of thought—and its inspiration guarantees that it is untainted by sinful bias. Human knowledge, then, from Van Til's standpoint, should begin with understanding and accepting the system of Truth presented in the Bible, and then all subsequent beliefs one encounters are to be assessed in terms of biblical presuppositions, so that beliefs that do not cohere with the biblical system are rejected. We might call his approach a Reformed "biblical coherence theory of truth" or a "biblical idealism."

Those committed to historic Christianity ought to find much to applaud in Van Til's thought. Some version of these assumptions would seem to be necessary to engage in worldview thinking and criticism and elimination of beliefs that really do not belong in an orthodox Christian system of thought.

However, his allegiance to Scripture combined with his implicit commitment to a coherentist epistemology led him in practice to require virtually perfect consistency between (his understanding of) biblical teaching and the thought of others. Though he acknowledged theoretically that non-Christians can understand truth (Van Til, 1972), he found it difficult to affirm any truth that was derived from nonbiblical systems of thought. And because he was Reformed (and believed that Reformed theology was the purest expression of biblical thinking), he also vigorously criticized non-Reformed theologies, like Roman Catholicism and Arminianism (and even other Reformed theologies insofar as they were not more thoroughly Reformed—according to his understanding). As Frame (1995), his former pupil, has suggested, Van Til's overall theoretical system was better than his use of it in practice. His strong coherentism got in the way of his own doctrine of common grace (1972) and kept him from appreciating fully the truth or knowledge found in systems different from Christianity, as well as Christian systems that differed from his own.

One must appreciate Van Til's rigorous desire to think biblically and in accordance with God's thoughts. Yet human thought cannot be evaluated solely by coherentist criteria (Alston, 1996; Audi, 1998; Frame, 1987). The fact is that most of a person's beliefs can be true while some of them (even basic beliefs or presuppositions) may be false (in fact, that is likely to be an apt description of the belief system of most humans). Only God's mind is perfectly coherent. Furthermore, because God is the ultimate source of all truth, it does him no service to ignore or minimize knowledge that those outside the faith have obtained. On the contrary, God's glory is mysteriously fostered when he gives good to those who misuse it (Mt 5:43-48). While Christianity has always taught that beliefs derived from Scripture should have an axiological priority over one's other beliefs, the Bible cannot be approached as if it were the only legitimate source of beliefs. For one thing, we could not make sense of any statement in the Bible were it not that we had many years of exposure to a language system and culture, information from others and everyday experiences by which to interpret statements like "Our Father who is in heaven," "The Lord is my shepherd," and "I am the bread of life." To live a meaningful, mature human life of any kind, humans must form beliefs through perception, action, memory, introspective consciousness, reasoning and the testimony of others (a category of which the biblical authors form an important subset) (Audi, 1998; Plantinga, 1993b, 2000). Scientific research makes use of a number of these God-ordained, extrabiblical sources of knowledge (Frame, 1987, 1995; Plantinga, 1993b, 2000; Poythress, 2006), so Christians seeking to understand the created order must take the created order seriously—and well-done research on and sound thinking about it—while always interpreting it in light of biblical presuppositions. Where Van Til was so good was in his identification of a system's false presuppositions that contradicted biblical ones. But his rigid biblical coherentism often made it difficult for Van Til to identify the remaining truth present in lesser systems than his own.

Van Til's Influence on the BCM

Van Til was a philosopher/apologist, so he did not think much about the contribution of the natural world (and research on it) to human thought (see Stoker, 1971), whereas Christian counseling is concerned with an empirical entity—human beings—that have been subjected to a great deal of research in the twentieth century, most of it done by non-Christians. Jay Adams does not really refer to philosophy in his works, but he approaches secular psychology (and other Christian approaches to counseling) in a manner nearly identical to Van Til's approach to non-Christian and non-Reformed systems of thought. With Van Til, Adams sees all non-Christian systems as fundamentally opposed to God (Adams, 1970, 1973, 1979, 2003). So "their presuppositional stance must be rejected totally" (1970, p. xviii), and "all concepts, terms and methods used in counseling need to be re-examined biblically. Not one thing can be accepted from the past (or the present) without biblical warrant" (1970, p. xviii). After citing Van Til positively, he concludes his introduction to his first important counseling book, *Competent to Counsel*, with the following nuanced statement:

> The conclusions in this book are not based upon scientific findings. My method is pre-suppositional. I avowedly accept the inerrant Bible as the Standard of all faith and practice. The Scriptures, therefore, are the basis, and contain the criteria by which I have sought to make every judgment. Two precautions must be suggested. First, I am aware that my interpretations and applications of Scripture are not infallible. Secondly, I do not wish to disregard science, but rather I welcome it as a useful adjunct for the purposes of illustrating, filling in generalizations with specifics, and challenging wrong human interpretations of Scripture, thereby forcing the student to restudy the Scriptures. However, in the area of psychiatry, science largely has given way to humanistic philosophy and gross speculation. (p. xxi)

This quote is very telling. On the one hand, Adams seeks to be thoroughly grounded in Scripture regarding everything he believes. This is foundational for a genuinely Christian system of soul care. Moreover, he speaks favorably of a science of human nature; this would seem to be an important concession. But then, like most of his followers, he goes on to talk about the relevant science in a way that suggests it is not knowledge-constitutive. It is no more than an "adjunct" that does not provide information that can substantially contribute to one's understanding of human nature and soul care. Rather, one's understanding of such matters should come from Scripture, and science is useful only for illustration, filling in specifics to the generalizations obtained from Scripture, and perhaps challenging wrong interpretations of Scripture. But he is careful not to base his book (and presumably his understanding) on "scientific findings." Why is that? As a good Van Tillian presuppositionalist, he bases his system solely on biblical teaching. It is hard to see how, with *these* presuppositions, Adams could support a constitutive role to empirical research and rational theory-building in his model of psychology and soul care. He ends, significantly, by discrediting most of the field of psychiatry in his day by suggesting it was largely based on humanist and speculative thought.

In theory, Adams (like Van Til) believed that "elements" of truth could be found in non-Christian systems (see Adams, 1973, p. 76; 2003). But in practice, Adams made very little positive reference to anything from secular psychiatry or psychology (see his remarks in Powlison, 1993), and just about the only exceptions are citations of non-Christians used to refute other non-Christians. Otherwise, the pervasive thrust of his work demonstrates a profound antipathy to anything from secular sources, including scientific research. Also analogous to Van Til, he (Adams, 1975b, 2003) was extremely critical of other Christian approaches to soul care that he believed were not as consistently biblical as was his. This approach to secular and other Christian thought is best explained by his adherence to a biblical coherence theory of truth, just like Van Til's.

As we have already noted, progressive biblical counseling advocates have been gradually moving away from some of the more extreme positions of their founder; whereas the traditionalists have been less critical of him. Regarding the material in this appendix, it is likely that most traditional biblical counselors do not knowingly subscribe to Adams's presuppositionalism (though the more well-informed do), let alone a biblical coherence theory of truth (or, for that matter, Adams's Reformed theology). However, the fundamentalism of many traditionalists comports well with Van Tillian epistemological idealism, since fundamentalism similarly requires that all one's beliefs be derived from the Bible and that one reject all beliefs belonging to "the world." This alone helps make sense of the comprehensive rejection (in practice) and vehement critique of the theory, research and technique of secular psychology and counseling. Consider, for example, Mack's (1997) approving citation of Pratt (a theologian profoundly influenced by Van Til):

> Extrabiblical statements that seem to reflect biblical truth must be regarded as false because, as Richard Pratt states, "they are not the result of voluntary obedience to God's revelation." "Beyond this," Pratt continues, "the statements are falsified by the non-Christian framework of meaning and therefore lead away from the worship of God. If nothing else, the mere commitment to human independence falsifies the non-Christian's statements." (p. 45)

This is quite an assertion by a noted TBC leader that exemplifies an extreme biblical coherentism. But it contradicts common sense, biblical and otherwise. Even statements that "seem to" reflect biblical truth—if uttered by non-Christians—are false. One could not trust non-Christian physicians and mechanics, if such a framework were followed through consistently. If something like this position is in fact implicitly embraced by others in TBC, it is easy to see why statements by non-Christian psychologists that aim at the description of human nature, presumably of some importance to Christians—like self-representations, causes and experience of psychopathology, and social dynamics—are virtually never cited: they are all false, simply because of the non-Christian framework of meaning within which they were uttered. Such a radical coherentism/idealism commits a serious epistemological blunder and a logical fallacy (the genetic)—bordering on relativism and akin to Kantian antirealism—for it necessarily rejects descriptive assertions made by non-Christian psychologists about psychological reality, not on rational, empirical or biblical grounds, but simply on the basis of their false presuppositions, which may or may not influence those assertions.

As stated above, according to a correspondence theory of truth, beliefs are true if they correspond to the way the world is; this approach, therefore, places a high priority on empirical investigation. All Christian psychologists ought to follow the BCM's example by beginning with a biblically based worldview, so that they read secular psychology texts using a hermeneutic of suspicion regarding its antithetic bias. However, a Christian worldview and epistemology also require Christians to take seriously knowledge about God's creation derived from careful research, regardless of the source. Only in this way will the knowledge of the Christian counseling community become increasingly comprehensive and sophisticated, so that its understanding of human nature corresponds more closely to the way human nature is, the way God understands it, more than it would without this research. According to Frame (1987; a student of Van Til who developed what could be called a "softer" presuppositionalism), the formation of true beliefs about reality requires the use of multiple perspectives: the situational (truth derived from studying facts in the real world, which we might call the empirical), the existential (truth derived from personal, lived experience; the phenomenological) and the normative (truth derived from God's authority expressed through his word). Frame believes that all three perspectives are necessary to form a comprehensive human knowledge, even in theology. And if these three perspectives are necessary in theology, how much more are they necessary for sciences that have as their object creatures that are accessible to empirical investigation, like individual human beings.

Revealing some internal inconsistency, Van Til himself taught (1977, pp. 1-

3) that Christian epistemology requires an appreciation of the One (coherence of all truth in God's mind) and the Many (correspondence to the facts as known by God). Theoretically, Van Til himself argued that to think God's thoughts after him, God's children should make use of whatever resources he has given for that purpose, the Bible primarily, but also all other legitimate resources, subordinate to the Bible. This has been the typical position of the Augustinian branch of historic Christianity.

Over the centuries, most Christians have affirmed some version of a correspondence theory of truth that assumes that humans (even fallen humans) can accurately understand some aspects of the creation and the way the universe really is (Butterfield, 1957; Gilson, 1940; Henry, 1976; Holmes, 1977; Lindberg & Numbers, 1986; McGrath, 2001, 2002; Nash, 1988; Pearcey, 2004; Pearcey & Thaxton, 1994; Poythress, 2006; Ramm, 1954; Young, 1954). Usually, the correspondence theory of truth has been held in conjunction with some form of realism (likewise favored by the church over idealism, e.g., Augustine, Thomas Aquinas, Calvin, and, in the present, Alston, 1996; McGrath, 2002; Plantinga, 1993b, 2000). One version of contemporary Christian realism asserts that humans can have warranted true beliefs about many things, because of a belief in the basic reliability of the cognitive equipment humans possess that was designed by God for forming knowledge in appropriate settings (Plantinga, 1993b, 2000).

At the same time, historic Christian realism recognizes that sin distorts human understanding, but not so much as to make it impossible to know things about human beings and not equally in all areas of thought (an approach we might term, with McGrath, 2002, "Christian critical realism"). Sin has most seriously compromised human understanding of religious matters (though even here, the *sensus divinitatis* is still functioning somewhat in most humans, Calvin, 1960; Plantinga, 2000), whereas perception and mathematical reasoning are generally little affected by sin. As we noted above, the closer we get to God and the core issues of life, the worse sin's effects on knowledge become. Non-Christian psychotherapists are positively blind regarding the most important beliefs about psychotherapy: its final end (the glory of God), its imminent goal (conformity to Christ) and its only ultimate means (the Holy Spirit), so the BCM is prophetic when pointing out these kinds of inadequacies in secular psychotherapy—inadequacies of such importance that they do indeed constitute an alternative form of soul healing to Christianity. However, the profound skepticism of TBC regarding secular psychological theory and research, evident in its pervasive lack of positive citation of virtually any non-Christian psychology literature, betrays an extreme biblical idealism common among fundamentalists that is foreign to the critical realism regarding human knowledge about human beings common to historic Christianity. Christians have no need to throw out the baby of God's creation grace evident in secular psychology, along with the "worldly," antithetical bathwater of its non-Christian assumptions and distortions.

Appendix 2

Toward a Christian Semiotics for a Christian Psychology

SEMIOTICS IS A RATHER COMPLEX FIELD OF STUDIES that experienced significant conceptual advances in the 20th century. However, the majority of its 20th century leaders were largely shaped by Kantian or post-Kantian (antirealist) assumptions. As a result, many Christians have tended to be skeptical of the value and validity of semiotics. For reasons that should be evident in the book, I consider this an unfortunate (but somewhat understandable) prejudice. The following is an attempt to offer a distinctive Christian reinterpretation of a few aspects of semiotic theory to demonstrate how a Christian model of semiotics might differ from a secular model.

The influential father of modern continental semiotics, Saussure (1966), taught that a sign was a dyadic entity and consisted of a *signifier* (the material aspect of a sign, e.g., a spoken word or a visual representation) and that which it *signified* (the mental content to which the material aspect referred). A sign is composed of these two aspects—they are two sides of the same coin. Independently of Saussure, Pierce (1958), an early herald of pragmatism, was the progenitor of modern American semiotics, and he suggested that signs can have a triadic structure. According to him, many signs include three components: the *representamen* (Saussure's *signifier;* e.g., a word like "sharp"), the *interpretant* (Saussure's *signified;* the specific meaning of the word, e.g., "very savvy"), as well as the *object* (the actual referent in the universe, which is represented by the word and its meaning, e.g., a trait of a particular individual, as in "He's sharp"). Pierce's model then is able to take into account the existence of extrahuman reality, an important, realist advantage over Saussure's model.

Those influenced by Saussure will point to the fact that some words (like *therefore*) do not have an objective referent, a point that reveals that not all signs are triadic. But Saussure's dyadic model of semiotics was an expression of a neo-Kantian, structuralist approach to human knowledge that avoided reference to the object, since, following Kant's antirealism, we only have access to our own mental/linguistic constructions of the world, not to the world itself. Saussure's stance has led to the decisively social constructivist approach to signs that came to dominate modern/postmodern semiotic theory throughout the twentieth century and has given semiotics a bad name among other, more realist thinkers, since Saussure's model is unable to take into its accounts the obvious referential capacity of so much of human speech. This fatal absence, effectively removing reality from the frame of semiotic theory, has severely compromised the ability of contemporary semiotic theory to make sense of science—in spite of its rich potential. Only a triadic semiotic model like Pierce's can do justice to language and the human mind's capacity to refer to and represent the extrahuman nature of reality (including social and psychological reality). As already noted, Christians have historically tended to utilize a realist epistemology (see Alston, 1996; Plantinga, 1993b, 2000). Therefore, a Christian semiotic will be more likely to take up a triadic model of the sign, than a dyadic, out of a respect for God and the reality he created.

Saussure and his heirs extended his dyadic model beyond the single sign to encompass the entire linguistic system and the semantic system, a move that was inevitable and desirable. Hjelmslev (1961), Greimas (1982, 1983) and Barthes (1967) have referred to the field of all signifiers (all words) as the "expression plane" (or discourse plane) and the field of all signifieds (all human thought) as the "content plane" (or semantic plane).

Now let us apply this distinction to *science*. Each science entails a specialized vocabulary—a set of relevant expressions—that are used to label their respective mental meanings, signifiers that refer to their signifieds—a set of corresponding content: concepts of the features of the object of the science and their lawful interrelations and relations with other objects. A Saussurian thinker might suppose that a science consists of nothing more than its discourse and the content or concepts that its discourse expresses. But a Piercian would presumably be more likely to point out that a science's discourse aims at a description of an actual object (an observation that, on the face of it, seems quite compelling). Since Christians tend to respect extrahuman reality, let us extend the Saussurian semiotic system of two planes and posit an "object plane": the field of all objects to which signifiers/signifieds refer. Such objects could be material or immaterial, real or ideal, and the science of psychology is interested in all these, with reference to the specific object of its investigations: "individual human beings." Material objects of interest in psychology include DNA sequences and neural networks, and immaterial objects include traits, emotion schemes and personality disorders, to name a few. Ideal objects are important for soul care and include such things as the goal of human maturation and ethical standards. (Fictional objects, by contrast, are another class, common in literature but not usually intentionally a part of scientific discourse. On the contrary, put negatively, science aims at eliminating fictional objects or features from its discourse. Scientific literature is by definition supposed to be *nonfiction.*)

A semiotic model that is fitting for Christian psychology and soul care will lie some distance from the antirealist assumptions of Saussurian semiotics. A Christian view of science sees it as a finite and therefore an inevitably compromised enterprise, further corrupted by the noetic effects of sin. But Christians historically have been able to recognize the limitations of human knowing without subscribing to a thoroughgoing epistemological relativism, like that which has characterized twentieth-century continental semiotics. Consequently, Christians generally share the realist epistemological aspirations of most scientists, whatever their worldview.

But in addition to the above considerations, a Christian framework also contains the assumption that God is the omniscient and wise knower and appraiser of all things and relations, who knows the true value of all things in relation to everything else (most importantly, the value of his own triune being). As a result, a Christian semiotics must consider God's mind and heart to be, perhaps we should call it, a "divine plane" for all signs: the field of God's comprehensive and exhaustive understanding of the way things actually are. God's mind and heart provide the ultimate semiotic frame of reference and source of all meaning, and they are the measure of all human understanding and appraisal (the content plane) of and human communication (the expression plane) regarding the creation (the object plane), including the variance of the first two from his perfect understanding, appraisal and communication in Christ and Scripture. The divine plane, of course, is absent from nontheistic semiotic discourse, but it is foundational to the kind of Christian semiotics developed by Augustine, Berkeley and Edwards.

According to a Christian understanding of science, God's involvement in scientific knowing provides its gracious support and makes possible its validity. A particular science is a gift of God's creation grace (and redemptive or regenerative grace, in the case of specifically Christian scientific activity), and it consists of discipline-relevant signs that exist along all four semiotic planes.

The divine plane is the ultimate plane in a Christian semiotic scheme, since every created object is itself the expression or signifier of that plane: God's originating content (his understanding and appraisal). Moreover, some relevant portions of that content are not supplied with the object itself (e.g., its relative value); therefore, God also expressed himself in special, supplementary discourse, known as the Bible. But both nature and Scripture are expressions of the mind and heart of God.

According to historic Christianity, the goal of scientific activity is reconstructive: to know and appraise something in accordance with the way God does (Frame, 1987; Van Til, 1969). A semiotic way of describing the goal of a Christian science of psychology is discourse (expression plane) regarding the human understanding and appraisal (content plane) of individual human beings (the object plane of humans but the expression plane for God), with God's comprehensive understanding and appraisal providing the source and measure for the human knowledge.

Another distinctive of Christian semiotics compared with secular semiotic theory is a belief in the existence of individual personal agents as meaning-full authors or actors. Contemporary secular semioticians (and their postmodern siblings) are reticent to acknowledge the reality of personal agents or selves, preferring to focus on linguistic systems and texts, out of which human life is constructed. However, a Christian approach assumes that God and human beings made in his image are unique kinds of beings, personal agents that have a special set of features that distinguish them from other beings. According to Christianity, God is a personal agent who is the source of and model for human personal agents, and upon reflection we realize further that God has ordained that human personal agents emerge out of the interpersonal and semiodiscursive landscape within which they are raised. Moreover, God has himself spoken into this landscape by means of the prophets and apostles, and relates to his people in large measure through their words. Finally, the God of the Bible is a covenant-making God. A covenant is a very special type of discourse that binds two or more personal agents together by means of their unique capacities to promise and act. God's covenantal relationship with his people, expressed in the covenantal documents of the Old and New Testaments, provides the ultimate interpersonal/semiotic context within which those people develop into mature personal agents.

Furthermore, given the nature of personal agents, the content and object planes (i.e., human knowledge of the object) have a depth dimension. Humans may understand at various levels of "depth": information may be memorized, understood, embraced and cherished. Content can be understood in the mind and, more deeply, in the heart. Christian soul care seeks to help humans internalize God's understanding and appraisal of them, in all of that comprehensiveness, as deeply as humanly possible. And the transformation of the object—the human being—is most fully realized only as God's understanding and appraisal of them is expressed in virtuous human action through the course (or the narrative) of their lives. The rest of the book is an exposition of this paragraph.

References

Abbott, C. (1999). *Julian of Norwich: Autobiography and theology.* Suffolk, U.K.: D. S. Brewer.

Adams, J. E. (1970). *Competent to counsel.* Grand Rapids, MI: Zondervan.

Adams, J. E. (1973). *Christian counselor's manual.* Grand Rapids, MI: Zondervan.

Adams, J. E. (1975a). *The use of the Scriptures in counseling.* Grand Rapids, MI: Baker.

Adams, J. E. (1975b). *Your place in the counseling revolution.* Grand Rapids, MI: Baker.

Adams, J. E. (1979). *More than redemption.* Phillipsburg, NJ: Presbyterian & Reformed.

Adams, J. E. (1982). Integration. *Journal of Pastoral Practice, 6*(1), 3-7.

Adams, J. E. (1986). *How to help people change.* Grand Rapids, MI: Zondervan.

Adams, J. E. (2003). *Is all truth God's truth?* Stanley, NC: Timeless Texts.

Adams, R. M. (1987). A modified divine command theory of ethical wrongness. In *The virtue of faith and other essays in philosophical theology* (pp. 97-122). New York: Oxford University Press.

Adams, R. M. (1999). *Finite and infinite goods: A framework for ethics.* New York: Oxford University Press.

Addis, L. (1995). Methodological holism. In R. Audi (Ed.), *The Cambridge dictionary of philosophy* (p. 492). Cambridge: Cambridge University Press.

Aidarova, A. (1982). *Childhood development and education.* Moscow: Progress.

Akmanjian, A., Demers, R. A., & Harnish, R. M. (1984). *Linguistics: An introduction to language and communication* (2nd ed.). Cambridge, MA: MIT Press.

Alexander, A. (1967). *Thoughts on religious experience.* Edinburgh: Banner of Truth. (Original work published 1844)

Alexander, F., & Selesnick, S. (1968). *The history of psychiatry.* New York: New American Library.

Alford, J. A. (1992). *The scriptural self.* In B. S. Levy (Ed.), *The Bible in the Middle Ages: Its influence on literature and art* (pp. 1-22). Binghamton, NY: Center for Medieval and Early Renaissance Studies.

Al-Issa, I. (1999). Abnormal psychology. In D. B. Benner & P. C. Hill (Eds.), *Baker encyclopedia of psychology and counseling* (pp. 27-31). Grand Rapids, MI: Baker.

Allen, J. J. (1993). *Inner way: Eastern Christian spiritual direction.* Grand Rapids, MI: Eerdmans.

Allen, J. J. (1994). *Inner way: Eastern Christian spiritual direction.* Grand Rapids, MI: Eerdmans.

Allender, D. B. (1999). *The healing path.* Colorado Springs, CO: Waterbrook.

Allender, D. B. (2005). *To be told.* Colorado Springs, CO: Waterbrook.

Allender, D. B., & Longman, T., III. (1990). *Emotions: The cry of the soul.* Colorado Springs, CO: NavPress.

Allender, D. B., & Longman, T., III. (1993). *Bold love.* Colorado Springs, CO: NavPress.

Allender, D. B., & Longman, T., III. (1995). *Intimate allies.* Wheaton, IL: Tyndale House.

Allport, G. W. (1950). *The individual and his religion.* New York: Macmillan.

Allport, G. W. (1961). *Pattern and growth in personality.* New York: Holt, Rinehart & Winston.

Almy, G. L. (2000). *How Christian is Christian counseling?* Wheaton, IL: Crossway.

Alspaugh, J. E. (1978). Serving the learning-disabled counselee. *The Journal of Pastoral Practice, 2,* 49-56.

Alston, W. P. (1991). *Perceiving God.* Ithaca, NY: Cornell University Press.

Alston, W. P. (1992). Conceptual analysis and psychological theory. In S. Koch & D. E. Leary (Eds.), *A century of psychology as science* (pp. 638-53). Washington, DC: American Psychological Association.

Alston, W. P. (1993). *The reliability of sense perception.* Ithaca, NY: Cornell University Press.

Alston, W. P. (1996). *A realist conception of truth.* Ithaca, NY: Cornell University Press.

Aman, C. J., Roberts, R. J., & Pennington, B. F. (1998). A neuropsychological examination of the underlying deficit in attention deficit hyperactivity disorder: Frontal lobe versus right parietal lobe theories. *Developmental Psychology, 34,* 956-69.

American Psychiatric Association. (2000). *Diagnostic and statistical manual of mental disorders* (4th ed.-Text Revision). Washington, DC: Author.

Ames, W. (1983). *The marrow of theology.* Durham, NC: Labyrinth

Amorth, G. (1999). *An exorcist tells his story.* San Francisco: Ignatius.

Anderson, C. A. (2000). Violence and aggression. In A. E. Kazdin (Ed.), *Encyclopedia of psychology* (Vol. 8, pp. 162-69). New York: Oxford University Press.

Anderson, C. A., Krull, D. S., & Weiner, B. (1996). Explanations: Processes and consequences. In E. T. Higgins & A. W. Kruglanski (Eds.), *Social psychology: Handbook of basic principles* (pp. 271-96). New York: Guilford.

Anderson, H. (1997). *Conversation, language, and possibilities.* New York: Basic Books.

Anderson, J. R. (1981). *Cognitive skills and their acquisition.* Hillsdale, NJ: Erlbaum.

Anderson, J. R. (1983). *The architecture of cognition.* Cambridge, MA: Harvard University Press.

Anderson, N. T. (1990). *The bondage breaker.* Eugene, OR: Harvest House.

Anderson, N. T. (1997). *Victory over darkness.* Ventura, CA: Regal.

Anderson, N. T., Zuehlke, T. E., & Zuehlke, J. S. (2000). *Christ-centered therapy.* Grand Rapids, MI: Zondervan.

Anderson, R. J., Hughes, J. A., & Sharrock, W. W. (1986). *Philosophy and the human sciences.* London: Croom Helm.

Anderson, R. S. (1982). *On becoming human.* Grand Rapids, MI: Eerdmans.

Anderson, R. S. (1990). *Christians who counsel: The vocation of wholistic therapy.* Grand Rapids, MI: Zondervan.

Anderson, R. S. (2000). *Soul-care: A theology of personal empowerment and spiritual healing.* Pasadena, CA: Fuller Seminary Bookstore.

Anderson, R. S. (2001). *The shape of practical theology.* Downers Grove, IL: InterVarsity Press.

Anderson, R. S. (2003). *Spiritual caregiving as secular sacrament: A practical theology for professional caregivers.* London: Jessica Kingley Publishers.

Anderson, S. W., Bechara, A., Damasio, H., Tranel, D., & Damasio, A. R. (2002). Impairment of social and moral behavior related to early damage in human prefrontal cortex. In J. T. Cacioppo, G. G. Berntson, R. Adolphs, C. S. Carter, R. J. Davidson, M. K. McClintock, B. S. McEwen, M. J. Meaney, D. L. Schacter, E. M. Sternberg, S. S. Suomi & S. E. Taylor (Eds.), *Foundations in social neuroscience* (pp. 333-44). Cambridge, MA: MIT Press.

Anderson, W. E. (1980). Editor's introduction. In *The works of Jonathan Edwards, 6, Scientific and philosophical writings.* New Haven, CT: Yale University Press.

Apel, K.-O. (1984). *Understanding and explanation: A transcendental-pragmatic perspective.* Cambridge, MA: MIT Press.

Archer, M. S. (1995). *Realist social theory: The morphogenetic approach.* Cambridge: Cambridge University Press.

Aristotle. (1985). *Nichomachean ethics* (T. Irwin, Trans). Indianapolis: Hackett.

Arndt, A. F., & Gingrich, F. W. (1957). *A Greek-English lexicon of the New Testament and other early Christian literature.* Chicago: University of Chicago Press.

Aronson, E. (1988). *The social animal* (5th ed.). New York: W. H. Freeman.

Ashcraft, M. H. (2005). *Cognition* (5th ed.). Englewood Cliffs, NJ: Prentice-Hall.

Ashcroft, M. H. (1994). *Human memory and cognition.* New York: HarperCollins.

Asher, M., & Asher, M. (2004). *The Christian's guide to psychological terms.* Bemidji, MN: Focus.

Aspinwall, L. G., & Staudinger, U. M. (Eds.). (2003). *A psychology of human strengths: Fundamental questions and future directions for a positive psychology.* Washington, DC: American Psychological Association.

Athanasius. (1954). On the incarnation of the Word. In E. R. Hardy (Ed.), *Christology of the later fathers* (pp. 55-110). Louisville, KY: Westminster John Knox.

Atwood, J. D. (Ed.). (1996). *Family scripts.* Washington, DC: Taylor & Francis.

Audi, R. (1993). *Action, intention, and reason.* Ithaca, NY: Cornell University Press.

Audi, R. (1998). *Epistemology: A contemporary introduction to the theory of knowledge.* New York: Routledge.

Augustine. (1942). *Confessions.* New York: Sheed & Ward.

Augustine. (1948). *Basic writings of Saint Augustine* (W. J. Oates, Ed.). New York: Random House.

Augustine. (1950). *City of God* (G. G. Walsh, D. B. Zema, G. Monahan & D. J. Honan, Trans.). (Abridged ed.). New York: Doubleday.

Augustine. (1978). *Faith, hope and charity* (L. A. Arand, Trans.). New York: Newman Press.

Augustine. (1997). *On Christian teaching*. Oxford: Oxford University Press.

Aumann, J. (1985). *Christian spirituality in the Catholic tradition*. San Francisco: Ignatius; London: Sheed & Ward.

Austin, J. L. (1962). *How to do things with words*. Cambridge, MA: Harvard University Press.

Azari, N. P., Nichel, J., Wunderlich, G., Niedeggen, M., Hefter, H., & Tellman, L., (2001). Neural correlates of religious experience. *European Journal of Neuroscience, 13,* 649-52.

Babler, J. (1999). A biblical critique of the DSM-IV. *Journal of Biblical Counseling, 18,* 25-29.

Backus, W., & Chapian, M. (2000). *Telling yourself the truth*. Minneapolis: Bethany House.

Bacote, V. E. (2005). *The Spirit in public theology: Appropriating the legacy of Abraham Kuyper*. Grand Rapids, MI: Baker.

Bainton, R. H. (1950). *Here I stand: A life of Martin Luther*. New York: Pierce & Smith.

Bainton, R. H. (1955). *Here I stand: A life of Martin Luther*. Nashville: Abingdon.

Baker, A. (2005, October). *Counseling children who have been sexually abused*. Paper presented at the meeting of the National Association of Nouthetic Counselors, Grand Island, NY.

Baker, D. L. (1991). *Two testaments, one Bible* (rev. ed.). Downers Grove, IL: InterVarsity Press.

Bakhtin, M. M. (1981). *The dialogic imagination: Four essays*. Austin, TX: University of Texas Press.

Bakhtin, M. M. (1986). *Speech genres and other late essays*. Austin: University of Texas Press.

Ball, R. A., & Goodyear, R. K. (1993). Self-reported professional practices of Christian psychotherapists. In E. L. Worthington Jr. (Ed.), *Psychotherapy and religious values* (pp. 171-82). Grand Rapids, MI: Baker.

Balswick, J. O., King, P. E., & Reimer, K. S. (2005). *The reciprocating self: Human development in theological perspective*. Downers Grove, IL: InterVarsity Press.

Baltes, P. B. & Smith, J. (1990). Towards a psychology of wisdom and its ontogenesis. In R. J. Sternberg (Ed.), *Wisdom: Its nature, origins, and development* (pp. 87-120). Cambridge: Cambridge University Press.

Balthasar, H. U. (1982-1991). *The glory of the Lord: A theological aesthetics*. (Vols. 1-7). San Francisco: Ignatius.

Balthasar, H. U. (1986). *Prayer*. San Francisco: Ignatius.

Balthasar, H. U. (1988-1998). *Theo-drama* (Vols. 1-5). San Francisco: Ignatius.

Balthasar, H. U. (1989a). *Christian meditation*. San Francisco: Ignatius.

Balthasar, H. U. (1989b). *The word made flesh*. San Francisco: Ignatius.

Bandura, A. (1986). *The social foundations of thought and action*. New York: Prentice Hall.

Bandura, A. (1989). Human agency in social cognitive theory. *American Psychologist, 44,* 1175-84.

Bandura, A. (1999). Social cognitive theory of personality. In L. A. Pervin & O. P. John (Eds.), *Handbook of personality* (2nd ed., pp. 154-96). New York: Guilford.

Banfield, J. F., Wyland, C. L., MacRae, C. N., Münte, T. F., & Heatherton, T. F. (2004). The cognitive neuroscience of self-regulation. In R. F. Baumeister & K. D. Vohs (Eds.), *Handbook of self-regulation: Research, theory, and applications* (pp. 62-82). New York: Guilford.

Banich, M. T. (1997). *Neuropsychology: The neural bases of mental function.* Boston: Houghton Mifflin.

Barkow, J. H., Cosmides, L., & Tooby, J. (1992). *The adapted mind: Evolutionary psychology and the generation of culture.* New York: Oxford University Press.

Bar-On, R., & Parker, J. D. A. (2000). *The handbook of emotional intelligence.* San Francisco: Jossey-Bass.

Barr, J. (1980). *The scope and authority of the Bible.* Philadelphia: Westminster Press.

Barth, K. (1936). *Church dogmatics 1.1.* (G. W. Bromiley & T. F. Torrance, Trans.). Edinburgh: T & T Clark.

Barth, K. (1956). *Church dogmatics 4.1* (G. W. Bromiley, Trans.). Edinburgh: T & T Clark.

Barth, K. (1957). *Church dogmatics 2.1* (T. H. L. Parker, W. B. Johnston, H. Knight & J. L. M. Haire, Trans.). Edinburgh: T & T Clark.

Barth, K. (1960). *Church dogmatics 3.2* (H. Knight, G. W. Bromiley, J. K. S. Reid, R. H. Fuller, Trans.). Edinburgh: T & T Clark.

Barth, K. (1981). *The Christian life.* Grand Rapids, MI: Eerdmans.

Barth, M. (1974). *Ephesians.* Garden City, NY: Doubleday.

Barthes, R. (1967). *Elements of semiology.* New York: Hill and Wang.

Battino, R. (2002). *Metaphoria: Metaphor and guided metaphor for psychotherapy and healing.* Carmarthen, UK: Crown House Publishing.

Baumeister, R. F. (1991). *Meanings of life.* New York: Guilford.

Baumeister, R. F., & Vohs, K. D. (Eds.). (2004). *Handbook of self-regulation: Research, theory, and applications.* New York: Guilford.

Bavinck, H. (1951). *The doctrine of God.* Grand Rapids, MI: Eerdmans.

Bavinck, H. (1956). *Our reasonable faith.* Grand Rapids, MI: Eerdmans.

Bavinck, H. (1981). *Foundations of psychology* (J. Vandenborn, Trans.). Translation project was an unpublished master's thesis. Calvin College, Grand Rapids, MI.

Bavinck, H. (1989). Common grace (R. Van Leeuwen, Trans.). *Calvin Theological Journal, 24,* 59-61.

Bavinck, H. (2003). *Reformed dogmatics. Vol. 1: Prolegomena* (J. Vriend, Trans.). Grand Rapids, MI: Baker.

Bavinck, H. (2004). *Reformed dogmatics. Vol. 2: God and creation* (J. Vriend, Trans.). Grand Rapids, MI: Baker.

Bavinck, H. (2006). *Reformed dogmatics. Vol. 3: Sin and salvation in Christ* (J. Vriend, Trans.). Grand Rapids, MI: Baker.

Baxter, L. R., Schwartz, J. M., Bergman, K. S., Szuba, M. P., Guze, B. H., Mazziotta, J. C., Alazraki, A., Selin, C. E., Feng, H. K., Munford, P., & Phelps, M. E. (1992). Caudate glucose metabolic rate changes with both drug and behavior therapy for obsessive-compulsive disorder. *Archives of General Psychiatry, 40,* 681-89.

Baxter, R. (1974). *The reformed pastor.* Edinburgh: Banner of Truth Trust. (Original work published 1656)

Baxter, R. (1981). What are the best preservatives against melancholy and overmuch sorrow? In S. Annesley (Ed.), *Puritan sermons: 1659-1689. Vol. 3* (pp. 253-92). Wheaton, IL: Richard Owen Roberts. (Original work published 1682)

Baxter, R. (1990). *The practical works of Richard Baxter: Vol. 1.* Ligonier, PA: Soli Deo Gloria.

Baxter, R. (2002). *The practical works of Richard Baxter: Vol. 2.* Ligonier, PA: Soli Deo Gloria.

Bayer, O. (2003). *Living by faith: Justification and sanctification.* Grand Rapids: Eerdmans.

Beck, A. T. (1976). *Cognitive therapy and the emotional disorders.* New York: International Universities Press.

Beck, A. T., & Emery, G. (1985). *Anxiety disorders and phobias: A cognitive perspective.* New York: Basic Books.

Beck, A. T., Rush, A. J., Shaw, B. F., & Emery, G. (1979). *Cognitive therapy of depression.* New York: Guilford.

Beck, J. R. (1999). *Jesus and personality theory: Exploring the five-factor model.* Downers Grove, IL: InterVarsity Press.

Beck, J. R. (2002). *The psychology of Paul: A fresh look at his life and teaching.* Grand Rapids, MI: Kregel.

Beck, J. R., & Demarest, B. (2005). *The human person in theology and psychology: A biblical anthroplogy for the twenty-first century.* Grand Rapids, MI: Kregel.

Beck, J. S. (1995). *Cognitive therapy: Basics and beyond.* New York: Guilford.

Beck, R. (2006). Communion and complaint: Atachment, object-relations, and trianglar love perspectives on relationship with God. *Journal of Psychology and Theology, 34,* 43-52.

Beck, R., & McDonald, A. (2004). Attachment to God: The attachment to God inventory, tests of working model correspondence. *Journal of Psychology and Theology, 32,* 92-100.

Beeke, J. R. (2004). *Puritan reformed spirituality.* Grand Rapids, MI: Reformation Heritage. Beilby, J. (Ed.). (2002). *Naturalism defeated?* Ithaca, NY: Cornell University Press.

Beit-Hallahmi, B., & Argyle, M. (1997). *The psychology of religious behavior, belief and experience.* London: Routledge.

Bellah, R. N., Madsen, R., Sullivan, W. M., Swidler, A., & Tipton, S. M. (1985). *Habits of the heart: Individualism and commitment in American life.* New York: Harper & Row.

Benjamin, L. S. (2003). *Interpersonal reconstructive therapy: Promoting change in nonresponders.* New York: Guilford.

Benner, D. G. (1983). The incarnation as a metaphor for psychotherapy. *Journal of Psychology and Theology, 11,* 287-94.

Benner, D. G. (1988). *Psychotherapy and the spiritual quest.* Grand Rapids, MI: Baker.

Benner, D. G. (1990). *Healing emotional wounds.* Grand Rapids, MI: Baker.

Benner, D. G. (2003). *Surrender to love.* Downers Grove, IL: InterVarsity Press.

Benner, D. G. (2004a). *Sacred companions: The gift of spiritual friendship and direction.* Downers Grove, IL: InterVarsity Press.

Benner, D. G. (2004b). *The gift of being yourself: The sacred call to self-discovery.* Downers Grove, IL: InterVarsity Press.

Benson, B. E. (2002). *Graven ideologies: Nietzsche, Derrida & Marion on modern idolatry.* Downers Grove, IL: InterVarsity Press.

Bergin, A. E. (1980). Psychotherapy and religious values. *Journal of Consulting and Clinical Psychology, 48,* 95-105.

Bergin, A. E. (1988). Three contributions of a spiritual perspective to counseling, psychotherapy, and behavior change. *Counseling and Values, 32,* 21-31.

Bergin, A. E., & Garfield, S. L. (Eds.). (1971). *Handbook of psychotherapy and behavior change.* New York: Wiley.

Bergin, A. E., & Garfield, S. L. (Eds.). (1994a). *Handbook of psychotherapy and behavior change* (4th ed.). New York: Wiley.

Bergin, A. E., & Garfield, S. L. (1994b). Overview, trends, and future issues. In A. E. Bergin & S. L. Garfield (Eds.), *Handbook of psychotherapy and behavior change* (4th ed., pp. 821-30). New York: Wiley.

Berkeley, G. (1929). Alciphron. In M. W. Calkins (Ed.). *Berkeley: Essay, principles, dialogues* (pp. 345-400). New York: Charles Scribner's Sons.

Berkhof, L. (1939). *Systematic theology.* Grand Rapids, MI: Eerdmans.

Berkhof, H. (1962). *Christ and the powers.* Scottdale, PA: Mennonite Publishing House.

Berkhof, H. (1979). *Christ: The meaning of history.* Grand Rapids, MI: Baker.

Berkouwer, G. C. (1952a). *Faith and sanctification.* Grand Rapids, MI: Eerdmans.

Berkouwer, G. C. (1952b). *The providence of God.* Grand Rapids, MI: Eerdmans.

Berkouwer, G. C. (1962). *Man: The image of God.* Grand Rapids, MI: Eerdmans.

Berkouwer, G. C. (1971). *Sin.* Grand Rapids, MI: Eerdmans.

Berkouwer, G. C. (1975). *Holy Scripture.* Grand Rapids, MI: Eerdmans.

Bernard of Clairvaux. (1953). *St. Bernard of Clairvaux seen through his selected letters.* Chicago: Henry Regnery.

Bernard of Clairvaux. (1983). *The love of God and spiritual friendship.* Portland, OR: Multnomah.

Bernstein, R. J. (1971). *Praxis and action.* Philadelphia: University of Pennsylvania Press.

Bernstein, R. J. (1980). *The restructuring of social and political theory.* Philadelphia: University of Pennsylvania Press.

Bernstein, R. J. (1985). *Beyond objectivism and relativism: Science, hermeneutics, and praxis.* Philadelphia: University of Pennsylvania Press.

Bertalanffy, L. (1976). *General systems theory.* New York: George Braziller.

Beutler, L. E., & Bergan, J. (1991). Value change in counseling and psychotherapy: A search for scientific credibility. *Journal of Counseling Psychology, 38,* 16-24.

Beutler, L. E., & Clarkin, J. F. (1990). *Systematic treatment selection: Toward targeted therapeutic interventions.* New York: Brunner/Mazel.

Beutler, L. E., & Harwood, T. M. (2000). *Prescriptive psychotherapy: A practical guide to systematic treatment selection.* New York: Oxford University Press.

Beutler, L. E., Malik, M., Alimohamed, S., Harwood, T. M., Talebi, H., Noble, H., & Wong, E. (2003). Therapist variables. In M. J. Lambert (Ed.), *Bergin and Garfield's handbook of psychotherapy and behavior change* (pp. 227-306). New York: Wiley & Sons.

Bhaskar, R. (1986). *Scientific realism and human emancipation.* London: Verso.

Bhaskar, R. (1997). *A realist theory of science* (2nd ed.). London: Verso.

Bhaskar, R. (1998). *The possibility of naturalism: A philosophical critique of the contemporary human sciences* (3rd ed.). London: Routledge.

Bird, A. (2000). *Thomas Kuhn.* Princeton, NJ: Princeton University Press.

Bloesch, D. (1978). *Essentials of evangelical theology, Vol. 1: God, authority, and salvation.* New York: Harper & Row.

Bloom, B. S. (Ed.). (1956). *Taxonomy of educational objectives handbook I: Cognitive domain.* New York: Longman.

Board of Publications. (1976). *Psalter hymnal.* Grand Rapids, MI: Christian Reformed Church.

Bobgan, M., & Bobgan, D. (1985). *How to counsel from Scripture.* Chicago: Moody Press.

Bobgan, M., & Bobgan, D. (1987). *Psychoheresy: The psychological seduction of Christianity.* Santa Barbara, CA: EastGate.

Bobgan, M., & Bobgan, D. (1989a). *Prophets of psychoheresy, Vol. I.* Santa Barbara, CA: EastGate.

Bobgan, M., & Bobgan, D. (1989b). *Prophets of psychoheresy, Vol. II.* Santa Barbara, CA: EastGate.

Bobgan, M., & Bobgan, D. (1994). *Against biblical counseling: For the Bible.* Santa Barbara, CA: EastGate.

Bobgan, M., & Bobgan, D. (2004). *Christ-centered ministry versus problem-centered counseling.* Santa Barbara, CA: EastGate.

Boisen, A. T. (1936). *The exploration of the inner world.* New York: Harper & Row.

Boivin, M. J. (2002). Finding god in prozac or finding prozac in God: Preserving a Christian view of the person amidst a biopsychological revolution. *Christian Scholar's Review, 32*(2), 161-78.

Bonaventure. (1946). *Breviloquium.* St. Louis, MO: B. Herder.

Bonaventure. (1978). *The soul's journey into God. The tree of life. The life of St. Francis.* New York: Paulist Press.

Bonger, B., & Beutler, L. E. (1995). *Comprehensive textbook of psychotherapy: Theory and practice.* New York: Oxford University Press.

Bonhoeffer, D. (1955). *Ethics*. New York: Macmillan.

Bonhoeffer, D. (1966). *Christ the center*. New York: Harper & Row.

Bonhoeffer, D. (1985). *Spiritual care*. Philadelphia: Fortress.

Bookman, D. (1994a). The Godward focus of biblical counseling. In J. F. MacArthur & W. A. Mack (Eds.), *Introduction to biblical counseling* (pp. 154-72). Dallas: Word.

Bookman, D. (1994b). The scriptures and biblical counseling. In J. F. MacArthur & W. A. Mack (Eds.), *Introduction to biblical counseling* (pp. 63-96). Dallas: Word.

Boston. T. (n. d.). *Human nature in its fourfold state*. Grand Rapids, MI: Associated Publishers and Authors. (Original work published 1720)

Boszormenyi-Nagy, I., & Spark, G. (1973). *Invisible loyalties*. New York: Harper & Row.

Bouchard, T. J., Jr., Lykken, D. T., McGue, M., Segal, N. L., & Tellegen, A. (1990). Sources of human psychological differences: The Minnesota study of twins reared apart. *Science, 250,* 223-28.

Bouissac, P. (Ed.). (1998a). *Encyclopedia of semiotics*. New York: Oxford University Press.

Bouissac, P. (1998b). Neurosemiotics. In P. Bouissac (Ed.), *Encyclopedia of semiotics* (pp. 446-47). New York: Oxford University Press.

Bouma-Prediger, S. (1990). The task of integration: A modest proposal. *Journal of Psychology and Theology, 18,* 21-31.

Bowen, M. (1978). *Family therapy in clinical practice*. Narthvale, NJ: Jason Aronson.

Bowlby, J. (1969/1982). *Attachment and loss: Vol. 1. Attachment*. New York: Basic Books.

Boyce, J. P. (1887). *Abstract of systematic theology* (Reprint ed.). Hanford, CA: den Dulk Christian Foundation.

Boyd, G. A. (1997). *God at war*. Downers Grove, IL: InterVarsity Press.

Braaten, C. E. (1984). Prolegomena to Christian dogmatics. In C. A. Braaten & R. W. Jenson (Eds.), *Christian dogmatics* (pp. 1-78). Philadelphia: Fortress.

Bradley, R., & Swartz, N. (1979). *Possible worlds: An introduction to logic and its philosophy*. Indianapolis: Hackett.

Bradley, S. J. (2000). *Affect regulation and the development of psychopathology*. New York: Guildford.

Braine, D. (1992). *The human person: Animal & spirit*. Notre Dame, IN: University of Notre Dame Press.

Braumann, G. (1975). Form. In C. Brown (Ed.), *Dictionary of New Testament theology, Vol. 1* (pp. 703-10). Grand Rapids, MI: Zondervan.

Bray, G. L. (1996). *Biblical interpretation: Past and present*. Downers Grove, IL: InterVarsity Press.

Bray, G. L. (2002). Has the Christian doctrine of God been corrupted by Greek philosophy? In D. S. Huffman & E. L. Johnson (Eds.), *God under fire: Modern scholarship reinvents God* (pp. 105-18). Grand Rapids, MI: Zondervan.

Breshears, G., & Larzelere, R. E. (1981). The authority of scripture and the unity of revelation: A response to Crabb. *Journal of Psychology and Theology, 9,* 312-17.

Brett, G. S. (1953). *Brett's history of psychology*, R. S. Peters (Ed.). London: George Allen & Unwin.

Briggs, R. S. (2001). *Words in action: Speech act theory and biblical interpretation: Toward a hermeneutic of self-involvement.* Edinburgh: T & T Clark.

Bright, P. (Ed.). (1999). *Augustine and the Bible.* Notre Dame, IN: University of Notre Dame Press.

Brinton, C. (1967). Enlightenment. In P. Edwards (Ed.), *The encyclopedia of philosophy, Vol. 2* (pp. 519-25). New York: Macmillan.

Brody, A. L., Saxena, S., Stoessel, P., Gillies, L. A., Fairbanks, L. A., Alborzian, S., Phelps, M. E., Huang, S. C., Wu, H. M., Ho, M. L., Ho, M. K., Au, S. C., Maidment, K., & Baxter, L. R. (2001). Regional brain metabolic changes in patients with major depression treated with either paroxetine or interpersonal therapy. *Archives of General Psychiatry, 58,* 631-40.

Broger, J. (1991). *Self-confrontation manual.* Palm Desert, CA: Biblical Counseling Foundation.

Bronfenbrenner, U. (1979). *The ecology of human development.* Cambridge, MA: Harvard University Press.

Brooke, J. H. (1991). *Science and religion: Some historical perspectives.* Cambridge: Cambridge University Press.

Brooks, T. (1980). *The works of Thomas Brooks* (Vols. 1-6). Edinburgh: Banner of Truth Trust. (Original work published 1861-1867)

Brown, C., & Augusta-Scott, T. (2006). *Narrative therapy: Making meaning, making lives.* Thousand Oaks, CA: Sage.

Brown, P. (1967). *Augustine of Hippo.* Berkeley: University of California Press.

Brown, W. P. (2002). *Character & Scripture: Moral formation, community, and biblical interpretation.* Grand Rapids, MI: Eerdmans.

Brown, W. S. (1998). Cognitive contributions to the soul. In W. S. Brown, N. Murphy & H. N. Malony (Eds.), *Whatever happened to the soul? Scientific and theological portraits of human nature* (pp. 99-126). Minneapolis: Augsburg Fortress.

Brown, W. S., Murphy, N., & Malony, H. N. (1998). *Whatever happened to the soul? Scientific and theological portraits of human nature.* Minneapolis: Augsburg Fortress.

Browning, D. S. (1966). *Atonement and psychotherapy.* Philadelphia: Westminster Press.

Browning, D. S. (1983). *Religious ethics and pastoral care.* Philadelphia: Fortress.

Browning, D. S. (1987). *Religious thought and the modern psychotherapies.* Minneapolis: Augsburg.

Browning, D. S. (1990). *A fundamental practical theology: Descriptive and strategic proposals.* Minneapolis: Fortress.

Browning, D. S. (2000). *From culture wars to common ground.* Louisville: Westminster John Knox.

Browning, D. S. (2003). *Marriage and modernization: How globalization threatens marriage, and what to do about it.* Grand Rapids, MI: Eerdmans.

Browning, D. S. (2006). *Christian ethics and the moral psychologies.* Grand Rapids, MI: Eerdmans.

Browning, D. S., & Cooper, T. D. (2004). *Religious thought and the modern psychotherapies* (2nd ed.). Minneapolis: Augsburg Fortress.

Brueggeman, W. (1997). *Theology of the Old Testament.* Minneapolis: Fortress.

Brueggeman W., Plancher, W. C., & Blount, B. K. (2002). *Struggling with Scripture.* Louisville, KY: Westminster John Knox.

Bruner, J. S. (1983). *Children's talk.* New York: Norton.

Brunner, E. (1939). *Man in revolt.* New York: Charles Scribner's Sons.

Brunner, E. (1946). *Revelation and reason.* Philadelphia: Westminster Press.

Bucci, W. (1997). *Psychoanalysis & cognitive science: A multiple code theory.* New York: Guilford.

Buckley, E. (1994). *Why Christians can't trust psychology.* Eugene, OR: Harvest House.

Bufford, R. K. (1981). *The human reflex: Behavioral psychology in biblical perspective.* San Francisco: Harper & Row.

Bufford, R. K. (1988). *Counseling and the demonic.* Waco, TX: Word.

Bugental, D. B., & Goodnow, J. J. (1998). Socialization processes. In W. Damon (Series Ed.) & N. Eisenberg (Vol. Ed.), *Handbook of child psychology: Vol.3. Social, emotional, and personality development* (5th ed., pp. 389-462). New York: John Wiley & Sons.

Bugental, J. F. T. (1965). *The search for authenticity.* New York: Holt, Rinehart and Winston.

Bugental, J. F. T. (1981). *The search for authenticity* (Enlarged ed.). New York: Irvington.

Bunyan, J. (1977). *The works of John Bunyan.* Grand Rapids, MI: Baker. (Originally published 1682)

Burke, K. (1945). *A grammar of motives.* Berkeley: University of California Press.

Burn, S. M. (2004). *Groups: Theory and practice.* Belmont, CA: Thomson Wadsworth.

Burns, J. P. (1989). Grace: The Augustinian foundation. In B. McGinn & J. Meyendorff (Eds.), *Christian spirituality: Origins to the twelfth century* (pp. 331-49). New York: Crossroad.

Burton, R. (1875). *Anatomy of melancholy.* New York: W. J. Widdleton. (Original work published 1621)

Buss, D. (1999). *Evolutionary psychology: The new science of the mind.* Boston: Allyn & Bacon.

Butterfield, H. (1957). *The origins of modern science 1300-1800* (Rev. ed.). New York: Free Press.

Bynum, C. W. (1979). *Docere verbo et exemplo: An aspect of twelfth-century spirituality* (Harvard Theological Studies, No. 31). Missoula, MT: Scholars Press.

Cacioppo, J. T., Berntson, G. G., Adolphs, R., Carter, C. S., Davidson, R. J., McClintock, M. K., McEwen, B. S., Meaney, M. J., Schacter, D. L., Sternberg, E. M., Suomi, S. S., & Taylor, S. E. (2002). *Foundations in social neuroscience.* Cambridge, MA: MIT Press.

Cacioppo, J. T., Berntson, G. G., Ernst, J. M., & Ito, T. A. (2000). Social neuroscience. In A. E. Kazdin (Ed.), *Encyclopedia of psychology* (Vol. 7, pp. 353-55). New York: Oxford.

Cacioppo, J. T., Berntson, G. G., Larsen, J. T., Poehlmann, K. M., & Ito, T. A. (2000). The psychophysiology of emotion. In M. Lewis & J. M. Haviland-Jones (Eds.), *Handbook of emotions* (2nd ed., pp. 173-91). New York: Guilford.

Cacioppo, J. T., Berntson, G. G., Sheridon, J. F., & McClintock, M. K. (2002). Multilevel integrative analyses of human behavior: Social neuroscience and the complementing nature of social and biological approaches. In J. T.Cacioppo, G. G. Berntson, R. Adolphs, C. S. Carter, R. J. Davidson, M. K. McClintock, B. S. McEwen, M. J. Meaney, D. L. Schacter, E. M. Sternberg, S. S. Suomi, & S. E. Taylor (Eds.), *Foundations in social neuroscience* (pp. 21-46). Cambridge, MA: MIT Press.

Calkins, S. D. (2004). Early attachment processes and the development of emotional self-regulation. In R. F. Baumeister & K. D. Vohs (Eds.), *The handbook of self-regulation* (pp. 324-55). New York: Guilford.

Calvin, J. (1960). *The institutes of the Christian religion.* Philadelphia: Westminster Press. (Originally published 1559)

Calvin, J. (1979). *Calvin's commentaries* (Reprint ed.). Grand Rapids, MI: Baker.

Cameron, A. (1991). *Christianity and the rhetoric of empire: The development of Christian discourse.* Berkeley: University of California Press.

Cameron, M. (1999). Sign. In A. D. Fitzgerald (Ed.), *Augustine through the ages* (pp. 793-98). Grand Rapids, MI: Eerdmans.

Campbell, S. B., Pierce, E. W., March, C. L., Ewing, L. J., & Szumowski, E. K. (1994). Hard-to-manage preschool boys: Symptomatic behavior across contexts and time. *Child Development, 65,* 836-51.

Canning, S. S., Case, P. W., Kruse, S. L. (2001). Contemporary psychological scholarship and "the least of these": An empirical review. *Journal of Psychology and Christianity, 20,* 205-23.

Canning, S. S., Pozzi, C. F., McNeil, J. D., & McMinn, M. R. (2000). Integration as service: Implications of faith-praxis integration for training. *Journal of Psychology and Theology, 28,* 201-11.

Cantor, N. (1990). From thought to behavior: "Having" and "doing" in the study of personality and cognition. *American Psychologist, 45,* 735-50.

Capps, D. (1981). *Biblical approaches to pastoral counseling.* Philadelphia: Westminster Press.

Capps, D. (1987). *Deadly sins and saving virtues.* Philadelphia: Fortress.

Capps, D. (1990a). Bible, pastoral use and interpretation of. In R. J. Hunter (Ed.), *Dictionary of pastoral care and counseling* (pp. 82-85). Nashville: Abingdon.

Capps, D. (1990b). *Reframing: A new method in pastoral care.* Minneapolis: Fortress.

Capps, D. (1993). *The depleted self: Sin in a narcissistic age.* Minneapolis: Fortress.

Capps, D. (1995). *Agents of hope: A pastoral psychology.* Minneapolis: Fortress.

Carey, G. (2003). *Human genetics for the social sciences.* Thousand Oaks, CA: Sage.

Carlsen, M. B. (1996). Metaphor, meaning-making, and metamorphosis. In H. Rosen & K. T. Kuehlwein (Eds.), *Constructing realities: Meaning-making perspectives for psychotherapists*. San Francisco: Jossey-Bass.

Carpenter, J. (1998). *Revive us again*. Oxford: Oxford University Press.

Carson, D. A. (1991). *The gospel according to John*. Grand Rapids, MI: Eerdmans.

Carson, D. A. (2000). *The difficult doctrine of the love of God*. Downers Grove, IL: InterVarsity Press.

Carter, C. S. (2002). Neuroendocrine perspectives on social attachment and love. In J. T. Cacioppo, G. G. Berntson, R. Adolphs, C. S. Carter, R. J. Davidson, M. K. McClintock, B. S. McEwen, M. J. Meaney, D. L. Schacter, E. M. Sternberg, S. S. Suomi & S. E. Taylor (Eds.), *Foundations in social neuroscience* (pp. 853-90). Cambridge, MA: MIT Press.

Carter, J. D. (1975). Adams' theory of nouthetic counseling. *Journal of Psychology and Theology, 3*(3), 143-55.

Carter, J. D., & Narramore, B. (1979). *Integration of psychology and theology*. Grand Rapids, MI: Zondervan.

Carter, J. D., Okamoto, T., Barnhurst, L., & Bheinheimer, R. (2003, June). The challenge of new integrated treatments for mood disorder patients. Paper presented at the national conference of the Christian Association for Psychological Studies, Anaheim, CA.

Carter, L., & Minirth, F. (1993). *The anger workbook*. Nashville: Thomas Nelson.

Carver, C. S. (2003). Self-awareness. In M. R. Leary & J. P. Tangney (Eds.), *Handbook of self and identity* (pp. 179-95). New York: Guilford.

Carver, C. S., & Scheier, M. F. (1981). *Attention and self-regulation: A control-theory approach to human behavior*. New York: Spring-Verlag.

Carver, C. S., & Scheier, M. F. (2002). Optimism. In C. R. Snyder & S. J. Lopez (Eds.), *Handbook of positive psychology* (pp. 231-43). Oxford: Oxford University Press.

Cary, P. (1999). Interiority. In A. D. Fitzgerald (Ed.), *Augustine through the ages: An encyclopedia* (pp. 454-56). Grand Rapids, MI: Eerdmans.

Case, R. (1998). The development of conceptual structures. In W. Damon (Series Ed.) & D. Kuhn & R. S. Siegler (Vol. Eds.), *Handbook of child psychology: Vol.2. Cognition, perception, and language* (5th ed., pp. 745-800). New York: John Wiley & Sons.

Cassian, J. (1985). *Conferences* (Colm Luibheid, Trans.). New York: Paulist.

Caussade, J.-P. (1986). *The joy of full surrender*. Brewster, MA: Paraclete.

Cavanagh, R. R. (1978). The term religion. In T. W. Hall (Ed.), *Introduction to the study of religion* (pp. 4-19). New York: Harper & Row.

Cayre, F. (1935). *Manual of patrology*. Philadelphia: Peter Reilly.

Chadwick, H. (1967). *The early church*. New York: Penguin.

Chalmers, A. F. (1982). *What is this thing called science?* (2nd ed.). St. Lucia, Australia: University of Queensland Press.

Chamblin, J. K. (1993). *Paul and the self: Apostolic teaching for personal wholeness*. Grand Rapids, MI: Baker.

Chan, S. (1998). *Spiritual theology: A systematic study of the Christian life*. Downers Grove, IL: InterVarsity Press.

Chang, E. C., & Sanna, L. J. (Eds.). (2003). *Virtue, vice, and personality: The complexity of behavior*. Washington, DC: American Psychological Association.

Chapman, M. D. (2002). Introduction: The past, present and future of liberal theology. In M. D. Chapman (Ed.), *The future of liberal theology* (pp. 3-17). Hants, UK: Ashgate.

Charry, E. T. (1997). *By the renewing of your minds: The pastoral function of Christian doctrine*. New York: Oxford University Press.

Childs, B. (1992). *Biblical theology of the Old and New Testaments*. Minneapolis: Fortress.

Chisholm, R. M. (1986). *Brentano and intrinsic value*. New York: Cambridge University Press.

Cicchetti, D., & Walker, E. F. (2003). *Neurodevelopmental mechanisms of psychopathology*. New York: Cambridge University Press.

Clark, L. A., & Watson, D. (1999). Temperament: A new paradigm for trait psychology. In L. A. Pervin & O. P. John (Eds.), *Handbook of personality* (pp. 399-423). New York: Guilford.

Clarkin, J. F., & Levy, K. N. (2004). The influence of client variables on psychotherapy. In M. J. Lambert (Ed.), *Bergin and Garfield's handbook of psychotherapy and behavior change* (5th ed., pp. 194-226). New York: John Wiley & Sons.

Clinebell, H. J., Jr. (1966). *Basic types of pastoral counseling*. Nashville: Abingdon.

Clinton, T., & Ohlschlager G. (2002). Competent Christian counseling: Definitions and dynamics. In T. Clinton & G. Ohlschlager (Eds.), *Competent Christian counseling* (pp. 36-68). Colorado Springs, CO: Waterbrook.

Clinton, T., & Sibcy, G. (2002). *Attachments: Why you love, feel, and act the way you do*. Brentwood, TN: Integrity.

Clore, G. C. (1994). Why emotions are felt. In P. Ekman & R. J. Davidson (Eds.), *The nature of emotion: Fundamental questions* (pp. 103-11). New York: Oxford University Press.

Cloud, H., & Townsend, J. (1995). *Boundaries*. Grand Rapids, MI: Zondervan.

Cloud, H., & Townsend, J. (2001). *How people grow: What the Bible reveals about personal growth*. Grand Rapids, MI: Zondervan.

Clouser, R. A. (1991). *The myth of religious neutrality*. Notre Dame, IN: University of Notre Dame Press.

Coe, J. H. (1999). Beyond relationality: Musings towards a pneumadynamic approach to personality and psychopathology. *Journal of Psychology and Christianity, 18*, 109-28.

Cohen, I. B. (Ed.). (1990). *Puritanism and the rise of modern science: The Merton thesis*. New Brunswick, NJ: Rutgers University Press.

Cole, M., & Scribner, S. (1978). *Mind in society: The development of higher psychological processes. L. S. Vygotsky*. Cambridge, MA: Harvard University Press.

Collier, A. (1994). *Critical realism: An introduction to Roy Bhaskar's philosophy*. London: Verso.

Collins, G. (1969). *Search for reality: Psychology and the Christian.* Wheaton, IL: Key Publishers.

Collins, G. (1977). *The rebuilding of psychology: An integration of psychology and Christianity.* Wheaton, IL: Tyndale House.

Collins, G. (1980). *Christian counseling: A comprehensive guide.* Waco, TX: Word.

Collins, G. (1981). *Psychology and theology: Prospects for integration.* Nashville: Abingdon.

Collins. G. (1993). *The biblical basis of Christian counseling for people helpers.* Colorado Springs, CO: NavPress.

Collins, G. (1994). *The biblical basis of Christian counseling.* Waco, TX: Word.

Collins, G. (2000). An integration view. In E. L. Johnson & S. L. Jones (Eds.), *Psychology and Christianity: Four views* (pp. 102-29). Downers Grove, IL: InterVarsity Press.

Colquhoun, J. (1965). *Repentance.* Edinburgh: Banner of Truth Trust. (Original work published 1826)

Colquhoun, J. (1998). *Spiritual comfort.* Ligonier, PA: Soli Deo Gloria. (Original work published 1814)

Congar, Y. M.-J. (1968). *A history of theology.* Garden City, NY: Doubleday.

Conn, W. E. (1981). *Conscience: Development and self-transcendence.* Birmingham, AL: Religious Education Press.

Connell, G. (1985). *To be one thing: Personal unity in Kierkegaard's thought.* Macon, GA: Mercer University Press.

Cook, W. R., & Herzman, R. B. (1983). *The medieval world view.* New York: Oxford University Press.

Cooper, J. W. (2000). *Body, soul, and life everlasting.* Grand Rapids, MI: Eerdmans.

Cooper, T. D. (2006). *Paul Tillich and psychology.* Macon, GA: Mercer University Press.

Corduan, W. (1991). *Mysticism: An evangelical option?* Grand Rapids, MI: Zondervan.

Corey, G. (1991). *Theory and practice of counseling and psychotherapy* (4th ed.). Pacific Grove, CA: Brooks/Cole.

Cotterell, P., & Turner, M. (1989). *Linguistics and biblical interpretation.* Downers Grove, IL: InterVarsity Press.

Counts, W. M. (1973). The nature of man and the Christian's self-esteem. *Journal of Psychology and Theology, 1,* 67-78.

Cozolino, L. (2002). *The neuroscience of psychotherapy: Building and rebuilding the human brain.* New York: Norton.

Crabb, L. J., Jr. (1975). *Basic principles of biblical counseling.* Grand Rapids, MI: Zondervan.

Crabb, L. J., Jr. (1977). *Effective biblical counseling.* Grand Rapids, MI: Zondervan.

Crabb, L. J., Jr. (1981). Biblical authority and Christian psychology. *Journal of Psychology and Theology, 9,* 305-11.

Crabb, L. J., Jr. (1987). *Understanding people: Deep longings for relationship.* Grand Rapids, MI: Zondervan.

Crabb, L. J., Jr. (1988). *Inside out.* Colorado Springs, CO: NavPress.

Crabb, L. J., Jr. (1991). *Men and women: Enjoying the difference.* Grand Rapids, MI: Zondervan.

Crabb, L. J., Jr. (1993). *Finding God.* Colorado Springs, CO: NavPress.

Crabb, L. J., Jr. (1997). *Connecting: A radical new vision.* Waco, TX: Word.

Crabb, L. J., Jr. (1999). *The safest place on earth.* Colorado Springs, CO: Waterbrook.

Crabb, L. J., Jr. (2002). *The pressure's off.* Colorado Springs, CO: Waterbrook.

Crabb, L. J., Jr. (2003). *Soul-talk.* Nashville: Integrity.

Crabb, L. J., Jr. (2006). *The PAPA prayer: The prayer you've never prayed.* Nashville: Integrity.

Crabb, L., & Allender, D. B. (1996). *Hope when you're hurting.* Grand Rapids, MI: Zondervan.

Craik, F. I. M., & Lockhart, R. S. (1972). Levels of processing: A framework for memory research. *Journal of Verbal Learning and Verbal Behavior, 11,* 671-84.

Craik, F. I. M., Moroz, T. M., Moscovitch, M., Stuss, D. T., Winocur, G., Tulving, E., & Kapur, S. (2002). In search of the self: A positron emission tomography study. In J. T. Cacioppo, G. G. Berntson, R. Adolphs, C. S. Carter, R. J. Davidson, M. K. McClintock, B. S. McEwen, M. J. Meaney, D. L. Schacter, E. M. Sternberg, S. S. Suomi, & S. E. Taylor (Eds.), *Foundations in social neuroscience* (pp. 189-201). Cambridge, MA: MIT Press.

Craik, F. I. M., & Tulving, E. (1971). Depth of processing and the retention of words in episodic memory. *Journal of Experimental Psychology, 104,* 268-94.

Crocker, J., & Park, L. E. (2003). Seeking self-esteem: Construction, maintenance, and protection of self-worth. In M. R. Leary & J. P. Tangney (Eds.), *Handbook of self and identity* (pp. 291-313). New York: Guilford.

Cushman, P. (1995). *Constructing the self, constructing America: A cultural history of psychotherapy.* Reading, MA: Addison-Wesley.

Damasio, A. (1994). *Descartes' error: Emotion, reason, and the human brain.* New York: Putnam.

Damon, W. (1988). *The moral child.* New York: Free Press.

Damon, W. (Ed.). (1998). *Handbook of child development* (5th ed., 4 vols.). New York: John Wiley & Sons.

Danaher, W. J., Jr. (2004). *The trinitarian ethics of Jonathan Edwards.* Louisville, KY: Westminster John Knox.

Daniel, S. H. (1994). *The philosophy of Jonathan Edwards.* Bloomington: Indiana University Press.

Danielou, J. (1969). *God's life in us.* New York: Dimension.

Danielou, J. (1996). *Prayer: The mission of the church.* Grand Rapids, MI: Eerdmans.

Danziger, K. (1979). The social origins of modern psychology. In A. R. Buss (Ed.), *Psychology in social context* (pp. 27-45). New York: Irvington.

Danziger, K. (1990). *Constructing the subject: Historical origins of psychological research.* New York: Cambridge University Press.

Danziger, K. (1998). *Naming the mind: How psychology found its language.* London: Sage.

d'Aquili, E. G., & Newberg, A. B. (1999). *The mystic mind: Probing the biology of religious experience.* Minneapolis: Fortress.

Davidson, D. (1980). *Actions and events.* Oxford: Oxford University Press.

Davidson, R. J. (1992). Anterior cerebral asymmetry and the nature of emotion. *Brain and Cognition, 6,* 245-68.

Davies, H. (1970). *Worship and theology in England, Vol. 1: From Cranmer to Hooer, 1534-1603.* Princeton, NJ: Princeton University Press.

Davies, H. (1990). *The worship of the American puritans.* New York: Peter Lang.

Davis, E. P., Bruce, J., & Gunnar, M. R. (2002). The anterior attention network: Associations with temperament and neuroendocrine activity in six-year-old children. *Developmental Psychobiology, 40,* 43-56.

Deason, G. B. Reformation theology and the mechanistic conception of nature. In D. C. Lindberg & R. L. Numbers (Eds.), *God and nature: Historical essays of the encounter between Christianity and science* (pp. 167-91). Berkeley: University of California Press.

Deci, E. L., & Ryan, R. M. (1985). *Intrinsic motivation and self-determination in human behavior.* New York: Plenum Press.

Deci, E. L., & Ryan, R. M. (Eds.). (2002). *Handbook of self-determination research.* Rochester, NY: University of Rochester Press.

Deely, J. (1998). Augustine of Hippo. In P. Bouissac (Ed.), *Encyclopedia of semiotics* (pp. 51-53). New York: Oxford University Press.

Delitzsch, F. (1966). *A system of biblical psychology.* Grand Rapids, MI: Baker.

Deloache, J. S., Miller, K. F., & Pierroutsakos, S. L. (1998). Reasoning and problem solving. In W. Damon (Series Ed.), D. Kuhn & R. S. Siegler (Vol. Eds.), *Handbook of child psychology: Vol. 2. Cognition, perception, and language* (5th ed., pp. 801-50). New York: Wiley.

Dembski, W. A. (1998). *The design inference.* New York: Cambridge University Press.

Dembski, W. A. (2002). *Intelligent design: The bridge between theology and science.* Downers Grove, IL: InterVarsity Press.

Dembski, W. A. (2006). http://www.designinference.com/documents/2006.05. christian_theodicy.pdf

DeMent, B. H., & Smith, E. W. (1988). Repent. In G. W. Bromiley (Ed.), *International standard Bible encyclopedia* (Vol. 4, pp. 135-37). Grand Rapids, MI: Eerdmans.

Dempster, S. G. (2000). Prophetic books. In T. D. Alexander, B. S. Rosner, D. A. Carson & G. Goldsworthy (Eds.), *New dictionary of biblical theology* (pp. 122-26). Downers Grove, IL: InterVarsity Press.

Dempster, S. G. (2004). *Dominion and dynasty: A biblical theology of the Hebrew Bible.* Downers Grove, IL: InterVarsity Press.

Derrida, J. (1976). *Of grammatology.* Baltimore: Johns Hopkins University Press.

Derrida, J. (1978). *Writing and difference.* Chicago: University of Chicago Press.

Derrida, J. (1981). *Positions* (A. Bass, Trans). Chicago: University of Chicago Press.

DeVries, M. (1982). Beyond integration. *Journal of psychology and Christianity, 2,* 320-25.

DeYoung, P. A. (2003). *Relational psychotherapy: A primer.* New York: Brunner Routledge.

Diamond, J. (2002). *Narrative means to sober ends: Treating addiction and its aftermath.* New York: Guilford.

Diener, E., & Diener, C. (1996). Most people are happy. *Psychological Science, 7,* 181-85.

Diener, E., & Lucas, R. E. (1999). Personality and subjective well-being. In D. Kahneman, E. Diener & N. Schwarz (Eds.), *Well-being: The foundations of hedonic psychology* (pp. 213-29). New York: Russell Sage.

Dies, R. R. (1995). Group psychotherapies. In A. S. Gurman & S. B. Messer (Eds.), *Essential psychotherapies: Theory and practice* (pp. 488-522). New York: Guilford.

Dionysius the Areopagite. (1920). *The divine names & the mystical theology.* London: SPCK.

Dobson, E. G. (1997). The Bible and the mission of the church. In E. Hindson & H. Eyrich (Eds.), *Totally sufficient: The Bible and Christian counseling* (pp. 237-47). Eugene, OR: Harvest House

Dobson, J. C. (1970). *Dare to discipline.* Wheaton, IL: Tyndale House.

Dobson, J. C. (1979). *Hide or seek.* Old Tappan, NJ: Revell.

Dockery, D. S. (1995). *Christian Scripture: An evangelical perspective on inspiration, authority, and interpretation.* Nashville: Broadman & Holman.

Doctrinal Standards of the Christian Reformed Church. (1976). *Psalter hymnal.* Grand Rapids, MI: Board of Publications of the Christian Reformed Church.

Doherty, W. J. (1995). *Soul searching: Why psychotherapy must promote moral responsibility.* New York: Basic Books.

Dooyeweerd, H. (1960). *In the twilight of Western thought.* Phillipsburg, NJ: Presbyterian & Reformed.

Dooyeweerd, H. (1979). *Roots of Western culture: Pagan, secular, and Christian options.* Toronto: Wedge.

Dooyeweerd, H. (1984). *A new critique of theoretical thought.* Jordan Station, ON: Paideia.

Draper, J. W. (1874). *History of the conflict between religion and science.* New York: D. Appleton.

Driscoll, M. S. (1993). Interiority, interior life. In M. Downey (Ed.), *The new dictionary of Catholic spirituality* (pp. 544-47). Collegeville, MN: Liturgical Press.

Duce, P. (1998). *Reading the mind of God: Interpretation in science and theology.* Leicester, UK: Apollos.

Dueck, A. (1995). *Between Jerusalem and Athens: Ethical perspectives on culture, religion, and psychotherapy.* Grand Rapids, MI: Baker.

Dueck, A., & Lee, C. (Eds.). (2005). *Why psychology needs theology: A radical-reformation perspective.* Grand Rapids, MI: Eerdmans.

Dueck, A., & Parsons, T. D. (2004). Integration discourse. Modern and postmodern. *Journal of Psychology and Theology, 32,* 232-47.

Dunn, J. D. G. (1988). *Romans 9-16*. Waco, TX: Word.

Dunn, J. D. G. (1998). *The theology of Paul the apostle*. Grand Rapids, MI: Eerdmans.

Durkin, K. (1995). *Developmental social psychology*. London: Blackwell.

Duval, S., & Wicklund, R. A. (1972). *A theory of objective self-awareness*. New York: Academic Press.

Dweck, C. S. (2000). *Self-theories: Their role in motivation, personality, and development*. Philadelphia: Taylor & Francis.

D'Zurilla, T., & Nezu, A. (1999). *Problem-solving therapy: A social competence approach to clinical interventions* (2nd ed.). New York: Springer.

Eccles, J. C., & Robinson, D. N. (1984). *The wonder of being human: Our brain and our mind*. New York: Free Press.

Eck, B. E. (1996). Integrating the integrators: An organizing framework for a multifaceted process of integration. *Journal of Psychology and Christianity*, 15, 101-15.

Eco, U. (1976). *A theory of semiotics*. Bloomington: Indiana University Press.

Edwards, J. (1959). *Religious affections*. New Haven, CT: Yale University Press. (Original work published 1746)

Edwards, J. (1960). *The nature of true virtue*. Ann Arbor: University of Michigan Press.

Edwards, J. (1969). *Charity and its fruits*. Edinburgh: Banner of Truth. (Original work published 1738)

Edwards, J. (1971). Observations on the trinity. In P. Helm (Ed.), *Treatise on grace and other posthumously published writings including observations on the trinity*. Greenwood, SC: Attic Press.

Edwards, J. (1974). *The works of Jonathan Edwards* (Vols. 1-2). Edinburgh: Banner of Truth Trust. (Original work published 1834)

Edwards, J. (1980). *The works of Jonathan Edwards: Vol. 6. Scientific and philosophical writings* (W. E. Anderson, Ed.). New Haven, CT: Yale University Press.

Edwards, J. (1989). *Ethical writings* (P. Ramsey, Ed.). New Haven, CT: Yale University Press.

Edwards, J. (1993). *The works of Jonathan Edwards: Vol. 11. Typological writings*. New Haven, CT: Yale University Press.

Edwards, J. (1994). *The works of Jonathan Edwards: Vol. 13. The "miscellanies," a-500: The Works of Jonathan Edwards*. New Haven, CT: Yale University Press.

Edwards, J. (1998). The end for which God created the world. In J. Piper (Ed.), *God's passion for his glory* (pp. 125-251). Wheaton, IL: Crossway. (Original work published 1765)

Edwards, J. (2003). *The works of Jonathan Edwards: Vol. 21. Writings on the trinity, grace, and faith* (S. H. Lee, Ed.). New Haven, CT: Yale University Press.

Egan, G. (1990). *The skilled helper: A systematic approach to effective helping* (4th ed.). Pacific Grove, CA: Brooks/Cole.

Egan, H. D. (1993a). Affirmative way. In M. Downey (Ed.), *The new dictionary of Catholic spirituality* (pp. 700-704). Collegeville, MN: Liturgical Press.

Egan, H. D. (1993b). Negative way. In M. Downey (Ed.), *The new dictionary of Catholic spirituality* (pp. 14-17). Collegeville, MN: Liturgical Press.

Eichrodt, W. (1961). *Theology of the Old Testament.* Philadelphia: Westminster Press.

Ekman, P. (1992). Are there basic emotions? *Psychological Review, 99,* 550-53.

Ekman, P. (1993). Facial expression and emotion. *American Psychologist, 48,* 384-92.

Eldridge, J. (2000). *The journey of desire.* Nashville: Thomas Nelson.

Ellingworth, P. (1993). *The epistle to the Hebrews.* Grand Rapids, MI: Eerdmans.

Elliott, R., Greenberg, L. S., & Lietaer, G. (2004). Research on experiential psychotherapies. In M. J. Lambert (Ed.), *Bergin and Garfield's handbook of psychotherapy and behavior change* (5th ed., pp. 493-540). New York: John Wiley & Sons.

Ellis, A. (1962). *Reason and emotion in psychotherapy.* New York: Lyle Stuart.

Ellis, A. (1973). *Humanistic psychotherapy: The rational-emotive approach.* New York: Julian.

Ellis, A. (1998). *Rational emotive behavior therapy: A therapist's guide.* New York: Impact.

Emlet, M. R. (2002). Let me draw you a picture: Understanding the influences of the human heart. *Journal of Biblical Counseling, 20*(2), 47-52.

Emlet, M. R. (2004). Obsessions and compulsions: Breaking free of the tyranny. *Journal of Biblical Counseling, 22*(2), 15-26.

Emmons, R. A. (1986). Personal strivings: An approach to personality and subjective well-being. *Journal of Personality and Social Psychology, 51,* 1058-68.

Emmons, R. A. (1997). Motives and goals. In R. Hogan, J. Johnson & S. Briggs (Eds.), *Handbook of personality psychology* (pp. 486-511). San Diego: Academic.

Emmons, R. A. (1999). *The psychology of ultimate concerns: Motivation and spirituality in personality.* New York: Guilford.

Encyclopedia of Marxism. (2006). http://www.marxists.org/glossary/terms/s/u.html.

Epstein, S. (1984). Controversial issues in emotion theory. In P. Shaver (Ed.), *Review of Personality and Social Psychology* (Vol. 5). Beverly Hills, CA: Sage.

Epstein, S. (1990). Cognitive-experiential self-theory. In L. Pervin (Ed.), *Handbook of personality: Theory and research* (pp. 165-92). New York: Guilford.

Epstein, S. (1994). Integration of the cognitive and the psychodynamic unconscious. *American Psychologist, 49,* 709-24.

Epstein, S. (1998). *Constructive thinking: The key to emotional intelligence.* New York: Praeger.

Erikson, E. H. (1959). *Identity and the life cycle.* New York: International Universities Press.

Erikson, E. H. (1962). *Young man Luther.* New York: Norton.

Erikson, E. H. (1963). *Childhood and society* (2nd ed.). New York: W. W. Norton.

Erikson, E. H. (1968). *Identity: Youth and crisis.* New York: W. W. Norton.

Erickson, M. J. (1983-1985). *Christian theology.* Grand Rapids, MI: Eerdmans.

Erickson, M. J., Helseth, P. K., & Taylor, J. (2004). Reclaiming the center: *Confronting evangelical accomodation in postmodern times.* Wheaton, IL: Crossway.

Eron, J. B., & Lund, T. W. (1996). *Narrative solutions in brief therapy.* New York: Guilford.

Evans, C. S. (1977). *Preserving the person.* Downers Grove, IL: InterVarsity Press.

Evans, C. S. (1989). *Wisdom and humanness in psychology: Prospects for a Christian approach.* Grand Rapids, MI: Baker.

Evans, C. S. (1990). *Søren Kierkegaard's Christian psychology.* Grand Rapids, MI: Baker.

Evans, G. R. (1985). *The language and logic of the Bible: The road to reformation.* Cambridge: Cambridge University Press.

Evans, R. I. (Ed.). (1975). *Carl Rogers: The man and his work.* New York: E. P. Dutton.

Everly, G. S., Jr., & Lating, J. M. (2002). *A clinical guide to the treatment of the human stress response* (2nd ed.). New York: Kluwer/Plenum.

Eyrich, H. A. (1979). The frigid wife in a good marriage. *The Journal of Pastoral Practice, 3* (3), 31-33.

Fairbairn, W. R. D. (1952). *An object-relations theory of the personality.* New York: Basic Books.

Farley, E. (1982). *Ecclesial reflection: An anatomy of theological method.* Philadelphia: Fortress.

Farnsworth, K. E. (1985). *Whole-hearted integration: Harmonizing psychology and Christianity through word and deed.* Grand Rapids, MI: Baker.

Farone, S. V., Tsuang, M. T., & Tsuang, D. W. (1999). *Genetics of mental disorders: A guide for students, clinicians, and researchers.* New York: Guilford.

Fay, B. (1987). *Critical social science.* Ithaca, NY: Cornell University Press.

Feinberg, J. S. (Ed.). (1988). *Continuity and discontinuity: Perspectives on the relationship between the Old and New Testaments.* Westchester, IL: Crossway.

Ferguson, E. (1993). *Backgrounds of early Christianity* (2nd ed.). Grand Rapids, MI: Eerdmans.

Ferguson, S. B. (1981). *The Christian life.* Edinburgh: Banner of Truth Trust.

Ferguson, S. B. (1987). *John Owen on the Christian life.* Edinburgh: Banner of Truth Trust.

Ferguson, S. B. (1988). How does the Bible look at itself? In H. M.Conn (Ed.), *Inerrancy and hermeneutic: A tradition, a challenge, a debate* (pp. 47-66). Grand Rapids, MI: Baker.

Ferguson, S. B. (1996). *The Holy Spirit.* Downers Grove, IL: InterVarsity Press.

Ferguson, T. J., Stegge, H., & Damhuis, I. (1991). Children's understanding of guilt and shame. *Child Development, 62,* 827-39.

Ferrari, M., & Sternberg, R. J. (Eds.). (1998a). *Self-awareness: Its nature and development.* New York: Guilford.

Ferrari, M., & Sternberg, R. J. (1998b). The development of mental abilities and styles. In W. Damon (Series Ed.) & D. Kuhn & R. S. Siegler (Vol. Eds.), *Handbook of child psychology: Vol. 2. Cognition, perception, and language* (5th ed., pp. 899-945). New York: John Wiley.

Fischer, K. W., & Bidell, T. R. (1998). Dynamic development of psychological structures in action and thought. In W. Damon (Series Ed.) & R. M. Lerner (Vol. Ed.), *Handbook of child psychology: Vol. 1. Theoretical models of human development* (5th ed., pp. 467-562). New York: John Wiley & Sons.

Fiske, S. T., & Taylor, S. E. (1984). *Social cognition*. New York: Random House.

Fitzpatrick, E. (1999). *Love to eat, hate to eat: Breaking the bondage of destructive eating habits.* Eugene, OR: Harvest House.

Flavell, J. H., & Miller, P. H. (1998). Social cognition. In W. Damon (Series Ed.) & D. Kuhn & R. S. Siegler (Vol. Eds.), *Handbook of child psychology: Vol.2. Cognition, perception, and language* (5th ed., pp. 851-98). New York: John Wiley & Sons.

Fonagy, P. (2002). Psychoanalytic theory from the viewpoint of attachment theory and research. In J. Cassidy & P. R. Shaver (Eds.), *Handbook of attachment: Theory, research, and clinical applications* (pp. 595-624). New York: Guilford.

Ford, D. F. (1999). *Self and salvation: Being transformed.* Cambridge: Cambridge University Press.

Forde, G. O. (1988). The Lutheran view. In D. Alexander (Ed.), *Christian spirituality: Five views of sanctification* (pp. 13-46). Downers Grove, IL: InterVarsity Press.

Forward, M. (2000). Culture, religious faiths, and race. In J. Woodward & S. Pattison (Eds.), *The Blackwell reader in pastoral and practical theology* (pp. 248-56). London: Blackwell.

Foucault, M. (1970). *The order of things* (A. Sheridan, Trans.). New York: Random House.

Foucault, M. (1972). *The archaeology of knowledge* (A. Sheridan, Trans.). New York: Pantheon.

Foucault, M. (2005). *The hermeneutics of the subject*. New York: Palgrave Macmillan.

Fowers, B. J. (2000). *Beyond the myth of marital happiness.* San Francisco: Jossey-Bass.

Fowles, D. C. (1993). Biological variables in psychopathology: A psychobiological perspective. In P. B. Sutker & H. E. Adams (Eds.), *Comprehensive handbook of psychopathology* (2nd ed., pp. 57-82). New York: Plenum.

Frame, J. (1987). *The doctrine of the knowledge of God.* Phillipsburg, NJ: Presbyterian & Reformed.

Frame, J. (1995). *Cornelius Van Til: An analysis of his thought.* Phillipsburg, NJ: Presbyterian & Reformed.

Frame, J. (2002). *The doctrine of God.* Phillipsburg, NJ: Presbyterian & Reformed.

Francis, D. D., & Meaney, M. J. (2002). Maternal care and the development of stress responses. In J. T. Cacioppo, G. G. Berntson, R. Adolphs, C. S. Carter, R. J. Davidson, M. K. McClintock, B. S. McEwen, M. J. Meaney, D. L. Schacter, E. M. Sternberg, S. S. Suomi & S. E. Taylor (Eds.), *Foundations in social neuroscience* (pp. 763-73). Cambridge, MA: MIT Press.

Francis de Sales (1949). *Introduction to the devout life.* New York: Harper & Brothers.

Francis, F. M. (1997). *Biblical exegesis and the formation of Christian culture.* Cambridge: Cambridge University Press.

Frankl, V. E. (1963). *Man's search for meaning*. Boston: Beacon Press.

Frazer, J. G. (1967). *The golden bough.* London: Macmillan. (Original work published 1922)

Freedman, J., & Combs, G. (1996). *Narrative therapy: The social construction of preferred realities.* New York: Norton.

Freeman, P. N. (2003). An abuse survivor learns to show mercy to her abuser. *Journal of Biblical Counseling, 21*(3), 42-45.

Freud, S. (1938). The interpretation of dreams. In A. A. Brill (Ed.), *The basic writings of Sigmund Freud* (pp. 181-552). New York: Random House.

Fries, G. (1978). Logos. In C. Brown (Ed.), *Dictionary of New Testament theology* (Vol. 3, pp. 1081-87) Grand Rapids, MI: Zondervan.

Frijda, N. H. (1994). Emotions are functional, most of the time. In P. Ekman & R. J. Davidson (Eds.), *The nature of emotion: Fundamental questions* (pp. 112-22). New York: Oxford University Press.

Friston, K. J. (2005). Models of brain function in neuroimaging. In S. T. Fiske, A. E. Kazdin & D. L. Schacter (Eds.), *Annual review of psychology, 56* (pp. 57-89). Palo Alto, CA: Annual Revews.

Froeb, K. (2006). Sublation. http://www.hegel.net/en/sublation.html.

Fromm, E. (2000). *The art of loving.* San Francisco: Harper.

Fromm-Reichmann, F. (1960). *Principles of intensive psychotherapy.* Chicago: University of Chicago Press.

Gadamer, H.-G. (1975). *Truth and method.* New York: Sheed & Ward.

Gadamer, H.-G. (1976). *Philosophical hermeneutics* (D. E. Linge, Trans.). Berkeley: University of California Press.

Gaebelein, F. E. (1954). *The pattern of truth.* New York: Oxford University Press.

Gaffin, R. B., Jr. (1971). Gerhardus Vos and the interpretation of Paul. In E. R. Geehan (Ed.), *Jerusalem and Athens: Critical discussions on the theology and apologetics of Cornelius Van Til* (pp. 228-36). Phillipsburg, NJ: Presbyterian & Reformed.

Gaffin, R. B., Jr. (1987). *Resurrection and redemption: A study in Paul's soteriology* (2nd ed.). Phillipsburg, NJ: Presbyterian & Reformed.

Gagnon, R. A. J. (2002). *The Bible and homosexual practice: Texts and hermeneutics.* Nashville: Abingdon.

Gallagher, S. (2000). *At the altar of sexual idolatry.* Dry Ridge, KY: Pure Life Ministries.

Ganz, R. (1993). *Psychobabble: The failure of modern psychology and the biblical alternative.* Wheaton, IL: Crossway.

Garfield, S. L., & Bergin, A. E. (1994). Introduction and historical overview. In A. E. Bergin & S. L. Garfield (Eds.), *Handbook of psychotherapy and behavior change* (4th ed., pp. 3-18). New York: Wiley.

Gauvain, M. (2001). *The social context of cognitive development.* New York: Guilford.

Gazzaniga, M. (Ed.). (2000). *The new cognitive neurosciences* (2nd ed.). Cambridge, MA: MIT Press.

Geertz, C. (1983). *Local knowledge: Further essays in interpretive anthropology.* New York: Basic Books.

Geisler, N. L., & Anderson, J. K. (1987). *Origin science: A proposal for the creation-evolution controversy.* Grand Rapids, MI: Baker.

Geldenhuys, J. N. (1958). Authority and the Bible. In C. F. H. Henry (Ed.), *Revelation and the Bible* (pp. 371-86). Grand Rapids, MI: Baker.

Gendlin, E. T. (1996). *Focusing-oriented psychotherapy: A manual of the experiential method.* New York: Guilford.

Gerkin, C. V. (1979). *Crisis experience in modern life: Theory and theology in pastoral care.* Nashville: Abingdon.

Gerkin, C. V. (1984). *The living human document: Revisioning pastoral counseling in a hermeneutical mode.* Nashville: Abingdon.

Gerkin, C. V. (1997). *An introduction to pastoral care.* Nashville: Abingdon.

Gerstner, J. H. (1979). The view of the Bible held by the church: Calvin and the Westminster divines. In N. L. Geisler (Ed.), *Inerrancy* (pp. 385-412). Grand Rapids, MI: Zondervan.

Ghorbani, N., Bing, M. N., Watson, P. J., Davison, H. K., & LeBreton, D. L. (2003). Individualist and collectivist values: Evidence of compatibility in Iran and the United States. *Personality and Individual Differences, 35*, 431-47.

Ghorbani, N., Watson, P. J., Krauss, S. W., Bing, M. N., & Davison, H. K. (2004). Social science as dialogue: Narcissism, individualist and collectivist values, and religious interest in Iran and the United States. *Current Psychology: Developmental, Learning, Personality, and Social, 23*, 111-23.

Gilson, E. (1940). *The spirit of medieval philosophy.* New York: Charles Scribner's Sons.

Gilson, E. (1965). *The philosophy of St. Bonaventure.* Paterson, NJ: St. Anthony Guild Press.

Gilson, E., & Langan, T. (1963). *Modern philosophy: Descartes to Kant.* New York: Random House.

Giorgi, A. (1970). *Psychology as a human science.* New York: Harper & Row.

Girard, R. (1987). *Things hidden since the foundation of the world* (S. Bann & M. Metteer, Trans.). Stanford, CA: Stanford University Press.

Girard, R. (1996). *The Girard reader.* New York: Crossroad.

Glaser, W. (1965). *Reality therapy.* New York: Harper & Row.

Goehring, M. (1995). Listening prayer: Perceiving the unseen and unheard real. *Journal of Psychology and Christianity, 14*, 318-29.

Goffman, E. (1959). *The presentation of the self in everyday life.* Garden City, NY: Doubleday.

Goldberg, A. (2002). *The executive brain: Frontal lobes and the civilized mind.* New York: Oxford University Press.

Goldhaber, D. E. (2000). *Theories of human development.* Mountain View, CA: Mayfield.

Goldstein, T. (1980). *Dawn of modern science.* Boston: Houghton Mifflin.

Goldsworthy, G. (2000). *Preaching the whole Bible as Christian Scripture.* Grand Rapids, MI: Eerdmans.

Gollwitzer, P. M. (1996). The volitional benefits of planning. In P. M. Gollwitzer & J. A. Bargh (Eds.), *The psychology of action: Linking cognition and motivation to behavior* (pp. 287-311). New York: Guilford.

Gollwitzer, P. M., & Bargh, J. A. (Eds.). (1996). *The psychology of action: Linking cognition and motivation to behavior.* New York: Guilford.

Goodnow, J. J. (1997). Parenting and the transmission and internalization of values: From social-cultural perspectives to within-family analyses. In J. E. Grusec & L. Kuczynski (Eds.), *Parenting and children's internalization of values: A handbook of contemporary theory* (pp. 333-61). New York: John Wiley & Sons.

Goppelt, L. (1981). *Theology of the New Testament.* Grand Rapids, MI: Eerdmans.

Gore, R. J., Jr. (2002). *Covenantal worship: Reconsidering the Puritan regulative principle.* Phillipsburg, NJ: Presbyterian & Reformed.

Gorman, M. J. (2001). *Cruciformity: Paul's narrative spirituality of the cross.* Grand Rapids, MI: Eerdmans.

Gorsuch, N. J. (2001). *Introducing feminist pastoral care and counseling.* Cleveland: Pilgrim Press.

Gorsuch, R. L. (1988). Psychology of religion. *Annual Review of Psychology, 39,* 201-21.

Gorsuch, R. L. (2002). *Integrating psychology and spirituality?* Westport, CT: Praeger.

Gottman, J. M. (1999). *The marriage clinic.* New York: W. W. Norton.

Gouwens, D. J. (1996). *Kierkegaard as religious thinker.* New York: Cambridge University Press.

Grace, C. R. (2001). Special issue: Evolutionary psychology and intelligent design—part 1. *Journal of Psychology and Theology, 29*(4).

Grace, C. R. (2002). Special issue: Evolutionary psychology and intelligent design—part 2. *Journal of Psychology and Theology, 30*(1).

Grant, B. W. (2001). *A theology for pastoral psychotherapy: God's play in sacred spaces.* New York: Haworth.

Green, J. B., & Palmer, S. L. (Eds.). (2005). *In search of the soul: Four views of the mind-body problem.* Downers Grove, IL: InterVarsity Press.

Greenberg, J., & Cheselka, O. (1995). Relational approaches to psychoanalytic psychotherapy. In A. S. Gurman, & S. B. Messer (Eds.), *Essential psychotherapies: Theory and practice* (pp. 55-84). New York: Guilford.

Greenberg, L. S., Elliott, R., & Lietaer, G. (1994). Research on experiential psychotherapies. In A. E. Bergin & S. L. Garfield (Eds.), *Handbook of psychotherapy and behavior change* (4th ed., pp. 509-42). New York: Wiley.

Greenberg, L. S., & Paivio, S. C. (1997). *Working with emotions in psychotherapy.* New York: Guilford.

Greenberg, L. S., & Van Balen, R. (1998). The theory of experience-centered therapies. In L. S. Greenberg, J. C. Watson & G. Lietaer (Eds.), *Handbook of experiential psychotherapy* (pp. 3-27). New York: Guilford.

Greenberg, L. S., Watson, J. C., & Lietaer, G. (1998). *Handbook of experiential psychotherapy.* New York: Guilford.

Greenwood, J. D. (Ed.). (1991). *The future of folk psychology: Intentionality and cognitive science.* New York: Cambridge University Press.

Gregory Nazianzus (1956). The theological orations. In E. R. Hardy (Ed.), *Christology of the later fathers* (pp. 128-214). Louisville, KY: Westminster John Knox.

Gregory the Great. (1950). *Pastoral care.* New York: Newman Press.

Greimas, A. J. (1982). *Semiotics and language: An analytical dictionary* (L. Crist, D. Patte, J. Lee, E. McMahon, G. Phillips & M. Renstorf, Trans.). Bloomington: Indiana University Press.

Greimas, A. J. (1983). *Structural semantics: An attempt at a method.* Lincoln: University of Nebraska Press.

Greimas, A. J. (1990). *The social sciences, a semiotic view.* Minneapolis: University of Minnesota Press.

Greimas, A. J. (1991). *The semiotics of passion.* Minneapolis: University of Minnesota Press.

Grenier, H. (1950). *Thomistic philosophy* (J. P. E. O'Hanley, Trans.). Charlottetown, Canada: St. Dunstan's University.

Grenz, S. J. (1998). *Welcoming but not affirming: An evangelical response to homosexuality.* Louisville, KY: Westminster John Knox.

Grenz, S. J. (2001). *The social God and the relational self: A trinitarian theology of the imago Dei.* Louisville, KY: Westminster John Knox.

Gribomont, J. (1989). Monasticism and asceticism: Eastern Christianity. In B. McGinn & J. Meyendorff (Eds.), *Christian spirituality: Origins to the twelfth century* (pp. 89-112). New York: Crossroad.

Griffith, P. J. (1999). *Religious reading: The place of reading in the practice of religion.* New York: Oxford University Press.

Groeschel, B. (1993). *Spiritual passages.* New York: Crossroads.

Grolnick, W. S., Deci, E. L., & Ryan, R. M. (1997). Internalization within the family: The self-determination theory perspective. In J. E. Grusec & L. Kuczynski (Eds.), *Parenting and children's internalization of values: A handbook of contemporary theory* (pp. 135-61). New York: John Wiley & Sons.

Grove, D. J., & Panzer, B. I. (1989). *Resolving Traumatic Memories: Metaphors and Symbols in Psychotherapy.* New York: Irvington.

Grudem, W. (1995). *Systematic theology.* Grand Rapids, MI: Zondervan.

Grusec, J. E., & Kuczynski, L. (Eds.). (1997). *Parenting and children's internalization of values: A handbook of contemporary theory.* New York: John Wiley & Sons.

Guibert, J. (1953). *The theology of the spiritual life.* New York: Sheed and Ward.

Gundry, R. H. (2002). *Jesus the Word according to John the sectarian.* Grand Rapids, MI: Eerdmans.

Guntrip, H. (1957). *Psychotherapy and religion.* New York: Harper & Brothers.

Gustafson, J. (1981, 1984). *Ethics in a theocentric perspective* (2 vols.). Chicago: University of Chicago Press.

Guthrie, D. (1957). *The pastoral epistles.* Grand Rapids, MI: Eerdmans.

Guy, J. D., Jr. (1980). The search for truth in the task of integration. *Journal of Psychology and Theology, 8,* 27-34.

Haan, N., Bellah, R. N., Rabinow, P., & Sullivan, W. M. (1983). *Social science as moral inquiry.* New York: Columbia University Press.

Haberlandt, K. (1999). *Human memory: Exploration and application.* Boston: Allyn and Bacon.

Habermas, J. (1971). *Knowledge and human interests.* Boston: Beacon Press.

Habib, M., & Demonet, J.-F. (2000). Dyslexia and related learning disorders: Recent advances from brain imaging studies. In J. C. Massiotta, A. W. Toga & R. S. J. Frackowiak (Eds.), *Brain mapping: The disorders* (pp. 459-84). San Diego: Academic Press.

Hales, S. W., Sorenson, R., Jones, J., & Coe, J. (April, 1995). Psychotherapists and the religious disciplines: Personal beliefs and professional practice. Paper presented at the conference of the Christian Association for Psychological Studies, Virginia Beach, VA.

Hall, T. W., & Porter, S. L. (2004). Referential integration: An emotional information processing perspective on the process of integration. *Journal of Psychology and Theology, 32,* 167-80.

Hamilton, N. G. (1998). *Self and others: Object relations theory in practice.* New York: Jason Aronson.

Hamilton, V. P. (1990). *The book of Genesis: Chapters 1-17.* Grand Rapids, MI: Eerdmans.

Hanson, A. T. (1982). *The pastoral epistles.* Grand Rapids, MI: Eerdmans.

Hare, J. E. (2002). *Why bother being good? The place of God in the moral life.* Downers Grove, IL: InterVarsity Press.

Hare, J. E. (2001). *God's call: Moral realism, God's commands, and human autonomy.* Grand Rapids, MI: Eerdmans.

Haroutunian, J. (1958). *Calvin: Commentaries.* Philadelphia: Westminster Press.

Harre, R. (1979). *Social being.* Cambridge, MA: Harvard University Press.

Harre, R. (1983). *Personal being.* Cambridge, MA: Harvard University Press.

Harre, R., & Gillett, G. R. (1994). *The discursive mind.* San Diego: Sage.

Harre, R., & Langenhove, L. (1999). *Positioning theory.* London: Blackwell.

Harrison, E. F. (1988). Holiness. In G. W. Bromiley (Ed.), *International standard Bible encyclopedia* (Vol. 2, pp. 725-29). Grand Rapids, MI: Eerdmans.

Hart, D. B. (2003). *The beauty of the infinite: The aesthetics of Christian truth.* Grand Rapids, MI: Eerdmans.

Harter, S. (1999). *The construction of the self: A developmental perspective.* New York: Guilford.

Hasker, W. (1983). *Metaphyscis.* Downers Grove, IL: InterVarsity Press.

Hasker, W. (1992). Faith-learning integration: An overview. *Christian Scholar's Review, 21,* 234-48.

Hasker, W. (1999). *The emergent self.* Ithaca, NY: Cornell University Press.

Hassin, R. R., Uleman, J. S., & Bargh, J. A. (Eds.). (2004). *The new unconscious.* New York: Oxford University Press.

Hauerwas, S. (1974). *Vision and virtue.* Notre Dame, IN: Fides.

Hauerwas, S. (1983). *The peaceable kingdom.* Notre Dame, IN: University of Notre Dame Press.

Hauerwas, S. (1990). *Naming the silences: God, medicine, and the problem of suffering.* Grand Rapids, MI: Eerdmans.

Hauerwas, S. (1993). *Unleashing the scripture: Freeing the Bible from captivity to America.* Nashville: Abingdon.

Hayes, S. C., Follette, W. C., & Follette, V. M. (1995). Behavior therapy: A contextual approach. In A. S. Gurman & S. B. Messer (Eds.), *Essential psychotherapies: Theory and practice* (pp. 128-81). New York: Guilford.

Heard, W. J. (1993). Eschatologically oriented psychology: A new paradigm for the integration of psychology and Christianity. In D. A. Carson & J. D. Woodbridge (Eds.), *God and culture* (pp. 106-33). Grand Rapids, MI: Eerdmans.

Heckhausen, H. (1991). *Motivation and action* (P. K. Leppmann, Trans.). Berlin: Springer-Verlag.

Heckhausen, J., & Dweck, C. (Eds.). (1998). *Motivation and self-regulation across the life-span.* New York: Cambridge University Press.

Heidegger, M. (1962). *Being and time* (J. Macquarrie & E. Robinson, Trans.). New York: Harper & Row.

Hellman, J. A. W. (1988). The spirituality of the Franciscans. In J. Raitt (Ed.), *Christian spirituality: High Middle Ages and Reformation* (pp. 31-49). New York: Crossroad.

Hendrix, H. (1993). *Keeping the love you find.* New York: Atria.

Hendrix, H. (2001). *Getting the love you want: A guide for couples.* New York: Owl Books.

Henry, C. F. H. (Ed.). (1958). *Revelation and the Bible.* Grand Rapids, MI: Baker.

Henry, C. F. H. (1976). *God, revelation, and authority: Vol. 1. God who speaks and shows: Preliminary considerations.* Waco, TX: Word.

Henry, M. (n. d.). *Commentary on the whole Bible: Vol. 6.* New York: Fleming H. Revell.

Henry, W. P., Strupp, H. H., Schact, T. E., & Gaston, L. (1994). Psychodynamic approaches. In A. E. Bergin & S. L. Garfield (Eds.), *Handbook of psychotherapy and behavior change* (4th ed., pp. 467-508). New York: Wiley.

Hibbs, C. (1991). The church as a multigenerational relational system. In H. Vande Kemp (Ed.), *Family therapy: Christian perspectives* (pp. 109-34). Grand Rapids, MI: Baker.

Hilgard, E. R. (1986). *Divided consciousness: Multiple controls in human thought and action.* New York: John Wiley.

Hill, C. E., & James, F. A., III. (2004). *The glory of the atonement.* Downers Grove, IL: InterVarsity Press.

Hiltner, S. (1943). *Religion and health.* New York: Macmillan.

Hiltner, S. (1949). *Pastoral counseling.* New York: Abingdon-Cokesbury.

Hiltner, S. (1958). *Preface to pastoral theology.* Nashville: Abingdon.

Hiltner, S. (1972). *Theological dynamics.* Nashville: Abingdon.

Hiltner, S., & Colston, L. G. (1961). *The context of pastoral counseling.* New York: Abingdon.

Hindson, E., & Eyrich, H. (1997). *Totally sufficient: The Bible and Christian counseling*. Eugene, OR: Harvest House.

Hirsch, E. D. (1967). *Validity in interpretation*. New Haven, CT: Yale University Press.

Hjelmslev, L. (1961). *Prolegomena to a theory of language* (F. J. Whitfield, Trans.). Madison: University of Wisconsin Press.

Hodge, C. (1995). *Systematic theology* (Reprint ed.). Grand Rapids, MI: Eerdmans.

Hodge, R., & Kress, G. (1988). *Social semiotics*. Ithaca, NY: Cornell University Press.

Hoekema, A. (1975). *The Christian looks at himself*. Grand Rapids, MI: Eerdmans.

Hoffman, M. L. (2000). *Empathy and moral development: Implications for caring and justice*. Cambridge: Cambridge University Press.

Hogan, R., Johnson, J., & Briggs, S. (1997). *Handbook of personality psychology*. San Diego: Academic Press.

Holifield, E. B. (1983). *A history of pastoral care in America: From salvation to self-realization*. Nashville: Abingdon.

Holifield, E. B. (1990). Paul Tillich. In R. J. Hunter (Ed.), *Dictionary of pastoral care and counseling* (p. 1277). Nashville: Abingdon.

Holmes, A. (1977). *All truth is God's truth*. Downers Grove, IL: InterVarsity Press.

Holmes, J. (1996). *Attachment, intimacy, and autonomy*. New York: Jason Aronson.

Holmes, J. (1998). Defensive and creative uses of narrative in psychotherapy: An attachment perspective. In G. Roberts & J. Holmes (Eds.), *Narrative in psychotherapy and psychiatry* (pp. 49-68). New York: Oxford University Press.

Holmes, S. R. (2001). *God of grace & God of glory: An account of the theology of Jonathan Edwards*. Grand Rapids, MI: Eerdmans.

Holquist, M. (1990). *Dialogism* (2nd ed.). London: Routledge.

Holton, G. (1973). *Thematic origins of scientific thought: Kepler to Einstein*. Cambridge, MA: Harvard University Press.

Hooykaas, R. (1972). *Religion and the rise of modern science*. Grand Rapids, MI: Eerdmans.

Hopkins, G. M. (1953). *Poems and prose of Gerard Manley Hopkins*. New York: Penguin.

Horton, M. S. (2002). *Covenant and eschatology: The divine drama*. Louisville, KY: Westminster John Knox.

Horton, M. S. (2005). *Lord and servant: A covenant Christology*. Louisville, KY: Westminster John Knox.

Hougen, J. (2002). *Transformed into fire*. Grand Rapids, MI: Kregel.

House, P. R. (1998). *Old Testament theology*. Downers Grove, IL: InterVarsity Press.

Howard, G. S. (1992). Behold our creation! What counseling psychology has become and might yet become. *Journal of Counseling Psychology, 39*, 419-42.

Howard-Snyder, D., & Moser, P. K. (2002). *Divine hiddenness*. Cambridge: Cambridge University Press.

Howe, L. T. (1995). *The image of God: A theology for pastoral care and counseling*. Nashville: Abingdon.

Howsepian, A. A. (1997). Sin and psychosis. In R. C. Roberts & M. R. Talbot (Eds.), *Limning the psyche: Explorations in Christian psychology* (pp. 264-81). Grand Rapids, MI: Eerdmans.

Hughes, P. E. (1977). *A commentary on the epistle to the Hebrews.* Grand Rapids, MI: Eerdmans.

Hughes, P. E. (1984). *Lefevre: Pioneer of ecclesiastical renewal in France.* Grand Rapids, MI: Eerdmans.

Hunsinger, D. V. D. (1995). *Theology and pastoral counseling: A new interdisciplinary approach.* Grand Rapids, MI: Eerdmans.

Hunt, D., & McMahon, T. A. (1985). *The seduction of Christianity: Spiritual discernment in the last days.* Eugene, OR: Harvest House.

Hunter, R. J. (Ed.). (1990). *Dictionary of pastoral care and counseling.* Nashville: Abingdon.

Hurley, J. B., & Berry, J. T. (1997a). The relation of Scripture and psychology in counseling from a pro-integration position. *Journal of Psychology and Christianity, 16,* 323-45.

Hurley, J. B., & Berry, J. T. (1997b). Response to Welch and Powlison. *Journal of Psychology and Christianity, 16,* 350-62.

Husserl, E. (1961). *Ideas: General introduction to pure phenomenology* (W. R. B. Gibson, Trans.). New York: Collier. (Original work published 1913)

Hyde, J. S. (1990). *Understanding human sexuality* (4th ed.). New York: McGraw-Hill.

Hyde, T. S., & Jenkins, J. J. (1973). Recall of words as a function of semantic, graphic and syntactic orienting tasks. *Journal of Verbal Learning and Verbal Behavior, 12,* 471-80.

IABC. (n. d.). *The sufficiency of Scriptures: Affirmations and denials.* Oklahoma City, OK: International Association of Biblical Counselors.

Ignatius. (1964). *The spiritual exercises of St. Ignatius.* New York: Doubleday.

Ingram, J. A. (1995). Contemporary issues and Christian models of integration: Into the modern/postmodern age. *Journal of Psychology and Theology, 23,* 3-17.

Ingram, J. (1997). Modern and postmodern issues in Christian psychology: An integrative transmodern proposal. *Journal of Psychology and Theology, 25,* 315-28.

Ingram, R. E., & Price, J. M. (Eds.). (2001). *Vulnerability to psychopathology: Risk across the lifespan.* New York: Guilford.

Izard, C. E. (1977). *Human emotions.* New York: Plenum.

James, W. (1890). *Principles of psychology.* New York: Henry Holt.

Jeeves, M. A. (1976) *Psychology and Christianity: The view both ways.* Downers Grove, IL: InterVarsity Press.

Jeeves, M. A. (1997). *Human nature at the millennium.* Grand Rapids, MI: Baker.

Jeeves, M., Berry, R. J., & Atkinson, D. (1984). *Free to be different.* Grand Rapids, MI: Eerdmans.

Jeffries, D. L. (1996). *People of the Book: Christian identity and literary culture.* Grand Rapids, MI: Eerdmans.

Jensen, J. P., & Bergin, A. E. (1988). Mental health values of professional therapists: A national interdisciplinary survey. *Professional Psychology: Research and Practice, 14,* 290-97.

Jensen, P. (2002). *The revelation of God.* Downers Grove, IL: InterVarsity Press.

Jenson, R. W. (1988). *America's theologian: A recommendation of Jonathan Edwards.* New York: Oxford University Press.

Jenson, R. W. (1997). *Systematic theology: Vol. 1. The triune God.* New York: Oxford University Press.

Jewett, P. K. (1985). *Election and predestination.* Grand Rapids, MI: Eerdmans.

John of the Cross. (1959). *Dark night of the soul.* New York: Image.

John of the Cross. (1964). *The complete works of St. John of the Cross.* Westminster, MD: Newman Press.

Johnson, E. L. (1987). Sin, weakness, and psychopathology. *Journal of Psychology and Theology, 15,* 218-26.

Johnson, E. L. (1992). A place for the Bible in psychological science. *Journal of Psychology and Theology, 20,* 346-55.

Johnson, E. L. (1996a). The call of wisdom: Adult development within Christian community, part I: The crisis of modern theories of post-formal development. *Journal of Psychology and Theology, 24,* 88-95.

Johnson, E. L. (1996b). The call of wisdom: Adult development within Christian community, part II: Toward a covenantal constructivist model of post-formal development. *Journal of Psychology and Theology, 24,* 96-103.

Johnson, E. L. (1997a). Christ, the Lord of psychology. *Journal of Psychology and Theology, 25,* 11-27.

Johnson, E. L. (1997b). Human agency and its social formation. In R. C. Roberts & M. R. Talbot (Eds.), *Limning the psyche: Explorations in Christian psychology* (pp. 138-64). Grand Rapids, MI: Eerdmans.

Johnson, E. L. (1998a). Whatever happened to the human soul? A brief Christian genealogy of a psychological term. *Journal of Psychology and Theology, 26,* 16-28.

Johnson, E. L. (1998b). Where are the Pharisees today? *Reformation and Revival Journal, 7,* 37-48.

Johnson, E. L. (2000). Describing the self within redemptive history. *Journal of Psychology and Christianity, 19,* 5-24.

Johnson, E. L. (2002). Can God be grasped by our reason? In D. S. Huffman & E. L. Johnson (Eds.), *God under fire: Modern scholarship reinvents God* (pp. 72-103). Grand Rapids, MI: Zondervan.

Johnson, E. L. (2003). How God is good for the soul. *Journal of Christianity and Psychology, 22,* 78-88.

Johnson, E. L. (2007). Toward a philosophy of science for Christian psychology. *Edification, 1,* 1-20.

Johnson, E. L., & Burroughs, C. S. (2000). Protecting one's soul: A Christian inquiry into defensive activity. *Journal of Psychology and Theology, 28,* 175-89.

Johnson, E. L., & Jones, S. L. (2000). A history of Christians in psychology. In E. L. Johnson & S. L. Jones (Eds.), *Psychology and Christianity: Four views* (pp. 11-53). Downers Grove, IL: InterVarsity Press.

Johnson, E. L., & Langberg, D. M. (in press). *The words of life: The unique content of Christian soul care.* Downers Grove, IL: InterVarsity Press.

Johnson, E. L., & Sandage, S. (1999). A postmodern reconstruction of psychotherapy: Orienteering, religion, and the healing of the soul. *Psychotherapy, 36,* 1-15.

Johnson, P. (1953). *Psychology of pastoral care.* New York: Abingdon-Cokesbury.

Johnson-Laird, P. N., & Oatley, K. (2000). Cognitive and social construction in emotions. In M. Lewis & J. M. Haviland-Jones (Eds.), *Handbook of emotions* (2nd ed., pp. 458-75). New York: Guilford.

Johnston, W. (Ed.). (1973). *The cloud of unknowing.* New York: Doubleday.

Jonas, H. (1966). *The phenomenon of life.* Chicago: University of Chicago Press.

Jones, L. G. (1995). *Embodying forgiveness: A theological analysis.* Grand Rapids, MI: Eerdmans.

Jones, R. D. (2003). Redeeming the bad memories of your past sins. *Journal of Biblical Counseling, 22,* 40-47.

Jones, S. L. (1986). Relating the Christian faith to psychology. In S. L. Jones (Ed.), *Psychology and the Christian faith* (pp. 15-33). Grand Rapids, MI: Baker.

Jones, S. L. (1994). A constructive relationship for religion with the science and profession of psychology. Perhaps the boldest model yet. *American Psychology, 49,* 184-99.

Jones, S. L. (1997). The meaning of agency and responsibility in light of social science research. In R. C. Roberts & M. R. Talbot (Eds.), *Limning the psyche: Explorations in Christian psychology* (pp. 186-205). Grand Rapids, MI: Eerdmans.

Jones, S. L., & Butman, R. E. (1991). *Modern psychotherapies: A comprehensive Christian appraisal.* Downers Grove, IL: InterVarsity Press.

Jones, S. L., Butman, R. E., & Mangis, M. W. (1991). Contemporary psychodynamic psychotherapies. In S. L. Jones & R. E. Butman, *Modern psychotherapies: A comprehensive Christian appraisal* (pp. 92-118). Downers Grove, IL: InterVarsity Press.

Jones, S. L., & Kwee, A. W. (2005). Scientific research, homosexuality, and the church's moral debate: An update. *Journal of Psychology and Christianity, 24,* 304-16.

Jones, S. L., & Yarhouse, M. A. (2000). *Homosexuality: The use of scientific research in the church's moral debate.* Downers Grove, IL: InterVarsity Press.

Joy, D. M. (1997). *Bonding: Relationships in the image of God.* Nappanee, IN: Evangel Publishing House.

Julian of Norwich. (1977). *Manifestations of divine love.* Garden City, NY: Doubleday.

Julian, R. (1998). *Righteous sinners: The believer's struggle with faith, grace, and works.* Colorado Springs, CO: NavPress.

Jung, C. (1968). *Analytical psychology: Its theory and practice.* New York: Random House.

Jüngel, E. (1983). *God as the mystery of the world* (D. L. Guder, Trans.). Grand Rapids, MI: Eerdmans.

Kagan, J. (1998). Biology and the child. In W. Damon (Series Ed.) & N. Eisenberg (Vol. Ed.), *Handbook of child psychology: Vol. 3. Social, emotional, and personality development* (5th ed., pp. 177-236). New York: John Wiley & Sons.

Kahneman, D. (1999). Objective happiness. In D. Kahneman, E. Diener & N. Schwarz, (Eds.), *Well-being: The foundations of hedonic psychology* (pp. 3-25). New York: Russell Sage Foundation.

Kahneman, D., Diener, E., & Schwarz, N. (Eds.). (1999). *Well-being: The foundations of hedonic psychology.* New York: Russell Sage Foundation.

Kaslow, N. J., & Celano, M. P. (1995). The family therapies. In A. S. Gurman & S. B. Messer (Eds.), *Essential psychotherapies: Theory and practice* (pp. 343-402). New York: Guilford.

Kass, L. R. (1994). *The hungry soul: Eating and the perfecting of our nature.* Chicago: University of Chicago Press.

Kaufman, E. (1994). *Psychotherapy of addicted persons.* New York: Guilford.

Kaufman, G. (1993). *In face of mystery: A constructive theology.* Cambridge, MA: Harvard University Press.

Kegan, R. (1982). *The evolving self: Problem and process in human development.* Cambridge, MA: Harvard University Press.

Kellemen, R. W. (2005a). *Soul physicians: A theology of soul care and spiritual direction.* Taneytown, MD: RPM Books.

Kellemen, R. W. (2005b). *Spiritual friends: A methodology of soul care and spiritual direction.* Taneytown, MD: RPM Books.

Kelly, E. W., Jr. (1995). Counselor values: A national survey. *Journal of Counseling and Development, 73,* 648-54.

Kelsey, M. (1982). *Christo-psychology.* New York: Crossroad.

Kelsey, M. (1986). *Christianity as psychology: The healing power of the Christian message.* Minneapolis: Augsburg.

Kemper, T. D. (2000). Social models in the explanation of emotions. In M. Lewis & J. M. Haviland-Jones (Eds.), *Handbook of emotions* (2nd ed., pp. 45-58). New York: Guilford.

Kernberg, O. (1976). *Object relations theory and clinical psychoanalysis.* New York: Jason Aronson.

Kernberg, O. (1996). A psychoanalytic theory of personality disorders. In J. F. Clarkin & M. F. Lenzenweger (Eds.), *Major theories of personality disorder* (pp. 106-40). New York: Guilford.

Keyes, L. M., & Haidt, J. (Eds.). (2003). *Flourishing: Positive psychology and the life well-lived.* Washington, DC: American Psychological Association.

Kierkegaard, S. (1938). *Purity of heart is to will one thing.* New York: Harper & Row. (Original work published 1847)

Kierkegaard, S. (1946a). *The concept of dread.* Princeton, NJ: Princeton University Press. (Original work published 1834)

Kierkegaard, S. (1946b). *Works of love*. Princeton, NJ: Princeton University Press. (Original work published 1847)

Kierkegaard, S. (1962). *The point of view for my work as an author*. New York: Harper & Row. (Original work published 1848)

Kierkegaard, S. (1980). *The sickness unto death*. Princeton, NJ: Princeton University Press. (Original work published 1849)

Kierkegaard, S. (1985). *Philosophical fragments*. Princeton, NJ: Princeton University Press. (Original work published 1844)

Kierkegaard, S. (1988). *Stages on life's way* (H. W. Hong & E. H. Hong, Trans.). Princeton, NJ: Princeton University Press. (Original work published 1845)

Kierkegaard, S. (1990). *For self-examination. Judge for yourselves!* (H. V. Hong & E. H. Hong, Trans.). Princeton, NJ: Princeton University Press. (*For self-examination* originally published 1851; *Judge for yourselves!* originally published 1875)

Kierkegaard, S. (1992). *Concluding unscientific postscript*. Princeton, NJ: Princeton University Press. (Original work published 1846)

Kierkegaard, S. (1993). *Upbuilding discourses* (H. W. Hong & E. H. Hong, Trans.). Princeton, NJ: Princeton University Press. (Original work published 1847)

Kihlstrom, J. F. (2002). To honor Kraelpelin. . . : From symptoms to pathology in the diagnosis of mental illness. In L. E. Beutler & M. L. Malik (Eds.), *Rethinking the DSM: A psychological perspective* (pp. 279-304). Washington, DC: American Psychological Association.

Kihlstrom, J. F., Beer, J. S., & Klein, S. B. (2003). Self and identity as memory. In M. R. Leary & J. P. Tangney (Eds.), *Handbook of self and identity* (pp. 68-90). New York: Guilford.

Kim, J. (1984). Concepts of supervenience. *Philosophy and Phenomenological Research, 45,* 153-76.

Kimball, D. R., & Holyoak, K. J. (2000). Transfer and expertise. In E. Tulving & F. I. M. Craik (Eds.), *The Oxford handbook of memory* (pp. 109-22). New York: Oxford University Press.

Kinneavy, J. L. (1971). *A theory of discourse*. New York: W. W. Norton.

Kirkpatrick, L. A. (1992). An attachment-theoretical approach to the psychology of religion. *International Journal for the Psychology of Religion, 2,* 3-28.

Kirwin, W. T. (1984). *Biblical concepts for Christian counseling*. Grand Rapids, MI: Baker.

Klein, W. W., Blomberg, C. L., & Hubbard, R. L., Jr. (1993). *Introduction to biblical interpretation*. Dallas: Word.

Klemke, E. D., Hollinger, R., & Kline, A. D. (1988). *Introductory readings in the philosophy of science*. Buffalo, NY: Prometheus.

Klerman, G. L., & Weissman, M. M. (1993). *New applications of interpersonal psychotherapy*. Washington, DC: American Psychiatric Press.

Kline, M. G. (1972). *The structure of biblical authority*. Grand Rapids, MI: Eerdmans.

Kline, M. G. (1999). *Images of the Spirit*. Eugene, OR: Wipf & Stock.

Kochanska, G. (1991). Socialization and temperament in the development of guilt and conscience. *Child Development, 62,* 1379-92.

Kochanska, G. (1993). Toward a synthesis of parental socialization and child temperament in early development of conscience. *Child Development, 64,* 325-47.

Kochanska, G. (1995). Children's temperament, mothers' discipline, and security of attachment: Multiple pathways to emerging internalization. *Child Development, 66,* 597-615.

Kochanska, G., & Aksan, N. (1995). Mother-child mutually positive affect, the quality of child compliance to requests and prohibitions, and maternal control as correlates of early internalization. *Child Development, 66,* 236-54.

Kochanska, G., Murray, K., Jacques, T. Y., Koenig, A. L., & Vandegeest, K. A. (1996). Inhibitory control in young children and its role in emerging internalization. *Child Development, 67,* 490-507.

Koenig, H. G., McCullough, M. E., & Larson, D. B. (2001). *Handbook of religion and health.* Oxford: Oxford University Press.

Kohut, H. (1971). *The analysis of the self.* New York: International Universities Press.

Kohut, H. (1977). *The restoration of the self.* New York: International Universities Press.

Kohut, H. (1984). *How does analysis cure?* Chicago: University of Chicago Press.

Kok, J. H. (1998). *Patterns of the Western mind.* Sioux Center, IA: Dordt College Press.

Kopp, C. B. (1982). Antecedents of self-regulation: A developmental perspective. *Developmental Psychology, 18,* 199-204.

Kosslyn, S. M., & Koenig, O. (1992). *Wet mind: The new cognitive neuroscience.* New York: Free Press.

Kristeva, J. (1974). *Revolution in poetic language.* New York: Columbia University Press.

Kristeva, J. (1980). Desire in language: A semiotic approach to literature and art (A. Jardine, T. A. Gora & L. S. Roudiez, Trans.). Oxford: Blackwell.

Kristeva, J. (1986). *The Kristeva reader.* New York: Columbia University Press.

Kristeva, J. (1987). *In the beginning was love: Psychoanalysis and faith* (A. Goldhammer, Trans.). New York: Columbia University Press.

Kruglanski, A. W. (1996). Goals as knowledge structures. In P. M. Gollwitzer & J. A. Bargh (Eds.), *The psychology of action: Linking cognition and motivation to behavior* (pp. 597-617). New York: Guilford.

Kruis, J. G. (1994). *Quick Scripture reference for counseling* (2nd ed.). Grand Rapids, MI: Baker.

Kruschwitz, R. B., & Roberts, R. C. (1987). *The virtues: Contemporary essays on moral character.* Belmont, CA: Wadsworth.

Kuhl, J. (1985). Volitional mediators of cognition-behavior consistency: Self-regulatory processes and action versus state orientation. In J. Kuhl & J. Beckmann (Eds.), *Action control: From cognition to behavior.* Berlin: Springer-Verlag.

Kuhn, T. S. (1962). *The structure of scientific revolutions.* Chicago: University of Chicago.

Kuhn, T. S. (1970). *The structure of scientific revolutions* (2nd ed.). Chicago: University of Chicago Press.

Kuhn, T. S. (1977a). *The essential tension: Selected studies in scientific tradition and change.* Chicago: University of Chicago Press.

Kuhn, T. S. (1977b). Second thoughts on paradigms. In F. Suppe (Ed.), *The structure of scientific theories* (pp. 459-82). Urbana: University of Illinois Press.

Kuyper, A. (1898a). *Lectures on Calvinism.* New York: Fleming H. Revell.

Kuyper, A. (1898b). *Principles of sacred theology* (J. H. DeVries, Trans.). New York: Charles Scribner & Sons.

Kuyper, A. (1998). Common grace in science. In J. D. Braat (Ed.), *Abraham Kuyper: A centennial reader* (pp. 441-60). Grand Rapids, MI: Eerdmans.

LaCugna, C. M. (1991). *God for us: The Trinity of Christian life.* San Francisco: Harper.

Ladd, G. E. (1974). *The theology of the New Testament.* Grand Rapids, MI: Eerdmans.

Lakatos, I. (1970). Falsification and the methodology of scientific research programmes. In *Criticism and the growth of knowledge.* Cambridge: Cambridge University Press.

Lake, F. (1966). *Clinical theology.* London: Darton, Longman & Todd.

Lambert, M. J. (Ed.). (2004). *Bergin and Garfield's handbook of psychotherapy and behavior change* (5th ed.). New York: John Wiley & Sons.

Lane, A. N. S. (1999). *John Calvin: Student of the church fathers.* Grand Rapids, MI: Baker.

Lane, R. D. (2000). Levels of emotional awareness: Neurological, psychological, and social perspectives. In R. Bar-On & J. D. A. Parker (Eds.), *The handbook of emotional intelligence* (pp. 171-91). San Francisco: Jossey-Bass.

Lane, T. S., & Tripp, P. D. (2006a). *How people change.* Greensboro, NC: New Growth Press.

Lane, T. S., & Tripp, P. D. (2006b). *Relationships: A mess worth making.* Greensboro, NC: New Growth Press.

Lane, W. L. (1991). *Word biblical commentary: Vol. 4. Hebrews 1-8.* Dallas: Word.

Langberg, D. M. (1997). *Counseling survivors of sexual abuse.* Wheaton, IL: Tyndale House.

Langberg, D. M. (1999). *On the threshold of hope.* Wheaton, IL: Tyndale House.

Langley, K. (2002). Genre-sensitive use of the Psalms in counseling. *Journal of Biblical Counseling, 20,* 38-45.

Larsen, R. J., & Prizmic, Z. (2004). Affect regulation. In R. F. Baumeister & K. D. Vohs (Eds.), *Handbook of self-regulation: Research, theory, and applications* (pp. 40-61). New York: Guilford.

Larzelere, R. E. (1980). The task ahead: Six levels of integration of Christianity and psychology. *Journal of Psychology and Theology, 8,* 3-11.

Lasch, C. (1979). *The culture of narcissism.* New York: Norton.

Lawless, C. (2002). *Discipled warriors: Growing healthy churches that are equipped for spiritual warfare.* Grand Rapids, MI: Kregel.

Lazarus, A. A. (1989). *The practice of multimodal therapy* (paperback ed.). Baltimore: Johns Hopkins Press.

Leary, M. R. (2002). When selves collide: The nature of the self and the dynamics of interpersonal relationships. In A. Tesser, D. A. Stapel & J. V. Wood (Eds.), *Self and motivation: Emerging psychological perspectives* (pp. 119-45). Washington, DC: American Psychological Association.

Leary, M. R., & Tangney, J. P. (2003). *Handbook of self and identity.* New York: Guilford.

Lecerf, A. (1949). *An introduction to reformed dogmatics.* London: Lutterworth.

LeDoux, J. E. (1996). *The emotional brain: The mysterious underpinnings of emotional life.* New York: Touchstone.

LeDoux, J. E. (1997). Emotion: Clues from the brain. *Annual Review of Psychology, 46,* 209-35.

Lee, C. (2004). Agency and purpose in narrative therapy: Questioning the postmodern rejection of metanarrative. *Journal of Psychology and Theology, 32,* 221-31.

Lee, D. J. (1993). Introduction. In D. J. Lee (Ed.), *Storying ourselves: A narrative perspective on Christians in psychology.* Grand Rapids, MI: Eerdmans.

Lee, S. H. (2005). Grace and justification by faith alone. In S. H. Lee (Ed.), *The Princeton compantion to Jonathan Edwards* (pp. 130-46). Princeton, NJ: Princeton University Press.

Lehrer, K. (1992). Coherentism. In J. Dancy & E. Sosa (Eds.), *A companion to epistemology* (pp. 67-70). New York: Blackwell.

Lerner, R. M. (1998). Theories of human development: Contemporary perspectives. In W. Damon (Series Ed.) & R. M. Lerner (Vol. Ed.), *Handbook of child psychology: Vol. 1. Theoretical models of human development* (5th ed., pp. 1-24). New York: John Wiley & Sons.

Lester, A. D. (1983). *Coping with anger: A Christian guide.* Philadelphia: Westminster Press.

Lester, A. D. (1995). *Hope in pastoral care and counseling.* Louisville, KY: Westminster John Knox.

Lester, A. D. (2003). *The angry Christian: A theology for care and counseling.* Louisville, KY: Westminster John Knox.

Levinas, E. (1981). *Otherwise than being or beyond essence* (Alphonso Lingis, Trans.). The Hague: Martinus Nijhoff.

Levitin, K. (1982). *One is not born a personality: Profiles of Soviet education psychologists.* Moscow: Progress.

Levy, B. S. (Ed.). (1992). *The Bible in the Middle Ages: Its influence on literature and art.* Binghamton: State University of New York at Binghamton.

Levy, M. (1972). *Modernization: Latecomers and survivors.* New York: Basic Books.

Levy, T. M. (Ed.). (2000). *Handbook of attachment interventions.* New York: Academic Press.

Lewis, C. S. (1949). *Transposition and other addresses.* Longdon: Geoffrey Bles.

Lewis, C. S. (1952). *Mere Christianity.* London: Fontana.

Lewis, G. R., & Demarest, B. A. (1996). *Integrative theology.* Grand Rapids, MI: Zondervan.

Lewis, M., & Brooks-Gunn, J. (1979). *Social cognition and the acquisition of self.* New York: Plenum Press.

Lewis, P. (1975). *The genius of Puritanism.* Haywards Heath, UK: Carey.

Lidov, D. (1998). Semiosis. In P. Bouissac (Ed.), *Encyclopedia of semiotics* (pp. 561-63). New York: Oxford University Press.

Lindberg, D. C., & Numbers, R. L. (Eds.). (1986). *God & nature: Historical essays on the encounter between Christianity and science.* Berkeley: University of California Press.

Lindberg, D. C., & Numbers, R. L. (Eds.). (2003). *When science and Christianity meet.* Chicago: University of Chicago Press.

Lints, R. (1993). *The fabric of theology: A prolegomenon to evangelical theology.* Grand Rapids, MI: Eerdmans.

Little, B. R. (1999). Personality and motivation: Personal action and the conative evolution. In LA. Pervin & O. P. John (Eds.). *Handbook of personality: Theory and research* (2nd ed., pp. 501-24). New York: Guilford.

Litz, B. T. (1992). Emotional numbing in combat-related post-traumatic stress disorder: A critical review and reformulation. *Clinical Psychology Review, 12,* 417-32.

Livingston, J. C. (1993). *Anatomy of the sacred.* Englewood Cliffs, NJ: Prentice-Hall.

Livingstone, D. N., Hart, D. G., & Noll, M. A. (1999). *Evangelicals and science in historical perspective.* New York: Oxford University Press.

Loder, J. E., Jr. (1998). *The logic of the Spirit: Human development in theological perspective.* San Francisco: Jossey-Bass.

Loehlin, J. C. (1992). *Genes and environment in personality development.* Newbury Park, CA: Sage.

Logue, A. W. (1993). *The psychology of eating and drinking* (2nd ed.). New York: Freeman.

Louf, A. (2002). *Grace can do more: Spiritual accompaniment and spiritual growth.* Kalamazoo, MI: Cistercian.

Louth, A. (1986). Augustine. In E. Jones, G. Wainwright & E. Yarnold (Eds.), *The study of spirituality* (pp. 134-45). New York: Oxford.

Loux, M. (1998). *Metaphysics: A contemporary introduction.* New York: Routledge.

Lubac, H. (1969). *Augustinianism and modern theology.* New York: Herder.

Luborsky, L. (1984). *Principles of psychoanalytic psychotherapy: A manual for supportive-expressive treatment.* New York: Basic Books.

Luria, A. R. (1979). *The making of mind: A personal account of Soviet psychology.* Cambridge, MA: Harvard University Press.

Luria, A. R., & Yudovich, F. I. (1971). *Speech and the development of mental processes in the child.* Middlesex, UK: Penguin.

Luther, M. (1955). *Luther: Letters of spiritual counsel.* Philadelphia: Westminster Press.

Luther, M. (1962). *Luther's early theological works.* Philadelphia: Westminster Press.

Luther, M. (1989). *Martin Luther's basic theological writings.* Minneapolis: Fortress.

Lyotard, J.-F. (1984). *The postmodern condition: A report on knowledge.* Minneapolis: University of Minnesota Press.

MacArthur, J. F., Jr. (1991). *Our sufficiency in Christ.* Dallas: Word.

MacArthur, J. F., Jr. (1994a). Rediscovering biblical counseling. In J. F. MacArthur & W. A. Mack (Eds.), *Introduction to biblical counseling* (pp. 3-19). Dallas: Word.

MacArthur, J. F., Jr. (1994b). Frequently asked questions about biblical counseling. In J. F. MacArthur & W. A. Mack (Eds.), *Introduction to biblical counseling* (p. 368). Dallas: Word.

MacArthur, J., & Mack, W. A. (1994). *An introduction to biblical counseling.* Waco, TX: Word.

MacCulloch, D. (2003). *The reformation: A history.* New York: Viking.

MacIntyre, A. (1977). Epistemological crises, dramatic narratives, and the philosophy of science. *Monist, 60,* 453-472.

MacIntyre, A. (1984). *After virtue* (2nd ed.). Notre Dame, IN: University of Notre Dame Press.

MacIntyre, A. (1988). *Whose justice? Which rationality?* Notre Dame, IN: University of Notre Dame Press.

MacIntyre, A. (1990). *Three rival versions of moral inquiry.* Notre Dame, IN: University of Notre Dame.

Mack, W. A. (1978). Biblical help for overcoming despondency, depression. *The Journal of Pastoral Practice, 2,* 31-48.

Mack, W. A. (1979). *A homework manual for biblical counselors, Vol. 1. Personal and interpersonal problems.* Phillipsburg, NJ: Presbyterian & Reformed.

Mack, W. A. (1980). *A homework manual for biblical counselors, Vol. 2. Family and marital problems.* Phillipsburg, NJ: Presbyterian & Reformed.

Mack, W. A. (1994a). Biblical counseling and inducement. In J. F. MacArthur & W. A. Mack (Eds.), *Introduction to biblical counseling* (pp. 268-83). Dallas: Word.

Mack, W. A. (1994b). Developing a helping relationship with counselees. In J. F. MacArthur & W. A. Mack (Eds.), *Introduction to biblical counseling* (pp. 173-87). Dallas: Word.

Mack, W. A. (1994c). Implementing biblical instruction. In J. F. MacArthur & W. A. Mack (Eds.), *Introduction to biblical counseling* (pp. 284-99). Dallas: Word.

Mack, W. A. (1994d). Providing instruction through biblical counseling. In J. F. MacArthur & W. A. Mack (Eds.), *Introduction to biblical counseling* (pp. 250-67). Waco, TX: Word.

Mack, W. A. (1997). What is biblical counseling? In E. Hindson & H. Eyrich (Eds.), *Totally sufficient: The Bible and Christian counseling* (pp. 25-55). Eugene, OR: Harvest House.

Mack, W. A., & Johnston, W. E. (2005). *A Christian growth and discipleship manual. A homework manual for biblical living: Vol. 3.* Minnesota: Focus.

Mackay, D. (1982). *The clockwork image.* Downers Grove, IL: InterVarsity Press.

Macmurray, J. (1957). *The self as agent.* London: Faber and Faber.

Maddox, D. B. (1994). Union with Christ: The implications for biblical counseling. In

J. F. MacArthur & W. A. Mack (Eds.), *Introduction to biblical counseling* (pp. 116-29). Dallas: Word.

Madtes, P., Jr., & Hyndman, A. (1997). What about biomedical research? In E. Hindson & H. Eyrich (Eds.), *Totally sufficient: The Bible and Christian counseling* (pp. 165-89). Eugene, OR: Harvest House.

Magnavita, J. (1999). *Relational therapy for personality disorders.* New York: Wiley.

Mahalik, J. R. (1995). Practitioners' value-orientation: Examination of core values and influence of theoretical orientation. *Counseling and Values, 39,* 228-39.

Mahaney, C. J., & Boisvert, R. (1992). *This great salvation: Unmerited favor, unmatched joy.* Gaithersburg, MD: Sovereign Grace Ministries.

Mahrer, A. R. (1983). *Experiential psychotherapy: Basic practices.* New York: Brunner/Mazel.

Mahrer, A. R. (1998). How can impressive in-session changes become impressive postsession changes? In L. S. Greenberg, J. C. Watson & G. Lietaer (Eds.), *Handbook of experiential psychotherapy* (pp. 201-25). New York: Guilford.

Malik, M. L., & Beutler, L. E. (2002). The emergence of dissatisfaction with the DSM. In L. E. Beutler & M. L. Malik (Eds.), *Rethinking the DSM: A psychological perspective* (pp. 3-16). Washington, DC: American Psychological Association.

Maloney, M. P. (1990). Psychological evaluation and diagnosis. In R. J. Hunter (Ed.), *Dictionary of pastoral care and counseling* (pp. 366-71). Nashville: Abingdon.

Mandler, J. (1998). Representation. In W. Damon (Series Ed.) & D. Kuhn & R. S. Siegler (Vol. Eds.), *Handbook of child psychology: Vol. 2. Cognition, perception, and language* (5th ed., pp. 255-308). New York: John Wiley.

Manning, B. (2002). *Abba's child.* Colorado Springs, CO: NavPress.

Marion, J.-L. (1991). *God without being.* Chicago: University of Chicago Press.

Markowitsch, H. J. (2000). Neuroanatomy of memory. In E. Tulving & F. I. M. Craik (Eds.), *The Oxford handbook of memory* (pp. 465-84). New York: Oxford University Press.

Markus, H., & Nurius, P. (1986). Possible selves. *American Psychologist, 41,* 954-69.

Marsden, G. M. (1994). *The soul of the American university: From Protestant establishment to established nonbelief.* New York: Oxford University Press.

Marsden, G. M. (2003). *Jonathan Edwards: A life.* New Haven, CT: Yale University Press.

Martin, J. (1994). *The construction and understanding of psychotherapeutic change.* New York: Teachers College Press.

Martin, J., Sugarman, J., & Thompson, J. (2003). *Psychology and the question of agency.* Albany: State University of New York Press.

Martin, M. (1986). *Self-deception and morality.* Lawrence: University Press of Kansas.

Maslow, A. H. (1954). *Motivation and personality.* New York: Harper & Brothers.

Maslow, A. H. (1968). *Toward a psychology of being* (2nd ed.). New York: D. Van Nostrand.

May, R. (1953). *Man's search for himself.* New York: W. W. Norton.

May, R. (1967). *Psychology and the human dilemma.* Princeton, NJ: D. Van Nostrand.

May, R. (1969). *Love and will.* New York: W. W. Norton.

Mayer, J. D. (2005). A tale of two visions: Can a new view of personality help integrate psychology? *American Psychologist, 60,* 294-307.

Mayer, J. D., & Salovey, P. (1997). What is emotional intelligence? In P. Salovey & D. J. Sluyter (Eds.), *Emotional development and emotional intelligence* (pp. 3-31). New York: Basic Books.

McAdams, D. P. (1993). *The stories we live by: Personal myths and the making of the self.* New York: Guilford.

McAdams, D. P. (1999). Personal narratives and the life story. In L. A. Pervin & O. P. John (Eds.), *Handbook of personality: Theory and research* (2nd ed., pp. 478-500). New York: Guilford.

McAdams, D. P., & Pals, J. L. (2006). A new big five: Fundamental principles for an integrative science of personality. *American Psychologist, 61,* 204-17.

McCabe, L. A., Cunnington, M., & Brooks-Gunn, J. (2004). The development of self-regulation in young children: Individual characteristics and environmental contexts. In R. F. Baumeister & K. D. Vohs (Eds.), *The handbook of self-regulation* (pp. 340-56). New York: Guilford.

McCarthy, M. (2000). Spirituality in a postmodern era. In J. Woodward & S. Pattison (Eds.), *The Blackwell reader in pastoral and practical theology* (pp. 192-206). London: Blackwell.

McCrae, R. R., & Costa, P. T., Jr. (1990). *Personality in adulthood.* New York: Guilford.

McConnell, T. I. (2005). The influence of idealism on the apologetics of Cornelius Van Til. *Journal of the Evangelical Theological Society, 48,* 557-88.

McCullough, L., Kuhn, N., Andrews, S., Kaplan, A., Wolf, J., & Hurley, C. L. (2003). *Treating affect phobia: A manual for short-term dynamic psychotherapy.* New York: Guilford.

McCullough, M. E., Pargament, K. I., & Thoresen, C. E. (Eds.). (2000). *Forgiveness: Theory, research, and practice.* New York: Guilford.

McCullough, M. E., Sandage, S. J., & Worthington, E. L., Jr. (1997). *To forgive is human: How to put your past in the past.* Downers Grove, IL: InterVarsity Press.

McDargh, J. (1983). *Psychoanalytic object relations theory and the study of religion: On faith and the imaging of God.* Lanham, MD: University Press of America.

McDonald, A., Beck, R., Allison, S., & Norsworthy, L. (2005). Attachment to God and parents: Testing the correspondence vs. compensation hypotheses. *Journal of Psychology and Christianity, 24,* 21-28.

McGee, R. S. (1990). *Search for significance* (2nd ed.). Houston: Rapha.

McGinn, C. (2000). *The mysterious flame: Conscious minds in a material world.* New York: Basic Books.

McGrath, A. E. (1988). *Reformation thought: An introduction.* London: Blackwell.

McGrath, A. E. (1990). *A life of John Calvin.* Oxford: Blackwell.

McGrath, A. E. (1995). *Evangelicalism and the future of Christianity.* Downers Grove, IL: InterVarsity Press.

McGrath, A. E. (1999a). *Christian spirituality.* London: Blackwell.

McGrath, A. E. (1999b). *Reformation thought: An introduction* (3rd ed.). London: Blackwell.

McGrath, A. E. (2001). *A scientific theology: Vol. 1. Nature.* Grand Rapids, MI: Eerdmans.

McGrath, A. E. (2002). *A scientific theology: Vol. 2. Reality.* Grand Rapids, MI: Eerdmans.

McGrath, A. E. (2003). *A scientific theology: Vol. 3. Theory.* Grand Rapids, MI: Eerdmans.

McHoul, A. (1998). Text. In P. Bouissac (Ed.), *Encyclopedia of semiotics* (pp. 609-11). New York: Oxford University Press.

McKenzie, W., & Monk, G. (1997). Learning and teaching narrative ideas. In G. Monk, J. Winslade, K. Crocket & D. Epston (Eds.), *Narrative therapy in practice: The archaeology of hope* (pp. 82-120). San Francisco: Jossey-Bass.

McMinn, M. R. (1988). *Your hidden half.* Grand Rapids, MI: Baker.

McMinn, M. R. (1991). *Cognitive therapy techniques in Christian counseling.* Waco, TX: Word.

McMinn, M. R. (1996). *Psychology, theology, and spirituality in Christian counseling.* Wheaton, IL: Tyndale House.

McMinn, M. R. (2001, August). Connection, not logic: Relational cognitive therapy and Christianity. Paper presented at the meeting of the American Association of Christian Counselors, Nashville.

McMinn, M. R. (2004). *Why sin matters.* Wheaton, IL: Tyndale House.

McMinn, M. R. (2006). *Christian counseling* (Video from the Spirituality APA Psychotherapy series). Washington, DC: American Psychological Association.

McMinn, M. R., & Campbell, C. D. (2007). *Integrative psychotherapy: Toward a comprehensive Christian approach.* Downers Grove, IL: InterVarsity Press.

McMinn, M. R., & Dominquez, A. W. (2005). *Psychology and the church.* Nova Science Publishers.

McQuilkin, J. R. (1977). The behavioral sciences under the authority of scripture. *Journal of the Evangelical Theological Society, 20,* 31-44.

Mead, G. H. (1934). *Mind, self, and society from the standpoint of a social behaviorist.* Chicago: University of Chicago Press.

Meichenbaum, D. (1977). *Cognitive-behavior modification: An integrative approach.* New York: Plenum.

Meisel, A. C., & del Mastro, M. L. (Eds.). (1975). *The rule of St. Benedict.* New York: Doubleday.

Meissner, W. W. (1987). *Life and faith: Psychological perspectives on religious experience.* Washington, DC: Georgetown University Press.

Meissner, W. W. (1991). *What is effective in psychoanalytic therapy: The move from interpretation to relation.* New York: Jason Aronson.

Merleau-Ponty, M. (1962). *Phenomenology of perception* (C. Smith, Trans.). London: Routledge.

Merleau-Ponty, M. (1963). *The structure of behavior* (A. L. Fisher, Trans.). New York: Beacon Press. (Original work published 1942)

Merrell, F. (1991). *Signs becoming signs: Our perfusive, pervasive universe.* Bloomington: Indiana University Press.

Merton, T. (1951). *The ascent to truth.* New York: Harcourt, Brace.

Merton, T. (1955). *No man is an island.* San Diego: Harcourt Brace Jovanovich.

Merton, T. (1960). *Spiritual direction and meditation.* Collegeville, MN: Liturgical Press.

Metcalfe, J. (2000). Metamemory: Theory and data. In E. Tulving & F. I. M. Craik (Eds.), *The Oxford handbook of memory* (pp. 197-214). New York: Oxford University Press.

Metzger, B. M. (1965). *The New Testament: Its background, growth, and content.* Nashville: Abingdon.

Milbank, J. (1990). *Theology and social theory: Beyond secular reason.* London: Blackwell.

Milbank, J. (1997). *The word made strange: Theology, language, culture.* London: Blackwell.

Milbank, J. (2005). *The suspended middle: Henri de Lubac and the debate concerning the supernatural.* Grand Rapids, MI: Eerdmans.

Miller, D. T., & Prentice, D. A. (1996). The construction of social norms and standards. In E. T. Higgins & A. W. Kruglanski (Eds.), *Social psychology: Handbook of basic principles* (pp. 799-829). New York: Guilford.

Miller, D. T., & Ross, M. Self-serving biases in attribution of causality: Fact or fiction? *Psychological Bulletin, 82,* 213-25.

Miller, G. A., Galanter, E., & Pribram, K. H. (1960). *Plans and the structure of behavior.* New York: Henry Holt.

Miller, W. R. (1999). *Integrating spirituality into treatment.* Washington, DC: American Psychological Association.

Miller, W. R., & C'de Baca, J. (2001). *Quantum change: When epiphanies and sudden insights transform ordinary lives.* New York: Guilford.

Miller, W. R., & Delaney, H. D. (2005). *Judeo-Christian perspectives on psychology: Human nature, motivation, and change.* Washington, DC: American Psychological Association.

Minsky, M. (1988). *The society of mind.* New York: Simon & Schuster.

Minuchin, S. (1974). *Families and family therapy.* Cambridge, MA: Harvard University Press.

Mischel, W., & Aydouk, O. (2004). Willpower in a cognitive-affective processing system. In R. F. Baumeister & K. D. Vohs (Ed.), *The handbook of self-regulation* (pp. 99-129). New York: Guilford.

Mischel, W., & Shoda, Y. (1999). Integrating dispositions and processing dynamics within a unified theory of personality: The cognitive-affective personality system. In L. A. Pervin & O. P. John (Eds.), *Handbook of personality* (2nd ed., pp. 197-218). New York: Guilford.

Mischel, W., Shoda, Y., & Ridriguez, M. L. (1989). Delay of gratification in children. *Science, 44,* 933-38.

Mischel, W., Shoda, Y., & Smith, R. E. (2004). *Introduction to personality: Toward an integration.* New York: Wiley.

Mohler, R. A. (n.d.). *Homosexuality and the Bible.* Louisville, KY: Southern Baptist Theological Seminary.

Molnar, P. D. (2000). Karl Barth. In T. A. Hart (Ed.), *The dictionary of historical theology* (pp. 53-58). Grand Rapids, MI: Eerdmans.

Monk, G., Winslade, J., Crocket, K., & Epston, D. (Eds.). (1997). *Narrative therapy in practice: The archaeology of hope.* San Fancisco: Jossey-Bass.

Monod, A. (1962). *Adolphe Monod's farewell.* London: Banner of Truth.

Montgomery, J. W. (Ed.). (1976). *Demon possession.* Minneapolis: Bethany.

Moo, D. J. (1993). The law of Christ as the fulfillment of the law of Moses: A modified Lutheran approach. In S. N. Gundry (Ed.), *Five views on law and gospel* (pp. 319-76). Grand Rapids, MI: Zondervan.

Moon, G. W. (2004). *Falling for God.* Colorado Springs, CO: Shaw.

Moon, G. W., & Benner, D. G. (Eds.). (2002). Special issue: Psychotherapy and spiritual direction, Part I. *Journal of Psychology and Theology, 30.*

Moon, G. W., & Benner, D. G. (2004). Spiritual direction and Christian soul care. In G. W. Moon & D. G. Benner (Eds.), *Spiritual direction and the care of souls* (pp. 11-30). Downers Grove, IL: InterVarsity Press.

Moreland, J. P. (2001). *Universals.* Montreal, Quebec: McGill-Queens University Press.

Moreland, J. P., & Craig, W. L. (2003). *Philosophical foundations for a Christian worldview.* Downers Grove, IL: InterVarsity Press.

Moreland, J. P., & Rae, S. B. (2000). *Body and soul: Human nature and the crisis in ethics.* Downers Grove, IL: InterVarsity Press.

Moreno, J. L. (1977). *Who shall survive? Foundations of sociometry, group psychotherapy, and sociodrama.* Boston: Beacon.

Morgan, J. (1999). The Puritan thesis revisited. In D. N. Livingstone, D. A. Hart & M. A. Noll (Eds.), *Evangelicals and science in historical perspective* (pp. 43-74). New York: Oxford University Press.

Moroney, S. (1999). *The noetic effects of sin.* Lanham, MD: Lexington Books.

Morrow, T. W. J. (1988). Systematic theology. In S. B. Ferguson & D. F. Wright (Eds.), *New dictionary of theology* (p. 671). Downers Grove, IL: InterVarsity Press.

Morson, G. S., & Emerson, C. (1990). *Mikhail Bakhtin: Creation of a prosaics.* Stanford, CA: Stanford University Press.

Morton, A. (2002). *The importance of being understood: folk psychology as ethics.* New York: Routledge.

Moshman, D. (1998). Cognitive development beyond childhood. In W. Damon (Series Ed.) & D. Kuhn & R. S. Siegler (Vol. Eds.), *Handbook of child psychology: Vol. 2. Cogni-*

tion, perception, and language (5th ed., pp. 947-77). New York: John Wiley.

Mounce, R. H. (1986). Kerygma. In G. W. Bromiley (Ed.), *The international standard Bible encyclopedia* (Vol. 3, pp. 9-10). Grand Rapids, MI: Eerdmans.

Mouw, R. J. (1990). *The God who commands.* Notre Dame, IN: University of Notre Dame Press.

Mouw, R. J. (1992). *Uncommon decency: Christian civility in an uncivil world.* Downers Grove, IL: InterVarsity Press.

Mouw, R. J. (1994). *Consulting the faithful.* Grand Rapids, MI: Eerdmans.

Mouw, R. J. (2000). *The smell of sawdust.* Grand Rapids, MI: Zondervan.

Mouw, R. J. (2001). *He shines in all that's fair.* Grand Rapids, MI: Eerdmans.

Muller, R. A. (1995). Grace, election, and contingent choice: Arminius's gambit and the Reformed response. In T. R. Schreiner & B. A. Ware (Eds.), *The grace of God, the bondage of the will.* Grand Rapids, MI: Baker.

Muller, R. A. (2003). *Post-Reformation Reformed dogmatics* (4 Vols.). Grand Rapids, MI: Baker.

Murphy, G. (1949). *Historical introduction to modern psychology.* New York: Harcourt, Brace.

Murphy, N. (1998). Non reductive physicalism: Philosophical issues. In W. S. Brown, N. Murphy & H. N. Malony (Eds.), *Whatever happened to the soul? Scientific and theological portraits of human nature* (pp. 127-76). Minneapolis: Augsburg.

Murphy, N., & Ellis, G. F. R. (1996). *On the moral nature of the universe: Theology, cosmology, and ethics.* Minneapolis: Augsburg.

Murphy, N., Kallenberg, B. J., & Nation, M. T. (Eds.). (1997). *Virtues and practices in the Christian tradition.* Notre Dame, IN: University of Notre Dame Press.

Murphy, R. E. (1996). *The tree of life: An exploration of biblical wisdom literature.* Grand Rapids, MI: Eerdmans.

Murray, A. (1985). *The Andrew Murray Collection.* Uhrichsville, OH: Barbour.

Murray, J. (1953). The attestation of Scripture. In N. B. Stonehouse & P. Woolley (Eds.), *The infallible word: A symposium* (pp. 1-53). Grand Rapids, MI: Eerdmans.

Murray, J. (1955). *Redemption accomplished and applied.* Grand Rapids, MI: Eerdmans.

Murray, J. (1977). Common grace. In *Collected writings of John Murray: Volume 2. Select lectures in systematic theology* (pp. 93-122). Edinburgh: The Banner of Truth Trust.

Murray, M. J. (2002). Deus absconditus. In D. Howard-Synder & P. K. Moser (Eds.), *Divine hiddenness* (pp. 62-82). Cambridge: Cambridge University Press.

Myers, D. G. (1978). *The human puzzle: Psychological research and Christian belief.* New York: Harper & Row.

Myers, D. G. (1993). *The pursuit of happiness.* New York: Avon.

Myers, D. G. (1996). On professing psychological science and Christian faith. *Journal of Psychology and Christianity, 15,* 143-49.

Myers, D. G. (2000). The levels-of-explanation approach. In E. L. Johnson & S. L. Jones (Eds.), *Psychology and Christianity: Four views.* Downers Grove, IL: InterVarsity Press.

Myers, D. G. (2001). *Social psychology* (7th ed.). New York: McGraw-Hill.

Myers, D. G. (2003). *Psychology* (7th ed.). New York: Worth.

Myers, D. G., & Jeeves, M. A. (1987). *Psychology through the eyes of faith.* New York: Harper & Row.

Myers, D. G., & Scanzoni, L. D. (2005). *What God has joined together? A Christian case for gay marriage.* San Francisco: Harper.

Narramore, C. M. (1960). *The psychology of counseling: Professional techniques for pastors, teachers, youth leaders, and all who are engaged in the incomparable art of counseling.* Grand Rapids, MI: Zondervan.

Narramore, S. B. (1973). Perspectives on the integration of psychology and theology. *Journal of Psychology and Theology, 1,* 3-17.

Narramore, S. B. (1984). *No condemnation: Rethinking guilt motivation in counseling, preaching, and parenting.* Grand Rapids, MI: Zondervan.

Nash, R. H. (1982). *The word of God and the mind of man.* Grand Rapids, MI: Zondervan.

Nash, R. H. (1988). *Reason and faith.* Grand Rapids, MI: Zondervan.

Naugle, D. K. (2002). *Worldview: The history of a concept.* Grand Rapids, MI: Eerdmans.

Neilsen, S. L., Johnson, W. B., & Ellis, A. (2001). *Counseling and psychotherapy with religious persons: A rational emotive behavior therapy approach.* Mahway, NJ: Lawrence Erlbaum.

Nevius, J. (1892). *Demon possession and allied themes.* Chicago: Fleming H. Revell.

Newton, J. (1985). *The works of John Newton.* Edinburgh: Banner of Truth Trust. (Original work published 1820)

Nicolosi, J. (1997). *Reparative therapy of male homosexuality: A new clinical approach.* New York: Jason Aronson.

Niebuhr, H. R. (1951). *Christ and culture.* New York: Harper & Bros.

Niebuhr, R. R. (2005). Being and consent. In S. H. Lee (Ed.), *The Princeton companion to Jonathan Edwards* (pp. 34-43). Princeton, NJ: Princeton University Press.

Niederhoffer, K. G., & Pennebaker, J. W. (2002). Sharing one's story: On the benefits of writing or talking about emotional experience. In C. R. Snyder & S. J. Lopez (Eds.), *Handbook of positive psychology* (pp. 573-83). Oxford: Oxford University Press.

Nielsen, S. L., Johnson, W. B., & Ellis, A. (2001). *Counseling and psychotherapy with religious persons: A Rational Emotive Behavior Therapy approach.* Mahwah, NJ: LEA.

Noll, M. A. (1995). *The scandal of the evangelical mind.* Grand Rapids, MI: Eerdmans.

Noll, M. A., & Nystrom, C. (2005). *Is the Reformation over? An evangelical assessment of contemporary Roman Catholicism.* Grand Rapids, MI: Baker.

Norcross, J. D., & Goldfried, M. R. (Eds.). (1992). *Handbook of psychotherapy integration.* New York: Basic Books.

Norcross, J. D., & Goldfried, M. R. (Eds.). (2005). *Handbook of psychotherapy integration* (2nd ed.). New York: Oxford University Press.

Norris, J. (2001). Augustine and sign in *Tractatus in Iohannis Euangelium.* In F. Van Fleteren & J. C. Schnaubelt (Eds.), *Augustine: Biblical exegete* (pp. 215-31). New York: Peter Lang.

Nöth, W. (1990). *Handbook of semiotics*. Bloomington: Indiana University Press.

Nussbaum, M. C. (1994). *The therapy of desire: Theory and practice in Hellenistic ethics*. Princeton, NJ: Princeton University Press.

Nussbaum, M. C. (2001). *Upheavals of thought: The intelligence of emotions*. Cambridge: Cambridge University Press.

Oates, W. E. (1953). *The Bible in pastoral care*. Philadelphia: Westminster Press.

Oates, W. E. (Ed.). (1959). *An introduction to pastoral counseling*. Nashville: Broadman.

Oates, W. E. (1962). *Protestant pastoral counseling*. Philadelphia: Westminster Press.

Oates, W. E. (1986). *The presence of God in pastoral counseling*. Waco, TX: Word.

Ochsner, K. N., & Gross, J. J. (2004). Thinking makes it so: A social cognitive neuroscience approach to emotion regulation. In R. F. Baumeister & K. D. Vohs (Eds.), *Handbook of self-regulation: Research, theory, and applications* (pp. 229-55). New York: Guilford.

Oden, T. C. (1966). *Kerygma and counseling: Towards a covenant ontology for secular psychotherapy*. Philadelphia: Westminster Press.

Oden, T. C. (1967). *Contemporary theology and psychotherapy*. Philadelphia: Westminster Press.

Oden, T. C. (1972). *The intensive group experience: The new pietism*. Philadelphia: Westminster Press.

Oden, T. C. (1984). *Care of souls in the classic tradition*. Philadelphia: Fortress.

Oden, T. C. (1987-1992). *Systematic theology: Volumes 1-3*. San Francisco: Harper.

Oden, T. C. (1989). *First and Second Timothy and Titus*. Louisville, KY: John Knox.

Oden, T. C. (1990). *After modernity—What?* Grand Rapids, MI: Zondervan.

Oden, T. C. (2003). *The rebirth of orthodoxy: Signs of new life in Christianity*. San Francisco: Harper.

O'Donnell, J. J. (1999). Bible. In A. D. Fitzgerald (Gen. Ed.), *Augustine through the ages: An encyclopedia* (pp. 99-103). Grand Rapids, MI: Eerdmans.

O'Donohue, W. (1989). The (even) bolder model: The clinical psychologist as metaphysician-scientist-practitioner. *American Psychologist, 44*, 153-64.

O'Donovan, O. (1980). *The problem of self-love in St. Augustine*. New Haven, CT: Yale University Press.

O'Donovan, O. (1986). *Resurrection and moral order: An outline for evangelical ethics*. Grand Rapids, MI: Eerdmans.

Oglesby, W. B., Jr. (1980). *Biblical themes for pastoral care*. Nashville: Abingdon.

Olson, D. R. (1994). *The world on paper: The conceptual and cognitive implications of writing and reading*. Cambridge: Cambridge University Press.

Olson, R. E., & Hall, C. A. (2002). *The trinity*. Grand Rapids, MI: Eerdmans.

Olson, R. P. (1997). *The reconciled life: A critical theory of counseling*. Westport, CT: Praeger.

Olthuis, J. H. (1997). Face to face: Ethical asymmetry or the symmetry of mutuality? In

J. H. Olthuis (Ed.), *Knowing otherwise: Philosophy at the threshold of spirituality.* New York: Fordham University Press.

Olthuis, J. H. (2001). *The beautiful risk: A new psychology of loving and being loved.* Grand Rapids, MI: Zondervan.

Orlinsky, D. E., Ronnestad, M. H., & Willutzki, U. (2004). Fifty years of psychotherapy process-outcome research: Continuity and change. In M. Lambert (Ed.), *Bergin & Garfield's handbook of psychotherapy and behavior change* (5th ed., pp. 307-89). New York: John Wiley & Sons.

Orr, J. (1904). *A Christian view of God and the world.* New York: Charles Scribner's Sons.

Osborne, G. R. (1991). *The hermeneutical spiral: A comprehensive introduction to biblical interpretation.* Downers Grove, IL: InterVarsity Press.

Osterhaven, M. E. (1971). *The spirit of the Reformed tradition.* Grand Rapids, MI: Eerdmans.

Owen, J. (1954). *The Holy Spirit: His gifts and power.* Grand Rapids, MI: Kregel.

Owen, J. (1967). *The works of John Owen* (Vols. 1-16). Edinburgh: Banner of Truth Trust. (Original work published 1850-1853)

Packer, J. I. (1973). *Knowing God.* Downers Grove, IL: InterVarsity Press.

Packer, J. I. (1974). Introduction. *The reformed pastor.* Edinburgh: Banner of Truth Trust.

Packer, J. I. (1980). *Beyond the battle for the Bible.* Westchester, IL: Cornerstone.

Packer, J. I. (1988). Scripture. In S. B. Ferguson, D. F. Wright & J. I. Packer (Eds.), *New dictionary of theology* (pp. 627-31). Downers Grove, IL: InterVarsity Press.

Packer, J. I. (1990a). *A quest for godliness: The Puritan vision of the Christian life.* Wheaton, IL: Crossway.

Packer, J. I. (1990b). Introduction. *A Christian directory* by Richard Baxter. Ligonier, PA: Soli Deo Gloria.

Packer, J. I. (1992). *Rediscovering holiness.* Ann Arbor, MI: Servant.

Paivio, A. (1990). *Mental representations: A dual coding approach.* New York: Oxford University Press.

Palmer, G. E. H., Sherrard, P., & Ware, K. (Eds.). (1979-1984). *The philokalia.* London: Faber and Faber. (Original work published 1782)

Palmer, R. E. (1969). *Hermeneutics.* Evanston, IL: Northwestern University Press.

Paloutzian, R. F., Richardson, J. T., & Rambo, L. R. (1999). Religious conversion and personality. *Journal of Personality, 67,* 1047-79.

Panksepp, J. (1994). The cleareast physiological distinctions between emotions will be found among the circuits of the brain. In P. Ekman & R. J. Davidson (Eds.), *The nature of emotion: Fundamental questions* (pp. 258-60). New York: Oxford University Press.

Pannenberg, W. (1985). *Anthropology in Christian perspective* (M. J. O'Connell, Trans.). Philadelphia: Westminster Press.

Pargament, K. I. (1997). *The psychology of religion and coping.* New York: Guilford.

Pargament, K. I., Kennell, J., Hathaway, W., Grevengoed, N., Newman, J., & Jones, W.

(1988). Religion and the problem-solving process: Three styles of coping. *Journal for the Scientific Study of Religion, 27*, 90-104.

Parker, J. D. A. (2000). Emotional intelligence: Clinical and therapeutic implications. In R. Bar-On & J. D. A. Parker (Eds.), *The handbook of emotional intelligence* (pp. 490-504). San Francisco: Jossey-Bass.

Parsons, T., & Shils, E. A. (1951). *Toward a general theory of action*. New York: Harper & Row.

Pascal, B. (1941). *Pensées/Provincial letters*. New York: Random House.

Patterson, S. (1999). *Realist Christian theology in a postmodern age*. Cambridge: Cambridge University Press.

Patton, J. (1983). *Pastoral counseling: A ministry of the church*. Nashville: Abingdon.

Patton, J. (1990). Pastoral counseling. In R. J. Hunter (Ed.), *Dictionary of pastoral care and counseling* (pp. 849-54). Nashville: Abingdon.

Patton, J. (1993). *Pastoral care in context: An introduction to pastoral care*. Louisville, KY: Westminster John Knox.

Pauw, A. P. (2001). *The supreme harmony of all: The trinitarian theology of Jonathan Edwards*. Grand Rapids, MI: Eerdmans.

Payne, L. (1991). *Restoring the Christian soul*. Grand Rapids, MI: Baker.

Payne, L. (1994). *Listening prayer*. Grand Rapids, MI: Baker.

Payne, L. (1995). *The healing presence: Curing the soul through union with Christ*. Grand Rapids, MI: Baker.

Payne, L. (1996). *Healing homosexuality*. Grand Rapids, MI: Baker.

PDM Task Force. (2006). *Psychodynamic Diagnostic Manual*. Silverspring, MD: Alliance of Psychoanalytic Organizations.

Pearce, S. S. (1996). *Flash of insight: Metaphor and narrative in therapy*. Boston: Allyn & Bacon.

Pearcey, N. R. (2004). *Total truth: Liberating Christianity from its cultural captivity*. Wheaton, IL: Crossway.

Pearcey, N. R., & Thaxton, C. B. (1994). *The soul of science: Christian faith and natural philosophy*. Wheaton, IL: Crossway.

Pelzer, D. (1995). *A child called "it."* Deerfield Beach, FL: HCI.

Pennebaker, J. W. (1997). *Opening up: The healing power of expressing emotions* (Rev. ed.). New York: Guilford.

Pennington, B. F. (2002). *The development of psychopathology: Nature and nurture*. New York: Guilford.

Pennington, M. B. (1980). *Centering prayer*. Garden City, NY: Image Books.

Perner, J. (2000). Memory and theory of mind. In E. Tulving & F. I. M. Craik (Eds.), *The Oxford handbook of memory* (pp. 297-313). New York: Oxford University Press.

Pervin, L. A., & John, O. P. (1999). *Handbook of personality* (2nd ed.). New York: Guilford.

Peterson, C., & Seligman, M. E. P. (Eds.). (2004). *Character strengths and virtues: A hand-*

book and classification. New York: Oxford University Press.

Petrovsky, A. V. (1985). *Studies in psychology: The collective and the individual.* Moscow: Progress.

Petty, F., Chae, Y., Kramer, G., Jordan, S., & Wilson, L. (1994). Learned helplessness sensitizes hippocampal norepinephrrine to mild stress. *Biological Psychiatry, 35,* 903-8.

Piaget, J. (1954). *The construction of reality in the child.* New York: Basic Books.

Pieper, J. (1966). *The four cardinal virtues.* Notre Dame, IN: University of Notre Dame Press.

Pierce, C. S. (1958). *The collected papers of Charles Sanders Pierce: Vols. 1-6.* Cambridge, MA: Harvard University Press.

Pinker, S. (1999). *How the mind works.* New York: W. W. Norton.

Piper, J. (1986). *Desiring God: Meditations of a Christian hedonist.* Sisters, OR: Multnomah.

Piper, J. (1991). *The pleasure of God.* Sisters, OR: Multnomah.

Piper, J. (1993). *Let the nations be glad! The supremacy of God in missions.* Grand Rapids, MI: Baker.

Piper, J. (1995). *Living by faith in future grace.* Sisters, OR: Multnomah.

Piper, J. (1996). *Desiring God: Meditations of a Christian hedonist.* Portland, OR: Multnomah.

Piper, J. (1998). *God's passion for his glory.* Wheaton, IL: Crossway.

Piper, J. (2002). God's glory is the goal of biblical counseling. *Journal of Biblical Counseling, 20,* 8-21.

Piper, J. (2005, February 9). Thoughts on the sufficiency of Scripture. *The Bethlehem Star.*

Plantinga, A. (1968). *God and other minds.* Ithaca, NY: Cornell University Press.

Plantinga, A. (1981). Is belief in God properly basic? *Nous, 15,* 41-51.

Plantinga, A. (1983). Advice to Christian philosophers. *Faith and Philosophy, 1,* 1-13.

Plantinga, A. (1993a). Divine knowledge. In C. S. Evans & M. Westphal (Eds.), *Christian perspectives on religious knowledge* (pp. 40-66). Grand Rapids, MI: Eerdmans.

Plantinga, A. (1993b). *Warrant and proper function.* New York: Oxford University Press.

Plantinga, A. (2000). *Warranted Christian belief.* New York: Oxford University Press.

Plantinga, A. (2003). Two (or more) kinds of Scripture scholarship. In C. Bartholomew, C. S. Evans, M. Healy & M. Rae (Eds.), *Behind the text: History and biblical interpretation* (pp. 19-57). Grand Rapids, MI: Zondervan.

Plantinga, C., Jr. (1995). *Not the way it's supposed to be: A breviary of sin.* Grand Rapids, MI: Eerdmans.

Plantinga, C., Jr. (2002). *Engaging God's world: A Christian vision of faith, learning, and living.* Grand Rapids, MI: Eerdmans.

Plass, R. E. (2002). *A theological and empirical assessment of narcissism in theological students: A pilot study.* Unpublished doctoral dissertation, Southern Baptist Theological Seminary, Louisville, KY.

Plato. (1961). *Plato: The collected dialogues.* Princeton, NJ: Princeton University Press.

Plutchik, R. (1994). *The psychology and biology of emotion*. New York: HarperCollins.

Polanyi, M. (1958). *Personal knowledge*. Chicago: University of Chicago Press.

Polanyi, M. (1966). *The tacit dimension*. Garden City, NY: Doubleday.

Polkinghorne, D. E. (1988). *Narrative knowing and the human sciences*. Albany: State University of New York.

Popper, K. R., & Eccles, J. C. (1977). *The self and its brain*. Berlin: Springer.

Povinelli, D. J., & Prince, C. G. (1998). When self met other. In M. Ferrari & R. J. Sternberg (Eds.), *Self-awareness: Its nature and development* (pp. 37-106). New York: Guilford.

Powlison, D. (1988). Crucial issues in contemporary biblical counseling. *The Journal of Pastoral Practice, 9*, 3-10.

Powlison, D. (1992). Integration or inundation? In M. Horton (Ed.), *Power religion* (pp. 191-218). Chicago: Moody Press.

Powlison, D. (1993). Twenty-five years of biblical counseling: An interview with Jay Adams and John Bettler. *Journal of Biblical Counseling, 12*, 8-13.

Powlison, D. (1994a). Biblical counseling in the twentieth century. In J. F. MacArthur & W. A. Mack (Eds.), *Introduction to biblical counseling* (p. 44-60). Dallas: Word.

Powlison, D. (1994b). Frequently asked questions about biblical counseling. In J. F. MacArthur & W. A. Mack (Eds.), *Introduction to biblical counseling* (p. 365-66). Dallas: Word.

Powlison, D. (1995a). Idols of the heart and "Vanity Fair." *Journal of Biblical Counseling, 13*, 35-50.

Powlison, D. (1995b). *Power encounters*. Grand Rapids, MI: Baker.

Powlison, D. (1996a). *Competent to counsel? The history of a conservative protestant anti-psychiatry movement*. Unpublished doctoral dissertation, University of Pennsylvania.

Powlison, D. (1996b). How shall we cure troubled souls? In J. H. Armstrong, (Ed.), *The coming evangelical crisis: Current challenges to the authority of scripture and the gospel* (pp. 207-25). Chicago: Moody Press.

Powlison, D. (1997). Does biblical counseling really work? In E. Hindson & H. Eyrich (Eds.), *Totally sufficient: The Bible and Christian counseling* (pp. 57-97). Eugene, OR: Harvest House.

Powlison, D. (1999a). Counsel Ephesians. *Journal of Biblical Counseling, 17*(2), 2-11.

Powlison, D. (1999b). *Pornography: Slaying the dragon within*. Phillipsburg, NJ: Presbyterian & Reformed.

Powlison, D. (2000). Affirmations & denials: A proposed definition of biblical counseling. *Journal of Biblical Counseling, 19*(1), 18-25.

Powlison, D. (2002). Do you see? In D. Powlison & W. P. Smith (Eds.), *Counsel the Word* (2nd ed., pp. 2-6). Glenside, PA: Christian Counseling & Educational Foundation.

Powlison, D. (2003). *Seeing with new eyes: Counseling and the human condition through the lens of Scripture*. Phillipsburg, NJ: Presbyterian & Reformed.

Powlison, D. (2004). Is the "Adonis complex" in *your* Bible? *Journal of Biblical Couseling, 22*(2), 42-58.

Powlison, D. (2005). *Speaking truth in love*. Phillipsburg, NJ: Presbyterian & Reformed.

Poythress, V. (1980). Mathematics. *Journal of Christian Reconstruction, 1*.

Poythress, V. (1987). *Symphonic theology: The validity of multiple perspectives in theology.* Grand Rapids, MI: Zondervan.

Poythress, V. S. (2006). *Redeeming science: A God-centered approach.* Wheaton, IL: Crossway.

Pratt, M. L. (1977). *Toward a speech act theory of literary discourse*. Bloomington: Indiana University Press.

Preus, R. D. (1979). The view of the Bible held by the church: The early church through Luther. In N. L. Geisler (Ed.), *Inerrancy* (pp. 357-84). Grand Rapids, MI: Zondervan.

Price, D. J. (2002). *Karl Barth's anthropology in light of modern thought*. Grand Rapids, MI: Eerdmans.

Prickett, S. (1986). *Words and* the Word*: Language, poetics and biblical interpretation*. Cambridge: Cambridge University Press.

Priolo L. (2005). Presupposition four: The Bible and psychology. *Journal of Moder Ministry, 2*(1), 61-70.

Prochaska, J. O. (1979). *Systems of psychotherapy: A transtheoretical analysis*. Chicago: Dorsey.

Prochaska, J. O. (1995). An eclectic and integrative approach: Transtheoretical therapy. In S. Gurman & S. B. Messer (Eds.), *Essential psychotherapies: Theory and practice* (pp. 403-40). New York: Guilford.

Prochaska, J. O., & Norcross, J. C. (2006). *Systems of psychotherapy: A transtheoretical analysis* (6th ed.). San Diego: Wadsworth.

Propp, V. (1968). *Morphology of the folktale* (L. Scott, Trans.). Austin: University of Texas Press.

Propri, J. (2005, October). *Counseling fear, anxiety, and panic attacks*. Paper presented at the meeting of the National Association of Nouthetic Counselors, Grand Island, NY.

Propst, L. R. (1988). *Psychotherapy in a religious framework*. New York: Human Sciences Press.

Propst, L. R. (1992). The comparative efficacy of religious and nonreligious cognitive-behavioral therapy for the treatment of clinical depression in religious individuals. *Journal of Consulting and Clinical Psychology, 60*, 94-103.

Pruyser, P. W. (1976). *The minister as diagnostician: Personal problems in pastoral perspective.* Philadelphia: Westminster Press.

Pruyser, P. W. (1990). Religious evaluation and diagnosis. In R. J. Hunter (Ed.), *Dictionary of pastoral care and counseling* (pp. 371-73). Nashville: Abingdon.

Purves, A. (2001). *Pastoral theology in the classical tradition*. Louisville, KY: Westminster John Knox.

Purves, A. (2004). *Reconstructing pastoral theology: A christological foundation.* Louisville, KY: Westminster John Knox.

Quine, W. V. (1963). *From a logical point of view* (2nd ed.). New York: Harper & Row.

Quine, W. V. (1976). *The ways of paradox and other essays.* Cambridge, MA: Harvard University Press.

Quine, W. V., & Ullian, J. S. (1978). *The web of belief* (2nd ed.). New York: Random House.

Quinn, S. L. (1994). Frequently asked questions about biblical counseling. In J. F. MacArthur & W. A. Mack (Eds.), *Introduction to biblical counseling* (p. 371-72). Dallas: Word.

Rabbinowitz, A. (2000). Psychotherapy with Orthodox Jews. In P. S. Richards & A. E. Bergin (Eds.), *Psychotherapy and religious diversity* (pp. 237-58). Washington, DC: American Psychological Association.

Rainer, T. S. (2001). *Surprising insights from the unchurched.* Grand Rapids, MI: Zondervan.

Ramm, B. (1954). *The Christian view of science and Scripture.* Grand Rapids, MI: Eerdmans.

Ranew, N. (1995). *Solitude improved by divine meditation.* Morgan, PA: Soli Deo Gloria. (Original work published 1839)

Ratzsch, D. (1986). *Philosophy of science: The natural sciences in Christian perspective.* Downers Grove, IL: InterVarsity Press.

Reagan, C. E. (1996). *Paul Ricoeur: His life and his work.* Chicago: University of Chicago Press.

Reid, J. S. K. (1957). *The authority of Scripture: A study of Reformation and post-Reformation understanding of the Bible.* London: Methuen.

Reid, T. (1969). *Essays on the intellectual powers of man.* Cambridge, MA: MIT Press. (Original work published 1785)

Reis, H. T., & Patrick, B. C. (1996). Attachment and intimacy: Component processes. In E. T. Higgins & A. W. Kruglanski (Eds.), *Social psychology: Handbook of basic principles* (pp. 523-64). New York: Guilford.

Renaut, A. (1997). *The era of the individual: A contribution to a history of subjectivity* (M. B. DeBevoise & F. Philip, Trans.). Princeton, NJ: Princeton University Press.

Rescher, N. (1995). Idealism. In J. Kim & E. Sosa (Eds.), *A companion to metaphysics* (pp. 227-29). New York: Blackwell.

Reventlow, H. G. (1985). *The authority of the Bible and the rise of the modern world.* Philadelphia: Fortress.

Richard of St. Victor. (1979). *The twelve patriarchs. The mystical ark. Book three of the trinity.* New York: Paulist Press.

Richards, F. A., & Commons, M. L. (1984). Systematic, metasystemic, and cross-paradigmatic reasoning: A case for stages of reasoning beyond formal operations. In M. L. Commons, F. A. Richards & C. Armon (Eds.), *Beyond formal operations, Vol. 1: Late adolescent and adult cognitive development* (pp. 92-119). New York: Praeger.

Richards, P. S., & Bergin, A. E. (1997). *A spiritual strategy for counseling and psychotherapy.* Washington, DC: American Psychological Association.

Richards, P. S., & Bergin, A. E. (2000). *Handbook of psychotherapy and religious diversity.* Washington, DC: American Psychological Association.

Richardson, F. C., Fowers, B. J., & Guignon, C. B. (1999). *Re-envisioning psychology: Moral dimensions of theory and practice.* San Francisco: Jossey-Bass.

Richardson, R. (2005). *Experiencing healing prayer: How God turns our hurts into wholeness.* Downers Grove, IL: InterVarsity Press.

Ricoeur, P. (1965a). *Fallible man.* Chicago: Regney.

Ricoeur, P. (1965b). *Freud and philosophy.* New Haven, CT: Yale University Press.

Ricoeur, P. (1966). *Freedom and nature: The voluntary and the involuntary* (E. V. Kohak, Trans.). Evanston, IL: Northwestern University Press.

Ricoeur, P. (1967). *The symbolism of evil* (E. Buchanan, Trans.). Boston: Beacon Press.

Ricoeur, P. (1974). Structure, word, event. In D. Ihde (Ed.), *The conflict of interpretations: Essays in hermeneutics.* Evanston, IL: Northwestern University Press.

Ricoeur, P. (1977). *The rule of metaphor.* Toronto: University of Toronto Press.

Ricoeur, P. (1981a). What is a text? In J. B. Thompson (Ed.), *Paul Ricoeur: Hermeneutics and the human sciences* (pp. 145-64). Cambridge: Cambridge University Press.

Ricoeur, P. (1981b). The model of the text: Meaningful action considered as text. In J. B. Thompson (Ed.), *Paul Ricoeur: Hermeneutics and the human sciences* (pp. 197-221). Cambridge: Cambridge University Press.

Ricoeur, P. (1984-1988). *Time and narrative: Vol. 1-3* (K. Blamey & D. Pellauer, Trans.). Chicago: University of Chicago Press.

Ricoeur, P. (1992). *Oneself as another.* Chicago: University of Chicago Press.

Ricoeur, P. (1995). *Figuring the sacred: Religion, narrative, and imagination.* Minneapolis: Augsburg Fortress.

Ridderbos, H. (1975). *Paul: An outline of his theology.* Grand Rapids, MI: Eerdmans.

Ridderbos, H. (1978). *Studies in Scripture and its authority.* Grand Rapids, MI: Eerdmans.

Riding, R. J., & Raynor, S. (1998). *Cognitive styles and learning strategies: Understanding style differences in learning and behavior.* New York: David Fulton Publishers.

Rieff, P. (1966). *The triumph of the therapeutic: Uses of faith after Freud.* New York: Harper & Row.

Ringenberg, W. C. (1984). *The Christian college.* St. Paul: Christian College Consortium.

Rist, J. M. (1997). *Augustine: Ancient thought baptized.* New York: Cambridge University Press.

Ritzema, R. J. (1979). Attribution to supernatural causation: An important component of religious commitment? *Journal of Psychology and Theology, 7,* 286-93.

Ritzema, R. J., & Young, C. (1983). Causal schemata and the attribution of supernatural causality. *Journal of Psychology and Theology, 11,* 36-43.

Riviere, C. (1987). Soul: Concepts in primitive religions. In M. Eliade (Ed.), *The encyclo-*

pedia of religion (Vol. 13, pp. 426-31). New York: Macmillan.

Rizzuto, A.-M. (1979). *The birth of the living God: A psychoanalytic study.* Chicago: University of Chicago Press.

Roberts, R. C. (1987). Psychotherapeutic virtues and the grammar of faith. *Journal of Psychology and Theology, 15,* 191-204.

Roberts, R. C. (1988). What an emotion is: A sketch. *The Philosophical Review, 97,* 183-209.

Roberts, R. C. (1993). *Taking the word to heart.* Grand Rapids, MI: Eerdmans.

Roberts, R. C. (1995). Virtue, virtues. In D. J. Atkinson, D. F. Field, A. F. Holmes & O. O'Donovan (Eds.), *New dictionary of Christian ethics & pastoral theology* (p. 881). Downers Grove, IL: InterVarsity Press.

Roberts, R. C. (1997). Parameters of a Christian psychology. In R. C. Roberts & M. R. Talbot (Eds.), *Limning the psyche: Explorations in Christian psychology* (pp. 74-100). Grand Rapids, MI: Eerdmans.

Roberts, R. C. (2000). A Christian psychology view. In E. L. Johnson & S. L. Jones (Eds.), *Psychology and Christianity: Four views* (pp. 148-77). Downers Grove, IL: InterVarsity Press.

Roberts, R. C. (2001). Outline of Pauline psychotherapy. In M. R. McMinn & T. R. Phillips (Eds.), *Care for the soul* (pp. 134-63). Downers Grove, IL: InterVarsity Press.

Roberts, R. C. (2003). *Emotions: An essay in aid of moral psychology.* New York: Cambridge University Press.

Roberts, R. C. (2007). *Spiritual emotions: A psychology of Christian virtues.* Grand Rapids, MI: Eerdmans.

Robertson, O. P. (1980). *The Christ of the covenants.* Phillipsburg, NJ: Presbyterian & Reformed.

Rockland, L. H. (1989). *Supportive therapy: A psychodynamic approach.* NY: Basic Books.

Roger, J. (1986). The mechanistic conception of life. In D. C. Lindberg & R. L. Numbers (Eds.), *God and nature: Historical essays on the encounter between Christianity and science* (pp. 277-95). Berkeley: University of California Press.

Rogers, B. (1998). *Pascal: In praise of vanity.* London: Phoenix.

Rogers, C. (1951). *Client-centered therapy.* Boston: Houghton Mifflin.

Rogers, C. (1961). *On becoming a person.* Boston: Houghton Mifflin.

Rogers, C. R. (1972). *Becoming partners: Marriage and its alternative.* New York: Delacorte.

Rogerson, J. (1988). The Old Testament. In P. Avis (Ed.), *The history of Christian theology: Vol. 2. The study and use of the Bible* (pp. 3-152). Grand Rapids, MI: Eerdmans.

Rogoff, B. (1990). *Apprenticeship in thinking: Cognitive development in social context.* New York: Oxford University Press.

Rogoff, B. (2003). *The cultural nature of human development.* New York: Oxford University Press.

Rohls, J. (1998). *Reformed confessions: Theology from Zurich to Barmen.* Louisville, KY: Westminster John Knox.

Roseman, I. J., & Smith, G. A. (2001). Appraisal theory: Assumptions, varieties, controversies. In K. Scherer, A. Schorr & T. Johnstone (Eds.), *Handbook of emotions* (2nd ed., pp. 397-416). New York: Guilford.

Rosenau, P. M. (1992). *Post-modernism and the social sciences*. Princeton, NJ: Princeton University Press.

Rosenthal, D. M. (Ed.). (1991). *The nature of mind*. New York: Oxford University Press.

Rosenthal, H. G. (1993). *Encyclopedia of counseling*. New York: Accelerated Development.

Rothbart, M. K., & Bates, J. E. (1998). Temperament. In W. Damon (Series Ed.) & N. Eisenberg (Vol. Ed.), *Handbook of child psychology: Vol. 3. Social, emotional, and personality development* (5th ed., pp. 105-75). New York: John Wiley.

Rothbart, M. K., Posner, M. I., & Hershey, K. L. (1995). Temperament, attention, and developmental psychopathology. In D. Cicchetti & D. J. Cohen (Eds.), *Developmental psychopathology: Vol. 1. Theory and methods* (pp. 315-42). New York: John Wiley & Sons.

Rowan, J. (1990). *Subpersonalities: The people inside us*. London: Routledge.

Rowe, C. E., Jr., & Mac Isaac, D. S. (1989). *Empathic attunement: The "technique" of psychoanalytic self psychology*. New York: Jason Aronson.

Rowe, D. C. (1994). *The limits of family influence: Genes, experience, and behavior*. New York: Guilford.

Rowe, D. C. (1997). Genetics, temperament, and personality. In R. Hogan, J. Johnson & S. Briggs (Eds.), *Handbook of personality psychology* (pp. 369-86). San Diego: Academic Press.

Runner, E. (1982). *The relation of the Bible to learning*. Jordan Station, ON: Paideia.

Russell, J. A. (1980). A circumplex model of affect. *Journal of Personality and Social Psychology, 39,* 1161-78.

Rutherford, S. (1984). *Letters of Samuel Rutherford*. Edinburgh: Banner of Truth Trust. (Original work published 1664)

Ryan, R. M., & Deci, E. L. (2000). Self-determination theory and the facilitation of intrinsic motivation, social development, and well-being. *American Psychologist, 55,* 68-78.

Ryan, R. M., & Deci, E. L. (2003). On assimilating identities to the self: A self-determination theory perspective on internalization and integrity within cultures. In M. R. Leary & J. P. Tangney (Eds.), *Handbook of self and identity* (pp. 253-72). New York: Guilford.

Rybash, J. M., Hoyer, W. J., & Roodin, P. A. (1986). *Adult cognition and aging*. New York: Pergamon.

Ryken, L. (1992). *Words of delight: A literary introduction to the Bible* (2nd ed.). Grand Rapids, MI: Baker.

Ryken, L., Wilhoit, J. C., & Longman, T., III. (1998). *Dictionary of biblical imagery*. Downers Grove, IL: InterVarsity Press.

Ryken, P. G. (1999). *Thomas Boston as preacher of the fourfold state*. Carlisle, UK: Paternoster.

Ryle, G. (1949). *The concept of mind*. New York: Barnes & Noble.

Saarni, C. (2000). The social context of emotional development. In M. Lewis & J. M. Haviland-Jones (Eds.), *Handbook of emotions* (2nd ed., pp. 306-24). New York: Guilford.

Salovey, P., Bedell, B. T., Detwelier, J. B., & Mayer, J. D. (2000). Current directions in emotional intelligence research. In M. Lewis & J. M. Haviland-Jones (Eds.), *Handbook of emotions* (2nd ed., pp. 504-22). New York: Guilford.

Sandage, S. J. (1998). Power, knowledge, and the hermeneutics of selfhood: Postmodern wisdom for Christian therapists. *Mars Hill Review, 15,* 65-73.

Sanford, J. (1987). *The kingdom within: The inner meaning of Jesus' sayings.* New York: Harper & Row.

Sanford, J. (1989). *Dreams: God's forgotten language.* New York: Harper & Row.

Sapolsky, R. M., Uno, H., Rebert, C. S., & Finch, C. E. (1990). Hippocampal damage associated with prolonged glucocorticoid exposure in primates. *The Journal of Neuroscience, 10*(9), 2897-902.

Sarbin, T. T. (Ed.). (1986). *Narrative psychology: The storied nature of human conduct.* New York: Praeger.

Saussure, F. de (1966). *Course in general linguistics.* New York: McGraw-Hill.

Scalise, C. J. (1996). *From Scripture to theology: A canonical journey into hermeneutics.* Downers Grove, IL: InterVarsity Press.

Schacter, D. L., Wagner, A. D., & Buckner, R. L. (2000). Memory systems of 1999. In E. Tulving & F. I. M. Craik (Eds.), *The Oxford handbook of memory* (pp. 627-43). New York: Oxford University Press.

Schaeffer, F. A. (1968). *Escape from reason.* Downers Grove, IL: InterVarsity Press.

Schafer, R. (1980). Narration in the psychoanalytic dialogue. *Critical Inquiry, 7,* 29-53.

Schafer, R. (1983). *The analytic attitude.* New York: Basic Books.

Schafer, R. (1992). *Retelling a life: Narration and dialogue in psychoanalysis.* New York: Basic Books.

Scharff, J., & Scharff, D. (1998). *Object relations individual therapy.* New York: Jason Aronson.

Scheler, M. (1961). *Man's place in nature* (H. Meyerhoff, Trans.). New York: Beacon Press. (Original work published 1928)

Schellenberg, J. L. (1993). *Divine hiddenness and human reason.* Ithaca, NY: Cornell University Press.

Schmidt, T. E. (1995). *Straight and narrow? Compassion and clarity in the homosexuality debate.* Downers Grove, IL: InterVarsity Press.

Schneider, K. (1998). Existential processes. In L. S. Greenberg, J. C. Watson & G. Lietaer (Eds.), *Handbook of experiential therapy* (pp. 103-20). New York: Guilford.

Schneider, K. J., & May, R. (1995). *The psychology of existence: An integrative, clinical perspective.* New York: McGraw-Hill.

Schneiders, S. M. (1989). Scripture and spirituality. In B. McGinn & J. Meyendorff (Eds.),

Christian spirituality: Origins to the twelfth century (pp. 1-22). New York: Crossroad.

Schore, A. N. (1999). *Affect regulation and the development of the self.* Mahwah, NJ: Lawrence Erlbaum.

Schore, A. N. (2003). *Affect dysregulation and the disorders of the self.* New York: Norton.

Schreiner, S. E. (1991). *The theater of his glory: Nature and the natural order in the thought of John Calvin.* Durham, NC: Labyrinth Press.

Schreiner, T. R. (1998). *Romans.* Grand Rapids, MI: Baker.

Schreiner, T. R. (2001). *Paul: Apostle of God's glory in Christ.* Downers Grove, IL: InterVarsity Press.

Schutz, A. (1967). *The phenomenology of the social world* (G. Walsh & F. Lehnert, Trans.). Evanston, IL: Northwestern University Press. (Original work published 1960)

Schwab, G. M. (2003). Critique of "habituation" as a biblical model of change. *Journal of Biblical Counseling, 21*(2), 67-83.

Schwartz, J. M., Stoessel, P. W., Baxter, L. R., Martin, K. M., & Phelps, M. E. (1996). Systematic changes in cerebral glucose metabolic rate after successful behavior modification treatment of obsessive-compulsive disorder. *Archives of General Psychiatry, 53,* 109-13.

Schweder, R. A., & Haidt, J. (2000). The cultural psychology of the emotions: Ancient and new. In M. Lewis & J. M. Haviland-Jones (Eds.), *Handbook of emotions* (2nd ed., pp. 397-416). New York: Guilford.

Schweiker, W. (2002). Images of Scripture and contemporary theological ethics. In W. C. Brown (Ed.), *Character and Scripture: Moral formation, community, and biblical interpretation* (pp. 34-54). Grand Rapids, MI: Eerdmans.

Schweizer, E. (1968). Pneuma. In G. Friedrich (Ed.), *Theological dictionary of the New Testament* (Vol. 6, pp. 332-455). Grand Rapids, MI: Eerdmans.

Schwöbel, C., & Gunton, C. E. (1991). *Persons divine and human.* Edinburgh: T & T Clark.

Scola, A. (1995). *Hans Urs von Balthasar: A theological style.* Grand Rapids, MI: Eerdmans.

Scott Kelso, J. A. (1995). *Dynamic patterns.* Cambridge, MA: MIT Press.

Scougal, H. (1976). *The life of God in the soul of man.* Minneapolis: Bethany. (Originally published 1680)

Seamands, D. A. (1981). *Healing of damaged emotions.* Wheaton, IL: Victor.

Seamands, D. A. (1985). *Healing of memories.* Wheaton, IL: Victor.

Searle, J. R. (1970). *Speech acts.* Cambridge: Cambridge University Press.

Searle, J. R. (1995). *The construction of social reality.* New York: Simon & Schuster.

Searle, J. R. (1998). *Mind, language and society: Philosophy in the real world.* New York: Basic Books.

Sebeok, T. A. (1994). *Signs: An introduction to semiotics.* Toronto: University of Toronto Press.

Seligman, M. E. P. (1991). *Learned optimism.* New York: Alfred A. Knopf.

Seligman, M. E. P., & Buchanan, G. (1994). *Explanatory style*. Mahwah, NJ: Lawrence Erlbaum.

Seligman, M. E. P., & Csikszentmihalyi, M. (2000). Positive psychology: An introduction. *American Psychologist, 55,* 5-14.

Sellars, R. W. (1916). *Critical realism*. Chicago: Rand-McNally.

Sellars, R. W. (1932). *The philosophy of physical realism*. New York: Macmillan.

Shapere, D. (1977). Scientific theories and their domains. In F. Suppe (Ed.), *The structure of scientific theories* (pp. 518-65). Urbana: University of Illinois Press.

Shaw, M. C. (1988). *The paradox of intention: Reaching the goal by giving up the attempt to reach it*. Atlanta: Scholars Press.

Shedd, R. P. (1958). *Man in community: A study of St. Paul's application of Old Testament and early Jewish conceptions of human solidarity*. London: Epworth.

Shepherd, T. (1990). *The parable of the ten virgins*. Morgan, PA: Soli Deo Gloria. (Original work published 1659)

Sherman, N. (1989). *The fabric of character: Aristotle's theory of virtue*. Oxford: Oxford University Press.

Shorr, J. E. (1974). *Psychotherapy through imagery*. New York: Intercontinental Medical Book.

Shorr, J. E., Sobel, G. E., Robin, P., Connella, J. A. (1980). *Imagery: Its many dimensions and applications*. New York: Plenum.

Shotter, J. (1993). *Conversational realities: Constructing life through language*. London: Sage.

Shults, F. L. (2003). *Reforming theological anthropology: After the philosophical turn to relationality*. Grand Rapids, MI: Eerdmans.

Shults, F. L., & Sandage, S. J. (2003). *The faces of forgiveness: Searching for wholeness and salvation*. Grand Rapids, MI: Baker.

Shults, F. L., & Sandage, S. J. (2006). *Transforming spirituality: Integrating theology and psychology*. Grand Rapids, MI: Baker.

Sibbes, R. (1961). *Light from heaven*. Wilmington, DE: Sovereign Grace Publishers.

Sibbes, R. (1973). *Works of Richard Sibbes, Vol. 1*. Edinburgh: Banner of Truth Trust. (Original work published 1862-1864)

Sibbes, R. (1981). *Works of Richard Sibbes, Vol. 3*. Edinburgh: Banner of Truth Trust. (Original work published 1862-1864)

Sibbes, R. (1983). *Works of Richard Sibbes, Vol. 4*. Edinburgh: Banner of Truth Trust. (Original work published 1862-1864)

Siegel, D. J. (1999). *Developing mind: Toward a neurobiology of interpersonal experience*. New York: Guilford.

Silver, D. (1983). Psychotherapy of the characterologically difficult patient. *Canadian Journal of Psychiatry, 28,* 513-21.

Skinner, E. A. (1999). Action regulation, coping, and development. In J. B. Brandtstädter & R. M. Lerner (Eds.), *Action and self-development* (pp. 470-500). Thousand Oaks, CA: Sage.

Slade, A. (1999). Attachment theory and research: Implications for the theory and practice of individual psychotherapy with adults. In J. Cassidy & P. R. Shaver (Eds.), *Handbook of attachment: Theory, research, and clinical applications* (pp. 575-94). New York: Guilford.

Slamecka, N. J., & Graf, P. (1978). The generation effect: Delimitation of a phenomenon. *Journal of Experimental Psychology: Human Learning and Memory, 4,* 592-604.

Slife, B. (2004). Theoretical challenges to therapy practice and research: The constraint of naturalism. In M. J. Lambert (Ed.), *Bergin and Garfield's handbook on psychotherapy and behavior change* (5th ed., pp. 44-83). New York: Wiley.

Small, D. H. (1968). *After you've said I do.* Ada, MI: Fleming Revell.

Smedes, L. B. (1983). *Union with Christ* (Rev. ed.). Grand Rapids, MI: Eerdmans.

Smith, B. (1977). A look at psychosomatic relations. *The Journal of Pastoral Practice, 1,* 81-89.

Smith, B. (1979). Migraine headaches. *The Journal of Pastoral Practice, 3,* 57-64.

Smith, E. M. (1996). *Genuine recovery: Orientation and overview of the basic principles of theophostic ministry.* Campbellsvile, KY: Alathia.

Smith, E. M. (2003). *Healing life's deepest hurts: Let the light of Christ dispel the darknes of your soul.* Ann Arbor, MI: Servant.

Smith, H. W. (1952). *The Christian's secret of a happy life.* Westwood, NJ: Fleming H. Revell.

Smith, J. A. (2003). *Qualitative psychology: A practical guide to research methods.* Thousand Oaks, CA: Sage.

Smith, J. E. (1959). Introduction to *Religious affections.* New Haven, CT: Yale University Press.

Smith, J. K. A. (2000). *The fall of interpretation: Philosophical foundations for a creation hermeneutic.* Downers Grove, IL: InterVarsity Press.

Smith, W. T. (2004). Getting the big picture of relationships. *Journal of Biblical Counseling, 22,* 2-14.

Smock, T. K. (1999). *Physiological psychology: A neuroscience approach.* Upper Saddle River, NJ: Prentice Hall.

Snyder, C. R. (Ed.). (2000). *Handbook of hope.* San Diego: Academic.

Snyder, C. R., & Lopez, S. J. (2002). *Handbook of positive psychology.* New York: Oxford University Press.

Sommers, C., & Sommers, F. (1989). *Vice & Virtue in everyday life* (2nd ed.). San Diego: Harcourt Brace Jovanovich.

Sorenson, R. L. (1994). Reply to Cohen. *Journal of Psychology and Theology, 22,* 348-51.

Sorenson, R. L. (1996a). "Where are the nine?" *Journal of Psychology and Theology, 24,* 179-96.

Sorenson, R. L. (1996b). The tenth leper. *Journal of Psychology and Theology, 24,* 197-211.

Sorenson, R. L. (1997). Is psychotherapy dead? *Journal of Psychology and Christianity, 17,* 110-24.

Sorenson, R. L. (2004). *Minding spirituality.* Hillsdale, NJ: Analytic Press.

Southard, S. (1989). *Theology & therapy: The wisdom of God in a context of friendship.* Waco, TX: Word.

Spearritt, P. (1986). Benedict. In E. Jones, G. Wainwright & E. Yarnold (Eds.), *The study of spirituality* (pp. 148-60). New York: Oxford.

Spence, D. P. (1982). *Narrative truth and historical truth: Meaning and interpretation in psychoanalysis.* New York: W. W. Norton.

Sperling, M., & Berman, W. (Eds.). (1994). *Attachment in adults: Clinical and developmental perspectives.* New York: Guilford.

Spero, M. H. (1992). *Religious objects as psychological structures: A critical integration of object relations theory, psychotherapy, and Judaism.* Chicago: University of Chicago Press.

Sphar, A. R., & Smith, A. (2003). *Helping hurting people: A handbook on reconciliation-focused counseling and preaching.* Lanham, MD: University Press of America.

Spiegel, J. (1996). The theological orthodoxy of Berkeley's immaterialism. *Faith and philosophy, 13*(2), 216-35.

Spiegel, J. (2002). Does God take risks? In D. S.Huffman & E. L. Johnson (Eds.), *God under fire* (pp. 187-210). Grand Rapids, MI: Zondervan.

Spiegel, J. (2005). *The benefits of providence: A new look at divine sovereignty.* Wheaton, IL: Crossway.

Spilka, B., Hood, R. W., Jr., Hunsberger, B., & Gorsuch, R. (2003). *The psychology of religion: An empirical approach* (3rd ed.). New York: Guilford.

Spykman, G. (1992). *Reformational theology: A new paradigm for doing dogmatics.* Grand Rapids, MI: Eerdmans.

Staniforth, M. (Ed.). (1968). *Early Christian writings.* New York: Penguin.

Stanley, C. (2001). I crashed hard. In *The desert experience: Personal reflections on finding God's presence and promise in hard times* (pp. 125-42). Nashville: Thomas Nelson.

Stark, R. (2003). *For the glory of God: How monotheism led to reformations, science, witch-hunts, and the end of slavery.* Princeton, NJ: Princeton University Press.

Steck, C. (2001). *The ethical thought of Hans Urs von Balthasar.* New York: Crossroad.

Steiner, G. (1989). *Real presences.* Chicago: University of Chicago Press.

Steiner, G. (2001). *Grammars of creation.* New Haven, CT: Yale University Press.

Stern, D. N. (1985). *The interpersonal world of the infant: A view from psychoanalysis and developmental psychology.* New York: Basic Books.

Sternberg, R. J. (2005). *Unity in psychology: Possibility or pipedream?* Washington, DC: American Psychological Association.

Sternberg, R. J., & Ben-Zeev, T. (2001). *Complex cognition: The psychology of human thought.* New York: Oxford University Press.

Sternberg, R. J., & Zhang, L.-F. (Eds.). (2001). *Perspectives on thinking, learning, and cognitive styles.* New York: Lawrence Erlbaum.

Stevenson, L. (1974). *Seven theories of human nature.* Oxford: Oxford University Press.

Stewart, J. (1975). *A man in Christ* (Reprint ed.). Grand Rapids, MI: Baker.

Stiver, D. R. (2001). *Theology after Ricoeur: New directions in hermeneutical theology*. Louisville, KY: Westminster John Knox.

Stock, B. (1996). *Augustine the reader: Meditation, self-knowledge, and the ethics of interpretation*. Cambridge, MA: Harvard University Press.

Stoker, H. (1973). Reconnoitering Cornelius Van Til's theory of knowledge. In E. R. Geehan (Ed.), *Jerusalem and Athens* (pp. 25-70). Phillipsburg, NJ: Presbyterian & Reformed.

Stone, H. W. (1996). *Theological context for pastoral caregiving: Word in deed*. New York: Haworth.

Stout, J. (1981). *The flight from authority: Religion, morality, and the quest for autonomy*. Notre Dame, IN: University of Notre Dame Press.

Stout, J. (1988). *Ethics after Babel: The languages of morals and their discontents*. Boston: Beacon Press.

Street, J. (2005). Counseling in the blended family vortex. *Journal of Modern Ministry, 2*(2), 91-104.

Street, J. (2005, October). *A biblical view of child development for biblical counselors*. Talk presented at the meeting of the National Association of Nouthetic Counselors, Grand Island, NY.

Strife, B. D. (2004). Theoretical challenges to therapy practice and research: The constraint of naturalism. In M. J. Lambert (Ed.), *Bergin and Garfield's handbook of psychotherapy and behavior change* (5th ed., pp. 44-83). New York: John Wiley & Sons.

Stump. E. (1995). Non-Cartesian substance dualism and materialism without reductionism. *Faith and Philosophy, 12,* 508-31.

Sullivan, H. S. (1953). *The interpersonal theory of psychiatry*. New York: Norton.

Suppe, F. (1977). Exemplars, theories and disciplinary matrixes. In F. Suppe (Ed.), *The structure of scientific theories* (pp. 483-99). Urbana: University of Illinois Press.

Swindoll, C. (2003). *Grace awakening*. Nashville: Thomas Nelson.

Talbot, M. R. (1997). Starting from Scripture. In R. C. Roberts & M. R. Talbot (Eds.), *Limning the psyche: Explorations in Christian psychology* (pp. 102-22). Grand Rapids, MI: Eerdmans.

Talbot, M. R. (2002). Does God reveal who he actually is? In D. S. Huffman & E. L. Johnson (Eds.), *God under fire: Modern scholarship reinvents God* (pp. 43-70). Grand Rapids, MI: Zondervan.

Tamburello, D. E. (1994). *Union with Christ: John Calvin and the mysticism of St. Bernard*. Louisville, KY: Westminster John Knox.

Tan, S. Y. (1987a). Cognitive-behavior therapy: A biblical approach and critique. *Journal of Psychology and Theology, 15,* 103-12.

Tan, S. Y. (1987b). Intrapersonal integration: The servant's spirituality. *Journal of Psychology and Christianity, 6,* 34-39.

Tan, S. Y. (1991). *Lay Counseling: Equipping Christians for a helping ministry.* Grand Rapids, MI: Zondervan.

Tan, S. Y. (1996). Religion in clinical practice: Implicit and explicit integration. In E. P. Shafranske (Ed.), *Religion and the clinical practice of psychology* (pp. 365-90). Washington, DC: American Psychological Association.

Tan, S. Y. (1999). Cognitive-behavior therapy. In D. G. Benner & P. C. Hill (Eds.), *Baker encyclopedia of psychology* (2nd ed., pp. 215-18). Grand Rapids, MI: Baker.

Tan, S. Y. (2001). Integration and beyond: Principled, professional, and personal. *Journal of Psychology and Christianity, 20,* 18-28.

Tan, S. Y. (2003). *Rest: Experiencing God's peace in a restless world.* Vancouver, BC: Regent College.

Tan, S. Y., & Dong, N. J. (2000). Psychotherapy with members of Asian American churches and spiritual traditions. In P. S. Richards & A. E. Bergin (Eds.), *Psychotherapy and religious diversity* (pp. 421-44). Washington, DC: American Psychological Association.

Tan, S. Y., & Ortberg, J., Jr. (2004). *Coping with depression* (2nd ed.). Grand Rapids, MI: Baker.

Tangney, J. P., & Dearing, R. L. (2002). *Shame and guilt.* New York: Guilford.

Tanquerey, A. (1930). *The spiritual life: A treatise on ascetical and mystical theology.* Tournai, Belgium: Society of St. John the Evangelist, Desclee.

Taylor, C. (1964). *The explanation of behavior.* London: Routledge & Kegan Paul.

Taylor, C. (1985a). *Human agency and language.* New York: Cambridge University Press.

Taylor, C. (1985b). Self-interpreting animals. In *Human agency and language: Philosophical papers 1* (pp. 45-76). Cambridge: Cambridge University Press.

Taylor, C. (1985c). The concept of a person. In *Human agency and language: Philosophical papers 1* (pp. 97-114). Cambridge: Cambridge University Press.

Taylor, C. (1985d). What is human agency? In *Human agency and language: Philosophical papers 1* (pp. 15-44). Cambridge: Cambridge University Press.

Taylor, C. (1989). *The sources of the self: The making of the modern identity.* New York: Oxford University Press.

Taylor, C. (1991). *The ethics of authenticity.* Cambridge, MA: Harvard University Press.

Taylor, G. J., & Bagby, R. M. (2000). An overview of the alexithymia construct. In R. Bar-On & J. D. A. Parker (Eds.), *The handbook of emotional intelligence* (pp. 40-66). San Francisco: Jossey-Bass.

Taylor, S. E., & Brown, J. D. (1988). Illusion and well-being: A social psychological perspective on mental health. *Psychological bulletin, 103,* 193-210.

Teresa of Ávila. (1961). *Interior castle.* Graden City, NY: Doubleday.

Tesser, A., & Martin, L. (1996). The psychology of evaluation. In E. T. Higgins & A. W. Kruglanski (Eds.), *Social psychology: Handbook of basic principles* (pp. 400-432). New York: Guilford.

Theissen, G. (1987). *Psychological aspects of Pauline theology* (J. P. Galvin, Trans.). Philadelphia: Fortress.

Thiessen, T. (2000). *Providence and prayer.* Downers Grove, IL: InterVarsity Press.

Thiselton, A. (1980). *Two horizons.* Grand Rapids, MI: Eerdmans.

Thiselton, A. C. (1992). *New horizons in hermeneutics.* Grand Rapids, MI: Zondervan.

Thomas à Kempis. (1864). *The imitation of Christ.* Boston: E. P. Dutton.

Thomas Aquinas. (1945). *Basic writings of Saint Thomas Aquinas.* New York: Random House.

Thomas, R. M. (2001). *Folk psychologies across cultures.* Thousand Oaks, CA: Sage.

Thompson, C. W. (2004). *Loving homosexuals as Jesus would: A fresh Christian approach.* Downers Grove, IL: InterVarsity Press.

Thompson, J. (1994). *Modern trinitarian perspectives.* Oxford: Oxford University Press.

Thompson, J. G. (1988). *The psychobiology of emotions.* New York: Plenum.

Thompson, R. A. (1998). Early sociopersonality development. In W. Damon (Series Ed.) & N. Eisenberg (Vol. Ed.), *Handbook of child psychology: Vol. 3. Social, emotional, and personality development.* (5th ed., pp. 25-104). New York: John Wiley & Sons.

Thorndike, E. L. (1905). *Elements of psychology.* New York: A. J. Seiler.

Thorne, C. G., Jr. (1974). Bonaventure. In J. D. Douglas (Ed.), *The new international dictionary of the Christian church* (p. 142). Grand Rapids, MI: Zondervan.

Thornton, E. E. (1964). *Theology and pastoral counseling.* Englewood Cliffs, NJ: Prentice-Hall.

Thurneysen, E. (1962). *A theology of pastoral care.* Richmond, VA: John Knox.

Tillich, P. (1951). *Systematic theology: Vol. 1.* Chicago: University of Chicago Press.

Tillich, P. (1957a). *Dynamics of faith.* New York: Harper & Row.

Tillich, P. (1957b). *Systematic theology: Vol. 2.* Chicago: University of Chicago Press.

Timpe, R. L. (1999a). Self-actualization. In D. G. Benner & P. C. Hill (Eds.), *Baker encyclopedia of psychology and counseling* (2nd ed., pp. 1073-75). Grand Rapids, MI: Baker.

Timpe, R. L. (1999b). Christian psychology. In D. G. Benner & P. C. Hill (Eds.), *Baker encyclopedia of psychology and counseling* (2nd ed., pp. 193-198). Grand Rapids, MI: Baker.

Tjeltveit, A. C. (1999). *Ethics and values in psychotherapy.* New York: Routledge.

Toga, A. W., & Mazziotta, J. C. (Eds.). (2000). *Brain mapping: The systems.* San Diego: Academic Press.

Tomkins, S. S. (1962-1963). *Affect, imagery, consciousness* (Vols. 1-2). New York: Springer.

Tompkins, P., & Lawley, J. (2000). *Metaphors in mind: Transformation through symbolic modeling.* London: Developing Company.

Torrance, T. F. (1969). *Theological science.* Oxford: Oxford University Press.

Torrance, T. F. (1984). *Transformation & convergence in the frame of knowledge: Explorations in the interrelations of scientific and theological enterprise.* Grand Rapids, MI: Eerdmans.

Torrance, T. F. (1989). *A Christian frame of mind.* Downers Grove, IL: InterVarsity Press.

Torrey, E. F., Taylor, E. H., Gottesman, I. I., & Bowler, A. E. (1995). *Schizophrenia and manic-depressive disorder: The biological roots of mental illness as revealed by the landmark study of identical twins*. New York: Basic Books.

Toulmin, S. (1972). *Human understanding*. Princeton, NJ: Princeton University Press.

Toulmin, S., & Leary, D. E. (1992). The cult of empiricism in psychology and beyond. In S. Koch & D. E. Leary (Eds.), *A century of psychology as science* (pp. 594-617). Washington, DC: American Psychological Association.

Tournier, P. (1962). *Guilt and grace*. New York: Harper & Row.

Tournier, P. (1965). *The healing of persons*. New York: Harper & Row.

Tracy, D. (1975). *Blessed rage for order*. Minneapolis: Seabury.

Tracy, D. (1981). *The analogical imagination*. New York: Crossroad.

Tripp, P. D. (2001). *Age of opportunity* (2nd ed.). Phillipsburg, NJ: Presbyterian & Reformed.

Tripp, P. D. (2002). *Instruments in the Redeemer's hands: People in need of change helping people in need of change*. Phillipsburg, NJ: Presbyterian & Reformed.

Tripp, P. D. (2004a). *Midlife and the grace of God.* Wapwallopen, PA: Shepherd Press.

Tripp, P. D. (2004b). Identity and story: A counseling transcript. *Journal of Biblical Counseling, 22*(2), 59-67.

Tulving, E. (2002). Episodic memory: From mind to brain. In S. T. Fiske, D. L. Schacter & C. Zahn-Waxler (Eds.), *Annual review of psychology, Vol. 53*. Palo Alto, CA: Annual Reviews.

Turner, J. (1985). *Without God, without creed: The origins of unbelief in America*. Baltimore: Johns Hopkins University Press.

Tweedie, D. F., Jr. (1961). *Logotherapy and the Christian faith: An evaluation of Frankl's existential approach to psychotherapy from a Christian viewpoint*. Grand Rapids, MI: Baker.

Tyson, P., & Tyson, R. I. (1990). *Psychoanalytic theories of development*. New Haven, CT: Yale University Press.

Underhill, E. (1990). *Mysticism*. New York: Doubleday.

Ury, M. W. (2001). *Trinitarian personhood*. Eugene, OR: Wipf & Stock.

Van Inwagen, P. (1993). *Metaphysics*. Boulder, CO: Westview.

Van Leeuwen, M. S. (1982). *The sorcerer's apprentice: A Christian looks at the changing face of psychology.* Downers Grove, IL: InterVarsity Press.

Van Leeuwen, M. S. (1985). *The person in psychology.* Grand Rapids, MI: Eerdmans.

Van Til, C. (1953). Nature and Scripture. In N. B. Stonehouse & P. Wooley (Eds.), *The infallible Word.* Grand Rapids, MI: Eerdmans.

Van Til, C. (1955). *The defense of the faith.* Philadelphia: Presbyterian & Reformed.

Van Til, C. (1967). *The doctrine of Scripture*. denDulk Christian Foundation.

Van Til, C. (1969). *A Christian theory of knowledge*. Phillipsburg, NJ: Presbyterian & Reformed.

Van Til, C. (1971). Response to "Vos and the interpretation of Paul." In E. R. Geehan

(Ed.), *Jerusalem and Athens* (pp. 237-41). Phillipsburg, NJ: Presbyterian & Reformed.

Van Til, C. (1972). *Common grace and the gospel.* Phillipsburg, NJ: Presbyterian & Reformed.

Van Til, C. (1977). *A survey of Christian epistemology.* Phillipsburg, NJ: Presbyterian & Reformed.

Van Til, H. (1959). *The Calvinistic concept of culture.* Grand Rapids, MI: Baker.

Vaillant, G. E. (1992). *Ego mechanisms of defense.* New York: American Psychiatric Association.

Vande Kemp, H. (1991). *Family therapy: Christian perspectives.* Grand Rapids, MI: Baker.

Vandenbos, G. R., Cummings, N. A., & DeLeon, P. H. (1992). A century of psychotherapy: Economic and environmental influences. In D. K. Freedheim (Ed.), *History of psychotherapy: A century of change* (pp. 65-102). Washington, DC: American Psychological Association.

Vander Goot, M. (1985). *Piaget as visionary thinker.* Bristol, IN: Wyndam Hall.

Vander Goot, M. (1987). Has modern psychology secularized religion? In T. J. Burke (Ed.), *Man and mind: A Christian theory of personality* (pp. 43-64). Hillsdale, MI: Hillsdale College Press.

Vanhoozer, K. J. (1998). *Is there a meaning in this text?* Grand Rapids, MI: Zondervan.

Vanhoozer, K. J. (2000). The voice and the actor: A dramatic proposal about the ministry and minstrelsy of theology. In J. G. Stackhouse Jr. (Ed.), *Evangelical futures: A conversation on theological method* (pp. 61-106). Grand Rapids, MI: Baker.

Vanhoozer, K. J. (2002). *First theology: God, Scripture & hermeneutics.* Downers Grove, IL: InterVarsity Press.

Vanhoozer, K. J. (2004). The atonement in postmodernity: Guilt, goats and gifts. In C. E. Hill & F. A. James III (Eds.), *The glory of the atonement* (pp. 367-404). Downers Grove, IL: InterVarsity Press.

Vanhoozer, K. J. (2005). *The drama of doctrine.* Louisville, KY: Westminster John Knox.

Varela, F. J., & Shear, J. (1999). First-person accounts: Why, what, and how. In F. J. Varela & J. Shear (Ed.), *The view from within: First-person approaches to the study of consciousness.* Thorverton, UK: Imprint Academic.

Varillon, F. (1983). *The humility and suffering of God.* New York: Alba.

Venema, H. I. (2000). *Identifying selfhood: Imagination, narrative, and hermeneutics in the thought of Paul Ricoeur.* Albany: State University of New York Press.

Venning, R. (1965). *The plague of plagues.* Edinburgh: Banner of Truth Trust. (Originally published 1669)

Vernick, L. (2005). *Getting over the blues.* Eugene, OR: Harvest House.

Viney, W., & King, D. B. (1998). *A history of psychology: Ideas and context* (2nd ed.). Boston: Allyn & Bacon.

Vitz, P. C. (1988). *Sigmund Freud's Christian unconscious.* New York: Guilford.

Vitz, P. C. (1990). The use of stories in moral development: New psychological reasons for an old education method. *American Psychologist, 45,* 709-20.

Vitz, P. C. (1992a). Narratives and counseling, Part 1: From analysis of the past to stories about it. *Journal of Psychology and Theology, 20,* 1-10.

Vitz, P. C. (1992b). Narratives and counseling, Part 2: From stories of the past to stories for the future. *Journal of Psychology and Theology, 20,* 11-19.

Vitz, P. C. (1994). *Psychology as religion:The cult of self-worship.* Grand Rapids, MI: Eerdmans.

Vitz, P. C. (1999). *Faith of the fatherless: The psychology of atheism.* Dallas: Spence.

Vitz, P. C., & Gartner, J. (1984). Christianity and psychoanalysis, Part 1: Jesus as the Anti-Oedipus. *Journal of Psychology and Theology, 12,* 4-14.

Voetius, G., & Horrnbeeck, J. (2003). *Spiritual desertion.* Grand Rapids, MI: Baker.

Vohs, K. D., & Baumeister, R. F. (2004). Understanding self-regulation: An introduction. In R. F. Baumeister & K. D. Vohs (Ed.), *The handbook of self-regulation* (pp. 1-12). New York: Guilford.

Volf, M. (1998). *After our likeness: The church as the image of the Trinity.* Grand Rapids, MI: Eerdmans.

Volf, M. (2002). Theology for a way of life. In M. Volf & D. C. Bass (Eds.), *Practicing theology* (pp. 245-63). Grand Rapids, MI: Eerdmans.

Volf, M., & Bass, D. C. (2002). *Practicing theology: Beliefs and practices in Christian life.* Grand Rapids, MI: Eerdmans.

Von Hildebrand, D. (1991). *Transformation in Christ: On the Christian attitude.* San Francisco: Ignatius.

Vondra, J. I., Shaw, D. S., Swearingen, L., Cohen, M., & Owens, E. B. (2001). Attachment stability and emotional and behavioral regulation from infancy to preschool age. *Development and Psychopathology, 13,* 13-33.

Vos, G. (1949). *Biblical theology.* Grand Rapids, MI: Eerdmans.

Vos, G. (1972). *The Pauline eschatology.* Grand Rapids, MI: Eerdmans.

Vos, G. (1980a). The eschatological aspect of the Pauline conception of the Spirit. In R. B. Gaffin (Ed.), *Redemptive history and biblical interpretation: The shorter writings of Geerhardus Vos* (pp. 91-125). Phillipsburg, NJ: Presbyterian & Reformed.

Vos, G. (1980b). The range of the Logos title in the prologue to the fourth gospel. In R. B. Gaffin (Ed.), *Redemptive history and biblical interpretation: The shorter writings of Geerhardus Vos* (pp. 59-90). Phillipsburg, NJ: Presbyterian & Reformed.

Vygotsky, L. (1978). *Mind in society: The development of higher psychological processes.* Cambridge, MA: Harvard University Press.

Wall, A. (1998). Fiction. In P. Bouissac (Ed.), *The encyclopedia of semiotics* (pp. 239-41). New York: Oxford University Press.

Wall, J., Browning, D. S., Doherty, W. J., & Post, S. (2002). *Marriage health and the professions: If marriage is good for you, what does this mean for law, medicine, ministry, therapy, and business.* Grand Rapids, MI: Eerdmans.

Wallace, R. S. (1953). *Calvin's doctrine of the word and sacrament.* Edinburgh: Oliver and Boyd.

Walsh, B., & Middleton, J. R. (1984). *The transforming vision: Shaping a Christian worldview.* Downers Grove, IL: InterVarsity Press.

Walsh, R., & Shapiro, S. L. (2006). The meeting of meditative disciplines and western psychology: A mutually enriching dialogue. *American Psychologist, 61,* 227-39.

Waltke, B. K. (2004). *The book of Proverbs* (2 vols.). Grand Rapids, MI: Eerdmans.

Wangerin, W., Jr. (1998). *Whole prayer: Speaking and listening to God.* Grand Rapids, MI: Zondervan.

Ward, B. (1986). Gregory the Great. In E. Jones, G. Wainwright & E. Yarnold (Eds.), *The study of spirituality* (pp. 277-79). New York: Oxford.

Ward, T. (2002). *Word and supplement: Speech acts, biblical texts, and the sufficiency of Scripture.* Oxford: Oxford University Press.

Ware, B. A. (2005). *Father, Son, & Holy Spirit: Relationships, roles, and relevance.* Wheaton, IL: Crossway.

Ware, K. (2000). *The inner kingdom.* Crestwood, NY: St. Vladimir's Seminary Press.

Warfield, B. B. (1915). Inspiration. In J. Orr (Ed.), *The international standard Bible encyclopedia* (Vol. 3, pp. 1473-83). Chicago: Howard-Severance.

Warfield, B. B. (1970a). The church doctrine of inspiration. In S. G. Craig (Ed.), *The inspiration and authority of the Bible.* Phillipsburg, NJ: Presbyterian & Reformed.

Warfield, B. B. (1970b). *The inspiration and authority of the Bible.* Phillipsburg, NJ: Presbyterian & Reformed.

Watson, F. (1994). *Text, church and world: Biblical interpretation in theological perspective.* Grand Rapids, MI: Eerdmans.

Watson, J. B. (1925). *Behaviorism.* New York: People's Institute.

Watson, P. J. (1993). Apologetics and ethnocentrism: Psychology and religion within an ideological surround. *The International Journal for the Psychology of Religion, 3,* 1-20.

Watson, P. J. (1998). Girard and integration: Desire, violence, and the mimesis of Christ as foundation for postmodernity. *Journal of Psychology and Theology, 26,* 311-321.

Watson, P. J. (2002, April). Toward a Christian post-postmodernism: Ideology, epistemological scapegoating, and the tasks of an empirical Christian psychology. Invited paper presented at Christian Association of Psychological Studies Convention, Chicago, IL.

Watson, P. J. (2004). After postmodernism: Perspectivism, a Christian epistemology of love, and the ideological surround. *Journal of Psychology and Theology, 32,* 248-61.

Watson, P. J. (2005, April). Christian psychological research and practice in a post-postmodern future: Framing psychology and religion within an ideological surround. Presented at the annual meeting of the Christian Association for Psychological Studies, Dallas.

Watson, P. J., Hood, R. W., Jr., & Morris, R. J. (1988). Existential confrontation and religiosity. *Counseling and Values, 33,* 47-54.

Watson, P. J., Hood, R. W., Jr., Morris, R. J., & Hall, J. R. (1985). Religiosity, sin, and self-esteem. *Journal of Psychology and Theology, 13*, 116-28.

Watson, P. J., Milliron, J. T., Morris, R. J., & Hood, R. W., Jr. (1994). Religion and rationality: II. Comparative analysis of rational-emotive and intrinsically religious rationalities. *Journal of Psychology and Christianity, 13*, 373-84.

Watson, P. J., Milliron, J. T., Morris, R. J., & Hood, R. W., Jr. (1995). Religion and the self as text: Toward a Christian translation of self-actualization. *Journal of Psychology and Theology, 23*, 180-89.

Watson, P. J., Morris, R. J., & Hood, R. W., Jr. (1987). Antireligious humanistic values, guilt, and self-esteem. *Journal for the Scientific Study of Religion, 26*, 535-46.

Watson, P. J., Morris, R. J., & Hood, R. W., Jr. (1988a). Sin and self-functioning, Part 1: Grace, guilt, and self-consciousness. *Journal of Psychology and Theology, 16*, 254-69.

Watson, P. J., Morris, R. J., & Hood, R. W., Jr. (1988b). Sin and self-functioning, Part 2: Grace, guilt, and psychological adjustment. *Journal of Psychology and Theology, 16*, 270-81.

Watson, P. J., Morris, R. J., & Hood, R. W., Jr. (1988c). Sin and self-functioning, Part 3: The psychology and ideology of irrational beliefs. *Journal of Psychology and Theology, 16*, 348-61.

Watson, P. J., Morris, R. J., & Hood, R. W., Jr. (1989). Sin and self-functioning, Part 5: Antireligious humanistic values, individualism, and the community. *Journal of Psychology and Theology, 17*, 157-72.

Watson, P. J., Morris, R. J., & Hood, R. W., Jr. (1990). Intrinsicness, self-actualization, and the ideological surround. *Journal of Psychology and Theology, 18*, 40-53.

Watson, P. J., Morris, R. J., & Hood, R. W., Jr. (1992). Quest and identity within a religious ideological surround. *Journal of Psychology and Theology, 20*, 376-88.

Watson, P. J., Morris, R. J., & Hood, R. W., Jr. (1994). Religion and rationality: I. Rational-emotive and religious understandings of perfectionism and other irrationalities. *Journal of Psychology and Christianity, 13*, 356-72.

Watson, P. J., Morris, R. J., Hood, R. W., Jr., Milliron, J. T., & Stutz, N. L. (1998). Religious orientation, identity, and the quest for meaning in ethics within an ideological surround. *The International Journal for the Psychology of Religion, 8*, 149-63.

Watson, P. J., Morris, R. J., Loy, T., Hamrick, M. B., & Grizzle, G. (in press). Beliefs about sin: Adaptive implications in relationships with religious orientation, self-esteem, and measures of the narcissistic, depressed, and anxious self. *Edification.*

Watson, R. I., & Evans, R. B. (1991). *The great psychologists: A history of psychological thought.* New York: HarperCollins.

Watson, T. (n.d.). *A body of divinity.* Grand Rapids, MI: Sovereign Grace Publishers.

Weber, O. (1981). *Foundations of dogmatics: Vol. 1* (D. L. Guder, Trans.). Grand Rapids, MI: Eerdmans.

Webster, C. (1986). Puritanism, separatism, and science. In D. C. Lindberg & R. L. Numbers (Eds.), *God and nature: Historical essays on the encounter between Christianity and science* (pp. 192-217). Berkeley: University of California Press.

Webster, J. B. (1988). Karl Barth. In S. B. Ferguson & D. F. Wright (Eds.), *New dictionary of theology* (pp. 76-80). Downers Grove, IL: InterVarsity Press.

Webster's new collegiate dictionary (8th ed.). (1974). Springfield, MA: Merriam-Webster.

Wegner, D. M. (2002). *The illusion of conscious will.* Cambridge, MA: MIT Press.

Welch, E. T. (1997a). What's the brain got to do with it? In E. Hindson & H. Eyrich (Eds.), *Totally sufficient: The Bible and Christian counseling* (pp. 147-63). Eugene, OR: Harvest House.

Welch, E. T. (1997b). *When people are big and God is small: Overcoming peer pressure, codependency, and the fear of man.* Phillipsburg, NJ: Presbyterian & Reformed.

Welch, E. T. (1998). *Blame it on the brain.* Phillipsburg, NJ: Presbyterian & Reformed.

Welch, E. T. (2000). *Depression: The way up when you are down.* Phillipsburg, NJ: Presbyterian & Reformed.

Welch, E. T. (2001a). Addictions: New ways of seeing, new ways of walking free. *The Journal of Biblical Counseling, 19,* 19-30.

Welch, E. T. (2001b). *Addictions: A banquet in the grave.* Phillipsburg, NJ: Presbyterian & Reformed.

Welch, E. T. (2002). How theology shapes ministry: Jay Adams's view of the flesh and an alternative. *Journal of Biblical Counseling, 20*(3), 16-25.

Welch, E. T. (2003). Motives: Why do I do the things that I do? *Journal of Biblical Counseling, 22*(1), 48-56.

Welch, E. T. (2004a). *Depression: A stubborn darkness.* Winston-Salem, NC: Punch.

Welch, E. T. (2004b). Self-injury: When pain feels good. *Journal of Biblical Counseling, 22*(2), 31-35.

Welch, E. T., & Powlison, D. (1997a). "Every common bush afire with God": The Scripture's constitutive role for counseling. *Journal of Psychology and Counseling, 16,* 303-22.

Welch, E. T., & Powlison, D. (1997b). Response to Hurley and Berry. *Journal of Psychology and Christianity, 16,* 346-49.

Weldon, J., & Ankerberg, J. (2005a). Visualization: God-given power or new age danger? (Part One). Retrieved from http://equip.org/free/DN388-1.htm.

Weldon, J., & Ankerberg, J. (2005b). Visualization: God-given power or new age danger? (Part Two). Retrieved from http://equip.org/free/DN388-2.htm.

Wells, S. (2004). *Improvisation: The drama of Christian ethics.* Grand Rapids, MI: Baker.

Wells, T., & Zaspel, F. (2002). *New covenant theology.* Frederick, MD: New Covenant Media.

Welton, G. L., Adkins, A. G., Ingle, S. L., & Dixon, W. A. (1996). God control: The fourth dimension. *Journal of Psychology and Theology, 24,* 13-25.

Werner, H. (1957). The concept of development from a comparative and organismic point of view. In D. B. Harris (Ed.), *The concept of development* (pp. 125-48). Minneapolis: University of Minnesota Press.

Werner, H., & Kaplan, B. (1956). The developmental approach to cognition: Its relevance to the psychological interpretation of anthropological and ethnolinguistic data. *American Anthropologist, 58,* 866-80.

Wertsch, J. V. (1985). *Vygotsky and the social formation of mind.* Cambridge, MA: Harvard University Press.

Wertsch, J. V. (1991). *Voices of the mind.* Cambridge, MA: Harvard University Press.

Wertsch, J. V. (1998). *Mind as action.* New York: Oxford University Press.

Westen, D., & Heim, A. K. (2003). Disturbances of self and identity in personality disorders. In M. R. Leary & J. P. Tangney (Eds.), *Handbook of self and identity* (pp. 643-66). New York: Guilford.

Westermann, C. (1995). *Roots of wisdom.* Louisville, KY: Westminster John Knox.

Westphal, M. (1990). Taking St. Paul seriously: Sin as an epistemological category. In T. P. Flint (Ed.), *Christian philosophy* (pp. 200-226). Notre Dame, IN: University of Notre Dame Press.

Westphal, M. (1993). *Suspicion and faith: The religious uses of modern atheism.* Grand Rapids, MI: Eerdmans.

Wetsel, D. (2003). Pascal and holy writ. In N. Hammond (Ed.), *The Cambridge companion to Pascal* (pp. 162-81). Cambridge: Cambridge University Press.

Whaling, F. (1981). The development of the word "theology." *Scottish Journal of Theology, 34,* 289-312.

White, A. R. (1970). *Truth.* New York: Doubleday.

White, G. M. (2000). Representing emotional meaning: Category, metaphor, schema, discourse. In M. Lewis & J. M. Haviland-Jones (Eds.), *Handbook of emotions* (2nd ed., pp. 30-44). New York: Guilford.

White, J. (1979). *Parents in pain.* Downers Grove, IL: InterVarsity Press.

White, J. (1982). *The masks of melancholy.* Downers Grove, IL: InterVarsity Press.

White, J. (1987). *Putting the soul back in psychology.* Downers Grove, IL: InterVarsity Press.

White, M. (2007). *Maps of narrative practice.* New York: Norton.

White, M., & Epston, D. (1990). *Narrative means to therapeutic ends.* New York: Norton.

Wiker, B., & Witt, J. (2006). *A meaningful world: How the arts and sciences reveal the genius of nature.* Downers Grove, IL: InterVarsity Press.

Wilbur, K. (2000). *Integral psychology: Consciousness, spirit, psychology, therapy.* Boston: Shambhala.

Wilson, R. M. (2000). Gnosticism. In T. A. Hart (Ed.), *The dictionary of historical theology* (pp. 229-31). Grand Rapids, MI: Eerdmans.

Wilson, S. D. (1990). *Released from shame.* Downers Grove, IL: InterVarsity Press.

Wilson, S. D. (1998). *Into Abba's arms: Finding the acceptance you've always wanted.* Wheaton, IL: Tyndale House.

Wilson, S. D. (2001). *Hurt people hurt people.* Grand Rapids, MI: Discovery House.

Wimberly, E. P. (1994). *Using Scripture in pastoral counseling.* Nashville: Abingdon.

Winn, J. K. (2003). Jesus rewrites our stories: Counseling in a crisis pregnancy center. *Journal of Biblical Counseling, 21*(3), 46-57.

Winter, D. G., & Barenbaum, N. B. (1999). History of modern personality theory and research. In L. A. Pervin & O. P. John (Eds.), *Handbook of personality* (2nd ed., pp. 3-30). New York: Guilford.

Winter, R. (1986). *The roots of sorrow.* Wheaton, IL: Crossway.

Winter, R. (2005). *Perfecting ourselves to death: The pursuit of excellence and the perils of perfectionism.* Downers Grove, IL: InterVarsity Press.

Wise, C. A. (1951). *Pastoral counseling: Its theory and practice.* New York: Harper & Brothers.

Wise, C. A. (1980). *Pastoral psychotherapy: Theory and practice.* New York: Jason Aronson.

Wolfe, D. L. (1987). The line of demarcation between integration and pseudointegration, In H. Heie & D. L. Wolfe (Eds.), *The reality of Christian learning* (pp. 3-12). Grand Rapids, MI: Eerdmans.

Wolitzky, D. L. (1995). The theory and practice of traditional psychoanalytic psychotherapy. In A. S. Gurman & S. B. Messer (Eds.), *Essential psychotherapies: Theory and practice.* New York: Guilford.

Wolterstorff, N. (1970). *On universals.* Chicago: University of Chicago Press.

Wolterstorff, N. (1975). *Reason within the bounds of religion.* Grand Rapids, MI: Eerdmans.

Wolterstorff, N. (1995). *Divine discourse: Philosophical reflections on the claim that God speaks.* Cambridge: Cambridge University Press.

Wolterstorff, N. (2001). The promise of speech-act theory for biblical interpretation. In C. G. Bartholomew (Ed.), *After Pentecost: Language and biblical interpretation* (pp. 73-90). Grand Rapids, MI: Zondervan.

Wolterstorff, N. (2004). *Educating for shalom: Essays on Christian higher education* (C. W. Joldersma & G. G. Stronks, Eds.). Grand Rapids, MI: Eerdmans.

Woltiers, A. M. (1985). *Creation regained: Biblical basics for a reformational worldview.* Grand Rapids, MI: Eerdmans.

Wood, A. S. (1969). *Captive to the word, Martin Luther: Doctor of sacred Scripture.* Grand Rapids, MI: Eerdmans.

Wooley, P. (1946). The relevancy of Scripture. In N. B. Stonehouse & P. Woolley (Eds.), *The infallible word: A symposium* (pp. 188-207). Grand Rapids, MI: Eerdmans.

Work, T. (2002). *Living and active: Scripture in the economy of salvation.* Grand Rapids, MI: Eerdmans.

Worthington, E. L. (1989). *Marriage counseling: A Christian approach to counseling couples.* Downers Grove, IL: InterVarsity Press.

Worthington, E. L., Jr. (Ed.). (1993). *Psychotherapy and religious values.* Grand Rapids, MI: Baker.

Worthington, E. L. (1994). A blueprint for intradisciplinary integration. *Journal of Psychology and Theology, 22,* 79-86.

Worthington, E. L. (Ed.). (1998). *Dimensions of forgiveness: Psychological research and theo-*

logical perspectives. Philadelphia: Templeton Foundation Press.

Worthington, E. L. (Ed.). (2000). *Christian marital counseling: Eight approaches to helping couples*. Resource Publications.

Worthington, E. L., Jr., Sandage, S. J., & Berry, J. W. (2000). Group interventions to promote forgiveness: What researchers and clinicians ought to know. In M. E. McCulough, K. I. Pargament & C. E. Thoresen (Eds.), *Forgiveness: Theory, research, and practice* (pp. 228-53). New York: Guilford.

Wright, D. F. (1988). Theology. In S. B. Ferguson, D. F. Wright & J. I. Packer (Eds.), *New dictionary of theology* (pp. 680-81). Downers Grove, IL: InterVarsity Press.

Wright, C. J. H. (2006). *The mission of God.* Downers Grove, IL: InterVarsity Press.

Wright, G. H. (1971). *Explanation and understanding*. Ithaca, NY: Cornell University Press.

Wright, N. H. (1986). *Self-talk, imagery, and prayer in counseling*. Waco, TX: Word.

Yalom, I. D. (1975). *The theory and practice of group psychotherapy* (2nd ed.). New York: Basic Books.

Yalom, I. D. (2002). *The gift of therapy.* New York: HarperCollins.

Yarhouse, M. A., & Burkett, L. A. (2003). *Sexual identity: A guide to living in the time between the times*. Lanham, MD: University Press of America.

Yarhouse, M. A., Butman, R. E., & McRay, B. W. (2005). *Modern psychopathologies: A comprehensive Christian appraisal.* Downers Grove, IL: InterVarsity Press.

Yates, T. P. (1997). *The supremacy of God in counseling: A leadership training program in illustrated Bible application.* Unpublished doctoral disseration, Westminster Theological Seminary, Glenside, PA.

Yeoman, W. (1964). St. Bernard of Clairvaux. In J. Walsh, & P. J. Kenedy (Eds.), *Spirituality through the centuries* (pp. 100-123). New York: P. J. Kenedy.

Young, E. J. (1957). *Thy word is truth.* Grand Rapids, MI: Eerdmans.

Young, F. (1997). *Biblical exegesis and the formation of Christian culture.* Cambridge: Cambridge University Press.

Young, J. E., Klosko, J. S., & Weishaar, M. E. (2003). *Schema therapy: A practitioner's guide.* New York: Guilford.

Young, W. C. (1954). *A Christian approach to philosophy.* Grand Rapids, MI: Baker.

Zelazo, P. D., Muller, U., Frye, U., & Overton, W. F. (2004). *The development of executive function*. New York: Blackwell.

Zimmermann, J. (2004). *Recovering theological hermeneutics: An incarnational-trinitarian theory of interpretation*. Grand Rapids, MI: Eerdmans.

Zinchenko, V. (1982). Preface. In K. Levitin (Ed.), *One is not born a personality: Profiles of Soviet education psychologists* (pp. 7-12). Moscow: Progress.

Zizioulas, Z. D. (1991). On being a person: Towards an ontology of personhood. In C. Schwöbel & C. E. Gunton (Eds.), *Persons, divine and human* (pp. 33-46). Edinburgh: T & T Clark.

Name Index

Subject Index

Scripture Index